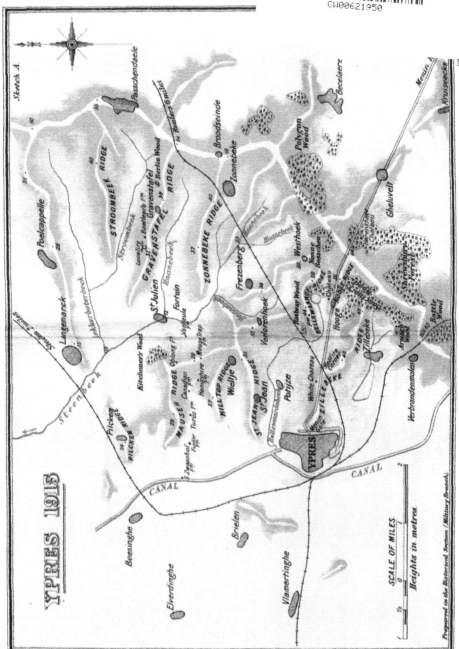

Prepared in the Historical Section (Military Branch).

HISTORY OF THE GREAT WAR

MILITARY OPERATIONS

THE BATTLE-FRONT OF THE B.E.F.
26TH DECEMBER 1914.

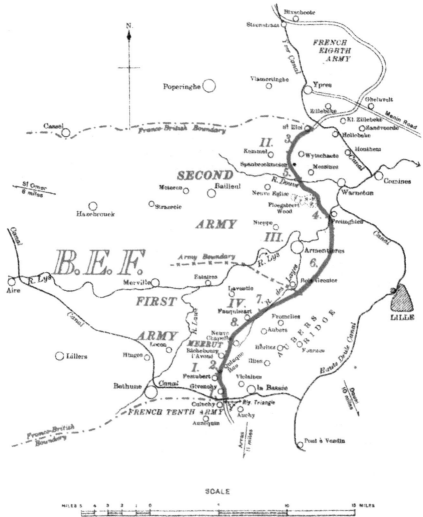

SCALE

MILES 5   4   3   2   1   0   10   15 MILES

Ordnance Survey, 1927.

HISTORY OF THE GREAT WAR

BASED ON OFFICIAL DOCUMENTS

BY DIRECTION OF THE HISTORICAL SECTION OF THE
COMMITTEE OF IMPERIAL DEFENCE

MILITARY OPERATIONS

FRANCE AND BELGIUM, 1915

WINTER 1914–15 : BATTLE OF NEUVE CHAPELLE : BATTLES OF YPRES

COMPILED BY

BRIGADIER-GENERAL J. E. EDMONDS

C.B., C.M.G., R.E. (Retired), p.s.c.

AND

CAPTAIN G. C. WYNNE

THE KING'S OWN YORKSHIRE LIGHT INFANTRY

MAPS AND SKETCHES COMPILED BY

MAJOR A. F. BECKE

R.A. (Retired) Hon. M.A. (Oxon.)

The Naval & Military Press Ltd

in association with

The Imperial War Museum
Department of Printed Books

Published jointly by

The Naval & Military Press Ltd

Unit 10 Ridgewood Industrial Park,

Uckfield, East Sussex,

TN22 5QE England

Tel: +44 (0) 1825 749494

Fax: +44 (0) 1825 765701

www.naval-military-press.com

www.military-genealogy.com

www.militarymaproom.com

and

The Imperial War Museum, London

Department of Printed Books

www.iwm.org.uk

PREFACE

IT was intended to include in this volume the whole war-year 1915, that is from the close of " First Ypres " in November 1914 to the dying down of the Battle of Loos in November 1915.[1] In spite of compression and the re-writing of several chapters, it became evident as the compilation proceeded that, if the whole twelve months were dealt with, the volume would be too bulky. On the other hand, to have reduced the narrative further would have rendered it obscure: it is impossible properly to depict the dangers of the situation or to do justice to the troops without going into a certain amount of detail. This was particularly the case in the battles of " Second Ypres ", where such was the shortage of men that small detachments had to do the work of battalions, and battalions hold the fronts of brigades. In other battles, too, the errors and delays of quite small forces compromised the success of whole divisions and corps. The first typescript was there-fore divided to form two volumes.

This volume contains an account of the winter of 1914–1915, and of the Allied plans for the spring campaign in 1915 ; a chapter on the expansion of the Army and the development of the supply of munitions up to the forma-tion of the Ministry of Munitions ; and the narratives of the Battle of Neuve Chapelle, and of the Battles of Ypres 1915, that long series of combats which, beginning with the first gas attack on 22nd April, lasted until 25th May. The next volume will continue the story of 1915 with the Battles of Aubers Ridge and Festubert ; the further ex-pansion of the Army ; the development of the Allied plans ; the Battle of Loos ; and the retirement of Field-Marshal Sir John French.

[1] The first of the volumes on 1918, which it was hoped might be issued before that on 1915, has unfortunately taken far longer to compile than was anticipated ; owing to unforeseen circumstances, it is impossible to say at present when it will be ready.

The year 1915 is not one on which the Nation or the Army can look back with satisfaction. It was the year of the disappointments of Gallipoli, the retreat from Ctesiphon, the overwhelming of the Serbs, and the great retirement of the Russian Armies from Poland and Galicia. Nor was there any substantial success achieved by French or British in the Western theatre to counterbalance these reverses. In that theatre the enemy undoubtedly had the best of the fighting. The B.E.F., forced to take over more of the front than its strength justified, and disastrously short of heavy guns and artillery ammunition, could not take the offensive as a whole. Small as it was, to comply with the requests of our Ally for active assistance, it had to be divided into two wings, one defensive and one offensive. But, in spite of this division of labour, the wing that carried out the attacks never had the reserves and the weight behind it essential for the attainment of an important success, while the defensive wing was hard put to it to hold its own. In both wings, old divisions, and the new as they arrived in France, had to discover by bitter experience the methods of the new warfare.

Its very misfortunes and mistakes make 1915 particularly worthy of study. In the remembrance of the final victory, we are apt to forget the painful and weary stages by which it was reached, and the heavy cost in our best lives during these stages. There is more to be learnt from ill-success—which is, after all, the true experience—than from victories, which are often attributable less to the excellence of the victor's plans than to the weakness or mistakes of his opponent. The story of 1915—though it has days in it at " Second Ypres " nearly as critical as that of 1914—has not the thrill of victory which even the partial successes of that year evoked, and is often very sad reading.

It must be borne in mind that many of the words used had in 1915 a value quite different to what they acquired later in the war. A " trench " was a slight narrow excavation with steep sides and six to nine feet wide traverses, lacking duck-boards and drainage and revetment worth the name. A " dug-out " was merely a hole in the ground with splinter-proof covering. A " trench mortar " was a length of brass tubing, inaccurate and dangerous to the firer. A " hand-grenade " was similarly an improvised weapon, set in action by a match or cigarette, or, at best, by a friction lighter. Artillery fire produced isolated craters, not the "small-pox" appearance of the Somme, the "confluent small-pox" of Vimy, or the complete devastation of 1918. An aeroplane photograph was a blurred picture, on which little else but trenches could be picked out. Mining had scarcely begun. The Signal Service at the front, with its wireless, buried lines, earth circuits, pigeons, etc., was in the making. Air warfare and anti-aircraft defences were in their infancy. Camouflage, flash and sound ranging, Lewis guns, Mills bombs, Stokes mortars, not to say Tanks, were still in the experimental stage. The possibilities of strategy, as the Dardanelles proved, were limited by want of means to carry out what were obviously the best and most effective strokes. The tactical conduct of battles was hampered not only by the difficulties of communication, but by the incomplete training of the reinforcements and the new units, and the inexperience of the staffs. Commanders had to handle, under novel conditions, far larger bodies of troops than they had ever been allowed to contemplate, and to do so with the aid of officers who had had little or no staff training.

Without the large leaven of trained men which the French and German Armies had available in raising their new formations—a quarter to a half being old soldiers—the new British Armies arose and took the field. But, as the narrative in this volume and the Gallipoli volume will show, the baptism of fire of the Canadian Division at Ypres, of the Australians and New Zealanders at Gallipoli, of the Territorials and new divisions everywhere, was a very severe one. Too many of the bravest and best perished, seeking to compensate by valour for lack of experience and the shortage of munitions, to the hazard of the final victory and the detriment of the future of the nation.

It is to 1915 rather than to 1914 or the later years of the war that we must look for lessons as regards raising troops, organizing munition supply and conducting operations with newly formed divisions. It was not indeed until Loos had been fought that there was sufficient experience on which to compile instructional pamphlets of any value.

During the fighting of 1914, which was more or less open, higher commanders, assisted by their liaison officers, could keep touch of a battle by actual vision; but from

1915 onwards it was impossible for any individual to see more than a very restricted portion of the field with his own eyes, and even in this portion the troops might be hidden from his view in trenches : he was either too near and concerned in some small part of the front, or too far away to see anything but turmoil. The artillery fire was such that dust and smoke concealed the progress of an attack even from brigadiers and battalion commanders fairly close up in observation posts ; and the heavy shelling cut the telephone wires by which they sought to transmit what information they were able to obtain. An account of a battle has therefore to be compiled from a medley of disconnected reports and descriptions of isolated actions, often contradictory; for units did not know what was happening on their right and left. In putting these fragments together the historian is forced to depict a battle with a kind of orderliness and in a series of phases which were not apparent during the actual events : it is quite impossible to describe on paper—as for instance the Battle of Waterloo can be described—the organized confusion of modern warfare.

The narrative is based on the British official records, but even to a greater extent than in previous volumes, I have been assisted by the loan of private diaries and regimental narratives and papers, and by the additions and corrections furnished by officers who have kindly read the chapters in typescript or in proof. To these friends, particularly to those who sent me valuable documents and maps, kept by them as souvenirs, I again offer my sincere thanks, and the apology that considerations of space have prevented me from including the whole of the material that they so generously provided. As all concerned may not have seen the draft or proofs, I ask, as I did in previous volumes, that any further information available, or any corrections thought necessary, should be sent to the Secretary of the Historical Section, Committee of Imperial Defence, 2 Whitehall Gardens, London, S.W.1.[1]

Owing to distance, I have not been in direct communication with officers of the 1st Canadian Division, except the General Officer Commanding and the G.S.O. 1. The history of the Canadian divisions and the corps they eventually constituted, has not yet been written, and only one

[1] A list of Addenda and Corrigenda to "1914" Volume II. and a few further amendments to Volume I. are issued with the present volume. I tender my best thanks to the readers who kindly furnished them.

Canadian regimental history, " The 13th Royal High-landers of Canada 1914–1919 ", is concerned with a unit that served in the Canadian Division at " Second Ypres ".[1] Colonel A. Fortescue Duguid, D.S.O., the Director of the Historical Section of the Department of National Defence, Ottawa, has, however, very kindly sent me material and given me all the help possible, and during a visit to England suggested a number of amendments to the text.

As regards the operations of the French, the British records are fairly complete. General Putz, commanding the Détachement d'armée de Belgique on the British left at Ypres, forwarded at the time copies of all operation orders, intelligence bulletins and reports to the V. Corps or Second Army headquarters. The reports of the inter-views of Generals Joffre and Foch with Sir J. French are available. But various points remained to be cleared up, and in this General Girard, Director of the Historical Section of the French General Staff, has rendered every assistance possible. Besides answering many questions, both verbally and in writing, he furnished a typescript copy of the French official account of the Battles of Ypres 1915, and advance copies of the disposition maps.

For the Belgian operations and the account of the Belgian batteries serving with the British at Ypres, I am obliged to Colonel Merzbach of the Historical Section of the Belgian General Staff. " Les Combats de Steen-straat " by Commandant " Willy Breton " of the Belgian Army, recommended by him, was found most valuable.

The battles which are described in the text were some-what difficult to piece together, inasmuch as many of the British war diaries are very short, and others are missing. The work of compilation was greatly facilitated by clues found in information from the German side. This informa-tion was courteously supplied, as in previous volumes, by General Freiherr Mertz von Quirheim, the Director of the German *Reichsarchiv*, Berlin, which has custody of the war records. He not only answered all questions, but furnished operation orders, and a short narrative of the Battles of Ypres. An account of these battles written by the late General Balck, is printed in Schwarte's " Der grosse Krieg ". " Der deutsche Landkrieg ", Volume II., was found of considerable use. From those two sources and from German regimental histories it has been possible

[1] There is also an excellent history of Princess Patricia's Canadian Light Infantry, which served in the 27th Division.

to give a brief picture of the battles as seen from the German side.

The maps, as in previous volumes, have been divided into " Sketches " bound in the volume, which it is hoped will be sufficient for the ordinary reader, and " Maps " for the use of students, issued in a separate case. Compiled independently by Major Becke, they formed a most useful check on the text.

As in the case of the volumes previously issued, I have received very great assistance in the compilation of this volume from the staff of the Historical Section (Military Branch) : from Mr. E. A. Dixon and Mr. A. W. Tarsey in the collection of material, and from Captain W. Miles in revision and preparation for the press. I have again had the benefit of invaluable criticism from Mr. C. T. Atkinson of Exeter College, formerly in charge of the Branch, and my brother-in-law, Mr. W. B. Wood, M.A. Captain G. C. Wynne, my particular assistant, has given me great help throughout : the labour of compiling Chapters III. to VII. (Munitions and Neuve Chapelle) in their first form was his, and my share in them has only been to cut them down and adapt their length to the space available. I feel that it is only fair that his name should appear on the title page.

J. E. E.

NOTES

THE location of troops and places is given from right to left of the front of the Allied Forces, unless otherwise stated. Thus, even in retreat, they are described from east to west. In translations from the German they are left as in the original, but otherwise enemy troops also are enumerated in relation to the British front.

To save space and bring the nomenclature in line with " Division ", " Infantry Brigade " has in the text been abbreviated to " Brigade ", as distinguished from Cavalry Brigade and Artillery Brigade.

The convention observed in the British Expeditionary Force is followed as regards the distinguishing numbers of Armies, Corps, Divisions, etc., of the British and Allied Armies, *e.g.* they are written in full for Armies, but in Roman figures for Corps, and in Arabic for smaller formations and units, except Artillery Brigades, which are Roman ; thus : Fourth Army, IV. Corps, 4th Cavalry Division, 4th Division, 4th Cavalry Brigade, 4th Brigade, IV. Brigade R.F.A.

German formations and units, to distinguish them clearly from the Allies, are printed in italic characters, thus : *First Army, I. Corps, 1st Division.*

The usual Army abbreviations of regimental names have been used in the narrative : for example, " 2/R. West Kent " or " West Kent " for 2nd Battalion The Queen's Own (Royal West Kent Regiment) ; K.O.Y.L.I. for the King's Own Yorkshire Light Infantry ; K.R.R.C. for the King's Royal Rifle Corps. To avoid constant repetition, the " Royal " in regimental titles is sometimes omitted : for instance, the Royal Warwickshire are occasionally called " the Warwickshire ".

Abbreviations employed occasionally are :—
B.E.F. for British Expeditionary Force ;
G.H.Q. for British General Headquarters ;

G.Q.G. for French Grand Quartier Général (usually spoken
"Grand Q.G.");

O.H.L. for German *Oberste Heeresleitung* (The Supreme
Command). *N.B.*—"G.H.Q." in German means
Grosses Haupt-Quartier, that is the Kaiser's
Headquarters, political, military and naval, as
distinguished from O.H.L.

Officers are described by the rank which they held at
the period under consideration.

The German practice, rarely followed in English, of
writing surnames, when no rank or title is prefixed, has
been adopted, *e.g.* " Kluck " and not " von Kluck ".

Time in German narratives and orders, which in the
period dealt with was one hour earlier than British, has
been corrected to our standard, unless it has specifically
stated against it, " German time ".

MAPS AND SKETCHES

THE end papers, and sketches A and B, have been provided to show the chief ridges in the Ypres Salient and the various stages of the Battles of Ypres. It will be sufficient for the ordinary reader to refer to these for the form of the ground in the Salient and for the line at various periods; but for military students a layered map of Ypres and neighbourhood (Map 4) will be found in the map volume. This can be laid on the table with the appropriate situation maps on top of it.

The situation maps and sketches give the position of the troops at the close of the day for the date they bear. On most occasions, therefore, for the first movements, it will be necessary to use the map marked with date of the previous day.

Endeavour has been made to insert on the maps all the places mentioned in the text, but to avoid overcrowding some small localities are omitted, and adequate description is then given in the text to enable the reader to fix their position with reference to a marked and well-known place.

The spelling of the place names has again given considerable trouble, particularly that of the Belgian names. Their spelling varies on different authoritative maps. Thus " Keerselare " is found on the Belgian 1/20,000, but " Keerselaere " on the 1/40,000. The " Noordhofwyk " of the Belgian 1/40,000 is rendered more correctly on the 1/20,000 as " Noordhofwijk ". In this volume, except on Map 4 which is an extract from maps prepared during the war, the spelling used in the latest edition of the Belgian Institut Cartographique Militaire has been followed for Belgian names, and that used on the French 1/80,000 for French. (The French 1/80,000 and 1/200,000 are taken as the authorities for the spelling of French names in the French Official History.)

The accents in French and Belgian place names have been omitted, with the exception of the accent on a final or penultimate *e*.

A list of place-names describing the position of small and not-well-known localities is provided in this volume.

CONTENTS

CHAPTER I

CHAPTER II

CHAPTER III

CHAPTER IV

CHAPTER V

CHAPTER VI

CHAPTER VII

CHAPTER VIII

THE BATTLES OF YPRES 1915. EVENTS IN THE SECOND ARMY
1ST TO 21ST APRIL 1915, PREVIOUS TO THE BATTLES :

CHAPTER IX

THE BATTLES OF YPRES 1915 (*continued*). THE BATTLE OF
GRAVENSTAFEL RIDGE :

CHAPTER X

THE BATTLES OF YPRES 1915 (*continued*). BATTLE OF GRAVEN-
STAFEL RIDGE (*concluded*). 23RD APRIL :

CHAPTER XI

CHAPTER XII

CHAPTER XIII

CHAPTER XIV

CHAPTER XV

CHAPTER XVI

CHAPTER XVII

CHAPTER XVIII

TABLE OF APPENDICES

SKETCHES AND MAPS

SKETCHES

(Bound in Volume)

MAPS

(In Separate Case)

LIST OF PLACE-NAMES WITH THEIR LOCATION*

A

Abancourt, 27 m. south-west of Amiens.
Abbeville, on the Somme, 26 m. north-west of Amiens.
Abeele, 9¾ m. W. by S. of Ypres.
Adinkerke, on coast between Nieuport and Dunkirk.
Aire, 10 m. south-east of St. Omer.
Annequin, 4 m. ESE. of Bethune.
Ardoye, 16 m. north-east of Ypres.
Argonne, district west of Verdun, between Meuse and Aisne.
Armagh Wood, 2¾ m. SE. by E. of Ypres.
Arques, 2 m. south-east of St. Omer.
Aubers, 2 m. NE. by E. of Neuve Chapelle.
Audruicq, 11½ m. north-west of St. Omer.
Augustovo Forest, formerly in Russia, close to German frontier, 100 m. south-east of Königsberg.
Aulnoye, 27 m. east of Cambrai.
Auxi le Chateau, 29 m. W. by S. of Arras, and 25 m. east of the mouth of the Somme.

---

* A list of this kind has been published in Tome X. of the French Official History of the War, and seems worthy of imitation, as it may save the reader's time in consulting the Sketches—on which it was impossible to insert all the names—and in his subsequent study of the appropriate map. The lesser known localities are described with reference to well-known ones. In the present list the centres Arras, Armentieres, Bethune, Ypres, St. Omer and Amiens, and, for battle purposes, Neuve Chapelle and Wieltje (2 miles north-east of Ypres), are mainly used. Distances are measured from the centre of these towns and villages.

NOTE.—In choosing the index word, disregard the article the, and l', le, la, les; *e.g.* la Bassée is indexed under Bassée, and The Dump is under Dump.

B

Bailleul, 10 m. SSW. of Ypres.
Bank Farm, ¾ m. SSE. of St. Julien (*q.v.*).
Bassée, la, 7 m. east of Bethune.
Beaucamps, 6½ m. WSW. of Lille.
Becque du Biez, stream flowing into Lys just above Armentieres.
Belle Alliance Farm, 1 m. W. by N. of Wieltje.
Bellewaarde, Ridge and Lake, just north of Hooge (*q.v.*).
Berlin Wood, ½ m. east of Gravenstafel (*q.v.*).
Bixschoote, 5¼ m. N. by W. of Ypres.
Blendecques, 2¼ m. S. by E. of St. Omer.
Boesinghe, on canal 3½ m. north of Ypres.
Boetleer's Farm, ½ m. W. by N. of Gravenstafel (*q.v.*).
Bois du Biez, ½ m. south-east of N. Chapelle.
Bois Grenier, 2½ m. south of Armentieres.
Brandhoek, 4¼ m. west of Ypres.
Brickstacks, 6 m. E. by S. of Bethune, south of railway.
Brielen, 2 m. north-west of Ypres.
Brique, la, 1 m. NNE. of Ypres.
Broodseinde, on Passchendaele ridge east of Zonnebeke (*q.v.*).
Brulots, les, ½ m. SE. by S. of Neuve Chapelle.
Bruges, 29 m. NNE. of Ypres.

C

Calonne, on the Lys, 6½ m. N. by W. of Bethune.
Cameron Lane, 1¼ m. NNW. of N. Chapelle.
Cambrai, 45 m. ENE. of Amiens.
Canadian Farm, 1 m. north-west of Wieltje.
Carency, 6½ m. N. by W. of Arras.
Cassel, 18 m. W. by S. of Ypres.
Caterpillar, The, just south of Hill 60 (Ypres).
Chapelle St. Roche, 1¾ m. WNW. of la Bassée.
Chantilly, 24 m. N. by E. of Paris.
Chapigny, 1¼ m. N. by E. of Neuve Chapelle.
Chocolat Menier Corner, in British front line, 1¼ m. south-west of Port Arthur (*q.v.*).
Chateau des Trois Tours, just west of Brielen (*q.v.*).

Cliqueterie Farm, 1a, 2 m. east of N. Chapelle.
Clonmel Copse, 1 m. SSE. of Hooge.
Clytte, 1a, 5 m. south-west of Ypres.
Comines, 8 m. south-east of Ypres.
Colne Valley, Canadian Farm towards South Zwaanhof Farm (see Sketch A).
Courtrai, 17 m. E. by S. of Ypres.
Crescent Redoubt, just south of Port Arthur (*q.v.*).
Croix Marmuse, 4¾ m. WNW. of N. Chapelle.
Cross Roads Farm, ½ m. north-west of Wieltje.
Crouy, on the Somme, 11 m. below Amiens.
Cuinchy, 5 m. E. by S. of Bethune, south of the canal.

D

Deule, Canal and River, flows north and south, 12 m. east of Bethune.
Dickebusch, and Lake, 3 m. south-west of Ypres.
Dinant, on the Meuse, 15 m. south of Namur.
Dixmude, 13 m. north of Ypres.
Dochy Farm, ⅝ m. S. by W. of Gravenstafel (*q.v.*).
Don, on Deule canal, 12½ m. E. by N. of Bethune.
Douai, 15 m. ENE. of Arras.
Douve, River, joins the Lys at Warneton, 7 m. S. by E. of Ypres.
Drie Grachten, on the canal, 8 m. north of Ypres.
Duck's Bill, in British front line (after the battle), ½ m. NNE. of Neuve Chapelle.
Dump, The, just west of Hill 60 (Ypres).

E

Edgware Road, enters N. Chapelle from south-west.
Eksternest (Westhoek), ⅞ m. north-east of Hooge (*q.v.*).
Elverdinghe, 3⅞ m. NW. by N. of Ypres.
Estaires, on the Lys, 7 m. WSW. of Armentieres.

Etaples, on coast, 15 m. south of Boulogne.
Eu, near coast, 40 m. W. by N. of Amiens.

F

Fauquissart, 2 m. NNE. of N. Chapelle.
Ferme Deleval, 2¾ m. north-east of N. Chapelle.
Ferme du Biez, 1⅛ m. SSE. of N. Chapelle.
Festubert, 4½ m. E. by N. of Bethune.
Fletre, 4 m. W. by N. of Bailleul (*q.v.*).
Fontinettes, les, railway junction on southern side of Calais.
Fournes, 12 m. ENE. of Bethune.
Fort Englos (Lille), 5 m. south-east of Armentieres.
Fortuin, just south-east of St. Julien.
Fortuinhoek, ½ m. south-east of St. Julien.
Fouquereuil, 2 m. south-west of Bethune.
Frelinghien, 3 m. north-east of Armentieres.
Frevent, 21 m. west of Arras.
Frezenberg, 3 m. ENE. of Ypres.
Fromelles, 11 m. NE. by E. of Bethune.
Furnes, 18½ m. NW. by N. of Ypres.
Fusilier Farm, 2¼ m. north of Ypres.

G

Gamaches, 33½ m. W. by N. of Amiens.
Gheluvelt, 4⅞ m. E. by S. of Ypres.
Ghent, 39 m. ENE. of Ypres.
Givenchy, 5 m. east of Bethune.
Glimpse Cottage, 2½ m. N. by W. of Ypres.
Goldfish Chateau, 1½ m. west of Ypres.
Gorlice, 75 m. south-east of Cracow (Galicia).
Gravenstafel, 5 m. NE. by E. of Ypres.
Groenen Jäger (Cabaret), 2 m. WSW. of Ypres.

H

Haanebeke, a stream which joins the Steenbeek at St. Julien (*q.v.*).

Halpegarbe, 1½ m. south-east of N. Chapelle.

Hampshire Farm, ¾ m. NNW. of Wieltje.

Haut Pommereau, 1⅜ m. east of N. Chapelle.

Havre, 100 m. W. by S. of Amiens.

Hazebrouck, 14 m. NNW. of Bethune.

Hell Fire Corner, railway crossing 1½ m. E. by S. of Ypres.

Herenthage Woods, 1 m. ESE. of Hooge (*q.v.*).

Herlies, 10 m. ENE. of Bethune.

Hesdigneul, 2¾ m. south-west of Bethune.

Het Sas, lock on canal 4½ m. north of Ypres.

Hill Top Ridge, ½ m. north-west of Wieltje.

Hill 28, ½ m. north-west of Frezenberg (*q.v.*).

Hill 29, top of Mauser Ridge, ¼ m. north of Turco Farm (*q.v.*).

Hill 33, ½ m. NW. by N. of Verlorenhoek (*q.v.*).

Hill 37, 2 m. ENE. of Wieltje.

Hill 60, 2⅝ m. south-east of Ypres.

Hirson, 64 m. ESE. of Arras, and 37 m. S. by E. of Mons.

Hollebeke, 4 m. SE. by S. of Ypres.

Hooge, 2½ m. E. by S. of Ypres.

Houthem, 5½ m. south-east of Ypres.

Houthulst Forest, 8 m. N. by E. of Ypres.

Hue, le, 2¼ m. south-east of N. Chapelle.

I

Illies, 9 m. E. by N. of Bethune.

Ingelmunster, 17 m. ENE. of Ypres.

J

Juliet Farm, ⅝ m. WSW. of St. Julien (*q.v.*).

K

Kattestraat, 2¾ m. SE. by E. of Dixmude (q.v.).
Keerselare, ¾ m. N. by E. of St. Julien (q.v.).
Kemmel, 5¼ m. SW. by S. of Ypres.
Kitchener's Wood, ⅝ m. west of St. Julien (q.v.).
Klein Zillebeke, 3¼ m. south-east of Ypres.
Knocke, Old fort of, on the canal 10 m. north of Ypres.
Kruisstraat, ⅞ m. south-west of Ypres.

L

Lacouture, 5 m. north-east of Bethune.
Lancashire Farm, 2⅛ m. north of Ypres.
Langemarck, 4½ m. NNE. of Ypres.
Laventie, 9 m. north-east of Bethune.
Layes, Riviere de, drainage channel on east side of N. Chapelle.
Ledeghem, 10½ m. east of Ypres.
Lekkerboterbeek, stream which joins the Steenbeek 1¼ m.
    below St. Julien (q.v.).
Lens, 10 m. N. by E. of Arras.
Lestrem, 7 m. NNE. of Bethune.
Ligny le Grand, 2 m. ESE. of N. Chapelle.
Ligny le Petit, 1⅛ m. south-east of N. Chapelle.
Limbourg Appendix, the narrow 30-mile-long strip of Nether-
    lands territory which stretches down to Maastricht between
    Germany and Belgium.
Lizerne, on the canal 5 m. NNW. of Ypres.
Lobes, les, 4½ m. west of N. Chapelle.
Locality C, defence work 1⅜ m. E. by N. of St. Julien (q.v.).
Locon, 3 m. NNE. of Bethune.
Lodz (Poland), 80 m. south-west of Warsaw.
Loisne, River, enters the R. Lawe 4¾ m. NE. by N. of
    Bethune.
Longpré, on the Somme, 16 m. NW. by W. of Amiens.
Longuyon, 22 m. NNE. of Verdun.
Longwy, 31 m. NNE. of Verdun.
Lorgies, 7½ m. E. by N. of Bethune.
Lowicz (Poland), 50 m. W. by S. of Warsaw.
Lys, River, flows through Armentieres and joins the Schelde
    at Ghent.

M

Maison du Passeur (Wit Huis), on the canal $6\frac{1}{2}$ m. north of Ypres.
Marloie, 27 m. south-east of Namur.
Marquillies, 10 m. E. by N. of Bethune.
Masuria, district in south-east corner of East Prussia.
Mauquissart, 1 m. NE. by N. of Neuve Chapelle.
Mauser Ridge, $1\frac{3}{8}$ m. north-west of Wieltje.
Menin, 11 m. ESE. of Ypres.
Merville, 8 m. north of Bethune.
Messines, 6 m. south of Ypres.
Mezieres, on the Meuse, 50 m. below Verdun.
Missy, on the Aisne, 5 m. east of Soissons.
Moated Grange (Ferme Vanbesien), $\frac{7}{8}$ m. north of N. Chapelle.
Moorslede, $8\frac{1}{4}$ m. ENE. of Ypres.
Morteldje (now **Moortelje**) **Estaminet,** 1 m. north-west of Wieltje.
Mottes Farm, les, $1\frac{1}{2}$ m. north-east of N. Chapelle.
Moulin du Pietre (Pietre Mill), $1\frac{1}{4}$ m. NE. of N. Chapelle.
Mouse Trap Farm, $\frac{1}{2}$ m. north of Wieltje.

N

Nameless Houses, $\frac{3}{4}$ m. north-east of N. Chapelle.
Neuf Berquin, 9 m. N. by E. of Bethune.
Neuve Chapelle, $7\frac{1}{2}$ m. ENE. of Bethune.
Neuville St. Vaast, 5 m. north of Arras.
Nieuport, at the mouth of the Yser, 20 m. north of Ypres.
Nonne Bosschen, a wood $1\frac{1}{4}$ m. E. by N. of Hooge (*q.v.*).
Noordschote, 8 m. NNW. of Ypres.
Noyon, 38 m. south-east of Amiens.

O

Oblong Farm, 1 m. north of Wieltje.
Oostroosebeke, 20 m. E. by N. of Ypres.
Orchard, The, $\frac{5}{8}$ m. north of N. Chapelle.
Ouderdom, $4\frac{3}{4}$ m. WSW. of Ypres.
Oxelaere, just south of Cassel, $18\frac{1}{2}$ m. W. by S. of Ypres.

P

Passchendaele, 7 m. NE. by E. of Ypres.
Perenchies, $4\frac{1}{2}$ m. E. by S. of Armentieres.
Perthes (Champagne), 22 m. E. by S. of Rheims.
Petit Bois, west of Wytschaete, $4\frac{3}{8}$ m. S. by W. of Ypres.
Picantin, 3 m. NNE. of N. Chapelle.
Pietre, 1 m. ENE. of N. Chapelle.
Pietre, le, $2\frac{3}{8}$ m. NE. by E. of Neuve Chapelle.
Pilckem, $3\frac{1}{2}$ m. north of Ypres.
Pilly, le, $3\frac{3}{4}$ m. east of N. Chapelle.
Ploegsteert Wood, 3 m. north of Armentieres.
Plouich, le, $2\frac{3}{4}$ m. ENE. of N. Chapelle.
Poelcappelle, $5\frac{3}{4}$ m. NE. by N. of Ypres.
Poix, 16 m. WSW. of Amiens.
Pola, Austrian port, 55 m. south of Trieste.
Polygon Wood, $4\frac{1}{2}$ m. east of Ypres.
Pommereau, Bas, $1\frac{5}{8}$ m. E. by N. of Neuve Chapelle.
Pommereau, Haut, $1\frac{3}{8}$ m. east of N. Chapelle.
Pont a Vendin, 14 m. NNE. of Arras.
Pont du Hem, $2\frac{1}{4}$ m. north-west of N. Chapelle.
Pont Levis, 2 m. east of Bethune.
Pont Logy, $\frac{1}{2}$ m. W. by N. of Neuve Chapelle.
Poperinghe, 7 m. west of Ypres.
Port Arthur, $\frac{1}{2}$ m. SSW. of N. Chapelle.
Potijze, $1\frac{1}{4}$ m. NE. by E. of Ypres.
Proven, 10 m. WNW. of Ypres.
Pypegaale, $1\frac{1}{4}$ m. W. by N. of Steenstraat (*q.v.*).

Q

Quadrilateral, German trench-work 1 m. NNE. of N. Chapelle.
Quinque Rue, la, 5 m. E. by N. of Bethune.

R

Racecourse Farm, 1¼ m. N. by W. of Wieltje.
Railway Triangle, 6 m. E. by S. of Bethune.
Railway Wood, 2 m. east of Ypres.
Richebourg l'Avoué, 1½ m. south-west of N. Chapelle.
Richebourg St. Vaast, 2 m. W. by S. of Neuve Chapelle.
Road Triangle, immediately north of N. Chapelle.
Roubaix, sister town of Lille, lying north-east of it.
Rouges Bancs, 3¾ m. north-east of N. Chapelle.
Rouge Croix, 1½ m. north-west of N. Chapelle.
Roulers, 13 m. NE. by E. of Ypres.
Rue d'Enfer, enters Aubers (2 m. ENE. of N. Chapelle) from west.
Rue des Berceaux, 1½ m. WSW. of N. Chapelle.
Rue du Bacquerot, enters Rouge Croix (q.v.) from east.
Rue du Bois, road running south-west from Port Arthur (q.v.).
Rue Tilleloy, passes through Fauquissart (2 m. NNE. of N. Chapelle).
Russie Farm, la, ¾ m. ESE. of N. Chapelle.
Ryveld, 16 m. W. by S. of Ypres.

S

Sainghin, 5 m. SE. by E. of Lille.
St. Eloi, 2¾ m. south of Ypres.
St. Jean, 1¼ m. north-east of Ypres.
St. Julien, 3¼ m. north-east of Ypres.
St. Nazaire, 240 m. WSW. of Paris.

St. Pol, 17 m. south-west of Bethune.
St. Quentin, 45 m. E. by S. of Amiens.
St. Vith, 33 m. south-east of Liege.
Salomé, 9 m. east of Bethune.
Sanctuary Wood, south-east of Hooge.
Shrewsbury Forest, 3¼ m. ESE. of Ypres.
Signpost Lane, ½ m. N. by W. of Neuve Chapelle.
Smith–Dorrien Trench, just east of N. Chapelle.
Soissons, on the Aisne, 55 m. north-east of Paris.
Souchez, 7 m. N. by W. of Arras.
South Zwaanhof Farm, on the canal 2½ m. north of Ypres.
Spanbroekmolen, 1⅛ m. south-west of Wytschaete (*q.v.*).
Spree Farm, ¼ m. SSE. of St. Julien (*q.v.*).
Staden, 10 m. NE. by N. of Ypres.
Steenbeek, name sometimes given to the stream flowing from
    St. Julien northwards.
Steenstraat, on the canal, 5¼ m. north of Ypres.
Steenvoorde, 14 m. W. by S. of Ypres.
Strazeele, 4 m. east of Hazebrouck.
Stroombeke, stream 5 m. north-east of Ypres.
Struyve Farm (Hindenburg Farm), ½ m. north of Turco
    Farm (*q.v.*).
Sunken Road, ½ m. N. by E. of Neuve Chapelle.

T

Tannenberg, in East Prussia, 90 m. south of Königsberg.
Tarnow, 40 m. east of Cracow (Galicia).
Thielt, 22 m. ENE. of Ypres.
Thiennes, 11½ m. south-east of St. Omer.
Thionville, on the Moselle, 15 m. north of Metz.
Thorn, formerly in East Prussia, 140 m. SW. by S. of
    Königsberg.
Tombe Willot, la, 5½ m. west of N. Chapelle.
Touquet, le, 3 m. north-east of Armentieres.
Tourcoing, sister town, NNE. of Lille.
Touret, le, 3¾ m. NE. by E. of Bethune.
Trivelet, 2 m. NE. by N. of Neuve Chapelle.
Turco Farm, 2¼ m. N. by E. of Ypres.

V

Valenciennes, 35 m. east of Arras.
Vandenberghe Farm, 1 m. WNW. of Wytschaete (*q.v.*).
Vanheule Farm, ½ m. SW. by S. of St. Julien (*q.v.*).
Verlorenhoek, 2½ m. ENE. of Ypres.
Vieille Chapelle, 5 m. NE. by N. of Bethune.
Vimy, 6 m. NNE. of Arras.
Violaines, 6½ m. east of Bethune.
Visé Bridge, over the Meuse, 8 m. NE. by N. of Liege.
Vlamertinghe, 2¾ m. west of Ypres.
Voormezeele, 2⅜ m. S. by W. of Ypres.

W

Warneton, on the Lys, 6 m. NE. by N. of Armentieres.
Wavrin, 13 m. E. by N. of Bethune.
Welch Farm, in the fork roads, 1¼ m. NNW. of Wieltje.
Westhoek, ⅞ m. north-east of Hooge (*q.v.*).
Wervicq, on the Lys, 8½ m. south-east of Ypres.
White Chateau, 1¼ m. east of Ypres.
Wieltje, 2 m. north-east of Ypres.
Wisques, 3⅓ m. SW. by S. of St. Omer.
Wit Huis (Maison du Passeur), on the canal, 6½ m. north of Ypres.
Witte Poort Farm, 2 m. east of Ypres.
Woesten, 5½ m. north-west of Ypres.
Woevre, district east of Verdun.
Wulverghem, 6½ m. S. by W. of Ypres.
Wytschaete, 4½ m. south of Ypres.

Z

Zandvoorde, 5 m. south-east of Ypres.
Zeebrugge, on coast, 13 m. ENE. of Ostend.

Zillebeke, 2 m. SE. by E. of Ypres.
Zonnebeke, 5 m. ENE. of Ypres.
Zouave Wood, $\frac{1}{4}$ m. south of Hooge (*q.v.*).
Zuydschoote, 5 m. NW. by N. of Ypres.
Zwarteleen, $2\frac{3}{4}$ m. south-east of Ypres.
Zwaanhof Farms (**N.** and **S.**), on canal, $2\frac{1}{2}$ m. north of Ypres.

LIST OF FOREIGN BOOKS

TO WHICH MORE THAN A SINGLE REFERENCE IS MADE

BAQUET : " Souvenirs d'un Directeur de l'Artillerie ". By General Baquet. (Paris : Charles-Lavauzelle.)
The author was Director of Artillery at the French Ministry of War, November 1914 to May 1915.

BAVARIA : " Die Bayern im grossen Kriege 1914–1918 ". Herausgegeben vom Bayerischen Kriegsarchiv. (Munich : Verlag des Bayerischen Kriegsarchiv.)
An official account of the operations of the Bavarian forces.

BINDING : " Aus dem Kriege ". By Rudolf G. Binding. (Frankfurt am Main : Rütten & Loenig.)
Diary and reminiscences of the war. The author was an officer of divisional cavalry in the *XXVI. Reserve Corps* in 1914–15.

FALKENHAYN : " General Headquarters 1914–1916 and its Critical Decisions ". By General Erich von Falkenhayn. (English translation, Hutchinson & Co., 21s.)
Falkenhayn was Prussian Minister of War in 1914 ; and Chief of the General Staff from September 1914 to August 1916, when he was superseded by Field-Marshal von Hindenburg. The book deals mostly with the successes of the Russian theatre of war, but contains much of importance as regards decisions in the West.

FRENCH ORDER OF BATTLE : " Les Armées françaises dans la Grande Guerre ". Tome X. Premier et deuxième volumes. (Paris : Imprimerie Nationale.) Ministère de la Guerre. État-Major de l'Armée. Service Historique.
This is an official work giving a summary in diary form of the composition and services of all formations down to and including divisions. From it an order of battle for any date in the war can be constructed.

GERMAN CONDUCT OF WAR : " Die deutsche Kriegführung und das Völkerrecht ". Issued by the German Ministry of War in 1919. (Berlin : Mittler.)
An official German apologia for alleged breaches of international law and usage.

GERMAN DIVISIONS : "Composition et historiques des divisions allemandes ".
A French official publication, translated as " Histories of the two-hundred and fifty-one Divisions of the German Army which participated in the War 1914–1918 ". (Washington : Government Printing Office.) It gives the composition, movements, engagements and station, year by year, of every German division.

HANSLIAN : "Der chemische Krieg ". By Dr. R. Hanslian und Fr. Bergendorff. (Berlin : Mittler.)
This is a manual of gas warfare. Dr. Hanslian was Staff Chemist and Gas Officer of the *XXII. Reserve Corps.*

HIERL : "Der Weltkrieg in Umrissen ", Vols. I., II. and III. By Lieut.-Colonel Constantin Hierl. (Charlottenburg : Verlag "Offene Worte ".)
An important summary of and commentary on the war, used, it is understood, for instructional purposes in the Reichswehr.

KÖSTER : "Die stille Schlacht ". By Dr. Adolf Köster. (Munich : Langen.)
This deals with the period February to September 1915. The author was Kriegsberichterstatter (official press correspondent) at German Great Headquarters.

MERMEIX : "Au Sein des Commissions ". By Mermeix. (Paris : Libraire Ollendorff.)
An account of the relations between the French Government, Parliament and the Army, before and during the war, right back to the Dreyfus Case. The " Commissions " mentioned in the title are the Committees of the Senate and the Chamber of Deputies on Army Affairs.

MÜLLER-BRANDENBURG : "Von der Marne zur Marne ". By Müller-Brandenburg. (Berlin : Verlag für Socialwissenschaft.)
A study of the causes of the loss of the war by a well-known Socialist pamphleteer, who served 46 months at the front in the artillery, eventually as a battery commander.

" OPÉRATIONS FRANCO-BRITANNIQUES DANS LES FLANDRES 1914– 1915 ". By " Ch.K." (? Captain Ch. Kuntz). (Paris : Charles-Lavauzelle.)
A brief account, with commentary.

PALAT : "La Grande Guerre sur le Front Occidental ". Vol. IX. By General Palat. (Paris : Berger-Levrault.)
A valuable unofficial compilation as regards the movements of the French. The ninth volume describes the December battle of 1914 and the offensives of 1915. The author is best known by his pseudonym, " Pierre Lehautcourt ".

REGIMENT NO. ....
These are the regimental war histories of German units. Nearly all of them are in the series " Erinnerungsblätter deutscher Regimenter ", published by Gerhard Stalling of Oldenburg. The history of the *5 Westfälisches Infanterie-Regiment Nr. 53*, for instance, is quoted as " Regiment No. 53 ". The volumes in the series are of varying length and

value ; some give detailed accounts of the fighting with extracts from the reminiscences of combatants ; others merely reproduce the official war diaries.

S. und G. : " Die Schlachten und Gefechte des grossen Krieges 1914–18 zusammengestellt vom grossen Generalstab ". (Berlin : Sack.)

An official list of the battles, compiled by the Great General Staff, showing the formations, etc., engaged in each, and giving lists of the higher commanders. It has an excellent index.

SCHWARTE : " Der deutsche Landkrieg Vol. II." Edited by General M. Schwarte. (Leipzig : Barth.)

This volume covers the period spring 1915 to the winter of 1916–17. The chapters are by various hands. That on " Second Ypres " is by the late Lieut.-General Balck.

SCHWARTE ORGANISATION : " Der Organisation der Kriegführung ". Edited by General M. Schwarte. (Leipzig : Barth.) Three volumes.

A complete account of the organization of the German Army and its institutions during the war.

SCHWARTE TECHNIK : " Die Technik im Weltkrieg ". Edited by General M. Schwarte. (Berlin : Mittler.)

An encyclopædic work, dealing with war material, naval, military and air, used in the war, and the application of science.

STEENSTRAAT : " Les Combats de Steenstraat, Avril-Mai 1915 ". By Commandant Willy Breton. (Paris : Berger-Levrault.)

A semi-official account of " Second Ypres " from the Belgian side, with sketch maps.

VOGEL : " 3,000 Kilometer mit der Garde-Kavallerie ". By Hofprediger Dr. Vogel. (Leipzig : Velhagen & Klasing.)

The author was chaplain of the *Guard Cavalry Division;* and the book is practically a war diary of the division.

WRISBERG : " Wehr und Waffen 1914–1918 ". By Generalmajor Ernst von Wrisberg. (Leipzig : Koehler.)

This gives an account of man power and munitions in Germany. The author was head of the principal department of the Prussian War Ministry. It is one of three volumes written by him under the general title, " Erinnerungen an die Kriegsjahre im Königlich - Preussischen Kriegsministerium ". (Recollections of the war years in the Prussian War Ministry.) The others, " Heer und Heimat " (Army and Homeland) and " Der Weg zur Revolution 1914–1918 " (The Way of Revolution), are concerned, respectively, with mobilization, the expansion of the army and supply of munitions, and the growth of the revolutionary movement as reported by the political bureau of the War Ministry.

Note.—The first volume of the series " Military Operations, France and Belgium 1914, Mons, the Retreat to the Seine, The Marne, The Aisne, August-October 1914 ", is quoted as " 1914 " Vol. i. ; The second volume " Antwerp, La Bassée, Armentières, Messines, and Ypres, October-November 1914 ", as " 1914 " Vol. ii.

CALENDAR OF PRINCIPAL EVENTS

Extracted from " Principal Events 1914–1918 " compiled by The Historical Section of the Committee of Imperial Defence, London. His Majesty's Stationery Office. 10s. 6d. net.

Western Theatre.	Other Theatres.	Naval Warfare and General Events.
	DECEMBER 1914	
	1st. *Austrian:* Second German offensive against Warsaw (begun 16th November) continues. Battle of Lodz.	8th. Battle of Falkland Islands.
14th. December fighting in Flanders begins.	2nd. *Austrian:* Battle of Limanova-Lapanow. Austrian offensive in Galicia begins.	
	Serbian: Belgrade occupied.	
	4th-8th. *Mesopotamia:* First Action of Qurna.	
	15th. *Serbian:* End of second Austrian invasion.	
	15th. *Austrian:* End of Battles of Lodz and Limanova-Lapanow.	18th. British protectorate over Egypt proclaimed.
	17th. *Turkish:* Beginning of Turkish offensive in Caucasus.	
20th. First Battle of Champagne begins.		
20th-21st. Defence of Givenchy.		
	JANUARY 1915	21st. First aeroplane raid on England near Dover.
		28th. End of organized rebellion in South Africa.
First Battle of Champagne continues.	*Turkish:* Operations in Caucasus continue.	14th. Swakopmund (German South-West Africa) occupied.
		19th. First airship raid on England.
		24th. Action of the Dogger Bank.
25th. First Action of Givenchy.		28th. British War Council decide on Naval expedition against Dardanelles.

xli

CALENDAR OF PRINCIPAL EVENTS—(continued)

Western Theatre.	Other Theatres.	Naval Warfare and General Events.
	FEBRUARY 1915	
First Battle of Champagne continues.	3rd-4th. Egypt : Turkish attack on Suez Canal.	15th. Mutiny of an Indian battalion at Singapore.
	4th. Russian : Winter Battle in Masuria begins.	18th. German submarine blockade of Great Britain begins.
	19th. Dardanelles : First Naval attack.	
	22nd. Russian : Winter Battle in Masuria ends.	
	MARCH 1915	
First Battle of Champagne continues.	12th. Dardanelles : General Sir Ian Hamilton appointed Commander-in-Chief.	
10th-18th. Battle of Neuve Chapelle.		
17th. First Battle of Champagne ends.	18th. Dardanelles : Second Naval attack.	
	22nd. Austrian : Capitulation of Przemysl.	
	25th. Dardanelles : General Liman von Sanders appointed to command Turco-German forces.	
	APRIL 1915	
17th. Fighting at Hill 60 begins.	12th. Cameroons : Advance on Yaunde begins.	20th. Armenian revolt begins at Van.
22nd. Battles of Ypres 1915 begin.	12th-14th. Mesopotamia : Battle of Shaiba.	
22nd-23rd. Battle of Gravenstafel. First Gas attack.		

25th. *Dardanelles* : Landing at Cape Helles and Anzac.
26th. *Russian* : German Baltic offensive begins.
28th. *Dardanelles* : First Battle of Krithia.

MAY 1915

2nd. *Russian* : Battle of Gorlice-Tarnow (Austro-German offensive) begins.

4th. Italy denounces the Triple Alliance.

6th-8th. *Dardanelles* : Second Battle of Krithia.

7th. "Lusitania" sunk.

13th. *German South-West Africa* : Windhuk occupied.

19th-21st. *Dardanelles* : Defence of Anzac.

23rd. Italy declares war against Austria.

24th. *Austrian* : Battle of Przemysl begins. Italians cross Austrian frontier at midnight 24th-25th.

26th. Mr. Winston Churchill, First Lord of the Admiralty, resigns.

31st. *Mesopotamia* : Second Action of Qurna, Advance up the Tigris.

24th-30th. Battle of St. Julien.

1st-4th. Battle of St. Julien (continued).

8th-13th. Battle of Frezenberg Ridge.
9th. Battle of Aubers Ridge. Second Battle of Artois begins (ends 18th June).

15th-25th. Battle of Festubert.

24th-25th. Battle of Bellewaarde Ridge. End of Battles of Ypres 1915.

CHAPTER I

THE LAST WEEKS OF 1914

23RD NOVEMBER TO 31ST DECEMBER

(Sketch 1)

THE twelve months following the close of the battles of
" First Ypres " in October and November 1914 brought
little but disillusion and disappointment. The failure of
the enemy in the Marne campaign, and the defeat of his
attempt to break through at Ypres had put fresh hope in
the hearts of the Allies. Having survived the dangerous
initial stages of the war, when they were unready and
strategically surprised, they not unnaturally believed that
their chance had now come, and that a vigorous offensive
would enable them to drive the invader from French and
Belgian soil and obtain a decisive victory. Such expectation proved fallacious. Although Italy entered the war
on the side of the Entente in April 1915,[1] the great successes
of the year—the driving of the Russians out of Poland
and Galicia, and the conquest of Serbia — fell to the
enemy. The offensives of the Allies in the battles of
Woevre, Artois, Neuve Chapelle, Aubers Ridge and
Festubert in the spring, and of Champagne, Artois and
Loos in the autumn, resulted in heavy losses, without
any compensating gain. They brought no relief to the
Russians or to the Serbians. The expedition to the
Gallipoli peninsula failed to establish communication with
Russia by way of the Dardanelles and Bosphorus, and
succeeded neither in forcing Turkey to quit the enemy ranks,
nor in forming a pro-Entente group of Balkan nations to
menace the southern flank of the Central Powers.

In April-May 1915 the first use of poison gas—a weapon

[1] The secret agreement was signed 26th April. Italy declared war
against Austria on 23rd May.

forbidden by The Hague rules and by a special Hague Convention [1]—at Ypres and at Gorlice-Tarnow gave indication that the Germans would stop short of nothing, either fair means or foul, in order to achieve final victory. This appreciation was further emphasized by the development of submarine warfare and the sinking at sight of passenger ships. [2]

For the British nation the period was one of grave anxiety, but tireless preparation: the forging of material and the raising and training of new forces. The Old Army had been practically annihilated and the New Armies were not ready; the vast material resources required were only in course of production.

The effects of this unreadiness for action will become manifest as the story proceeds. Yet in spite of it, the British Expeditionary Force had not only to fight in its own defence, but also to take part in offensive battles in co-operation with the French. A great part of France—and a most valuable part—was in possession of the enemy; the withdrawal of German forces from the West to Russia undoubtedly offered an opportunity that might never recur; so General Joffre could not possibly let his Armies sit still and make no effort to drive the weakened invaders from French territory. The instructions from the Secretary of State for War to Sir John French [3] directed him to support and co-operate with the French Army and conform, as far as possible, to the plans and wishes of our Ally. He was subject to constant insistence and pressure from Generals Joffre and Foch to take the offensive. Apart from this, a factor which naturally had much influence on the British Commander-in-Chief, was his knowledge that the French Army and the French public at every opportunity expressed the opinion that the British Empire was not making its utmost effort for the common cause. They complained that the British troops had accomplished very little. Appreciated purely from the British point of view the situation seemed to demand something more than patient waiting until the British Expeditionary Force was completely ready to strike. It had for several months been constantly hammered by the enemy; the depression of some of the troops during the winter of 1914-15 was

---

[1] See Note II. at end of Chapter IX.
[2] S.S. " Lusitania " was sunk off Queenstown on 7th May 1915 ; the first hospital ship was sunk on 30th March 1916.
[3] See " 1914 " Vol. I. Appendix 8

evident. It was of the utmost importance as regards moral that our men should see that the enemy could be paid back in kind and was not going to have things all his own way. These various motives for offensive action tended to induce Sir John French to concur in General Joffre's plans, although, theoretically, it might have been wiser to have waited until the New Armies were trained, and guns and munitions provided. Fortunate it was that the choice of the German Supreme Command in 1915 to stand on the defensive in the West and take the offensive in the East removed the danger of serious attack. It gave the Allies the initiative in France, and allowed the British the time and leisure that they required to equip, organize, and train their new forces.[1]

But throughout 1915 the scarcity of war material, the small number of trained troops in comparison with the front to be held, and the uncertainty regarding reinforcements—some of which, together with precious munitions, were despatched to other theatres of war—made the task of the British Commander-in-Chief in France and his principal commanders immeasurably more difficult than it should have been. It is not unfair to say that in 1914 and 1915 these officers never had the means which would enable them either to conduct defence or undertake offence with reasonable confidence.

For the British leaders of all ranks, the year 1915 was a period of education and instruction. It taught them the handling of hastily trained troops and improvised formations, the employment of the new instruments of war, and the methods to be used in the attack of well-defended, continuous field positions. Neuve Chapelle, Aubers, Festubert and Loos were most valuable lessons in the staging of an offensive and in the comprehension of the enemy's methods. These battles were definite steps to the preparation for the campaign of the Somme in 1916, and as such it is but fair to regard them. The most important result, perhaps, was that the divisions of the New Armies, partially trained as they were, learnt that man for man, unit for unit, they were more than a match for the Germans. After 1915 the troops at the front, as they saw the arrival of the Kitchener divisions, the processions of heavy guns and the huge accumulations of ammunition, never despaired of winning the war.

[1] See Note II. at end of Chapter : " The German Decision to break " off the Flanders Offensive ".

A Period of Recuperation

23rd November to 13th December 1914

Sketch 1.   By the 22nd November, the date on which the Battles of Ypres 1914 came officially to an end, the redistribution, in progress since the 15th, of the line in Flanders between the French and British, had been completed. The Expeditionary Force now held a compact front of some twenty-one miles from Givenchy, near the La Bassée canal, to a point opposite Wytschaete. On either flank it had French troops, who thus occupied the Ypres salient.[1] The British line was held in succession from the right by the Indian Corps (Lieut.-General Sir James Willcocks), 2 miles ; the IV. Corps (Lieut.-General Sir Henry Rawlinson) 6 miles ; the III. Corps (Lieut.-General Sir William Pulteney) 10 miles ; the II. Corps (General Sir Horace Smith-Dorrien), with a cavalry division attached, 3 miles. The I. Corps (General Sir Douglas Haig) and the rest of the Cavalry Corps (Lieut.-General Sir Edmund Allenby) were in reserve behind the centre.

For nearly three weeks the exhaustion of both sides, coupled with bad weather, led to a lull in the operations. Shelling, sniping and bombing went on with varying degrees of intensity ; the British carried out several successful minor night operations in the last week of November ; and the German *112th Regiment* on the 23rd captured eight hundred yards of trenches east of Festubert from the Indian Corps. These were recovered by a counter-attack which lasted throughout the night.[2] Otherwise the enemy near Ypres was quiescent and observed to be digging a series of lines of defence, and to be erecting more and more wire, so that it became a jest that wiring was his national game.[3] The question of rear lines also occupied the attention of the Allies. Throughout the Battles of Ypres the Engineer-in-Chief (Br.-General G. H. Fowke), had had the matter in hand. Now a limited amount of digging, which served to mark out back lines, was done by battalions

---

[1] See " 1914 " Vol. II. p. 458.

[2] For gallantry in these operations, Lieut. F. A. de Pass, 34th Poona Horse, who was killed, and Naik Darwan Sing Negi, 1/39th Garhwal Rifles, were awarded the Victoria Cross. The losses of the Indian Corps were 58 British and Indian officers and 866 other ranks.

[3] Falkenhayn, p. 35, apologizes for the departure from the accepted German principle that only one line of defence should be constructed.

of the Territorial Force as they arrived and before they joined formations at the front; by French Territorials; and by civilian labour. There was no material for the construction of revetments, dug-outs, or even obstacles, such little as was available being required for the front trenches.

In spite of considerable lethargy and a marked disinclination on the part of the infantry to dig, the British front trenches were gradually improved and connected up. This was particularly necessary in the case of the parts of the line taken over from the French, where, as a rule, closed groups of trenches and support trenches separated by intervals had systematically been made. There was leisure to dig some elementary communication trenches, which at last permitted of reliefs being carried out by daylight. In Ploegsteert wood, the first " duck boards " were improvised. Picks and shovels, and other tools, however, were so scarce that one divisional C.R.E., speaks of them in his official diary as " worth their weight " in gold ". Supervision of work was difficult and slow, as it had to be carried out mainly at night. It imposed heavy labour on the senior officers, since owing to casualties the company commanders were as a rule young and inexperienced, and a battalion commander—still less a brigadier—could hardly inspect the whole of his front during the hours of darkness of a single night. The naming of trenches and posts, begun by the G.O.C. 11th Brigade, Br.-General A. Hunter-Weston, on the Aisne became a general custom.

Re-equipping and refitting of units went on apace. The most urgent matter was the organization of arrangements to enable the men to have a thorough wash, and to provide them, at least, with clean underclothing. Of this, however, there was not sufficient to give every one a change. Divisional schemes were therefore devised by which a first batch of men, after getting a bath in tubs provided in washhouses, factories and other large buildings taken over for the purpose, received new underclothing. Their original garments were then washed and issued to the next succeeding batch, and so on. There was no change of uniform to be had, so the khaki jackets, trousers and great coats were ironed, in order to destroy insect life, whilst the men were in the baths. Warm clothing in the shape of " Coats warm British " and goat-skin jerkins, and " comforts " were received in good quantities. A much appreciated ration of rum was issued. Entertainments for the men were also started, the first being inaugurated in Armentières with the help of artistes imported from Paris.

The improvement and widening of the narrow pavé Belgian roads was carried out with the assistance of French Territorials, Belgian troops and local labour. The building of huts for the men, to supplement the very dirty and insufficient local accommodation, and the erection of standings and shelters for horses, were undertaken mainly by the Engineers, with assistance from the troops. Charcoal burning, in order to furnish fuel for keeping the troops on duty in the trenches more or less warm, was put in hand. Though the rubbing of whale oil on the feet as a provision against frost bite in the water-logged trenches was recommended in General Routine Orders, no supply of this prophylactic was received for many weeks to come ; and worse than this there was a shortage of boots.

TRENCH STORES, AMMUNITION, REINFORCEMENTS, SCHOOLS

Plenty of timber and guncotton was available, but the quantities of other trench stores, particularly sandbags, that came to hand were very far from sufficient ; and when small quantities did reach railhead, there was no transport to bring them up.[1] A number of steel loophole plates sent out, each requiring a carrying party of six men, found no favour with the troops and were little used.

The Signal Service, under Br.-General J. S. Fowler, was fairly well equipped with stores for communication down to brigade headquarters. On arrival of G.H.Q. at St. Omer it had, with fine intuition, begun building, on permanent poles towards the front, open lines which were to do service for more than four years. Now the demand for cable for field telephones and lines up to the trenches, and for artillery service far outran anything that had ever

---

[1] By the end of January 1915, in which month one million sandbags arrived—a year later the issue was 30 millions for the month—the situation had greatly improved.

Engineer parks had been abolished in the years of peace succeeding the South African War, and by the 1914 regulations engineer stores were to be drawn on indent from the Ordnance. It soon became necessary to revert to the former system and reinstitute engineer parks and workshops. Similarly the Army Service Corps had to improvise workshops and depôts for the repair of its motor vehicles and storage of spare parts. The centralized system inaugurated in peace time for the issue and repair of all stores and equipment proved unworkable under the stress of war.

been contemplated, and could only gradually be satisfied. The divisional ammunition columns were made the intermediate echelon for the supply to the artillery. The first attempts at securing safety for cable lines by burying them in shallow trenches were made in some sectors, and these elementary efforts eventually developed into a highly organized system when the proper cables and instruments became available.

The Indian Corps, by virtue of its early initiation into trench warfare, had taken the lead, under its Chief Engineer, Br.-General H. C. Nanton, R.E., in the manufacture of trench mortars, grenades, periscopes and other trench appliances, which the troops were driven to improvise. Little of this nature had been received from home. The official returns show that the average number of hand-grenades issued to France weekly in November, was 70, and of rifle grenades, 630. The Commander-in-Chief in October asked for a minimum of 4,000 and 2,000 per month, respectively; but even this very moderate total had not been reached by March 1915. The favourite patterns of the improvised hand-grenades were the " jam pot ", " the Battye bomb ", and the " hairbrush ".[1]

[1] The recipe for making the " jam pot " hand-grenade of the period was : take a tin jam pot, fill it with shredded guncotton and tenpenny nails, mixed according to taste. Insert a No. 8 detonator and short length of Bickford's fuze. Clay up the lid. Light with a match, pipe, cigar or cigarette, and throw for all you are worth. During the winter a French cardboard friction lighter was obtained ; but this, unless secured by a tack, functioned almost at a touch, and was useless in wet weather.

The " Battye bomb " was so-called from Captain B. C. Battye, R.E., of the 21st Company Sappers & Miners, who initiated its manufacture in some iron works in Bethune—which afterwards developed into the " First " Army Workshops ". The pattern was based on the design of a rifle-grenade made by Major R. L. McClintock, R.E., at Bangalore before the war. It consisted of a cast-iron cylinder about 4 inches long and 2 inches in diameter, closed at one end, with serrations about half an inch square on the outside to facilitate its break up. The bombs, which were of a convenient size and weight to throw, were filled with an explosive, generally ammonal, and closed by a wooden plug, through a central hole in which detonator and fuze were inserted. The Nobel fuze igniter, of which large quantities were available in Pas de Calais coal mines, was used ; it was ignited by a light blow, and adapted to military purposes by the addition of a cap and safety pin.

In the " hairbrush " grenade a slab of guncotton was made fast by wires to a flat piece of wood of hairbrush shape, which afforded a convenient handle for throwing. It was ignited in the same way as the " jam pot " pattern.

As may well be imagined, the first and third of these extemporized missiles proved far from reliable. At a demonstration before more than forty generals and their staffs, when the officer in charge threw a " hairbrush ", only the stick went forward, the charge dropped to the ground. Some spectators fled, others crouched to the ground, but no explosion

Of trench mortars, twelve 3·7-inch experimental weapons are recorded as sent to France towards the end of December 1914, with 545 rounds of ammunition. They proved inaccurate, and the arrangement of the ammunition was conducive to premature explosion. An experimental 5-inch mortar was reported to be unsuitable, and a rifled 4-inch to have too many defects, which local efforts failed to remedy. Forty old Coehorn mortars, bearing the cypher of Louis Philippe, were, by the initiative of Lieut.-Colonel A. Rawlinson, obtained from the French. After infinite difficulties as regards ammunition—for the spherical shell propelled by black powder would not serve—they were, " faute de mieux ", actually used in battle at Neuve Chapelle and Aubers.[1] All the trench mortars improvised by the troops were more or less dangerous to use, and the firer was recommended to pull the lanyard from behind the cover of a traverse. They were evolved out of brass or steel tube of 88 mm., 93 mm. and 95 mm. bore, purchased locally, usually secured to a flat base, and aimed by adjusting a pair of legs. Ammunition proved even a greater difficulty than the mortar ; the flash of discharge was usually relied on to ignite a piece of time fuze attached to a " jam pot " or more elaborate shell.[2]

---

took place. After an interval, a search was made, and the charge was found—under the person of a general.

The first 48 Mills hand-grenades—which became the Service pattern No. 5 (until superseded by an improved Mark No. 23 in 1917)—were sent over by the War Office for trial on 15th March ; by the beginning of July 1916 the output was 800,000 weekly. In the interval, before it was manufactured in mass, ten other patterns of hand-grenades were sent out in small quantities from home, but very few during the first two quarters of 1915 : Hale's Service and Hale's Mexican Percussion ; Royal Laboratory's Light and Heavy patterns, with friction igniter ; Double Cylinder, Light and Heavy patterns, with Nobel fuze lighter ; Hairbrush with spring lighter (a copy of the German) ; the Pitcher, Ball and Oval grenades, with friction lighter (which was useless in wet weather).

At this period, the Germans had the " Stick Grenade ", with its own friction lighter, that was used throughout the war ; an iron ball grenade, with service friction lighter, too heavy to be thrown far, but very effective ; a percussion " Disc " grenade that was somewhat dangerous to handle ; and improvised " Stick " and " Hairbrush " grenades with the service spring lighter. The " Egg " grenade did not appear until 1917.

Periscopes were not issued officially in the B.E.F. until the end of January 1915, and then only one per battery.

[1] From Colonel Rawlinson's nickname, they were called " Toby " mortars.

[2] The whole output of trench mortars in the United Kingdom in 1915 was : 1st Quarter, 75, 2nd Quarter, 225, 3rd Quarter, 121, 4th Quarter, 524. The last total includes 304 Stokes mortars, of which 200 were issued to training centres in November 1915. The difficulty was not so much in the manufacture of mortars as of the ammunition ; of this, the output

As a substitute for trench mortars, among other devices catapults, actuated by a very strong spring, were tried. They sometimes threw a hand-grenade 40 or 50 yards, but occasionally sent it straight up into the air to descend on the mechanic. They were hard to conceal and, being impartial in action, did not find favour with the troops.

On the 21st December Sir John French telegraphed home that special measures must be taken to put the British Army on a level with the enemy by expediting the manufacture of both grenades and mortars ; but throughout 1915 the principal source of supply was the output of the Royal Engineer Army workshops and Ordnance workshops at Havre. Eventually, the last named, at great risk, were able to turn out 1,400 extemporised bombs per day for the 95 mm. steel trench mortars.

Gun ammunition was still very short. When, on the 16th-18th November, the II. Corps took over the Messines— Wytschaete sector, the 3rd Division had only 363 rounds per field gun and the 5th Division, 323 ; with a reserve of 6,828 in the park. The III. Corps reported a total of 45,551 for the field artillery, roughly 300 rounds per gun and howitzer, instead of the regulation number laid down (viz., 528 for field guns, and 280 for field howitzers, with 472 and 520, respectively, in reserve on the lines of communication).[1] Thus for these two corps there was in the field only about three-fifths of the regulation amount calculated on the experience of the Boer War, and really little more than a day's supply in a modern battle. For the I. Corps, there was even less, and little in reserve on the lines of communication.

As regards men, the situation was improving in the matter of numbers, and by the middle of December, the Army was reinforced up to about three-quarters of its establishment.[2] Of the officers, about one-third had joined

for the four quarters was 8,816, 42,753, 176,785, and 182,880 ; in the 1st Quarter of 1916 it was over a million, and in the 2nd Quarter, over two millions.

The Germans had three service trench mortars (*Minenwerfer*) light, medium and heavy, before the outbreak of war. (Wrisberg, " Wehr und "Waffen ", 1914–18, p. 75.) Schwarte, "Organization ", i. p. 162, states that only 160 had been issued at outbreak of war. The Chief Superintendent of Ordnance Factories, Woolwich, considered the form of their ammunition unsafe, and they were not copied.

[1] War Establishments, Part I. p. 5.

[2] The 1st Division when it returned to the line on 20th December averaged 20 officers and 840 men per battalion ; the 2nd Division, 19

since the outbreak of war. By the end of the year practically all the Army Reservists and the pre-war Special Reservists had been used up ; and although there was no lack of recruits for the old battalions—splendid material in spite of the attraction of the New Army—they took time to train. On the other hand, some of the drafts of partially trained Special Reservists and old soldiers sent to France were reported to have neither the physique nor the will to fight.[1] Many of these disappeared from the ranks during the hardships of the winter, but that some such men remained must not be forgotten in reviewing the fighting and the situation in the early half of 1915. Fortunately many convalescents, wounded in the early days of the campaign, began to return to their units.

By the middle of December there were twenty-two Territorial Force battalions and six Yeomanry regiments in France, and one more battalion and part of another regiment arrived before the close of the year.[2] There were then in France six Special Reserve siege or railway companies and six Territorial field companies of the Royal Engineers. The latter were sent to divisions to give to each of them three field companies instead of two. No complete Territorial Force division reached France until March 1915, although four had gone abroad to India and Egypt.

Other reinforcements which had landed or were in sight were the 1st Indian Cavalry Division (Major-General M. F. Rimington), which concentrated at Orleans on 16th November,[3] and the 2nd Indian Cavalry Division,

---

officers and 885 men ; the 3rd and 5th Divisions at the end of November, 22 officers and 770 men ; the divisions of the III. Corps somewhat less, and the 7th Division, a lower number still.

[1] On 16th December, Sir John French complained to the War Office that some of the reinforcements sent out were over 50 years of age, and had not fired a rifle since the South African War ; he mentioned two battalions which had been filled up chiefly by men of this class. Some Special Reservists of a Highland battalion could not speak or understand English. See also Chapter III.

[2] See "1914" Volume II., Appendices 2 and 4. Nineteen of the battalions were attached to Regular brigades before the end of the year 1914. Two of the Yeomanry regiments went to the 7th and 8th Divisions as divisional troops : the others were posted to cavalry brigades, so that an 8th Cavalry Brigade could be formed, making the 3rd Cavalry Division up to three brigades.

[3] It sailed from Bombay on 16th October, and arrived at Marseilles on the 7th November. On the 26th November divisional headquarters and the Ambala Brigade were sent up to Hinges, but the other two brigades were delayed by sickness amongst the horses and did not reach the front until 8th-10th December.

which arrived there a month later.[1] The Sirhind Brigade rejoined the Lahore Division from Egypt, detraining west of Bethune on the 5th and 6th December. The 27th Division (Major-General T. D'O. Snow, formerly commanding the 4th Division), mainly composed of troops drawn from overseas garrisons, completed disembarkation on the 23rd December.[2]

In addition to the general training of all new units and formations when they arrived in France, the development of schools of instruction—which was eventually to have so large a scope—was begun in the winter of 1914–1915. On the 22nd November 1914 the Machine-Gun School, with Major C. D'A. B. S. Baker-Carr, a retired officer of the Rifle Brigade as commandant, was established at Wisques, close to St. Omer. He had to begin by training six instructors ; but the first class of 8 officers and 100 other ranks joined on 14th December 1914. By the end of May 1915 some 280 officers, N.C.O.'s and men were passing through the school monthly. This number was not sufficient to meet demands, as in February 1915 the allotment of machine guns per battalion was increased from two to four. In June, therefore, the school was expanded to take two classes of 500 each per month, and in the same month a separate Lewis Gun School was established.

To provide officers efforts were being made at home by the O.T.C., Inns of Court, and Universities ; and, both at home and in France, by the Honourable Artillery Company. In addition a Cadet School was organized at Bailleul on 1st December 1914, with Major H. N. R. Cowie,[3] 1/Dorsetshire as commandant. At first it took for a month's intensive training 40 cadets ·whose initial instruction had been begun in the Artists' Rifles, converted by Sir J. French into an O.T.C. Battalion on its arrival in France. In March the School was moved to Blendecques, near

---

[1] It left Bombay on 19th November—its Secunderabad Brigade having sailed with the Indian Corps—reached Marseilles 14th-16th December, and Orleans 20th-24th December, but did not reach the front until 1st-4th January 1915. Major-General G. A. Cookson assumed command on 14th December 1914.

[2] For Order of Battle see Appendix 4. It arrived at the front without howitzers and heavy battery. Its field artillery consisted of three brigades of three batteries of 4-guns, as did that of the 28th Division, the next formed. These 18 batteries (72 guns) were created by expanding nine 6-gun batteries (54 guns) brought home from India, and adding the extra guns, equipment, horses and men required. In March each artillery brigade throughout the two divisions received a fourth battery, made up in France by reducing some batteries from six to four guns.

[3] Killed at Hill 60 ; see Chapter XVI.

St. Omer, and by May was turning out 200 cadets a month.[1]

THE VISIT OF HIS MAJESTY THE KING

During the period between 30th November and 5th December 1914, His Majesty the King paid his first visit to his Army in France, and was able to see practically all his troops, except those actually in the trenches. After inspecting hospitals at Boulogne, he visited G.H.Q., where the Maharaja of Jodhpur, the Maharaja of Kishangarh, Maharaja Sir Pertab Singh, the Maharaja of Bikanir, and Malik Umar Hyat Khan then with the Army in France, assembled to meet him. Accompanied by H.R.H. the Prince of Wales, he motored to the areas of all the corps, seeing troops of every division, and heavy batteries in action. Whilst at Merville, IV. Corps headquarters, the President of the Republic, M. Poincaré and the Président du Conseil des Ministres, M. Viviani, with General Joffre, arrived to call on His Majesty. He subsequently saw General Foch and the French army and corps commanders most intimately connected with the British Expeditionary Force—Generals de Maud'huy, d'Urbal, Conneau, de Mitry, Maistre, Dubois and Grossetti—and conferred decorations on them. His Majesty then paid a visit to the King of the Belgians, who met him at Adinkerke on the frontier, near Dunkirk, and conducted him to Furnes (13 miles east of Dunkirk) where a review of Belgian troops was held.[2]

---

[1] The following partial list will give some idea of the Schools gradually organized in France :

G.H.Q. : Lewis Gun and Light Trench Mortar, Machine Gun, Wireless, Cadet, and Royal Engineers ; and a Staff College Course, each winter.

Army : Artillery, Infantry, Signal, Scouting, Observation and Sniping, Mine, Trench Mortar, Anti-Gas.

Corps : Infantry, Bombing and Trench Mortar, Lewis Gun, Anti-Gas.

Cavalry Corps : Equitation, Signal.

Miscellaneous : Ammunition School of Instruction, Anti-Aircraft, Bridging, Cookery, Intelligence, Labour Corps Officers, Machine-Gun Corps, Light Railway (Forward), Mechanical Transport, Officers commanding Field and Army troops R.E., Young Officers, R.A.M.C., Tank Tactics, Transportation Units, Chaplains.

[2] His Majesty's message to his troops is given in Note I. at the end of the Chapter.

The December Fighting in Flanders

14th to 24th December 1914 [1]

From the 23rd November onwards, movements of German transport to the rear had been observed, and occasionally columns of troops had been caught on the march by the British artillery ; but it was some time before the Intelligence Branch could state with any certainty what divisions had left the British front.   On the 3rd December the movement of the *48th Reserve Division* (*XXIV. Reserve Corps*) and *26th Division* was, however, ascertained, and two days later part of the *26th Division* was identified in Poland.   On 9th December information was received from Russia that the *II. Corps*, *XIII. Corps* (*26th Division* and *25th Reserve Division*), *XXIV. Reserve Corps*, and most of the cavalry divisions had been transferred from the Western to the Eastern theatre.[2] This was correct, but the Russian General Staff reported also the transfer of the *XV. Corps*, *XXIII. Reserve* and *XXVI. Reserve Corps*, which had not taken place.   The continued presence of these formations on the Western front was fully established by the British Intelligence.   Actually, by the early part of December, eight divisions and four cavalry divisions had left,[3] and the situation was :

Allies.	*Germans.*
Béthune—Annequin—La Bassée Road [4]	
Indian Corps	*29th Division*
IV. Corps	*VII. Corps*
III. Corps	*XIX. (Saxon) Corps*

---

[1] The operations 14th-24th December have no special name in the French and British " Battle Nomenclature ", but a battle-honour is given for the " Attack on Wytschaete " on 14th December.   In the German they are officially known as the " December battle in Flanders " (S.u.G. p. 72).   The front of this battle is given as Arras to the Comines canal.

[2] See Volume II. p. 450, fn. 2.

[3] Including the *III. Reserve Corps* which proceeded to Russia on the 2nd December, its absence being noticed on the 6th.   Winckler's composite *Guard Division* remained in the north until the end of December ; it then rejoined the *Guard Corps* in Artois.   After a rest the whole corps proceeded to Galicia in April 1915.

[4] The Indian Corps took over Cuinchy (south of the La Bassée canal) and Givenchy from the French during the 11th and 12th December.

Allies.   *Germans.*

River Douve

II. Corps
{ *6th Bavarian Reserve*
Division
quarter of *II. Bavarian*
Corps

Wytschaete Hospice

French XVI. Corps
„ IX. Corps
„ XXXII. Corps [1]
„ XX. Corps
„ 87th Territorial Division
„ 89th Territorial Division
{ three-quarters of *II. Bavar-*
ian Corps
XXVII. Reserve Corps
XXVI. Reserve Corps
37th Landwehr Brigade
XXIII. Reserve Corps
XXII. Reserve Corps (part of)

Old Fort of Knocke (10 miles north by west of Ypres)

Belgian Army
Brigade of the French 81st
Territorial Division
{ *XXII. Reserve Corps* (part of)
Marine Corps [2]

Sea

Thus opposite the ten British and Indian divisions (including the I. Corps in reserve) were 6¼ German divisions; opposite the ten French divisions were 8¾ German; opposite the six weak Belgian divisions (32,000 rifles) with a French detachment—the equivalent of, say, four divisions—were 3¼ German divisions.

Map 1.   Towards the end of October it had been proposed, on the initiative of Mr. W. S. Churchill, the First Lord of the Admiralty, to make an attack up the Belgian coast in order to recover Ostend and Zeebrugge and prevent these ports from being used as torpedo and submarine bases. The French 42nd Division from Nieuport was to be employed in co-operation with Admiral Hood's squadron; but the severe fighting in front of Ypres during November had made such a move impossible. On the 7th December Mr. Churchill visited G.H.Q., and the scheme for recovering the coast up to the Dutch frontier was again discussed. The advantages that would accrue from such a move to both the British Navy and the Army were beyond doubt.

[1] Went out of the line 30th December.
[2] This had to guard against landings on the coast and, besides two divisions, included torpedo boats, submarines and aircraft.

As the new proposals involved shifting the British Ex- Dec. peditionary Force to the left of the line and therefore affected our Allies, a formal suggestion for their consideration was made on the 9th December to the French Government through the British Ambassador. Lord Kitchener promised the 27th Division as reinforcement for the operation. The French Government did not regard the plan with any enthusiasm, and referred it, as a military question, to their Commander-in-Chief ; and when he discussed it with Sir John French, General Joffre was not inclined to acquiesce. He had already made arrangements for a general offensive in the north to take place on the 14th December, and the operation proposed would in no way assist it.   The corps commanders to whom Sir John French spoke of the scheme were also opposed to it, and—in view of the weather and other conditions— suggested the recovery of the Wytschaete—Messines ridge as more feasible and more important from the military standpoint.   The plan was discussed in London on the 8th January but laid aside as likely to be costly in life and requiring more troops and ammunition than could at the moment be provided.[1]   On the 13th January however, on the suggestion of Sir John French, a final decision was postponed until the beginning of February.   The operation was eventually dropped, General Joffre strongly disapproving of it as a "mouvement eccentrique".   An advance up the coast could be no easy task, since the country between Nieuport and Zeebrugge for eight to nine miles inland—except for a very narrow belt of dunes, along which the Field-Marshal thought to make his main thrust —consists of dead-flat grass meadows without a vestige of cover, intersected and divided by drainage canals and wet ditches, where, with the water-level only a few inches below the surface, entrenching is impossible.   A landing from the sea near the ports, as was proposed and prepared for in 1917, does not seem to have been discussed.   Such a landing was possibly feasible in 1914 in good weather, before elaborate defences of the Flemish coast had been developed by the Germans.

A British proposal was made at this time for the amalgamation of the Belgian and British Armies, with a

[1] Sir John French asked for fifty Territorial Force battalions ; for 50 rounds per day per field gun for 10 to 20 days ; and for a sufficient number of heavy guns with a liberal supply of artillery ammunition of all kinds, but especially high-explosive.   At this time the output of field gun ammunition was only 13 rounds per gun per day.

Dec. view to obtaining the maximum effect from them. It broke down owing to the opposition of the Belgian and French Governments.

There remained, therefore, General Joffre's scheme. On the 30th November, in view of the information that the enemy was reducing his strength on various parts of the front, he had issued a warning order to the French Armies. He directed them to be ready to take the offensive in all sectors where it seemed possible, whilst providing adequate defences in other sectors, particularly broad zones of barbed wire. On the 7th December he addressed a letter to General Foch, forwarding a copy to Sir John French, in which he pointed out that the enemy's withdrawals were now so obvious and his resistance at certain parts of the front so slight, that it was necessary for the B.E.F. and the French Eighth Army (General d'Urbal) to proceed to partial attacks in the Yser district and around Ypres without waiting for the completion of the final preparations. The French Second (General de Castelnau) and Tenth (General de Maud'huy) Armies between the Oise and the La Bassée canal were to attack in conjunction with the troops in Flanders.

At the same time General Joffre sent precise orders to the French Fourth Army (General de Langle de Cary) in Champagne to be ready to attack northwards, while the Third Army (General Sarrail) covered its right. On the right of the Third again, the First Army (General Dubail) and the Detachment of the Vosges were to continue to make methodical progress. On the Aisne, to the west of the Fourth Army, the Fifth (General Franchet d'Esperey) and Sixth (General Maunoury) were to make diversions. All these moves were preliminary to a large scheme of operations that General Joffre was maturing, but did not disclose at the time.[1] In an interview with Sir John French, General Joffre explained his plan for the operations in Artois and Flanders. He asked that on the 14th December the British might attack all along their front, but strongly against Warneton—Messines, when d'Urbal's Eighth Army on their left would take the offensive against the front Wytschaete—Hollebeke.

General d'Urbal [2] in his orders for this operation which

---

[1] It will be dealt with in Chapter V.

[2] His Eighth Army consisted of the IX. XVI. XXXII. and XX. Corps, the 38th Division and the Groupement Hély D'Oissel (87th and 89th Territorial Divisions, the 7th Cavalry Division and the Fusiliers Marins Brigade).

were communicated to the British, directed the XVI. Dec. (General Grossetti) and XXXII. Corps (General Humbert) to carry out a surprise attack in the direction of Houthem, south of the Comines canal; and the right half of the IX. Corps (General Dubois) to advance similarly towards Zandvoorde and Gheluvelt. The rest of his forces were to demonstrate.

Sir John French's instructions,[1] issued at 7 P.M., on 12th December, were a little more explicit. In them it was stated that the objective was the line Le Touquet (on the Lys, opposite Frélinghien)—Warneton—Hollebeke, the French being responsible for the capture of Hollebeke and Wytschaete, the British for Messines and Warneton. The British attack was to be made by the II. and III. Corps— the right of the latter being held back—whilst the IV. and Indian Corps were to carry out active local operations with a view to containing the enemy on their front. The I. Corps and 1st Indian Cavalry Division were held in reserve. Admiral Hood's squadron was to co-operate on the coast, but this naval assistance was withdrawn after the 16th, as the operations were not considered worth the risk involved.[2]

Little space need be given to the account of the fighting on the 14th December and the following days. At a conference on the 12th with the general officers commanding the corps and divisions concerned, Sir John French considerably diluted the orders issued from his G.H.Q., and the operation became, not a simultaneous offensive, but an attack of divisions in succession from the left, gradually spreading southwards. He impressed on every commander that he was not on any account to get ahead of his neighbours in the attack—everybody was to wait for the man on his left. The attack was to be made in three stages. First, Wytschaete and the small wood [2] west of it were to be captured by the French and the 3rd Division; then Spanbroekmolen by the II. Corps; and finally Messines by the II. Corps, from the west, and the III. Corps, from the south. At first only the 3rd Division next to the

[1] Appendix 7.
[2] The First Lord telegraphed to Sir John French on 20th December : " We'are receiving requests almost daily from French for Naval support " on the Belgian coast. We regret inability to comply. The small vessels " alone cannot face the shore batteries, and to expose battleships to " submarine risks, unless in support of a land attack of first importance, " is unjustifiable ".
[3] Marked " Petit Bois " on the 1/40,000 map.

Dec. French was to push the attack with the " utmost determination " ; the 5th Division on its right was not to attack
at all with infantry, but " by activity in the trenches to
" convey the impression that an attack is going to be
" delivered ". Similarly, during the early stages of the
attack, the III. Corps was to " make demonstrations
" against the enemy with the object of holding him to his
" trenches ". As the III. Corps had a ten-mile front, it
could not be expected to do much more. No wire cutting
by the artillery was contemplated, and for crossing the
enemy's obstacles wire cutters and mattresses were provided or had to be improvised. In other respects, too,
no attempt at a properly arranged artillery preparation
on a considerable scale was made. The amount of support
to be given by the guns was left to the discretion of the
divisional commanders. The Commander-in-Chief, however, gave definite orders for the placing of the heavy guns
well back behind the line. The officers as they left the
conference felt that it had not been inspiring, and their
feelings were reflected in the course of the operations.

No progress was made on the 14th. The French XVI.
Corps next to the British did not succeed in capturing any
of the enemy's defences. In the 3rd Division (Major-
General J. A. L. Haldane), next to the French, the leading
companies of the 1/Gordon Highlanders (Major A. W. F.
Baird) and 2/Royal Scots (Lieut.-Colonel R. C. Dundas) of
the 8th Brigade (Br.-General W. H. Bowes) left their
trenches at 7.45 A.M. In crossing the 200 to 300 yards of
No Man's Land, they encountered heavy rifle and machine-
gun fire. The Gordons got within 50 yards of the German
line, but with uncut wire in front of them could get no
nearer. The Royal Scots were successful in reaching the
first trench on a front of 200 yards and took prisoner 42
men of the *5th Bavarian Reserve Regiment (II. Bavarian
Corps)* and captured two machine guns ; but could make
no further headway.[1] In this position the two battalions
remained until dark, when they were relieved by the
supporting battalions, the 2/Suffolk, with the 10/Liverpool
attached, and 4/Middlesex.[2]

The first objectives, Wytschaete and the wood west of
it, not being secured, and further action depending on this,

---

[1] Private H. H. Robson, 2/Royal Scots, was awarded the V.C. for
rescuing wounded under fire until rendered helpless by two wounds.
[2] The 1/Gordon Highlanders lost 7 officers and 248 other ranks out of
9 and 550, and the 2/Royal Scots, 6 officers and 97 other ranks.

no other attack took place on the 14th, and the shelling Dec.
of the German line brought far heavier retaliation.

The operations were continued in a half-hearted way
on the 15th and 16th. With the German trenches and
wire practically intact and the ground hopelessly deep in
mud, even the most determined troops could not advance.
On the 17th neither the French XVI. Corps nor the British
II. Corps moved, and the fighting died down, after the
French IX. Corps had advanced by sapping a hundred
yards on the Menin road and equally small progress had
been made near Klein Zillebeke and Bixschoote.

General Joffre now determined to discontinue the
attack in the north except near Arras, south of the British,
where the ground was harder, and begged Sir John French
to give what assistance he could. In consequence, at
10.40 P.M., on the night of the 17th, a G.H.Q. Operation
Order [1] was issued announcing that it was " the intention
" of the Commander-in-Chief to attack vigorously all
" along the front to-morrow with the II., III., IV. and
" Indian Corps ". In the details of the order, however, the
II. Corps was told merely to resume its attack in conjunction with the French XVI. Corps, and the III., IV. and
Indian Corps were directed to " demonstrate and seize any
" favourable opportunity which may offer to capture any
" enemy's trenches on their front ". No more than forty
rounds per 18-pdr. gun and twenty rounds per 4·5-inch
howitzer were allowed for the operation. Fog, however,
interfered with the main French offensive near Arras, and
near Ypres the Germans counter-attacked the French
XVI. Corps, so the British II. Corps did not move.

In the other corps the demonstrations ordered resulted
in six attacks being made in the 8th, 7th, 4th and two
Indian Divisions, by small bodies varying in strength from
a few companies to two battalions. Such ground as was
gained had to be relinquished, in most cases within a few
hours, either as a result of enemy counter-attacks, or owing
to the impossibility of consolidating—that is, fortifying the
position won—in the water-logged ground. In the close fighting the superiority of the German hand-grenades was very
marked. The casualties in these attacks were heaviest in
the IV. Corps, the 7th Division losing 37 officers and 784 other
ranks, and the 8th Division 17 officers and 240 other ranks.[2]

---

[1] Appendix 8.

[2] On the 19th December Lieut. P. Neame, R.E., who went up to
superintend consolidation by a battalion of the 23rd Brigade won the

20 Dec.　The British operations in Flanders were now formally brought to an end and further enterprises left to corps arrangements. The French operations in Flanders and Artois were also stopped, and the others, elsewhere than in Champagne, suspended.[1]

Sketch 1.　The German retaliation for the Allied offensive in Flanders came on the 20th December, and, as usual, against a weak spot in the line. At daylight on this day the whole front of the Indian Corps was severely bombarded by heavy artillery and trench mortars. At 9 A.M., ten small mines were exploded under the British trenches in front of Givenchy, followed immediately by infantry attacks, with much bombing, on Givenchy and the front northward to La Quinque Rue.[2] It soon became evident that the attack was a serious one. Givenchy, held by the

---

Victoria Cross for saving the situation by standing on the parapet and counter-bombing so effectually that he enabled the battalion to get clear.

The Victoria Cross was also awarded, for conspicuous bravery, on the same day, to Lieut. W. A. McC. Bruce, 59th Scinde Rifles and Private J. Mackenzie, 2nd Scots Guards, both subsequently killed : to the first for encouraging his men to hold on all day, though himself wounded ; and to the second for rescuing a wounded man after others had failed.

Private A. Acton, 2/Border Regt., and Private James Smith, 3/attached 2/Border Regiment (20th Brigade, 7th Division) were awarded the Victoria Cross for bringing in on 21st December, by daylight under heavy fire, wounded lying in No Man's Land.

[1] In Champagne, beginning on the 20th December, the French Fourth Army had attacked on a front of 20 miles east of Rheims, in the so-called " Winter Battle in Champagne ". The German front line of defences was captured after heavy fighting ; but otherwise the results were disappointing. According to French battle nomenclature the First Battle of Champagne lasted from 20th December 1914 to 17th March 1915 ; the German official " S. und G." pp. 74-82 discriminates between different periods, and makes the classification : 20th to 30th December 1914, " 1st Battle of Perthes " ; 31st December 1914 to 7th January 1915, " Trench warfare in Champagne " ; 8th to 13th January, " 2nd Battle of Perthes " ; 14th to 31st January, " Trench warfare in Champagne " ; 1st to 5th February, " 3rd Battle of Perthes " ; 6th to 15th February, " Trench warfare in Champagne " ; 16th to 19th February, " 4th Battle of Perthes " ; 21st February to 20th March, " Winter battle in Champagne ".

[2] The report of the German VII. Corps on this operation was subsequently captured. The mines were charged, with only 50 kg. (110 lbs.) each, from sap-heads driven close to the British line. An attempt to fire 300 kg. (660 lbs.) under a house held by the British, failed. The attack was carried out by two battalions of the 57th Regiment and four engineer companies on a 990 yard front, well supported by 8-inch howitzers and numerous Minenwerfer. It is claimed that 19 British officers and 815 other ranks were taken prisoner, with a German loss of 250 killed, 462 wounded in hospital and 459 slightly wounded. The last are not always counted in the casualty lists. (" 8th Bavarian Regt.", p. 100. " Lightly " wounded who remained with the troops [that is did not leave the corps " area] were often not entered in the casualty lists.") The figures give some idea of the additions that may have to be made to the German official losses before they can be compared with the British.

1/Manchester, was in danger, the trenches on either side 20 Dec. being lost, and in the front east of Festubert a pocket three hundred yards deep was made by the enemy.

At 2.30 P.M., G.H.Q. ordered an infantry brigade of the I. Corps to be sent to assist the Indian Corps ; at 3.17 P.M., another brigade, and at 8.25 P.M., two field companies. In compliance with these orders the 1st (Guards) Brigade (which included the London Scottish) reached Bethune at 3 A.M., on the 21st, and the 3rd Brigade (with the 4/Royal Welch Fusiliers, T.F.) at 7.30 A.M. Both brigades rested and then, soon after 12 noon, moved to the attack—the former with its left on Givenchy—reported still held by the 1/Manchester—and the latter with its right on the village, against the enemy's pocket near Festubert. The 2nd Brigade, despatched later in motor buses by G.H.Q. order, reached Le Touret (2½ miles west of Richebourg L'Avoué) at 3 P.M. It was at once ordered to retake the left sector of the Indian front near " the Orchard " (about a mile north-east of Festubert) which had been lost that morning. The three brigades of the 1st Division (now under Major-General R. C. B. Haking) [1] moved through the Indian troops, but were delayed in heavy water-logged ground by machine-gun fire. It was dark before they reached the neighbourhood of Givenchy, which the 1/Manchester, practically surrounded and despairing of assistance, had just evacuated. With the assistance of a company of the French 142nd Territorial Infantry which was on the ground, the 1st (Guards) Brigade recovered the village. But the concerted attack of the brigades was interrupted, and though most of the ground lost by the Indian Corps was retaken, a piece on the left, in front of Festubert, was not recovered, and the isolation of the three brigades in the dark made the position somewhat difficult. During the afternoon the G.O.C. Indian Corps had reported that his troops were quite tired out and unable to fight any more, and that they must be relieved at once or the consequences would be disastrous. At 6.30 P.M., therefore, G.H.Q. directed the I. Corps to replace the Indian Corps, which was to be gradually withdrawn into

[1] Major-General Sir D. Henderson, at the urgent request of the Secretary of State for War, had on the 19th December been recalled to resume command of the Royal Flying Corps. Br.-General H. R. Davies (Oxfordshire Light Infantry) took over the 5th Brigade, Br.-General H. C. Lowther (Scots Guards) received command of the 1st (Guards) Brigade, vice Lieut.-Colonel D. L. MacEwen, who had temporarily held it after the death of Br.-General FitzClarence. The 3rd Brigade was under Br.-General R. H. K. Butler (Lancashire Fusiliers).

Dec. reserve, leaving details to be arranged between the two corps commanders.[1] Although Lieut.-General Anderson stated that some of his men would not stay in the trenches any longer, the Meerut Division was retained to hold one and three-quarter miles on the left of the corps front, where a new line slightly in rear of the old trenches had been organized. General Haig took over formally from Sir J. Willcocks at 1 P.M., on the 22nd.[2]

Measures were immediately taken to bring up the 2nd Division, the 5th and 6th Brigades being conveyed by motor buses. At 9.45 P.M., the I. Corps issued instructions for the organization of the line into three divisional sectors. General Haking (with the 1st Division less the 2nd Brigade, but plus the 6th Brigade), General Monro (2nd Division, less the 5th and 6th Brigades but plus the 2nd Brigade), and General Anderson (Meerut Division) were placed in charge of them. The 5th Brigade remained in corps reserve at Locon. General Haig laid down that the first object to be aimed at was to establish the I. Corps in good trenches as a preliminary to taking the offensive later. Fortunately the day was fairly quiet, and by night time the Lahore Division had been entirely withdrawn.

The relief of the Meerut Division was gradually taken in hand by the I. Corps, and completed by 9 P.M. on the 27th, when the whole Indian Corps went into reserve. Its casualties since it came into the line had been 9,579.[3] The losses of the 1st Division in the operations for relieving it were 1,682.

THE FORMATION OF ARMIES

Sketch 1.   The British Expeditionary Force now consisted of eleven divisions and five cavalry divisions. It was decided

---

[1] Appendix 9.

[2] The failure of the Indian Corps to hold the line in which it had been for two months is attributed to : general ignorance of trench warfare and bombing, shortage of technical troops owing to a weak establishment, heavy casualties, lack of engineer stores, and too many troops exposed to shelling in the front trenches. It must be recalled that the climate and conditions of ground in a Flanders winter reacted adversely on the natives of a hot climate. Further there was in the Indian Corps at the time a lack of suitable clothing and of the accustomed special rations.

[3]

	Killed.	Wounded.	Missing.
British Officers	104	148	40
Indian ,, . . .	39	96	31
British Other Ranks . . .	349	1,246	566
Indian ,, ,, . .	905	4,370	1,685
	1,397	5,860	2,322

to reorganize it for fighting purposes into two Armies and **Dec.** on the evening of the 25th December instructions were issued for the change to take effect from 12 noon next day. The new order of battle was as follows :

First Army, under General Sir D. Haig :
  I. Corps (Lieut.-General Sir C. C. Monro) ;
  IV. Corps (Lieut.-General Sir H. S. Rawlinson) ;
  Indian Corps (Lieut.-General Sir J. Willcocks).

Second Army, under General Sir H. L. Smith-Dorrien :
  II. Corps (Lieut.-General Sir Charles Fergusson) ;
  III. Corps (Lieut.-General W. P. Pulteney) ;
  27th Division (Major-General T. D'O. Snow).

Cavalry Corps, under Lieut.-General Sir E. H. H. Allenby ;
Indian Cavalry Corps, under Major-General M. F. Rimington.

Major-General Horne took over the 2nd Division from General Monro : Major-General Haldane had a few days earlier succeeded General Wing in the 3rd Division.

Christmas 1914 was further marked by the gift from H.R.H. Princess Mary of a box of cigarettes or tobacco and a pipe to every officer and man of the B.E.F., and the institution at the end of December of the Military Cross (M.C.).

During Christmas day there was an informal suspension of arms during daylight on a few parts of the front, and a certain amount of fraternization. Where there had been recent fighting both sides took the opportunity of burying their dead lying in No Man's Land, and in some places there was an exchange of small gifts and a little talk, the Germans expressing themselves confident of early victory. Before returning to their trenches both parties sang Christmas carols and soldier songs, each in its own language, ending up with " Auld Lang Syne " in which all contingents joined. On part of the front where there happened to be two Irish battalions, the Germans suggested the prolongation of the cessation of fighting, naturally without result. There was to be an attempt to repeat this custom of old time warfare at Christmas 1915, but it was a small and isolated one, and the fraternization of 1914 was never repeated.

NOTE I.

Special Order of the Day by His Majesty the King

Officers, non-commissioned officers and men : I am very glad to have been able to see my Army in the Field.

I much wished to do so in order to gain a slight experience of the life you are leading. I wish I could have spoken to you all, to express my admiration of the splendid manner in which you have fought and are still fighting against a powerful and relentless enemy.

By your discipline, pluck and endurance, inspired by the indomitable regimental spirit, you have not only upheld the tradition of the British Army, but added fresh lustre to its history. I was particularly impressed by your soldierly, healthy, cheerful appearance.

I cannot share in your trials, dangers and successes, but I can assure you of the proud confidence and gratitude of myself and of your fellow countrymen.

We follow you in our daily thoughts on your certain road to victory.

GEORGE R.I.
December 5th 1914.

General Headquarters.

NOTE II.

The German Decision to break off the Flanders Offensive

General von Falkenhayn has stated [1] that at the beginning of November 1914, the Supreme Command could not conceal from itself that a thorough-going success was not to be obtained in Flanders. He gives as the reasons for this view the importance of the inundations formed by the Belgians and the constant access of fresh strength to the Allies. The heavy German losses in the West, especially at Ypres, had placed a powerful lever in the hand of the supporters of Hindenburg-Ludendorff and the school which asserted "the war must be won in the East ", and their plea for decisive action there was strengthened by the appeals of the Austrians for assistance, and the fear that if it were not given at once they might drop out of the war. Falkenhayn himself was convinced that the final victory must be obtained in the West ; but the pressure on him became so great that he had to yield. It was decided to stand on the defensive in France and despatch seven divisions, besides cavalry, from Flanders to the East, followed in January by three newly-raised corps, and one old corps replaced in France by a new corps. On 19th December 1914, according to Field-Marshal Conrad von Hötzendorf, Chief of the General Staff of the Austro-Hungarian Army, Falkenhayn had determined to renew the offensive in France after driving the Russians behind the Vistula. He said to the Austrian, in reply to the latter's arguments for pressing the campaign against the Russians to a decision : " We cannot wait so long. " We want (wollen) to begin our offensive in France at the beginning " of February ".[2] The fatal error of the decision to go to Russia

[1] Falkenhayn, pp. 33-4, 53-7.
[2] Conrad's " Aus meiner Dienstzeit ", v. p. 820. The conversation is reported at length, covering 5½ pages. Falkenhayn remained un-

is now recognized, as the following opinion of a well-known German general shows : " There is no doubt as to what the proper course " should have been in the spring of 1915. The Regular British " Army had suffered heavily in the battles of 1914, and could only " be reinforced gradually by volunteers from the United Kingdom " and Dominions, hardly trained as soldiers. The British Army " should have been so defeated that it could never develop into an " efficient ' million army '. It should have been like a newly-sown " field struck by a heavy hailstorm, which never recovers to bear a " full crop ; the result would have been certain if such storms of " hail and battle had been repeated several times in 1915, when " their fury would have been intensified by the hatred of the British " which justly filled every German heart." [1]

Falkenhayn, though he turned the German Armies towards Russia, remained of the opinion not only that a victory there would not win the war, but that it was impossible to obtain a decisive victory. He trusted, however, that " the success would be big enough " to check the enemy for a long time ". Such success was not obtained, and although the Germans conquered Poland and recovered Galicia in 1915, this could not prevent the Russian offensives of 1916. Just as the two corps sent from France in August 1914 failed to be in time for Tannenberg, the reinforcements for the East despatched from Ypres arrived too late to take part in the Lodz campaign, 14th-24th November. In these operations, under the direction of Hindenburg who had been appointed " Commander-in-Chief, East " on 1st November, Mackensen with the German *Ninth Army* attacked the northern flank of the Russian armies which had pursued after the abortive German-Austrian attack on Warsaw. The Germans gained a little ground, but the Russians suffered no disaster, and a large body of Germans only narrowly escaped capture east of Lodz by " the break-through of Brzeziny " on the 23rd-24th November.

The winter battle of Masuria, 7th-21st February 1915, carried out with the German *Eighth Army* and newly formed *Tenth Army,* achieved a tactical success by the capture of the greater part of the Russian Tenth Army in the Augustovo Forest, but it brought no change in the general situation.

Though the December fighting in Flanders is officially recognized in Germany by the award of battle names, as earlier mentioned, practically nothing has been written about it. The fullest account [2] says little more than that the Germans maintained their position and regained some unimportant loss of ground by counter-attacks. It is however stated that on the Givenchy—Festubert front, on the 21st 23rd December, that is after the I. Corps came up, " the " fighting was the heaviest on the West front during the winter of " 1914/15 ". The loss of the two villages, after they had been gained from the Indian Corps, is admitted, but is attributed to the numerical superiority of the British artillery.

convinced that the defeat of Russia would bring about the end of the war, as Conrad admits he himself believed, and said : " Without England "possibly, but not with England, and that props up (*stutzt*) France ". Where in France Falkenhayn meant to attack does not appear.

[1] General von Moser's " Das militärisch und politisch Wichtigste vom Weltkrieg ", pp. 24-5 (January 1926).

[2] Schwarte, i. p. 415.

CHAPTER II

AFFAIRS OF CUINCHY : FIRST ACTION OF GIVENCHY :
AFFAIR OF ST. ELOI [1]

(Sketch 1)

Sketch 1. DURING December and January [2] reinforcements from
the United Kingdom had gradually brought most of the
units of the Expeditionary Force up to war establishment,[3]
and in addition, several new formations had swelled its
ranks. The 27th Division, which, as already mentioned,
had arrived on the 23rd December, took over trenches from
the French 32nd Division on the nights of the 5th/6th and
6th/7th January, extending the British left from the
Kemmel—Wytschaete road northwards to St. Eloi.[4] It
was followed in the middle of January by the 28th Division,[5]

---

[1] These are the names assigned by the Battles Nomenclature Committee.

[2] On 25th January, Lieut.-General Sir W. R. Robertson succeeded
Lieut.-General Sir A. Murray as Chief of the General Staff of the B.E.F.,
the latter proceeding to London to become first Deputy C.I.G.S. and, in
September 1915, C.I.G.S. Major-General E. M. Perceval succeeded Major-
General H. H. Wilson as Sub-Chief, the latter being appointed Chief Liaison
Officer with French G.Q.G. Major-General J. P. Du Cane became Artillery
Adviser at G.H.Q. vice Major-General W. F. L. Lindsay, who went to
command the 50th (Northumbrian) Division.

[3] 23,575 reinforcements arrived during December 1914, and 23,815
during January 1915, but the G.O.C. First Army was compelled to report
that his troops were short of officers and N.C.O.'s of experience, and that
in some battalions neither the training of companies nor the general
cohesion came up even to a moderate standard of efficiency. The vast
majority of the trained men had fallen before the enemy in 1914. (See
also pp. 9-10.)

[4] The 27th Division, which had to make a 17-mile march to reach the
trenches, and whose troops were wearing only indifferent foreign service
boots—no new ones being available—suffered very severely from trench
feet. The French trenches taken over by the 27th and 28th Divisions
were in an exceedingly poor state, both as regards protection and drainage.

[5] The 28th Division, under Major-General E. S. Bulfin, consisted of

26

which extended the front northwards again from St. Eloi **Feb.**
to the Ypres—Zandvoorde road, taking over on the nights
of the 1st/2nd and 2nd/3rd February the front of the
French 31st Division, the remaining division of the French
XVI. Corps.[1] The 27th and 28th Divisions were organized
on 18th February into the V. Corps under Lieut.-General
Sir H. C. O. Plumer.

On 15th February the Canadian Division [2] commenced
to assemble in the Hazebrouck—Strazeele area, and on 27th
February the first of the Territorial divisions, the North
Midland (46th),[3] concentrated north of Cassel. Both
these formations required further training, and initiation
into continental warfare, but were available in case of
urgent need. In addition, a further number of Territorial
battalions arrived independently, and were attached, one
by one, to Regular infantry brigades. Thus by the end
of February there were in all 48 Territorial battalions in
France.

Whilst plans for 1915 were under consideration [4] the
British Expeditionary Force had no easy time. January
was a month of rain, snow and flood, and, although shelling
and incessant sniping continued by day, the maintenance
and repair of the trenches absorbed most of the attention
and energies of the opposing forces. The greater part
of the twenty odd miles of British front from Cuinchy in
the south to the Kemmel—Wytschaete road, south-east of
Ypres, lay in the flat low-lying meadows of the basin of

Regular battalions from India and overseas that had not been incorporated
in the 27th Division. Its artillery was formed like that of the 27th
Division, see footnote p. 11. The R.E. and divisional troops were mostly
Territorial Force formations. (See Order of Battle, Appendix 4.)

[1] There now remained two French corps, the IX. and XX., holding
the front between the British left, the Ypres—Zandvoorde road, and the
Belgian right about Steenstraat, a distance of 16 miles, and on 4th February
the British 2nd Cavalry Division took over 1,400 yards of the IX. Corps
front on the left of the 28th Division. There were behind this sector of
the front two French Territorial divisions, 87th and 89th, and three French
cavalry divisions, the 4th, 5th and 7th.

[2] See Order of Battle, Appendix 4. The Canadian Division was
commanded by Lieut.-General E. A. H. Alderson. The first Canadian
contingent, which included more than a division, reached England on
14th October 1914, and after training at Salisbury Plain during the winter,
the division embarked at Avonmouth for St. Nazaire in February. The
offer of troops by the Government of Canada, and the organization of the
Canadian Expeditionary Force have been narrated in "1914", Volume II.

[3] The North Midland Division was commanded by Major-General
Hon. E. J. Montagu-Stuart-Wortley, and was composed of men of Derby-
shire, Lincolnshire, Leicestershire, Nottinghamshire and Staffordshire.

[4] See Chapter IV.

Jan. the Lys and the Flanders plain. Here, throughout the
winter months, the clayey sub-soil holds up the water two
feet or less below the surface, so that the trenches were
perpetually water-logged. The Lys rose 7 feet, and in
places spread out to over one hundred yards in width :
the dike called the Rivière de Layes became a running
stream. Some trenches which could not be pumped out
and kept dry had to be abandoned ; in places the troops
occupied only isolated sectors of the fire trenches, dammed
at each end and bailed dry, a system of cross-fire from
posts on these "islands" being relied upon for defence ;
and breastworks sometimes took the place of trenches.
Even then the men in many parts of the line stood knee-
deep in mud and water, and had to be relieved twice
a day. There were many sick and heavy casualties from
frozen feet.[1]

The enemy's guns dominated the situation and added
to the general misery. Owing to the shortage of ammunition the British artillery could do little to moderate
his fire. At this period, the available allowance for the
field artillery was limited to four rounds per gun per day,
whilst the enemy not only seemed to have plenty of his own
manufacture, but fired captured ammunition found in the
French and Belgian fortresses.[2] One British commander
went so far as to direct his guns to fire what rounds they
had low over the heads of the infantry so that the
men in the trenches might be led to imagine that they
were getting some support. Nor had the British a
sufficient proportion of guns. When the 27th and 28th
Divisions took over from the French XVI. Corps, it was
found that this corps had been backed up by one hundred
and twenty 75-mm. guns, twenty-four 90-mm. guns and
six 120-mm. guns, whereas the British divisions had only
seventy-two 18-pdrs.[3] between them. The French had
practically held their front by artillery covered by an
outpost line, whereas the British were forced, owing to
lack of guns, to occupy the trenches more thickly, and
accept the cost in life and limb.

Indications that the Germans were beginning to mine

---

[1] Thus during January the two British corps of the First Army
averaged 2,144 officers and men daily absent sick, and the Second
Army about the same ; in succeeding weeks the numbers fell to about
half.

[2] See, however, Chapter III. as to German ammunition difficulties.

[3] The fourth battery per brigade did not join these divisions until
March.

on a definite system became apparent.[1]   The strength of Jan.
the British field companies R.E. was insufficient to take
counter-measures on an adequate scale and it was therefore
decided to organize special Tunnelling Companies.   They
were formed of professional miners and tunnellers with a
small Regular personnel, but it was not until the latter
part of February that the first batch of tunnellers arrived
in France.[2]

CUINCHY AND GIVENCHY

The front was never at rest ; but the principal combats
took place in two areas, the first in the neighbourhood of
the Brickstacks—a number of low rectangular blocks of
burnt brick, just south-west of the Railway Triangle in
front of Cuinchy, near the La Bassée canal.   The second
was near St. Éloi, south of Ypres.   Both happened at
the time to be weak spots, being held respectively by
the 1st Division, so terribly cut up at Ypres in November
1914, and by newly arrived divisions already severely
wasted by the winter conditions.   Regimental officers were
in agreement that none of the German attacks could have
succeeded had the British infantry been capable of the
" mad minute " rapid fire of the original B.E.F.

Near Cuinchy on the 1st January the Germans captured
a machine-gun post and some observation posts held by
the 2nd Brigade on the railway embankment, in front of
the general line.   A small counter-attack made at 10 P.M.
by part of the 2/K.R.R.C. failed to dislodge the intruders,
and another attempt by the 1/Scots Guards at 4 A.M. next
morning, though at first successful, was eventually driven
back, five out of the six officers in the action having become
casualties.   The posts were recaptured on the 10th, and
held against three counter-attacks, but regained by the
enemy on the 12th.   Early on the 25th January a deserter
brought notice of an enemy attack on a larger scale against
Cuinchy, now held by the 1st Brigade, and the French
on its right ;   and against Givenchy, held by the 3rd
Brigade.   An attack did take place an hour and a half
later, units of the German *84th Brigade (XIV. Corps)*
advancing south, and units of the *79th Brigade (VII. Corps)*

[1] On 21st February the enemy, by means of mines destroyed the
front trench of the 16th Lancers in Shrewsbury Forest north of Klein
Zillebeke—the 2nd Cavalry Division at the time holding 1,400 yards of
the French IX. Corps line.   The reserve squadron at once counter-attacked,
and only 40 yards of ground in depth and 100 yards long were lost, but
the casualties in the regiment were 10 officers and 47 other ranks.

[2] See Note at end of Chapter.

Jan. north of the canal. The fighting that took place was very instructive as regards the use of reserves to counter-attack, but can only be summarized here. In both cases the Germans penetrated to the keeps, or strong points, behind the support line, and there were stopped. North of the canal at Givenchy an immediate counter-attack was made by the local reserves,[1] the enemy was driven back, and the lost trenches were recovered.[2] Seventy-two prisoners were taken and 135 Germans buried. South of the canal there was delay in making a counter-attack, and although one was eventually carried out by part of the 1st Division reserve, the lost trenches were not recovered, and the British line south of the canal now formed a re-entrant, with a strong point at its apex. On the 29th the Germans made two further efforts to push their advantage here, but they failed before the stout defence of the 2/Royal Sussex and 1/Northamptonshire of the 2nd Brigade, which had relieved the 1st. On the 1st February the enemy captured, but was unable to retain, an advanced post on the railway embankment.[3] He left 32 prisoners behind. On the 4th February the 2nd Division relieved the 1st on this front, and two days later the 4th (Guards) Brigade, under Lord Cavan, having secured a good jumping-off place during the night, successfully pushed forward the left of the line, straightening it out and also improving the position on the right so as to make a better junction with the French. The German counter-attacks failed, although a large party approached the British line, shouting " Don't shoot, we are engineers ".[4]

St. Eloi

Near St. Eloi, the divisions of the V. Corps had little peace, possibly because the enemy realized they were new

[1] Each of the four battalions (1/South Wales Borderers, 2/Welch, 1/Gloucestershire, 2/R. Munster Fusiliers) had two companies in front line, one in local reserve and one in brigade reserve.

[2] There was one curious incident in which history repeated itself. When the enemy broke through on the left of the 1/Gloucestershire—the old 28th, which had fought back to back at Alexandria 1801, an action commemorated by its back and front cap badges—part of the battalion manned the rear, as well as the front face of the trenches, in order to deal with the Germans behind them.

[3] Lce.-Corporal M. O'Leary, 1/Irish Guards, received the V.C. for capturing two enemy barricades practically by himself, killing 8 Germans and capturing 2, on this day.

[4] This is a legitimate ruse, as the foe can, by taking proper precautions—e.g. challenging and allowing only one man to approach—avoid being deceived.

to the front. The 83rd Brigade of the 28th Division was Feb.-
attacked on the 4th February, soon after it had relieved Mar.
the French, and before it had made the trenches defensible,
and the 2/East Yorkshire suffered considerably. The lost
trenches were recovered, but local fighting with fairly
heavy casualties went on for a good many days. The
82nd Brigade of the 27th Division, next on the right of
the 28th, underwent a similar experience on the 14th and
15th. On the 18th February, the infantry brigades of the
28th Division, depleted by sickness, were relieved by the
9th, 13th and 15th Brigades as a temporary measure;
but the 27th Division remained in the line, and on 28th
February carried out a successful minor attack with parties
of Princess Patricia's Canadian Light Infantry.[1]

On the 14th March the Germans made a surprise attack
at 5 P.M. on a larger scale at St. Eloi, firing two mines.
They captured the village, the trenches near it, and the
" Mound " (an artificial heap of earth about thirty feet
high, and perhaps half an acre in extent, on the western
side of the knoll south of the village) from the 80th
Brigade of the 27th Division. There was severe hand-to-
hand fighting, in which the 2/King's Shropshire L.I. and
4/Rifle Brigade particularly distinguished themselves. An
immediate counter-attack could not be made, as owing
to the heavy shelling no reserves were kept near at hand ;
but after midnight one was carried out by Br.-General
J. R. Longley (82nd Brigade) with the 1/Royal Irish and
1/Leinster of his own brigade and the 4/K.R.R.C. of the
80th. He recovered the village and the trenches, although
part of the latter had to be evacuated at daylight, after
Lieut.-Colonel G. F. R. Forbes of the Royal Irish had been
wounded. The " Mound ", which gave good observation,
was not recaptured, the Germans having at once consolidated their position on it. A further German offensive
on the 17th was repulsed with great loss.

Sir John French, considering that the enemy was
showing too much initiative, issued a memorandum on
5th February in which he called attention to the importance
of constant activity and offensive methods, although
standing on the defensive. Thus he gave official authority
to what were known in the army as " raids ", local attacks
on a small scale to gain ground, take advantage of any
tactical or numerical inferiority on the part of the enemy,

---

[1] Lieut.-Colonel F. D. Farquhar (Coldstream Guards), who had brought
the " Patricia's " to France, had been killed on the 20th.

and capture prisoners for "identification" purposes, *i.e.* to determine what units were on a particular front.[1]

In all their attacks of entrenchments the Germans made great use of their trench mortars (*Minenwerfer*), and their general equipment of service material for trench warfare gave them an immense advantage over the British and French. In the earlier combats of the first months of 1915, it almost appeared as if the inexperienced British drafts that filled the ranks of the old battalions would not be the equals of the Germans in close fighting. Any fear, however, that such a condition of affairs was characteristic wore off as the weeks passed by. The British infantry and engineers, with improvised material, began to establish that moral superiority over the enemy, both above and below ground which they never again lost; whilst the artillery, which still had a good percentage of fully trained men, managed to hold their own, even when ammunition was lowest, and seldom failed to give assistance to their comrades of the other arms.

In closing this summary account of the winter period, it may be recorded that the very strict censorship of the letters of officers and soldiers was in March 1915 slightly relaxed by the introduction of the " green envelope ". A certain number of these were issued to every unit, and were in great request, as enclosures in them, though liable to censorship at the base, were free from examination regimentally, provided a certificate on the back was signed that the contents referred to nothing but private and family matters.

An account of the British lines of communication in 1915 is given in Note III. which follows this chapter.

NOTE I.

FORMATION OF TUNNELLING COMPANIES R.E.

The British Army had no organization for mining, although all officers and the majority of the men of the Royal Engineers received a short training in military mining ; and in 1907, consequent upon the experience of the siege of Port Arthur, an extensive mining

---

[1] See Note II. at end of Chapter. The first recorded "raid"— although earlier patrol work closely approached the nature of a raid— appears to be that carried out on the night of the 3rd/4th February 1915 by Lieut. F. C. Roberts, with 25 men of the 1/Worcestershire (24th Brigade, 8th Division), under the instructions of Major E. C. F. Wodehouse, commanding the battalion.

scheme had been carried out at Chatham. After the first battles of Ypres 1914 operations were evidently developing into siege warfare, and it was equally evident that the R.E. Field and Siege Companies had far too much other work in hand to provide personnel for mining. On 3rd December Lieut.-General Sir Henry Rawlinson asked for a special battalion for sapping and mining, and on the 28th, Major J. Norton Griffiths (now Sir John Norton-Griffiths, Bt., K.C.B., D.S.O.) of 2/King Edward's Horse, suggested the employment of " clay-kickers ", men specially skilled in tunnelling in clay, and the War Office was asked to send out 500. The Armies were instructed to proceed with offensive sapping and mining with such suitable personnel as they could find in the ranks, formed into " Brigade Mining Sections ". In February 1915, after some discussion, it was definitely decided to create eight Tunnelling Companies, formed partly, as suggested, by drafts of special men recruited in the United Kingdom, and partly by transfers of men of the mining trades already serving in units at the front. Twelve more companies were formed later in the year, and one more in 1916, when the men of the Brigade Mining Sections were absorbed into them or sent back to their original units. The first Canadian Tunnelling Company was formed in France in December 1915, two others arrived in March 1916, and a New Zealand and three Australian Tunnelling Companies arrived in March and May 1916.

NOTE II.

G.H.Q. MEMORANDUM ORDERING RAIDS

General Staff. G.H.Q.
British Army in the Field,
Operations Section.
No. O.A. 447.
Date, 5th Feb. 1915.

First Army.
Second Army.
Cavalry Corps.
Indian Cavalry Corps.

The Field-Marshal Commanding-in-Chief desires me again to draw attention to the importance of constant activity and of offensive methods in general in dealing with the enemy immediately opposed to us.

2. For reasons known to you, we are for the moment acting on the defensive so far as serious operations are concerned, but this should not preclude the planning and making of local attacks on a comparatively small scale, with a view to gaining ground and of taking full advantage of any tactical or numerical inferiority on the part of the enemy. Such enterprises are highly valuable, and should receive every encouragement, since they relieve monotony and improve the moral of our own troops, while they have a corresponding detrimental effect on the moral of the enemy's troops and tend in a variety of ways to their exhaustion and general disquiet.

3. Further, as you are well aware, enterprises of this nature constitute the most effective form of defence, since by throwing

upon the enemy anxiety for his own security, they help to relieve our own troops from the wearying and demoralising effects produced by expected attacks on the part of the enemy.

4. These minor operations should, of course, not be of an aimless character but should be based on a specific object, have a reasonable chance of success, and be commensurate with the losses likely to be entailed. They should be methodically initiated in accordance with the instructions of the Army Commanders, and must invariably be well thought out beforehand, and careful preliminary arrangements made for their execution.

5. By the publication to neighbouring troops of short accounts of successful and meritorious work, by promptly bringing to the notice of the Commander-in-Chief the brave deeds of individuals, and by other similar means, the endeavour should be to create throughout the different formations and units of the Army a keen spirit of rivalry and emulation.

6. The Commander-in-Chief would be glad if you would give this matter your special attention, and issue the necessary instructions to give effect to his wishes.

W. R. ROBERTSON.
Lieut.-General.
Chief of the General Staff.

NOTE III.

BRITISH LINES OF COMMUNICATION IN 1915 [1]

(In continuation of Note II. on p. 260 of " 1914," Volume II.)

Map 2 of " 1914," Vol. I.   The continuous growth of the Expeditionary Force in the winter of 1914 and the very large increase in strength anticipated when the New Armies should begin to arrive made it necessary to examine closely the possibility of maintaining through the ports of Havre, Rouen and Boulogne the force expected to be in the field in the ensuing spring.

Accordingly on 1st December the Inspector - General of Communications wrote to the Quartermaster-General, B.E.F. enclosing tables showing the maximum numbers which it was estimated could be supplied through the three ports, and the numbers, just twice as large, which were expected to be in the country before long. He proposed an examination by a party of representatives of various Directorates of the capacities of Calais and Dunkirk. To this, however, the Q.M.G. replied that the C-in-C did not consider the time ripe for a reconnaissance of additional base ports.

On 23rd December the I.G.C. again wrote to the Q.M.G. pointing out that it took six weeks or so to get a new base port into working order and urging that immediate steps be taken. By this time the Belgians were already installed at Calais ; as regards Dunkirk it was known that for various reasons the French were not anxious to permit of its use as a British base, there were also naval objections, and the General Staff considered that it was too near to the front, which as yet was not a stable one. So many considerations—political, naval and military, and questions of shipping, supply of

---

[1] Contributed by Colonel A. M. Henniker, C.M.G., R.E.

the civil population, etc., etc.—entered into the question, that it was not until early in April 1915 that an arrangement was come to with the French under which the British were to share Calais with the Belgians ; Dunkirk they were not to use at all. The actual lay out of the British installations at Calais was begun early in April and the regular daily loading of supply trains, in June.

A few months later the French consented to railway material destined for the Railway Stores Depôt and Wagon Erecting Yard at Audruicq (between St. Omer and Calais) being landed at Dunkirk on condition that everything was loaded direct from ship to rail and no British installation established there.

Up to about the end of 1914 the main bases of supply for the army had been Havre and Rouen, Boulogne being used at first mainly for individual passengers, mails, ammunition and wounded. But the general growth in the traffic and the development of Boulogne as a base for supplies soon showed the necessity of a re-arrangement and reorganization of the railway communications on the L. of C. By February 1915 the main requirements of a comprehensive scheme were beginning to emerge, and work was already in active progress on parts of it. The new arrangements came into force in part on 6th May and wholly (except that the daily loading of supply trains at Calais did not actually commence until the middle of June) on 28th May.

The main feature of these arrangements consisted in the establishment of two separate lines of communication, each fed by its own group of base ports and serving its own group of railheads. The Northern L. of C. starting from Boulogne and Calais, served a group of railheads used by the Second Army and Cavalry Corps ; the Southern L. of C. based on Havre, Rouen and Dieppe, served another group of railheads used by the First Army and Indian Cavalry Corps. The dividing line between the two groups of railheads was drawn east and west immediately north of the station of Thiennes (between Béthune and Hazebrouck).

On the Northern L. of C. trains from Boulogne were made up at the small and inconvenient marshalling yard at the Bassin Loubet in the docks. The bulk of the traffic from Boulogne travelled via Calais (avoiding the line of Les Fontinettes), St. Omer and Hazebrouck, and returned by the same route ; but a few trains travelled via the single line Hesdigneul-Arques. Traffic from Calais was marshalled at a new regulating station known as Rivière Neuve constructed during May and June just outside Calais, and then joined the stream of traffic from Boulogne, travelling to the front via St. Omer and Hazebrouck. The detrainment regulating station for reinforcements and new units was Hazebrouck.

On the Southern L. of C. large extensions were made at Abbeville to provide a larger and more satisfactory regulating station. West of Abbeville, until the Poix viaduct was repaired, trains from Rouen travelled via Abancourt, Gamaches and Longpré ; trains to Rouen travelled from Abbeville via Eu, Gamaches and Abancourt. North of Abbeville trains travelled to railheads via Etaples, St. Pol and Béthune (Fouquereuil), returning via St. Pol, Frévent and Auxi le Chateau. The detrainment regulating station of the Southern L. of C. was Béthune.

On both lines of communication the stations actually used as railheads varied almost from day to day and the general arrangements on the L. of C. did not remain the same for any long period. Early in 1916 the supply by rail was organized in *four* lines of communication.

A considerable number of improvements to stations and lines were carried out during 1915 by the British railway troops, who also began to operate railway yards and lines, *e.g.* first doubling and then, from 1st November, working the Hazebrouck—Ypres line.

CHAPTER III

MUNITIONS, RECRUITING AND MAN POWER IN 1915

MUNITIONS

THE Expeditionary Force had been seriously hampered at the battles of La Bassée, Armentières, Messines and Ypres, 1914, and during the winter of 1914–15 by the small number of heavy guns available, by the short supply of ammunition both for heavy and for field artillery, and by the general lack of trench stores and material of war. The British forces in all theatres, and their Allies, were to remain thus handicapped and inferior to the Armies of the Central Powers in respect of munitions throughout 1915 and well on into 1916. The result of this grave disadvantage on the operations in Flanders, as well as on those in Gallipoli, was far-reaching both as regards moral effect and material loss. The matter, although essentially technical, is inseparably connected with the history of the campaigns ; so that it seems desirable to explain how the deficiencies arose, and why, in spite of the immense resources of the British Empire, they were not immediately met. Without bearing in mind the munitions question, the difficulties of the British commanders cannot be fairly appreciated, nor the necessity fully realized for some balance of the available man power between the home front and the fighting front during a great war. Throughout operations in 1915 a careful tally of ammunition expenditure had to be kept by the General Staff of the B.E.F., and on more than one occasion—*e.g.* at Aubers and Festubert in May—the Chief of the General Staff had to report to the Commander-in-Chief—to use the phrase current at the time—" the battle must now cease " for lack of ammunition.[1]

[1] The French, though they had not to supply an army greatly increased by the improvisation of new divisions, had much the same difficulties as ourselves. (See General Baquet's "Souvenirs d'un Directeur de l'Artil-

The War Office plans for the increase of the output of munitions formed during 1914, the support afforded to them by the Cabinet and the difficulties encountered owing to lack of plant and suitable buildings, and still more owing to the unrestricted enlistment of skilled men, have been mentioned in the Introductory Chapter of the previous volume. By the spring of 1915 the orders placed by the War Office in the United Kingdom, either by direct contract, or sub-contract through the armament firms, had involved over 2,500 manufacturers in the production of munitions; in the United States the house of J. Pierpont Morgan & Company, of New York, had been appointed commercial agents for the British Government, and as regards much of the material required, for the Allied Governments also, in order to obviate competition. But the need of skilled labour for the armament firms at home had become the crux of the situation. Much of the new plant required had become available, but the hands to operate it were wanting. The delivery of munitions had fallen much behind what had been contracted for, and it became clear that not one-fourth part of what had been ordered would be ready at the specified time. The Secretary of State was averse from taking any steps or making any restriction that might affect recruiting, but, nevertheless, a beginning

---

lerie ", and Mermeix's " Au Sein des Commissions ". The latter has many valuable appendices giving statistics.) The causes of their difficulties, somewhat different from ours, were : the general mobilization for duty in the field of masters, managers and workmen regardless of their highly skilled services being required for the manufacture of munitions ; the lack of raw material in iron and coal due to the loss of the Briey Basin ; and complete want of preparation for expansion of factories.

As regards guns and general war material, the Germans never had any serious difficulties, for they entered the war well equipped ; but as regards ammunition, they were not so well prepared. General von Falkenhayn, the Chief of the German General Staff, has written : " By " mid-September [1914] the spectre of the shortage of ammunition was " already apparent. Consumption exceeded peace-time estimates many " times over. . . . Only those who held responsible positions in the " Supreme Command during the winter of 1914–1915 can form any " estimate of the difficulties that had to be overcome. Almost every shot " had to be counted, and the failure of a single ammunition train or any " other slight accident threatened to render whole sections of the front " defenceless ". But he concludes, " as early as spring 1915 the Supreme " Command was relieved of any serious anxiety with regard to ammunition " supply ". (Falkenhayn, pp. 11 and 44-5.)

General von Wrisberg, head of the General War Department of the German Ministry of War, whose " Wehr und Waffen " and " Heer und Heimat " give a full account of the organization of munition manufacture and labour in Germany, states in " Wehr und Waffen ", p. 15 : " A serious " want of guns and material, that would have had an injurious effect on " the front and the operations, never occurred, not even temporarily ".

had been made in this direction.   The War Office, through March.
the ordnance factories and armament firms, had issued
exemption certificates and badges to workmen whose
technical knowledge and skill were urgently required in the
production of war material.   Thus such men might remain
at work without incurring the reproach of being called
shirkers.   This protection, however, did not touch the
employés of the smaller sub-contracting firms, nor of those
engaged in manufacturing new plant, machinery and
machine tools, and in erecting the extensions to munition
factories.   Efforts were also made to get back to their
original employment skilled workmen who were already
serving; but the measures taken had very little result.[1]

The call on private firms not engaged on Government
work to release skilled engineers for munitions work was
also a failure.   This was due to the objections of the men
themselves to transfer, the difficulties of housing them when
transferred, the jealousy occasioned by the advantages that
the large firms obtained by the flow of labour directed to
them, in fact the general unpopularity of the scheme.   An
alternative proposal was made to allot work to places
where labour could be found, and where existing premises
and plant could be converted to munition manufacture, and
of grouping firms together for co-operative work—that is,
spreading armament work all over the country.   Although
thoroughly sound and eventually exploited to the utmost,
it did not promise immediate results.   Moreover the regular
armament firms had machinery standing idle for want of
hands, and the need of munitions was pressing.

On the 16th March 1915, therefore, by an amendment
of the Defence of the Realm Act, the Secretary of State
for War took powers to compel manufacturers to undertake
Government work if they had the necessary machinery, to
permit the transfer of their skilled labour if they had not,
and to give priority to Government work if they were
engaged on private contracts.   Before using these extensive powers Lord Kitchener first tried appeal and persua-
sion.   The firms affected were canvassed ; posters and
advertisements were issued calling for volunteers for munition work.   But neither masters nor men approved of the
scheme.   The results of the campaign were insignificant,

---

[1] By July 1915, the first date on which reliable figures are obtainable,
841 skilled engineers had been brought back on the "individual release"
system, and 4,184 by means of the "bulk" system, that is, by ordering
men of certain specified trades to be picked out.   The scheme applied
only to men still in the United Kingdom.

and at the end of March the munition workshops were still greatly undermanned. An official census of the machinery available for the manufacture of war material showed only one-fifth was being used for night shifts, and most of the remainder for only eight hours out of the twenty-four. A War Office committee, known as the " Armaments Output Committee ", was therefore appointed on 31st March 1915 to enquire into the best means of putting the Amendment Act into force.

All this time the most obvious remedies for lack of hands, which had already been applied in France and Germany—the dilution of skilled labour by unskilled, and the employment of women—were practically beyond the reach of manufacturers in consequence of the restrictions imposed by Trade Union rules.[1] To permit of such employment, fool-proof automatic machinery had been devised by the manufacturers, and where it could be done with safety, specifications had been made more elastic and the rigour of inspection reduced by the War Office.

The Trade Union rules in question were the prohibition of semi-skilled or unskilled men doing the work of skilled men ; prohibition of women doing men's work ; limitation of one man to one machine ; limitation of a man's output ; prohibition of union men working with non-union men ; demarcation of trades, that is to say the limitation of a tradesman to a particular class of work. By the rules, for instance, the working of a row of machines by semi-skilled persons under superintendence of a skilled operator was forbidden.

It will be appreciated what it meant to organized labour to surrender the result of long years of negotiation, and at times of open strife between the unions and the employers, and especially to relinquish them at a moment when the armament firms were thought to be making enormous profits. At first neither Lord Kitchener, nor the Board of Trade, nor the Government could bring about an agreement. On the 4th February, 1915, therefore, the Prime Minister appointed a " Committee on production " in engineering and shipbuilding establishments engaged " on Government work " to enquire and report how the productive power of the engineering establishments working

---

[1] Between the outbreak of war and 15th March 1915 only some 2,000 women and 30,000 unskilled males were taken on for armament work. Of the 78,946 women who volunteered between 16th March and 4th June 1915, only 1,816, owing to restrictions, could be engaged.

for Government purposes could be made fully available.[1] **March.**
Unfortunately the efforts of the committee towards con-
ciliation coincided with an outbreak of industrial unrest,
caused mainly by the rise in the cost of food, and based on
a demand for an all round increase of wages by reason
of the profits that employers were believed to be making.
In January there had been only ten labour disputes outstanding; in February there were 47 fresh ones, and in
March another 74.

As a result of the reports of the committee, the Cabinet
recognized that the profits of the employers, who stood
to gain all the financial benefits from the removal of Trade
Union restrictions, were the only real obstacle in the way,
and they were prepared to limit such profits. On the 11th
March representatives of the thirty-five workmen's as-
sociations concerned were invited to a conference at the
Treasury, and at a preliminary meeting these representatives
appointed a delegation of seven to act for them. As a
result of the conference an agreement was come to that
certain restrictions should be temporarily abrogated, and
dilution by semi-skilled and female labour permitted,
provided the persons so employed should be the first to
be affected by any discharges either during or after the
war. On their part the Government gave a written pledge
to limit the profits of all important firms engaged wholly
or mainly upon engineering and ship-building for war
purposes, and promised to use their influence to secure
the restoration of previous conditions as soon as the war
came to an end. No legal powers were immediately taken
to enforce the agreement, and though it eventually formed
the basis of the relations between the Government, the
employers and the unions for the rest of the war, it was
not received by the workers with much approbation or
sympathy. It was not indeed until 15th June, 1915,
under pressure of a Munitions of War Bill, the stipulations
of which are given later on, that the Treasury agreement
was definitely accepted by ballot of the members of the
Amalgamated Society of Engineers and other unions
concerned.

The War Office Armaments Output Committee [2] when

[1] The members were Sir George Askwith, Sir Francis Hopwood and
Sir George Gibb.
[2] Its members were : Lord Kitchener ; Major-General Sir S. Von
Donop, Master-General of the Ordnance ; Sir Herbert J. Walker, Chairman of the Railways Executive Committee ; Sir Algernon Firth, President

March. appointed on 31st March and asked " to take the necessary " steps to provide such additional labour as may be " required to secure that the supply of munitions shall " be sufficient to meet all requirements ", had a most difficult and delicate task before it. As the Committee was the direct and immediate forerunner of the Ministry of Munitions, its career and expansion and the evolution of its policy are of special interest. It did not last long as a separate and independent body. On the 8th April the Government formed the Munitions of War Treasury Committee—sometimes called " the Super-Committee "— to direct and give Cabinet sanction to the work of the War Office Armaments Output Committee. Mr. Lloyd George was appointed its chairman, and its members were Mr. A. J. Balfour, Mr. E. S. Montagu, Mr. A. Henderson, with Mr. G. M. Booth of the Output Committee, and representatives of the War Office, Admiralty and Board of Trade. Thus by its composition it was the first outward sign of the appreciation of the paramount fact that the production of munitions was no longer a matter for the War Office and Admiralty alone, but was about to affect the general trade of the country and involve the whole fabric of its industries.

The Output Committee began by endeavouring to provide a compromise between the War Office plan for manning the new plant of the recognized armament firms, and the alternative policy of the Board of Trade for encouraging co-operative groups and spreading the Government munition contracts. Within a week the committee decided on a division of the country into " A " and " B " areas. An " A " area comprised the district within a 20 miles radius of any one of the Royal Ordnance Factories or recognized armament firms. Such an area was to be treated as a preserve for the concentration of the flow of labour to such factories and firms. All other districts where engineering facilities existed were designated " B " areas, and in these the alternative policy of forming co-operative groups and allotting direct contracts to them was to be permitted. A more important step than the definition of the areas was the organization of central and local authorities to control them, as these were to form the framework on which the Ministry of Munitions

of the Associated Chambers of Commerce ; Mr. George M. Booth, Director of the Booth Steamship Co., etc., and Mr. Allan Smith, Secretary of the Engineering Employers' Federation.

was later to build. The central authority was nominally the Output Committee; but at first it consisted of practically only two members of this Committee, with a few clerks, in Room 367 at the War Office. The local authorities were the armament committees in the areas. These were of two types, corresponding to their work; in " A " areas, their main duties were the transfer of labour; in " B " areas, they organized co-operative groups, and contained for that purpose representatives of the Board of Trade, the employers and the Trade Unions. Both the War Office and the Board of Trade gave the fullest support to the Area Scheme, and facilities were afforded to members of the co-operative groups to visit the armament factories and obtain courses of instruction at them. But as regards the most pressing matter, the provision of hands to man existing machinery in the areas, the Output Committee failed owing to the labour difficulties already mentioned.

In the middle of April therefore Lord Kitchener sent for Colonel Sir Percy Girouard—an engineer officer who had been his director of railways in the Soudan and South Africa, and after being a colonial governor, was now at the age of 48 managing director of Armstrong's works at Elswick—to advise him personally, in conjunction with Mr. Booth, on the means for increasing the munitions output.[1] Sir P. Girouard had originally been an ardent supporter of the plans for assisting the armament firms, but after consultation with members of the Output Committee, both he and they modified their views. On the 20th April it was unanimously agreed that on the one hand the Area Scheme was impracticable, and on the other that a more extensive method of production must be organized than at present conceived by the armament firms. The main reasons for the abandonment of the Area Scheme were first, that sufficient skilled supervision to make " B " areas successful was not available; and, secondly, that the thirteen " A " areas contained a very large proportion of the surplus engineering capacity of the country, which was thus excluded from employment in " B " areas.

The 20th to 26th April was spent by Sir P. Girouard and Mr. Booth in visiting the local armament committees, and at Leeds they found the most promising solution of

[1] In September 1914 the Secretary of the Committee of Imperial Defence had suggested that Sir P. Girouard should be put at the head of an " emergency armament multiplication committee or department to set " on foot and develop the maximum possible output of guns, rifles and " ammunition etc."; but nothing came of this at the time.

the problem. This was to select a suitable factory in an area and concentrate workmen and machinery in it under one management and one supervision staff. It was the first step towards the realization of a national factory in each of the great munition areas.

Sir P. Girouard was invited by Mr. Lloyd George on the 26th April to lay his views before the Super-Committee of which he was now made a member. In so doing he gave it as his opinion that the co-operative group system was unworkable, in that the policy that relied on twenty or thirty groups of small firms in widely separated towns to produce munitions was uneconomical, apart from the difficulties of supervision and inspection. He proposed that the " A " areas should be enlarged and that the local armament committees should become the controlling agents on behalf of the Government and bring together, as far as possible under one roof, all the resources both in men and machinery in their respective areas. Large factories controlled by Government would thus be established in all the important engineering centres of the country, and whilst they were being equipped, the staffs could be sent to existing factories for instruction.

Sir P. Girouard's proposal was approved in principle by the Super-Committee, and it was later suggested that " the armament firms should build, organize, administer " and work the new factories which were to be outside of, " but if possible close to their own works ; also that they " should supervise the factories being built and organize " the labour and the supervising staffs, so that when the " buildings were ready the labour and staff could at once " be got to work in the new factories ".

The Government accepted the scheme on the 28th April, and Lord Kitchener appointed Sir P. Girouard and Mr. Booth to carry it out, as far as might be found practicable. He authorized them to act in all matters covered by the scheme without further reference to him. It will be observed that the proposals followed the principles adhered to by the War Office from the beginning, of the gradual expansion of the armament firms as opposed to spreading the work over the whole country. It was different, however, in that the new extensions were to be regarded as State factories, although, following the War Office plan, the capital outlay was either to be paid to the firm outright or included in the price of the orders that were to be placed. It also put an end to the system of sub-contracting which had caused resentment in many May. quarters.

The Output Committee, which Sir P. Girouard and Mr. Booth now controlled, ceased to be a departmental organization under the Master-General of the Ordnance. With the new powers conferred on it, it became not only the intermediary between the War Office and the local armament committees, but the recognized central department of the Government " for controlling the whole of our Imperial "output of munitions". It first turned its attention to the organization of the new national factories. It gave extensive powers for this purpose to the local armament committees, which were each asked to nominate an executive board of management. The local committees were authorized to rent and convert suitable premises, hire or purchase machinery, appoint staffs and engage labour. They set to work to do so with the greatest enthusiasm. Buildings in many cases were lent free of rent by large firms, towns and municipalities. In some cases the boards of management found it advisable to employ small contractors ; thus makers of biscuits, cutlery, jewellery, paper bags and such like became the manufacturers of various items of munitions for these local boards.[1]

Before the end of May twenty-five local armament committees had been set up, and contracts for shells and fuzes to a considerable amount had been placed by them for the War Office. Forty more were sanctioned between June and September.

To co-ordinate the work of the armament committees and their boards of management, an " Organization of National Manufacture Branch " of the Output Committee was established, and a special section formed to deal with the supply of labour.

Labour as ever was the root of all difficulties. To cope with the thorny question of the transfer of skilled engineers from commercial to munition work the Output Committee followed the lead of the North-East Coast Armament Committee. It appealed directly to the men themselves to volunteer, instead of through their employers or their trade unions, dealing afterwards with any objections raised by their masters. Volunteers for three months were to be allowed travelling and subsistence allowances,

[1] It is understood that the German stick hand-grenades were manufactured almost entirely by the toy industry, and artillery fuzes by the watch and clock makers.

May. guaranteed against wage reduction, and enrolled in a formation called the " King's Squad ". The result of this appeal, carried out by leaflets, placards and the newspapers, exceeded expectation, and within a fortnight 5,200 men had been entered. In June therefore, the scheme was enlarged and the name changed from " King's Squad " to " War Munition Volunteers ". By mid-July a body of over 100,000 fresh workers had been collected, from which the various boards of management, as well as the armament firms, were able to select such men as they required.

Another measure adopted by the Output Committee was devised to prevent recruiting for the army from interfering with munition work, for during the period January to May 1915 approximately 10,000 men had been drawn from the engineering trades for the fighting forces. On the 12th May the Committee secured that certain trades essential to the munition industry were barred from enlisting. It also took up with fresh vigour the schemes for the release of skilled men already serving, and for a more comprehensive system of the issue of badges. In addition a mission was sent to Canada early in May to arrange for the transfer of labour on a small scale. By the first fortnight in July a thousand skilled engineers had been imported in this way ; but the supply was found to be limited owing to the increasing number of contracts placed in the Dominion by the British Government.[1] Offers of assistance in men from Australia, New Zealand and South Africa were declined in view of the difficulties connected with testing the applicants, transport and distance.

Sir P. Girouard in a report to Mr. Lloyd George in April had drawn attention to the lack of arrangements to

[1] In Canada from September 1914 till November 1915 the Shell Committee, formed at the instance of Lieut.-General Sir Sam Hughes, the Minister of Militia, acted as the agents and contractors of the British Government. Its members were Colonel (afterwards Major-General) A. Bertram, Major-General Benson (Master-General of Ordnance), Colonel Harston (Inspector-General of Arms and Ammunition), Lieut.-Colonel Lafferty (Superintendent of Quebec Arsenal) and Messrs. G. W. Watts, T. Cantley and E. Carnegie. The Committee began by producing 18-pdr. shell shrapnel. In 1914, 3,000 were supplied ; in January 1915, 30,000. The total shipments in 1915 of 15-pdr. and 18-pdr. shrapnel and 18-pdr. and 4·5-inch high explosive shells amounted to over 5¼ millions. After the formation in England of the Ministry of Munitions the Committee was in November 1915 superseded by the Imperial Munitions Board, constituted on the lines of a company board, which acted as the representatives of the Ministry of Munitions in Canada. Mr. J. W. Flavelle was appointed Chairman and General Bertram, Vice-Chairman.

secure a flow of raw materials for the manufacture of May. munitions. On the 29th April a sub-committee was therefore appointed to investigate the sources of supply of the various classes of material. The Output Committee soon after was in a position to take control of the distribution of what was available, and to ascertain what fresh sources of supply were required. Early in July it formed a " Raw Material Department " and the Government then began to purchase raw material. Similarly on the 5th May the " Machine Tool Department " of the Output Committee was organized to control the supply and demand of machinery.

A further problem which confronted the Output Committee, as labour, material and machinery were not unlimited, was the co-ordination of munition requirements and the maintenance of proper proportion in the supply of all the various requirements of an army in the field. For instance, it was useless to have a good supply of heavy shell if there were no lorries to convey it to the troops. A balance too, not to say the prevention of competition, was required between the needs of the Army and the Navy. The Output Committee therefore obtained the appointment of a Joint Committee of the War Office and Admiralty to co-ordinate the requirements of these two services.

In the Armaments Output Committee a great central authority had now been established, with the legal powers and administrative machinery needed to organize the home front for military purposes. But more than this was necessary. It could not be permitted that the supply of labour in the country should be wholly absorbed for purely war ends in the supply of recruits to the fighting forces and of workmen to munition production. In a memorandum drafted by Mr. A. J. Balfour for the Committee of Imperial Defence, dated 1st January 1915, it was pointed out that the continuation of overseas trade must be considered, and " the maintenance of exports sufficient " to enable us to import and of trade actively sufficient " to enable us to borrow . . . not from the point of view " of national wealth, present or prospective, but from that " of national production required merely as an instrument " of military success in this war ". An united control and organization of the whole potential energy and the industries of the country was demanded. The Armaments Output Committee offered the framework of such an

May- office, but it was a departmental creation, though it derived
June. its authority from the Treasury Super-Committee. On the
26th May 1915 the Prime Minister, Mr. Asquith, announced
that a new Department of State, to be called the Ministry
of Munitions, was to be formed. Mr. Lloyd George would
be at the head of it. The Output Committee thereupon
ceased in name to exist, and in the course of the following
days its personnel moved from the War Office to No.
6 Whitehall Gardens.

The new ministry began its legal existence on the
9th June with the passing of the Ministry of Munitions
Act. It was organized on the 1st July 1915 into four
departments : " Secretariat and Labour " ; " Munitions
Supply " ; " Explosives Supply " and " Engineer Muni-
tions ".[1] Sir P. Girouard became Director-General and
Mr. G. M. Booth, a Deputy Director-General of Munitions
Supply.

Before this ministry began operations, the Munitions
of War Act, which was to invest it with the greater part
of its powers, became law. Its enactments applied to all
controlled establishments, that is, all factories employed
on munition work which the Minister of Munitions considered advisable to place under Government control.
Part I. prohibited strikes and lock-outs, and laid down a
system of arbitration ; Part II. gave legal sanction to the
agreement made between the Government, the employers
and the Trade Unions at the Treasury Conference on
17th-25th March, by which the trade union restrictions
limiting production were suspended, provided that employers' profits were properly controlled and the union
restrictions restored after the war. The profits of controlled firms, when the Government themselves were not
the employers, were limited to the average net profit of
the firm concerned for the two financial years preceding
the outbreak of war. The Bill, unfortunately did not
limit profiteering by private contractors, and this omission
opened the way to much subsequent strife. By Part III.
the powers given by the Defence of the Realm Amendment
Act of the 16th March to compel manufacturers to execute

---

[1] Up to this time engineer and trench stores (not grenades), mining
apparatus, explosives for engineer purposes and such like had been dealt
with, under the Master-General of the Ordnance, by the Department of
the Director of Fortifications and Works (Major-General G. K. Scott-
Moncrieff), the branch, F.W.3, under Colonel L. Jackson, being principally
concerned. Colonel Jackson was now transferred to the Ministry of
Munitions, and became Director-General of Trench Warfare Supply.

Government work and permit transfer of workmen, were July. extended to allow of skilled men and machinery being taken to fill the State-owned, State-erected, State-controlled and State-equipped national munition factories. The passage of the Munitions of War Act through the House of Commons was made the occasion for an attack on the Secretary of State for War, on the Master-General of the Ordnance, and on the War Office in general. This was followed by a campaign in the Press. The blame for failure to be ready in all respects can hardly be laid on the shoulders of Lord Kitchener, who had never served at the War Office before the war, and indeed had seldom been in England since he was a subaltern. At the trial of General Stessel in St. Petersburg in 1908 a thoughtful Russian remarked : " We are trying not the defender of " Port Arthur but the Russian people ", and similarly it may be suggested that the unreadiness for a great war was not the fault of the Army and Navy, or of any department or officer of State, but was the consequence of the want of forethought of the whole body of British electors, their representatives and their Ministers. A proper system of expansion of war industries could not have been elaborated in Great Britain during the leisure of peace, or provision made in advance for the abrogation in war of trade safeguards endurable only under the peace conditions of a very prosperous community ; for the whole spirit of the country was opposed to preparations for a great war.

Ten months were still to elapse before the activities of the Ministry of Munitions could bring effective aid to the fighting troops, and thus throughout 1915 the conduct of operations required that a constant watch should be kept on the expenditure of munitions. It was not until April 1916 that the deliveries under the first contracts for gun ammunition made by the new Ministry took place, and it was not until 1917 that all anxiety on the part of the military leaders was removed. Until the former date the great and constant increase in production of war material of all kinds—not only for the original six divisions, but for the Territorial divisions, which had not been expected to take part in a Continental war, and for the divisions of the New Army—was due to the foresight of the War Office in expanding the armament factories, and placing large contracts both at home and overseas in the first months of the war. That the supply of munitions was for long unequal to the demand, and that the expansions of the first years proved

July. inadequate to cope with it, may fairly be attributed to its unprecedented nature, and to the habits of economy ingrained in peace time in the War Office, which were only slowly and unwillingly discarded by the officials concerned.

The formation of a Ministry of Munitions was completed by the passing of the National Registration Act in the following month. The entire adult population was to be classified according to age, physical fitness, trade and residence, so that the man and woman power of the country could be organized as a single force working behind and feeding the battle front. It had the result, that in three years, by July 1918, three-fifths of the workers of Great Britain, male and female, were engaged on production and distribution work for the British and Allied Governments. During the first ten months of the war in spite of the shortage of labour and machinery, and notwithstanding the lack of housing accommodation and other inconveniences, the loyalty and devotion of the staff and workers of the Royal Ordnance Factories and the recognized armament firms had managed to increase their output ten to twentyfold. In the three years that followed British brains and hands were to build up an entirely new industry at a speed and on a scale that were unprecedented, and of an efficiency that was unrivalled in any of the belligerent countries. It not only met the most varied requirements of the development of modern warfare, but was finally a main factor in the defeat of the nation's enemies.[1]

RECRUITING AND EXPANSION OF THE ARMY IN 1915

A short account of Lord Kitchener's call to arms and the beginning of the expansion of the army was given in the previous volume.[2] A few more particulars to continue the story into 1915 are briefly recorded here. The actual arrivals of the new divisions in the theatre of war are mentioned in their proper sequence in the narrative of the operations.

The recruiting standard which had been raised on 10th September 1914 in order to check the enormous influx of recruits, for whom there were available neither uniforms, nor arms nor accommodation, was on the 11th October 1914

[1] Some statistical details of the supply and expenditure of munitions are given in the Note at the end of this Chapter.
[2] "1914," Vol. II., Introduction.

reduced to 5 ft. 5 ins. height. On the 5th November it **Aug.** was still further lowered to 5 ft. 3 ins.; at this it remained. No further attempt was made to limit the number of volunteers. During the eight months, November 1914 to June 1915, an average of 125,000 men a month enlisted for the Army and the Territorial Force. But the actual numbers per month varied greatly, being for instance 156,290 in January and 87,896 in February. Lord Kitchener's appeal on the 19th May for 300,000 produced no special result, the May numbers being 10,000 above and the June 10,000 below the average.

On 15th July 1915 the National Registration Act, already mentioned, came into force. It marked the beginning of a definitely organized plan of obtaining recruits, and formed a stage on the way to conscription which was introduced seven months later on 2nd March 1916. The Act was not a purely military measure; for under it the occupation and the capacity for other employment of every man and woman in Great Britain between the ages of 15 and 65 were registered on the card system. Thus it became possible to discover how many persons were engaged in each trade, and after giving consideration to the comparative needs of munitions, agriculture, etc., to decide how many workers of military age could be withdrawn from them for the army. As regards certain trades it was ruled that no workers, not even those of military age, could be spared. These trades were termed " reserved occupations ", and the cards of the men in them were " starred ".[1]

The registration was carried out on the 15th August 1915, and a month later, when the register was complete, the local authorities were directed to hand the cards of all men between the ages of 18 and 41 to the recruiting staffs of the districts. These men, except such as were " starred ", were then canvassed by the agents of the Parliamentary Recruiting Committee.[2] At the same time all the usual methods of propaganda : the press, cinemas, hoarding advertisements and recruiting marches, were vigorously set going again. On the 11th October Lord Derby was appointed Director-General of Recruiting and on the 16th he laid the " Derby Scheme " before the Parliamentary Committee and the Joint Labour Recruiting Committee.

[1] The total number starred was 1,605,629 : by October 1918 the number had risen to 2,574,860.
[2] See " 1914," Vol. II.

Under this scheme men were still allowed to enlist immediately; but others who chose merely to attest, with the obligation to come up if called on, were classified into 46 groups, according to age and married or single state.[1] An assurance was given on behalf of the Government by Mr. Asquith that unless the bulk of single men came in under the scheme, compulsory service for them would be introduced before married men who had attested were called to the colours.

The groups were opened on the 23rd October and when on the 15th December recruiting for them was closed, no less than 2,184,979 men had attested and 215,431 had enlisted for immediate service. The total enlistments for the Army and Territorial Force, which in the five last months of 1914 had been 1,186,337, in 1915 were 1,280,362.

Of the Dominion forces during 1915, the 2nd Canadian Division was organized in May, and the 3rd so far developed that it came into official existence at the end of the year. The New Zealand and Australian Division was formed in January 1915 and the 2nd Australian Division in August. South Africa in 1915 had over 40,000 men in the field in German South-West Africa, and after the capitulation of the Germans there on 9th July 1915, a force was formed for service in East Africa. Three new Indian divisions, the 10th, 11th, and 12th, were organized in 1915.

At home the First New Army of six divisions had been constituted on 21st August 1914 and followed within the month by the Second and Third. A Fourth[2] and Fifth were added in the middle of 1915. The divisions of the first three Armies were each concentrated in a definite training area. The units of the 1915 Armies on the other hand had to carry out their training in the districts where they were raised, scattered in billets and camps, and they were not, speaking generally, assembled in divisions until the first eighteen new divisions had left the country.

The story of the conversion of between six and seven hundred thousand civilians into soldiers, their equipment, and their organization into units, and the assembly of

---

[1] The first 23 groups included all single men between 18 and 41, a group for each year; the married men were similarly comprised in the remaining 23 groups.

[2] The original Home Fourth Army was constituted at the same time as the Third, but later its units were utilized for depôt and drafting purposes. The second Fourth and the Fifth Armies were composed of units raised by special committees, etc., and were not taken over by the War Office for administration until organized and equipped, but not armed.

these units into brigades and divisions is in itself an epic. There is no room to do it justice here and it must be studied in the histories of the various units and divisions, and in the volumes from the pens of some of those who "joined up".

Such was the emergency in France in the winter of 1914–1915 that instead of being used as training cadres, a framework on which to build the new battalions and batteries, the last units of Regular soldiers from oversea stations were formed into the 27th, 28th and 29th Divisions. The first two of them were sent to Flanders as soon as possible. Of the destination of the 29th more will be said. Thus there was only a very small leaven of trained officers and non-commissioned officers for the New Armies, and these when from foreign stations or the Reserve not always up to date. Battalions were built up on a nucleus of two or three officers and a dozen N.C.O.'s or less—in one case of one officer, born overseas and 23 years of age. One artillery brigade began life with a retired colonel and four second lieutenants ; a battery was constructed on a cadre of an ex-Volunteer infantry major and a band sergeant. Specialist units like Engineers, Army Service Corps and Field Ambulances had fewer troubles ; for men with professional qualifications were abundant and only required an initiation into the use of arms, the military methods of obtaining and accounting for stores and money, the differences between military and civil practice, the care of their men, simple movements, and working with other troops.

Every kind of equipment, uniform, even clothing, was at first lacking ; staves and sticks were used for rifles, water pipes for gun drill. Great was the jubilation when a few condemned rifles arrived or an old gun was unearthed from a museum : no service rifles or guns were available for training until November 1914 and then only a few. The lack of training manuals which could be understood and correctly acted on without explanation by an expert was a grave cause of delay and error.

The general methods by which officers were appointed were mentioned in the previous volume, but it must be realized that the New Army had to train its own regimental officers and N.C.O.'s. In time of peace, just before the war, with complete cadres of officers, N.C.O.'s and specialists, and recruits who had done their barrack square drills, it took just eleven months—at high pressure—to work through the course of training from squad drill to divisional exercises. In 1914–1915 with a superior class of recruit and the incentive of a foe at our gates, but with a staff of instructors wholly inadequate as regards numbers and without proper equipment, it was hoped to complete the training of the new divisions in six months. And the miracle was very nearly brought to pass. The extraordinary results attained in the leisure allowed us by our enemies will appear in the following pages, but that many of the new units were sent into battle before they were fit for the great ordeal, or their officers fully competent to handle them, will be evident. Further, it could not be expected that the units of the old Regular Army would, in 1915, be of the same fighting value as before. They had been watered down by reinforcements, first of half-trained Special Reservists (the successors of the old Militia), and time-expired re-enlisted soldiers past military age, and then by recruits attested since the opening of hostilities. Thus the old battalions were mere simulacra, bearing the glorious names of their former selves it is true, but except for being the immediate inheritors of tradition and experience, hardly better trained than the new units. It has been said—with only too much truth—that the New Armies never saw the Old Army: its men were dead and disabled before ever Kitchener's men set foot in France.

The new divisions deserved and required specially skilled handling, but here again the sudden expansion of the military forces caused difficulty. The brigade and divisional staffs were formed of retired officers, convalescent wounded officers, and others available at home. Fully qualified officers to fill these posts and all the other numerous staff appointments rendered necessary by the increase in the number of divisions at home and overseas, could not be found. Good-will, intelligence, and capacity for work, could not compensate for lack of training and inherited experience ; a class of specialist staff officers gradually arose, *i.e.* officers who understood the routine of one branch or department of the staff only.

It was with such extemporized staffs, formations and soldiers that the battles of 1915 were to be fought. And whereas it had long been recognized that hastily trained infantry require more than the normal proportion of artillery, over the whole Army lay the shadow of lack of guns and shortage of ammunition.

NOTE

Some Statistical Details of Munition Supply and
Expenditure [1]

HEAVY ARTILLERY

The British Army entered the war with 4 heavy guns, 60-pdrs., per division ; " the German heavy artillery according to plan, took " into the field at the outbreak of hostilities about 2,000 [heavy] " pieces of which three-fifths were on modern gun-recoil carriages. " [This would give the 104 divisions nearly 20 heavy guns each " instead of the British 4.] In the home fortresses were about " another 2,200 heavy guns of older patterns, exclusive of those on " fixed mountings (mostly modern coast defence weapons or behind " armour) ". [2]

By February 1917, the total number of German heavy guns in the field reached its maximum, 7,130.[3]

Although as early as September 1914 the British War Office appointed a committee of experts to discuss the provision of heavy artillery, by June 1915 the total in the B.E.F., in France, excluding the nearly worthless 4·7-inch guns [4] was, 15-inch howitzer, three ; 9·2-inch howitzer, fourteen ; 8-inch howitzer, four ; 6-inch howitzer (old), forty ; 6-inch guns, eight ; and divisional 60-pdrs., thirty-six ; [5] total 105. By October 1918, the total was 2,200.

FIELD ARTILLERY

As regards the lighter forms of artillery the B.E.F. was sufficiently provided, although at first old 15-pdrs. and Horse Artillery 13-pdrs. had to be used in the Territorial divisions instead of 18-pdrs., and the old 5-inch howitzer instead of the 4·5. But the deliveries for the new divisions fell behind the contracted times. Thus on 1st July 1915 only 803 of the 2,148 18-pdrs. had been delivered, and 165 out of 530 4·5-inch howitzers.

ARTILLERY AMMUNITION

As the campaign progressed the supply of ammunition rather than guns was the real difficulty, as will be pointed out from time to time in the narrative. And it was the manufacture of the fuzes, not of the actual shell—which it was easy to produce—that caused delay. By the end of May less than half the contract delivery of No. 80 fuze for the 18-pdr. had been made (870,000 instead of 1,770,000), and those for other natures of gun were equally behindhand. The difficulty in the provision of fuzes continued right on through 1916. Thus during the twelve weeks ending 29th January

---

[1] Hand grenades and trench mortars have been dealt with in Chapter I.
[2] Wrisberg iii. p. 53.   [3] Wrisberg iii. p. 56.
[4] The 4·7-inch Q.F. gun (on travelling carriage), firing a 45-lb. shell, was obsolete (see " 1914," Vol. II. p. 164 footnote), having been replaced by the 60-pdr. Its shooting had always been irregular and its shells unreliable, but the thin driving bands of the American-made shells used in 1915 made it even less dependable. Nevertheless, by going in to short range, the batteries managed to render important service.
[5] Only 37 out of 96 ordered for 1st July 1915 had been delivered.

1916, 10 million shell were delivered, but only 3½ million complete rounds could be sent overseas. Eight months later, in August 1916, there were 25 million 18-pdr. shell lying in stock awaiting fuzes. Throughout 1915 it may be said that the resources in ammunition were totally inadequate for sustained operations, as Sir John French was compelled from time to time to remind the War Office. To show the actual increase in production the case of the 18-pdr. will be taken—other types increased in much the like proportion :—

July 1914 production	.	. 3,000 rounds per month	
Sept. ,,	,,	. 10,000	,, ,,
Nov. ,,	,,	. 45,000	,, ,,
Jan. 1915	,,	. 93,000	,, ,,
March ,,	,,	. 174,000	,, ,,
April ,,	,,	. 225,000	,, ,,

But as the number of divisions and guns also rose, the actual receipts in France for the four weeks ending 28th April, though 200,000, amounted only to 10·6 per gun per day. For the 4·5-inch howitzers the figure was but 8·2 ;[1] for the 9·2-inch, 5 ; and for the 15-inch howitzer, one round per gun per day.

The production of ammunition had been complicated by the need experienced for an increased supply of high-explosive shell. At the outbreak of war the 18-pdr. fired shrapnel only, the 4·5-inch howitzer was allotted 70 per cent shrapnel and 30 per cent H.E. The experimental H.E. ammunition for the 18-pdr. issued in October 1914 proved so effective that a proportion of 50 per cent of it was requested by Sir John French. To convert the machinery which was making shrapnel to the manufacture of H.E. ammunition was out of the question ; for such a step would have reduced the supply of the former without producing any of the new shell for at least ten weeks. As it was, the introduction of a new type of shell delayed the delivery of the H.E. ammunition already contracted for. By May 1915, of the 481,000 rounds 18-pdr. H.E. ordered only 52,000 had been received, and of the 220,000 rounds 4·5-inch only 73,772. It turned out as the result of experience that G.H.Q. France considered the effect of small H.E. shell had been over-estimated and that it was inadequate to demolish deep and elaborate field entrenchments, for which heavy artillery was necessary. On 19th April 1915 G.H.Q. requested that the proportion of H.E. for the 13-pdr. and 18-pdr. guns should be lowered from 50 to 30 per cent. This view it maintained and in the preliminary bombardment at the battle of the Somme 24th June to 1st July 1916, inclusive, the British 18-pdr. fired 1,022,296 rounds, of which only 247,766, less than 25 per cent, were H.E. When, eighteen months afterwards, on the 10th January 1918, the scale of weekly requirements of 18-pdr. shell was fixed by the Ministry of Munitions, the quantities were :—shrapnel, 391,000 and H.E. 252,000 (including 17,000 chemical and 20,000 smoke shell) : that is about 33 per cent were pure H.E.

The campaign against the military authorities in England towards

---

[1] In February 1915 the British Commander-in-Chief in France limited the expenditure of 18-pdr. shell (no H.E. available) to 10 rounds per gun per day and the 4·5-inch howitzer to 8. In April the allotment was reduced to 3 rounds (no H.E.) for the 18-pdr. and 4·5-inch howitzer. (See Chapter XI.)

the later part of May 1915,[1] in which they were accused of starving the Army in France of H.E. ammunition was based on a misapprehension. What the B.E.F. lacked was heavy guns firing H.E. shell not H.E. for the field artillery which can accomplish little against material objects. There were at the time in France 1,263 field guns and howitzers but only, as before stated, 105 heavy guns and howitzers.

The strain on munition supply at this period was increased by the opening of naval and military operations against the Dardanelles. The output of ammunition was comparatively so meagre that it was not sufficient for France, and of necessity offensive operations in both theatres were starved. In summing up the situation on 12th June Sir John French wrote that the general result of the shortage of artillery ammunition had been (1) to cause anxiety during the operations on the Aisne in September 1914 ; (2) to make this anxiety acute during the later phases of the first battle of Ypres ; (3) to necessitate during the winter of 1914–15 the exercise of an economy that made it difficult to maintain a satisfactory moral amongst the infantry in the trenches ; and (4) to limit the scope of our offensive efforts during the spring of the year, to make them spasmodic, and to separate them by considerable intervals of time.

The trouble lay not in the lack of material or machinery, but in the failure to organize labour. Had it been possible to execute all contracts made there would have been at the end of May 1915, not 10 but 45 rounds a day for the 18-pdr., and 288 heavy guns and howitzers instead of 105.

RIFLES

The reserve of rifles was nominally 600,000,[2] and when war broke out the weekly output of the Enfield Government Factory was 1,000 new rifles and 600 bayonets. By the end of September the reserve had been depleted by 30,000 to make good the wastage of the first six weeks' fighting, and by 70,000 required to arm the Indian Corps at Marseilles. Of the 600,000 rifles required for the New Armies only 400,000 could be supplied, and these included 200,000 " training rifles " which were useless at the front. Of the 400,000 needed by the Territorial Force, only 240,000 had been found by mid-December 1914, but within the next few months a further 160,000 " training rifles ", or rifles of a foreign pattern, chiefly Japanese, became available.

The production of rifles takes longer to organize than that of any article of the soldier's outfit, and lack of them was a main factor in limiting the number of men put into the fighting line in 1915. Though foreign rifles were available in small quantities the difficulty

[1] The leading article in the *Daily Mail*, entitled the " Tragedy of the Shells ", is dated 21st May.

[2] The principles approved by the Army Council in 1913 to govern the stock of rifles were that

(a) A rifle should be held for every man of the Regular Army, Reserve, Special Reserve and Territorial Force. The total was put at 625,000.

(b) A reserve of 150,000 rifles resighted for Mark VII. ammunition and 100,000 resighted for Mark VI. ammunition.

This made a total of 875,000. As a matter of fact, there were 1,241,018 rifles and 66,111 carbines in possession of the troops or in stock in August 1914.

of providing another pattern of ammunition was a serious objection to their purchase. One hundred thousand Ross rifles were ordered in Canada on 15th September 1914, but none were received until the late autumn of 1915. By 21st October 1914, 781,000 Service rifles had been ordered for delivery by 1st July 1915, and 400,000 were then added at the suggestion of the Cabinet Committee on Munitions.[1] But only a small proportion of them was actually delivered to time. In November 200,000 rifles were ordered in America and a further contract for 1,500,000 was signed in April 1915, but the effect of all these arrangements was not felt until many months later.

MACHINE GUNS

At the outbreak of war there were 1,963 machine guns in the service and in reserve, all, except 105 Vickers, of the Maxim and Maxim Converted patterns. Fortunately Messrs. Vickers were engaged on contracts for their weapon for the Russian and Italian Governments, and were therefore able to accept an order for 192 given by the War Office on the 11th August 1914. In the first weeks of September this total was increased to 1,792 to be delivered by July 1915, at the rate of 50 a week. In November the order was further expanded to 200 a week or all the firm could produce. In February 1915 a contract for 2,000 was placed in America.

An order for 250 Lewis guns was given early in August 1914 and then a further order for 1,250 ; but, as the gun was only in an experimental stage when the war broke out, the company was not ready to manufacture before the 11th November.

Owing to general difficulties caused by shortage of labour, there were very considerable delays, and by July 1915 instead of 1,792 Vickers and 1,500 Lewis guns contracted for—a total of 3,292— only 1,022 and 621 had been delivered, a total of 1,643.

SMALL ARMS AMMUNITION

There was a total reserve of approximately 400 million rounds of small arms ammunition in the United Kingdom in August 1914, the authorized reserve having been increased in 1913. In spite of all endeavours to augment the output, this reserve had actually fallen at the end of the first eight months of war to some two millions, although the musketry practice of New Armies and other troops at home had, for a time, been considerably restricted, and the home output was actually rising from 26 million rounds a month in September 1914 to 93 million in May and 101 million in June 1915. Large orders were placed in America in September and October 1914, and the first supplies began to arrive in December 1914. In the next twelve months 150 million rounds were sent over. By the end of May 1915, the prospective deliveries for 1916 were approximately 300 million rounds a month.

[1] See " 1914," Vol. II.

CHAPTER IV

PLANS FOR OPERATIONS IN 1915

THE GENERAL PLAN

(Sketches 1 and 2)

TOWARDS the end of the year 1914 the British Government Dec. had become alarmed at the reports of large transfers of German troops from the Western to the Eastern theatre of war ; at the rumours of a shortage of ammunition in Russia ; and at the possibility of a decisive German success in the East enabling the Supreme Command to resume the offensive in Flanders with large numerical superiority. Sir John French was directed to put these views before General Joffre, and to enquire what he was prepared to do should this possibility develop into serious fact. Accordingly, the British commander-in-chief sought an interview with him at Chantilly on 27th December. At this time the Russians were holding their own well, although they had been forced, by Mackensen's attack from Thorn on 11th November against the exposed right flank of their advance from Warsaw, to retire ; to give up a belt of territory on their Polish front averaging fifteen miles in width ; and to evacuate Lodz (6th December) and Lowicz (16th December). Established now on a good line, they still retained the greater part of Poland, and occupied nearly all Galicia. General Joffre professed himself not in the least nervous about the situation, and firmly refused to consider the consequences of a Russian defeat. According to the notes of the interview made by the staff officer who accompanied Sir John French, the French commander-in-chief thought the British Cabinet " affolé ".[1] He admitted

---

[1] General Joffre subsequently somewhat changed his attitude and during the early months of 1915 several times expressed apprehension lest the Germans should call a halt in the East and bring back troops to France.

Dec. that the Russians had only about six weeks' supply of ammunition, but seemed satisfied that the shortage was merely temporary. He was sending two experts to Russia to explain the methods by which the French had greatly increased their own production, and to advise as to the improvement of the Russian output.

In the Balkans for the moment he thought all was well, as the Serbs had expelled the Austrians from their country and recaptured Belgrade on the 15th December. Ultimately, as they were much exhausted, they might require help, particularly if the attitude of Bulgaria changed for the worse ; but a military success of the Allies would certainly decide Tzar Ferdinand not to cast in his lot against them.

It was obvious that General Joffre was convinced that the final victory could only be achieved in France, and therefore rightly felt that it mattered little what happened in the minor theatres. Nevertheless, it seemed to the British Government that there was small prospect of any decision, and none of an immediate decision, on the Western front. Both belligerents had failed in their attempts to penetrate the line of their adversaries. There was naturally the strongest objection to seeing the New Armies thrown away and shattered in the attempt to accomplish the impossible feat, as it seemed, of breaking through the German defences in France. Various views were tentatively put forward, all having the exploitation of British sea power as a factor. The First Sea Lord, Admiral Lord Fisher, favoured the Baltic. The Secretary of the Committee of Imperial Defence, in a paper that he drew up at the request of the Prime Minister, considered that, failing the discovery of new weapons or methods of attack for use in France, we must go elsewhere ; that Germany could be most easily affected through Turkey ; and that in conjunction with Greece and Bulgaria three corps ought to be sufficient to capture Constantinople.[1] Mr. Lloyd George went further, and in a paper suggested that, leaving a large reserve near the coast in case of emergency, the whole of the rest of the B.E.F. might be taken from France and despatched to a new theatre.

The effect of these views on the general policy of the

[1] It was by the throwing in of a strategic reserve of exactly this strength that the Germans achieved their three great successes in 1917 : the defeat of the Kerenski offensive, the passage of the Dwina and capture of Riga, and Caporetto.

war is exhibited in a letter of 2nd January 1915 from Lord Jan.
Kitchener to Sir John French in which he said :—" I
" suppose we must now recognize that the French Army
" cannot make a sufficient break through the German lines
" to bring about the retreat of the German forces from
" Northern Belgium. If that is so, then the German lines
" in France may be looked on as a fortress that cannot be
" carried by assault and also that cannot be completely
" invested, with the result that the lines may be held by
" an investing force, whilst operations proceed elsewhere ".[1]

Once officially recognized, the problem as to whether
anything effective could be accomplished elsewhere opened
a large field of possibilities. After the project for an
advance towards Zeebrugge in co-operation with the fleet
had been laid aside,[2] the question of an alternative was
the principal subject of discussion at the meetings of the
War Council in London on 7th and 8th January 1915.
The question resolved itself into determining how to employ
the New Armies then in training in this country. Various
suggestions were put forward. The principal one and the
only one considered in detail was that the Central Powers
should be attacked from the southern flank by way of
Austria, where a decisive effect might be easily produced.
Austria, it was argued, was the weakest part of the hostile
combination ; she had been defeated in battle by both
Russians and Serbs and had already suffered heavily.
There were great racial antagonisms in the Austro-
Hungarian Empire ; in the southern part the population
was largely Slav and anti-German, and no doubt a British
expeditionary force landing there would receive a sym-
pathetic greeting. In the advance inland it would en-
counter a nation inferior in military efficiency to Germany ;
and if the campaign was successful probably Italy and
Rumania would enter the war on the side of the Entente.
The withdrawal of Austrian troops from the north, from
the Russian front, to meet the new menace from the
south would materially assist the Russian plan—the inva-
sion of Silesia. Communications were the main difficulty
in such an operation, but as sea bases Ragusa and Salonika
were mentioned.

In reply to this suggestion, Lord Kitchener explained
that the General Staff had already carefully examined an
operation in south-eastern Europe from three points of
view ; an attack upon Austria from the northern Adriatic

---

[1] For Sir J. French's views see p. 65.   [2] See p. 15.

Jan. assuming Italy to be an ally; an attack on Austria in
co-operation with the Serbian Army using Salonika as a
base; and an attack on Turkey. A landing in the northern
part of the Adriatic would be very dangerous owing to
Austrian submarines, unless the naval base at Pola were
first reduced, and this would be an operation of the first
magnitude. Ragusa was impossible as a base owing to
the difficulties of its hinterland, the ease with which the
port could be destroyed by the enemy and the lack of
sufficient roads; it had also been provided with artillery
defences since the outbreak of war. Salonika could only
be used if Greece were an ally, and in any case there
was, leading northwards to Serbia, only a single line of
railway, which would be constantly liable to destruction
by local bands.

An attack against Turkey by way of the Dardanelles
appeared to be the most promising operation from the
southern flank, as the Navy could take part in it.

The desirability of such an attack was increased by
an appeal from the Russian Government that had reached
the British Government a few days previously, on 2nd
January, and contained a definite request that the pressure
on the Caucasus front should be relieved by a demonstration against Turkey.[1] Lord Kitchener stated he had
already written to the First Lord of the Admiralty on
the subject, suggesting that the Dardanelles was the only
place where a demonstration might have some effect.
Many members of the Council, however, agreed that a
definite attack against the Dardanelles would, if successful, be most helpful. Apart from relieving the Turkish
pressure on the Caucasus front it would put Constantinople
under our control, and open direct communication with
Russia through the Black Sea. This would enable Russia
to resume exports, particularly of wheat, and thereby
restore her exchange which had fallen rapidly and was
causing much financial embarrassment. It would also
influence more than any other project the attitude of the
Balkan States in our favour.[2]

[1] The Turkish Third Army had advanced from Erzeroum in November,
and in December Enver Pasha himself, with a number of German staff
officers, arrived to take charge. It was evident that this was to be the
main Turkish campaign. The operations actually ended in a complete
fiasco, owing to the difficulty of communications, bad weather, and the
general incompetence of Enver and his satellites.
[2] The steps leading to the initiation of the Dardanelles expedition will
be found related at greater length in the volume on that campaign.

As a result of these discussions, the Government decided Jan. that the main theatre for the British Army should be the Western Front as long as the French required armed support ; but should the result of the next offensive indicate that no serious advance in the West was possible, then the British troops should be sent to some other theatre.

A Sub-Committee appointed by the War Council [1] met later in the day to investigate the employment of a military force in a new theatre of war. On the conclusion of their deliberations, there was general agreement that at the moment the most important place in which to create a diversion was the Balkan Peninsula. In co-operation with the Serbian Army, the object of the diversion would be to draw into the war the various Balkan States and forestall a German advance across the Danube into Serbia, which seemed imminent. For such an expedition Salonika was proposed as being the best place for disembarkation of troops.

In response to the Russian appeal for help Lord Kitchener had promised the Grand Duke Nicholas to make a demonstration against Turkey, though he offered little hope that it would seriously reduce the number of Turkish troops in the Caucasus. On the 19th January, however, after a decision had been taken at a War Council meeting on the 13th, a further communication was made to the Russian commander-in-chief and brought to the notice of the French Naval authorities by the First Lord of the Admiralty. In it the project for a naval attack on the Dardanelles was broached. The Grand Duke replied with enthusiasm, and the French also sent a favourable reply, promising co-operation. Preparations therefore were put in hand for a naval expedition, to take place about the middle of February, and on the 28th January the British Government definitely decided that the attack should be made.

By the end of January the situation therefore was that this naval expedition against the Dardanelles was being rapidly pushed forward, but that no military commitments were as yet made in any European theatre of war outside the Western Front. In the event of a decision to send a military expedition to the Balkans, it was considered that

[1] The Chairman of the Sub-Committee was Lord Kitchener ; the members were :—Mr. D. Lloyd George, Mr. A. J. Balfour, Mr. W. S. Churchill and Lieut.-General Sir J. Wolfe-Murray (C.I.G.S.), with Major-General C. E. Callwell (Director of Military Operations) in attendance.

Feb. the force should contain Regular troops only. The 29th Division, made up with the last of the British Regular battalions from overseas garrisons, and now assembling in the Midlands, was mentioned as the only division of this category available.

On the 19th February, at a time when the crisis in the Eastern European theatre happened to be at its worst,[1] although the Caucasus danger seemed to be over,[2] a meeting of the War Council was held to discuss further measures by which to assist the Russian Armies. Their losses had been exceedingly heavy both in men and material, and there was much anxiety for the future owing to lack of artillery, rifles and ammunition. This last difficulty had been acute since the declaration of war by Turkey at the end of October had closed the Dardanelles, leaving only two unreliable trade routes open.

The Prime Minister considered the most effective way to help the situation would be to strike a blow at the Dardanelles. Lord Kitchener agreed, but with certain reservations. He feared that if a sufficiently decisive defeat was inflicted on the Russians, the Germans would be in a position to bring back masses of troops very rapidly to France and there would be a great demand for reinforcements on the Western Front. He therefore considered that it would be a most serious decision to send the 29th Division, the only remaining Regular division, to the East, and was inclined to substitute for it the Australians and New Zealanders, as the garrison of Egypt was sufficient without them to repel any attacks on the Suez Canal. This reservation was eventually overruled, other members considering it essential that some Regular troops should

---

[1] The Russian offensive set in motion by the Grand Duke Nicholas early in January had driven the Austrians from the Carpathian passes and threatened to invade the plains of Hungary. Before the initial success could be consolidated the Central Powers launched two strong counter-attacks, one in the north, in East Prussia, and the other in the south towards the Carpathians. In East Prussia they forced back the Russians across the frontier and enveloped almost the entire Tenth Army in the Augustovo Forest. In the Carpathians three Prussian divisions rallied the retreating Austrians and attacked the invaders, whose supply difficulties along the bad ice-covered roads and through the deep snow of the high lying forests became increasingly worse as they advanced. After bitter fighting the Russian front broke, and the tactical failure was followed by a hasty and disastrous retreat back through the Carpathian passes. About the middle of February it seemed that the passes themselves would have to be abandoned.

[2] The Turks had been defeated at the battle of Sarikamish (29th December 1914–2nd January 1915).

be used for the expedition. The 29th Division was **Feb.** therefore ordered to prepare for embarkation for the Mediterranean; but it did not leave until the 15th March.

Sir John French was at once informed that instead of the 29th Division, the 46th (North Midland) Division, the best Territorial division then available, would be sent. It embarked on the 24th February and concentrated in France as we have seen, on the 27th.

THE PLANS FOR A COMBINED FRANCO-BRITISH OFFENSIVE EARLY IN MARCH 1915

Throughout the discussions both General Joffre and Sir John French had strongly deprecated the idea of sending French or British troops to any theatre of war other than the Western Front.   Although the French War Council approved of the British proposal for an advance in the Balkans, General Joffre was opposed to any French troops taking part.   Sir John French had represented a similar point of view when he personally attended the meeting of the War Council in London on the 13th January. He was optimistic and did not admit the impossibility of breaking through the German lines by direct attack. He had already written to the War Office on the 3rd January, " in view of numbers and German commitments " in Russia, it seems of the utmost importance that we " should strike at the earliest possible moment with all " our available strength ".   Breaking through, he urged, was chiefly a question of larger supplies of ammunition, especially of high explosive for destroying the defences ; and until the impossibility of breaking through on the Western Front was proved, there could, he said, be no question of making an attempt elsewhere.[1]

General Joffre, like Sir John French, considered it incumbent on the Western Powers, with their forces gaining daily in numbers and material, to take every advantage of the situation in an effort both to relieve the German pressure against Russia and, if possible, break through the German defences in France.

General von Falkenhayn's change of plans and the operations in Russia had led to 8 infantry and 6 cavalry

---

[1] Sir John French considered that although a victory of the Franco-British Armies in the West might force back the Germans to the Rhine, the ultimate decision of the war would have to be gained on the Eastern front.   Reply to Lord Kitchener, 2nd January 1915.

Feb. divisions being withdrawn from the Western Front during the last two months of 1914 to reinforce the 32 German divisions on the Eastern Front, and had also absorbed for the same purpose 12 infantry divisions of the new formations created at the German depôts after the outbreak of war. Instead of increasing as the months passed, the number of German divisions on the Western Front had therefore diminished from 106 in November 1914 to 98 in January 1915, and these below establishment.[1] Not only did the operations on the Russian front take away much of the man-power of Germany destined for the Western Front, but also a large quantity of artillery, ammunition and material. Thus towards the end of January, after local attacks at Soissons,[2] in the Argonne and near Verdun, the Germans found themselves compelled to adopt a purely defensive attitude in France and Belgium. General Joffre therefore wished to begin operations as soon as the weather and the conditions of the ground permitted. Although the War Councils in London and Paris had been discussing the possibilities of operations in some new theatre, the French and British General Staffs at Chantilly and St. Omer began to prepare elaborate plans for a 1915 campaign in France. In view of the situation on the Western Front and the subsequent failures of the French and British offensives in 1915, the wisdom of the decision to make trial elsewhere—provided that surprise was ensured—can hardly be questioned. But once the decision was reached, and British troops were to be detached for the purpose, all attacks in the West on a large scale—at any rate by the B.E.F.—should have been prohibited; for in 1915 there were neither the munitions nor the men to sustain two serious efforts with any hope of bringing either of them to a successful conclusion.

In forming their offensive plans the French General Staff were naturally greatly influenced by the importance

[1] The Germans had received no important reinforcements beyond the influx of the 1914 class of recruits, which had brought the strength of the normal infantry company to about 180 men, still 60 below establishment. It was estimated that at this period the average German corps contained about 80 per cent of its war establishment.

[2] On the 7th January the French on the Aisne holding the old front of the British 5th and 4th Divisions from Missy to Crouy and around Soissons, on the northern bank, had attempted to improve their position. The Germans replied by a counter-attack, and, a flood carrying away the French bridges, they were successful in gaining possession of the entire bridgehead, except in the small loop of the river just east of Soissons. The French lost over 5,000 prisoners and 35 guns. (Palat, ix. p. 81.)

of reducing the great German salient which bulged forward Map 2 of "1914," Vol. I. between Rheims and Amiens ; for it menaced communication between Paris and the north, and at Noyon its apex was within fifty-five miles of the capital. It was obvious that the enemy could not hold this salient if his lines of supply to it were cut. With the same views as those of General Foch three years later, the French plan aimed at the railways, and took into special consideration the long German communications through the occupied territory of Northern France. In the case of the German Armies holding the southern part of the line from the Swiss frontier through Alsace to the east of Rheims, sufficient roads and railways lay, generally speaking, directly behind them across the Rhine into Germany. On the other hand, the enemy Armies holding the two hundred miles of front between Rheims and the North Sea were in a salient, the northern side of which was a neutral frontier, and were dependent on long and circuitous communications that had to pass from the Rhine crossings at Cologne and Düsseldorf through a gap, limited on the north by the "Limburg Appendix", between the Dutch frontier and the Ardennes,[1] a block of ravines and forests, some eighty miles in breadth and sixty from north to south, lying immediately behind the centre of the German battle front. South of the Ardennes there was one double line now in enemy hands which, starting from the German railway system at Thionville, ran parallel to the German-French frontier through Longuyon, Mezières and Hirson and thence to Valenciennes. Only 12 miles from the defences of Verdun, although most valuable and useful, it obviously could not be depended on as a main artery by the Germans, albeit of immense value for shifting troops from one part of the front to another. After passing the "Limburg Appendix", and, in the case of the southern line after reaching Hirson, the railways and the main roads open out into the flat spaces of Central Belgium, and thence

---

[1] See "1914," Vol. I. Map 2. There were three double-line railways in this gap after the Visé bridge over the Meuse north of Liége, and a line to it, had been built early in 1915. Only one double-line railway crossed the Ardennes, from south-east to north-west, forming an important transversal : it ran from Luxembourg to Marloie, whence it bifurcated to Liége and Namur. Twelve miles west of this line, and nearly parallel, was a single line running from Longwy to Dinant. Another single line from St. Vith, in Germany, ran south-west to about the centre of the Longwy-Dinant line, but there stopped. The other lines in the Ardennes were under the normal gauge. (Extracted from Kretzschmann's " Die Wiederherstellung der Eisenbahnen auf dem westlichen Kriegsschauplatz".)

Feb. spread westwards to the plain of Flanders and southwards across the plain of Douai towards Paris.

The most vulnerable part of the northern lines of supply, two hundred miles in length from the Rhine, lay in the plain of Douai, which contains the important communication centres of Valenciennes, Aulnoye, Douai, Cambrai and St. Quentin. The plain itself, some thirty miles across, forms a natural gateway from the north into France, hemmed in on its eastern side by the Ardennes, and on the western limited by the Artois plateau,[1] a great square-shaped area of rolling upland, fifty to sixty miles in length and breadth, that reaches westwards to the English Channel (Boulogne—Abbeville).

Three lines of operation against these enemy communications offered prospects of decisive results. An advance from the Artois plateau eastwards, driving the Germans from its western border, north and south of Arras, and thence across the plain of Douai, would reach the centres of the communications of the German forces in the Noyon salient between Rheims and Arras. An advance from the Champagne about Rheims northwards against the Mezières-Hirson railway and subsequently the railways in the gap between the Ardennes and Holland,[2] would threaten the lines of supply of all the German Armies between Rheims and the North Sea. Thirdly, an advance from the Verdun—Nancy front northwards, through the Rhine provinces of the left bank, would sever the German communications close to the Rhine crossings and, in addition, would carry the war into the enemy's country.

With these three possible offensives in view, a number of local operations had, as already mentioned, taken place in November and December in Artois, in Champagne and in Alsace. In view of the experience gained, General Joffre decided, whilst continuing the attacks in Champagne, to prepare offensives both on the Artois plateau and on the Verdun—Nancy front. The attack from the Artois plateau was to be delivered in co-operation with that in Champagne, both being directed against the communica-

---

[1] The name Artois, though obsolete, is used in the French and British documents regarding these operations, and is therefore repeated here. At the time of the French Revolution in 1789, when the provinces of France were changed into departments, the Province of Artois was split up into the Departments of the Somme and the Pas de Calais.

[2] It was in an attempt to pass through the Ardennes and reach this that the French Third and Fourth Armies failed so grievously in August 1914, largely owing to the unsuitability of the ground for great operations.

tions and lines of retreat of the German Armies between **Feb.**
Rheims and the North Sea. General Joffre confidently
expected that a continued pressure on these fronts would
gradually weaken, and in a few months effectively break,
the enemy line. As soon as the Germans began to yield,
the offensive from the Verdun—Nancy front would be
delivered, in order to threaten and, if possible, cut the
German lines of retreat from Belgium across the Rhine.

In its essentials this scheme was the basis of all the
offensive operations that were to be carried out by the
Franco-British Armies on the Western Front in 1915. It
contained, too, the germ of the greater plan that, three
years later, was to bring victory. Sir John French desired
to co-operate as effectively as possible with the French.
He also particularly wished to foster an offensive spirit in
the Expeditionary Force after its trying and enervating
experiences of a severe winter in the trenches. On the
8th February he issued to Army commanders a memorandum in which he discussed the possibility of undertaking
offensive operations.

The trenches of the British First Army from Cuinchy **Sketch 1.**
astride the La Bassée canal and northwards through
Givenchy and Neuve Chapelle to Bois Grenier lay in the
mud of the Lys valley. In front of them, however, at a
distance of from one to four miles, was the long low elevation of Aubers ridge, some twenty miles in length, stretching
from La Bassée northwards to the west of Lille, and
forming the watershed between the Lys on the west and
the upper reaches of the river Deule (Canal de la Haute
Deule) on the east. Its top forms a comparatively flat
plateau of open arable land, and, though it never rises
more than forty feet above the plain, this is sufficient to
give a good command for many miles, both beyond La
Bassée in the south and beyond Lille in the north. With
its drier surface and its advantages for observation, this
ridge lay as a tempting bait opposite the front of the First
Army sitting in the wet meadows below.

The British Second Army continued the line of the
First northwards from Bois Grenier, eastward of Armentières to the semi-circle of hills that surround Ypres on
its eastern side. Here, particularly in the Kemmel sector,
were the only commanding positions on the British front ;
but these advantages were outweighed by the enemy being
in possession of Messines ridge. The previous fighting had
shown that defects of infantry positions could be remedied

Feb. by artificial means, but had abundantly proved that nothing could replace or compensate for the tactical advantage of high ground for steady and continuous artillery observation of the enemy's position.

Tactically therefore an offensive by the Second Army against the Messines—Wytschaete ridge to prepare the way for an advance to the river Lys and the northern defences of Lille was favoured. Strategically, however, an offensive by the First Army had greater prospects of bringing about the capture of Lille, which was regarded as a necessary prelude to any considerable advance by the B.E.F. The ground between the Lys river and the northern defences of Lille is flat, offering no facilities for attack and many for defence, whereas from Aubers ridge direct observation could be obtained on the railways leading from the east and south-east into Lille, and on the town itself. For this reason alone the capture of Aubers ridge was of determining importance. But, in addition, an offensive against it would be in direct co-operation with and receive full support from the prospective French offensive from the Artois plateau ; and together the two attacks would threaten the rail, road and canal junction of La Bassée from north and south. Apart from these strategical considerations, the great benefit to be gained by an advance out of the water-logged trenches of the Lys valley on to the drier ground of Aubers ridge was clearly apparent. On the 15th February, taking these various facts into consideration, and being of opinion that the divisions of the First Army were in better condition to carry out an attack than those of the Second, Sir John French asked General Haig to draft a scheme for an offensive with the La Bassée—Aubers ridge as his objective. On the 16th February a memorandum from General Joffre to Sir John French gave fresh stimulus to the British plan. " Among " various offensives [it said] which are in course of prepara- " tion by the French Armies, I contemplate an attack by " the [Tenth] Army of General de Maud'huy. The object " of this operation would be to enable this Army :

" to debouch with its right from Arras ;
" to capture with its centre the heights of Vimy (7½
" miles s.s.w. of Pont à Vendin), thus dominating the
" whole of the Douai region ;
" to hold with its left the high ground about Lens (3½
" miles s.s.w. of Pont à Vendin) and Pont à Vendin".

He suggested that the British should participate by

carrying out an offensive in the direction of La Bassée and **Feb.**
the neighbouring ridge. He believed that such an attack
could be pushed across the ridge as far as the Haute Deule
canal without encountering much resistance. If carried
out at the same time as that of the French Tenth Army it
would effectively prolong the fighting line and constitute
a general offensive on a front of some seventy miles from
Arras by Pont à Vendin to near Lille.

The minor enterprise already in preparation by British
G.H.Q. now assumed greater importance. The French
Tenth Army was to capture Vimy ridge and the northern
foothills of the Artois plateau between Lens and La
Bassée, whilst the British First Army occupied Aubers
ridge from La Bassée towards Lille. When this continuous
barrier had been secured preparations could be made
behind it for a more powerful offensive into the plain of
Douai. An advance of from ten to fifteen miles into the
plain would suffice to cut the network of roads and railways
that supplied the German Armies in the Noyon salient
between Rheims and Arras.

Decision of British G.H.Q. to take the Offensive Independently

The arrangements for the combined offensive were,
from the French point of view, dependent on the relief by
British troops of the French IX. and XX. Corps north of
Ypres, according to an agreement made between General
Joffre and Sir John French on the 21st January at Chantilly.[1] One of these corps was required to strengthen the
French mass of attack on the Arras—La Bassée front, and
the other to extend the French front to the north of the
La Bassée canal, where it would take over the front of
the British I. Corps. Sir John French, who expected the
29th Division and the 1st Canadian Division from the
United Kingdom during the first fortnight of February,
agreed to carry out this relief as soon as their arrival
permitted.

This agreement had been modified by a letter from
General Joffre, asking that the offensive of the French
Tenth Army from the Artois plateau should be supported
by an offensive of the British First Army north of
the La Bassée canal, for which purpose the British
I. Corps could remain in its position north of the canal.

[1] Appendix 10.

Feb. This, General Joffre explained, would simplify the arrangements for the relief of the French troops north of Ypres.
The French XX. Corps, instead of moving down to take
over the front of the British I. Corps might remain where
it was.   The relief of the French IX. Corps he still insisted
on.   It was " absolutely indispensable for carrying out
" satisfactorily the projected attack of the Tenth Army.
" Without its support the latter will not have adequate
" reserves to undertake an effective operation.   The relief
" of the IX. Corps is, in fact [he wrote] the necessary
" condition for an offensive by the French Tenth Army ".

At this juncture Sir John French was informed that
the 29th Division was no longer available.   He considered
that its substitute, the 46th (North Midland Territorial)
Division, would require some weeks training in trench
warfare before it could be asked to take over a sector of
the battle front.   The other division about to arrive in
France, 1st Canadian Division, was earmarked for taking
over part of the front of the First Army to enable that
Army to take the offensive in co-operation with the French.
Sir John French had therefore to reconsider the situation.
The alternatives open to him were either to stick to his
plan, or, abandoning his offensive, relieve the French IX.
Corps.   He considered that the forces at his disposal did not
permit him to do both.   He decided on the former course,
suggesting to General Joffre that the relief of the French
IX. Corps should be postponed until after the conclusion
of the combined offensive.   He held out the prospect that
the First Army would be ready about the 7th March.
General Joffre meantime had increased his demands.   On
the 18th February he had asked that in addition to attacking north of La Bassée and taking over the line at Ypres,
the British should also advance from Armentières along
the Lys.   In reply to the British commander-in-chief, he
merely repeated that the relief of the French IX. Corps
was essential for the offensive of the French Tenth Army.

Here, in a state of deadlock, the matter rested until
the 28th February, when General Haig visited General de
Maud'huy,[1] commanding the French Tenth Army, at his
headquarters, St. Pol, in order to settle the arrangements
for mutual co-operation during the battle.   General de
Maud'huy received General Haig warmly, but said that he
had comparatively few troops for the front that he was

---

[1] His corps had been next to General Haig's on the Aisne, when they
were both corps commanders.

holding, and gave him to understand that unless the Feb. French IX. Corps were relieved from about Ypres, the Tenth Army would be unable to give any support to a British offensive north of the La Bassée canal except by the heavy artillery already in position south of the canal. "The net result of this information", General Haig wrote to Sir John French, summarizing his interview, " is that our proposed offensive action must be considered " an entirely independent operation ".

Although General Joffre did not inform G.H.Q. until the 7th March of the definite postponement of the offensive of the French Tenth Army, such a decision was now to be expected. In any case, however, Sir John French determined to carry out the offensive that was being prepared by the First Army. The failure of the British to accomplish anything in the " December Battle " in Flanders [1] had undoubtedly impressed the French very unfavourably, and it is more than probable that they did not think that the Field-Marshal was in earnest. Until the Battle of Neuve Chapelle was fought there is small doubt but that they were of opinion that the B.E.F. might be helpful to hold the line and act defensively, but would be of little use to drive the Germans out of France.

[1] See p. 17.

CHAPTER V

THE PLAN

Sketch 1. THE stretch of country over which the First Army was to deliver its offensive had already been a battle ground between British and Germans. Four months previously,[2] in October 1914, during the extension of the front to the North Sea, the II. Corps under General Sir H. Smith-Dorrien, in its advance eastwards from Béthune, had occupied Aubers ridge on the 17th October, and by the evening of that day was precariously established along it, from Le Pilly near Fournes on the left south-westwards by Herlies and Illies to Violaines and Givenchy, its right astride the La Bassée canal in touch with the French. The arrival of German reinforcements had held up any further advance from this line. Then on the 20th October the German *Sixth* and *Fourth Armies* had begun their great general offensive on the whole front from Arras to Ypres and the sea, and the *XIII. Corps* attacking from Lille, threatened to envelop the left flank of the II. Corps, exposed by the failure of Conneau's Cavalry Corps to keep level with it. General Smith-Dorrien had therefore to wheel his corps back off the ridge into the meadow land of the Lys, withdrawing the left flank some three miles to Fauquissart, whilst the right remained stationary about Givenchy. The Germans followed up, and on the 26th attacked the new line, putting their main weight against

---

[1] Map 2 is reproduced from the operations map in use at the time. For reference the numbers in circles were employed instead of the usual map squares.
[2] See " 1914," Volume II. p. 77.

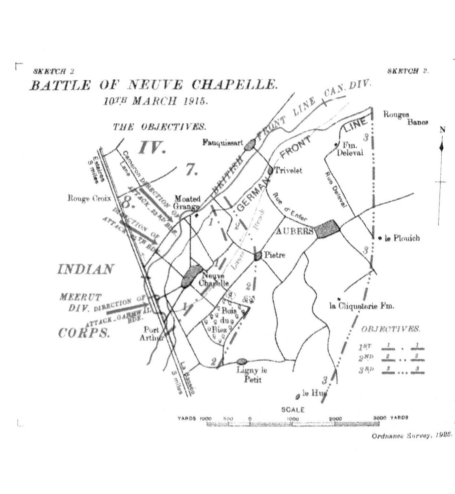

BATTLE OF NEUVE CHAPELLE.
10TH MARCH 1915.

THE OBJECTIVES.

Ordnance Survey, 1925.

the trenches east of Neuve Chapelle village, the nearest Feb.
point of the line to Aubers ridge. After twenty-four
hours' heavy fighting, the whole of the II. Corps front was
maintained with the exception of a stretch of 2,000 yards
east of Neuve Chapelle. Here the Germans succeeded
in breaking in and capturing the village, from which
counter-attacks failed to dislodge them. The fresh line Sketch 2.
occupied after the fighting ran immediately west of the
village. It joined on to the original front at the cross
roads to the south, where the defences formed a small
salient, which received the name of " Port Arthur ",[1] and
on the north near the Moated Grange (Ferme Vanbesien).
No further attempt was made in 1914 to recapture Neuve
Chapelle and regain the old trench-line east of it, called
the Smith-Dorrien trench.

General Haig, in his appreciation of the situation sub-
mitted to G.H.Q. on 12th February 1915, recommended
that the offensive towards Aubers ridge should begin by
the capture of Neuve Chapelle, which lay about the centre
of the front of the First Army. The German defences
there formed a salient, which enabled convergent artillery
fire to be brought to bear on them from Port Arthur to
the Moated Grange, and presented an attack frontage of
two thousand yards, a suitable place at which to break in.
In fact, an advance on either side would be difficult until
the Neuve Chapelle salient had been reduced or neutralized.
All the winter the Germans holding it had been able to
enfilade the British lines right and left, but had escaped
the disadvantage of exposure to convergent fire because
the British had little artillery ammunition wherewith to
shell them.

The plan proposed by General Haig was therefore to
capture Neuve Chapelle as the first objective, and establish
a line east of the village along the original Smith-Dorrien
trench. Every effort was then to be made to enlarge the
gap created in the enemy's front, by attacking simultaneously to the left and right of it and progressing towards the
line Herlies—Illies on the Aubers ridge, thereby threatening the enemy's communications between La Bassée and
Lille. For this purpose General Haig asked that the First
Army should be reinforced by at least a corps [2] and as
many heavy guns and howitzers as possible. He expected

---

[1] The point is now marked by the Café de la Bombe, which bears the
words " Port Arthur " painted under its name.
[2] Only one division, the 1st Canadian, was available.

Feb. at the time that the French would co-operate on the immediate right of the First Army by a movement against La Bassée from the south.

On the 15th February Sir John French approved General Haig's plan and directed him to be ready to carry it out as soon after the 9th March [1] as the weather and the condition of the ground permitted. It was useless to attack before the ground dried, for with water 18 inches below the surface it was impossible to entrench and secure any position that might be captured.

In order to concentrate all possible strength of men, guns and ammunition for the operations of the First Army, Sir John French decided to postpone any independent action by the Second Army, which, however, was to assist by containing the enemy on its front. For this purpose, its centre and left, the II. and V. Corps, were to undertake minor enterprises and act as if an offensive were about to be launched from the high ground east of Ypres. On its right, the III. Corps, east of Armentières, was to make active demonstrations towards the front Pérenchies—Fort Englos, the outer line of the Lille defences, with the ulterior motive of preparing a way for an eventual attack on Lille.

As a general reserve for the offensive of the First Army, Sir John French decided to retain at his own disposal the Cavalry Corps, the Indian Cavalry Corps and the 46th (North Midland) Division.

The details of the scheme of attack as the first offensive from a trench system were the subject of several conferences and many instructions in the First Army. As regards numbers, General Haig could scarcely hope for more favourable circumstances in which to take the offensive. Owing to the depletion of the German ranks on the Western Front for the operations in Russia, only three and a half corps of the German *Sixth Army* [2] faced the six corps of the B.E.F. (First and Second Armies) then in France. Of these only the German *VII. Corps* of two divisions lay opposite to the six divisions of the First Army on the thirteen-mile frontage between the La Bassée canal and Bois Grenier.[3]

---

[1] In accordance with the notice given to General Joffre (see p. 72).

[2] The German *Sixth Army*, under Crown Prince Rupprecht of Bavaria, consisted in all of eight corps, and held the line from Bapaume, south of Arras, to the Ypres—Menin road. On its right, the *Fourth Army* continued the line to the Belgian coast, whilst on its left the *Second Army* held the front down to south of the Somme.

[3] See Note II. at end of Chapter.

The British reserves were small: only one infantry and Feb. five cavalry divisions would be in general reserve, but the Germans also had no extensive reserve formations.[1] Reinforcements could certainly be collected from other parts of the long German line; but the Intelligence Section, General Staff, G.H.Q., calculated that by this means not more than about 4,000 additional rifles might be expected within twelve hours, that is by the evening of the first day of the battle, and a further 16,000 by the evening of the second day.[2]

As a general principle, General Haig laid down that the infantry was to advance as rapidly as possible in order to take full advantage of the sudden and heavy preliminary bombardment which he hoped would surprise and temporarily demoralize the Germans holding the front defences. He pointed out that any delay in getting forward would enable the Germans to bring up reserves and guns sufficient to hold a fresh position, the attack of which would entail a fresh bombardment and a renewed infantry assault. The intention, therefore, was " to sur- " prise the Germans, carry them right off their legs, and " push forward at once to the Haute Pommereau—Aubers " ridge ". In making preparations for the attack, the G.O.C. First Army directed that the following points should be specially considered :—the placing of guns in position gradually and secretly ; the unostentatious registration of targets, and practice in wire-cutting ; arrangements for bringing up the attacking troops to the assembly positions ; the passage through the British wire ; study of the ground to locate the enemy's machine guns and wire, and for the correction of maps ; the following up of the assaulting parties by mountain and machine guns ; the running of some telephone lines underground and the use of lamps for signalling ; the possibility of massing the improvised trench mortars against important localities ; the running out of saps to support the attack ; and measures to combat possible enemy mines.

For fighting the German batteries throughout the whole

[1] The only reserve of the German *Sixth Army* was a brigade of the *2nd Guard Division* in rear of the left flank opposite Arras, and the newly constituted *58th Division*, formed on the 7th March at Cambrai, consisting of three surplus regiments taken from other divisions (the *24th* and *26th Reserve*).

[2] This estimate, which assumed that conditions with regard to roads and railways would be favourable and that no local reserves would be retained by subsidiary actions, was to prove, as will be seen, substantially correct.

Feb. period of the assault, the divisional and corps artillery were
to be assisted by the heavy batteries of the First Army and
by units of the general reserve of artillery (afterwards
called the Heavy Artillery Reserve),[1] placed at the disposal
of the First Army by G.H.Q. for the duration of the battle.

The battle was to begin by the capture of Neuve
Chapelle as a distinct operation. This included the
assault of the German front defence system west of the
village, the storming of the village itself, and the consolidation of the Smith-Dorrien trench along its eastern
edge. The bombardment was to begin at 7.30 A.M., an
hour after sunrise, by which time it was considered that
the final registration of targets would have been carried
out and that the light would be sufficient for accurate
observation. Thirty-five minutes were to be allotted for
the first phase of the bombardment.[2] During this period
passages were to be cut through the German wire entanglement by 18-pdr. batteries firing shrapnel; other
field gun batteries were to fire on the trenches right
and left of the actual front of attack and on certain
selected areas; whilst the howitzer batteries demolished
the German front and support trenches. At 8.5 A.M. the
artillery would lift to its next objective, Neuve Chapelle
village, and the strong points to the north and south;
the 6-inch howitzers would concentrate on the village
itself, which was also to be the target of three 9·2-inch
howitzers throughout the first and second phases, whilst
the 18-pdr. and 13-pdr. batteries were to form a belt of
fire east of the village covering rather more than the front
of attack. This second phase of the bombardment was to
last thirty minutes.

At 8.5 A.M. also, immediately the artillery had lifted

[1] See Note I. at end of Chapter.

[2] Although experiments were carried out in a back area with live shell
against specially made entanglements, there was much difference of opinion
as to the number of shells required to destroy a given length of the German
position. At first, it was suggested that the bombardment would have
to last 2½ hours to complete its work, but on the 3rd March, at a meeting
of all the C.R.A.'s concerned and some battery commanders, the duration
of the bombardment, both for cutting the wire and destroying the German
trenches, was fixed at 35 minutes. It was the expressed opinion at that
time (before the No. 106 fuze was introduced) that shrapnel was preferable
to H.E. for wire destruction, as it cut the wire clear of the posts and left
it lying in small pieces, whereas H.E. left it broken but still an entanglement. General Haig directed his corps commanders to consider and
report to him their proposed allotment of artillery for (1) destroying enemy
wire and front trenches, (2) protecting flanks, (3) forming a " curtain "
behind the enemy's front trench to prevent reinforcements coming up,
(4) neutralizing the enemy's artillery and machine guns.

from the German front defences, the infantry was to Feb.
move forward from the breastworks and trenches and,
crossing the two hundred yards of No Man's Land, carry
out the assault before the Germans could recover from
the effects of the bombardment. Three infantry brigades
(one of the Indian Corps and two of the IV. Corps)
were detailed for this first assault on a frontage of 2,000
yards. On reaching the line of the German support
trenches, some two hundred yards beyond the front trench,
the leading troops of these three brigades were to wait
till the end of the 30-minute bombardment of the village.
At 8.35 A.M. the attack against the village was to be
launched and the advance continued through it to the
line of the Smith-Dorrien trench.

The occupation of this line, from the German defences
opposite the Port Arthur salient on the right, along the
eastern edge of Neuve Chapelle village to the German
defences about the Moated Grange on the left, would
conclude the opening stage of the battle.

From this point onwards the operations were to
assume more extensive proportions. Having broken in
on a front of 2,000 yards, it was intended gradually to
widen this gap by the vigorous and sustained pressure of
ever-increasing numbers. The second stage of the battle
was therefore to consist of an offensive by the remainder
of the Indian and IV. Corps on the whole five-mile frontage
held by them. At a time to be decided by mutual agreement between the two corps commanders according to
the situation, the whole of their two corps (less the three
original assaulting brigades) would advance across the
mile of flat broken country that separated them from
Aubers ridge, and thence on to the ridge itself. The final Sketch 2.
objective of the Indian Corps was to be the front Le Hue—
La Cliqueterie Farm (exclusive), and that of the IV. Corps
from La Cliqueterie Farm northwards through Le Plouich,
including the village of Aubers, to Rouges Bancs. On
reaching the final objective patrols were to be sent forward
to Herlies, Illies and the La Bassée—Lille road. The
British front would thus be firmly established on the ridge.

This second stage of the operation was to be supported
by a further artillery bombardment, particularly of various
known strong points about the Bois du Biez, at Pietre
and near Aubers village.

It was hoped that the effect of the break-in on the
front of the Indian and IV. Corps would extend rapidly

March. to the flanks and weaken the German defences opposite
the I. Corps to the south, and the Canadian Division to
the north.   These two formations therefore whilst assisting
the initial stage of the operation by fire and demonstrations,
were to be ready to take advantage of any weakening of
Sketch 1. the enemy on their front by assuming a vigorous offensive,
the I. Corps in the direction of Violaines, covering the right
flank of the Indian Corps, and the Canadian Division
towards Fromelles, covering the left flank of the IV. Corps.
In this manner it was hoped that the battle would eventually
involve a general advance of the First Army out of the mud
of the Lys valley on to the drier ground of Aubers ridge.

To reap the full benefit of success, the Cavalry Corps
and the Indian Cavalry Corps in general reserve, were to
be ready to advance through the gap in the enemy's front
opposite Neuve Chapelle village as soon as a passage
across the German trenches could be prepared.   Their
subsequent action was to take the form of a right wheel
along the ridge into the open country behind the German
lines between Neuve Chapelle and La Bassée.

Sketch 2.   When at the end of February it was realized that no
considerable assistance was to be expected from the French,
the British plan was not altered ; but General Haig had
to be prepared to limit its scope.   Taking into account the
available supply of ammunition, which would only permit
of the operations lasting at most three or four days,[1] it
was apparent that if there were no French support it
might become necessary to halt and establish a new
defensive line before the top of Aubers ridge had been
gained.   At a conference with corps and divisional commanders on 5th March [2] General Haig therefore fixed on
three alternative intermediate positions which the assaulting units were to be prepared to put in a state of defence :
first, the line of the German front trenches ; secondly, the
line of the Smith-Dorrien trench east of Neuve Chapelle ;
and, thirdly, a line along the eastern edge of the Bois du
Biez to Aubers village.   These successive lines were to be
so organized—by parties of infantry and engineers which
had moved forward behind the assaulting lines—that they
might be used either as rallying centres from which to
resist possible German counter-attacks, or as intermediate
lines of defence.

[1] See p. 37.
[2] The First Army Operation Order (Appendix 11) was issued on 8th
March.

The Preparations

The material preparations for the offensive were begun Feb.
during the last days of February,[1] allowing ten days for
completion, short indeed in comparison with the five Map 1.
months taken up in making ready for the Battle of the Sketches
Somme in the following year. The three corps of the First 1 and 2.
Army, from right to left, the I., Indian and IV., at that
time occupied a frontage of thirteen miles (23,000 yards)
from Cuinchy in the south to Bois Grenier, and this was
considered to be too extensive for the delivery of a strong
and continued offensive against an entrenched enemy. To
enable two of these corps, the Indian and IV., to assemble
an adequate force in depth opposite the principal objective,
Neuve Chapelle, they were closed up to a narrower frontage.
To this end, the I. Corps took over the front (2,000 yards)
of the right brigade of the Indian Corps between La
Quinque Rue and Chocolat Menier Corner ($1\frac{1}{4}$ miles south-
west of Port Arthur); and to strengthen the IV. Corps
front, the Canadian Division was attached to the First
Army to take over the frontage (4,000 yards) of the 7th
Division from Bois Grenier northwards. The Indian Corps
frontage was thus reduced to 3,300 yards[2] and that of the
IV. Corps to 5,000 yards. These reliefs were carried out by
the 28th February. At the same time in order to place the
right of the Indian Corps directly opposite its objective,
the southern end of Neuve Chapelle village, that corps took
over 800 yards of front from the IV. Corps, from the Port
Arthur salient (inclusive) northwards to a point where the
British line crossed the La Bassée—Estaires road.

This re-arrangement of the First Army gave its two
assaulting corps considerable depth, and allowed of their
forming reserves. It was therefore considered that the
operation could be carried through without further reinforcement from the general reserve under the Commander-
in-Chief.

The arrangements for the assembly and disposition of
the infantry and artillery presented many difficulties to
the divisional and brigade staffs concerned. This was but

---

[1] On 22nd February the B.E.F. suffered a heavy loss by the death of
Br.-General John Edmond Gough, V.C., General Haig's Chief of the
Staff, as the result of a wound from a sniper's bullet received two days
previously whilst visiting his old battalion, the 2/Rifle Brigade, in the
front line. He was succeeded as Br.-General General Staff First Army,
by Br.-General R. H. K. Butler, commanding the 3rd Brigade.

[2] The Indian Corps had only one division in the front line.

March. the natural result of the establishment of trench warfare ; for it had introduced conditions in offensive operations very different to anything that had been anticipated in the previous peace training of the British Army. Movements that formerly had been the chief factors in its training, such as the approach march, the deployment for battle, the gradual advance and the building up of the firing line within assaulting distance of the enemy's position, were now unnecessary. All these preliminary stages had to be carried out under cover of darkness before the battle opened, and the action now began at what in the training manuals had been considered its final stage : the assault with the bayonet. As a result, those responsible for planning the preliminaries for a battle which was the first trench offensive were faced by problems for which neither their training nor experience had actually prepared them, and consequently much of their work at this period was experimental.

The three infantry brigades detailed to carry out the assault [1] were withdrawn into rest billets on the 2nd March. Here they rehearsed the first phase of the operation in every detail. Each officer was given a clearly defined objective and a definite responsibility, and each individual was instructed where he was to go, what his duty was, and where he was to stop. The officers of the assaulting units also visited the front trenches to see their places of assembly and lines of advance. Owing to the difficulty of finding adequate cover for the troops immediately prior to the assault, it was found necessary to construct additional trenches and lines of breastworks—" forming-up trenches " —as close as possible to the front line ; in later phases of the war, when No Man's Land was wide, they were often dug in front of the line, and then called " jumping-off trenches ". Dummy breastworks and screens were also erected at other parts of the front of the First Army, so as to mislead the enemy as to the intended sector of assault.

Advanced depôts, or " dumps " as they came to be called, were established at short intervals and close up to the breastworks on the front of attack. These contained rations, entrenching tools and such engineer stores as would be necessary to place the captured positions in a state of defence. Magazines were also constructed for storing ammunition and bombs. The supply of stores

[1] Appendix 2 (Order of Battle). Appendices 12-15 (Operation Orders : Indian Corps, Meerut Div., IV. Corps, and 8th Div.).

and ammunition was greatly facilitated by the laying of light tramlines [1] to within a few hundred yards of the front line. The roads leading up to the front of the First Army were also improved, and, in anticipation of a successful advance, working parties of over one thousand men [2] were detailed for repairing the roads into Neuve Chapelle.

The entire artillery of both the Indian and the IV. Corps was to be concentrated principally opposite the German defences of Neuve Chapelle. It was to be assisted by two 6-inch howitzer batteries, one 6-inch gun battery, three 9·2-inch howitzers, and two 15-inch howitzers [3] from G.H.Q. Heavy Artillery Reserve, and six 13-pdr. R.H.A. batteries drawn from the Indian cavalry divisions.[4]

The guns to support the first stage of the offensive were disposed in the form of a horseshoe facing the village. The 18-pdr. batteries for wire-cutting were placed at ranges varying between 1,300 and 2,000 yards from the German lines, whilst the howitzer and heavy batteries were at 3,000 to 5,000 yards. By this time the positions of most heavy and siege batteries had been fixed by survey, and the ranges and bearings of all prominent points in the German area accurately ascertained.[5] A feature of

---

[1] These tramlines had wooden rails and sleepers, and proved most useful in transporting material of all kinds to the trenches. The work was done at night, and the employment of wooden instead of steel rails greatly minimized the noise. The trucks had iron wheels taken from the Béthune tramways. The 8th Division pushed its tramlines into Neuve Chapelle during the night of the first day of battle.

[2] The 125th Rifles and 1 company of the 34th Sikh Pioneers from Lahore Division.

[3] Only one 15-inch (under the superintendence of Admiral (retired) Sir Roger Bacon) arrived in France in time for the battle. " Its ammuni- " tion was faulty and there was not much of it ".

[4] Appendix 2. The actual total heavy artillery (including the armament of the armoured train " Churchill ") at the disposal of First Army in the battle was :—
　　33, 4·7-inch guns ; 24, 6-inch howitzers ; 5, 6-inch guns ;
　　　3, 9·2-inch howitzers ; 1, 15-inch howitzer.
It was the first time that a battery of 9·2-inch howitzers (Major C. W. Collingwood) was used in battle. Two howitzers arrived just before the 10th March, and joined the experimental one already in France. The tractors were Holt caterpillars, and the whole of the transport was mechanical.

[5] This had been carried out by the Ranging Section R.E. under Captain H. St. J. L. Winterbotham, R.E., working under Major E. M. Jack, R.E., of the Topographical Subsection General Staff G.H.Q., better known as " Maps ". The Ranging Section was originally sent out to France in November 1914 for the purpose of ascertaining the location of hostile targets by fixing the position of an aeroplane at the moment it dropped a smoke bomb (or other signal) over them. When wireless signalling proved a superior method, the Section was on 25th January utilized for survey work in the field.

March. historical interest was the issue for the first time of an artillery time-table, that gave to each battery a definite purpose and target for each of the various phases of the bombardment.[1] It was the first time also that objective maps (with the later well-known " Red Line ", " Blue Line ", etc.) were prepared, and the first time that a barrage was ordered.[2] All subsequent attacks to the end of the war were, indeed, based on the methods developed in the First Army for Neuve Chapelle. The construction of platforms for the guns and the arrangements for anchorage of the 18-pdrs.[3] in the muddy ground offered many difficulties. The platforms were made chiefly of bricks, planks and hurdles, and the most reliable anchorage was obtained by placing a loosely-filled sandbag under each wheel and a heavy log of wood across the end of the trail, with filled sandbags packed between this log and the spade, and all round the trail.

In the flat low-lying country, the provision of observation stations was also difficult. They were practically limited to two crow's-nests, constructed about Rouge Croix, a mile from the British front line, and some high strawstacks which were hollowed out and turned into semi-protected observatories. For the forward observers, the principal look-outs both for the Indian and IV. Corps artillery were, to begin with, in the houses near Pont Logy ($\frac{3}{4}$ mile N.N.W. of Port Arthur).

To guarantee accurate fire under such conditions, and to allow for a certain amount of bad weather in the preliminary period, the artillery staff recommended that all batteries detailed for the bombardment should begin to take up their positions ten days prior to the operation. Although the first of the new batteries arrived on the first day of March and were in position by the 5th, two 6-inch howitzer batteries, due from the United Kingdom on the 1st, did not reach the battle zone till the afternoon of the 9th, the day before the battle, a delay which was to have unfortunate results.[4]

---

[1] Appendix 16.
[2] See Chapter VI.
[3] The 18-pdr. carriage was not stable enough to ensure that many rounds could be fired without re-laying, and accuracy was the main factor in wire cutting.
[4] See Chapter VI. On the 26th February the War Office informed G.H.Q. that the 59th and 81st Siege Batteries forming the 7th Siege Brigade (6-inch howitzers) would embark on 1st March. On 2nd March they wired that the brigade had not embarked on 1st, but would do so on 5th. On 3rd March G.H.Q. wired to the War Office that it was

For the supply of ammunition for the battle, G.H.Q. March. based its calculations on the assumption that it was undesirable to reduce the stock of ammunition in France below an amount equivalent to that laid down in " War Establishments " to be carried in the various ammunition echelons, from the park to the battery, both inclusive, or, in other words, that the amount to be regarded as disposable should not exceed the number of rounds available in rear of the parks on the lines of communication. This quantity was considered adequate for a three or four days' battle.[1]

The Royal Flying Corps carried out reconnaissances and observations for the artillery on a scale hitherto unprecedented, despite the unfavourable weather.[2] It also photographed from the air the proposed zone of operations to a depth of some fifteen hundred yards. Thus there were available for the first time, although the first efficient

---

of the greatest importance that the brigade should embark as soon as possible ; nevertheless it did not embark till the 5th, arriving at Estaires on the morning of the 9th.

[1]   APPROXIMATE AMOUNT OF AMMUNITION AVAILABLE FOR
ARTILLERY OF THE FIRST ARMY

Gun or Howitzer.	H.E. or Lyddite.	Shrapnel.	Total.	Average Rounds per Gun or Howitzer for First Army.
13-pdr. gun (60) . .	. .	36,000	36,000	600
18-pdr. gun (324) .	4,000	128,840	132,840	410
4·5-inch howitzer (54) .	10,500	1,000	11,500	212
60-pdr. gun (12) . .	2,400	3,000	5,400	450
4·7-inch gun (32) . .	3,700	10,300	14,000	437
6-inch howitzer (28) .	6,000	2,000	8,000	285
6-inch gun (4) . .	500	1,100	1,600	400
9·2-inch howitzer (3) .	1,000	. .	1,000	333
Pack (2·75-inch) (12) .	. .	6,000	6,000	500
15-inch howitzer (1) .	(Probably not more than 35 to 40 rounds)			

The armament of H.M.A.T. " Churchill " and ammunition therefor are not included in the above.

[2] A programme was prepared for bombing enemy headquarters and railway centres to prevent enemy reserves from being brought up. Up to Neuve Chapelle dropping bombs from aeroplanes had been spasmodic, and carried out only occasionally by pilots or observers primarily engaged on other duties. Unfortunately bad weather interfered but, on the 10th, Furnes, believed to be a divisional headquarters, was bombed at 7 A.M., and Courtrai station and Menin junction were attacked about 3 P.M., and at the former two trains were hit. On the 11th visibility was too poor, and on the 12th the weather too stormy.

March. air cameras did not arrive until February, photographic maps giving the trace of the German trenches. These were only shown in outline without the details achieved later, but a great advance in aerial reconnaissance had been made. The trenches were reproduced on skeleton maps (1 in 5,000), and 1,500 copies sent to each corps. In addition, maps of the British trenches on a larger scale (1 in 40,000) were issued.

The thorough manner in which the secrecy of the preparations was maintained is shown by the fact that a tactical surprise was obtained. The Germans, though realizing the imminence of an offensive, were uncertain as to the point and direction of the assault until it was actually delivered.

NOTE I.

THE ORGANIZATION OF THE HEAVY ARTILLERY AND THE ARTILLERY COMMANDS

During the winter of 1914–15 the divisional heavy batteries, the 60-pdrs. and 4·7-inch, were withdrawn, and with the few 6-inch howitzer batteries formed into Army Artillery. It was contemplated that portions of it would be attached to divisions as required, and would fight under the divisional artillery commanders. The first heavy howitzer batteries to arrive in France were placed at the disposal of corps.

In February 1915, the heavier natures of tractor-drawn artillery (that is 8-inch and upwards) were organized as Reserve Heavy Artillery, and formed into groups, commanded by brigadier-generals. As required, groups were allotted to Armies. To avoid confusion in abbreviation, the name Reserve Heavy Artillery (R.H.A.) was soon changed to Heavy Artillery Reserve (H.A.R.).

Medium guns and howitzers were organized by brigades and allotted to corps, and by them to divisions.

In the spring and early summer of 1915, the 60-pdrs. and 4·7-inch batteries were withdrawn from the Army Artillery and added to the H.A.R. Groups. These groups then became responsible for counter-battery work, which, during the summer, was gradually developed. The battles of Festubert and Loos were fought under these conditions, and the experience thus gained disclosed the need for further alterations in the organization of the existing Heavy Artillery system, so as to ensure corps control and real liaison with the infantry.

It was decided to allot one H.A.R. Group definitely to each Army, under the title of " Army Heavy Artillery Group ", and to retain the remaining groups as H.A.R. under the C-in-C.

The system continued in force until June 1916, when sanction was given for the reorganization of the artillery—it took some time to carry it out—into three categories :—

Divisional artillery . 18-pdrs. and 4·5-inch howitzers.   March.
Corps artillery . . Medium artillery (60-pdrs., and 6-inch, 8-inch
                                 and 9·2-inch howitzers and 6-inch guns).
Army artillery. . The heaviest artillery.

When the First and Second Armies were formed in December 1914, an artillery major-general was attached to each as " Artillery Adviser ". He was not a commander nor a staff officer, but was in a purely advisory position, unless in the event of a concentration of artillery the Army commander decided to place him in command of it. In practice, the term artillery adviser soon fell into disuse, and the signature M.G.R.A. or B.G.R.A. was gradually adopted in the course of 1915. This continued until December 1916, when the title G.O.C. R.A. was definitely sanctioned, his command recognized, and a staff allotted to him.

In the corps, the Corps Artillery Adviser became G.O.C. R.A. in October 1915 for the purpose of co-ordination and exercising command as required.

At G.H.Q. the Artillery Adviser continued to bear that name until April 1917, when he became Major-General R.A.

NOTE II.

THE OPPOSING GERMAN FORCES

(Map 1 ; Sketch 3)

In March 1915 the German forces holding the line opposite the B.E.F. were, from south to north, the *VII.*, the *XIX.* and the *II. Bavarian Corps*, and the *30th Division* of the *XV. Corps*. This was reported in the Intelligence Summaries early in the month.

The *VII. Corps* that faced the three corps of the First Army, consisted of the *13th* and *14th Divisions*. They divided the 13-mile frontage between them, the *14th* occupying from the La Bassée canal to Neuve Chapelle village, and the *13th* from that village (exclusive) to Bois Grenier. The two divisions were weaker than the British Intelligence could know at the time ; [1] for on the 5th March each had been ordered to transfer one regiment (3 battalions) to a new division, the 50th, that was being formed at Hirson behind the Champagne front. They were thus reduced to 9-battalion divisions, a reorganization not adopted by the British until the winter of 1917–18. On the 7th and 8th March the *158th Infantry Regiment* of the *13th Division* from Fauquissart, and the *53rd Infantry Regiment* of the *14th Division* from opposite Neuve Chapelle had accordingly been taken out of the front line, the three remaining regiments of each division, with the help of the *11th Jäger Battalion*, the only

[1] In a Special Order of the Day to the First Army issued on the 9th March, it was correctly stated :—" We are now about to attack with 48 " battalions a locality held by three German battalions ". This order did not, however, reach the British and Indian battalions concerned until just before, or after the battle had begun. Thus many of the fighting troops did not know how few were the numbers in front of them, whilst the fire power of machine guns and artillery gave the impression that the enemy was very strong.

VII. Corps reserve, extending their front to fill the gaps.[1]   Actually
on the front of the *VII. Corps* there were therefore two weak German
against seven British divisions, or approximately 20,000 against
87,000 rifles.   But the enemy apparently possessed superiority in
trench mortars and machine guns, although not in heavy or field
artillery : ten heavy batteries only were identified on the front of
the Indian and IV. Corps.[2]   Of gun ammunition he had no lack.[3]
    In front of the Indian Corps, the *16th Infantry Regiment (14th
Division)* held the line with all its three battalions.   The two
battalions on the left, occupying the sector opposite Richebourg
l'Avoué from the Rue du Bois to the Port Arthur salient (exclusive),
were not attacked.   The battalion on the right continued the line
from the Port Arthur salient to Signpost Lane, a frontage of sixteen
hundred yards.   Its two left companies faced the four assaulting
battalions of the Garhwal Brigade between the salient and Pont
Logy, whilst its two right companies faced the 25th Brigade of the
IV. Corps.   The sector of 700 yards between Signpost Lane and the
Moated Grange (exclusive) to be assaulted by the 23rd Brigade, was
defended by two companies of the *11th Jäger Battalion*, the other
two companies of which were in reserve about Halpegarbe.   The
13th Infantry Regiment (13th Division) continued the line northwards
from the Moated Grange by Chapigny to Fauquissart, facing the
British 7th Division (IV. Corps).
    Actually to oppose the assault of the fifteen British battalions
(three infantry brigades) on the front between the Port Arthur
salient (inclusive) and the Moated Grange (exclusive) there were
therefore approximately $1\frac{1}{2}$ German battalions (six infantry companies) with two companies in reserve about Halpegarbe.

    [1] Similarly, and at the same period, many of the field artillery regi-
ments (*i.e.* the *22nd F.A.R.* of the *13th Divisional Artillery*) were reduced
from six-gun to four-gun batteries to provide the complement of field
batteries for the newly constituted divisions.
    [2] See Chapter VI. for details of German artillery.
    [3] See p. 38.

SKETCH 3.

BATTLE OF NEUVE CHAPELLE.
10TH MARCH 1915.
THE ASSAULT & THE SITUATION AT 10 A.M.

BRITISH :—
Positions at Zero
Line reached at 10 A.M.

German Strong
Points (unoccupied
at Zero)

Ordnance Survey, 1925.

Note.—The JULLUNDUR BDE.
(LAHORE DIV.) reached Rue
du Bereau ≈ 10th March
(1 mile west)

SCALE

0   500   1000   1500   2000 YARDS
YARDS 500   0   ½   1   MILE
0   1   2   3 miles

CHAPTER VI

THE BATTLE OF NEUVE CHAPELLE (*continued*)

10TH MARCH 1915

(Maps 1, 2 and 3 ; Sketches 3 and 4)

THE CAPTURE OF NEUVE CHAPELLE

THE eve of the battle was wet, rain with occasional light Map 1.
snow falling. As night approached, however, the wind Sketch 3.
changed to southward and the sky cleared, which seemed
to confirm the weather forecast, received during the
evening from England, indicating more settled conditions.
At 10 P.M. therefore the corps concerned were informed
by wire from First Army Headquarters that, failing
further instructions, the orders already issued for the
operations on the following day would hold good. It
was realized that if the weather played false, the mass of
the assaulting troops would have to remain all day in their
forming-up trenches, since the dangers and difficulties of
a withdrawal in daylight were too great. It was a risk
that could not be avoided. Between 11.30 P.M. and
1.30 A.M. the Garhwal Brigade, assaulting brigade of the
Indian Corps, marched from the area Vieille Chapelle—
Richebourg St. Vaast. It used two parallel routes, the communication trench alongside the Rue du Bois, and the next
road north of the Rue, and proceeded to the breastworks [1]
along the La Bassée—Estaires road from Port Arthur
(inclusive) to about four hundred yards south of Pont
Logy, and to the two new lines of breastworks west of the
road. At the same time, the 25th and 23rd Brigades, the

---

[1] The breastworks had a shallow trench behind them, but the cover
provided was mostly built up above ground with sandbags filled with
earth obtained from a ditch in front.

10 Mar. two assaulting brigades of the IV. Corps, marched from about Lestrem and Estaires to Rouge Croix and Pont du Hem (a mile N.N.W. of Rouge Croix) respectively, and thence across country to the trenches and breastworks along the Rue Tilleloy (which passes by Moated Grange) between a point four hundred yards north of Pont Logy and the Sunken Road. No unit had much more than five miles to march and all movements were timed so as to ensure the assembly positions being reached one hour before daylight, and to allow for the troops eating a hot meal provided en route. In the early hours before dawn there was a slight frost that temporarily hardened the muddy and sodden ground and helped the cross-country progress of the battalions.

Before the arrival of the assaulting troops, the units already holding the front defences had made room for them. The Bareilly Brigade on the front of the Indian Corps had closed mainly to the right; and the two battalions (2/Northamptonshire and 4/Cameron Highlanders) of the 24th Brigade on the front of the IV. Corps, had moved the one outwards and the other to the left, leaving vacant lengths of breastwork to which the assaulting battalions were guided. In front of the line where there were not convenient ditches for the purpose, a few short lengths of trench to be occupied by the two leading lines of the assaulting battalions had been dug, as jumping-off trenches. Small ladders had been placed at intervals behind the breastworks to assist the rear lines to climb over, and light portable footbridges had been prepared for crossing the ditches on the front of attack. During the night the front line troops had also stripped the wire from the trestles and posts of the British entanglements, and removed other obstacles within reach that might delay the advance.

By 4.30 A.M. the assaulting battalions were ready in position. As day broke it proved to be cold, damp and misty, and consequently unfavourable either for aerial reconnaissance or for artillery observation; but about sunrise—6.30 A.M.—the low clouds and mist began to clear and the weather showed signs of improvement. General Haig, from his advanced headquarters at Merville,[1] thereupon ordered the attack to be carried out as planned.

[1] To mislead spies he had a dummy headquarters marked with his flag, at Béthune. The Advanced Headquarters of the Indian Corps were

Apart from a few artillery ranging shots, the first hours of daylight were comparatively quiet, but on the stroke of 7.30 A.M. the air was rent by the sudden outburst of the general bombardment.

The destruction of the German obstacles and trenches was entrusted to the artillery of the Indian Corps, both Meerut and Lahore Divisional artillery, under Br.-General A. B. Scott, and the artillery of the IV. Corps, both 7th and 8th Divisional artillery under Br.-General A. E. A. Holland.[1] The ninety guns of five 18-pdr. brigades (IV., IX., XIII., XXXIII. and XLV. Brigades R.F.A.) were detailed for the work of cutting broad passages through the German wire, and 50 rounds per gun were allowed. The entanglement varied from six to fifteen yards in depth, and consisted of two or three rows of " knife rests " [2] with strands of thick barbed wire wound around the frames and pulled tight between them. In addition, nearer the German trenches, was a quantity of low wire on wooden posts. Time-shrapnel with a long corrector was used and although it was the first time such an operation had been carried out, and there was no chance of correcting the fire, with so many shells falling at once, within ten minutes the greater part of the demolition had been accomplished. The wire was lying on the ground in short strips, and formed at most of the places selected no serious impediment to the advance.

Simultaneously with the attack on the wire the remaining fifteen 18-pdr. batteries, and six 6-inch siege and six 4·5-inch field howitzer batteries, totalling sixty howitzers,[3] all that were available, opened on the front trenches. The German fire trench itself was two to three feet deep, with a fire-step, and was only kept habitable by constantly pumping out the water. The parapet, in reality a breastwork, was the chief protection and this, composed almost entirely of sandbags, was about four feet high and five to six feet across. It therefore gave adequate cover for normal purposes, but could not withstand a bombardment by high explosive howitzer shell. There was also a support trench,

---

at Croix Marmuse (5 miles W.N.W. of Neuve Chapelle), and those of the IV. Corps at Estaires.

[1] Appendices 2 and 16.

[2] Extemporized chevaux de frise made on a wooden frame, consisting of a horizontal bar, 25 to 30 feet long, with cross-pieces, 3 feet long, at either end, with barbed wire stretched between them.

[3] A 6-inch battery had four howitzers ; a 4·5-inch battery six howitzers.

10 Mar. a hundred yards in rear of the front trench, but this was so waterlogged that it was not tenable, and no attempt had been made by the enemy to make it so. In ignorance of this, orders were given for both fire and support trenches to be destroyed, and each 6-inch battery was allotted approximately two hundred yards frontage of each. The fire of the 4·5-inch howitzers was superimposed on that of the 6-inch howitzers to complete the destruction of the front and support and any neighbouring subsidiary trenches. Some 4·7-inch guns were also used to intensify the fire of the howitzers on certain strong points. The bombardment of the trenches and strong points lasted 35 minutes, during which period some three thousand shells[1] were expended with effective results, the German front trenches being practically obliterated and most of the defenders killed or buried. The only exception was a frontage of 400 yards on the left sector to be assaulted that had been allotted to the two siege batteries that had only arrived from the United Kingdom on the afternoon of the previous day.[2] They had not had time to complete the gun platforms, so that accurate fire was not possible, nor were they able to register targets or lay out lines to the forward observing officers. They failed therefore to do serious damage to the trenches assigned to them, with fatal consequences to the assaulting infantry, the left of the 23rd Brigade.[3]

At 7.40 A.M. the whole of the ten (18-pdr.) brigades, R.F.A., together with ten (13-pdr.) batteries R.H.A.,[4] formed a belt of fire 400 yards in depth east of the village in order to prevent the escape of the Germans from the front defences and the arrival of reinforcements to their support. This was the first time that an artillery barrier or " barrage "[5] had been put down to isolate an enemy force holding the objective of the infantry assault.

At the same time, the heavy artillery detailed for

---

[1] The 6-inch howitzer fired one round in two minutes ; the 4·5-inch howitzer fired two rounds in one minute.

[2] See p. 84.

[3] It also transpired that the 6-inch howitzers were placed too far back to be quite sure, at extreme range, of clearing the infantry or dealing with the German strong points behind the front line.

[4] Appendices 2 and 16.

[5] The French word " barrage " first appeared in this sense in the First Army report on the battle of Neuve Chapelle. For the origin of the term and practice see " 1914," Volume II. p. 91.

counter-battery work [1] began their fight with the German 10 Mar. batteries supporting the defence.[2]

At 8.5 A.M. the artillery lifted to a general line 300 yards further east, including the village of Neuve Chapelle. Simultaneously, the infantry, which had formed up in front of the trenches and breastworks during the bombardment, greatly impressed by the artillery fire, and confident that it had achieved its purpose, advanced across No Man's Land, nominally at a steady double, but actually as fast as the heavy mud of the fields would allow.

THE INDIAN CORPS

The Garhwal Brigade (Br.-General C. G. Blackader) was disposed for the assault with four battalions in the front line on a frontage of 600 yards between the Port Arthur salient (inclusive) and Pont Logy. The extra, fifth, battalion, the 3/London, was in brigade reserve.[3]

The assault of the 1/39th Garhwal Rifles (Lieut.-Colonel E. R. R. Swiney), the right battalion of the brigade, met with misfortune almost immediately. Its two leading companies were directed to attack straight to their front from the right face of the Port Arthur salient, but on leaving the trench, the left company mistook direction and bore right-handed, the right company conforming.[4] As a

---

[1] For counter-battery work and for assisting in the demolition of strong points behind the front defences, the heavy artillery at the disposal of the First Army was organized into two groups. See Appendices 2 and 16. Eight aeroplanes with wireless were available for observing fire.

The 15-inch howitzer (" Granny ") was ready to open fire at 6 A.M. on the 9th, but no registration was carried out, in order to conceal its presence. On the 10th registration was still impossible, owing to the mist, but during the first two phases of the bombardment it fired two unobserved rounds by the map at Aubers church, used by the Germans as an observation post.

The " Churchill " Train was in position at 9 P.M. on the 9th, and opened fire at 7.35 A.M. on the 10th at Aubers and the vicinity, also firing by the map.

[2] Active in the battle zone were the *7th* and *43rd Field Artillery Regiment* of the *14th Division* (nine 77 mm. field gun batteries and three 10·5 cm. howitzer batteries). In addition, certain batteries of the *13th Division* to the north were in a position to participate. These field batteries were assisted by part of the *VII. Corps* artillery, particularly the *7th* (*Foot*) *Artillery Regiment* (2 battalions of heavy field howitzers and a mortar battery) in position on Aubers ridge about Aubers and Pommereau.

[3] The brigade was confronted by two companies of the German *16th Infantry Regiment*.

[4] Owing to the heavy casualties amongst the officers of the 1/39th Garhwal Rifles, no copy of battalion orders has been found. Various explanations of the loss of direction have been suggested : that the leading mark, a prominent tree behind the German lines, was destroyed by artillery fire or obscured by smoke ; that the left was to be on the Layes

10 Mar. result, the attack of the Garhwalis was delivered southward of the intended flank of the offensive and therefore against a part of the German defences unprepared for assault by artillery bombardment. Before the mistake was realized, the two remaining Garhwali companies, less two platoons, had followed in support. Although the German wire had not been shattered, the Garhwalis forced a way through the obstacle in face of a heavy fire from the German trench beyond, cutting the wires and pulling away the knife rests like gates. After a sharp fight, the trench was entered on a front of two hundred yards and its occupants captured or killed. The Garhwali casualties were very heavy, all the six British officers who were in the assault being killed, and others, including an artillery observing officer, who attempted to replace them, wounded ; but the companies continued to hold the captured trench under their native officers.

The attack of the three remaining front battalions of the Garhwal Brigade—the 2/Leicestershire (Lieut.-Colonel H. Gordon), 2/3rd Gurkhas (Lieut.-Colonel V. A. Ormsby) and 2/39th Garhwal Rifles (Lieut.-Colonel D. H. Drake-Brockman)—was more easily successful. Advancing in lines of platoons at fifty paces distance they crossed rapidly and with little loss the 200 yards of No Man's Land. The remains of the German wire entanglement formed no obstacle and the front trench was entered before the survivors of its garrison could organize any resistance.[1] The assaulting lines then pressed on without delay to the support trench, the whole movement having taken less than fifteen minutes. Without waiting for the completion of the second phase of the bombardment, the period of 30 minutes fire on the village itself, the leading companies went on across the Port Arthur—Neuve Chapelle road, the two left battalions passing through the southern houses of the village. By 9 A.M. about two hundred prisoners and five machine guns had been captured, and the brigade objective, the line of the Smith-Dorrien trench, two hundred yards beyond the road, was reached. The trench was found to be full of water, and a position was therefore taken up some fifty yards in rear of it. Here the front

brook and a ditch which ran across the front was mistaken for this ; that the trench from which the companies jumped off bent round to the right and was not at right angles to the direction of attack.

[1] Rifleman Gobar Sing Negi, 2/39th Garhwal Rifles, was the first man to enter the main German trench. He was killed during this engagement, and posthumously awarded the Victoria Cross.

troops began to entrench, undisturbed except for occasional 10 Mar.
shrapnel, the Leicestershire along ,the Layes brook with
their right on the Lorgies road, and the 2/3rd Gurkhas
carrying on the line to the Brewery Road, a track, immediately east of Neuve Chapelle village, with the 2/39th
Garhwal Rifles some two hundred yards in rear. Unfortunately no attempt was made to push forward detachments
as covering troops or to locate the enemy positions in front.

Owing to the misdirection of the attack of the 1/39th
Garhwal Rifles, a gap of two hundred and fifty yards now
separated that battalion from the right of the Leicestershire on the Lorgies road. The bombardment had battered the intervening sector of the German front trench
and caused many casualties among its defenders, but the
survivors, about half a company (*10th Company, 16th
Infantry Regiment*), held out. As soon as he could appreciate the situation, Colonel Swiney telephoned at 8.45 A.M.
to brigade headquarters for a reinforcement of two companies with which to take the uncaptured portion of the
German front trench. He was informed that the 1/Seaforth
Highlanders (Lieut.-Colonel A. B. Ritchie) of the Dehra
Dun Brigade, in support, would assault it from the north
from behind the right of the Leicestershire. He was also
given to understand that as soon as the Seaforth attack
began to develop, he was to co-operate by a frontal assault
with any of the Garhwalis still in Port Arthur, and two
companies of the 3/London that were being sent forward
to him at once from brigade reserve.

In the meantime a number of the enemy from the
uncaptured part of the German position began to work
northwards along their trench and across the Port Arthur—
Neuve Chapelle road, behind the new front of the Leicestershire. The support company of that battalion wheeling
so as to face them, forced them back with bayonet and
hand-grenade [1] some hundred yards to the south of the
road. Here, however, the enemy trench had been bar-
ricaded, and the attack was unable to make further
progress.

THE IV. CORPS

The 25th Brigade (Br.-General A. W. G. Lowry Cole)
of the 8th Division, in battle for the first time in the war,

[1] Early in 1915 each infantry brigade had formed a " grenade company ", later called a bombing company, composed of thirty selected
men drawn from each of its battalions, who were trained by the field companies R.E., the original bombers. In the attack, as a rule, twenty bombers
accompanied each battalion, the remainder being held in brigade reserve.

10 Mar. was to assault the German defences on a frontage of four hundred yards between the Neuve Chapelle road (inclusive) and Signpost Lane (exclusive). Starting some seven hundred yards to the left of the Indian Corps and converging towards it, the brigade was to carry forward the advance to the eastern edge of Neuve Chapelle village.[1] At 8.5 A.M. the two leading battalions—the 2/R. Berkshire (Lieut.-Colonel E. Feetham) on the right, and the 2/Lincolnshire (Lieut.-Colonel G. B. McAndrew) on the left—moved forward to the assault, and were able to cross No Man's Land with little loss. Here, too, the wire entanglement had been completely shattered, and the Germans, demoralized by the suddenness and intensity of the bombardment, were unable to man the battered remnants of the front trench before the assault reached them. Moving in four lines of companies, the leading troops crossed the German front trench and continued without delay to the support trench, two hundred yards beyond. This they reached about 8.20 A.M., and there halted. As in the case of the three left battalions of the Garhwal Brigade they had demonstrated that a break-in was possible, and without severe losses.[2]

Whilst the artillery was carrying out the second phase of the bombardment, firing on the village itself, the two supporting battalions of the brigade—the 2/Rifle Brigade (Lieut.-Colonel R. B. Stephens) and 1/R. Irish Rifles (Lieut.-Colonel G. B. Laurie)—moved forward into position behind the captured line. At 8.35 A.M. this bombardment was completed, and the artillery lifted its fire to the east of the village. The two battalions thereupon advanced over the German support trench, and passed through the Berkshire and the Lincolnshire. They crossed the open ground towards the village in artillery formation, four lines of small columns each of half a platoon. Little opposition was encountered, though the mountain (pack) guns following the attack were put out of action, and the 2/Rifle Brigade entered Neuve Chapelle about 8.50 A.M., its front lines pressing on through the ruined cottages and across the main street out into the open fields beyond. Here the advance was brought to a standstill by the artillery barrage, then falling between the village and the

---

[1] It was opposed by the two right companies of the German *16th Infantry Regiment*.

[2] Among the killed was Lieut.-Colonel G. B. McAndrew of the Lincolnshire, who, when mortally wounded in the first advance, caused himself to be held up that he might see his men capture the German trenches.

Bois du Biez. On the right touch was gained with the 10 Mar. Garhwal Brigade entrenching slowly in bad ground.

The Royal Irish Rifles reached the Armentières road almost simultaneously with the Rifle Brigade. Pivoting on their own right at the northern road junction of the main street, the Irishmen now wheeled right-handed through the orchards and houses in the triangle of roads (Road Triangle) immediately north of the village. No British troops were, however, moving forward on their left. Thus on that flank parties of Germans from positions about a tiny group of houses known as Mauquissart, and the nameless group of houses 500 yards south of it, were able to take the later stage of this advance in enfilade with machine-gun and rifle fire, inflicting heavy losses. Nevertheless by 9.40 A.M. the Irish Rifles had occupied the Road Triangle and taken up a position on its eastern side in touch with the 2/Rifle Brigade on the right. They then swung back a company to guard their left flank.

The 25th Brigade had now reached the objectives assigned to it. Over fifty prisoners had been taken, and, apart from small isolated parties of survivors, many without rifles, making their way back to the Bois du Biez and towards Pietre, there was little sign of any enemy on the immediate front. Lieut.-Colonel R. B. Stephens, commanding the Rifle Brigade, sent word back to this effect, and asked whether a further advance should be made. Br.-General Lowry Cole replied that the 23rd Brigade, on the left, was held up and that until it got through, no further advance was practicable. The 25th Brigade, assisted by the 2nd Field Company R.E. sent forward for the purpose, therefore set to work constructing trenches and erecting wire.

The 23rd Brigade (Br.-General R. J. Pinney) was to assault with its two leading battalions on a front of four hundred yards, the 2/Scottish Rifles (Lieut.-Colonel W. M. Bliss) on the right and the 2/Middlesex (Lieut.-Colonel R. H. Hayes) on the left.[1] The 2/Devonshire (Lieut.-Colonel J. O. Travers) following in support behind the inner flanks of the two leading battalions, was to strengthen the new front along the Armentières road and enable the Middlesex both to extend their left towards the Moated Grange and clear the Orchard to their immediate front. The 2/West Yorkshire (Captain P. L. Ingpen) was in brigade reserve.

[1] They were faced by two companies of the *11th Jäger Battalion*.

10 Mar.   On the left, the bombardment of the two hundred yards of front opposite the Middlesex had been a failure as already mentioned, owing to the late arrival of the batteries concerned. The occupants of the German front trench, the greater part of a company of the *11th Jäger Battalion*, were scarcely affected ; and immediately the Middlesex left their trenches they were met by heavy machine-gun and rifle fire at point-blank range both from their front and left flank. The three leading waves were completely annihilated, and it was therefore decided at 8.30 A.M. to await the effect of another bombardment.[1]

On the right, although the bombardment had been successful, the assault of the 2/Scottish Rifles was also severely handled by the Germans holding out in front of the Middlesex. Advancing with its right on Signpost Lane, its right leading company reached the German front trench, but its left was stopped. Lieut.-Colonel Bliss was killed whilst bringing the survivors of the latter and the leading platoons of the Devonshire over to the right to exploit his success there, and nine other officers also fell. But by 10 A.M. further rushes had carried the line of Scottish Rifles and Devonshire forward another two hundred yards when, completely enfiladed from the left flank, the leading troops were barely able to hold on to the ground gained.

From brigade headquarters two hundred yards in rear of the British front trenches, Br.-General Pinney saw the delay and went forward to the Middlesex trench. After conferring with Lieut.-Colonels Hayes and Travers, he decided to close the rest of the Devonshire to the right, when they would work forward astride Signpost Lane behind the Scottish Rifles and, facing north, take in enfilade the Germans holding out in front of the Middlesex. Two companies of the West Yorkshire were ordered forward from brigade reserve to support this movement. At the same time he asked Major-General Davies, commanding the 8th Division, for a further bombardment of the un-captured sector of trench.

By 10 A.M., then, the central battalions of the assault had broken through on a front of sixteen hundred yards, had captured Neuve Chapelle village and reached their

---

[1] It was thought at first that the attack had succeeded in reaching the German trenches, as no one behind could see, and not a man returned. The dead bodies of the attackers were found lying in rows in the 11.15 A.M. advance.

objective, the Smith-Dorrien trench east of the village. 10 Mar.
On both flanks, however, the Germans continued to hold
portions of their front trench : on the right a sector of
two hundred and fifty yards in front of the Port Arthur
salient, and on the left a sector of two hundred yards in
front of the 2/Middlesex.

ACTION OF THE SUPPORTING BRIGADES

In the meantime the two supporting brigades—the
Dehra Dun Brigade of the Meerut Division, and the 24th
Brigade [1] of the 8th Division—were moving forward to
their positions of assembly behind the breastworks and
trenches of the British original front line, vacated earlier
in the morning by the assaulting brigades.

The Dehra Dun Brigade (Br.-General C. W. Jacob)
marched from its concentration area, one to two miles
behind the battle front, soon after 9 A.M. ; but the order
to assist the 1/39th Garhwal Rifles against the Germans
still holding out opposite the Port Arthur salient did not
reach Lieut.-Colonel A. B. Ritchie of the 1/Seaforth Highlanders until his arrival at the front breastwork on the
La Bassée—Estaires road at 11.45 A.M. He at once went
to Port Arthur, where Lieut.-Colonel Swiney explained the
situation, and then returned to his unit and gave the
necessary orders. Owing to these various delays, it was
1 P.M. before the two leading companies of the Seaforths
moved forward across No Man's Land behind the front of
the Leicestershire. Their orders were to advance from
the La Bassée—Estaires road and swing right-handed
pivoting on the northern end of the Port Arthur salient
in order to attack down the line of the German defences,
whilst a frontal assault by two companies of the 3/London
and the remainder of the 1/39th Garhwal Rifles was
delivered from Port Arthur itself. The progress of the
Highlanders across the difficult and intersected country
was, however, slow, and they soon came under heavy fire
from the German trench. Moreover, at 2.15 P.M. when
the advance southwards was about to begin, it was delayed
by another incident. Reports had led General Anderson,
commanding the Meerut Division, to believe that the

[1] Although two Territorial battalions were attached to the brigade only
three Regular battalions were available for the attack : the 2/Northampton-
shire and the 4/Camerons were holding the line, whilst the 5/Black Watch
was providing carriers and stretcher parties.

10 Mar. Seaforth attack had been made but was held up, and he therefore ordered the XLIII. Brigade R.F.A. (4·5-inch howitzers) to carry out a further bombardment of the trench in order to hasten its capture. The Highlanders, on realizing this, temporarily suspended their attack.

The remainder of the Dehra Dun Brigade, assembled about the original British front line at and south of Pont Logy, waited in readiness until the front was clear, Br.-General Jacob establishing his headquarters with the Garhwal Brigade, so as to ensure close touch.

The forward movement of the 24th Brigade (Br.-General F. C. Carter) had also been interrupted, whilst attempts were being made to clear the German front trench opposite the Middlesex. At 9.30 A.M. Br.-General Pinney had reported the situation to the 8th Division with a request for a further howitzer bombardment of the un-captured sector. This message reached General Davies at 9.40 A.M. ; and he took immediate action, with the result that, at 10.10 A.M., the XLV. Brigade (18-pdrs.), 31st Battery R.F.A. (4·5-inch howitzers) and the 4th Siege Battery (6-inch howitzers), were turned on to the trench in question. Further, as it was clear that the left flank of the 25th Brigade about the Road Triangle would be already dangerously exposed owing to the check to the 23rd Brigade, General Davies ordered the 24th Brigade to detail a battalion to fill the gap of five hundred yards between the inner flanks of the two first line brigades. At 10.20 A.M. the 2/East Lancashire (Lieut.-Colonel C. L. Nicholson, who was wounded during the day), the leading battalion of the 24th Brigade, was accordingly sent forward, and took up a position facing north-east astride the cross roads, at the junction of Signpost Lane and Armentières Road.

Whilst this was in progress the renewed artillery bombardment had taken place. It was exceedingly accurate and effective, and when at its conclusion the 23rd Brigade bombing section started working northwards along the trench from Signpost Lane, one officer and 64 men of the *11th Jäger Battalion* got up out of it and walking across No Man's Land surrendered to the Middlesex, who thereupon advanced and about 11.30 A.M. occupied the German trench.

Preparations were now made to attack the Orchard, believed to be a German strong point, which General Rawlinson had ordered to be taken as soon as possible at all costs. The Middlesex, who had suffered heavily earlier in the day, were reinforced by the remaining companies 10 Mar. of the West Yorkshire from brigade reserve, and the 1/Worcestershire (24th Brigade) was sent up from divisional reserve to be at the disposal of Br.-General Pinney. The position was then bombarded by the howitzers of the XXXVII. Brigade R.F.A. for half an hour, and shortly after noon the Middlesex and two companies of the West Yorkshire advanced. They found the Orchard neither defended nor even prepared for defence, and occupied it without loss. Two companies of the West Yorkshire now worked northwards from the Orchard towards the Moated Grange, which had been shelled throughout the morning by the 24th Brigade Trench Mortar Battery,[1] and the few German survivors, unable to get away under cover as their communication trenches had been destroyed, now surrendered. The Middlesex began to consolidate the German old front line, whilst sections of the 15th Field Company, R.E., with working parties of the 5/Black Watch, were sent up to put the Orchard and two captured groups of houses in Signpost Lane in a state of defence.

The advance to the Orchard enabled the Scottish Rifles —with only three officers still in action—and the Devonshire, the right of the 23rd Brigade, who had crossed the Armentières road, to establish themselves behind the line of the Smith-Dorrien trench, immediately north of the Road Triangle, where the Scottish Rifles joined up with the left flank of the 25th Brigade.

About 1 P.M., therefore, both the 23rd and 25th Brigades had reached their objectives. General Davies now ordered them to hold and consolidate the ground gained, and at 1.30 P.M. instructed the 24th Brigade—the order took half an hour to reach it—to reassemble as rapidly as possible with a view to a further advance.

Except for the failure to capture two hundred yards of the defences still held by the Germans in front of the Port Arthur salient, the first phase of the operations had now been completed. The whole of the village of Neuve Chapelle was in British hands, and being organized for defence by Lieut.-Colonel P. G. Grant, C.R.E. of the 8th Division, whilst the three assaulting brigades, assisted by their affiliated engineer companies were consolidating a

---

[1] This battery, from a position immediately behind the British front trench, fired 232 bombs during the morning into the German trenches about the Moated Grange.

10 Mar. defensive line east of the village.   Six previously selected localities behind the new front were put in hand as supporting points, and communication trenches were dug across No Man's Land to join up the British and German original front trenches.

THE DELAY IN FURTHER ADVANCE

General Haig, at Merville, had kept in constant communication with his corps commanders throughout the morning. At 9 A.M., hearing of the successful advance through the enemy front line, and of the Germans holding it having been killed, captured or scattered, he had asked Sir John French to move forward at least one cavalry brigade from the general reserve to a position behind the British front trenches.   The extent of front being considerable he wished to have some mounted men at hand to assist the infantry in keeping touch with the Germans, and for reconnaissance should they really have broken. At 11.15 A.M., the 5th Cavalry Brigade (2nd Cavalry Division) was accordingly ordered to Estaires.   General Haig then waited until the advance of the Indian and IV. Corps from the east of Neuve Chapelle towards Aubers ridge should create a favourable opportunity for a general offensive by the remainder of the First Army.   But several hours were still to elapse before a further advance was attempted.

In the case of the IV. Corps the check to the Middlesex had seriously affected General Rawlinson's plans.   Information was slow in arriving from the front.   He had believed the Orchard to be one of the strong points of the German defence, and did not know of its occupation until more than an hour after the event.   Until this point had been captured he did not consider an advance feasible from the Moated Grange.   The 7th Division had therefore been kept inactive, though there was no opposition on this part of the front, and General Capper begged to be allowed to push on.[1]   It was not until 1.15 P.M., when he heard that the Orchard was taken, that General Rawlinson ordered the division to be prepared to advance towards Aubers ridge.

---

[1] " At 12.5 P.M. the corps commander [General Rawlinson] spoke to " the G.O.C. 7th Division [General Capper] on the telephone, telling him " of the situation, and that he could not send his division forward until " Point 6 [the Orchard] had been taken ".

At 1.30 P.M. he sent a summary of the situation to 10 Mar. the First Army, stating that the leading brigade (21st) of the 7th Division was moving forward to a position near the Moated Grange and that it would advance as soon as the 24th Brigade, the reserve brigade of the 8th Division was ready to co-operate on its right. He proposed, he added, to give the order to advance on Aubers at 2 P.M. To this, General Haig wired his approval and, in order to exploit the operation to full advantage, placed the 20th Brigade (7th Division) then in First Army reserve, at the disposal of the IV. Corps.

The further advance of the Indian Corps had been dislocated in a somewhat similar manner by the situation in front of the Port Arthur salient. At 1.35 P.M. General Rawlinson telephoned to General Willcocks giving the situation on the IV. Corps front and stating his intention to advance on Aubers at 2 P.M. General Willcocks replied that the Meerut Division would not be ready by then, as the attack southwards (by the 1/Seaforth Highlanders) against the Germans still holding out in the front line had not yet been completed. As soon as the front was cleared, the Meerut Division would, he said, continue its advance on the Bois du Biez. General Rawlinson thereupon postponed the issue of his orders for the movement on Aubers, as he considered that the advance of the Indian Corps, to be effective, should be simultaneous with his own.

At 2.45 P.M., in reply to a message from First Army Advanced Headquarters to the effect that General Haig was most anxious for the further advance to be pushed on, General Rawlinson said that he was waiting for the Indian Corps, which was not ready. At that moment, however, General Willcocks, realizing that the situation was far from being as unfavourable as he had imagined, telephoned that he was sending forward another brigade (the Jullundur) and that he had ordered the Meerut Division to move on the Bois du Biez as soon as possible. General Rawlinson thereupon at 2.50 P.M. sent word to the First Army that he was about to issue his orders for the advance. General Haig then ordered the 5th Cavalry Brigade to march through Estaires to a position of readiness about Rouge Croix (1 mile west of the Moated Grange).

THE FIGHTING EAST OF THE VILLAGE

THE GERMAN SITUATION

The trace for a second line of defence along the whole of their Western battle front had already been planned on paper by the Germans. It was to be constructed some thousand yards behind the front system ; but the work had been greatly delayed owing to the scarcity of labour. The troops available were fully employed in maintaining in repair the front and communication trenches. This was especially the case in the Flanders sector, where the weather and high water level had made the conditions exceptionally difficult. Nevertheless a second line trench had been begun in places, and strong points partially prepared.[1]

Behind the Neuve Chapelle front, the second line trench was to run from Mauquissart southwards to the bridge, really only a brick culvert, over the Layes brook on the upper Neuve Chapelle—La Russie road, and thence along the western edge of the Bois du Biez to the Lorgies road. Strong points were to be made at every few hundred yards interval. One of these at Mauquissart was nearly complete, as also another among the nameless group of cottages 500 yards to the south, on the Mauquissart—Neuve Chapelle road. Close to the Layes bridge, on the Neuve Chapelle side of the brook, is a slight rise in the ground ; it is only a matter of a few feet, but sufficient to give a fair command on all sides. Here also a small closed work was under construction among the ruins of a cottage ; but a line of low willows and a few scattered trees in front made it difficult to locate from the British side. From here southwards to the Lorgies road the only defence was the conversion of the ditch along the western edge of the Bois du Biez into a trench ; but the wood itself, consisting chiefly of young oak-trees with a quantity of undergrowth, gave good cover.

These beginnings of a second line position and some small strong points a mile further east near the crest of

---

[1] " 17 Monate in englischer Kriegsgefangenschaft " by Lieut. Pult. The author was in the German *16th Regiment* and was taken prisoner at Neuve Chapelle.

Also " 17th Bav. Res. Regt." pp. 28-30 ; " 21st Bav. Res. Regt." p. 28, and statements of prisoners, First Army Intelligence Summary, March 1915.

Aubers ridge were the only defences behind the German **10 Mar.**
front line.[1]

The six German companies, about fourteen hundred
men, that had held the front trench and opposed the
first assault, had been practically annihilated, either
killed or taken prisoner.   Only a few stragglers managed
to get back through Neuve Chapelle, some retiring to the
Bois du Biez and others towards Pietre.

The two companies of the *11th Jäger Battalion*, the
only troops immediately available in support, coming
from Halpegarbe, behind the Bois du Biez, had been
unable to reach Neuve Chapelle before the British were
in possession of it.   About 9.30 A.M. they therefore
occupied and hurriedly improved the beginnings of the
second line trench in the centre and on their right flank,
especially the strong points at the bridge over the Layes
brook, at Mauquissart and at the nameless group of
cottages between.

The *13th Division*, that held the front northwards from
the Moated Grange, was already very extended owing to
the withdrawal from it four days previously of the *158th
Infantry Regiment*.[2]   Consequently it was unable to send
any considerable support.   The *13th Infantry Regiment*
that held the left of the divisional front from the Moated
Grange to Fauquissart moved forward its reserve battalion
from Fournes about 10 A.M. to form a defensive flank
north and east of the Moated Grange and prevent the
extension of the gap northwards.   In addition, two
companies had been sent from the supporting battalion
of the *15th Infantry Regiment*, that held the line on the
right of the *13th*, and they marched to Pietre to reinforce
the two companies of the *11th Jäger Battalion* about
Mauquissart.[3]

The delay in the British advance gave five clear hours
in which to strengthen the strong points, arm them with
machine guns, and make this part of the line into the
beginnings of a formidable position.   An effective crossfire
could now be brought to bear on any advance from the
front north of Neuve Chapelle.

[1] The villages on top of Aubers ridge, such as Herlies, Illies and
Halpegarbe, were also defended by trenches around their perimeters,
dating for the most part from the fighting on the ridge with the II. Corps
in October 1914.

[2] See p. 87.

[3] For German *VII. Corps* Orders for this movement see Note at end
of Chapter.   It will be noticed that such German reinforcements as arrived
during the morning went to the front attacked by the IV. Corps.

10 Mar. On the left flank, however, south of the Layes bridge, the front of the Bois du Biez lay open to attack. It was not until 6 P.M. that the arrival of two battalions from about Violaines (3 miles to the south of Neuve Chapelle), the supporting battalions of the *56th* and *57th Infantry Regiments*, filled this critical gap.[1]

THE IV. CORPS

General Rawlinson's orders for the advance of the IV. Corps on Aubers and Pietre, after his exchange of communications with the First Army, were sent out at 2.55 P.M.[2]

The 8th Division was to be directed on the nameless group of cottages between the Layes bridge and Mauquissart as a first objective and thence on Pietre.

The 7th Division was to advance through and north of Mauquissart with Pietre Mill (Moulin du Pietre) as a first objective and thence to the Rue d'Enfer, between Aubers and Trivelet (a mile north-west of Aubers), 700 yards beyond.

One brigade of each division was to be in first line ; the remaining brigades were to support and co-operate as the situation demanded. The leading brigades—the 24th Brigade of the 8th Division and the 21st Brigade of the 7th Division—were to cross the line of the Smith-Dorrien trench north of Neuve Chapelle at 3.30 P.M., which allowed very little time for orders to get down to battalions. Touch was to be maintained on the right with the Indian Corps, which was to advance simultaneously on the Bois du Biez. The artillery of the 7th Division, attached to the 8th Division for the first period of the operations, was now to revert to its own division according to the original arrangement. The artillery of both divisions was, however, to support the infantry advance, their fire being directed at first on the Mauquissart road and the Bois du Biez—Pietre road, with special attention to the strong points which had been reported at the Layes bridge and near Mauquissart. These points had not, however, been previously registered, and could not be clearly seen from any of the existing observation posts. The light, too, was already failing, and these disadvantages, together with the fact that most of the telephone cables communicating

---

[1] The *56th* and *57th Infantry Regiments*, holding the line from the Rue du Bois to the La Bassée canal, each had one battalion in support.
[2] Appendix 17.

from the forward observing officers with the batteries had **10 Mar.**
been cut, and the officers themselves killed or wounded,
made the bombardment ineffective.

For the attack of the 8th Division, General Davies had
earlier, at 1.30 P.M., ordered the 24th Brigade to assemble
astride Signpost Lane, whence it was to advance through
the inner flanks of the 23rd and 25th Brigades on the
divisional objectives.[1]   The assembly of the brigade along
Signpost Lane took longer than was anticipated, owing to
the fact that two battalions had been detached during the
morning to assist the 23rd Brigade and were in action.
Nevertheless when, at 3.55 P.M., the orders to advance
arrived, the brigade was ready in position.   The 1/Sherwood
Foresters (Major C. R. Mortimore, wounded during the
day) and 2/Northamptonshire (Colonel C. S. Prichard)
deployed along the line of the Armentières road, right and
left of the Signpost Lane cross roads.   There seemed no
sign of movement in the 7th Division : as will be seen, the
21st Brigade had moved forward at 2.30 P.M., but had been
halted.   Br.-General Carter, therefore, sent word to the
21st Brigade, first by runner and then by an officer, to
enquire if it were ready.   Two exchanges of messages took
place on this subject before the matter was cleared up,
and it was 5.30 P.M. before the two leading battalions
finally moved forward from the Armentières road.   By that
time thick clouds that had been gathering during the afternoon settled over the sodden battle area, so that darkness
came on early and movement across country became
very difficult.   After an advance of five hundred yards,
during which units in crossing several dykes became hopelessly intermingled, fire was opened on the brigade both
from the Layes bridge redoubt, to the right front, and
from the nameless group of cottages directly ahead.   It
was not considered advisable to attack in the existing
confusion of companies and the line was therefore halted
and reorganized.   The Sherwood Foresters now had their
right near the Layes bridge — La Russie road close to
the Mauquissart road junction, and their left on the Sunken
Road, a track leading back past the Orchard.   The
Northamptonshire were within two hundred yards of
the nameless group of cottages, and were separated by a
gap of two hundred yards from the left of the Sherwood
Foresters.   This gap was eventually filled by two companies of the 1/Worcestershire.   The 2/East Lancashire

[1] Appendix 17.

10 Mar. (Lieut.-Colonel C. L. Nicholson) and the rest of the Worcestershire (Lieut.-Colonel E. C. F. Wodehouse) remained in support about the line of the Smith-Dorrien trench, north of the Road Triangle. Thus the movement of the leading brigade of the 8th Division came to an end.

The position of the remainder of the division did not alter during the evening. The 25th Brigade continued to strengthen its position in front of Neuve Chapelle village and along the eastern side of the Road Triangle. Its casualties during the day's fighting had been 35 officers and 746 other ranks. The 23rd Brigade, which had had a total of 1,241 casualties, all ranks, during the day, mostly incurred by the Middlesex and Scottish Rifles during the first assault, occupied a line beyond the Armentières road, between the Road Triangle and the Orchard, in rear of the 24th Brigade.

The operations of the 7th Division were much like those of the 8th. After its very heavy losses at Ypres, it had barely 15 per cent of its original infantry, and was for all intents and purposes a new formation. Major-General Sir T. Capper ordered the 21st Brigade (Br.-General H. E. Watts) to assemble on a front between the Orchard and the Moated Grange. Thence it was to attack north-eastwards —it actually went more east than north-east—towards the divisional objectives,[1] supported by the 20th Brigade (Br.-General F. J. Heyworth). General Capper hoped that a successful advance by these two brigades to the Rue d'Enfer would take in rear and unsettle the Germans opposing the 22nd Brigade (Br.-General S. T. B. Lawford), the remaining brigade of his division, which was in position in the front trenches and breastworks north of the Moated Grange. At the first sign of weakness, therefore, the 22nd Brigade was to leave its trenches and advance north-eastward by the Ferme Deleval (1 mile north of Aubers) and across the left of the 21st Brigade, but keep touch by its own left with the right of the Canadian Division, in the British original front line.

About 2 P.M., before receiving these orders, the two leading battalions of the 21st Brigade, the 2/Royal Scots Fusiliers (Major J. H. W. Pollard) and the 2/Green Howards (Lieut.-Colonel W. L. Alexander), had moved forward to the line of the Armentières road, to a position of readiness between the Orchard and the Moated Grange.

---

[1] Appendix 17.

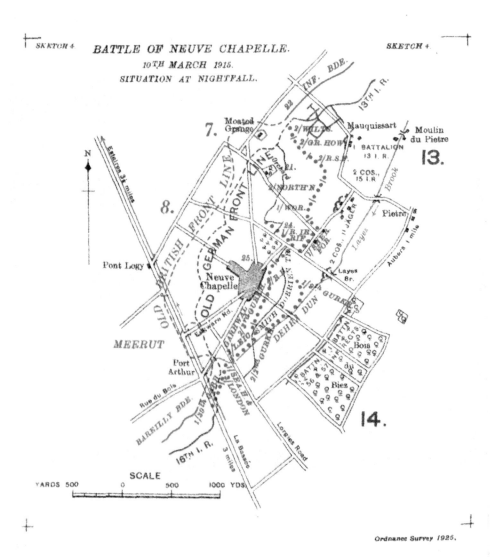

BATTLE OF NEUVE CHAPELLE.
10TH MARCH 1915.
SITUATION AT NIGHTFALL.

SCALE

YARDS 500   0   500   1000 YDS

Ordnance Survey 1925.

Meeting with no opposition in their movement across the 10 Mar. open over the British and German original trenches, they passed on across the Armentières road and through the left of the 23rd Brigade without a shot being fired. But at 2.45 P.M. they were stopped in consequence of a definite message from divisional headquarters and halted about two hundred yards beyond the road, the 2/Royal Scots Fusiliers east of the Orchard, with the 2/Green Howards on the left. The orders that reached them later stated that the advance would be continued as soon as the 24th Brigade came up into line. For reasons that have been given it was not until 5.30 P.M. that the 24th Brigade moved forward and it was therefore nearly 6 P.M. before the general advance began. This was over two hours later than the time appointed in corps orders.

In the gathering darkness progress across the ditches Sketch 4. and hedges was difficult and slow. The Royal Scots Fusiliers and Green Howards of the 21st Brigade were soon held up by fire, not only from the front but from the northern flank. To their left, the 2/Wiltshire,[1] the left supporting battalion of the brigade, working northwards from the Moated Grange up the line of the German defences,[2] led by bombing detachments, was at first very successful, and captured an officer and 180 men of the *13th Infantry Regiment.* After an advance of 200 yards it reached a wide ditch, where the Germans had hurriedly built up a flank position facing south, and here after a combat at close range and considerable casualties, including five officers, progress came to an end.

At 6 P.M. General Capper, the divisional commander, realizing the urgency of capturing the defended localities which were checking the 21st Brigade before the Germans could further organize their defence, sent a staff officer to Br.-General Watts to urge him to press the attack. Owing to the darkness, however, the latter considered that no good purpose would be gained by sending forward more troops. The area was already congested and units were hard to locate, as map identification was very difficult in the flat ground intersected by dykes, more than one dyke being mistaken for the Layes brook. Reports showed that the three battalions in his front line with only 5 or 6

---

[1] Under Captain R. M. T. Gillson until 2.30 P.M. when he was wounded and Captain E. L. Makin took command.

[2] At 2.50 P.M. First Army had telegraphed to General Rawlinson that " General Haig was particularly anxious that the IV. Corps should sweep " northwards up the German trenches north of the Moated Grange ".

10 Mar. officers apiece were too disorganized to rush the German positions in the dark with any chance of success.

At 7 P.M., on being informed of this, General Capper ordered the 21st Brigade, in reserve about Cameron Lane, north-east of Rouge Croix, to secure the line gained, to keep close touch with the troops on either flank and to reorganize with a view to resuming the attack early the following morning. The front line of the brigade, held by three battalions, was thus established on a curve corresponding approximately to the bend of the Mauquissart road. The 2/Bedfordshire (Major C. C. Onslow), the right supporting battalion of the brigade, halted east of the Orchard and in rear of the Royal Scots Fusiliers. The 2/Gordon Highlanders attached to the brigade for the operations,[1] remained about Cameron Lane in brigade reserve. The 2nd Highland and 55th Field Companies R.E., were sent forward to assist in strengthening the new front.

Except by fire, the 1/R. Welch Fusiliers (22nd Brigade) particularly assisting the 2/Wiltshire, the other two infantry brigades of the 7th Division were not engaged. The 20th was now ordered to bivouac about Cameron Lane, ready to turn out at short notice; the 22nd Brigade remained in its front line trenches and breastworks north of the Moated Grange. Thus the movement of both divisions of the IV. Corps came to an end.

THE INDIAN CORPS

General Willcocks's orders for the advance of the Indian Corps on the Bois du Biez, passed on through General Anderson, commanding the Meerut Division, reached the Dehra Dun Brigade at 3.30 P.M., the hour at which the advance should have begun. Br.-General C. W. Jacob had only three battalions with which to carry out the attack, as the 1/Seaforth Highlanders were attached to the Garhwal Brigade to clear up the situation in front of the Port Arthur salient. He was therefore to be supported by two battalions, 1/Manchester (Major B. D. L. G. Anley) and 47th Sikhs (Lieut.-Colonel H. L. Richardson), of the Jullundur Brigade (Br.-General E. P. Strickland).

---

[1] The 2/Gordon Highlanders of the 20th Brigade was attached to the 21st Brigade on 9th March, the 20th Brigade being allotted as Army reserve. As the 20th Brigade had rejoined the 7th Division during the first day of the battle, the Gordons were returned to it during the night 10th/11th March. Lieut.-Colonel H. P. Uniacke commanding was killed on the 13th March.

The three battalions had been waiting in readiness 10 Mar. behind the original front breastworks along the La Bassée —Estaires road, north of Port Arthur, and at 4 P.M. they moved forward in succession along and astride the Edgware Road (which enters Neuve Chapelle from the south-west), so as to give a wide berth to the Germans still in position opposite the Port Arthur salient. Before reaching the southernmost houses of Neuve Chapelle—where brigade headquarters were established—they turned right-handed across country for two hundred yards to the Port Arthur —Neuve Chapelle road, along which, as it offered a definite line, they deployed: the 2/2nd Gurkhas (Major E. R. P. Boileau) on the right, the 1/9th Gurkhas (Lieut.-Colonel G. T. Widdicombe) on the left, and the 4/Seaforth Highlanders (Lieut.-Colonel D. J. Mason MacFarlane) in support.

It was after 5 P.M. and getting dusk when the advance began. The line of the Layes brook 300 yards from the road, was reached without opposition. The stream, here about ten feet broad with nearly vertical banks and three or four feet of water in it,[1] was crossed on eight light bridges brought forward by the leading battalions, and the advance on a front of about six hundred yards was then continued to the Bois du Biez, four hundred yards away. A road and ditch border the southern edge of the wood, and there was a group of cottages, Les Brulots, at the south-west corner. Darkness had now set in, but a burning cottage gave the direction. By 6.30 P.M. the leading company of the 2/2nd Gurkhas had reached the road without difficulty and, occupying the cottages of Les Brulots, began to dig in at the edge of the wood. The 1/9th Gurkhas, on the left, were not so successful. The right of the battalion reached the wood, but the advance of the left was held up by enfilade fire from the redoubt at the Layes bridge on the left flank. Casualties were only slight, but as it was understood that the 8th Division (IV. Corps) was advancing on the left, the greater part of the battalion waited along the line of the Layes brook for the enemy to be cleared from their left flank.

German reinforcements were by now arriving in the

---

[1] The Layes brook is an old artificial drainage channel, said to have been dug by the farmers without expert assistance. As a result it has not a proper flow, the water sometimes going north, sometimes south. The drainage in this area was not got under control until the winter of 1915–16 when the Layes was connected with the Becque du Biez, the natural drainage channel that flows into the Lys, and lies a mile to the west of the Layes.

10 Mar. Bois du Biez to fill the gap in the line.[1] Whilst the
Gurkhas were beginning to establish themselves along the
western edge of the wood the enemy was entering it from
the other side. Gurkha scouts captured a scout of the
56th Infantry Regiment, who stated that two regiments
(in reality two battalions belonging to different regiments)
were collecting in the wood, and this was reported at
8 P.M. to brigade headquarters. Br.-General Jacob did
not consider his situation favourable for risking an action
in the wood. The left of his brigade was held up and,
as no British troops had advanced to right or left, both his
flanks were in the air. He therefore decided to withdraw
from the wood to the line of the Layes brook.

About 9 P.M., therefore, a position was taken up along
the western bank of the stream. The left was about four
hundred yards south of the Layes bridge with the flank
thrown back towards the trench of the 25th Brigade in
front of Neuve Chapelle village. The right was in touch
with the trench of the Leicestershire of the Garhwal
Brigade, which continued the line along the Layes brook
to the Lorgies road. The 4/Seaforth Highlanders, which
had supported the advance with two companies in rear
of each Gurkha battalion, helped to occupy the new front.
The two battalions (1/Manchester and 47th Sikhs) of the
Jullundur Brigade, that had been attached to the Dehra
Dun Brigade for the advance, were sent back to rejoin
their headquarters.

Whilst these events were taking place, the situation
in front of the Port Arthur salient had cleared. The
advance of the Dehra Dun Brigade at 5 P.M. towards the
Bois du Biez behind the right and rear of the Germans
still holding out in the two hundred yards of original
front, made their position desperate and, soon after, the
1/Seaforth Highlanders, from its position astride the
German original trenches north of the salient, moved
southwards in open order. Simultaneously Colonel Swiney,
commanding the troops in the Port Arthur salient, who
though wounded remained on the field, ordered the two
companies of the 3/London (Lieut.-Colonel A. A. Howell)

---

[1] Two battalions, the reserve battalions of the *56th* and *57th Infantry
Regiments* (*79th Brigade*, *14th Division*), with *79th Brigade* headquarters,
had marched during the day from about Violaines and Salomé, east of
La Bassée to Herlies and Halpegarbe. Here they awaited the dusk to
cover their movement down the exposed slope of the ridge to the Bois
du Biez. (Prisoners' Statements, First Army Intelligence Summaries,
March 1915.)

and the remainder (four platoons) of his own battalion— **10 Mar.**
1/39th Garhwal Rifles—to make a frontal assault on the
position.   This attack was carried out with great gallantry
under a heavy fire and at first many casualties were
suffered, particularly by the Londoners.   As the trench
was approached, however, the Germans, seeing themselves
attacked in front and flank, ceased their resistance and,
standing up, 3 officers and 80 men of the *16th Infantry
Regiment* surrendered.   The parapet of the German trench
was now reversed and the new line consolidated for defence
facing east, the flanks being connected up : the right flank
with the sector of trench captured in the morning by the
1/39th Garhwal Rifles and thence with the British front
line south of the Port Arthur salient, and the left flank
in touch with the new trench near the junction of the
Layes brook with the Lorgies road.

At nightfall the Garhwal Brigade had therefore two
battalions (1/39th Garhwal Rifles and the attached 1/Sea-
forth) [1] in front of and about the Port Arthur salient,
between the La Bassée and the Lorgies roads.   North of
the latter, in second line behind the Gurkhas of the Dehra
Dun Brigade, were the Leicestershire, the 2/3rd Gurkhas
and the 2/39th Garhwal Rifles, which still occupied the
position taken up during the morning behind the line of
the Smith-Dorrien trench and about the southern part of
Neuve Chapelle village.

The remaining brigade of the Meerut Division—the
Bareilly Brigade—continued to hold the original front
defences from the Port Arthur salient southward along
the Rue du Bois to the left of the I. Corps.   The casualties
of the division, which had borne all the fighting on the
front of the Indian Corps, were approximately one thousand
all ranks, practically all in the Garhwal Brigade and
1/Seaforth (Dehra Dun Brigade).

The Lahore Division had moved forward two of its
brigades during the day.   The Jullundur Brigade had
advanced to the Rue des Berceaux (1¼ miles west of Port
Arthur), and the Sirhind Brigade, in corps reserve, had
taken its place, 1½ miles in rear, about Vieille Chapelle
and La Couture.   The Ferozepore Brigade, in Army
reserve, had remained in billets in the villages south-west
of Merville, 8 miles behind the battle front.

[1] The survivors of the two companies of the 3/London rejoined
their unit in brigade reserve.

GENERAL RESULTS OF THE 10TH MARCH

As the result of the day's fighting, the Indian and
IV. Corps had together captured the German defences
on a front of four thousand yards, from the Port Arthur
salient (inclusive) to just beyond the Moated Grange, and
taken 748 prisoners.[1] They had occupied the whole of
Neuve Chapelle village, and had advanced to a maximum
depth of twelve hundred yards.

The general reserve at Sir John French's disposal[2] had
not participated in the day's fighting, and, with the
exception of the 5th Brigade of the 2nd Cavalry Division,
had not moved from its assembly position. During the
morning this brigade had been sent forward by Sir John
French, at General Haig's request, from Neuf Berquin
to a position of readiness between Estaires and Rouge
Croix. At 3.30 P.M., confident of a successful advance
of the Indian and IV. Corps from Neuve Chapelle on to
Aubers ridge before nightfall, General Haig had sent
orders to the remainder of the 2nd Cavalry Division to
follow the 5th Cavalry Brigade to Estaires. At 4.5 P.M.,
however, Sir John French, hearing of this, cancelled the
orders, as he had only put the 5th Cavalry Brigade at
General Haig's disposal. The remainder of the Cavalry
Corps—the 1st and 3rd Cavalry Divisions—remained in
their billeting areas, as did also the 46th (North Midland)
Division.

THE SUBSIDIARY ATTACKS

Sketch 1.   The subsidiary actions that had taken place during
the day to the right and left of the main attack had
accomplished little. In the I. Corps, on the right of the
Indian Corps, the preliminary bombardment on the front
of the right division, the 2nd (Major-General H. S. Horne),
which opened at 7.30 A.M. to synchronize with that of
the main attack, did not adequately prepare the position
for assault. Owing to difficulties in ranging in the mist[3]
and to the fact that the enemy's front trench was sited

---

[1] IV. Corps, 5 officers, 413 men ; Indian Corps, 8 officers, 322 men.
[2] The Cavalry Corps, the Indian Cavalry Corps, and the 46th (North
Midland) Division.
[3] In explanation of this failure Br.-General W. H. Onslow, C.R.A.
2nd Division, reported that " to allow for effect of temperature on cordite,
" fire was opened at increased range and the mist prevented satisfactory
" correction of the range during the bombardment ".

on the reverse side of a slight rise in the ground, neither **10 Mar.** the wire entanglement nor the front trench itself was sufficiently shelled. The first assault of the 6th Brigade (Br.-General R. Fanshawe) on a front of 750 yards east of Givenchy with Chapelle St. Roche and Violaines as objectives, therefore came under a heavy fire before No Man's Land was crossed, both from the front and from machine guns on both flanks. On the right the leading line of the 2/S. Staffordshire reached the German trench, but the supporting lines were held up, and shortly afterwards the men that had entered the trench were driven out by a bomb attack. Further efforts to recover the trench failed. In the centre the 1/King's was stopped by the entanglement through which no passable breach had been made. The leading men were killed on the wire itself in their endeavour to break through it, and after losing very heavily the battalion withdrew as best it could to its original trenches. On the left small parties of the 1/K.R.R.C. succeeded in entering the German position, but here, too, machine-gun fire prevented the supports from getting forward and the captured sector had to be abandoned.

After the failure of the first assault General Horne decided to make a second assault on a smaller sector of the front. After thirty minutes bombardment, at 2.15 P.M., the right and centre only were to attack, the left remaining in readiness to push forward if an opportunity occurred. The infantry assault was however again checked on the whole front, principally by machine-gun fire. A third assault planned to be made under cover of darkness, was forbidden by General Monro, the corps commander, and further operations were postponed.

The 1st Division (Major-General R. C. B. Haking), the left division of the I. Corps, occupied an exceptionally water-logged sector of the front over which an attack was not considered practicable. It therefore assisted the attacks both of the 2nd Division on its right and the Indian Corps on its left by a bombardment of the enemy's defences, and by periodic bursts of rifle fire so as to hold the enemy. At 4.15 P.M. General Haig ordered the I. Corps to send three battalions from the 1st (Guards) Brigade to operate on the right of the Indian Corps. It was intended that these battalions should widen the gap already made in the German front opposite Neuve Chapelle by advancing southwards from the Port Arthur salient, parallel to and

10 Mar. west of the Estaires—La Bassée road, so as to enfilade
and take in reverse the German defences as far as Richebourg l'Avoué. After the troops had been sent up, it
was however decided by the commanders on the spot, after
reference to General Willcocks, that it was inadvisable to
carry out this manœuvre, and the battalions were sent
back to their brigade.

On the extreme right, south of the La Bassée canal,
the French 58th Division (XXI. Corps) had co-operated
during the day by engaging with its artillery the enemy's
batteries south of the canal according to previous agreement.

North of the main attack the action of the Canadian
Division, between Fauquissart and Bois Grenier, and of
the III. Corps, the right corps of the Second Army, between
Bois Grenier and Ploegsteert Wood, was limited to demonstrations. At 7.30 A.M. the artillery of the Canadian
Division and III. Corps shelled the German wire and
defences in order to mislead the enemy as to the point of
attack and, from time to time for periods of 15 minutes,
the infantry opened bursts of machine-gun and rifle fire
followed by cheering as if about to assault. It was hoped
in this way to hold the enemy to his ground and to prevent
the despatch of reinforcements to the Neuve Chapelle
battle area.

The effect of these subsidiary actions, if any, was not
of long duration. By the afternoon the limits of the main
zone of operations had been clearly established and German
units had been sent in all haste from north and south to
fill the breach opposite Neuve Chapelle.

NOTE

THE GERMAN REINFORCEMENT DURING 10TH MARCH 1915 [1]

At 10 A.M., as soon as the news of the loss of Neuve Chapelle
village was confirmed at *VII. Corps* headquarters and the first
assault seemed to have been checked, General von Claer ordered
the recapture of the village and the original trenches beyond it.[2]

[1] " Die Bayern im grossen Kriege " ; " Das K.B. Reserve Inf. Regt.
" No. 21 " ; " Das K.B. Reserve Inf. Regt. No. 17 " ; " Das Feld Art.
" Regt. No. 22 "; First Army Intelligence Summaries, March 1915
(Statements of prisoners).

[2]   VII. CORPS OPERATION ORDER

11 A.M. [German time]
10.3.1915.

The 14th Infantry Division will reoccupy Neuve Chapelle. For this

Owing to the losses incurred by the front units, a counter-attack **10 Mar.** was, however, found impracticable, and all the troops sent up for the purpose were needed to hold the new line.

By the evening of the 10th all the battalions of the German *VII. Corps* were thus employed in holding its widely extended sector of defence between the La Bassée canal and Bois Grenier ; and the corps had no further troops with which to deliver a counter-stroke and regain its lost positions. The *XIX. Corps* to the north, holding from Bois Grenier past the front of Armentières to the foot of the Ypres hills was therefore called upon to send all available troops both to support the *VII. Corps* and to recapture Neuve Chapelle village. During the afternoon and evening one battalion each of the *104th, 133rd, 139th* and *179th (Saxon) Infantry Regiments* were sent by rail via Lille towards the new battle front.[1]

In addition to these reinforcements from the *XIX. Corps*, the *6th Bavarian Reserve Division* was placed by the *Sixth Army* at the disposal of the *VII. Corps* for the counter-offensive. This division had been withdrawn on 7th March from its position about Messines to Tourcoing and Roubaix, east of Lille, for a period of rest. It took up its rest billets on the morning of the 10th, but at 3 P.M. the orders were received for it to reinforce the German *VII. Corps* opposite Neuve Chapelle. Its infantry—the *12th* and *14th Bavarian Reserve Brigades*—entrained that evening, artillery and transport going by road. The trains, following at close interval, reached Wavrin and Don[2] after dark, between 7 and 10 P.M., so German accounts state, and if so escaped the observation of the British aeroplanes.[3] Shortly after midnight the leading brigade—the *14th*—marched westward to Halpegarbe. Operation orders had been issued at 9 P.M. that evening from *VII. Corps* advanced headquarters at Marquillies (4 miles south-east of Neuve Chapelle) for the counter-offensive to be delivered at 5 A.M. the next morning for the recapture of the lost positions.[4]

---

purpose it will have at its disposal the following units : the battalions of the 13th Infantry Division in corps reserve in Fournes [1 battalion 13th Infantry Regiment, 2 companies of 15th Infantry Regiment] and that of the 14th Infantry Division [1 battalion 56th Infantry Regiment], in Salomé [2 miles east of La Bassée], also the three field batteries in corps reserve of the 14th Field Artillery Brigade [these batteries—22nd Field Artillery Regiment—moved up from Beaucamps to Fromelles and Herlies]. Further reinforcements have been asked for from *Sixth Army*. Colonel von Campe has been ordered to support the counter-attack with heavy artillery and other available batteries.

[1] Men of the *106th* and *107th Regiments* were also identified. See Order of Battle (Appendix 3).

[2] Wavrin is 6¼ miles east of Neuve Chapelle, and Don is 1¼ miles south of Wavrin.

[3] Three trains, close together, were, however, seen arriving at Wavrin at 5 P.M.

[4]   VII. CORPS OPERATION ORDER

10 P.M. [German time] 10th March.

Major-General von Ditfurth [commanding *14th Infantry Division*] will carry out the attack on Neuve Chapelle. In case the troops at his disposal are not sufficient for the recapture of our former positions west of the village, the *14th Bavarian Reserve Infantry Brigade* is placed at General von Ditfurth's disposal. This brigade must be in position in the Bois

The *14th Divisional* artillery had also been strengthened by batteries of the *13th Divisional* artillery (four field batteries, *22nd F.A. Regiment,* two to Fromelles and two to Herlies, 1½ heavy field howitzer batteries, and half a 12 cm. battery). These had moved during the night to positions about Pietre and the Rue d'Enfer to support the new infantry position along the Mauquissart road. Of the artillery of the *6th Bavarian Reserve Division,* three heavy field howitzer batteries (*Bavarian Reserve Foot Artillery*) and two batteries of the *6th Bavarian Reserve Field Artillery Regiment* were moved up into the battle sector.

---

du Biez by 6 A.M. on the 11th, detailed instructions to be issued by General von Ditfurth.

To support the attack, two Bavarian heavy howitzer batteries will be placed at the disposal of Colonel von Campe. These batteries will be sent by road to Herlies and will take up a position at Le Plouich on the Herlies—Aubers road according to more detailed instructions to be issued by Captain Weidemann.

The remaining infantry of the *6th Bavarian Reserve Division* will stay in their billets from 7 A.M. onwards.

VON CLAER.

To *13th Infantry Division ;*
　　14th Infantry Division ;
　　6th Bavarian Reserve Division ;
　　VII. Corps Heavy Artillery.

SKETCH 5.

BATTLE OF NEUVE CHAPELLE.
11TH MARCH 1915.

The new German line & arrival of German reinforcements.

6 BAV. R. D.

12th Res Inf Bde at Wavrin
& Sainghin (4½ miles east).
14th Res Inf Bde at Illies
& Herlies (1½ miles east)

SCALE

Ordnance Survey, 1925.

VII.

AUBERS

Bas Pommereau

Ht Pommereau

Halpegarbe

Pietre

Mn du Pietre

les Mottes Farm

Rue du l'Enfer

13.

14.

Layes Brook

Lorgies Road

Layes Bridge

la Russie

Lagny le Petit

Pork

Bois

Rue du Bois

SMITH

TRENCH

BDE LORIERS

BATTS SYNDIC

BDE Armentieres

Smith Road

Neuve Chapelle

Port Arthur

IV.

INDIAN
MEERUT.
CORPS.

BRITISH

Mauquissart

2 COS. 13TH R.

1 BN 13TH R.

2 COS. II JÄGER

Chapigny BDE

INF. BDE

Mented Granges

7.

20.

24.

8.

25.

FRONT LINE

Pont Logy

Cameron Lane

Rue du Bacquerol

Rouge Croix

Estaires
3 miles

La Bassée
3 miles

Note:—
The DEHRA DUN BDE, moved back
at night towards Lannoere (2 miles east)

LAHORE DIVISION.
JULLUNDER BDE moved back
at night to Rue des Berceaux.
SIRHIND BDE moved forward at
night to Neuve Chapelle.
FEROZEPORE BDE Moved west
of the R. Lawe, (4 miles west).

CHAPTER VII

THE BATTLE OF NEUVE CHAPELLE (concluded)

11TH AND 12TH MARCH 1915

11TH MARCH 1915 : CONTINUATION OF THE ATTACK

(Map 1 ; Sketches 5, 6 and 7)

DURING the night the Germans continued to consolidate 10/11 March. their new front line. On the right, from opposite Chapigny Map 1. along the Mauquissart road to the Layes bridge redoubt, Sketch 5. low breastworks were thrown up between the strong points, and the whole front wired. The strong points themselves were improved, and armed with additional machine guns. On the left, a new line was taken up under cover of darkness two hundred yards in front of and parallel to the western edge of the Bois du Biez, the right on the Brewery Road—leaving an open field of fire to the machine-gun nest in the Layes bridge redoubt—and the left on the Lorgies road.[1]

Whilst the front line was being strengthened, the *14th Bavarian Reserve Brigade* was marching, under cover of darkness, from its detraining area [2] *via* Aubers ridge in order to take part in the counter-attack to recapture Neuve Chapelle. The intention was to reinforce the front line before daybreak and assault at dawn with the bayonet without artillery preparation.[3] The night was very dark,

---

[1] North of the Layes bridge redoubt the new German front was held by a battalion of the *13th Infantry Regiment*, all that remained (two companies) of the *11th Jäger Battalion*, and two companies of the *15th Infantry Regiment*. South of the redoubt to the Lorgies road were two battalions, one each of the *56th* and *57th Infantry Regiments*, and the *16th Infantry Regiment* carried on the line south of the road facing the Port Arthur salient.

[2] See p. 117.

[3] German *14th Division* operation order issued at 2.20 A.M. 11th March 1915.

119

11 Mar. however, causing unexpected delays, so that by the time the brigade reached Halpegarbe it was already growing light, and an advance in daylight down the slope of the Aubers ridge to the Bois du Biez exposed to the British artillery fire, was not considered practicable. The counterstroke was therefore postponed, the *14th Bavarian Reserve Brigade* assembling at Illies and Herlies, with the *12th Bavarian Reserve Brigade* in reserve 3 to 4 miles in rear about Wavrin and Sainghin.[1]

The new German line on the morning of the 11th was therefore held by approximately four battalions between Chapigny, north of the Moated Grange, and the Lorgies road, east of the Port Arthur salient. In reserve on Aubers ridge in the area Illies—Sainghin—Fournes—Aubers were twelve Bavarian battalions (*6th Bavarian Reserve Division*) and four Saxon battalions (from the *XIX. Corps*) ready for the counter-offensive.

General Haig's warning orders for the 11th, sent out to corps at 7 P.M. on the previous evening, were confirmed by an operation order issued at 11.30 P.M.[2] By that hour reports had reached him giving the general situation and the positions reached by the various units. Messages received from aeroplane observers during the day had accurately reported the movements of German units by road to the Neuve Chapelle battle zone, but no train movements on a large scale had been noticed. It was therefore assumed that the reinforcements consisted solely of *VII. Corps* units, and that no considerable force was as yet available from other parts of the line. It was on this information that General Haig decided to continue the offensive of the Indian and IV. Corps. The main attack was to be delivered by the IV. Corps with its 7th and 8th Sketch 2. Divisions. These were to press forward to Aubers ridge as far as the line La Cliqueterie Farm—Le Plouich—Rouges Bancs. The Indian Corps was to support the right of the IV. Corps by advancing through the Bois du Biez to the line Ligny le Grand (2000 yards east of Ligny le Petit)—La Cliqueterie Farm (inclusive). The advance was to begin at 7 A.M. at all points, and was to be pressed vigorously, as " from information received, it appears " that the enemy before us is in no great strength ".

---

[1] These brigades remained concealed in the villages and woods throughout the day. Their presence became known at British G.H.Q. the following morning (the 12th), when prisoners from them were captured.
[2] Appendix 18.

The I. Corps to the south was to continue its sub- 11 Mar.
sidiary attacks on the German trenches east of Givenchy
and " in co-operation with the right of the Indian Corps,
" attack southwards from about Richebourg l'Avoué with
" the object of capturing the German trenches in front of
" the I. Corps as far south as the La Bassée Canal ".[1]

Orders were issued from IV. Corps headquarters to the
7th and 8th Divisions shortly after midnight. The howitzer
brigades of both divisions, opening at 6.45 A.M., were for
fifteen minutes to bombard the strong points reported
along the Mauquissart road and near the Layes bridge.[2]
At 7 A.M., the time for the infantry assault, the howitzers
were to lift to the Pietre—Bois du Biez road, and the
18-pdr. and R.H.A. batteries would cover the infantry
advance by firing on certain allotted points between that
road and Aubers ridge. The Northern Group of heavy
batteries,[3] including the 15-inch howitzer and the guns of
the " Churchill " Armoured Train were to be directed
against the German artillery positions on Aubers ridge,
between Aubers and La Cliqueterie Farm.

The infantry advance was to be carried out in the Sketches
manner in which it had been hoped it would develop on 2 and 5.
the previous day. The leading brigades of the 8th and
7th Divisions (24th Brigade of the 8th and the 21st Brigade
of the 7th) were to advance eastwards and north-eastwards,
respectively. The gap that would quickly occur between
them was to be filled by the 20th Brigade of the 7th Division. The last-named brigade on leaving the Moated
Grange was at first to move eastwards, its right on Pietre,
where it would incline to the left and attack Aubers
village from the south-west. Its ultimate objective was
the line Le Plouich—east end of Aubers village—Ferme
Deleval. In the meantime, the 21st Brigade on its left
was to have reached a line Les Mottes Farm (1300 yards
north of Pietre)—Rue d'Enfer—Trivelet, thereby uncover-
ing the front of the 22nd Brigade, which still held the
British original trenches between the Moated Grange and
Chapigny. As the front of the 22nd Brigade was cleared,
this brigade was to assemble as 7th Division reserve
between the Moated Grange and Mauquissart, behind the
advancing 20th and 21st Brigades.

[1] This latter part of the order to the I. Corps was cancelled as the
result of a consultation between General Haking (G.O.C. 1st Div.) and
General Willcocks.

[2] The 6-inch howitzers, however, were unable to reach the Layes
bridge redoubt.   [3] Appendix 2.

11 Mar. On the front of the 8th Division the leading 24th Brigade, moving first towards Pietre and then north of La Cliqueterie Farm, was to be supported by the 25th Brigade. To enable the latter to move forward when necessary, the 23rd Brigade, which was to remain as 8th Division reserve along the Armentières road, was also to take over the trenches of the 25th Brigade in front of Neuve Chapelle and at the Road Triangle.

THE ACTION IN THE FORENOON

Sketch 5. Day broke dull and misty, making artillery observation and the registration of targets very difficult. At 6.45 A.M. the bombardment of the German strong points along the Mauquissart road was begun, but the continuous line of trenches, constructed during the night to connect the strong points, being as yet undetected, was not shelled at all. Thus the infantry assault had little chance of success.

On the front of the 7th Division attempts were made in vain by the 21st Brigade (Br.-General H. E. Watts) to advance at the conclusion of the bombardment, at 7 A.M. But in every case the leading troops were received at once by a heavy machine-gun and rifle fire, and the battalion commanders sent back reports that any advance was impracticable without an organized artillery preparation on a big scale along the whole front of assault.

The 20th Brigade (Br.-General F. J. Heyworth) moving forward at 7 A.M. from between the Moated Grange and the Orchard (inclusive), in column of platoons, preparatory to its advance on the right of the 21st Brigade, came under shell fire almost immediately from the batteries of the *13th Division* about Aubers and Le Pietre, and those of the *14th Division* further south. These enemy batteries, apprehending from reports the imminence of a renewed offensive, maintained an intense bombardment for three hours along the entire British front, chiefly in rear of the front line, on Neuve Chapelle village and northwards towards the Moated Grange. The advancing lines of the 20th Brigade, coming into this fire zone, lost heavily and slackened their pace. Some platoons worked forward by short rushes to the 21st Brigade line still in position facing Mauquissart, but the mass of the two leading battalions— the 1/Grenadier Guards on the right and the 2/Gordon Highlanders on the left—took what cover they could in

the ditches and disused, waterlogged trenches that inter-
sect the meadows between the Orchard and the Mauquissart
road. The brigade, unable to get forward, was ordered
by Br.-General Heyworth to halt and consolidate the line
reached. A report sent back by the Grenadiers gave their
position as astride the Layes brook, they, as others had
done, mistaking for it a broad ditch which ran athwart
their front. Now the Layes brook was east of the
Mauquissart road, and behind the German position. Thus
the report led the higher commanders to believe that the
German defences along that road had been broken through
in spite of the previous adverse reports. The divisional
artillery was therefore ordered to lengthen its range, and
it was not until nearly mid-day that the error was definitely
rectified. Of the two supporting battalions the 2/Scots
Guards on the right halted some five hundred yards in
rear of the brigade line, about the Orchard, and the
2/Border Regiment, on the left, moved up on the flank of
the 2/Gordons. The 6/Gordon Highlanders remained in
reserve in Cameron Lane. The 22nd Brigade remained
in the British original trenches north of the Moated
Grange.

On the front of the 8th Division, the attack of the
leading 24th Brigade had suffered the same fate as that
of the 21st Brigade. After advancing a few yards, the
leading lines of platoons of the Sherwood Foresters and
Northamptonshire were met by heavy rifle and machine-
gun fire and were unable to get forward. General Davies
thereupon ordered a second bombardment to be begun at
8.45 A.M., and a message was sent to the Northamptonshire
that at the conclusion of this bombardment the unnamed
group of cottages in front of them, at the Mauquissart—
Pietre road junction, must be captured. The Sherwood
Foresters were ordered to assist by a simultaneous attack
on the right. These messages, however, were never
delivered. The German bombardment, still in progress,
was so heavy that all telephone communication between
brigade headquarters and battalions had broken down
and messengers were unable to move across the open to
the front trenches.

The relief of the 25th Brigade by a battalion—2/West
Yorkshire—of the 23rd Brigade, took place early in the
morning, but owing to a misunderstanding the trenches
of the 2/Rifle Brigade, east of the Neuve Chapelle main
street, were not taken over. At 10.25 A.M., when this

11 Mar. additional relief was about to be carried out, orders were received from the 8th Division to be prepared to meet a counter-attack, for which, according to reports from the Indian Corps, Germans were collecting in the northern end of the Bois du Biez. The Rifle Brigade was therefore directed to remain in position. The rest of the 25th Brigade had assembled further east in the German original trenches at and south of Signpost Lane.

On the IV. Corps front from the Moated Grange to the Layes bridge—La Russie road, the attack had therefore failed and the general situation had not been appreciably altered.

Orders for the attack by the Meerut Division, on the right of the IV. Corps, were issued at 3 A.M. on receipt of Indian Corps operation orders.[1] The Dehra Dun Brigade (Br.-General C. W. Jacob) was to attack the Bois du Biez on a front Les Brulots—La Russie at 7 A.M., as soon as the 8th Division came up into line on its left. The attack was to be prepared by the artillery of the Meerut and Lahore Divisions, supported by the Southern Group Heavy Artillery. The Garhwal Brigade (Br.- General C. G. Blackader) was to place at the orders of Br.-General Jacob one battalion—2/39th Garhwal Rifles. This battalion, previously south of Neuve Chapelle village in support to the 2/3rd Gurkhas, had been moved during the night into position on the right of the Dehra Dun Brigade astride the Lorgies road, near the trenches of the 2/Leicestershire. When the brigade advanced the Garhwalis were to move forward on a front of four hundred yards in echelon on its right to protect the southern flank of the attack. The remainder of the Garhwal Brigade was to consolidate the position already held south of Neuve Chapelle village. The Bareilly Brigade on the right was to continue to hold its sector of the British original trenches.

The Lahore Division (less the Jullundur Brigade) was to be in Corps reserve. The Jullundur Brigade was to move forward to Neuve Chapelle, and thence advance in support of the Dehra Dun Brigade.

The bombardment, like that on the front of the IV. Corps, failed to prepare the German position for assault ; for it was directed against the western edge of the Bois du Biez and on the wood itself. Unfortunately no definite information had been received of the new German trench constructed during the night in front, half-way between

[1] Appendix 19.

the wood and the Layes brook. This trench, now the 11 Mar. main German defence, therefore remained untouched.

In the orders both of the Indian Corps and the Meerut Division the arrival of the 8th Division in line on the left was given as the signal for the advance of the Dehra Dun Brigade. No brigade of the 8th Division was mentioned, and Br.-General Jacob concluded that his attack was to await the arrival in line with it of the 25th Brigade on his immediate left rear, in front of Neuve Chapelle village. It will be remembered, however, that the 25th Brigade was in support and that the attack of the 8th Division was to be delivered by the 24th Brigade, which was five hundred yards north of the left flank of the Dehra Dun Brigade, and already practically level with it, though this could not be seen in the mist. So, after a preliminary move which drew heavy infantry fire, the Dehra Dun Brigade awaited in vain the arrival of the 25th Brigade on its left. At 8 A.M., Br.-General Jacob sent his brigade-major (Major H. A. Walker) to the 2/Rifle Brigade, the right battalion of the 25th Brigade, to enquire the reason of the delay. He was informed that, as yet, the battalion had received no orders to advance, and the last instructions were definite : to consolidate and hold the position. In the meantime, the 1/9th Gurkhas, the left battalion of the Dehra Dun Brigade, had reported that no advance was possible without support on the left flank, owing to enfilade fire from the Layes bridge redoubt. The German trench beyond the Layes brook was also reported to be strongly held with machine guns and rifles, while the breadth, 10 feet, of the brook, made it a serious obstacle to cross under fire. Owing to the mist, it was difficult for the artillery to range on the new trench. Br.-General Jacob, after he himself had been over to the 2/Rifle Brigade, considered therefore that in the circumstances an attack was not feasible, and for the time-being the Dehra Dun Brigade stood fast.

The Jullundur Brigade moved forward to Neuve Chapelle, taking cover in and about the village. Otherwise the situation on the front of the Indian Corps remained unchanged.

The breaking of all communications with the front line battalions by the German artillery bombardment and the time (two to three hours) taken by runners to get back with reports, made it difficult for the corps and divisional commanders to take any action during the morning. Their

11 Mar. task was further complicated by the inaccuracy of some of the reports received, due chiefly to the difficulty of picking up landmarks in this flat, featureless district. It was hoped, nevertheless, that the German counter-attack from the Bois du Biez, reported as imminent at about 10 A.M., would, when repulsed, offer a favourable opportunity for a general advance, if followed up immediately. Orders were issued to brigades to be prepared accordingly. It seems, however, that no such attack was contemplated by the Germans. The two battalions—supposed to be two regiments—holding the Bois du Biez sector were fully employed in manning the new trench line in front of the wood and preparing the western edge of the wood itself for defence. To check the reported preparations for a German counter-attack, the fire of two hundred British guns was nevertheless directed on the wood, with the result in any case that further movement there quickly ceased.

THE ACTION IN THE AFTERNOON

At 12.19 P.M., as no further information of the counter-attack had been received, General Rawlinson decided to continue the frontal attack against the Mauquissart road. He telegraphed to the 7th and 8th Divisions :—" It is " most important that the buildings at the Moulin du " Pietre and at the Mauquissart—Pietre cross roads [the " unnamed group of cottages] should be captured without " further delay. Lose no time in getting guns on to them " and assaulting the buildings with infantry ".

In view of this message, General Capper (7th Division) sent orders to the 21st Brigade to the effect that artillery (XXXV. Brigade R.F.A.) would destroy a nest of machine guns reported in an orchard half-way between Chapigny and Mauquissart, and that the northern houses of Mauquissart would be shelled. This bombardment, beginning at 2 P.M., would last one hour, when the 21st Brigade was to assault and break through the enemy's line along the Mauquissart road. The 20th and 22nd Brigades were to back up the assault by a general advance on the lines already ordered for the 7 A.M. attack.

The fact that the Germans were holding a continuous trench line, in addition to the strong points along the Mauquissart road, was not yet fully appreciated by the higher commanders. In any case, however, the difficulty of passing orders rapidly to and along the firing line to individual companies prevented the organization of another united assault. Isolated attempts to get forward were made by such companies as received the order, but heavy machine-gun and rifle fire from the German position quickly checked them. This second attack was therefore a failure, and the position of the brigades of the 7th Division remained unchanged for the remainder of the day.

General Davies (8th Division), on receipt of the IV. Corps message, replied to General Rawlinson that he would order a new bombardment of the Mauquissart road between the Mauquissart—Pietre cross roads and the Layes bridge redoubt, to be followed by an infantry assault. Indian Corps headquarters were informed and General Willcocks agreed to order the Dehra Dun Brigade to push on as soon as the 24th Brigade came up into line on its left. This plan was confirmed by an order from General Haig at 1.8 P.M. to the effect that the Indian Corps would connect with the right of the leading brigade of the 8th Division, that the road junction at La Russie was to be secured by the IV. Corps and the Bois du Biez by the Indian Corps, and that the attack should be pressed vigorously.

Corps instructions were issued in this sense. General Davies informed General Rawlinson that he doubted any success from the attack, owing to the difficulty of carrying out an effective bombardment of the new German position, but the latter urged that the Mauquissart—Pietre cross roads must be taken. General Davies thereupon ordered the bombardment to begin at 1.45 P.M., to last half an hour. At its conclusion the 24th Brigade was to assault the German position in front of it and advance to the Pietre—Bois du Biez road. General Willcocks was informed, and he ordered arrangements to be made for a simultaneous advance by the Dehra Dun Brigade at 2.15 P.M. The order for the attack of the 24th Brigade reached the brigade headquarters [1] at 1.42 P.M., leaving only 33 minutes to pass it on to the front battalions, twelve hundred yards away. Br.-General Carter therefore ordered the Worcestershire to send forward at once two support companies, in the hope that they would be able to reach the front line in time and carry the Northamptonshire, Sherwood Foresters and remainder of the Worcestershire forward with them. Thus only two companies of the brigade

[1] 24th Brigade headquarters at this time were in a ruined house near the junction of Signpost Lane with the Rue de Tilleloy.

11 Mar. actually received the order to attack. The two Worcestershire companies, two hundred yards east of the Armentières road, did not themselves receive this order till
2.20 P.M., that is five minutes after the bombardment had
finished. They at once advanced, and soon came under
heavy machine-gun and rifle fire. Only a few men were
able to cover the four hundred yards of open ground
separating them from the front line trenches, but these
were able to pass on the order. The Northamptonshire
did not attack. They had already attempted to do so
and had been stopped in the first ten yards by heavy
enfilade machine-gun fire, their strength being reduced to
12 officers and 320 other ranks. In a message sent back
to brigade headquarters by the battalion commander—
Colonel Prichard—at 2.50 P.M., he said :—" I received a
" note from the Worcestershire, ' We have *got* to advance.
" ' Will you give the order?' I answered ' No! it is a
" ' mere waste of life, impossible to go 20 yards much less
" ' 200 yards. The trenches have not been touched by
" ' the artillery. If artillery cannot touch them the only
" ' way is to advance from right flank. A frontal attack
" ' will not get near them ' ". The two front Worcestershire companies began to advance, but the leading lines
were shot down at once and the effort was not continued.
The Sherwood Foresters, after three attempts to push
forward, managed to occupy two dilapidated farm buildings,
one hundred yards apart, on the Mauquissart road and
between the opposing lines. This small success, however,
cost them considerable casualties, their strength being
reduced to 11 officers and 680 men.

General Willcocks's order for the attack of the Dehra
Dun Brigade at 2.15 P.M. reached the brigade headquarters
by signal message at 2.10 P.M. and it was therefore impossible
to inform units in time. Hasty instructions were nevertheless sent out ordering that an attack should be made as
arranged for 7 A.M., and that the signal for advance, as before,
would be the arrival of the 2/Rifle Brigade (25th Brigade),
the right battalion of the 8th Division, in line with the
1/9th Gurkhas. On receipt of these orders two companies of
the 4/Seaforth Highlanders, the support battalion, whose
commanding officer, Lieut.-Colonel Mason MacFarlane had
shortly before been wounded, got up and doubled forward,
coming under heavy machine-gun fire, and had to crowd
into the Gurkha trenches to get cover. The two front
battalions—the 2/2nd and 1/9th Gurkhas—waited, however,

for the Rifle Brigade. As the 25th Brigade showed no sign of movement, Br.-General Jacob again sent his brigade-major to the headquarters of the 2/Rifle Brigade to find out why the battalion had not advanced. There he learnt from Lieut.-Colonel R. B. Stephens that nothing was known about the 2.15 attack, and his instructions were not to attack without orders. On hearing this Br.-General Jacob reported the matter to the Meerut Division. He added that he could see no chance of a success under the present conditions with both his flanks exposed, and that in view of the many casualties that were being incurred from enfilade fire from the left flank, he wished, after dark, to withdraw his brigade behind the line of the Garhwal Brigade.

In the meantime, as no progress by the 24th Brigade could be noticed, General Davies decided to employ the 25th Brigade, and at 2.50 P.M. ordered it to attack eastward in co-operation with the Dehra Dun Brigade to its right front, to capture the Layes bridge redoubt and to advance to La Russie. He gave permission that the whole brigade might be used for this operation. Br.-General Lowry Cole, on the arrival of these orders at 3.20 P.M., went forward to his leading battalion, 2/Rifle Brigade, to arrange the attack. On reaching battalion headquarters, he was informed that the brigade-major of the Dehra Dun Brigade had just left and it was understood that the Dehra Dun Brigade was not going to advance. There was no direct communication between this brigade and the 25th; but through divisional channels the information was obtained that no further attack was to be made by the Meerut Division. After a personal reconnaissance, Br.-General Lowry Cole decided that it would be useless to attack single-handed with the 25th Brigade and informed the division accordingly.

Br.-General Jacob's request for the withdrawal of the Dehra Dun Brigade after dark was sanctioned and at nightfall the trenches along the western side of the Layes brook were evacuated by the 2/2nd and 1/9th Gurkhas. The whole of the Dehra Dun Brigade, composed now of these two battalions and 4/Seaforth Highlanders and 2/39th Garhwal Rifles, was subsequently withdrawn to behind the La Bassée—Estaires road. At the conclusion of the move- Sketch 6. ment, the trenches of the Garhwal Brigade again formed the British front line. On the right, the survivors of the 1/39th Garhwal Rifles and the 1/Seaforth Highlanders [1]

---

[1] The 1/Seaforth Highlanders had remained attached to the Garhwal Brigade.

11 Mar. held the German original trenches in front of the Port Arthur salient, between the La Bassée—Estaires and the Lorgies roads. At the point where the latter is crossed by the Layes brook was the right of the Leicestershire, who with the 2/3rd Gurkhas carried on the line east of Neuve Chapelle village to the Brewery Road. The latter battalion was in touch with the 2/Rifle Brigade, the right battalion of the IV. Corps that carried on the line along the eastern edge of the village.

The position of the units holding the front of the IV. Corps was not materially altered during the night.

The failure to make any advance during the 11th March was attributed chiefly to the difficulties of getting information back from the front line as to the position and extent of the new German trenches that had been dug overnight. It was also due to the inability of the artillery to range on them, where known, owing partly to the mist that covered the battle zone throughout the day, and partly to the constant cutting by the German artillery fire of telephone cables connecting the forward observing officers with the batteries. For these reasons, the heavy batteries and howitzers had been compelled to resort to ranging by the map without being able to observe their fire, and a large proportion of ammunition was consequently expended with doubtful result.[1] It was clear that until the new German position could be prepared for assault by an effective bombardment, the prospects of a successful advance by the infantry were negligible.

General Haig visited the battle front early in the evening and ordered guns to be brought up in places, particularly on the left flank (7th Division), closer to the German position preparatory to a resumption of the offensive at 10.30 A.M. on the following morning.

12TH MARCH 1915 : THE GERMAN COUNTER-ATTACK

Sketch 6. At dusk on the 11th the Germans reinforced their front line with six battalions : two Saxon battalions on either flank, about Pietre and Mauquissart and facing the Port Arthur salient respectively, and two Bavarian battalions in the centre about the Bois du Biez. During the night their

---

[1] Map shooting by the artillery was still at this time in its infancy : guns had not been calibrated, weather reports were not sent out to batteries, and maps were not sufficiently exact for artillery fire without observation and good communications.

SKETCH 6

BATTLE OF NEUVE CHAPELLE.

12TH MARCH 1915.

The German Counter-attacks, 5 A.M.– Noon.

Ordnance Survey, 1925

SCALE

YARDS 500   0   500   1000   1500   2000 YARDS

¼   ½   ¾   MILE

troops were reorganized for the assault into two brigades.[1] 12 Mar.
It was to be delivered at 5 A.M. along the whole of the new
front from north of the Moated Grange to south of the
Port Arthur salient, in order to recapture Neuve Chapelle
village and the German original trenches beyond.   At
the same time the *6th Bavarian Reserve Division* moved
forward to a position of readiness in support.   The two
regiments of the *14th Bavarian Reserve Brigade* (less two
battalions already in the front line) marched from Herlies—
Illies (2 miles east of Halpegarbe), where they had been
concealed throughout the day, down from Aubers ridge to
a supporting position in and north of the Bois du Biez.
The night was pitch dark, and the assembly positions,
though only three to four miles distant, were not reached
until just before the hour of assault.   The other brigade
(the *12th*) of the *6th Bavarian Reserve Division*, moved forward to a position in reserve about Herlies and Halpegarbe.

A total of some sixteen thousand men were thus
assembled for the counter-stroke, approximately ten
battalions in the front line, four in support and six in
reserve.

At 4.30 A.M., before dawn, on the 12th March the
German artillery bombarded the whole front of the Indian
and IV. Corps.   Its shells, however, were badly ranged
and fell almost entirely behind the British front, about
the Moated Grange, the Armentières road, Neuve Chapelle
village and the Estaires—La Bassée road near the Port
Arthur salient.   The British front trenches were left
practically untouched, but in many cases troops waiting
in support suffered severely, particularly the Jullundur
Brigade near the Estaires—La Bassée road, which had
three hundred casualties from shell fire.

At 5 A.M. the German infantry moved forward to
counter-attack.   Day was beginning to break, but a thick
mist effectually covered from view the advancing lines
until they were some sixty yards from the British front
trenches.

As the enemy's assault developed into four separate
attacks on the different parts of the line, it will be convenient to describe it from that point of view.

The right attack [2] had the Moated Grange and the

---

[1] See Note at end of Chapter for German operation orders and
objectives.
[2] Made by units of the *13th* and *15th Infantry Regiments*, supported
by the *179th Saxons*.

German original trenches between it and Signpost Lane as its objective. It came up against the British 21st Brigade.

On the front of the 2/Wiltshire a number of old German trenches crossed the new British position, enabling the Germans to get forward to close quarters unseen. In spite of this disadvantage, and the distraction caused by the arrival of the morning's rations, the Wiltshire held up the assault except on the front of the left flank company, whose trench was rushed. The enemy was stopped by the support company, the trench recovered later on, and in it thirty prisoners were captured.[1] At 9.30 A.M. the attack against the Wiltshire was renewed, large numbers of Germans again moving forward along the old communication trenches towards them. To fight and drive the enemy back was a task that could best be carried out by the newly formed companies of trained bomb-throwers, and, on receipt of a message from the Wiltshire, Br.-General Watts, commanding the 21st Brigade, requested the loan of bombers from the 20th Brigade to check this attack. A detachment was at once sent from the brigade reserve of bombers.[2]

The attack against the 2/Green Howards completely failed. This battalion at once opened heavy machine-gun and rifle fire on the Germans, who were advancing in lines across the open, and none of them were able to come within thirty yards of the position. The attack soon ceased, the enemy leaving over one hundred dead in front of the Yorkshire trenches.

On the front of the 2/Royal Scots Fusiliers, the right battalion of the 21st Brigade, the enemy attack had a small, but fleeting, success in the sector of the right company, which had lost all its officers in the previous days' fighting. A counter-movement at once organized by two support companies of the 2/Bedfordshire and delivered frontally failed with heavy loss, but Captain C. C. Foss, leading a party of eight bombers of the battalion advanced over the open from the left of the Northamptonshire's

[1] Corporal W. Anderson of the 2/Green Howards—whose bombers had been sent to help the Wiltshire—was awarded the Victoria Cross for most conspicuous bravery. He led three men with bombs against a large party of the enemy who had entered the British trenches. He first threw his own bombs, then those in possession of his three men, who had been wounded, after which, although he was alone at the time, he opened rapid fire upon the Germans with great effect.

[2] See page 95.

trench and took the Germans in flank. After a number 12 Mar.
of bombs had been thrown, one officer and 48 men, 14 of
them wounded, surrendered.[1] Seeing this, some hundred
more survivors of the 5 A.M. German attack, lying out in
the shell holes and ditches in front of their main position,
got up, some with rifles and some without, and, after a
certain hesitation, returned to their trenches pursued by
bullets and losing heavily. The recaptured salient was
quickly consolidated by a company of the 2/Bedfordshire.

The right - centre German attack upon the 24th
Brigade was directed against the Road Triangle and the
northern part of Neuve Chapelle, its left on the church.[2]
Much of its cohesion and violence was, however, lost from
the outset owing to the fact that the final order giving
the hour of assault, sent by runner, did not reach the
front line units in time. These did not therefore attack
at the appointed hour, and the *21st Bavarian Reserve
Regiment*, moving forward across the Layes brook in support,
advanced through them, causing considerable confusion
and bad feeling. The front of the 24th Brigade was still
held by three battalions, the Northamptonshire on the
left, some two hundred yards from and facing the nameless
group of houses south of Mauquissart, the Worcestershire
in the centre, their right on the Sunken Road, and the
Sherwood Foresters on the right between that road and
the La Russie—Layes bridge road. It will be remembered that the Sherwood Foresters on the previous afternoon had occupied two dilapidated farm buildings on
the Mauquissart road—which later marked " the Duck's
Bill " of the Neuve Chapelle defences — and during the
night the front of this battalion, held by three companies,
had been established along the road and formed a considerable salient, one hundred yards in advance of the British
position. The 2/East Lancashire was in brigade reserve.

The Bavarian battalion which attacked the Worcestershire and Northamptonshire was stopped dead by rapid
fire. Further to the right the sister battalion made a
strong attack from two sides against the Sherwood
Foresters' salient, to the northern part of which the first
parties were able to approach unhindered, being mistaken
in the mist for a British listening post returning at daybreak. The garrisons of the two farms and the trenches

---

[1] Captain C. C. Foss, D.S.O., was awarded the Victoria Cross.
[2] Made by a battalion of the *133rd Saxon Regiment* and the remnants
of the *11th Jäger Battalion*.

12 Mar. near were rushed, and either killed, captured or driven out, and the remnants of the three companies of the Sherwood Foresters — who had lost nearly all their officers on the previous two days—intermingled with the Germans, were carried back towards the support company entrenched two hundred yards in rear. Other lines of Germans followed into the gap, but they were now caught in a pocket occupied on three sides. Fired on from the south by the West Yorkshire, fired on and then charged with bomb and bayonet on the initiative of the company commander by a reserve company of the West Yorkshire from the west, and by the flank company of the Worcestershire from the north, the Germans eventually ran back to their own trenches, leaving over four hundred dead between the Sherwood Foresters' front and support trenches. Further to the left, the Worcestershire, after stopping the Bavarian attack by fire, had charged with the bayonet. After a sharp hand-to-hand struggle in No Man's Land, they drove the Bavarians back to and through the nameless group of cottages near the Pietre—Mauquissart road junction. The Bavarian battalion suffered very severely and left six hundred dead in No Man's Land. The Worcestershire took up their position in the captured cottages, whilst, further to the right, the survivors of the Foresters, who had lost 16 officers and 342 other ranks, occupied a line behind their original front trench, which was full of dead, British and German. The line was wired during the night by the 15th Field Company R.E., and the Duck's Bill farm buildings occupied by a party of the Devons (23rd Brigade).[1]

The German attack against the centre and south part of Neuve Chapelle village was delivered from the front of the Bois du Biez, the right directed on the church, now a heap of brick rubble, and only distinguishable by the remains of the cemetery around it.[2] The Layes brook was crossed by plank bridges under cover of the mist, and the line of the evacuated Dehra Dun trench along the western bank was entered just as the night listening posts

---

[1] Private J. Rivers of the Sherwood Foresters, killed during the fighting, was awarded the Victoria Cross for two acts of great bravery that materially assisted in checking the attack. For German losses, see p. 151.

[2] The *57th* and part of the *56th Infantry Regiments*, together with the battalion of the *21st Bavarian Reserve Infantry Regiment* that had reinforced the line the previous evening, moved forward from the trench west of the Bois du Biez, supported by the three battalions of the *20th Bavarian Reserve Infantry Regiment*.

of the 2/3rd Gurkha Rifles, who had occupied it during 12 Mar. the night, were withdrawing to the main position. Shortly afterwards the attack developed from the line of the evacuated Dehra Dun trench and astride the Brewery road, the track leading from the Bois du Biez to Neuve Chapelle.

Two hundred yards separated the Germans from the British line along the eastern edge of the village. North of the Brewery road the front was defended by the 2/Rifle Brigade, the only battalion of the 25th Brigade still in the front line. The Garhwal Brigade continued it to the south, the 2/3rd Gurkhas on a frontage of four hundred yards, with the Leicestershire on its right as far as the Lorgies road. The front of the last-named unit was still along the Layes brook and slightly in advance of the Gurkhas, so that its left company, thrown back facing north, was in a position to enfilade any advance against the Gurkha position.

The reports brought back by the listening posts enabled the British trenches to be manned in good time; so that as soon as dim forms in helmets appeared through the mist about a hundred yards away, followed by a dense grey wave of men, a violent fusillade was opened on them at point-blank range. It checked not only the leading lines, but also those still unseen, moving forward in support, from the Bois du Biez. Few of the enemy got within ten yards of the British parapet, the mass of them being stopped forty to fifty yards away. After an hour of repeated efforts the attack was abandoned, the Germans leaving behind several hundred dead and wounded, used as a cover by the succeeding lines, on the front of nine hundred yards opposite the Rifle Brigade, 2/3rd Gurkhas and the Leicestershire, besides a large number of dead seen later between the brook and the Bois du Biez. The survivors withdrew to their original position in front of and in the Bois du Biez, except about a hundred who still remained west of the brook in the water-logged Smith-Dorrien trench, up to their waists in mud and water, or in the evacuated Dehra Dun trench.

The German left (southern) attack was delivered against the Port Arthur salient.[1] The survivors of the

[1] Part of the *56th Infantry Regiment* and three companies of the *16th Infantry Regiment*, that held the front facing the salient between the Lorgies and the La Bassée roads, were supported for the attack by parts of the two Saxon battalions, one each from the *104th* and *139th Infantry Regiments*, that had come forward the previous evening, the total attacking force being estimated at two thousand men.

12 Mar. 1/39th Garhwal Rifles and 1/Seaforth, in position in the German original trench fronting the salient, had before dawn received reports from listening posts of considerable movement in the German trenches. The battalions were therefore ready and the machine guns in the front line manned when, shortly afterwards, the firing of Very pistols into the mist revealed some hundred yards away three dense lines of advancing German infantry. Rapid fire was at once opened on them, and they were raked from end to end. The right of the attack was completely checked, no Germans, except one who crawled in and surrendered, getting within twenty yards of the British trenches, whilst over two hundred dead and wounded were left on the ground. The survivors hurriedly withdrew into the cover of the mist and their own trenches. The left of the attack managed to cross the La Bassée road and advance over the original No Man's Land, south of the Port Arthur salient, as if to envelop the right flank of the 1/39th Garhwal Rifles. But the 2/Black Watch (Bareilly Brigade), holding the salient and the British original trench near, met it with machine-gun and rifle fire, and most of the Germans disappeared back into the mist, a few only remaining in an old disused trench in No Man's Land. At 7 A.M. the brigade trench mortars were turned on to this party, and shortly afterwards some bombers of the Black Watch attacked it, and 2 officers and 70 men surrendered. In addition, 22 dead and 5 wounded were found in the trench, and of others who attempted to escape, 40 were shot either by the Black Watch or by the 1/39th Garhwal before they could regain their line. During this fighting the Garhwalis had worked southwards down the German original front trench as far as the La Bassée road. This line was now consolidated and a connecting trench dug linking it with the front line near the Crescent redoubt, a closed work 200 yards south of Port Arthur.

The complete repulse of the counter-stroke astride the Lorgies road and opposite the Port Arthur salient was greatly assisted by the carefully sited machine guns, twenty in all, of the Garhwal Brigade, under Captain J. T. Lodwick, 2/3rd Gurkhas, which gave a further proof of the devastating effect of concentrated machine-gun fire in the defence.[1]

[1] For further German information as regards the counter-attack, see Note at end of Chapter.

12TH MARCH 1915 : CONTINUATION OF THE ATTACK
EAST OF THE VILLAGE

The reports which reached First Army headquarters 12 Mar.
during the morning regarding the German counter-offensive Sketch6.
had been scanty, and gave little idea either of the large
German force engaged or of the losses it had sustained.
No immediate attempt was therefore made to follow up
the repulse and the enemy was thus given time to recover.[1]

General Haig's operation orders for the 12th[2] had
been issued at 11.45 P.M. on the 11th, and they were not
changed in any way in consequence of the counter-attack.
The offensive was to be continued in accordance with the
previous plan. To allow time for the capture by the
8th Division of the Layes bridge redoubt, that throughout
the previous day had so effectively prevented any advance
by the left of the Meerut Division, the assault of the IV.
Corps was to precede that of the Indian Corps. The bombardment by the IV. Corps artillery was to begin at 10 A.M.
and to last half-an-hour, when the infantry would assault
with the Pietre—La Russie (Bois du Biez) road as a first
objective. The Indian Corps was to assault half-an-hour
later with the Bois du Biez as its objective.

The weather conditions were no more favourable than
on the previous day. A thick haze continued to hang
over the battlefield, making the observation and registration of artillery targets impracticable, and at the same
time preventing aeroplanes either from assisting artillery
to range or from undertaking tactical reconnaissances
except at dangerously low altitudes of less than three
hundred feet. At 9.20 A.M., on an enquiry from First
Army headquarters, General Rawlinson stated that, owing
to the mist, the artillery had as yet been unable to register
some of the more important points in the German position,
particularly the Layes bridge redoubt and the neighbouring
trench along the Mauquissart road. General Haig therefore decided to postpone the offensive for two hours. At
11.20 A.M., although the registration was not satisfactory,
it was agreed after a further telephone consultation between

---

[1] The gaps in his ranks were rapidly replenished by the *12th Bavarian
Reserve Infantry Brigade*, the remaining brigade of the *6th Bavarian Reserve
Division*. The whole of this brigade, in position early in the morning as
VII. Corps reserve about Herlies and Halpegarbe, was thrown piecemeal,
by separate battalions and companies, into the front line during the
morning.
[2] Appendix 20.

12 Mar. First Army headquarters and the Indian and IV. Corps, that the attack should not be again postponed.

THE IV. CORPS

In the IV. Corps the bombardment was begun at noon and continued till 12.30 P.M., the hour of the infantry assault. On the right of the 8th Division, the 25th Brigade attacked from the northern front of Neuve Chapelle and from the Road Triangle, with two battalions, the 2/Rifle Brigade and 1/Royal Irish Rifles. The bombardment, however, had been ineffective, very few of the shells struck the trench, and the Layes bridge redoubt, in particular, was left untouched. The attack therefore failed after a short advance, both battalions losing heavily. It was estimated that the Layes bridge redoubt, which was heavily wired, was armed with at least fifteen machine guns, and it could be seen that the wire entanglement in front of it was little damaged. After a conference with the battalion commanders, Br.-General Lowry Cole informed divisional headquarters that he did not consider a frontal attack could succeed in daylight, and suggested waiting till dark.

The 24th Brigade (Br.-General F. C. Carter), next to the left, was still in the process of reorganizing after the repulse of the German counter-offensive in the early morning. On the right, the Sherwood Foresters and the right of the Worcestershire were unable to re-form in time for the attack. On the left of the brigade, the remainder of the Worcestershire and part of the Northamptonshire and East Lancashire, who had followed up the retreating Germans in the early morning and occupied part of the German trench along the Mauquissart road, had suffered considerably during the morning from frequent shelling by the British guns which were registering the German line there. The report of the advance to the road at this place did not reach the IV. Corps artillery till after midday, and its fire led at 10 A.M. to the captured sector of the German trench being evacuated. During this withdrawal, which was carried out very steadily under a crossfire of rifle and machine guns, Lieut.-Colonel E. C. F. Wodehouse, commanding the 1/Worcestershire, and his adjutant, were killed. The local commanders did not consider themselves sufficiently strong after this to retake and hold the German trench unless supported on the flanks, and as no subsequent advance was made on right or left, no attack was carried out after the noon bombardment.

The 23rd Brigade remained throughout the morning about the line of the Armentières road as 8th Division reserve.

The orders for the offensive of the 7th Division were that the 21st Brigade, holding the front trenches facing the Mauquissart—Chapigny road,[1] was to remain in position whilst the two leading battalions of the 20th Brigade, the 2/Scots Guards and 2/Border, advanced through it to the line of the road as their first objective. Unfortunately the order postponing the 10.30 A.M. attack did not reach these two battalions, for both the runners carrying the message were killed on the way. The Scots Guards, with the Border Regiment on their left, had therefore advanced from their assembly position through the front of the Green Howards and the left of the Royal Scots Fusiliers into No Man's Land. They were, however, faced by a large self-contained work, west of Mauquissart, the Quadrilateral, strongly held with machine guns. As there had been no artillery preparation, heavy losses were at once incurred, and the advance was checked after little more than a hundred yards had been covered. Twenty minutes later their commanders received the order, passed along from the flank battalions, postponing the infantry assault till 12.30 P.M. The leading companies of the Scots Guards and the Border Regiment therefore remained out in the open, taking cover in a slight depression, and awaited the artillery preparation.

The British bombardment was accurate and intense. From its position about the Rue du Bacquerot (passing through Rouge Croix) the 7th Division artillery was able to enfilade this sector of the German position, and it completely demoralized the defenders. The Scots Guards and the Border Regiment crept forward during the bombardment and, as soon as the fire ceased, rushed the Quadrilateral and the neighbouring trench. The Germans at once came out from cover, holding up their hands and waving handkerchiefs. Some four hundred prisoners of the *13th, 15th* and *179th (Saxon) Regiments*, with a quantity of material, were taken.

Simultaneously, on the left of the Border Regiment, the party of bombers, under Captain W. E. Nicol, 1/Grenadier Guards, sent forward from the 20th Brigade reserve of bombers earlier in the day to reinforce the Wiltshire,[2]

---

[1] Through the cross-roads south-west of Chapigny.   [2] See page 95.

12 Mar. supported by a company of the Wiltshire, advanced with
great gallantry along the disused communication trenches
in No Man's Land. They forced the Germans back to
their main trench, about forty yards of which was quickly
captured. This attack was so ably and rapidly carried
out that the Germans were taken unawares and surrendered
in considerable numbers to right and left along the main
trench.[1] Two more companies of the Wiltshire and two
platoons of the Green Howards were hurried forward and
the German trench was occupied in strength, some two
hundred prisoners (of the *13th* and *15th Infantry Regiments*)
being captured.

The new front of the 7th Division was now established
and consolidated within one hundred and fifty yards of, and
parallel to, the Mauquissart—Chapigny road. The right
flank of the Scots Guards, however, was exposed and efforts
of that battalion to advance to the road, north-west of
Mauquissart, were enfiladed from that flank and were unsuccessful. The 1/Grenadier Guards, supporting the Scots
Guards, lost direction in the labyrinth of trenches east of
the Orchard, and were unable to get forward.

The front units found great difficulty in sending back
information regarding the extent of the advance made,
and divisional headquarters had to rely mainly on messages
from artillery forward observing officers. At 1.10 P.M. it
was reported from this source that the Royal Scots Fusiliers
were approaching the cottages of Mauquissart, that British
troops had crossed the Mauquissart road [2] and that the
Germans were surrendering in large numbers. This, together
with other more or less conflicting reports, gave General
Capper the false impression that the Mauquissart road and
the buildings were practically, if not entirely, in British
hands. He thereupon ordered the 21st Brigade to press
on to the Rue d'Enfer (which leads into Aubers), and the
20th Brigade to advance to Pietre and attack Aubers
and Le Plouich ($\frac{1}{2}$ mile east of Aubers). These orders

[1] L/Cpl. W. D. Fuller, of 1/Grenadier Guards, was awarded the Victoria
Cross. Seeing a party of the enemy endeavouring to escape along a
communication trench he ran towards them, although quite alone, and
killed the leading man with a bomb ; the remainder, nearly fifty, finding
no means of avoiding his bombs, surrendered.

Private E. Barber, of the same battalion, was also awarded the
Victoria Cross. He ran in front of his grenade company and bombed
the enemy with such effect that a very large number of them surrendered.

[2] It appears that small parties of the Scots Guards and the Border
Regiment had advanced beyond the Quadrilateral and were taken prisoner.
These, moving as prisoners across the Mauquissart road, may have been
mistaken by the observers for advancing infantry.

assumed that the German position along the Mauquissart 12 Mar.
—Chapigny road had been broken through. The Germans,
however, had rapidly converted into a fire trench, facing
south, a communication trench along the northern side of
the road, the road itself being now in No Man's Land, and
the British position parallel to and one hundred and fifty
yards to the south of it. The trench in front of Mauquissart itself was still in German possession. The orders
could not therefore be carried out, nor was the actual
situation made clear to divisional headquarters till the
evening.

THE INDIAN CORPS

On the front of the Indian Corps the attack to be
delivered half an hour later than that of the IV. Corps,
was to be carried out by the Sirhind and Jullundur
Brigades, both of the Lahore Division, and under Br.-
General W. G. Walker, the senior brigadier. By his
orders issued at 9.20 A.M., the two brigades, the Sirhind
on the right and the Jullundur on the left, were to pass
through the line of the Garhwal Brigade at 11 A.M., after
half-an-hour's bombardment of the Bois du Biez, and
thence advance on a front of fifteen hundred yards with
the Bois as the first objective.

The message postponing the attack for two hours was
not received at Br.-General Walker's headquarters till
10.50 A.M., allowing only ten minutes to inform battalions.
The leading units were successfully stopped as they were
about to leave the trenches, a company of the 1/4th
Gurkhas, the right battalion of the Sirhind Brigade, reaching, and halting in, the front Garhwal trench. About
noon, seeing a number of Germans in front showing signs
of surrender, this company, together with the left company
of the 2/Leicestershire,[1] advanced across the open and
with little loss reached the Layes brook, halting in the
evacuated Dehra Dun trench. During this movement
they captured fifty Germans of the *16th Regiment*, and shot
about fifty others, who were running off. These were men
who had taken refuge in the Dehra Dun trench and in the
disused Smith-Dorrien trench, after the failure of the
German counter-attack in the morning.[2]

---

[1] Private W. Buckingham, of this battalion, was awarded the Victoria
Cross for conspicuous acts of bravery both on the 10th and 12th March,
and for rendering aid to the wounded whilst exposed to heavy fire.

[2] See page 135.

12 Mar.   At 1 P.M., after the half-hour bombardment, the remainder of the 1/4th Gurkhas with the 1/Highland L.I. of the same brigade on the left also moved forward towards the evacuated Dehra Dun trench, the Highland L.I. losing heavily from enfilade fire from the left flank, from the direction of the Layes bridge redoubt. Advancing by short rushes these two battalions, however, reached the trench and there awaited the arrival of the Jullundur Brigade, on the left, before continuing on across the Layes brook to the Bois du Biez. The three battalions of the Jullundur Brigade had, unfortunately, come under continuous machine-gun and rifle fire from the Layes bridge redoubt and suffered heavy loss as soon as ever they left their assembly trenches. Seeing that the 25th Brigade, the right brigade of the 8th Division, was unable to get forward, the 1/Manchester, the left battalion of the Jullundur Brigade, after an advance of a couple of hundred yards, halted in front of the last houses of Neuve Chapelle, astride the Brewery Road. As the Manchesters were directing the advance, the other two leading battalions of the brigade, the 47th Sikhs and 4/Suffolk, also halted. Thus no further progress was made and by 1.45 P.M. the situation on the Indian Corps front was again at a standstill.

FURTHER ATTACK ORDERED

In the meantime fuller details of the repulse of the German counter-offensive in the early hours had reached First Army headquarters, as well as the news of the many surrenders of German troops during the morning both on the front of the Indian and of the IV. Corps. At 1 P.M. reports from the IV. Corps were received to the effect that the 24th Brigade had occupied the road and the nameless group of houses at the Pietre—Mauquissart road-junction, and although as a fact, the captured sector of the German trench had been evacuated three hours earlier,[1] no message to that effect reached the First Army till the evening. An hour later (1.58 P.M.) a further report was received from the IV. Corps giving information of the successful advance on the front of the 7th Division, with the details that it had captured the Moulin du Pietre, east of Mauquissart and was pushing on towards Pietre and Les Mottes farm.

The impression gained at First Army headquarters

[1] See page 138.

from this misleading information was that the entire 12 Mar.
German position along the Mauquissart road had at last
been broken through. In order to take immediate advantage of the situation, General Haig, at 3.6 P.M., wired
to all commanders : " Information indicates that enemy
" on our front are much demoralized. Indian Corps and
" IV. Corps will push through the barrage of fire regardless
" of loss, using reserves if required ". In view of the
supposed situation, General Haig also asked Sir John
French to place at his disposal the 2nd Cavalry Division,
a request that was granted. The 5th Cavalry Brigade,
supported by two armoured motor cars, was thereupon
ordered at 2.50 P.M. to move by way of the Rue du
Bacquerot to the Moulin du Pietre, and co-operate there
with the 7th Division. The remainder of the 2nd Cavalry
Division was to move forward from about Estaires ready
to support its 5th Brigade. Even much later, at 6.20 P.M.,
General Haig telephoned to Sir John French asking that,
" in view of the promising situation, the 46th (North
" Midland) Division from the General Reserve might relieve
" the two left brigades of the Canadian Division, these two
" Canadian brigades to be massed in rear of the right
" Canadian brigade with a view to breaking through op-
" posite Rouges Bancs and co-operating with the advance
" of the 7th Division ". Similarly, for the right flank, he
directed the I. Corps to order its 1st Division to be prepared to co-operate with the advance of the Indian Corps.
The movement both by the Canadian and 1st Divisions,
was, however, necessarily dependent on the progress made
by the Indian and IV. Corps.[1]

On receipt of the 3.6 P.M. instructions from the First
Army, General Willcocks ordered the Lahore Division to
push forward to the Bois du Biez at all costs. The Sirhind
and Jullundur Brigades under Br.-General Walker were
already held up in the Dehra Dun trench west of the

---

[1] Under the misapprehension that the *6th Bavarian Reserve Division*,
identified from prisoners taken during the counter-attack in the early
morning, had come from the Ypres sector, British G.H.Q. ordered the
Second Army to make an attack as soon as possible to prevent the withdrawal of more German troops. This attack was delivered by the 7th
Brigade at 2.30 P.M., about Spanbroekmolen, two thousand yards north
of Wulverghem, but the bombardment was inaccurate and the wire not
cut. Consequently, the attack failed, the 3/Worcestershire losing 9 officers
and 169 other ranks, and the 1/Wiltshire 7 officers and 86 other ranks.

Lieut. C. G. Martin, 56th Field Co. R.E. (3rd Division), was awarded the
Victoria Cross for conspicuous gallantry, although wounded, when in com-
mand of a bombing party which he led into the enemy trenches near
Spanbroekmolen, holding them for 2½ hours until evacuation was ordered.

Layes brook and about Neuve Chapelle, whilst the Feroze-pore Brigade was still in reserve at Richebourg St. Vaast, two miles behind. Major-General H. D'U. Keary there-upon ordered the Ferozepore Brigade to Neuve Chapelle and told its commander, Br.-General R. G. Egerton, the senior brigadier of the division, to assume command of all three infantry brigades and organize an advance to the Bois.

The Ferozepore Brigade marched at 5 P.M. ; and about the same time General Haig rode forward to Indian Corps headquarters at Croix Marmeuse (5 miles west by north of Neuve Chapelle). Here he heard further details of the failure of the Sirhind and Jullundur Brigades to advance earlier in the afternoon, and on being told that the left could not get forward owing to the Layes bridge redoubt, he urged General Willcocks not to wait for it, but to push on with his right both against the southern part of the Bois du Biez and down the La Bassée road.[1] A staff officer was therefore despatched with further instructions to General Egerton, and, after delivering his message, asked to be informed at what hour the preliminary bombardment should begin. Not having yet seen the ground or knowing the condition of the Sirhind and Jullundur Brigades, General Egerton suggested 8.30 P.M., reserving, however, the right to alter the time as soon as he had had opportunity to appreciate the situation.

It was dark when, at 7.20 P.M., General Egerton found Sirhind Brigade headquarters. Br.-General Walker told him that the troops were exhausted and had suffered severely during the day, the Jullundur Brigade alone having at least eight hundred and eighty casualties, more than a quarter of its fighting strength, and that both brigades were held up by fire from the left flank and the left front. General Egerton came to the conclusion that it would not be possible to reorganize the brigades for an attack in a new direction against the south end of the Bois du Biez by 8.30 P.M. He telephoned to the Lahore Division asking for the bombardment to be postponed for two hours, till 10.30 P.M., at the same time giving his opinion that the attack ordered was not likely to succeed.

---

[1] At the same time, at the request of General Haig, the divisional cavalry regiments of the Lahore and Meerut Divisions, the 4th Cavalry and the 15th Lancers, were moved forward to Richebourg St. Vaast, with orders to push on as soon as the Bois du Biez was captured and advance to the east of the wood, reconnoitring towards Illies and Marquillies, and taking every opportunity to harass the enemy's retreat and destroy his transport.

General Willcocks, on being informed that the attack 12 Mar. had been postponed, cancelled it altogether, as he did not consider it feasible to make one with such a large body of troops by night over unreconnoitred ground.   The Jullundur and Ferozepore Brigades were then withdrawn, and the Sirhind Brigade took over the front line under the orders of the Meerut Division.

General Rawlinson (IV. Corps), on receipt of General Haig's instructions, at 3.20 P.M. went personally to the headquarters of both the 7th and 8th Divisions and urged Generals Capper and Davies to push on vigorously regardless of the enemy's fire.   He sent word to General Haig that the road to Pietre was not yet sufficiently clear to allow the cavalry to pass through, but that the 5th Cavalry Brigade should be kept at Pont du Hem (a mile northwest of Rouge Croix) ready to act at the first opportunity.

From 4.40 P.M. till dusk a continuous bombardment of the German position was maintained by the IV. Corps artillery, but as it was still uncertain whether the Mauquissart road had been occupied by British troops, the fire was directed to the east and north of the road.   The trenches and strong points along the road itself were still held by the Germans, so that actually the bombardment was ineffective.

On the front of the 8th Division, the 25th Brigade on the right, north of Neuve Chapelle, reported at 5.45 P.M. that the renewed assault had failed, that every man who rose to advance was shot down, but that a further attempt would be made under cover of darkness.[1]

The effort of the 23rd and 24th Brigades was on a larger scale.   Both these brigades were placed under Br.-General R. J. Pinney, the senior brigadier, and were ordered to push forward with every available man regardless of loss.   It was, however, 6.15 P.M. and dark before Br.-General Pinney had been able to collect the battalion commanders and explain his intentions.   These were that the 23rd Brigade, in reserve on the Armentières road, should advance and carry the 24th Brigade forward with it to the Pietre—La Russie road, as a first objective.

No proper reconnaissance had been made by the

___

[1] For conspicuous bravery on this occasion, Company-Sergeant-Major H. Daniels and Corporal C. R. Noble, both of the 2/Rifle Brigade, were awarded the Victoria Cross.   When their battalion was impeded in the advance by wire entanglements and subjected to a very severe machine-gun fire, these two men voluntarily rushed in front and succeeded in cutting some of the wire.   They were both wounded at once, and Corporal Noble died of his wounds.

12 Mar. battalion officers of the 23rd Brigade either of the ground to be crossed, the position of the 24th Brigade in front, or of the German trenches. Added to this, the night drew on rapidly, the low clouds and mist soon making the darkness intense. There was consequently great delay in crossing the ground between the Armentières road and the front trenches of the 24th Brigade. Though only a distance of 700 to 800 yards, it was 9.30 P.M. before the 2/Devonshire, the central battalion, reached the assaulting position, and even then the battalions on the flanks were not up. The 2/Scottish Rifles,[1] advancing from the Road Triangle on the right of the Devons, was unable to get in touch with them on the new alignment; whilst, on the left, the 4/Cameron Highlanders of the 24th Brigade lost its way, and about midnight appeared behind the centre. Br.-General Pinney hoped to be able to attack at 11.30 P.M., but the confusion of units was so great that battalion commanders asked for a two-hours postponement. During this interval it was discovered that a low blackthorn hedge, well wired, protected the German position, and had been demolished only in places by the previous bombardments. An officer went back to brigade headquarters for instructions, but had not returned at zero hour. As this time approached, the men, exhausted after three days and nights continuously under fire, had fallen asleep, and could only be aroused by use of force, a process made very lengthy by the fact that this part of the battlefield was covered with British and German dead, who, in the dark, were indistinguishable from the sleepers. No counter-orders having been received, at 1.30 A.M. the leading lines of the Scottish Rifles and the Devons, to right and left, respectively, of the Sunken Road, crossed the front trenches of the 24th Brigade and advanced towards the Mauquissart road. They had hardly started before the attack was brought to an end by a message from 8th Division—despatched at 10.15 P.M., but only received at 1.25 A.M. at brigade headquarters—ordering no advance to be made beyond the Mauquissart road. Br.-General Pinney, therefore, issued instructions to abandon further attempts to get forward. The left company of the Devons, being separated from the battalion by a wide dyke, did not hear

---

[1] Major G. T. C. Carter-Campbell had been wounded at 4 P.M. when the command of the 2/Scottish Rifles devolved on Lieut. W. F. Somervail (killed in October 1918), who had joined the Special Reserve in August 1914 and was the only officer left.

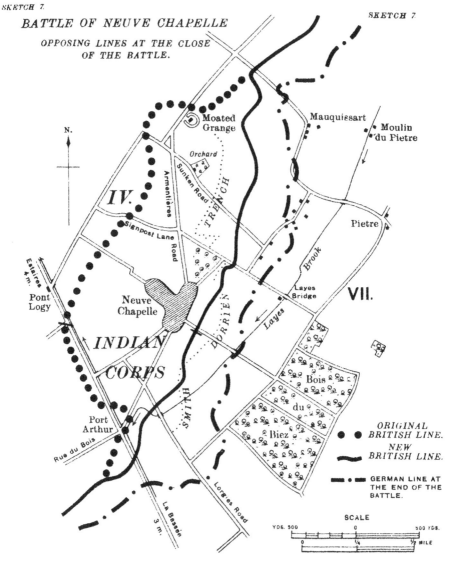

BATTLE OF NEUVE CHAPELLE

OPPOSING LINES AT THE CLOSE
OF THE BATTLE.

N.

Moated
Grange

Mauquissart

Moulin
du Pietre

Orchard

Armentières Road

Sunken Road

TRENCH

IV.

Signpost Lane

Pietre

Brook

Estaires
4 m.

Neuve
Chapelle

Layes
Bridge

DORRIEN

Layes

VII.

Pont
Logy

INDIAN

CORPS

SMITH

Bois

du

Port
Arthur

Biez

Rue du Bois

ORIGINAL
BRITISH LINE.

NEW
BRITISH LINE.

GERMAN LINE AT
THE END OF THE
BATTLE.

Longies Road

La Bassée
3 m.

SCALE

YDS. 500   0   500 YDS.

0   ¼   ½ MILE

Ordnance Survey 1925.

of this until it got close up to the enemy lines, and, being 12 Mar.
received by rifle fire at close range, had thirty casualties
before it could extricate itself.   The remaining hours of
darkness were spent in reorganizing the 23rd and 24th
Brigades, now thoroughly intermingled, in the 24th Brigade
trenches.   At 1.50 A.M. a further message, timed midnight,
from the 8th Division was received by Br.-General Pinney
to the effect that the division was to consolidate its present
position, the 23rd Brigade to take over the line of the
24th Brigade, and the latter to withdraw before daylight
into divisional reserve west of the Armentières road.   When
this order had been carried out, the front trenches of the
24th Brigade were occupied by the Scottish Rifles, astride
the Sunken Road, the Devons in the centre, and the
Middlesex, facing the southern houses of Mauquissart.
The West Yorkshire and the Cameron Highlanders (24th
Brigade) moved to positions in support.

The 7th Division at 3.25 P.M. had also received orders
to press forward regardless of loss.   Since, however, the
situation of the various units could not yet be established
owing to the mass of conflicting messages,[1] no further
orders were issued to battalions.   About 4 P.M. definite
reports received from some of the front battalion commanders showed that the Mauquissart road had not been
reached.   A staff officer was therefore sent forward to
find out the situation, and it was not until 6.40 P.M. that
a more accurate knowledge of the position of the front
units was obtained.   It was then clear that no 7th Division
unit had reached the Mauquissart road and that the only
result of the day's fighting had been the capture of the
Quadrilateral and of the neighbouring German trench.
General Capper therefore explained the situation to the
IV. Corps, adding that the troops in the front line had
been fighting continuously for thirty-six hours and had
suffered considerable losses.   He recommended the relief
of the front battalions and the reorganization of the
supporting battalions for an attack the following morning.
To this, General Rawlinson agreed.

POSTPONEMENT OF FURTHER ATTACK AND CONSOLIDA-
TION OF THE LINE

During the evening the reports received at First Army Sketch 7.
headquarters made it clear that the German defence line had

[1] See page 140.

12 Mar. not been so broken as was at first imagined. On the right, messages from the Indian Corps showed no further progress, whilst in the centre the 8th Division reported that the Layes bridge redoubt and the neighbouring trenches were strongly held and that no headway could be made against them. On the left, the 7th Division, at 7.34 P.M. reported that the progress made during the day had not been so great as previous messages had stated, that none of the Mauquissart—Chapigny road was in British possession, that the troops had been fighting hard all day and could not do much more, and there was no opportunity for cavalry to break through.

It was clear that the Germans had constructed a new position east of Neuve Chapelle which they were holding in strength. General Haig, at 10.40 P.M., after telephoning to headquarters of both the Indian and IV. Corps and still hearing that no further progress had been made, decided to cancel his previous instructions. He considered that further efforts to break through opposite Neuve Chapelle would be of no avail, and he therefore ordered [1] the front held to be established as a defensive line, and wired and secured against attack. The corps were informed that the general advance should not be continued the following morning without further orders, and that reliefs might be carried out. His intention was now to carry on the fight for Aubers ridge by assaulting the German line at some other point and thereby to regain the advantage of surprise. For this purpose he selected a part of the front on the Armentières road, astride the Fauquissart cross roads and a mile north of the Moated Grange. Since, however, there were no experienced troops in reserve, a division would have to be withdrawn from the front line for the operation, thereby delaying its commencement for several days.

Early on the 13th General Haig motored to Hazebrouck and explained his new plans to Sir John French. He said a week would be needed for the preparations, and suggested the 22nd March as the day of attack, given favourable weather. Sir John French approved of this plan.

On General Haig's return to First Army headquarters, orders were therefore issued for a preparatory redistribution of divisions ; the 8th Division to take over the whole front from the left of the Indian Corps (the southernmost

[1] Appendix 21.

cross roads of Neuve Chapelle village) to the right of the 13 Mar.
Canadian Division (at Fauquissart). The 7th Division
was to be withdrawn from the front with a view to taking
up a fresh position in rear of the Fauquissart road junction.

During the day (13th), however, the returns of gun
ammunition expended during the three days' fighting at
Neuve Chapelle that now reached British G.H.Q. showed
Sir John French that the needs of a modern battle were
greater than had been anticipated, and were not to be
easily met. The expenditure on the first battle day alone [1]
was a revelation as to the quantity required to break
through the German front line and support a subsequent
advance, and it was evident that the available supply
of ammunition was quite inadequate to maintain the
offensive. Taking the case of the 18-pdr. field gun, the
amount of ammunition with field units and in ammunition parks previous to the battle was 528 rounds per
gun, and there was a reserve of 220 rounds on the lines
of communication, giving a total of 748 rounds per gun
in France. On the first battle day, the 10th March,
132 rounds per gun had been fired, on the 11th March,
64 rounds per gun, and on the 12th, 49 rounds per gun,
a total of 245 rounds per gun for the three days' fighting,
that is a third of the total per gun, and in sum nearly
a sixth of the available 18-pdr. ammunition for the entire
British Expeditionary Force. To put it in another way,
the rate of production in England of complete 18-pdr.
ammunition was at this time $7\frac{1}{2}$ rounds per gun per day
and it would take 17 days to replace the 18-pdr. ammunition expended. The amount fired by the other types of
artillery was in approximately similar proportion.

Early on the 13th March Sir John French wired to
Lord Kitchener :—" Cessation of the forward movement is
" necessitated to-day by the fatigue of the troops, and,
" above all, by the want of ammunition. The First Army
" is consolidating and strengthening its new line. Further

---

[1] The ammunition fired on the 10th March by the principal types of
artillery employed *on the whole front* of the First Army was as follows :—

13-pdr. (60)	.	.	.	9,052 (150 rounds per gun)
18-pdr. (324)	.	.	.	41,810 (129 ,, ,,)
4·5-inch how. (54)	.	.	.	6,040 (112 ,, ,,)
60-pdr. (12)	.	.	.	523 (43 ,, ,,)
6-inch how. (28)	.	.	.	3,364 (120 ,, ,,)
6-inch gun (4)	.	.	.	175 (44 ,, ,,)
9·2-inch how. (3)	.	.	.	243 (81 ,, ,,)
15-inch how. (1)	.	.	.	12 (12 ,, ,,)

For the total available for the battle see p. 85.

13 Mar. " plans are being matured for a vigorous offensive ". Subsequent enquiries as to the ammunition available showed, however, that if the offensive operations were resumed there would be a risk of depleting the supplies beyond the limits of safety, and on the 15th March Sir John French decided that for the time-being the idea of continuing the offensive must be abandoned. General Haig was informed accordingly and at the same time Sir John French again wired to Lord Kitchener :—" The " supply of gun ammunition, especially the 18-pdr. and " 4·5-inch howitzer, has fallen short of what I was led to " expect and I was therefore compelled to abandon further " offensive operations until sufficient reserves are ac- " cumulated ".

Although the battle of Neuve Chapelle may be said to have ended on the night of the 12th March, a further local effort to press forward to the line of the Mauquissart— Chapigny road was made on the following morning (13th) at 9.30 A.M. by the 7th Division. This effort failed with heavy loss, particularly to the 6/Gordon Highlanders and 1/Grenadier Guards.

During the 13th and 14th the new front line was further consolidated by both sides,[1] and reliefs were carried out under cover of darkness. In the Indian Corps, the Lahore Division took over the front defences from the Meerut Division, the right in touch with the I. Corps south of Richebourg l'Avoué and the left on the Brewery Road, immediately east of Neuve Chapelle village, a total frontage of 3,500 yards. The Meerut Division was withdrawn into Indian Corps reserve about Locon.

The IV. Corps maintained the line with its 8th Division, from the Brewery Road, including the southern cross roads in Neuve Chapelle village, along the new front facing the length of the Mauquissart road to its junction with the Armentières road, near Chapigny, and thence along the original line of trenches to Fauquissart, a total frontage of 3,600 yards. The 7th Division was withdrawn into IV. Corps reserve to the area Laventie—Estaires—Pont du Hem (2 miles north-west of Neuve Chapelle).

---

[1] Orders issued by the German *VII. Corps* on the afternoon of the 12th directed the line held to be strengthened as a permanent position. To make good the losses of the *13th* and *14th Infantry Divisions* in the battle, the *6th Bavarian Reserve Division* was to occupy that part of the new line between Chapigny and the La Russie—Neuve Chapelle road, the *13th* and *14th Divisions* to north and south closing up their inner flanks accordingly.

The British casualties during the battle had been 583 officers and 12,309 other ranks.[1] The German losses had also been very heavy, probably about twelve thousand, including 30 officers and 1,657 other ranks taken prisoner.[2]

RETROSPECT OF NEUVE CHAPELLE

The battle of Neuve Chapelle was the first planned British offensive, and is therefore an important landmark in trench warfare. Both as regards attack and defence, it indicated the lines on which the battles of the new warfare would proceed and the difficulties that would be encountered. It demonstrated that a break-in was possible under certain conditions. Prepared with great care and minuteness by the First Army, the operations, beginning with a surprise, had a considerable initial success. But once this set piece was over, there came unforeseen delays. Command of the operations became slow and difficult, and the assistance of the infantry by the artillery was hampered by the breakdown of the telephone system. The vulnerability of our means of communication and methods of inter-communication in the

---

[1] These include over a thousand in the I. Corps and a hundred in the Canadian Division. The losses in the four attacking divisions were :—

	Officers.	Other Ranks.	Total.
7th Division	138	2,653	2,791
8th ,,	218	4,596	4,814
Meerut Division	103	2,250	2,353
Lahore ,,	85	1,609	1,694
	544	11,108	11,652

Drafts, it may be added, arrived from the Base during the battle and replaced a great part of the casualties.

[2] So many German regiments and detached units were involved, that it is difficult to obtain an accurate figure, nevertheless the *6th Bavarian Reserve Division*, by its own official statement, had casualties of 70 officers and 6,000 men on the 11th, 12th and 13th March, most of which occurred during the counter-offensive on the morning of the 12th. The *21st Bavarian Reserve Infantry Regiment*, alone, gives the losses of its three battalions for the three days, 11th, 12th and 13th March, making them 26 officers and 1,139 other ranks. The official German casualty lists also give the losses of the *14th Infantry Regiment (VII. Corps)*, that received the brunt of the first attempt, as 17 officers and 649 other ranks during the period 7th-12th March, most of which had occupied the line in front of Neuve Chapelle village. The casualties of the *13th Infantry Regiment*, that had held the front from Moated Grange northwards to Fauquissart, are given as 21 officers and 1,301 other ranks for the period 6th-27th March, most of which were incurred in the Neuve Chapelle fighting. Thus the losses for 18 out of 26 battalions amount to 108 officers and some 8000 men.

face of modern artillery, and the difficulty, under conditions of siege warfare, of getting reinforcements to the required positions at the proper time, up trenches already congested, exceeded all expectation and calculations. The enemy gained time to bring up reinforcements, and construct a retrenchment, to use the old word of siege warfare, behind the threatened breach. Thus equilibrium was very quickly re-established, mere repetition of the first effort only brought repetition of failure, and, for the moment, all hope of further progress vanished, except after renewed preparations and an entirely fresh attack.

Given that the front of attack was wide enough to make it impossible for the small local reserves of the defence to deal with the situation, success was shown to be a time problem, a question of whether a break-in—which, with adequate artillery preparation was always possible—could be converted into a break-through before the enemy could be certain of the point of attack and rush reinforcements to it. Unfortunately units that were successful were not ordered to assist, by pressing on, those that were held up, and there was a tendency on the first day to send in supports and reserves to repeat assaults that had failed, instead of employing them to exploit success. The enemy showed, as the British troops had shown at Ypres, the tremendous value of a few brave men holding on in strong points and isolated trenches.

The Allies were in reality confronted by siege-warfare, but by some mischance it was named and treated as " trench-warfare ", something little different to open warfare. The broad conception of their operations, indeed, varied little from that of open warfare as evolved in pre-war " doctrine " and laid down in pre-war manuals, where trenches and barbed wire did not exist. Trench-warfare came to be regarded as a special problem to be solved by " the bomb and the bayonet ", and the old lessons of siege-warfare were not applied. As an unkind critic said, every endeavour was made to convert what was in reality an " engineer and artillery war " into a " cavalry war " ; instead of gun and mine preparing a way for the infantry, it was the infantry which was expected to open a door for an inroad of horsemen against the enemy's rear. A fresh vocabulary was created to meet the supposed new conditions. Instead of using the old-fashioned word " breach ", the higher commands called upon the troops to make a " gap " ; a " retrenchment " became a "switch"; a "sap" was not made by sapping; "mining" was renamed "tunnelling"; "subsidiary" attacks, mere demonstrations that could not possibly be developed into a " break-through ", took the place not only of " false " attacks, but also of the minor attacks of old days[1]; and the new words were misleading.

The Germans stuck closer to the old methods, as will be seen from their procedure at " Second Ypres ".[2]

The result of the battle of Neuve Chapelle did not change the strategical situation on the Western Front; nevertheless certain definite and substantial advantages had been gained. It had shown that several months of trench warfare under the most adverse conditions had not affected the general spirit of the British Expeditionary Force. After the long spell of defensive warfare, the preparation and delivery of this first offensive battle on an organized scale was in itself a factor of marked value, giving a practical proof to the troops themselves that neither the enemy nor his entrenchments were invulnerable. For this reason alone it may be considered as the first step in the gradual establishment of that moral superiority over the enemy so essential to victory.

In addition to demonstrating to the Allies the earnest intentions of the British Government, the battle had also raised the prestige of the B.E.F. as an efficient instrument of war in the opinion of both friend and foe, as was soon made manifest. There is little doubt that the Germans had not regarded seriously either the British will or power to take the offensive. Although they expected Territorial divisions to take the field, even imagined them at " First Ypres " in 1914, they did not believe that the New Armies, in process of creation in the·United Kingdom, would ever be fit to send to France as fighting units, and they took it for granted that the British force in France would remain on the defensive, merely holding part of the front. For this reason they had been disposed to run great risks

---

[1] In the successful sieges of the Peninsula Wellington did not rely on one assault at the main breach or breaches, which, as often as not, failed because the enemy was ready. Besides actual false attacks, he executed minor ones intended to be driven home. Thus at Badajoz in 1812, there were two false attacks by Portuguese brigades, and three subsidiary attacks, on San Roque, the Castle, and San Vicente, by the 4th Division guards of the trenches, the 3rd Division, and a brigade of the 5th Division, respectively. The main assault by the 4th and Light Divisions on the great breach failed; but the subsidiary assaults were successful, and determined the fate of the day.
[2] Chapter X.

24 Mar. and, as has been seen, prior to the battle of Neuve Chapelle had thinned their defensive front facing the British sector of the line to an absolute minimum.   The battle had, however, been a revelation in this respect, and the Germans at once set about strengthening their defences and increasing the garrisons opposite the British front.   The French, too, had seemed to regard the rôle of the British Army primarily as that of taking over an increasing extent of frontage to relieve the French troops for offensive action.   Its participation in a French offensive was treated as a secondary and subsidiary part of its activities.   After the battle of Neuve Chapelle, however, the correspondence between the French and British General Staffs contained a fresh note of confidence and a more cordial desire on the French side for an effective co-operation in a combined offensive movement.

RESUMPTION OF THE PLAN FOR A COMBINED FRANCO-BRITISH OFFENSIVE

The negotiations between General Joffre and Sir John French for an offensive on a general front between Armentières and Arras, which had been temporarily broken off prior to the battle of Neuve Chapelle, were resumed by a letter from General Joffre to British G.H.Q. dated 24th March 1915.   The experiences gained in the recent fighting both on the French and British fronts, had, General Joffre wrote, made it necessary to postpone combined operations. " In a war such as we are now engaged in, where the " enemy occupies defensive positions organized in the " strongest manner, and, in addition, has sufficient men " and material for an energetic defence, our offensive can " only succeed under the following conditions : (1) the " possession on a large front of the necessary numerical " superiority ; (2) the possession and full use of adequate " material both for the destruction of supplementary " defences and for close fighting ; (3) the possession of " large reserves of ammunition both for heavy and for " field artillery ".   He considered that he would be unable to collect all the means necessary for such action on a front sufficiently large to produce a decisive result until the end of April.   Five to six weeks were therefore available for the necessary preparations ; and he asked Sir John French to arrange accordingly.   " It appears to me " to be extremely desirable that the British Armies should " be in a position to co-operate in this operation with the

" maximum of their power by assembling their effectives Mar.-
" and by saving and collecting their ammunition and other April.
" war material. . . . I am full of confidence that this
" offensive will inflict such a blow on the enemy that the
" greatest results may follow and that our movement may
" be an important step towards the final victory ". In
addition, General Joffre repeated his request that British
troops should relieve the French IX. and XX. Corps,
north of Ypres, as soon as possible, so that these two corps
might be reorganized with a view to participating in the
projected operation.

In his reply on the 1st April, Sir John French stated
that he had ordered an extension of the British line northwards as far as the Ypres—Poelcappelle road, and that he
had every reason to hope that this relief would be completed on or before the 20th April. He also hoped to be
" in a position to co-operate in the proposed combined
" offensive at the end of April with the whole of the British
" First Army which will, by then, have a strength of eight
" divisions ".

But until the British Government had formulated a military policy, had communicated it to Sir John French and had
informed him of the resources on which he could depend
it was impossible to make comprehensive plans for future
action, or even to agree to local plans for immediate action.
A new theatre of war had been opened at the Dardanelles,
and the original policy, the reconquest of Belgium and the
defeat of the German Armies in that theatre, seemed to be
undergoing eclipse. Beyond the arrival of the 47th (2nd
London) Division,[1] and a curt telegram that the South
Midland Division would embark for France during 28th to
30th March, there were no signs of substantial reinforcements, and during the month of March the Commander-in-
Chief could obtain no information as to when the New
Army divisions would be sent, or even if they were to be
sent at all.[2]

Nevertheless early in April preparations were begun by
the First Army for taking part in the combined offensive;

---

[1] The 47th (2nd London) Division T.F. (Major-General C. St. L. Barter)
began to arrive at Havre on the 16th March and concentrated in the
Bethune area by the 20th.

[2] When on the 8th April he asked on what date the next Territorial
division would arrive, he received the reply that the first of two would
embark on the following Monday. In response to his continued demands
for more troops, divisions were despatched to France as they were considered fit for the field, and even earlier.

12 Mar. but before they were completed a German attack in the neighbourhood of Ypres developed. This attack, which began on the 22nd April, was to influence considerably the Allied offensive plan, for it both withdrew troops from the intended battle area and used up much of the reserves of ammunition and material that were being accumulated.

NOTE

THE GERMAN COUNTER-ATTACK, 12TH MARCH 1915 [1]

On the evening of the 11th March the Germans reinforced their front line with six battalions. In the centre two battalions, one each from the *20th* and *21st Bavarian Reserve Infantry Regiments* (*6th Bavarian Reserve Division*), moved forward through the Bois du Biez into the front line west of the wood, reinforcing the two battalions, one each of the *56th* and *57th Infantry Regiments* (*79th Brigade*), already in position between La Russie and the Lorgies road. The right and left flanks were each reinforced by two Saxon battalions, two of the *133rd* and *179th Infantry Regiments* moving up to about Mauquissart and Pietre, and two of the *104th* and *139th Infantry Regiments* behind the *16th Infantry Regiment* facing the Port Arthur salient between the Lorgies and the La Bassée roads.

At 5.30 P.M. the orders for the counter-offensive on the following morning were issued from German *14th Division* headquarters.[2]

[1] " 17 Bav. Res. Regt." ; " 21 Bav. Res. Regt." ; " Bavarian Official History " ; Corps and divisional orders from the Reichsarchiv ; Prisoners' statements, First Army Intelligence Summaries.

[2] The previous orders for the counter-offensive, postponed from the morning of the 11th, were, it will be remembered, for an assault with the bayonet without artillery preparation. With this exception, there was no alteration of importance.

14TH DIVISIONAL OPERATION ORDER
6.30 P.M. 11th March.

1. The enemy holds the eastern edge of Neuve Chapelle.
2. The division will take Neuve Chapelle to-morrow.
3. For this purpose the division will be supported, in addition to the units of the *13th Infantry Division* already in position, by units of the *XIX. Corps*, *14th Bavarian Reserve Infantry Brigade*, the *16th Bavarian Reserve Infantry Regiment*, a Pioneer company of the *6th Bavarian Reserve Division*, and three more companies of the *13th Infantry Regiment* (*13th Infantry Division*).
4. Attack sectors :—
   (a) Sector under commander of *14th Bavarian Reserve Infantry Brigade*. Right boundary : Aubers—Big Farm [Moated Grange] north of Neuve Chapelle. Left boundary : La Russie—Neuve Chapelle church—Pont Logy.
   (b) Sector under commander of *79th Infantry Brigade*. Right in touch with left of (a) sector. Left boundary : Halpegarbe—Ferme du Biez—cross roads La Bassée—Pont Logy, Richebourg l'Avoué—Neuve Chapelle.
5. Troops available :—
   (a) Under *14th Bavarian Infantry Brigade*. In addition to troops already in position in the right sector will be the *14th Bavarian*

The front line units, reorganized into two brigades, were to assault 12 Mar. at 5 A.M. (6 A.M. German time) along the whole of the new front from north of the Moated Grange to south of the Port Arthur salient, in order to recapture the German original trenches including the village of Neuve Chapelle.

The two brigade assault sectors, north and south of the Layes bridge road were further sub-divided by the brigade commanders so that the assault actually developed as narrated in the text into four separate attacks, on the right, in the right centre, in the left centre, and on the left.

> *Reserve Infantry Brigade* (less 2 battalions), the three companies of the *13th Infantry Regiment*, and ⅓ *Bavarian Pioneer Company*. (b) Under the *79th Infantry Brigade*. In addition to troops already in position in the left sector will be the *16th Bavarian Reserve Infantry Regiment* and ⅓ *Bavarian Pioneer Company*.
>
> 6. Of the *14th Bavarian Reserve Infantry Brigade* 2 battalions will be at my disposal in Halpegarbe, covered from aeroplane view, from 5.30 A.M. onwards.
>
> 7. During the night 11th/12th the front line will be strengthened and any gaps filled up. The front line will work forward under cover of darkness to within assaulting distance of the enemy. The supporting lines will also move forward under cover of darkness in several waves so close to the front line that at 6 A.M. the whole can assault together (der einheitliche Sturm erfolgen kann). The preparatory movements must be completed by 5.30 A.M. By these measures the supporting lines in the rapid advance will be able to press on at once through the front line if, as may be expected, it is held up by enemy counter-attacks or by the street fighting in the village. Reserves will be brought forward by the commanders of sectors according to circumstances.
>
> 8. The objective of the attack is the recapture of the German positions west and north of Neuve Chapelle. Efforts will also be made to occupy the cross-roads La Bassée—Pont Logy, Richebourg l'Avoué—Neuve Chapelle.
>
> 9. The artillery, strengthened by the heavy batteries and other batteries of the *VII. Corps Artillery Reserve*, will keep under heavy fire throughout the day and the coming night the village of Neuve Chapelle, the enemy's position and the approach roads within the attacking zone. All the registered enemy batteries will also be kept under a regular and heavy fire.
>
> At 6 A.M. on the 12th the artillery will lift its fire on to the former enemy position north and south of Pont Logy and the approach roads. The fire will be regulated by Colonel Campe in unison with that of the southern group of the *13th Divisional Artillery* according to the instruction issued verbally.
>
> 10, 11, 12 and 13. (Engineer, Ammunition and Medical arrangements.)
>
> 14. I shall be at Divisional Battle Headquarters in the factory at Illies from 5 A.M. onwards.
>
>   VON DITFURTH.

CHAPTER VIII

THE BATTLES OF YPRES 1915 [1]

EVENTS IN THE SECOND ARMY 1st-21st APRIL 1915, PREVIOUS TO THE BATTLES

(Maps 4, 5 ; Sketches A, B, 8)

THE EXTENSION OF THE BRITISH FRONT

Sketch 1. DURING the first weeks of April, in deference to the wishes
Map 5. of General Joffre,[2] the British Expeditionary Force took
Sketch 8. over nearly five more miles of the French front which
lay to its left : the sector from the Ypres—Menin road
opposite Gheluvelt to the Ypres—Poelcappelle road beyond Zonnebeke. On the completion of this relief the
British again covered the town of Ypres as they had done
in October 1914. Their front, however, was now continuous, there were no French troops interpolated in it as
was the case during the Battles of Ypres 1914 ; and its
total length, from Cuinchy on the south side of the La
Bassée canal to the new northern boundary, was thirty
miles as against the nineteen miles held after the re-
division of the line between the Allies at the end of November 1914.[3] Opposite the new front, counting from south
to north, were the German *VII. Corps, 6th Bavarian
Division, XIX. Corps* (opposite Armentières), *II. Bavarian
Corps* (in front of Wytschaete), *XV. Corps* (opposite
Zillebeke), and the *XXVII. Reserve Corps* with the *38th
Landwehr Brigade* attached (between Gheluvelt and the
Ypres—Poelcappelle road).[4] Thus there were 11¼ German

---

[1] This is the official nomenclature. The battles of Ypres 1914 and
1915 are better known as " First Ypres " and " Second Ypres ", and these
titles are from time to time used in the text.

[2] See p. 155.   [3] For the portions taken over in January see p. 26.

[4] The attachment of *Landwehr* and *Ersatz* brigades to the *XXVII.*
Reserve and *XXVI.* Reserve Corps was not known at the time, although
the presence of the brigades was.

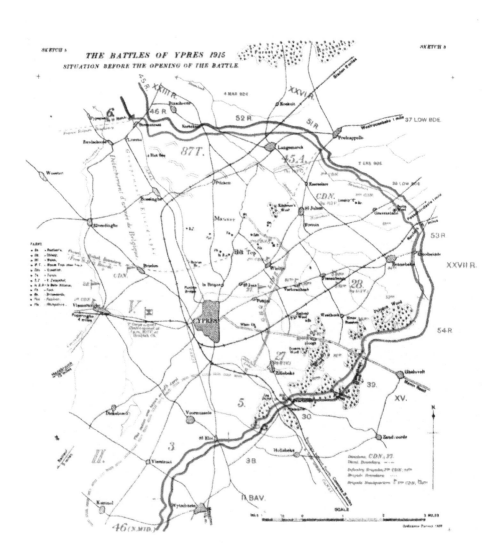

THE BATTLES OF YPRES 1915
SITUATION BEFORE THE OPENING OF THE BATTLE

divisions, apart from any general reserves, in line against April.
16 British.[1]

The extension of the British front to meet the French
wishes was carried out gradually by the Second Army—
the First Army was preparing another offensive—and by
the II. and V. Corps only of that Army, for the III. Corps
was already holding ten miles of front with two divisions.
To enable General Smith-Dorrien to cover the ground,
each of his three corps was augmented by a division. The
newly arrived South Midland Division (48th) was detailed
by G.H.Q. to the III. Corps ; [2] the North Midland (46th)
from the general reserve, to the II. Corps ; and the Canadian
Division, withdrawn from the First Army as from 7th
April, to the V. Corps. Between the 2nd and 8th April,
the 27th Division (V. Corps),[3] between the 8th and 11th
April, the 28th Division (V. Corps),[4] and between the 15th
and 17th April, the Canadian Division relieved in succession three French divisions, whose staffs and regimental
officers did everything possible to make the handing over
easy and methodical. There then remained between the
British and the Belgians, from the Franco-British boundary
line west of the Ypres—Poelcappelle road [5] to the canal at
Steenstraat [6]—that is on the northern side of the Ypres
salient—only two French divisions, the 45th (Algerian)
and 87th (Territorial), with a detachment of cavalry,[7] all

[1] 1st to 8th, 27th, 28th, Canadian, Lahore, Meerut, 46th (North
Midland), 47th (2nd London), and 48th (South Midland) Divisions.

[2] The South Midland Division (Major-General H. N. C. Heath), which
consisted of units drawn from the counties of Warwickshire, Worcestershire and Gloucestershire, and the Thames Valley, reached France during
the 29th/30th March, and arrived in the III. Corps area during the first
weeks of April. Its units were at once attached to brigades in the line
for training.

[3] The short sector it held was taken over by the 3rd Division which
extended its left.

[4] Its old sector in the line had previously been taken over by the 5th
Division, relieved on the right of the II. Corps by the North Midland.

[5] The line shown in Sketch 8 as the boundary is taken from the
G.H.Q. records, and differs in some details from the lines on the maps of
the French Historical Section and the V. Corps.

[6] At the close of the Battle of Ypres 1914 the Belgian right flank was
at Knocke, the junction of the Ypres—Yser canal with the Yser. On
26th January 1915, at the request of General Joffre, the Belgian Army
took over rather more than three miles of front from the French, down
to the Maison du Passeur (Wit Huis on pre-war maps, 1-1/4 miles north
of Steenstraat). A month later, at the request of General Foch, a further
extension was made down to Steenstraat (exclusive), making the total
4½ miles.

[7] The 45th Division (General Quiquandon) came into the line at Ypres,
relieving what remained of the 11th Division on 16th April, when the
Canadian Division was taking over next to it. It contained 9 battalions

April. under the command of General Putz.[1] Opposed to them were the German *XXVI. Reserve Corps*, with the *37th Landwehr* and *2nd Reserve Ersatz Brigades* attached, and from opposite Boesinghe northwards, part of the *XXIII. Reserve Corps.*

The French front trenches—or rather breastworks, as they were more above the ground than below—taken over, varied considerably ; some were good, some were reported on as in a deplorable condition, and dangerous both as regards safety and sanitation. They consisted of isolated groups of shallow fire and support trenches, with parapets in some cases only four feet thick at base, and not bullet proof ; they had good machine-gun posts, but few traverses, no parados, and only flimsily built dug-outs which afforded little more than shelter from the weather.

A very considerable amount of work had to be done—often with built-up sandbag breastworks, on account of the presence of water close to the surface—in order to make the fire trenches reasonably defensible ; the French had relied mainly on the very effective fire of their 75 mm. field guns, for which they had plenty of ammunition, to hold the front. The wire entanglements were usually very good, but there were no communication trenches except those connecting the front and support trenches, and these were rarely more than 2 to 2½ feet deep.[2] There were some unfinished subsidiary trenches and supporting points,[3] without much wire, behind the front position, and

of Zouaves, 2 of African L.I. and 3 of African Rifles (Tirailleurs Indigènes) a regiment of Chasseurs d'Afrique, and 10 batteries (4-gun) of artillery. The 87th (Territorial) Division (General Roy), it will be recalled, was in the fighting round Ypres in 1914, and had been in the area ever since.

[1] His command, organized on 4th April when General d'Urbal left, is referred to both as the " Détachement de Belgique " and the " Groupement d'Elverdinghe ". The former included the Nieuport groupement consisting of two infantry brigades, dismounted squadrons and cyclists of the 4th and 5th Cavalry Divisions, and 12 horse and field batteries, all under General de Mitry ; the latter name applied only to the troops between the British and the Belgians. General Putz's Chief of the Staff was Colonel Desticker, well known later as a member of the staff of Marshal Foch. There was no heavy artillery with the Elverdinghe groupement except the 120 mm. old pattern guns attached to the 87th (Territorial) Division.

[2] The history of the *215th Reserve Inf. Regt. (XXVI. Reserve Corps)*, p. 219, corroborates exactly the British impression of the French trenches : it states that when the Germans captured the French " fortress " near Steenstraat, which had held them back the whole winter, they found " a primitive sandbag parapet, hardly bullet-proof, miserable shelters . . . " only the French wire entanglements were strong and good ".

[3] One of the supporting points, known as " Locality C ", comes prominently into notice during the fighting. It was on the skyline on the

in the area held by the Canadians, there were also a few April. groups of old trenches which had been dug by the troops of General Dubois' IX. Corps during "First Ypres" as they fought their way forward north-eastwards from the line Zonnebeke—St. Julien—Langemarck over Gravenstafel ridge towards Passchendaele and Poelcappelle.[1] Here, too, lay a number of bodies, French and German, unburied since the same period, and an acrid smell of death infected the air, which even chloride of lime failed to make more than just endurable.

Far better prepared for defence than the front line and the supporting points was a second line, constructed by the French, but known to the British and referred to in this narrative as " G.H.Q. Line ".[2] It ran from Zillebeke Lake, where it was 1½ miles behind the front, northwards to a point half-a-mile east of Wieltje, where it was three miles behind the front ; thence it gradually turned north-westwards to join a line covering Boesinghe village and railway bridge. It consisted of well-constructed text-book redoubts, of some thirty yards face, with their flanks turned back, each for a garrison of about fifty men. These redoubts were from four to five hundred yards apart, and were eventually joined up by fire trenches. The line was exceedingly well sited from the point of view of a good field of fire, sometimes on a reverse, sometimes on a forward slope, but not overlooked owing to the general flatness of the ground. The real strength of the line lay in its wire, a continuous belt some six yards wide, with openings only at the transverse roads and tracks. There was no such thing as shell-proof cover in the Ypres district ; the dug-outs under the ramparts of the town were not yet made, and neither French nor British constructed more than

---

western part of Gravenstafel ridge, about 800 yards west of Boetleer's Farm. It is described as " consisting chiefly of a rather poor trench, " 200 yards long, facing north-east, built in the usual French thin parapet " style, with no depth, no thickness and no parados, and, in common with " the other supporting points, in a less than half-finished state, the trench " two feet deep. Along the front, about ten yards away, was a barbed " wire fence ". The same general line of trench elements extended with occasional gaps some 1,000 yards north-west along the top of the western end of the ridge. Another supporting point of the same description covered Gravenstafel, another was in the enclosure of Boetleer's Farm, whilst a fourth had been constructed between the last two named, but in front of them, half way down the forward slope to the Stroombeke.

    [1] See "1914" Vol. II. Sketches 8 and 9.
    [2] Its original designation was " G.H.Q. 2nd Line ", but there was no G.H.Q. 1st Line.

April. mere splinter-proofs : shallow holes in the ground—for three feet of digging usually found water—roofed with corrugated iron, logs or timber, on which was piled eighteen inches to three feet of earth.[1]

On the removal from the area of the French anti-aircraft guns, a weapon hardly yet possessed by the British, there was a great revival of German air activity ; [2] Ypres and Poperinghe and the villages round were bombed, and the number of enemy aeroplanes that came over to assist artillery registration greatly increased.

Although his front trenches were only one hundred and fifty to three hundred yards away, the enemy made no attempt to interfere, except by normal shelling, whilst the British were taking over the new front.[3] He appeared to be devoting his efforts to strengthening his line ; his wire entanglements grew every night, and every morning his parapets showed fresh signs of having been thickened. He sent out few patrols, and those few were unenterprising.

Even apart from the usual disabilities of a salient, the situation of the Allies at Ypres was, however, distinctly weak. They certainly possessed superior numbers, but were very inferior in heavy guns and means of artillery observation; and, in addition to this, there were two far from first-class French divisions interpolated between the British and the Belgians. There were no arrangements for unity of command of the three different contingents, and the two junctions were ill-chosen : that of the French and British at a shoulder of the salient, and that of the French and Belgians at the canal, where the two forces were on opposite sides of the water. The Germans could hardly select a better sector for attack.

---

[1] Thirty feet of undisturbed solid ground in the Ypres district was hardly heavy-shell proof.

[2] The pom-pom, firing a tiny 1-inch common shell, of very small range, with black powder burster, sent out as an anti-aircraft gun, had proved quite useless. Next the Royal Horse Artillery 13-pdr., mounted on a motor chassis, was tried, firing high-explosive shell or shrapnel ; but the high-explosive proved dangerous, occasionally bursting the gun. This difficulty was not overcome until April 1916, and meantime the far less efficient shrapnel was used. Even at the end of July 1915 less than half the divisions in France possessed an anti-aircraft section of two guns.

[3] Private R. Morrow, 1/Royal Irish Fusiliers (4th Division), was awarded the V.C. for rescuing on his own initiative and carrying to safety several men buried in trenches wrecked by shell fire on 12th April 1915.

THE WARNINGS OF A GAS ATTACK

On 14th April at 11.15 P.M., after four days' artillery 14 April.
activity, the enemy fired a mine at St. Eloi (4,000 yards
south of Ypres) and began a methodical bombardment.
An artillery barrage, in which the XI. Heavy Artillery
Brigade, as well as the divisional batteries of the II. Corps,
took part, was at once put down, and no infantry attack
followed ; but the incident attracted attention to that
quarter, and was possibly intended to have that result.[1]
Next day, however, the Second Army forwarded to G.H.Q.
the following report, brought by its liaison officer with
General Putz :—

"A reliable agent of the Détachement of the French
"Army in Belgium reports that an attack on the Ypres
"Salient has been arranged for night 15th/16th April.[2]
"A prisoner of the *234th Regiment, XXVI. Corps*, taken
"on 14th April near Langemarck reports that an attack
"had been prepared for noon 13th. Reserves have been
"brought up and passages have been prepared across old
"trenches existing in rear of the present German trenches
"to facilitate bringing forward artillery.

"The Germans intend making use of tubes with
"asphyxiating gas, placed in batteries of 20 tubes for
"every 40 metres along the front of the *XXVI. Corps*
"[then, as far as was known, in the line on either side of
"Langemarck, wholly opposite the French]. This prisoner
"had in his possession a small sack filled with a kind of
"gauze or cotton waste [cotton waste in a gauze bag]
"which would be dipped in some solution to counteract
"the effect of this gas.

"The German moral is said to have much improved
"lately, owing to the men having been told that there
"is not much in front of them.

"It is possible that the attack may be postponed, if

---

[1] In this combat the Belgian 97th and 99th Field Batteries took part.
On 10th February a provisional regiment of Belgian field artillery formed
of the II. and III. " Groupes " of the 6th Artillery Regiment, under
Lieut.-Colonel C. M. L. Dujardin, had been placed by King Albert at the
disposal of the V. Corps. It remained with the corps, doing most gallant
work in what appeared to be hopelessly open positions throughout the
Ypres fighting until 16th May, when it was replaced by six other batteries
forming the 7th Field Artillery Regiment, which served with the British
(its number being changed later to 13th) until the 17th May 1917.

[2] This was correct. All was ready for a gas attack on the 15th, but it
had to be postponed as the wind was not favourable. See Note I. at end
of Chapter IX.

14 April. " the wind is not favourable, so as to ensure that the gases " blow over our trenches ".[1]

In sending this very circumstantial information to the Second Army, General Putz told the liaison officer that he did not believe it ; for the prisoner, on further examination, had exhibited such great knowledge of the German position and defence arrangements, that he had come to the conclusion that the man had been primed and sent over with the intention to deceive. On the following day No. 6 Squadron of the R.F.C. was ordered to observe the German lines for the express purpose of verifying the presence of any special apparatus. Its reconnaissance failed to discover anything unusual ; [2] nor did flights on the following days reveal any sign of special concentration of troops, except that in the early morning of the 18th increased rolling stock at Wervicq gave indication of the possible arrival of reinforcements. On the 16th April further information came from Belgian sources [3]

[1] After searching the records it appears that the prisoner's story was not the first warning. The following was found in the Bulletin of the French Tenth Army (on the right of the B.E.F.) of the 30th March 1915 :

" Employment of Asphyxiating Gases by the Germans

" According to prisoners of the *XV. Corps*, there is a large supply along " the whole front in the neighbourhood of Zillebeke [this was where the " enemy first intended to use gas ; see Note I., Chapter IX.] of iron " cylinders, 1·4 metres long, which are stored a little in rear of the trenches " in bomb-proof shelters or even buried. They contain a gas which is " intended to render the enemy unconscious or to asphyxiate him. It " has not yet been made use of, but the pioneers have received instructions " regarding its employment ; the cylinder is laid on the ground pointing " towards the enemy and is opened by withdrawing the cap ; the gas is " forced out by its own pressure, and remains near the surface of the " ground ; in order that the operation may be without danger for the " operator a favourable wind is necessary. The pioneer detailed to open " the cylinder has a special apparatus attached to his head. All the men " are supplied with a cloth pad to be placed over the nostrils to prevent " the gas being breathed in. The inventor has been promoted lieutenant ".

No action seems to have been taken with regard to this warning.

For those who understood the German mentality, there was a further warning in the Wolff wireless communiqué of 17th April. This said : " Yesterday east of Ypres the British employed shells and bombs with " asphyxiating gas ". This, like the official accusation that the French aviators had violated German territory on 1st August 1914—since denied by Herr von Schoen, then the German Ambassador in Paris, and stigmatized as " false " (" Memoirs of an Ambassador ", p. 201)—merely meant that the Germans intended to do something of the kind themselves, and were putting the blame on their opponents in advance.

[2] Similarly, before the Battle of Loos, the Germans failed to notice signs of preparations for our gas attack. (Report of German *Second Army*, signed " von Below ", dated 11th October 1915, captured in 1916.)

[3] It was, like the original information, published in the (French) " Bulletin de Renseignements de la Détachement d'Armée de Belgique ".

that " the Germans have manufactured in Ghent 20,000 16 April.
" mouth protectors of tulle, which the men will carry in
" a waterproof bag 10 cm. by 17·5 cm. These mouth
" protectors, when soaked with a suitable liquid, serve
" to protect the men against the effects of asphyxiating
" gas ".

The three batteries of the XI. Heavy Artillery Brigade
fired on the German trenches on the 16th, 17th and 18th ;
but heavy artillery ammunition was so scarce that a
thorough bombardment to prepare for a raid of investiga-
tion, or to damage and destroy any gas cylinders there might
be, was deemed impracticable. As no German reinforcements seemed to have been brought up, and as no attack
took place on the night of the 15th/16th, the headquarters
of the Allied Armies paid no further attention to the
warnings. They were regarded by the French as a ruse
to prevent troops being withdrawn from Ypres for the
offensive in preparation near Arras, or an attempt to
inspire terror by the mere threat of some new form of
" frightfulness ". The relief of the French XX. Corps was,
as already related, proceeded with, the remainder of its
last division, the 11th, being replaced between the 16th
and 19th April by the 45th (Algerian), which contained
a large percentage of coloured troops.

Measures to meet the contingency of an attack on the
French were considered by the Second Army, but they
were of a tactical nature only. For instance, the brigade in
Army reserve was held in special readiness for part of the
15th and 16th. As the area threatened was clear of the
British front, and as the particular gas that might be
employed could not be guessed, no gas precautions were
suggested or ordered.[1]

Copies of this were sent to G.H.Q. The originals, dated 15th and 17th
April, and the translations circulated to the General Staff G.H.Q. are
preserved in the Intelligence files.

[1] It is difficult to reconstitute our ideas of " gas " before the attacks
in 1915. The word then meant little more to the soldier than a Chinese
stinkpot or the smell of the burst of an H.E. shell, of which the burghers
of the South African Republics had complained in 1899–1902. The gas
shell now known to have been tried by the enemy at Neuve Chapelle had
not been noticed. It was presumed, no doubt, that the effect of " gas "
would be trivial and local. At that date no British officer believed that
the enemy's leaders would deliberately depart from the usages of civilized
warfare. Whether the warnings were sent to London remains in doubt ;
letters and telegrams to the War Office seem to have been drafted, but
there is no record of their despatch or receipt. The information was
apparently referred to at a meeting on 15th April of the senior medical
officers of the V. Corps and of the divisions in it, for the rumour of an

April.   In the V. Corps, General Plumer, as his troops, being next
to the French, would be most affected by any mishap to
them, passed on the warning to his divisional commanders
" for what it was worth ". He moved two battalions in
reserve nearer to Ypres, and directed that battalions when
relieved from duty in the trenches should remain east of
Ypres. Further careful ground scrutiny as well as air
reconnaissance failed to reveal any preparations for an
attack. Thus, as nothing unusual occurred, the warning
seems to have been not only disregarded but forgotten,
though on the 18th April the V. Corps issued a reminder
that some kind of offensive action in retaliation for the
success of the II. Corps at Hill 60—the account of which
is now to be related—might be expected. Attention to
some degree was diverted from the actual front by the
bombardment of Ypres with a 17-inch howitzer, the huge
shells of which were fired in pairs, and travelled through
the air with a noise like a runaway tramcar on badly laid
rails. Having delay-action fuzes, they formed immense
craters. The real destruction of Ypres now began, and by
the 21st the shops and cafés which had reopened were
again closing down, and the inhabitants were leaving. The
Cloth Hall—which, though the roof had disappeared, was
still solid enough to house two battalions—and other
buildings, including General Bulfin's headquarters (28th
Division) had to be evacuated. Meantime, Hill 60 had
become the scene of heavy fighting, and this also served
to obliterate any remembrance of the rumours of a gas
attack from the minds of the officers who had been told of
them.

HILL 60

Map 4.   This eminence, which lies between Zwarteleen village
Sketch A. and the Comines—Ypres railway, is an artificial mound,
not a natural feature.[1] The earth excavated in making
the railway cutting nearby, where the line passes through
the Ypres ridge, had been deposited in three spoil heaps,
the highest of which became known to the British soldier

---

attack by asphyxiating gases is mentioned in the war diary of the A.D.M.S.
of the Canadian Division (who was present), though not in any other.
Arrangements were made for handling that night a thousand normal
wound cases of the V. Corps, but no special medical preparations were ordered.
    [1] Zillebeke and Dickebusch Lakes were also artificial, having been
excavated as reservoirs to supply the town and feed the moat of Ypres
and certain inundations. (" Histoire Militaire de la Ville d'Ypres ", by
J. J. J. Vereecke, 1858.)

as " Hill 60 ", from the ring contour marking it on the
large scale maps. " The Caterpillar ", on the opposite
side of the railway, was so named from its long irregular
shape, and " The Dump " was a conical mound west of
the Caterpillar. Situated on the very crest of the Ypres
ridge and providing observation all round, but particularly
good views towards Zillebeke and Ypres, Hill 60 was of
very considerable military importance. It had been
captured by the German *39th Division* (*XV. Corps*) from
the French on 10th December 1914, and when the British
28th Division, then in the II. Corps, took over the line in
February 1915, it continued the preparations that were in
progress for raiding the hill. These, at the instance of
G.H.Q., were elaborated into an attempt to recover it.
Mining was pushed on,[1] under the direction of Major D. M.
Griffith, R.E., assistant to the C.R.E. 28th Division, by
a party of officers and men with mining experience attached
to the 1st Northumbrian Field Company R.E. from the
1st and 3rd Battalions Monmouthshire Regiment (T.F.).
Probably, as events turned out, it would have been
wiser to have raided the defences and retired as originally proposed, forcing the enemy to keep a large garrison on the
hill exposed to fire if he wished to retain it. For Hill 60
when recaptured would form a small but pronounced
salient, exposed to attack on both sides : officers who knew
the ground were of opinion that it could not be held unless
the Caterpillar also was taken. In view of its value as an
observation post, the enemy was certain to make every
effort to retake the hill ; and unfortunately, in the spring
of 1915, he was far better equipped for such warfare, with
trench mortars, grenades, etc., than was the B.E.F.

The operations of the II. Corps against Hill 60 were
continued when the 5th Division relieved the 28th Division
in April, the Monmouthshire mining parties being left
behind, and, reinforced by the newly formed 171st Tunnelling Company R.E.[2] The 13th Brigade (Br.-General
R. Wanless O'Gowan) was selected to make the attack
above ground, and was brought out of the line for special

[1] The ground in the area being so waterlogged, there was difficulty in
selecting places to carry on mining : after trial had been made at St.
Eloi, at Hill 60 alone did it seem to be practicable.

There was a small French mine gallery, 3 feet by 2 feet in section in
existence ; a few " camouflets "—small defensive charges which shake up
the ground, but do not affect the surface—had been fired from it.

[2] See Note I. p. 32. The first draft of 38 specially enlisted miners
arrived on 9th April ; other men were transferred from the Royal Monmouth Siege Companies, R.E.

17 April. training.   On the night of the 16th/17th April the brigade took over part of the line opposite Hill 60 from the 15th Brigade without attracting the notice of the enemy.   It had the 1/R. West Kent (Major P. M. Robinson) and 2/K.O.S.B. (Lieut.-Colonel D. R. Sladen) in front line, with the 2/Duke of Wellington's (Lieut.-Colonel P. A. Turner) in support near Zillebeke Lake, and the 2/K.O.Y.L.I. (Lieut.-Colonel W. M. Withycombe) and Queen Victoria's Rifles (Lieut.-Colonel R. B. Shipley) in reserve.

The 17th April passed quietly, the weather was fine and sunny, and, as evening approached, there was complete stillness, not a shot being fired by either side.   Suddenly at 7.5 P.M. two pairs of mines and one single mine were exploded at 10 seconds interval.[1]   As the columns of earth from the explosion of the first pair rose into the air, the crash of bombardment broke the silence and the XV. and XXVII. Field Artillery Brigades and IX. Heavy Artillery Brigade, the 130th (Howitzer) Battery and the 48th Heavy Battery, with two batteries of French and three of Belgian artillery opened fire on all the approaches to the hill.   With the firing of the last mine, the storming party, C Company 1/Royal West Kent and sappers of the 1/2nd Home Counties Field Company R.E., climbed from their trenches and rushed forward.   In two minutes they reached the top of the slope and occupied the craters and what remained of the German trenches to the south-east.   The surprise was complete ; those of the German garrison, a company of the *172nd Regiment* (*XV. Corps*), who had survived the explosion were at once overwhelmed, some who resisted being bayoneted and twenty captured, with only seven casualties on the British side.   The supporting company of the R. West Kent and two companies of the K.O.S.B. as carrying and working party, with the machine-gun section of the Queen Victoria's Rifles, followed the storming party, and, fifteen minutes after the advance, reported that they were consolidating.

To retain the hill was another matter.   At first, on re-opening fire, the German artillery shot wildly and anywhere but at Hill 60 ; it then settled down to shelling the railway cutting south of the hill, the trenches on either side,

---

[1] In the north two of 2,000 lbs. of powder each ; in the centre two of 2,700 lbs. each ; and in the south one of 500 lbs. of gun-cotton.   The third gallery in which the last was placed, had run very close to some German mining, and further work on it had been stopped for fear of detection.   A charge was put in as a precaution in case the enemy broke through.

and the British batteries with what appeared to be lachry- 17-21
matory shell. The troops on the hill had had over three April.
hours for consolidation when, soon after midnight, the
K.O.S.B. began to relieve the R. West Kent; but before this
operation was completed the enemy's infantry delivered
three desperate counter-attacks, coming on in great waves,
and some individuals reaching the parapet. And it was soon
evident that his artillery was at last alive to the situation.
The Royal West Kent sent up their two reserve companies
in time to assist in repelling a further most determined
effort at 4.30 A.M. ; but when, at 8.30 A.M., the Duke of
Wellington's relieved the R. West Kent and the K.O.S.B.,
although the defence had not been seriously shaken,
the companies of these battalions, overwhelmed by high-
explosive and gas shell,[1] and enfiladed by machine-gun
fire, had been forced from the right half of the actual
crest nearest the railway cutting, and elsewhere back to
the crest. Very heavy shelling by the enemy and fighting
continued all day. A counter-attack at 6 P.M. by the
Duke of Wellington's [2] with the K.O.Y.L.I. as second wave,
placed the 13th Brigade again in possession of the whole
hill. In the lull during the night of the 18th/19th, the 13th
was relieved by the 15th Brigade (with the 1/East Surrey of
the 14th Brigade attached), the 1/East Surrey and the
1/Bedfordshire providing the front line. During the 19th, on
the evening of which day Queen Victoria's Rifles (13th
Brigade) were moved up in close support, the Germans only
bombarded the hill. They recommenced furious fighting
on the 20th, mainly by bombing, but with two definite
infantry attacks as it grew dark, at 6.30 and 8 P.M., and
they continued the struggle throughout the 21st, when
the 1/Devonshire (14th Brigade) relieved the two front
line battalions. All traces of trenches had by this time
disappeared. The surface of Hill 60 was a medley of
confluent mine and shell craters, strewn with broken
timber and wire : and in this rubbish heap it was im-

----

[1] Thus the British account. Nothing can, however, be found in the
German archives pointing to the use of gas shell as early as the 18th ;
the first mention in the *Fourth Army* records is on the 20th, when sixty
gas shells were fired at the hill. The use on this latter day is confirmed
by British artillery diaries. It would appear that the gas which was
smelt came from cylinders dug in on the hill ready for attack. See
Note I. at end of Chapter IX.

[2] Lieut.-Colonel P. A. Turner was wounded and his second in command,
Major W. E. M. Tyndall, died of wounds ; Major J. F. Joslin, commander
of the original assaulting party of the R. West Kent, was killed ; and
Lieut.-Colonel D. R. Sladen of the K.O.S.B. was wounded.

21-2 possible to dig without disturbing the body of some British
April. or German soldier.

On this day, the 21st, to distract enemy attention from the hill, and also from the preparations of the attack of the First Army designed for 8th May,[1] the 3rd and 46th Divisions (II. Corps) and the V. Corps carried out the semblance of preparations for attack by digging assembly trenches, cutting wire, shelling parapets, bombarding roads, and engaging enemy batteries. On the 22nd, however, British interest was diverted from the hill by the German gas attack on the French 45th Division, holding the line on the left of the British—the opening phase of the fighting, best known as the Second Battle of Ypres. Hill 60 was finally lost by the British on 5th May, partly in consequence of enfilade fire from the Caterpillar—which had not been attacked—but mainly in consequence of repeated gas attacks. To these reference will be made in proper sequence in connection with the battles of Ypres, as they form important landmarks in the history of gas fighting. In the end the struggle for the possession of the hill cost the 5th Division over 100 officers and 3,000 men.[2]

[1] The Battle of Aubers Ridge, actually fought on 9th May.

[2] Victoria Crosses were awarded to Lieut. G. R. P. Roupell, 1/East Surrey Regiment, for his magnificent example of courage and devotion on 20th April ; to Private E. Dwyer of the same battalion for gallantry in bombing and assistance under fire to wounded comrades ; to 2/Lieut. G. H. Woolley of the 9/London Regiment (Queen Victoria's Rifles)—the first Territorial officer to receive the V.C.—for defence on the night of the 20th/21st, when he was for a time the only officer on the hill ; and to 2/Lieut. B. H. Geary, 4/, attached 1/East Surrey Regiment, for conspicuous bravery and determination on 20th and 21st April.

CHAPTER IX

THE BATTLES OF YPRES 1915 (*continued*)

THE BATTLE OF GRAVENSTAFEL RIDGE[1]

(Maps 4, 5; Sketches A, B, 8, 9)

GENERAL SITUATION ON THE 22ND APRIL

ON 22nd April Lieut.-General Sir Herbert Plumer, com- Map 5. manding the V. Corps, had his headquarters in Poperinghe, Sketch 8. and his three divisions, the 27th, the 28th and the Canadian, were holding the southern two-thirds of the front of the salient covering Ypres, the northern third being occupied by the French. The Allied forces were practically on the line where the fighting had come to an end on 11th November 1914 at the close of " First Ypres ". The V. Corps front—nearly 10 miles in length—ran from the left of the II. Corps, a few hundred yards north of Hill 60, through Shrewsbury Forest, Herenthage Woods, Polygon Wood and the western end of Broodseinde village to a point on the Ypres—Poelcappelle road about half a mile south of Poelcappelle village. Behind this front were the partly finished supporting points, the so-called " subsidiary lines ", and the G.H.Q. Line, already described.

The 27th Division (Major-General T. D'O. Snow, head-quarters at Potijze) [2] occupied the sector on the right of

[1] The Battles Nomenclature Committee allotted four battle names to the Battles of Ypres 1915 :—" Battle of Gravenstafel Ridge, 22nd-23rd April " ; " Battle of St. Julien, 24th April-4th May " ; " Battle of Frezenberg Ridge, 8th-13th May " ; and " Battle of Bellewaarde Ridge, 24th-25th May ". Historically, there seems no reason for connecting Gravenstafel ridge with the fighting on the 22nd-23rd April, for both the German attack and the British counter-attacks took place well to the west of the ridge, as will be seen from the narrative. Keerselare—where the Canadian battle monument has been erected—would seem to be a more appropriate name.

[2] To its 81st Brigade were attached the 9/Royal Scots and 9/Argyll and Sutherland Highlanders ; and to its 82nd, the 1/Cambridgeshire (its

171

22 April. the corps, as far as the centre of Polygon Wood. It had—
after the routine moves for the 22nd had been completed
—all its three brigades, 82nd, 81st and 80th, in the line,
each with three battalions in front line; there were two
battalions in support in and behind Sanctuary Wood near
Hooge; in divisional reserve were two battalions north-
west of Ypres and one near Vlamertinghe. The 28th
Division [1] (Major-General E. S. Bulfin, headquarters in
Vlamertinghe chateau[2]) held the sector from Polygon
Wood to opposite Passchendaele, with 8½ battalions (3, 3,
and 2½ by brigades) in front line ; in brigade reserve, two
near Verlorenhoek ; and, in divisional reserve, three near
St. Jean (north-east of Ypres), and two battalions and a
half west of Ypres.

The Canadian Division [3] (Lieut. - General E. A. H.
Alderson, headquarters in the Chateau des Trois Tours
near Brielen, two miles north-west of Ypres) was on the
left of the corps. It had the 2nd and 3rd Canadian
Brigades in the line, each with two battalions in front
line, and one in brigade reserve ; and two battalions in
divisional reserve on either side of the canal, one being
between St. Jean and Ypres, the other along the western
bank east of Brielen, near a temporary bridge.

In Army reserve at Vlamertinghe was the 1st Canadian
Brigade.[4] The 13th Brigade (II. Corps) just brought out
for rest from the fighting at Hill 60, was also in the area,
south of Vlamertinghe.

The heavy guns supporting the V. Corps were three
4·7-inch batteries: the 2nd London and 1st North Midland Heavy Batteries, of the XIII. Brigade R.G.A., in
Kitchener's Wood (west of St. Julien) and Wieltje, respectively, and the 122nd Heavy Battery of the XI.
Brigade R.G.A. near Frezenberg.[5] The guns were all in

companies being distributed to the four Regular battalions). The
2/Cameron Highlanders (81st Brigade), lent to the 5th Division, was at
Hill 60. Princess Patricia's Canadian L.I. was the fifth battalion of the
80th Brigade.

[1] Attached to its 83rd Brigade were the 3/Monmouthshire and 5/King's
Own ; to its 84th, the 1/Monmouthshire and 12/London (Rangers) ; and
to its 85th, the 8/Middlesex. The 2/Northumberland Fusiliers (84th
Brigade) was lent to the 5th Division.

[2] Removed there after the shelling of Ypres on 20th April.

[3] See p. 27.

[4] Certain battalions of the divisional reserves could not be moved
without V. Corps approval, but there was no definite corps reserve until
23rd April.

[5] The other heavy units in the Salient were four 4·7-inch batteries each
of 4 guns :—71st, near Kruisstraat, just south of Ypres, and 121st, north-

the open. For observation purposes they had the assistance 22 April. of No. 6 Squadron Royal Flying Corps.[1]

The French on the left of the V. Corps had a 5-mile front from the Poelcappelle road to the canal at Steenstraat —actually a flank facing north at right angles to the general direction of the Allied line in Flanders. From Steenstraat the line was continued northwards along the canal by the Belgians. Of the French front, the 45th (Algerian) Division, on the Canadian left, held about one-third with three native battalions in the line, and the 87th Territorial Division, two-thirds, with $4\frac{1}{2}$ battalions (18 companies). Including troops in second line, there was a total of 12 French battalions and 10 batteries east of the canal. About a mile in rear of their front was a second position—the northern part of the G.H.Q. Line—not continuous, which covered Pilckem and Het Sas (on the canal); and a third line, also on the east bank of the canal, defended Boesinghe village and railway bridge.[2]

---

west of Bellewaarde Lake, both of the IX. Brigade R.G.A., firing south ; the 123rd (of the XI. Brigade R.G.A.) near Potijze, firing eastwards and south-eastwards ; the 110th, divided, 1 section behind Ypres and 1 near Kemmel, firing southwards. The 3rd Siege Battery of four old 6-inch howitzers came into action behind Dickebusch on the evening of the 23rd April registering St. Eloi mound.

Apart from the inherent defects of the 4·7-inch, the number of heavy guns was far too small, with the consequence that the divisional artillery had to cover very long fronts.

For the German heavy artillery see Note I. at end of Chapter.

[1] The disposition of the Royal Flying Corps on the Western front was :—

  1st Wing (Nos. 2, 3 and 16 Squadrons) with the First Army ;
  2nd ,, (,, 1, 5 ,, 6 ,,) ,, ,, Second ,,
  3rd ,, No. 4 Squadron with the III. Corps ;
    Nos. 7 and 8 Squadrons with G.H.Q.

The bulk of the aerial work at Ypres, therefore, fell to the squadrons of the 2nd Wing. Artillery observation was carried out by No. 1 Squadron for the II. Corps and No. 6 for the V. Corps. Strategic reconnaissance devolved on squadrons at G.H.Q., whilst the 1st Wing, under instructions from G.H.Q., assisted the Second Army squadrons by bombing railway stations and trains, mainly with the small 20-lb. bombs of the period. Defensive patrols flew between 9 A.M. and 1 P.M., and 5 P.M. and 6 P.M. From first to last during the battle the British machines were greatly outnumbered by the enemy.

[2] In the front line were the 1st and 2nd Battalions of the 1st Tirailleurs, a battalion of African L.I., 9 companies of the 74th Territorials, and 9 companies of the 73rd Territorials. In the second line of the 45th Division was the 1st Battalion of the 2nd bis Zouaves, of which half was behind the centre of the divisional front and the other on the Pilckem—Langemarck road, 550 yards east of Pilckem. Behind it was the " Bataillon Cail " of the 7th Zouaves. In second line of the 87th Division were one and a half Territorial battalions. One Zouave battalion guarded the bridges between Boesinghe and Ypres. The rest of the French troops were, according to a map supplied at the time, west of the canal, one

Sketch A.   The ground north-east and east of Ypres, very open
and passable for all arms, was, in April 1915, still under
cultivation.   From the Ypres ridge—on the crest of which
stand Broodseinde and Passchendaele, both in enemy
hands [1]—it falls gradually to the Ypres canal.   The area
at first sight seems to be a rolling plain, dotted with small
houses and cottages, and without any outstanding feature,
for the extreme difference in level never amounts to a
hundred feet ; [2] it comprises a series of long very gentle
slopes,[3] dipping down to narrow drainage ditches—for
the upper courses of the " beeks " are little more—then
rising slowly to the crests of low, straight, flat-topped
ridges.[4] In the tactical sense, however, it is by no means
featureless, and on examination its relief presents definite
characteristics.   Running from south-east to north-west
will be noticed a depression formed by the basin of the
Steenbeek, on which watercourse the village of St. Julien
is situated.   From the Ypres ridge, here running nearly
north and south, there project towards the Steenbeek
a number of long low spurs, amongst them Zonnebeke,
Gravenstafel, Stroombeek and Langemarck ridges,separated
one from the other by tributary drainage channels of the
Steenbeek.   In consequence of the divergence of the Ypres
ridge and the Steenbeek, the northern spurs are longer—
and lower—than the southern ones.   West of the Steenbeek, parallel to it and enclosing its basin on that side,
is a lower ridge, on which stand Verlorenhoek and Mouse
Trap Farm, called in this narrative by the name of the
latter locality.[5] This ridge is doubled in its southern

Zouave and two Territorial battalions near Boesinghe, the others further
back. The extra brigade, the 186th, of the 87th Division (normally,
173rd and 174th Brigades) was " détachement reserve ".

[1] The British line curved slightly back at Broodseinde, thus excluding
the cross roads.

[2] The best landmarks to-day for visitors to the area are the churches,
particularly the tall square tower of Zonnebeke church ; the large two-
storied villa that has replaced Hooge Chateau ; and a windmill on the toe
of Gravenstafel ridge near St. Julien.

[3] Just east of Bellewaarde Lake and on the eastern part of the reverse
slope of Gravenstafel ridge there are short stretches of slope 1 in 25, but
elsewhere the inclination is rarely more than 1 in 50, and over most of the
area considerably flatter.

[4] The general form of the ground will best be understood by reference
to Sketch A, which shows the main features, and on which the principal
localities are marked.

[5] Practically all the farm names shown on the present British maps
were bestowed during and after the battles of April-May 1915, and were
not on the maps in use at the time. In the orders and messages the
localities were described by map squares ; thus, throughout, " Mouse Trap

portion by the parallel Frezenberg ridge. Westward again beyond Mouse Trap ridge, towards the canal, are continuations of the spurs of the Ypres ridge, known as Bellewaarde, St. Jean, Hill Top, Mauser and Pilckem ridges. Thus there is a series of small ridges and depressions running east and west, intersected nearly at right angles by the Ypres ridge and the Frezenberg— Mouse Trap ridges, which often command and overlook them. Many of the valleys and depressions and their reverse slopes are, however, sheltered from ground observation, and afford cover, at any rate, from distant view. The low ground near Bellewaarde Lake, north of Hooge, the basin-lake depressions at Potijze and a similar minor depression at St. Julien are notable examples.

The villages on the actual battlefield were no more than a few cottages bordering the road passing through them, or, in the case of St. Julien and a few others, the cross roads, with an occasional church.[1] In addition to these agglomerations, there were a fair number of scattered

---

Farm " was officially called " farm in C.22.b ", and never by name. As map squares are not marked on the ground and are easily confused, this method did not suit the fighting troops. On the Belgian maps, from which the earlier British ones were derived, most of the farms are unnamed, indeed, have no names, as the present owners protest. When pressed, the inhabitants will do no more than admit that a farm is identified by its owner's name or the name of some former owner. Mouse Trap Farm was marked merely " Chateau " on the Belgian 1 : 20,000 ; it was known to the Belgians and French as " Chateau du Nord ", to the Germans as " Wieltje Chateau ", and to the British generally as " Shell Trap Farm ", but to some units as " Canadian Farm ", because the 3rd Canadian Brigade had its headquarters in it. As the name " Shell Trap " was considered of ill-omen, it was later changed by V. Corps orders to " Mouse Trap ". The farm now known as " Canadian Farm " was at first, with others, called " Moated Farm ", because it had a moat ; it also appears as " Oblong Farm ", a name later transferred to another east of it. " Turco Farm " appears in French accounts as " Mortalje Farm ", and was sometimes confused with the inn near-by shown on British maps as " Morteldje Estaminet " (its present signboard is Moortelje); during the battle it was called " French Farm ". The confusion of names has made the elucidation of the various accounts and narratives more than usually difficult. It should be noticed that many of the farms have not been rebuilt on exactly the same sites as they occupied in 1915, they are generally nearer to the main roads. Canadian Farm, for instance, is over three hundred yards from the remains of the old moat and buildings.

[1] The villages were all small, except Langemarck (7,438 inhabitants) and Boesinghe (2,263). Bixschoote had 932 inhabitants; St. Jean, 851 ; Brielen, 773 ; Zonnebeke, 769 ; St. Julien, Pilckem, Wieltje, Frezenberg, Gravenstafel, are merely mentioned as " hameaux " in the French " Notice Descriptive et Statistique sur les deux Flandres ". The Belgian Historical Section kindly ascertained that St. Julien, which was to become so celebrated, in 1914 contained, including outlying farms, 190 houses and 950 inhabitants.

22 April. farms—as a rule well built and surrounded by water, usually of the extent and nature of a moat—and the whole area was sprinkled with innumerable small isolated brick cottages and wood-and-plaster barns, rarely more than five hundred yards apart. Except the town of Ypres itself and where the French had fought, between Zonnebeke and St. Julien, and the British, further south, in 1914, the area was little damaged by war, the inhabitants were in their dwellings and the fields cultivated. There was only one rather large wood (Kitchener's Wood, west of St. Julien), in which respect the area was quite unlike the scene of the previous British fighting east and south-east of Ypres, the woods in which had provided such good cover from view.

Sketch B.   The Allied line lay just below the top of the Ypres ridge until about half-a-mile north of Broodseinde; crossed then to Gravenstafel ridge, and in front of it over the Stroombeek channel and the Stroombeek ridge, where this ridge flattens out, over the Lekkerboterbeek to the low Langemarck ridge ; and then in front of the village of that name westward over nearly level ground to the canal.

THE FIRST GAS ATTACK. THE ATTACK ON THE
FRENCH NEAR LANGEMARCK

Map 5.   The 22nd April was a glorious spring day. Air recon-
Sketch 9. naisance in the morning had disclosed considerable liveliness behind the German lines and some activity in the Houthulst Forest (2 miles north of Langemarck), where a column was seen on the march, though it tried to evade observation ; but there was nothing abnormal in this. In the forenoon there was considerable shelling of Ypres by 17-inch and 8-inch howitzers and lighter guns, and towards midday, of the roads leading into the town; but this gradually ceased and all was quiet again.

    Suddenly, at 5 P.M., a new and furious bombardment of Ypres by heavy howitzers was recommenced. The villages in front of Ypres, almost untouched until then, were also heavily shelled, and simultaneously French field-guns to the north-east of Ypres began a somewhat rapid fire, although the German field artillery was silent.[1] At first

---

[1] The German field batteries were silent from 5 to 5.10 P.M. in order not to disturb the gas clouds, and then opened with shrapnel. The infantry advanced at 5.20 P.M. At 6.15 P.M. batteries were switched on to the French guns. " Res. Field. Art. Regt. Nr. 46 ", p. 45.

YPRES, 1915.

BATTLE OF GRAVENSTAFEL RIDGE.
THE FIRST GAS ATTACK. 22ND APRIL.

N

A A Front on which the Gas was released

XXVII R.

53 R.

54 R.

38 LDW. BDE

2 ERS BDE

Poelcappelle

51 R.

XXVI R.

Koekuit

52 R.

Langemarck

Steenbeek

XXIII R.

Bixschoote

Kortekeer

46 R.

45 R.

87 T.

Het Sas

Steenstraat

Lizerne

Zuydschoote

CANAL

CDN.

Keerselare

St Julien

Fortuin

28

Graventafel

Hanebeek

Berlin Wd.

Kitchener's Wood

Mausers

Pilckem

Boesinghe

CANAL

Poelcappelle

Wieltje

Hill Top

St Jean

Pilckem

la Brique

YPRES

Frezenberg

Westhoek

Zonnebeke

Hooge

Polygon Wood

Brielen

Vlamertinghe

V.

Elverdinghe

Poperinghe 4 miles

SCALE

MILE 0 1 2 3 MILES

German Front Line at 5 p.m. before the Gas Attack.
French Front Line at 5 p.m. before the Gas Attack.

Ordnance Survey, 1926.

FARMS.

Bo. : Bosinor's
Ob. : Oblong
M.T. : Mouse Trap (Shell Trap)
Cdn. : Canadian
Ta. : Turco
S.Z. : S. Zwaanhof
la.B.A. : la Belle Alliance
Fs. : Fusilier's
Fo. : Fooling
Ha. : Hampshire

some officers who heard the firing surmised that the newly 22 April. arrived Algerian Division was " shooting itself in " ; but those who were on points of vantage saw two curious greenish-yellow clouds on the ground on either side of Langemarck in front of the German line. These clouds spread laterally, joined up, and, moving before a light wind, became a bluish-white mist, such as is seen over water meadows on a frosty night.[1] Behind the mist the enemy, by the sound of his rifle fire, was advancing. Soon, even as far off as the V. Corps report centre at " Goldfish Chateau " (2,000 yards west of Ypres railway station and five miles from Langemarck) a peculiar smell was noticed, accompanied by smarting of the eyes and tingling of the nose and the throat. It was some little time, however, before it was realized that the yellow clouds were due to the gas about which warnings had been received, and almost simultaneously French coloured troops, without officers, began drifting down the roads through the back areas of the V. Corps. Soon afterwards French Territorial troops were seen hurriedly crossing the bridges over the canal north of Ypres.[2] It was impossible to understand what the Africans said, but from the way they coughed and pointed to their throats, it was evident that, if not suffering from the effects of gas, they were thoroughly scared.[3]

[1] The gas attack was seen by many British observers, amongst them, General Smith-Dorrien, who was returning on foot to Ypres after a visit to Hill 60 ; the G.O.C. 27th Division from the observatory in the garden of his headquarters at Potijze ; and the G.O.C. Canadian Division, who was north-east of St. Julien visiting his batteries.

[2] Except a derelict barrel pier bridge, the only bridge in this area over the canal north of Ypres when the British took over was east of Brielen, and from engineer records appears to have been of solid timber trestles, with a canal barge in the centre. As it is often referred to in the narrative, it will, for convenience, be called the Brielen bridge. Two pontoon bridges were laid ½ to ¾ of a mile nearer Ypres by the 1st Bridging Train, at the junction of the Yser and Menin canals. Six other temporary bridges north of Ypres, one west of Ypres and five south of Ypres were constructed in the course of the month by the 59th Field Company R.E. (5th Division), 1st Canadian Field Company, and Cornwall, Wiltshire and Monmouth Army Troops Companies R.E. The construction and mainten- ance of all these bridges was very difficult, for although the high embank- ments on each side of the canal, formed of the earth excavated from the channel, sheltered them from view, the enemy peppered them with shrapnel and no work or repairs could be done on them during daylight. No bridge, however, was destroyed.

[3] Chlorine, the gas employed, has a powerful irritant action on the respiratory organs and all mucous membranes exposed to it, causing spasms of the glottis, a burning sensation in the eyes, nose and throat, followed by bronchitis and œdema of the lungs. Frequently there is evidence of corrosion of the mucous membranes of the air channels and of the cornea. Prolonged inhalation or exposure to a high concentration

22 April. Teams and wagons of the French field artillery next appeared retiring, and the throng of fugitives soon became thicker and more disordered, some individuals running and continuing to run until they reached Vlamertinghe and beyond. Although the " seventy-fives " were firing regularly, it was obvious that something very serious had happened, and this was emphasized when, about 7 P.M., the French guns suddenly ceased fire.

MEASURES TAKEN TO THROW BACK A FLANK

Immediately the attack took place, the G.O.C. 3rd Canadian Brigade, Br.-General R. E. W. Turner, who had the 15th and 13th Battalions in the line, next to the French, ordered up his reserve battalion, the 14th, then at St. Jean, to his headquarters at Mouse Trap Farm. The 2½ companies in St. Julien belonging to these three battalions were moved out to cover this village. The Canadian divisional artillery by General Alderson's order, was directed to assist the French. Almost all of the Algerians and Territorials were in flight, but the right of the 1/1st Tirailleurs on the immediate left of the Canadian Division, unaffected by the gas, remained in position—as did the 1/2nd *bis* Zouaves, who were in support. The Germans, however, pressed on fast through the gap, and some appeared within 300 or 400 yards of the Poelcappelle —St. Julien road and Mouse Trap Farm. These were held back by two platoons of the 13th Canadian Battalion north of Keerselare which fought until their last man had fallen, and by a company of the 14th at and east of Hampshire Farm. Their efforts to advance were finally stopped about 6.30 P.M. by the fire of two guns of the 10th Canadian Battery, which was in position 500 yards north of St. Julien, and a hundred yards east of the road.[1]

of the gas will cause death by asphyxia, or, if not fatal, produce cardiac dilatation and cyanosis (blueness of the skin) as a result of the injury to the lungs. It early became evident that the men who stayed in their places suffered less than those who ran away, any movement making worse the effects of the gas, and those who stood up on the fire step suffered less—indeed they often escaped any serious effects—than those who lay down or sat at the bottom of a trench. Men who stood on the parapet suffered least, as the gas was denser near the ground. The worst sufferers were the wounded lying on the ground, or on stretchers, and the men who moved back with the cloud.

[1] Lance-Corporal Frederick Fisher, 13th Battalion, was awarded, posthumously, the Victoria Cross, for most gallant conduct when in charge of a machine gun. After the four men with him, whilst covering the retirement of the battery, had become casualties, he obtained four

But it was evident that the Canadian line was in grave 22 April.
danger of envelopment.

The first reports that came back to General Alderson
gave the idea that all the French had disappeared, and
that the Canadian left had been driven back to St.
Julien.[1] He impressed on the 2nd and 3rd Brigades the
necessity of holding on, and placed one of his divisional
reserve battalions, the 16th (Canadian Scottish) at Br.-
General Turner's disposal. The other, the 10th Canadians,
then falling in as a working party, was also sent to report
to Br.-General Turner, but in marching up it found the
road blocked by fugitives, and for a time occupied the
sector of the G.H.Q. Line east and south-east of Wieltje.[2]
The 2nd Canadian Brigade (Br.-General A. W. Currie), in
line on the right of the 3rd, had been called upon for
support by Br.-General Turner at 7.10 P.M. The 7th
Battalion, in brigade reserve, was detailed to be in readiness, half at headquarters at Spree Farm, near the cross
roads 1,000 yards south-east of St. Julien, and half at the
cross roads south of Locality C, known as " Bombarded
cross roads ". A little later it was moved to Locality C,
behind the junction of the 2nd and 3rd Canadian Brigades.

At 8.25 P.M. Br.-General Turner reported that his
original line was still in place—the rumours that his
brigade had been forced back were fortunately erroneous
—supported between its left and St. Julien by the 2½
companies moved out from that village ; that the ground
between St. Julien and Mouse Trap Farm was not occupied
at all ; and that the three companies of the 14th Battalion
and the 3rd Field Co. held the G.H.Q. Line near the latter
point westward to Hampshire Farm. The right half of
the 1/2nd *bis* Zouaves soon after retired on the companies
of the 14th Battalion, taking up position on their right in
the G.H.Q. Line, whilst two companies of the 7th Zouaves
came up on their left front. Thus a line was now manned

---

others, and, getting the machine gun again in action, was soon afterwards
killed. (The date assigned to this incident in the London Gazette, the
23rd, is, according to the Canadian Historical Section, incorrect.)

[1] From 3rd Canadian Brigade, 6.25 P.M. : " Left of our subsection is
" retiring."

6.30 P.M. " Your wire to us is down. Our left driven back, and
" apparently whole line forced back to St. Julien."

7.10 P.M. " We are forced back on G.H.Q. Line ; attack coming
" from the west. No troops left."

[2] In the defence scheme the portion of the G.H.Q. Line roughly
between the Ypres—Verlorenhoek road and Canadian Farm was allotted
to the Canadian Division.

22 April. on the east and north of Mouse Trap Farm, and an important point in the open flank secured.

The first news of the German attack reached the Second Army headquarters at Hazebrouck through the V. Corps at 6.45 P.M. It was followed at 7.45 P.M. by a message reporting that the French were retiring, and that the left of the 3rd Canadian Brigade had been forced back to about Wieltje.[1] That a disaster had happened was soon afterwards confirmed by two telephone messages from General Putz, in which he said, first, that he had learned from air reports that two simultaneous attacks had been made on his force in which asphyxiating gases had been employed, and, secondly, that the French right was at Pilckem. This would leave a gap of over three thousand yards open to the enemy between the French and the Canadians. General Smith-Dorrien was faced with the danger to Ypres, and to all the troops and guns east of the town of a successful enemy attack from the north through the French. He at once (8 P.M.) placed the 1st Canadian Brigade, then in Army reserve near Vlamertinghe, at the disposal of V. Corps to help to re-establish the line. General Plumer, in his turn, at 8.15 P.M. handed back half the brigade, the 2nd (later known as the Eastern Ontario Regiment) Battalion and 3rd (Toronto) Battalion, to General Alderson, who ordered them to the assistance of the 3rd Canadian Brigade. From the reserve of the 28th Division, the 2/East Yorkshire, then in hutments about a mile west of Ypres, was also put at General Alderson's disposal, and was shifted northwards to his headquarters at Brielen.

Generals Snow and Bulfin, commanding the divisions on the right of the Canadians took action without waiting for orders, so that already parts of their reserves were on the move towards the threatened flank. In the 27th Division the 4/Rifle Brigade was ordered from divisional reserve north-west of Ypres to between Potijze and St. Jean ; the 2/K.S.L.I., from near Bellewaarde, was divided between divisional headquarters at Potijze and 80th Brigade headquarters at Verlorenhoek. Later one of the divisional engineer companies—2/Wessex—was sent to put Wieltje in a state of defence. Of the 28th Division, the 2/Buffs and the 3/Middlesex were in billets and bivouacs near St. Jean. These two battalions, the Middlesex having moved out on the initiative of Lieut.-Colonel E. W. R.

[1] This, of course, was a mistake, the brigade was still holding its original line.

Stephenson as soon as the stream of French fugitives began 22 April. to arrive, took up a position at St. Jean astride the cross roads leading north, with the 5/King's Own, which had been shelled out of its billets in Ypres, in reserve. Patrols were sent out to discover the nature of the gap in the French front. The 1/York and Lancaster Regiment, in reserve west of Ypres, was ordered to reinforce St. Jean, but did not arrive there until next morning. All four battalions were eventually, at 12.30 A.M. on the 23rd, placed at the disposal of the Canadian Division, which put them under the command of the senior officer, Colonel A. D. Geddes of the Buffs, to form the " Geddes Detachment ".[1] One half of the 3/Middlesex, however, under Major G. H. Neale, was ordered to secure, on both banks of the canal, the Brielen bridge, where it relieved the 2nd Canadian Field Co. General Bulfin sent forward the last two battalions of his divisional reserve, the 2/Cheshire and 1/Monmouthshire, near Verlorenhoek, to a covered position under Frezenberg ridge as a local reserve.

All these moves took time to carry out. Actually, towards 9 P.M., the long gap between the original left of the Canadian Division and the canal at Brielen bridge, 4½ miles measured straight, left open by the French retirement was held only at three places : at its extreme right on the Poelcappelle road by part of the 1/1st Tirailleurs and by a short flank thrown back by the 3rd Canadian Brigade ; by 2½ companies in trenches covering St. Julien ; and by the four companies of the 2nd *bis* and 7th Zouaves and the reserves of the 3rd Canadian Brigade around Mouse Trap Farm. This left three great gaps of 2,000 yards, 1,000 yards and 3,000 yards, the last with a single French machine-gun post at Fusilier Farm in it. Even when the various reinforcements arrived, the new flank would be little more than an outpost line, with hardly a trench or vestige of wire, and only four miles from the backs of the men in the front line of the 27th and 28th Divisions on the southern side of the salient.

Shortly before 9 P.M.—when there was still some light, the moon having just reached her first quarter—the 1/1st Tirailleurs on the left of the Canadians were attacked, and gave way, but 200 of them rallied, and were placed with six platoons of the 13th Canadians in the new flank or " throw back " along the Poelcappelle road, against the

---

[1] A brigade-major and a platoon of the 28th Divisional Cyclists were sent to him as staff and signal section, and arrived about 1.30 A.M.

22 April. stubborn defence of which the Germans had come to a halt. Br.-General Turner at this time called on Colonel Geddes for assistance, but the latter—this being before the formation of his Detachment—could detail to go to St. Julien only one company of his own battalion, the Buffs. This company (Captain F. W. Tomlinson), with two platoons of the 13th Canadians (under Major V. C. Buchanan)[1] from St. Julien was sent on to the front line, where it arrived shortly before daybreak, to find that the left company of the 13th Canadians had just fallen back to 500 yards east of the St. Julien— Poelcappelle road. On the arrival of these reinforcements, the original line was reoccupied, the Buffs extending to the road at the apex of the salient, before any withdrawal had been noticed by the Germans.

In view of their exposure, the III. Canadian Artillery Brigade north of St. Julien, and the CXVIII. Howitzer Brigade R.F.A. (serving with the Canadian Division) west of that place were moved back to the neighbourhood of St. Jean and La Brique.[2]

By 8.45 P.M. reports had come in to the V. Corps that the French had no flank at Pilckem, that both their first line and second line and the guns had been abandoned,[3] and that there were no formed bodies of French troops east of the canal, except at Steenstraat.[4] Thus it was clear

[1] Major Buchanan now became senior officer with the 13th Battalion, as Lieut.-Colonel F. O. W. Loomis was commanding at St. Julien.

[2] The attack caught the Canadian artillery at an unlucky moment. The 5th, 8th and 11th Field Batteries were in process of relief by the 2nd and 3rd when the attack began : they fought as composite units, and were not reunited in battery until the 4th May or after.

[3] The guns of the 2nd London Battery in Kitchener's Wood, in the French area, had also to be abandoned, the strikers and breechblocks being carried off when the German infantry reached the wood. There were only seven rifles in the battery, which were used to cover the retreat of the detachment. The Germans claim to have captured eight French batteries.

[4] This, except for four companies of Zouaves and the 1/1st Tirailleurs, was true. The Germans claim that the *XXIII. Reserve Corps* was actually on the west bank at Steenstraat and Het Sas. " F.A.R. Regt. No. 46 ", p. 46, states that by 8 P.M. the French " had been driven over " the canal as far as Boesinghe, and our infantry held the passages at " Steenstraat and Het Sas, and had reached a line 200 yards south of the " Boesinghe—Langemarck road, that is beyond Pilckem ". This is confirmed by " Reserve Regiment No. 215 ", p. 207. The report brought late at night by the V. Corps liaison officer was to the effect that the French held the western bank of the canal up to Boesinghe railway bridge, whence their front probably ran south-east. Nothing of this line could, however, be found, except the post of Fusilier Farm ; indeed, when day dawned, the enemy was seen on the low ridge south-east of Boesinghe, for the greater part of the *XXIII. Reserve Corps* had followed the French westward.

to General Plumer that the gap was not three thousand 22 April. yards, but eight thousand, and the way to Ypres was open to the enemy. Almost simultaneously, however, with these most unpleasant tidings came reports that the Germans were not pressing on, but had halted—as early, it was said, as 7.30 P.M.—and were digging in.[1] Covering their new line were outposts, which in taking up position came into collison at several points with the Canadians. But about 8.25 P.M. even rifle fire ceased. The enemy's pause gave the British precious time in which to bring up troops to meet the threatening danger and fill the gaps.

General Smith-Dorrien informed G.H.Q. at 9 P.M. that the position appeared somewhat grave ; and at 10 P.M. he suggested that representations should be made to General Foch to induce the latter to put in sufficient troops to restore the French situation,[2] as, up to the hour of reporting, General Quiquandon (45th Division) had been unable to do more than organize a counter-attack from Boesinghe towards Pilckem with six companies of a regiment placed at his disposal by General Putz. Soon after midnight, General Smith-Dorrien informed G.H.Q. that a new British flank had been formed facing north, and that General Quiquandon proposed to make an attack at 4.30 A.M.,[3]

[1] Among others, a message from the 3rd Canadian Brigade to the Canadian Division : timed 7.30 P.M., " Rifle fire has slackened and it is thought enemy is digging himself in ". Liaison officers reported that the battlefield, except for a few bullets, was quiet and peaceful. Several British officers expressed the opinion at the time that the Germans were stopped by running into their own gas. This would seem to be to some extent confirmed by Schwarte's phrase, ii. p. 259 : " the advance over "the ground covered with gas had not proceeded without checks ". From prisoners taken during the following days it was ascertained that they had not worn respirators or other protection, but that the gas had only made their eyes smart ; they averred, however, that the troops were afraid of advancing for fear of suffering bad effects from the gas. This, added to the stout resistance offered by the Canadians along the St. Julien road no doubt had an influence. The excuses offered by General Balck for not taking advantage of the long twilight are : first, that reserves to convert the break-in into a break-through were lacking ; and, secondly, that the effects of the new weapon of war were underestimated. (See Note I. at end of Chapter.)

[2] Towards midnight General Foch informed General Putz that " he " should (1) make sure of holding on to the line he occupied ; (2) organize " a base of departure for a counter-attack to regain the ground lost ; " (3) counter-attack ". To carry out the counter-attack, he ordered the 153rd Division of the XX. Corps (Tenth Army) to be sent to General Putz, and warned the Tenth Army that he might want more troops.

[3] A second infantry regiment and two field batteries were on their way to him from General Putz's reserve, so that nominally he had the equivalent of two complete brigades again, whilst the 186th Territorial Brigade was warned to stand by for transport to Woesten (1½ miles west of Elverdinghe) by bus, to be at his disposal.

22 April. in which troops on the new flank would co-operate under the command of Lieut.-General Alderson. The Cavalry Corps and the 50th (Northumbrian) Division,[1] in G.H.Q. reserve around Steenvoorde and Cassel, some fifteen to twenty miles west of Ypres, were warned to be ready to move.[2]

Very satisfactory news of the Belgians on the left of General Putz gradually came to hand, and it became certain that they were still in position. On the afternoon of the 22nd April their 6th Division (General de Ceuninck) held the bank of the Ypres canal from Steenstraat (exclusive) past the Maison du Passeur to Drie Grachten, a front of about two and a half miles. Observing the gas attack and retirement of the French, General de Ceuninck had given assistance with his artillery, and then had ordered a defensive flank to be formed along a communication trench, whilst reserves were moved up towards the gap. About 7.30 P.M.[3] the Germans (*46th Reserve Division*), having crossed the canal at Steenstraat, attacked the right of the Belgians, but were repulsed. Later, after bombardment with gas shell, other Germans actually reached the canal bank, and began an attempt to cross on the front of the Belgian 6th Division ; but they failed to get a single boat or raft into the water. By midnight the Belgian flank had been extended by detachments to Pypegaale, over a mile back from the canal, and General de Ceuninck was in a position to lend the French a battalion, afterwards increased to three, for their proposed counter-attack.

Soon after midnight enemy attacks were made against the fronts of the 27th and 28th Divisions. Although they completely failed and many German dead were found on the ground, they had the effect of making General Plumer hesitate to utilize all the reserves of these divisions on his threatened flank. Against the original Canadian front and the new flank there was no further movement during the night, but the enemy plastered the villages with shell and continued to bombard Ypres and all roads leading into it, the Ypres—Boesinghe road being reported practically impassable owing to fire.

---

[1] Commanded by Major-General W. F. L. Lindsay ; it had arrived in France only on 16th April. See Order of Battle (Appendix 4). Its infantry brigades, at this time called the Northumberland, York and Durham, and Durham L.I. will be referred to in the narrative as the 149th, 150th and 151st, their later titles.

[2] 1st Cavalry Division and six companies of the 150th Brigade, to travel by motor bus, were first warned.

[3] According to the German account, the fighting here continued late into the evening. See Note I. at end of Chapter.

THE MIDNIGHT COUNTER-ATTACK OF THE 10TH AND   **22 April.**
16TH CANADIAN BATTALIONS AGAINST KITCHENER'S WOOD

Towards 8 P.M. a French liaison officer sent to the Canadian Division had informed General Alderson that the 45th Division was going to counter-attack towards Pilckem, and asked for co-operation. In consequence, at 8.25 P.M., orders were sent to the 3rd Canadian Brigade, which reached it by orderly officers at 9.40, to counter-attack towards Kitchener's Wood [1] as soon as the reinforcements sent from the 1st Canadian Brigade were ready. The wood recaptured, the advance was to be continued, in co-operation with the French, and directed just east of Pilckem. It was, however, nearly midnight before the troops for the purpose had arrived.

The counter-attack was carried out by the two battalions of the 2nd and 3rd Brigades originally in divisional reserve : the 10th Canadians (Lieut.-Colonel R. L. Boyle), with the 16th (Lieut.-Colonel R. G. E. Leckie) in support. A true counter-attack, made soon after the enemy's advance, and carried out with decision, rapidity and courage, it had complete success ; but, as the French made no effort, all the ground regained could not be maintained. Although both units in the failing moonlight came under heavy machine-gun and rifle fire at 300 yards, and Colonel Boyle was mortally wounded, they not only reached the front of the wood, but passed right through it and beyond, taking prisoners from the *234th Reserve Infantry Regiment (51st Reserve Division)*. They were at once reorganized and began to dig in north-east of the wood, and the guns of the 2nd London Heavy Battery being found, a message was sent to bring up teams to remove them. The enemy, however, immediately opened heavy fire on the wood and its vicinity, and very soon the two Canadian battalions were reduced to 10 officers and a little over four hundred men. There was no hope of holding unsupported such an advanced position ; no news came of the French ; and when the 2nd Battalion (Lieut.-Colonel D. Watson) of the 1st Brigade arrived and, towards dawn, sent in one company to attack on the left, it was nearly exterminated. It was therefore decided to evacuate the forward position. No

---

[1] The Belgian name for this oak wood is Bois des Cuisiniers. Lying only a thousand yards west of St. Julien on the nearly flat forward slope of Mouse Trap ridge, with unseen access into it, it was a most dangerous locality to leave in enemy hands.

22/23 teams having arrived, the four guns of the 2nd London
April. Heavy Battery could not be removed, but their ammunition was destroyed. The line was then withdrawn to the
southern edge of the wood, where later, at 5 A.M., it was
prolonged on the right towards St. Julien by half of Lieut.-
Colonel R. Rennie's 3rd Battalion (1st Brigade), which had
arrived at Mouse Trap Farm at 1.15 A.M.

At 1.30 A.M. Colonel Geddes received instructions from
General Alderson—who had motored shortly before to
consult with General Plumer—to push forward from St.
Jean, and get in touch with the left of Br.-General Turner's
battalions, and, if possible, with the right of the French.
As the position of the latter was doubtful, General
Alderson also ordered the remaining two battalions of the
1st Canadian Brigade (Br.-General M. S. Mercer) [1]—the
1st and 4th Battalions leaving Vlamertinghe at 1.40 A.M.
—to march via Brielen, and take up a position east of the
canal in order to prevent the enemy from seizing the
bridges and cutting off Ypres from the north. His last
reserve, the divisional squadron, he sent on the western
bank to cover the Steenstraat road, down which he expected
the Germans might be marching. All batteries of the
Canadian Division were also warned to be ready to fire
northwards.

At 2 A.M. Br.-General Turner had again called on the
2nd Brigade for assistance, as the enemy was in strength
at Keerselare cross roads, a thousand yards north of St.
Julien. Keeping one company in Locality C, Br.-General
Currie despatched to him the remainder of the 7th Battalion (Lieut.-Colonel W. F. H. McHarg), which by 3 A.M.
was deployed, digging in and wiring between Keerselare
and St. Julien. Thus, before dawn, there were on the
flank between the apex of the front and Kitchener's Wood
(inclusive) : a company of the Buffs, some of the Tirailleurs,
3 companies of the 7th Battalion, and one company each of
the 14th and 15th Battalions.

Telephone communication between headquarters of the
28th and Canadian Divisions west of the canal and their
troops east of Ypres had already been broken several
times, and this was constantly to recur during the battle,
for the lines ran through Ypres and parallel to the flank, or,
as it should be called, the new front. Henceforward, the
most reliable channel of communication was over the

---

[1] Killed as a Major-General commanding the 3rd Canadian Division
on 2nd June 1916.

V. Corps lines to the 27th Division at Potijze. By the 22/23
efforts of the 27th, 28th and Canadian Signal Companies, April.
the cables, however often they were cut, were sooner or
later repaired, in spite of the heaviest fire. Although cars
could as a rule reach Wieltje, at times messages could
only be got through by runners, and liaison maintained
with the headquarters of General Snow and Br.-Generals
Currie and Turner in front of Ypres by mounted officers,
who galloped as far to the front as practicable. The 27th
Division headquarters at Potijze, situated behind the new
front, very soon became a focus of communications and
the point to which corps reinforcements and reserves were
directed.

To sum up the situation : before daylight on the 23rd
there were bodies of troops, amounting to some ten
battalions,[1] strung out to cover the gap from the original
Canadian left to the canal, under the orders of Br.-General
Turner and Colonel Geddes, with $3\frac{1}{2}$ battalions of General
Snow's division as reserve. The ten battalions did not
form a continuous line ; and, though some digging and
wiring was done, a few of them had only had time to move
out to the ground, where they lay down, or occupied such
rudimentary trenches as they found existing.

NOTE I

The Enemy Plan, and Events on the 22nd April 1915
from the German Side

In the spring of 1915 the German *Fourth Army*, commanded by Sketches
General-Colonel Duke Albrecht of Württemberg, with Major-General 1 and 8.
Ilse as Chief of the Staff, held a front from the Ypres—Comines
canal to the sea, with the *XV. Corps*, the new Reserve corps *XXVII.*,
XXVI., *XXIII.* and *XXII.* (half), with the *2nd Ersatz Brigade*
and *38th Landwehr Brigade* attached, and the *4th Ersatz Division*.
The *Marine Division* guarded the coast. The *37th Landwehr Brigade*
and the other half of the *XXII. Reserve Corps* (the *43rd Reserve
Division*), with the *Guard Cavalry Division*, were in reserve.[2]

[1] Twelve, if the two battalions of the 1st Canadian Brigade which
began crossing the canal at Brielen bridge at 4.20 A.M. on the 23rd are
counted.

[2] The heavy howitzers with the *XXIII. Reserve*, *XXVI. Reserve* and
XXVII. Reserve Corps on the battle front were :—one 42 cm. (17-inch) ;
20 8-inch and 72 5·9-inch ; guns : 4 5·2-inch ; 16 4-inch ; and 34 old or
captured weapons. With the *XV. Corps* were : howitzers, 4 8-inch ;
12 5·9-inch ; guns : 4 5·2-inch ; 2 4-inch and 14 old or captured guns.
To these on the 26th April was added a 15-inch long-range gun—effective
range, 36 miles (Schwarte ii. p. 363). This weapon should have taken
part in the attack on the 22nd by bombarding headquarters, but its
concrete platform had not sufficiently set.

" The battles of Ypres [1] which began on the 22nd April, had
" their origin on the German side solely in the desire to try the
" new weapon, gas, thoroughly at the front.

" When, towards the end of January 1915, the necessary pre-
" parations in the homeland had been completed, and a practical
" trial at the front could be taken in hand, the Supreme Command
" selected for the purpose the *XV. Corps* which was in position
" opposite the south-east portion of the Ypres Salient [Comines
" canal to the Menin road]. As a result of the meteorological
" observations, the Supreme Command believed that in the season
" approaching southern winds mainly were to be expected.[2] The
" trial had therefore to be made on a front facing north. The only
" portion of the German front line which complied in some measure
" with this condition was the sector of the *XV. Corps*.

" From a reply of the Supreme Command to the *XV. Corps*,
" which had demanded large quantities of ammunition in order to
" exploit and consolidate any success that might be gained at the
" trial, it may be concluded that any idea of a large operation near
" Ypres was completely wide of the intentions of the Supreme
" Command. The Supreme Command refused the request of the
" *XV. Corps*, with the hint that the corps had solely to try the new
" weapon ; should a success of any kind arise in consequence, the
" necessary ammunition would be allotted from time to time, as
" the situation required.

" The gas attack of the *XV. Corps* was to be arranged in co-
" operation, as regards time only, with a local, limited attack of
" the *XXVII. Reserve Corps*, which for some time had been intending
" to improve its position by a thrust towards the line Zonnebeke—
" Gravenstafel.

" The digging in of the gas cylinders in the sector of the *XV.*
" *Corps* front first approved was completed towards the middle of
" February. The sector was then several times increased in width ;
" so that by the 10th March the whole front of the *XV. Corps* was
" prepared for a gas attack.

" The date of this had, however, to be continually postponed,
" as the south or south-east wind required did not blow. During
" this period the gas cylinders, though dug in, were damaged several
" times by shell fire, and there were some casualties.

" On the 25th March the commander of the *Fourth Army* decided
" to carry out preparations for a gas attack at a second place on
" the Ypres Salient, and the sectors of the *46th Reserve Division*
" and of the *XXVI. Reserve Corps* [Poelcappelle to Steenstraat]
" were now selected. The] digging in of the cylinders was completed
" by 11th April. At first, however, there was no wind from the
" right direction.

" On the evening of the 17th April, Hill 60 in the sector of the
" *XV. Corps* was captured by the British after an explosion of mines.
" The fear expressed at the time that some of the gas cylinders dug
" in on Hill 60 had fallen into the hands of the enemy seems to
" have been groundless.[3]

[1] This (translated) account of the initiation of the attack and the first
day's operations has been very kindly furnished by the *Reichsarchiv*.
  [2] The German meteorologists were strangely mistaken.
  [3] Gas was noticed, but the smell was attributed to gas shell. See
page 169.

" The attack was finally carried out at 5 P.M. [British time] on
" the 22nd April ; it took place in the sector Poelcappelle—Steen-
" straat, and, according to the order of the *Fourth Army* issued on
" 8th April, had as its objective the capture of Pilckem ridge and
" the ground adjoining it on the east.

" In a complementary ' Instructions for the Attack on Pilckem ',
" issued on the 14th April, the *Fourth Army* stated that ' by capturing
" ' the high ground near Pilckem it may be expected that it will
" ' be impossible for the enemy to remain longer in the Ypres
" ' Salient. [This expectation was falsified.] The further objective
" ' of the attack would be the securing of the line of the Yser canal
" ' as far as Ypres.'

" No allotment of reserves was made to the *Fourth Army* by the
" Supreme Command either before the attack or during the fighting
" that continued on into May.[1] The *Fourth Army*, on its own
" initiative, had taken a division (*43rd Reserve Division*) from the
" sector of the *XXII. Reserve Corps* (Yser sector), and this on the
" 22nd April was stationed with three of its infantry regiments and
" a field artillery brigade in the area Roulers—Ingelmunster—
" Oostrosebeeke—Meulebeke—Ardoye. [An area the centre of
" which is 15 miles north-east of Ypres.] Its fourth infantry
" regiment was in the *XV. Corps* sector, and six batteries remained
" either in the old sector of the division or were distributed as anti-
" aircraft batteries. As further reserve there was the *Guard Cavalry*
" *Division* in the area [south of Bruges], and of this the Horse
" Artillery Brigade and Machine-Gun Squadron were employed in
" the fighting.

" In the course of the fighting various other units were with-
" drawn by the *Fourth Army* from sectors not immediately engaged
" in the battle and used in the Salient, viz., the reinforced *4th Marine*
" *Brigade* (*4th* and *5th Matrosen Regiments*, and the *I.* and *II.*
" *Landwehr Field Artillery Brigades X. Corps*), the *2nd Marine*
" *Infantry Regiment* and *207th Reserve Infantry Regiment* (*44th*
" *Reserve Division*) reinforced by a Marine infantry battalion.

" In accordance with the arrangements for the attack, the
" infantry was to advance 15 minutes after the discharge of the gas.

" The first objectives were :—

" *45th Reserve Division* . Steenstraat—Lizerne.
" *46th* ,, ,, . Lizerne—Het Sas—Pilckem (exclusive).
" *XXVI. Reserve Corps* . Line of high ground on the road Boe-
" singhe — Pilckem — Langemarck —
" Poelcappelle.

" The attack on the 22nd encountered considerable difficulties
" at Steenstraat ; here, for some unexplained reason, part of the
" gas cylinders were not discharged ; the *45th Reserve Division* had
" to fight hard for possession of Steenstraat, and the village was
" taken only late in the evening. The attack failed to go beyond
" the western exit of the village.

" The advance of the *46th Reserve Division* against the Ypres
" canal was likewise difficult ; but late in the evening it reached
" the canal everywhere, and at Het Sas, passed across it. The
" left flank got only as far as the steam mill east of Boesinghe.

" The attack of the *XXVI. Corps* succeeded best. In particular,
" the *52nd Reserve Division* as early as 5.30 P.M. reached Pilckem

[1] This confirms the British Intelligence reports of the period.

" and the Haanebeek.[1]   Soon after 6 P.M. the division was directed
" for the moment not to go beyond the southern slope of Pilckem
" ridge.

" The progress of the *51st Reserve Division* was a little more
" difficult, the gas cloud had not its full effect in the ruins of Lange-
" marck, or on either side of the road Poelcappelle—Keerselare.[2]
" Towards 6 P.M., however, Langemarck was traversed, and the
" division was ordered to get possession of the bridgehead over the
" Haanebeek [Steenbeek] south-east of Langemarck, and, if possible,
" to take St. Julien.[3]

" At the conclusion of the fighting on the 22nd April the *52nd*
" *Reserve Division* of the *XXVI. Reserve Corps* had reached the line :
" Ypres—Staden railway near the canal bridge—point 550 yards
" north of Zwaanhof—point 29 [500 yards north of Turco Farm]—
" south edge of the wood 880 yards west of St. Julien [Kitchener's
" Wood].   The *51st Reserve Division* had reached the two passages
" over the Haanebeek [Steenbeek] 1,300 yards south-west of
" Poelcappelle ".[4]

The following further particulars are given in Schwarte ii. and
various regimental histories.

As soon as the corps had been brought up to strength after their

---

[1] The various reaches and branches of the streams are sometimes
differently named on British and German maps.   On the British 1 : 40,000,
below St. Julien, the same watercourse is called first Steenbeek, then
Haanebeek, then St. Jansbeek, and, finally, Martjevaart.   Here the
Haanebeek means its lower course, marked Steenbeek on the maps
accompanying this volume.

[2] Thus in the original, and it seems to have been the intention of the
Fourth Army that the gas attack should have extended across the Poelcappelle road.   Why it did not, does not appear.   The cylinders east of
the road not opened on the 22nd were discharged on the 24th, as will be
seen.

[3] As in the case of the instructions given to the same division on the
evening of the 24th, to retake St. Julien, no attempt was made on the
22nd or 23rd to carry out the part of the order referring to the village,
for which, no doubt, the resistance offered near Keerselare and the counter-
attack against Kitchener's Wood by the Canadians must be thanked.
The German high commands on several other occasions issued counter-
orders of this kind, entirely upsetting the nature of the planned operations
already in progress.   The writing or telephoning of such counter-orders
is easy enough, but for the troops to execute them without lengthy preparation is another matter.   A good example is the case of the Crown Prince
at Verdun on 21st February 1916, when at dusk, at 4.30 P.M., 5.40 P.M.
and 6 P.M., to his three corps—which had orders to take the French first
line and then reconnoitre—he telephoned the messages " Take everything
to-day ", " Get as far forward as possible ", " Try to take the second
trench ".   As the whole of the first line even had not been captured, no
attention was paid to the messages, which would probably have taken the
whole night to reach the battalions in the front line.   See the German
official monograph, " Die Tragödie von Verdun ", p. 55.

[4] The Haanebeek [Steenbeek] is further from Poelcappelle than the
" 1,200 metres " of the typescript.   Possibly the passages 3,000 yards
south-west of Poelcappelle to the north-east of Kitchener's Wood are
meant.   There is one " passage ", a culvert, over the Lekkerboterbeek
1,300 yards south-west of Poelcappelle.   None of these small water-
courses offers a military obstacle, being at most ten feet wide, so that the
" passages " over them are not of importance.

losses in the battles of Ypres 1914, the reduction of the Ypres Salient, or " Ypres Bridgehead ", as the Germans called it, was taken into consideration by the *Fourth Army*. Its possession by the Allies, it was thought, offered great facilities for an offensive towards Brussels and Lille, whilst if it could be seized the German line would be shortened, the last piece of Belgian soil conquered, and the Allied flank threatened.[1] Proposals that the *Sixth Army*, south of the *Fourth*, should co-operate in an offensive and storm Mount Kemmel, after which it would be very easy to deal with the Salient and even to push on to Calais, fell through, and the *Fourth Army* was left to its own resources ; but it was sent reinforcements which brought the strength of its companies up to numbers between 180 and 250. The *XXVI. Reserve Corps* opposite the French suggested in December 1914, the capture of Langemarck and Pilckem ridge, and the consequent gain of the eastern bank of the canal as far up as Boesinghe railway bridge. The *XXIII. Reserve Corps*, which faced the Belgians, proposed to push westwards over the canal. Duke Albrecht accepted the former suggestion, doubtless as being more within his means. Preparations for the attack were immediately taken in hand. Besides the collection of material, a normal gauge railway to bring up super-heavy guns was constructed through Houthulst Forest, and narrow gauge lines were laid up to the front ; sidings and huts were built and roads improved by Belgian labour. None of these significant measures came to the knowledge of the Allies. Finally, the Supreme Command provided poison gas. The German commanders were not, however, enthusiastic about its employment, as it was dependent on a suitable wind, and, this in Flanders being a very uncertain factor, troops might have to be kept in position a long time awaiting a favourable moment. There was always the chance, too, of the secret leaking out—as it actually did, although the Allies paid no attention to the warning.

The *XXVI. Reserve Corps*' [2] orders for the attack were actually issued on 8th April,[3] and the gas cylinders must then have been in position ; but not for a fortnight did the opportunity come. Whatever the original intention, the gas was released in the evening, leaving but a short period of daylight to exploit the success.[4] Only

[1] Falkenhayn, p. 84, states that the Ypres attack and other activities on the Western front " were to cloak the transportation of troops to " Galicia ".

[2] Reinforced by the Horse Artillery Brigade of the *Guard Cavalry Division*, and an armoured train on the Langemarck—Staden railway. Vogel, pp. 24-28.

[3] These orders have been kindly furnished by the *Reichsarchiv*. The date of the preparations shows it was purely fortuitous that the gas attack struck coloured troops who only came into the line between the 9th and 16th.

[4] This was a usual procedure at German fortress manœuvres, when ground was gained by a rush just at dusk and immediately entrenched. The history (p. 191), of *No. 215 Reserve Infantry Regiment* (*XXIII. Reserve Corps*), which attacked towards Steenstraat, gives some interesting details which indicate that it was hoped to attack at dawn. It states that attack orders were issued at midnight of the 21st-22nd (British time) ; respirators were then examined to see if they were damp, sandbags removed from the gas cylinders, and the tubes laid over the parapet ; sortie steps were made, the ladders available divided, and passages cut in the wire by the engineers. At 5.20 A.M. orders were received that the attack would begin

a small gain of ground was planned, for the operation orders of the *XXVI. Reserve Corps* ran : " Objective : the seizure of the ridge " marked by the road, Boesinghe—Pilckem—Langemarck—Poel- " cappelle. After the objective is reached the troops are at once " to dig in, arranging for mutual flanking by means of supporting " points ". Further, the only additional reserves brought up to support the attack of the *XXVI*. and *XXIII. Reserve Corps* was the *4th Marine Brigade.*[1] As in the first use of tanks, no special tactics for the new weapon seem to have been thought out ; at any rate, no tactical instructions were issued. As far as it went, the effect of the gas was expected to be overwhelming ; the infantry, according to the orders were to follow behind the gas cloud with bayonets fixed, but rifles unloaded.[2]

The front of 6 km. (3¾ miles) [3] was organized with gas cylinders, 20 to a battery. 180,000 kilograms of chlorine were released, the flow lasting five minutes, and the effect on the flanks was thickened by gas shell.[4]

The *XXVI. Reserve Corps* were ordered to attack Langemarck with one division, whilst the other took the rest of the front, some three thousand yards, to Pilckem (inclusive) ; the *XXIII.*, on its right, had as objective, the railway line Pilckem—Boesinghe. This corps, however, swung westwards, and part crossed the canal and secured a strip on the western side up to the Boesinghe—Lizerne road from Het Sas to Steenstraat, including these localities, but not Lizerne. From Het Sas to Boesinghe the German line was on the eastern bank. In the course of the action the *51st Reserve Division* of the *XXVI*. wheeled towards the open Canadian flank along the Poelcappelle—St. Julien road, and the *52nd*, apparently, conformed. Thus a gap came into existence between the two corps, " into which " the *2nd Reserve Ersatz* and *38th Landwehr Brigades* were inserted ". The *37th Landwehr Brigade* was sent up from the reserve and ordered to dig a second line on Pilckem ridge.

---

at 5.45 A.M. At 5.30 A.M., however, there being no wind, the attack was postponed. The men remained packed in the trenches all day, but fortunately there was no artillery fire. As the sun began to set a wind got up, and at 4.40 P.M. definite orders were issued for the opening of the cylinders at 5 P.M.

[1] Schwarte, ii. p. 262. Müller-Brandenburg, " Von der Marne zur Marne ", p. 23, says " one composite brigade ".

[2] This order was disobeyed, see p. 177. " Reserve Regiment, No. 215 ", p. 193, says that when the French were seen bolting men jumped on to the parapet and opened independent fire.

[3] From a point 500 yards east of Langemarck to the canal at Steenstraat is just 6 km.

[4] Hanslian, pp. 11 and 63. Schwarte, " Technik ", pp. 280-1. 6,000 cylinders, half of the stock in commercial use, were requisitioned, and these were supplemented by manufacturing 24,000 new ones of half the normal size. Of the total provided, 30 per cent were used on 22nd April. According to Schwarte, iv. p. 489, the Germans began official experiments with gas in October 1914. Schwarte (" Technik ", pp. 280-1) and other authors state that it was first intended to load the gas into shell, but at the time the output of shell was small, and the Supreme Command doubted whether mass effect could be obtained by firing gas shell. Dr. Haber then suggested cloud gas.

NOTE II

THE USE OF POISON GAS

Lord Kitchener in his telegram to Sir John French when he heard of the first gas attack, said :—" The use of asphyxiating gases " is, as you are aware, contrary to the rules and usages of war ". Viscount Grey of Fallodon, in 1915 Secretary of State for Foreign Affairs, has written [1] that the use of " poison gas " by the Germans in April 1915 was " an offence not only against the rules of war, but " against all humane considerations ". The use both of poison and asphyxiating gas was in fact forbidden.

As regards poison, Article 23 (a) of the Rules attached to the Hague " Convention Respecting the Laws and Customs of War on " Land ", 1907, definitely forbids the use of " poison or poisoned " weapons ".[2] The preamble to the Convention further states : " Until a more complete code of the laws of war can be drawn up, " the High Contracting Parties deem it expedient to declare that, " in cases not covered by the rules adopted by them, the inhabitants " and belligerents remain under the protection and governance of " the principles of the law of nations ". Since it has been argued that the gas used was not " poisonous " but merely " asphyxiating ", it must be further pointed out that the use of cloud gas was inferentially, although not specifically, barred. A special Hague " Declaration respecting asphyxiating gases ", 1899, forbids " the " use of projectiles the *sole* object of which is the diffusion of " asphyxiating gases ". Thus the principle was established that asphyxiating gases solely and simply may not be used as a weapon of war. Even when contained in a shell a limitation was imposed. In the debate at The Hague in 1899 on the wording of the Declaration, the text was held to mean that the destructive effect of the projectile must be greater than the deleterious effect of the gas. Under this accepted interpretation cloud gas is obviously barred, as it has no separate destructive effect. German literature on the subject of the first gas attack speaks with two voices, one of pride that the Germans were the first to elaborate such an effective weapon as gas, and the other of exculpation, alleging that the Allies thought of gas first and that their intention to use it was merely anticipated. The only statement in support of this latter defence, which appears in most books on the subject, is an assertion that notice of the Allies' intention leaked out through the " Pall Mall Gazette ". Vain search, with the assistance of the editor, was made for such a statement. At last " Hanslian " p. 9 (published 1924), gave a date in a footnote which may be translated as follows : " We read in the " ' Pall Mall Gazette ' of 17th September 1914 for the first time of " the preparations of the enemy to use gas ". The only relevant statement in the number in question is the mention of a new *explosive* " Turpinite " (invented by M. Turpin), which was said to cause painless death to everyone within reach of its explosion. In

---

[1] " 25 Years, 1892–1915 ", ii. p. 102.

[2] The purely legal point of whether the Convention of 1899 or that of 1907 was in force—for all the belligerents had not ratified the latter—hardly arises, for the prohibition is included in both.

the " Daily Express " of the same date " Turpinite " is described as being fired in a 56-lb. shell, and killing everyone within 400 yards. There is no mention whatever in either newspaper of cloud gas or poison gas, or of any means forbidden by international agreement.[1]

If their idea of using gas dates from 17th September 1914 only, the Germans lost little time ; for in a memorandum of the German *Second Army*, dated St. Quentin 16th October 1914 (captured in April 1915), on the subject of the assault of fortified positions, it is stated :—the " arms at disposal of the pioneers for fighting at close " quarters " are (1) trench mortars ; (2) hand-grenades ; (3) rifle grenades ; (4) flame or asphyxiating gas projectors.

The official apologia issued by the German War Ministry and Supreme Command in 1917, entitled " Die deutsche Kriegführung " und das Völkerrecht (The German Conduct of War and International " Law)'', claims that before the war the French Army was in possession of and used a rifle-grenade, designed for fortress warfare, filled with bromic acid, and a hand-grenade, filled with a lachrymatory liquid called ethyl bromo-acetate. The date and place of their being used is not given, nor is it claimed that their " sole object " was the diffusion of asphyxiating or deleterious gases. The first use of gas in the war, apart from its incidental recognized use in combination with a shell, was by the Germans on the 22nd April 1915 at 5 P.M. near Langemarck, Belgium.[2] Some indication that they knew they were transgressing the laws and usages of war is provided by the fact that the German Government endeavoured to conceal the fact of the use of gas from their people and the world by omitting all allusion to it in their communiqués. That of the 23rd April 1915 is as follows :—" Yesterday we broke out of our front Steenstraat— " Langemarck against the enemy position north and north-east of " Ypres. In one rush our troops pressed forward on a nine-kilometre " frontage to the heights south of Pilckem, and eastward of them. " At the same time, after a stubborn fight, they forced the passage " of the Ypres canal at Steenstraat and Het Sas, where they " established themselves on the western bank''.[3] Even in some of the popular histories of the war issued since the cessation of hostilities, there is no mention of gas during the fighting at Ypres in 1915.[4]

[1] On the 1st July 1926 Professor Haber, the German expert responsible for the introduction of gas warfare, speaking at the Inter-Parliamentary Union in Berlin, said (as reported in " The Times " of 3rd July) that a mistake had been made in attributing the first use of gas to the Allies :— " In the early part of the war it was reported that British troops had " used gas shell. He had gone forward to make an examination and " found that picric acid had been used as an explosive, and the fumes " [complained of in South Africa 1899–1902] had been mistaken for gas ".

[2] The first use of cloud gas on the Russian front was on 2nd May 1915 at Skiernjewitze, according to Hierl, iii. p. 20.

[3] The Press translation of this communiqué must have given some little trouble to those who tried to read it with a map ; for the German word " davon " translated above as " of them " in the phrase " eastward of them ''—is turned into the name of a village, and the phrase rendered " eastward of Douon ''.

[4] *E.g.* the history issued in parts by the Kaiser Wilhelm Dankverein der Soldatenfreunde, edited by Lieut.-General Baron von Ardenne, Part 133, p. 12, *et seq.*

YPRES, 1915.
BATTLE OF GRAVENSTAFEL RIDGE.
Situation at Dawn, 23rd April, & the
British counter attacks in the morning.

SKETCH 16.

CHAPTER X

BATTLE OF GRAVENSTAFEL RIDGE [1] (*concluded*)
23RD APRIL

(Map 6 ; Sketches 10, 11)

DURING St. George's Day, the day following the gas attack, Map 6.
the British had leisure to improve their position, and Sketch
could even, with such small forces as might be collected, 10.
proceed to counter-attack. The French on their left,
having lost most of their artillery and received only trifling
reinforcements, could not make a serious effort to recover
the ground they had lost : indeed, they had difficulty in
carrying out even the first of General Foch's instructions—to make sure of holding the ground they still
occupied.

Although the weather was perfect and much air
reconnaissance behind the enemy front was carried out,
only small bodies of his troops were seen. The general
impression left by the air reports was that the movements
observed only represented the reinforcement of the troops
in front line by units of their own divisions brought up
from rest centres in rear, and this was substantially
correct. The position of the enemy's front line was located,
but not photographed.

In all of the three Allied armies protective measures
against gas were taken in hand. The first instructions
sent out were that the troops should hold wetted handkerchiefs or cloths over their mouths, or use respirators made
of lint and tape (proposed by Lieut.-Colonel N. C. Ferguson,
the A.D.M.S. of the 28th Division), damped in any case,
but, if possible, dipped in a solution of bicarbonate of
soda kept in buckets for the purpose.

[1] See footnote p. 171.

THE ADVANCE OF GEDDES'S DETACHMENT AND THE EARLY
MORNING COUNTER-ATTACK OF THE 1ST CANADIAN
BRIGADE AND 3/MIDDLESEX. THE ASSEMBLY OF
REINFORCEMENTS

23 April.   The British counter-operations begun in the night
were continued on the 23rd. Colonel Geddes at St. Jean
had received instructions from General Alderson at
1.50 A.M. to link up with the Canadians at Kitchener's
Wood and extend his left to get in touch with the French,
driving back any enemy forces which had penetrated
through the gaps. Later these instructions were amplified
to the effect that he was to counter-attack in co-operation
with other troops, but to dig in if he could not advance.
Colonel Geddes, in consequence, ordered forward all the
men he had—2¼ battalions. His plan was for the 2/Buffs
(now under Major R. E. Power)—less the company lent to
the 3rd Canadian Brigade—to advance and connect with
the flank of that brigade, and then extend to the left, and
for the 3/Middlesex (Lieut.-Colonel E. W. R. Stephenson),
less two companies guarding the bridges, to find the
French, and then extend to the right to join up with the
Buffs. His third unit, the 5/King's Own (Lieut.-Colonel
Lord R. F. Cavendish) was to move forward in the centre.
He directed the 1/York and Lancaster, which had left
Ypres at 1.15 A.M. to join him, to march to the north-west
of Wieltje and follow the King's Own in reserve. Colonel
Geddes had great difficulty—having only a small staff—
in finding the battalions of his improvised command, and,
in spite of an urgent message from the 3rd Canadian
Brigade that matters would become still more serious
unless he hastened, it was 4 A.M., and daylight, before the
Buffs, Middlesex and King's Own got under way. They
were supported after daybreak by the 122nd Heavy
Battery near Frezenberg, and from the west side of the
canal by the North Midland Heavy Battery, 365th Field
Battery (28th Division), and improvised batteries formed
from sections, both French and British, including Canadian,
that were out of the line for rest.[1]

Deploying half a mile north of Wieltje, where they
came in sight of the crest of Mauser ridge, the Buffs passed
northwards over the open, practically level, ground west

[1] One battery at least was formed of one French and one British
section.

of Mouse Trap Farm under furious machine-gun fire, 23 April. losing two officers and 80 men. After Major Power had communicated with Br.-General Turner, his two leading companies eventually took up position in some old trenches beyond the farm, where they found on their left towards Hampshire Farm a company of the 14th Canadians and men of the 7th Zouaves. Extending to the right, they got in touch with two other companies of the 14th Canadians, which were in G.H.Q. Line north and south of Mouse Trap Farm. These Canadians were subsequently sent towards St. Julien to dig a support line, when the remaining company of the Buffs took their place. The 5/King's Own was halted under shelter of Hill Top ridge.

Colonel Geddes's other unit, the headquarters half of the 3/Middlesex, which had orders to find the French right, and, having done so, to deploy to the right and gain touch with the rest of his force, moved forward from St. Jean between Hill Top and the Pilckem road. In the course of the advance, Lieut.-Colonel Stephenson found the 1st and 4th Canadian Battalions on his left. Br.-General Mercer had received orders from the Canadian Division at 4.15 A.M. to co-operate in the French counter-attack against Pilckem, with his left on the Pilckem road. He had immediately led his two battalions across the Brielen bridge, and they had begun the forward movement at 5.25 A.M., the 4th Battalion (Lieut.-Colonel A. P. Birchall) leading. The enemy could then be seen on the crest of Mauser ridge, 1,400 yards away, busily digging, and the Canadians soon came under fire. The two companies of the Middlesex on their right, being without information, first pushed an advanced guard on to Hill Top ridge, where it also drew rifle fire. These two companies, at the instance of Br.-General Mercer, joined in the counter-attack. Nothing, however, could be seen of the French—their movement had been put off owing to the battalions detailed not being in position. The British, nevertheless, persevered. Passing over the low western end of Hill Top ridge, Canadians and Middlesex entered the depression between it and Mauser ridge, known later in the war as "Colne Valley", without any artillery support except from one battery of the I. Canadian Field Artillery Brigade. They came under heavy fire. Half a mile of ground was covered, and a position gained behind a bank some six or seven hundred yards from the enemy, the last two hundred yards of advance across the bottom having been

23 April. under heavy enfilade fire, particularly from a spur of Mauser ridge, south-east of Boesinghe, supposed, in error, to be in French possession. The 1st Canadians (Lieut.-Colonel F. W. Hill) at about 7.15 A.M., reinforced and extended the line to the left, but further progress up the gentle glacis leading to the enemy's position proved impossible in spite of the most heroic attempts.

At 6.45 A.M. Colonel Mordacq (90th Brigade, 45th Division), who had been placed in charge of the French operations on the east bank, had 3½ battalions of Zouaves along the canal on the eastern side, and two more on the western side, about to cross. At 7 A.M. he began deploying them gradually, two companies first, for the ground over which his force had to advance, though enclosed in places, was dead flat and exposed to view. At 7.40 A.M., as the French seemed unable to get on, General Alderson sent orders to his 1st Brigade to dig in, but to advance again if the French did so. The 2½ battalions with Br.-General Mercer therefore entrenched as best they could in the hollow in front of the German position. Here in the course of the morning they were plastered with gas shell to such an extent that every man was coughing, had his eyes blinded by tears, and became temporarily useless. Fortunately the effect passed off when the shelling ceased.[1]

By the advance of Geddes's and Mercer's troops a fairly continuous line had now been completed from the old left flank of the 3rd Canadian Brigade to within twelve hundred yards of the canal. There was some hope that this gap, too, would soon be filled ; but the situation as revealed by intelligence reports was still most alarming, for 17½ British battalions (12 of them Canadian), including reserves (10½ were in front line and 7 in second), some already sadly reduced in numbers, supported by half the artillery of a division were facing, in the most indifferent of trenches, 42 German battalions (*XXVI. Reserve Corps, 2nd Ersatz, 37th* and *38th Landwehr Brigades*), which had a preponderance of at least five to one in divisional guns, apart from immense superiority in heavies.

As a result of the counter-attacks delivered during the night and in the early morning, and the strenuous resistance offered where he appeared, the enemy made no attempt to

---

[1] Tear gas was also used on other parts of the II. and V. Corps front during the day, particularly on the woods south of the Ypres—Menin road.

advance against the improvised British flank ; [1] indeed, 23 April. except for shelling, he did little during the whole day but slightly improve his position opposite the French on the west bank of the canal, and make another abortive attempt to cross the canal by boats and rafts on the front of the Belgian 6th Division. His guns continued, however, to bombard Ypres, and shelled—often using gas shell—the Belgian artillery which was assisting the French, and the whole front of the British V. Corps, particularly the apex of the front of the Canadian Division. The Germans were able to take both sides of this salient in reverse, whilst trench mortars and machine guns ensconced in the trenches of the former French front enfiladed the northern face at close range.

It was by now fully confirmed by the first tactical air reports of the day that the enemy north of Kitchener's Wood was in force and close up to the Canadian flank, and that west of the wood he had dug in and wired a strong position on Mauser ridge in front of Langemarck—Pilckem ridge, with a second position, prepared in places, running from the northern end of Kitchener's Wood to Pilckem.[2] Any further advance against the enemy without considerable reinforcements seemed out of the question ; for the counter-attacks initiated at the request of the French and the extension of the front to cover the gap left by them had consumed not only the resting battalions of the Canadian Division, but all the Second Army reserves except the 13th Brigade just brought from Hill 60 to south of Vlamertinghe for rest. The V. Corps reserve consisted only of a few battalions drawn from the 27th and 28th Divisions, which might require them back at any moment.

Anxiety was by no means lessened when at 9.15 A.M. the 3rd Canadian Brigade reported to the division that the retention of the left of its original line was endangered by

---

[1] The *XXVI. Reserve Corps* was ordered to continue the attack, " but " had to report several counter-attacks during the morning, and its right " flank on the canal suffered from heavy artillery fire from the west bank ". It therefore set about making preparations to attack with gas next day. See Note at end of Chapter.

[2] Most of the British battalions that attacked later in the day, until they actually advanced, seem to have thought that the enemy's front line was on Pilckem ridge itself. The first full definition recorded came from the 13th Brigade at 11.45 A.M. on the 24th :—south edge of Kitchener's Wood, just north of Oblong Farm, south of Race Course Farm (500 yards north-west of Oblong Farm), south of Welch Farm, thence along Mauser ridge.

23 April. fire from the captured French trenches, that the Germans had crossed the Poelcappelle—St. Julien road in rear of the trenches facing north-east and that St. Julien would become untenable unless the counter-attacks succeeded in recovering the lost French front line.   In reply, General Alderson suggested that a rear line should be prepared by the supports behind the threatened apex of the front and a retirement made to it, so as to blunt the angle.   A withdrawal of this kind was already in contemplation and, as we shall see, was eventually carried out at night.   But, in spite of bombardment and gas shell, the 15th and 13th Canadians on the original front, as well as the portions of these battalions employed to build up a flank, held on, though it was impossible to get supplies or ammunition to them, and they were short of drinking water and reduced to eating their iron ration.

To return to the left near Ypres, towards 9.30 A.M. touch was obtained by the 1st Canadian Brigade with the right of the Zouave detachment between it and the canal, and the line to the canal was thus completed.   But the French counter-attack, already postponed until 9 A.M., was now put off till 3 P.M., for so many French guns had been lost in the gas attack that, in spite of support given by the I. Brigade Canadian Field Artillery and the Belgian artillery, it was judged impossible to attempt one until fresh batteries had arrived.   At 9.30 A.M., too, came news that the 13th Brigade had been placed by the Second Army at the disposal of General Plumer, and was on its way to Brielen, but could not arrive until the afternoon. Meanwhile at 11 A.M. two battalions of the 27th Division from the corps reserve at Potijze [1] were temporarily allotted to the Canadian Division, and sent by it to Br.-General Turner, but immediately recalled to rejoin Colonel Geddes. To this officer was despatched also the 2/East Yorkshire from Brielen.   Thus, he had now seven battalions to command without the staff even of a brigade, and as late as 3 P.M. he was ignorant of the whereabouts of the two battalions sent back to him by Br.-General Turner.   In all 3½ battalions of the 27th Division, 5 battalions of the 28th, the

---

[1] The 2/Duke of Cornwall's L.I. (Lieut.-Colonel H. D. Tuson) and the 9/Royal Scots (Lieut.-Colonel A. S. Blair) from west of Ypres. They reached General Snow's headquarters at Potijze at 3 A.M. and 4.30 A.M., respectively. These two battalions, with the 4/Rifle Brigade and 2/K.S.L.I. (less 2 companies), all of the 27th Division reserve, which had been placed under Lieut.-Colonel Tuson to collect at Potijze, were held in corps reserve from 12.55 A.M. to 9.30 A.M. on the 23rd.

13th Brigade, and the 1st Canadian Brigade (Army 23 April. reserve) had been made available to fill the threatened flank.

The artillery in the Salient available to support the original Canadian front and the new flank were now one heavy battery (122nd) near Frezenberg, three batteries of the 28th Division (149th, 366th and 367th) between Frezenberg and Gravenstafel, the II. Canadian Artillery Brigade south of Fortuin, the III. between St. Jean and Wieltje, and two howitzer batteries near La Brique.

As far as movement was concerned, a lull now took place in the action. During the morning Sir John French paid a visit to General Foch at Cassel, who assured him that it was his intention to make good the original line and regain the trenches lost by the 45th and 87th Divisions. For this purpose he had ordered up large reinforcements, and troops from the north had already arrived to assist General Putz.[1] The British Commander-in-Chief agreed to co-operate in any counter-attack, but stipulated that if the position were not re-established within a limited time he should be free to withdraw his troops from their exposed and dangerous situation in the reduced Salient, now a pocket five miles deep and less than five miles across. He was apprehensive also lest the advance of the German *XXIII. Reserve Corps* across the canal near Steenstraat might enable it to drive a wedge between the French and Belgians. On his return to Hazebrouck, where his advanced headquarters had been established, he decided to continue to reinforce the Second Army, and directed General Smith-Dorrien that he should use some of the fresh troops to assist General Putz should the French have difficulty in preventing the further advance of the Germans west of the canal. He therefore placed at General Smith-Dorrien's disposal the infantry of the 50th (Northumbrian) Division,[2] then near Steenvoorde (4 miles east of Cassel), which had been warned at midnight to prepare to move; and at 12.15 P.M. its 150th (York and Durham) Brigade started in buses via Poperinghe to Vlamertinghe, to come under the orders of the G.O.C. 28th Division. Its

---

[1] Two battalions and three batteries arrived in the course of the afternoon from the Nieuport detachment of General Putz's own command.

[2] Its artillery personnel not being fully trained and its field guns short range 15-pdrs., and there being little room in the Salient, the divisional artillery was not sent up. The two 5-inch old pattern howitzer batteries (Nos. 4 and 5) and the heavy battery were, however, ordered up on the 5th May and went into action next day.

23 April. 149th (Northumberland) Brigade was ordered to march to Brandhoek (between the last-named two villages), there to occupy a defensive line, little more than traced, known as G.H.Q. 3rd Line. The 151st (Durham Light Infantry) Brigade, the third infantry brigade of the division, was assembled at Ryveld (2½ miles north-east of Cassel), and also placed under the 28th Division, but to be held as V. Corps reserve. The Cavalry Corps had already been directed by G.H.Q. to concentrate near Poperinghe, and at 11.40 A.M., at General Smith-Dorrien's urgent demand, the 1st Cavalry Division was put under his orders, and directed to the line Elverdinghe—Woesten (3½ miles and 5 miles, respectively, north-west of Ypres), to cover the left of the Second Army and ascertain the situation near Boesinghe and Lizerne, to which latter place the Germans were said to have penetrated. Later in the day the whole Cavalry Corps was handed over to the Second Army as mobile reserve. G.H.Q., at 2.15 P.M., further directed that the 10th and 11th Brigades of the 4th Division and the Lahore Division of the Indian Corps, then in billets in rest areas near Bailleul and Merville respectively, should be held in readiness to proceed northwards, and that the First Army should send a 60-pdr. battery to the Second Army, and also have two more Regular brigades ready at two hours' notice to move by train to the north.

The anxiety in the Second Army and V. Corps was greatly lessened, towards 1 P.M., by the actual arrival of the 1st Cavalry Division (Major-General H. de B. de Lisle) and the—though sadly attenuated—13th Brigade (Br.-General R. Wanless O'Gowan).

Sketch 11. THE AFTERNOON ATTACK OF GEDDES'S DETACHMENT AND THE 13TH BRIGADE, AND EVENTS OF THE AFTERNOON and NIGHT.[1]

Soon after the arrival of the 1st Cavalry Division and the 13th Brigade in the vicinity of Ypres, messages between General Smith-Dorrien's and General Plumer's headquarters crossed. Both generals were convinced that if the attack ordered by G.H.Q. was to be made at all, it must take place soon, although the French appeared to be doing

---

[1] The word " attack " has been used to distinguish the tactical operation, made 24 hours after the first German success, from the counter-attacks made earlier by the Canadians at Kitchener's Wood and near the canal.

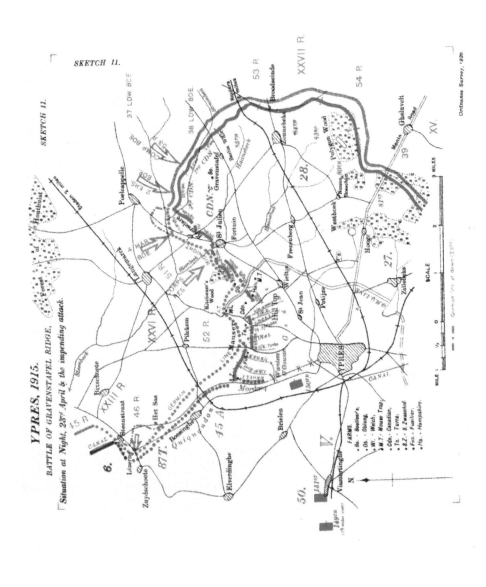

SKETCH 11.

YPRES, 1915.

BATTLE OF GRAVENSTAFEL RIDGE.

Situation at Night, 23rd April & the impending attack.

Ordnance Survey, 1925.

nothing to relieve the situation.[1] The more time the 23 April. Germans were given to entrench, the more difficult would it be to dislodge them. Orders were therefore issued by General Smith-Dorrien to the V. Corps at 2.40 P.M. for a general attack between Kitchener's Wood and the canal, through the existing line, towards Pilckem. It was to be under command of Br.-General Wanless O'Gowan (13th Brigade) who was given instructions by General Alderson at Canadian Division headquarters, where Generals Smith-Dorrien and Plumer were present. The four fresh battalions of Geddes's detachment were to advance east of and the 13th Brigade west of the Ypres—Pilckem road, for the Zouaves had retired to the canal bank again ; the 3rd Canadian Brigade to the north-east was to be ready to act if opportunity occurred. Actually, Colonel Geddes, who did not receive the orders placing him under the 13th Brigade until three-quarters of an hour after the attack had begun, acted independently.

General Putz now ordered the 45th Division to attack east of the canal from south to north in close liaison with the British, whilst the rest of his force, the 87th Territorial Division and the Nieuport detachment continued the fighting at Lizerne and Steenstraat.[2]

The time of starting was subsequently postponed from 3 P.M. until 4.15 P.M., as the 13th Brigade, which was to direct the movement, had been delayed, its road being occupied by French troops. This respite enabled Br.-General Wanless O'Gowan to ride forward to Brielen bridge and make a hasty reconnaissance on foot of the ground on which his brigade was to deploy. He found a complete gap again existed between the Pilckem road and the canal.

The attack to which the Second Army was committed by G.H.Q. order at the request of the French never had any prospect of success. The ground over which it took place was very open, broken only by a few widely separated hedges, except near the canal, where it was more enclosed, and it sloped gently up to the enemy's first position on Mauser ridge five to eight hundred yards away. The 13th Brigade was cheery, just having had a meal, but physically tired, as observers noticed when it crossed the canal, and the other battalions, though they had not

[1] General Foch, to show how much he had the matter at heart, twice went personally to General Putz's headquarters during the day to impress on him the necessity for action.
[2] The only artillery support, 3 batteries of 75's from Nieuport, was allotted to the Steenstraat attack.

23 April. had heavy fighting, had been on foot from the previous night. The sole reserves on the field, beyond battalion reserves, consisted of the 4/Rifle Brigade and half the 2/K.S.L.I. at Potijze, half the 14th Canadian Battalion digging a support line, and one company of the 7th in Locality C. Owing to the short time available, there was practically no preparation, no reconnaissance by battalions ; even the enemy's exact location was uncertain, and little could be done to arrange communication with the artillery (part of the 28th Division and Canadian field artillery and the 122nd and 123rd Heavy Batteries of the XI. Brigade) which had opened fire for a short time at 2.45 P.M., having been informed that the attack would take place at 3 P.M., but not of the postponement. There was no other preliminary bombardment, as ammunition was short. The batteries began firing again after the advance had started, and support improved as the operation proceeded.[1]

The right of the attack, under Lieut.-Colonel Tuson, was formed by units of the 27th Division, the 2/Duke of Cornwall's L.I., supported on the right rear by two companies of the 9/Royal Scots.[2] It moved so as to clear the left of the Buffs, who remained in position.[3] Next in the centre, to pass through the 1st and 4th Canadian Battalions, were three battalions of the 83rd Brigade (28th Division) under Colonel Geddes personally :—2/East Yorkshire and 1/York and Lancaster in front line, their left on the Pilckem road, with the 5/King's Own in reserve, though the last was soon moved up to fill a gap between the Cornwall L.I. and the East Yorkshire. On the left was the 13th Brigade, in which the 2/K.O.S.B. and 1/R. West Kent led, the 2/K.O.Y.L.I. and 9/London (Queen Victoria's Rifles), which were to be in second line, remaining on the west bank of the canal until the two former had cleared their front, when the Yorkshiremen followed in close support

[1] Of the seven German six-battalion brigades (*51st* and *52nd Divisions* and *2nd Reserve Ersatz*, and *37th* and *38th Landwehr Brigades*) there were probably four on the front of attack.

[2] Its other two companies had been recalled at 4.30 P.M., but, having gone on to St. Julien, had not arrived.

[3] The Zouaves near Hampshire Farm in the morning, and other French troops remaining, having exhausted their ammunition, had by now been withdrawn to rejoin their units. A few individual men, however, remained with the British units, refusing to leave the fight. The last of them, it is believed, was killed with the Northumberland Fusiliers on the 8th May. Blinded by a wound, he crawled on to the parapet, stood up, shouting defiance, and was there shot.

of the West Kent.[1]   Each battalion of the first line was 23 April. allotted five hundred yards of front, and was organized in five or six lines at wide intervals.   The general advance began at 4.25 P.M., Colonel Tuson's command on the right following half an hour later.

Directly the leading line of Geddes's and O'Gowan's men rose from the ground the enemy opened heavy gun and rifle fire; for in the clear light of the spring afternoon every single man was distinctly visible.   To British observers it seemed marvellous that a line of skirmishers should dare to stand up and move in broad daylight under such fire against a hidden enemy.   But dust and smoke soon hid the advancing troops alike from friend and foe.   Casualties among the officers were so serious that little information came back, and it became impossible to direct the battle.   When the 13th Brigade had advanced about five hundred yards from Brielen bridge, some four hundred Zouaves who had been lining the eastern bank of the canal, joined in the attack, but unfortunately masked the front of the West Kent, crowded that battalion towards the right, and for some time stopped its progress.   It, however, was resumed when the Zouaves soon afterwards withdrew.   This advance and retirement was the only sign of the offensive of the French 45th Division.

Undeterred by their previous losses and twelve hours under fire, the half battalion of the Middlesex and the 1st and 4th Canadian Battalions joined in the attack as the leading lines reached them.   But, except on the left in the enclosed ground near the canal, little progress could be made.   After advancing about two hundred yards up the gentle slope to the enemy's trenches, the leading battalions came under intense machine-gun and rifle fire at short range.   Some parties of the British got within two hundred yards of the main German position,[2] some within one hundred yards, whilst one small detachment of the East Yorkshire fought its way up to within thirty yards.   There was hand-to-hand fighting in the farms and cottages held by the Germans in advance of their position.   But about 7 P.M., broken by German fire, all movement came to an end.   The general line then ran from the south end of Kitchener's Wood to Hampshire

---

[1] The 2/Duke of Wellington's was left in reserve near Zillbeke Lake; on the 24th April it was moved to Hooge as reserve to the 82nd Brigade.
[2] In Turco Farm the D.C.L.I. found a German observer, who stuck to his post telephoning information until death.

23 April. Farm, and thence partly in German outpost trenches along the forward edge of the bottom of the depression (Colne valley) in front of Mauser ridge, via Turco Farm to the canal in front of South Zwaanhof Farm, where junction was made with the French.[1]

The French attack in the northern area had no better success. One made by the reserve of the 87th Division on Het Sas completely failed, and that from Lizerne on Steenstraat by the newly arrived Nieuport detachment,[2] supported by two Belgian batteries, made no appreciable progress.

When it grew dark, about 9.30 P.M., and movement again became possible, a new line in the Colne valley in rear of the high water mark of the attack, and about six hundred yards from the enemy, was organized by Br.-General O'Gowan and Colonel Geddes, with great difficulty owing to the confusion and mix-up of units ; and this, from Hampshire Farm westwards, remained the front, with a support line on Hill Top ridge, until the night of the 28th/29th, when a more forward line including Canadian Farm was secured. Undisturbed by the Germans, the troops dug in as best they could, for water two feet down forbade deep trenches. It was a miserable night ; some food in the shape of bread and bacon was got up, but not to all, and little ammunition arrived. A lamentable shortage of officers left the rank and file much to their own resources, but nothing deterred them from holding on. In the reorganization the two battalions of the 1st Canadian Brigade, with the few survivors of the half battalion of the Middlesex, were withdrawn into support and reserve of the 13th Brigade, and at 11.30 P.M. the 4/Rifle Brigade arrived at Brielen bridge [3] to reinforce the 13th Brigade on account of its heavy losses—which hardly left it an officer or a man who had fought at Mons and Le Cateau. The Rifle Brigade relieved Br.-General Wanless O'Gowan's two front line battalions, the K.O.S.B. and R. West Kent, allowing them to be withdrawn into reserve north-west of Brielen.

[1] The line of the 13th Brigade was through Fusilier Farm and Glimpse Cottage (400 yards east of South Zwaanhof) to South Zwaanhof Farm. The brigade received the special thanks of General Alderson : " Words " cannot express what the Canadians owe the 13th for their splendid " attack and the way they restored confidence ".

[2] Palat ix. p. 195.

[3] At 3.40 P.M. it had been sent, at the request of General Alderson, from 27th Divisional reserve, Potijze, to be at the disposal of 3rd Canadian Brigade south-west of Mouse Trap Farm.

Sir John French's promise to General Foch had been redeemed, the attack had been a magnificent display of discipline and courage : the offensive at all costs carried to an extreme. It certainly had the effect of stopping the enemy's advance [1] in this quarter, but the price paid had been very heavy, and actually no ground was gained that could not have been secured, probably without any casualties, by a simple advance after dark, to which the openness of the country lent itself. It is obvious now that it was a mistake to agree to whatever General Joffre's deputy wished, without regard to British ideas. The 1/York and Lancaster lost its commanding officer, Lieut.-Colonel A. G. Burt, killed, 13 officers and 411 other ranks ; the 2/East Yorkshire, 14 officers and 369 men (it was reduced to 7 officers and 280 men) ; the 2/K.O.S.B., 2/Duke of Cornwall's L.I. and 5/King's Own between 200 and 300 each ; the 1st and 4th Canadian Battalions lost, respectively, 11 officers and 393 other ranks, and 18 officers (including Lieut.-Colonel A. P. Birchall, killed) [2] and 436 other ranks. Lieut.-Colonel E. W. R. Stephenson of the Middlesex was killed, and only twenty men of his two companies remained : it was the end of the half battalion.[3] Late at night, on hearing of the losses, General Bulfin ordered the 150th (York and Durham) Brigade, then just west of Ypres at his disposal, to Brielen bridge to support the 13th Brigade, if required.

In the apex of the front opposite Poelcappelle, the original left of the V. Corps line, the 13th Canadians and Captain Tomlinson's company of the 2/Buffs had managed to hold out all day. But the position, forming an angle of 60°, and with its faces fired into from front and rear, and enfiladed both from the old French trenches and a communication trench only forty yards away, was obviously not permanently tenable, even if the rest of the front of the 3rd Canadian Brigade could be held. The enemy had begun to feel his way towards it already, making two attacks on it by bombing in the course of the afternoon. The suggestion to round off the angle by taking a line across it was therefore acted on. Reconnaissances for the purpose were undertaken during the afternoon, and after dusk a retirement was made to the

[1] See Note at end of Chapter.
[2] Lieut.-Colonel Birchall was an officer of the Royal Fusiliers employed with the Canadian forces.
[3] With the original advanced guard of 40 men, not engaged in the second attack, the survivors were formed into one company.

23 April. selected line. This started from a point about four hundred yards to the right of the apex, and ran westwards at 90°, instead of 60°, to join the trenches east of the Poelcappelle road near Keerselare, where Lieut.-Colonel W. F. H. McHarg's [1] 7th Battalion (less one company) was entrenched. The withdrawal was completed without a casualty. Immediately after the movement had been begun, just long enough after, however, to make its hastening unnecessary, the Germans started bombing from the west up the original front trench, but stopped a hundred yards short of the new alignment, and left the Canadians and Buffs to dig in in peace. Thus by morning they had formed such cover as it was possible to improvise with the portable entrenching implement.

General Situation on Night of 23rd April

At the close of the 23rd April, therefore, the situation of the right and centre of the V. Corps was unimpaired, and that of its left, except for the great extension of its front, had been slightly improved ; but this had been achieved at the expense of throwing into the fight every battalion in divisional and corps reserve, and the two brigades, 13th and 1st Canadian, of the Second Army reserve. These troops had formed a new front on the flank exposed by the disappearance of the French, but, there having been no time for even essential preparations, they had gained little ground. There were still no French troops east of the canal, except a few hundred Zouaves along the canal bank, and the safety of the divisions of the V. Corps, with the whole of the artillery east of Ypres, was still gravely imperilled. At 6.30 P.M. the good news had come to the Second Army through the 1st Cavalry Division—from the 1st Cavalry Brigade, which had reached and occupied Woesten—that the Germans had made practically no further progress against the French, though they still held bridgeheads at Het Sas and Steenstraat and the ground between, and were in the outskirts of Lizerne ; that the Belgian front was intact ; and that French Territorials were holding a third entrenched line north of Woesten to connect with the Belgians. Information was sent, too, direct by General Quiquandon that the situation near Boesinghe was in hand, and that he was confident of

---

[1] Lieut.-Colonel McHarg was mortally wounded whilst reconnoitring in front of his battalion during the afternoon.

being able to hold the Germans, if only on the line of the 23 April. canal. The Belgian position Steenstraat (exclusive)— Noordschote was, in fact, not only intact, but the situation had been improved by the arrival of reinforcements from the Belgian 1st Division, and the seven hundred yards gap between the Belgians and the French had been filled by extending the Belgian right to Lizerne.[1] The position on the west bank, however, was towards midnight seriously menaced by the capture of Lizerne by the German *XXIII. Reserve Corps.*

Late at night information was sent by G.H.Q. to the Second Army by telephone that one brigade, the 10th (Br.-General C. P. A. Hull) of the 4th Division, placed at General Smith-Dorrien's disposal, had left Bailleul for Locre en route for Vlamertinghe ; and that the French 153rd Division (General Deligny) [2] had been entrained, and would arrive at Cassel on the 24th. General Joffre, too, had given General Foch permission to draw, if necessary, on the reserves assembled behind the Tenth Army on the right of the B.E.F., on the understanding that any divisions taken would be returned in time to be employed in the projected offensive. Immediate measures to improve the situation seemed, however, imperative, and on receiving confirmation soon after midnight that there were no French east of the canal, except on the canal bank near Ypres, General Smith-Dorrien instructed his liaison officer at General Putz's headquarters to point this out and ascertain the general's intentions. The enemy had now seven bridges to his bridgehead on the west bank, and, pausing in his advance on the east side against the new British flank, seemed to be concentrating his efforts on making a breach between the French and Belgians and sweeping the former away. At 1.15 A.M. on the 24th, General Smith-Dorrien directed the Cavalry Corps to place the 1st Cavalry Division at the disposal of General Plumer, so as to enable the latter to deal with the new danger to his flank. What had begun as a local attack against the French had developed into a serious threat against the left flank of the Second Army, and thus of the whole of Sir John French's force.

---

[1] " Steenstraat ", p. 58.

[2] Formed 1st to 13th April. French Order of Battle, Tome X., ii. p. 841. One of its two infantry brigades was the 3rd Moroccan, containing one mixed Zouave and native Tirailleur regiment, and one regiment of " Zouaves de marche ".

The Tactics of "Second Ypres"

It may assist the comprehension of the further operations to point out here that the German procedure in the attack on 22nd April 1915, a short advance, after careful preparation, to a definite line selected beforehand—the so-called limited objective—is the clue to the whole battle of " Second Ypres ". It was the method that Sir Douglas Haig essayed with inadequate artillery at Festubert in the following month, and carried out successfully on a much greater scale in 1916 at the battles of the Somme. It was adopted by the enemy because the infantry available were insufficient in number and too inferior in quality to attempt to obtain a decision by mere weight of attack, as had been tried and had failed at " First Ypres ". As the narrative continues it will become evident to the reader that the German procedure approximated to the step by step operations of siege warfare, hardly modified from the old method of advance by " parallel " elaborated by Vauban, and actually practised in the attack of fortified positions at German manœuvres before the war. The British were driven back by overwhelming artillery fire, with the assistance from time to time of further discharges of gas, although shell fire was throughout the determining factor. Position after position was gained by the enemy, and the conquest immediately consolidated by trench and wire, the new " parallel " sometimes being actually the conquered position. Eventually the Germans came to a stop from lack of men and ammunition to continue the process, their resources being required elsewhere—to obtain a great strategic success in Russia, and to hold the Franco-British attacks further south. Such deliberate methods of advance are possible only when the attackers are very superior to the foe in heavy artillery, as they were at Ypres, and as they usually were in the great sieges of history. Otherwise, the siege must fail ; the chests of the bravest, as Napoleon said, are useless against ramparts.

To such deliberate procedure there are two replies possible. The first is the sortie or counter-attack before the enemy has had time to consolidate himself in his new " parallel ". An immediate reply is often imperative if the enemy has broken the ring of the defences at any point, and is in a position to widen the breach and thus envelop from a flank the remainder of the defenders. For the latter to sit still means that they will be rolled up, or shelled off the face of the earth when the enemy is ready for his next move. The other reply is a deliberately prepared attack with adequate numbers as soon as they are available, and with carefully arranged artillery co-operation. In the operations at Ypres in April, the choice was not left to the British higher commanders. The governing idea was that the French should restore the line lost by them, and that the British should assist. Thus Sir John French, apart from his desire to preserve unity of command whenever possible, was bound to his Ally's plan and wishes. General Foch ordered immediate counter-attacks, which General Putz was not in a position to execute, whilst the British whole-hearted attempts to carry out their share by means of offensive action, which was as a rule neither a true counter-attack nor a deliberately prepared attack, led to heavy losses without restoring the situation, although it made the enemy pause and rely more than ever on his artillery.

That the British operations were carried out mainly by infantry—rifles against heavy guns, as one commander described it—was not the fault of those who ordered them. They had not at their disposal the heavy artillery that the foe possessed to break down the way. Although it is an accepted maxim that new levies require a greater proportion of and better artillery than old and seasoned troops, there was little to support the brave but hastily trained infantry at Ypres except the 4·7-inch gun and 5-inch howitzer, the ancient and obsolete weapons of the South African War. There was little opportunity in the attacks for reconnaissance or preparation, and hardly time to write orders. It seemed to the British officers at the front that they were being sacrificed to gain time until the French were ready for a big spectacular effort; but this, even if ever intended, did not materialize. Whether a deliberate withdrawal to the canal should not have been made at once will be referred to later, when the question of retirement came up for discussion between the French and British commanders. In any case, it would seem that the disasters of the following days would never have taken place, and that a decent flank could have been formed had it not been for the heavy casualties incurred first in the counter-attacks and then in the attacks of the 23rd.

NOTE

THE GERMANS ON THE 23RD APRIL 1915

23 April. The following is the account kindly furnished by the *Reichsarchiv* :
Map 6. " At 9 A.M. [British time] the *Fourth Army* gave orders for the
Sketches " continuation of the attack. The *XXIII. Reserve Corps* was to
10, 11. " continue it in the direction of Poperinghe, the *XXVI. Reserve*
" *Corps* in a southern direction, with the right flank along the canal.
" The Army reserve (*43rd Reserve Division*) was allotted to the
" *XXIII. Reserve Corps.* The *XXVII. Reserve Corps* and the *XV.*
" *Corps* [opposite the original front of the British V. Corps and II.
" Corps] were at first only to hold the enemy to his ground by
" artillery fire, and local thrusts (*Vorstösse*) ; later the *XXVII.*
" *Reserve Corps* was to join in with the advance of the *XXVI.*
" *Reserve Corps.*
" The attack of the *XXIII. Reserve Corps* [against the French
" and Belgians] on 23rd again encountered extraordinary difficulties.
" Neither of the next objectives : for the *45th Reserve Division*,
" Lizerne ; for the *46th Reserve Division*, Boesinghe, could be
" attained. Only late on the night of the 23rd/24th did the *45th
" Reserve Division* capture Lizerne.
" The *XXVI. Reserve Corps* had to report several counter-
" attacks during the morning, and its right flank on the canal
" suffered from heavy artillery fire from the west bank. The corps
" brought forward its guns and prepared for an advance on the 24th.
" The gas cylinders not discharged on the 22nd were dug in in the
" sector of the *51st Reserve Division* in order to facilitate its attack.
" As regards the rest, on the 24th the *52nd Reserve Division* was to
" remain on the Pilckem heights and only take part in the attack
" with artillery. On its left flank the corps reserve (*102nd Reserve
" Brigade*) was interpolated, and was to advance west of the
" Haanebeek [Steenbeek] and support the attack of the *51st Reserve
" Division*. This latter, advancing via St. Julien and Fortuin, was
" to reach the ridge north of the Zonnebeke valley [Zonnebeke
" ridge]. During the evening of the 23rd there were several more
" counter-attacks against the position of the *XXVI. Reserve Corps*,
" which were all repulsed ".
The following additional particulars are taken from the account
in Schwarte ii. p. 262, written by the late Lieut.-General Balck,
who was present in command of a division of the *XXVI. Reserve
Corps*:
" In the early hours of the 23rd the *Fourth Army* ordered the
" attack to be continued by the *XXIII. Reserve Corps* in the direction
" of Poperinghe, to the line Boesinghe—Zuydschoote [a mile south-
" west of Steenstraat] and Pypegaale [in Belgian hands, 2,000 yards
" west of Steenstraat], and it placed *Brigade Runkel* (the staff of
" the *85th Reserve Brigade* and the *201st Reserve Regiment*), as well
" as the *4th Marine Brigade* with two batteries in the area Staden—
" Houthulst, at its disposal. The *XXVI. Reserve Corps* was ordered
" to gain more ground to the south, so as to attack in flank and rear
" the enemy troops still holding out in front of the *XXVII. Reserve
" Corps* and *XV. Corps*. . . .
" However desirable it was to exploit the success [of the 22nd],

" reserves to do so were lacking ; any further advance would have **23 April.**
" involved the troops in close fighting in the dark and on unknown
" ground. It would have been better on the 23rd to have pursued
" only one objective and thrown the enemy over the Yser. The
" situation would have been very different if the attack [on the
" 22nd] had been made in the early morning. Thus arose two
" divergent objectives [those proposed originally by the *XXIII.*
" *Reserve* and *XXVI. Reserve Corps* respectively] which were bound
" in the end to lead to failure, although the Allies were surprised
" by the direction of the attacks. The enemy dug in 500 yards from
" the front of the *XXVI. Reserve Corps* and there he was not attacked.
" In the *XXIII. Reserve Corps* there was some further fighting on
" the west bank. . . . No further progress was made ".

General Balck then quotes from the war diary of the *XXIII.
Reserve Corps* :—

" Unfortunately the infantry had become enfeebled by trench
" warfare and had lost its daring and its indifference to heavy losses
" and the disintegrating influence of increased enemy fire effect.
" The leaders and the brave-hearted fell, and the bulk of the men,
" mostly inexperienced reinforcements, became helpless and only too
" inclined to leave the work to the artillery and trench mortars ".

CHAPTER XI

THE BATTLES OF YPRES 1915 (*continued*)

BATTLE OF ST. JULIEN, 24TH-30TH APRIL

24TH APRIL

(Map 7; Sketch 12)

FIRST PHASE : THE GAS ATTACK ON THE 2ND AND 3RD
CANADIAN BRIGADES, AND THE LOSS OF THE APEX OF
THE FRONT, 4 A.M. TO 9 A.M.

Map 7.
Sketch
12.

AEROPLANE reconnaissances made from 4.30 A.M. onwards on the 24th April did not discover any German movements of importance. The only indication of the possible arrival of enemy reinforcements in the Ypres district during the night was the presence of thirty trains at Menin and seven at Ledeghem (4 miles north of Menin and 10 miles east of Ypres); but, as these trains consisted of covered coaches, they could have brought up little except infantry, and might be empties intended for the evacuation of wounded. Nevertheless, the II. Corps, south of the V. Corps and opposite Menin—Ledeghem was specially warned by General Smith-Dorrien to be on the watch for any signs of an attack. It was quite possible that the enemy was meditating a blow against the south-eastern face of the Ypres Salient, narrowed to a dangerous degree by the events of the 22nd April, and stripped of its central reserves to combat the new danger on its northern face. On the other hand in a memorandum sent off at 9.30 A.M.[1] the Chief of the General Staff, Lieut.-General Sir W. R. Robertson, directed the Second Army to make such dispositions as would secure its left, but without expecting much assistance from the French. He stated that, in

---

[1] Appendix 22.

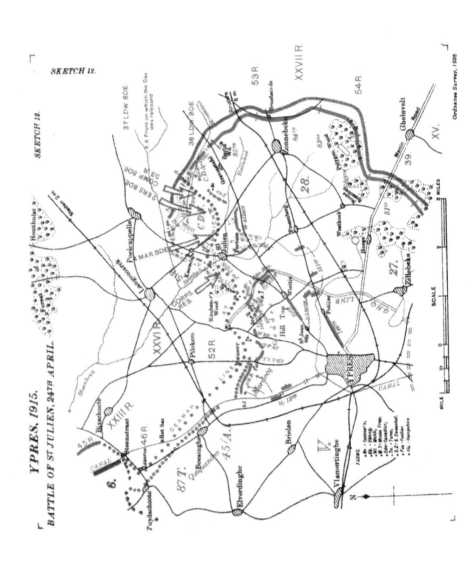

YPRES, 1915.

BATTLE OF ST. JULIEN, 24TH APRIL.

SKETCH 12.

Ordnance Survey, 1925.

Sir John French's opinion, vigorous action east of the 24 April. canal would be the best means of checking the enemy's advance westward through General Putz's troops.

The Germans, however, as they so often did, made their move first. The *XXIII. Reserve Corps*, having captured Lizerne from the French during the night (at 1.30 A.M. on the 24th), from this position of advantage at once endeavoured to turn the defensive flank of the Belgians. The attack at 3 A.M., though backed up by a large quantity of gas shell, was very gallantly met, and the Belgians not only held their flank, but, by extending it south-westwards round Zuydschoote (700 yards S.S.W. of Lizerne), outflanked the would-be enveloper and got touch again with the French.[1] The high-water mark of the German success across the canal had been reached. The French, under General Codet (commanding the 306th Brigade of the 153rd Division), counter-attacked against Lizerne at 8.30 A.M. and again at 2 P.M.; and, though they failed to enter the village, they closed round on three sides of it. Their attack against Het Sas made no progress,[2] but about 1.30 P.M. Colonel Mordacq's Zouaves advanced from the canal bank, and, passing through the 4/Rifle Brigade—the British left—took up a position in front, from the Ypres—Pilckem road to South Zwaanhof Farm on the canal.

The enemy also began operations early against the apex of the front of the Canadian Division, using gas; but on this occasion, although he had all the hours of daylight in which to exploit his success, he gained no such startling advantage as he had done against the coloured troops and elderly French Territorials on the evening of the 22nd April. At 4 A.M., after an hour's heavy bombardment with guns and trench mortars, cloud gas was released on a front of about a thousand yards [3] against

---

[1] " Steenstraat ", pp. 74-104.

[2] Throughout the fighting in the Het Sas—Steenstraat area, the Germans in defending the oblong area that they had gained on the west bank in the first rush—to which Steenstraat brewery and Lizerne were subsequently added as projections—had the great advantage that the ground on the east bank had a slight command over it and gave them precious artillery observation, if not a second tier of fire.

[3] According to the German records, it had been intended to discharge gas across and on both sides of the Poelcappelle—Ypres road, but it was discovered that west of the road there was no opposition likely within effective range of the gas, and therefore it was not released on the front of the right battalion of the attacking regiment. (Information supplied by the *Reichsarchiv*.)

24 April. the centre of the original Canadian front :—the 8th Battalion (Lieut.-Colonel L. J. Lipsett) [1] and the 15th Battalion [2] (Lieut.-Colonel J. A. Currie), of the 2nd and 3rd Canadian Brigades, respectively.[3] The wind being N.N.E., the gas drifted over the north-eastern face of the salient of the Canadian front, but behind and nearly parallel to the new north-western face, now held from the apex down to St. Julien by B Company of the Buffs, the 13th (Royal Highlanders of Canada), the 7th (1st British Columbia Regiment) and the 14th (Royal Montreal Regiment). Behind the gas followed the attacking waves of the *4th Reserve Ersatz Infantry Regiment*, which was supported by the rest of its brigade and a composite brigade of the *53rd Reserve Division* (*XXVII. Reserve Corps*).[4] A brigade of the *51st Reserve Division* and the *4th Marine Brigade* menaced the north-western face of the apex, the right of the attack extending across the Steenbeek, west of which a brigade of the *XXVI. Reserve Corps* later advanced.[5] Thus at least four six-battalion brigades enveloped both sides of the apex, held, from the right near Gravenstafel round by St. Julien to Kitchener's Wood, by the equivalent of eight battalions, with no more reserves than a company at Boetleer's Farm,[6] two com-

[1] A p.s.c. officer of the Royal Irish Regiment lent to the Canadian Government and serving at the outbreak of the war as G.S.O.2 of a military district. He was killed in September 1918 commanding the British 4th Division.

[2] The 8th was known as the Winnipeg Rifles, and the 15th as the 48th Highlanders of Canada.

[3] It will be recalled that only two battalions of the 2nd and one of the 3rd Brigade were in the original front line and apex : the others were on the new north-west front.

[4] See account of German operations in Note at end of Chapter. This brigade is called a composite brigade. Two such brigades seem to have been formed in the *XXVII.* to assist the *XXVI. Reserve Corps.* " Reserve Regiment No. 241 " speaks of " *Regiment Reussner* ", formed of two battalions of the *241st Reserve Regiment* and one of the *242nd* of the *53rd Reserve Division.* " Reserve Regiment No. 245 ", p. 29, mentions " *Regi-*" *ment Heygendorff*," formed of battalions of the *245th, 246th* and *247th Reserve Regiments* of the *54th Reserve Division*, and allotted to " *Brigade* " *Schmieden* ", which, " Reserve Regiment No. 242 ", p. 21, says was formed from units of the *53rd Reserve Division* to support the *51st.* The front of the *XXVII. Reserve Corps* was evidently combed bare to provide reinforcements.

[5] Some German accounts call it a composite brigade, some the *102nd Reserve Brigade.*

[6] This farm, which is often mentioned in the fighting of the 24th-26th April, was on the flat top of Gravenstafel ridge, one thousand yards west of Gravenstafel. It is shown on the sketches as " Bo ". It was known during the battle as " Farm at centre of D.8 ", or as " 8th Battalion headquarters ".

panies at Locality C, and two half-companies behind the Keerselare front.

Against the gas cloud, which came on rapidly like a fog bank, 15 feet high, from trenches on the same level only 100 to 200 yards off in the case of the 15th Battalion, and 200 to 300 yards away and on a slightly higher level in the case of the 8th Battalion, the Canadians had no protection but handkerchiefs, towels and cotton bandoliers wetted with water or any liquid available in the trenches.[1] Breathing with the mouth thus covered was most difficult, and great was the temptation to tear off the damp rags during the ten minutes that the gas flow lasted. Many men were overcome by the fumes, and collapsed, but the majority of those affected, the left (two-thirds) of the 8th Battalion, and three-quarters of the 15th, succeeded in manning the parapet and beating off the enemy. In spite of the complete surprise, only on the front of two platoons of the 15th did he eventually succeed in penetrating. This battalion, after close fighting and having all its eleven officers in the front line killed or taken prisoner, fell back to its second line, the old French trenches westward of Locality C. The two platoons of the 15th on the left alongside the company of the Buffs at the apex remained holding out. The 8th Battalion, too, on the right, stuck

---

[1] Respirators had been recommended, but as none could be expected from home for several days, divisions had set about making them for themselves. Only small quantities of the muslin, flannel, gauze and elastic required could be obtained locally, and officers were despatched to Paris to purchase material, which was made up in the small towns near the front. One division records it employed 17 French women with sewing machines ; another had lint bandages made in the convent at Poperinghe ; many were made in Hazebrouck. Some of these went up with the rations, but only on the evening of the 24th. The manufacture naturally took some time, and the troops were not all equipped with improvised respirators before May. On 26th April an experimental laboratory was organized at G.H.Q., and between 27th and 29th Professors Watson, Haldane and Baker arrived. The respirators, with gauze veiling for the eyes, at first found favour, and the " Daily Mail " called on the women of England to make a million. In the first week in May Major Cluny McPherson, Newfoundland Medical Corps, working with Professor Watson, sent to the War Office a sample helmet consisting of a bag of flannel with celluloid window, impregnated with a suitable solution. This type was considered greatly superior to the respirator, but as no supplies of it could come along until June, the manufacture of respirators was continued as a temporary measure. By 6th July the whole army was equipped with the bag, or, as it was called, " smoke helmet ". By November an improved pattern, the well-known " P " tube helmet, had been introduced. Between August and November 1916 the " small box respirator " was issued in succession to Armies. Special patterns for heavy artillery, anti-aircraft gunners, etc., were also prepared. Improvements in details to meet new gases devised by the enemy continued to be made until the end of the war.

24 April. to its position with the greatest gallantry, in spite of the effects of the gas and of the German attempts to bomb up its trenches from those captured from the 15th Battalion. It even drove back the bombers and recovered for a time part of the lost ground.

By 5 A.M. wounded and gassed men of the 15th Battalion were streaming past the rear of the 7th Battalion on the north-western face; but news of the gas attack had preceded them. At 4.30 A.M. Br.-General R. E. W. Turner (3rd Canadian Brigade), having no reserves, recalled the 10th and 16th Battalions (each only about two hundred men strong after their losses on the night of the 22nd/ 23rd) from Kitchener's Wood, directing the 2nd Battalion to relieve them. But these reinforcements could not arrive in time to help the threatened front, and they were eventually directed, the 10th Battalion to Locality C — it actually took position in the French trenches immediately west of that place, the survivors of the 15th being on its left—and the 16th to G.H.Q. Line, where half the 3rd Battalion already waited.

Little artillery support could be given to the 3rd Canadian Brigade, except by the II. Canadian Artillery Brigade—co-operating with the 2nd Canadian Brigade— which at ranges from 3,500 to 3,800 yards, was greatly instrumental in breaking up the attacks against both the 2nd and 3rd Canadian Brigades; and by the 122nd Heavy Battery at Frezenberg, which did yeoman service until the afternoon, when, the only infantry in front of it being German, it was withdrawn. The III. Canadian Artillery Brigade south of St. Jean, and the I. and other artillery units west of the canal were out of range, but in the course of the day parts of the I. and XX. Brigades R.F.A. of the 27th Division and XXI. and CXLVI. of the 28th, east of Ypres, gave assistance to the Canadian Division.

The Germans who had followed up the gas, stricken by fire they had not expected, paused and left the next move to their comrades on their right opposite the north-western face, whilst the shell of their heavy artillery pursued the retiring Canadians and pounded those still in position. The first onslaught on the north-western side, however, was heavily defeated by the fire of the 122nd Heavy Battery and of the 13th, 7th, 3rd and 2nd Canadians and the Buffs, who had a splendid target and took heavy toll, as some of the enemy—believed to be the *Marine Brigade*—came on over practically level ground in comparatively close formation. Towards 7 A.M. the 24 April. Germans accentuated their efforts on the north-western face between the apex and Kitchener's Wood. For a considerable time, however, this face held, although the Highlanders of the 13th Battalion were not only heavily attacked in front, but threatened in rear by the enemy, who had now pushed on through the gap left by the 15th Battalion. Eventually Major Buchanan [1] rightly judged that he must withdraw his men or be surrounded, and towards 9 A.M. ordered a retirement to the reserve line westwards of Locality C, where the remnant of the 15th Battalion was establishing itself, [2] and where his men would at any rate partly fill the gap between it and the 7th Battalion still in position. This retirement was carried out under heavy fire of all kinds, the 13th losing over half its strength. The order to retire unfortunately failed to reach Tomlinson's company of the Buffs and the two platoons of the 15th with it in the apex. Left isolated, they held out until after 9 A.M. when, with ammunition exhausted and most of the men wounded, they were surrounded and captured.

There was now a gap in the front from the left of the 8th Battalion, south-westwards to Locality C, a distance of nearly fifteen hundred yards; and there was little at first to defend it except cross fire, for the only infantry available to fill it was the company at Boetleer's Farm, the sole reserve of the 2nd Brigade.

The first news of the break in the front of the 3rd Brigade reached the Canadian Division headquarters at 6 A.M. in a message from the 2nd Brigade, timed 5.15 A.M., which said that the Germans had entered the 15th Battalion trenches with the assistance of gas and were working down them, but that the 8th Battalion had the situation in hand. At 6.30 A.M. the same brigade reported that the Germans had broken through to its left. It was not until 7.20 A.M. that General Alderson received a definite message from the G.O.C. 3rd Brigade that his right battalion (15th) was retiring, and that he had ordered the garrison of St. Julien (one company each of the 14th and 15th Battalions) to move out and counter-attack. This was confirmed by a message thrice repeated reporting the front broken, and

---

[1] Major V. C. Buchanan was killed on the Somme in command of the 13th Battalion.

[2] The losses of the 15th in the period 22nd-24th were 17 officers and 674 other ranks.

24 April. asking for support, as there were no reserves. At 7.40 A.M., therefore, General Alderson ordered two battalions (4/East Yorkshire and 4/Green Howards) of the 150th (York and Durham) Brigade (Br.-General J. E. Bush) from the canal bank to man the G.H.Q. Line athwart the Poelcappelle—Wieltje and Fortuin—Wieltje roads, in support of the 2nd and 3rd Brigades. An hour later he ordered the other two battalions of the 150th, then with the 13th Brigade, to rejoin their headquarters, with a view to the 150th Brigade relieving the 3rd Canadian Brigade.

The V. Corps heard of the break in the line, announced by the 7.20 A.M. message, at 7.40 A.M., but received no further definite news until 11.33 A.M., when the 27th Division reported that the Canadians were now holding from the original left of the 8th Battalion to Locality C, and thence to St. Julien and Kitchener's Wood—a sufficiently alarming message. General Plumer at once issued orders to the Canadian Division to take instant action to reconstitute the line. A quarter of an hour later the bad news seemed to be confirmed by the Canadian Division reporting that the two battalions of the 150th Brigade sent up to G.H.Q. Line were about to be used to counter-attack from St. Julien. General Plumer had by this time placed the 151st Brigade under the Cavalry Corps, which (less the 2nd Cavalry Division, at General Alderson's disposal since 3.30 A.M.) was then guarding the left flank west of the canal. The only other troops under his hand, the 10th and 149th Brigades, were still en route; thus he could do nothing more for the present to help the Canadians except to promise them the 10th Brigade when it arrived, should the reports that the 3rd Canadian Brigade was driven back on St. Julien prove correct, as they turned out to be.

SECOND PHASE : THE RENEWED ATTACK ON THE CANADIAN LINE AND LEFT FLANK :—LOCALITY C TO KITCHENER'S WOOD, 9 A.M. TO NOON

There was now a distinct pause in the action, due to the heavy losses of the German infantry and to the confusion of units resulting from a convergent attack. It was not until towards 11 A.M. that the enemy, having heralded his advance by heavy artillery fire which should have annihilated all opposition—for neither guns nor ammunition were lacking—again proceeded to close. Now in open formation, but still from two sides, he attacked the second Canadian position—a rough semi-circle passing 24 April. from Locality C towards the northern end of St. Julien, whence it ran in a large zigzag to Kitchener's Wood. His attack from the north-west up the valley of the Steenbeek towards St. Julien again waited until the northern one was under way.

There were now no reserves in the 3rd Canadian Brigade, except two platoons of the 7th Battalion east of St. Julien, and two of the 3rd Battalion west of it. As no reinforcements were appearing, the commanders of the 7th (Major V. W. Odlum), 14th (Lieut.-Colonel W. W. Burland) [1] and 15th (Lieut.-Colonel J. A. Currie), separated from their brigadier, met at the cross roads between Locality C and St. Julien, and decided to evacuate the exposed position on the western end and forward slope of Gravenstafel ridge, and "to take up position covering "Fortuin,[2] with left on St. Julien and right on Locality "C, and to hold that line until the situation could be "cleared up, reinforcements received and situation re-"established ".

The retirement of what may be called the right half of the 3rd Canadian Brigade began shortly after 11 A.M., the troops on the left edge of the semi-circle north of St. Julien moving first, heavily pressed by the Germans. Eastward of them the companies, in groups and small parties, disputed every yard of ground as they went back, utilizing every piece of cover and the remains of the old trenches constructed during "First Ypres ". The German account speaks of the stout resistance offered, particularly near Keerselare.[3] But no sooner did the Canadians make a pause in their retirement than 5·9-inch howitzer

[1] He was second in command ; the commanding officer, Lieut.-Colonel F. S. Meighen, had been placed in command of the troops in G.H.Q. Line.

[2] "Fortuin " here means the cross roads a thousand yards south-east of St. Julien. The name which comes into prominence in these days was during the battle generally used as a topographical expression to mean the area across which the name is written on the map, where there is a slight rise of ground, between the western end of Zonnebeke ridge and the Steenbeek south of St. Julien. It was of importance as commanding the Haanebeek valley east of St. Julien, and the eastern and southern exits from that village. There were a few houses on the roads which bound it on the south-west and south-east, which were known locally as Fortuinhoek (Fortuin Corner). Spree Farm, the original headquarters of the 2nd Canadian Brigade, was at the southern corner of the Fortuin area. It was destroyed by fire at 6 A.M., when headquarters were moved to Bank Farm, two hundred yards away.

[3] Captain E. D. Bellew, machine-gun officer of the 7th Canadian Battalion, received the Victoria Cross for conspicuous bravery and devotion to duty in the defence of Keerselare.

24 April. fire, directed by balloon and aeroplane observers, found them out. All approaches, roads, headquarters and localities, too, were bombarded with guns of larger calibre, shells falling even as far back as V. Corps headquarters in Poperinghe. Such was the position of vantage of the enemy round the Ypres Salient that he could fire from any point of the compass from north to south round by east, with equal facility and nearly perfect observation. There was relatively little to reply with. The heavy artillery with the whole V. Corps comprised only two batteries of old 6-inch howitzers and three batteries of equally obsolete 4·7-inch guns. This meagre artillery support was increased during the day by the arrival of a 9·2-inch howitzer of the 12th Siege Battery and the 108th Heavy Battery (60-pdrs.), which, under V. Corps control, took up position in a wood north-west of Vlamertinghe, the 9·2 being ordered to fire on important cross roads.[1]

Artillery ammunition, too, was very short, the allotment at the time being about three rounds per day per piece ; but this restriction was unheeded, and the batteries fired what they could procure.[2] The ammunition columns of the 27th, 28th and Canadian Divisions accomplished marvels in getting up filled wagons along the shelled roads into the fire zone.

It was now largely due to the assistance given by the artillery—in spite of its small numbers and ammunition difficulties, and in spite of the enemy's fire—that the enemy was prevented from pushing through the shattered front of the 3rd Canadian Brigade. Into the gap between the left of the 2nd Canadian Brigade and Locality C, and forming virtually its sole defence, fired—in addition to the

---

[1] It fired an average of 30 rounds a day for seven days, and then was out of action for a time on account of mounting defects.

[2] The precise ammunition allotment at the time per gun per day in the Second Army was :—13-pdr., 2 ; 18-pdr., 3 (no H.E. available) ; 4·5-inch howitzer, 3 (1 may be lyddite) ; 4·7-inch, 10 (no lyddite available) ; 6-inch howitzer, 3 (1 may be H.E.).

The actual daily average expenditure during the battles 22nd April to 14th May, according to the records of four divisional artilleries, was :—

	18-pdr. Shrapnel.	H.E.	4·5 inch how. H.E.
27th Division	42·3	16·8	23·3
28th ,, ...	43·5	24·2	8·8
Canadian Division (to 4th May only)	69·7	84·0	17·1
4th Division (from 5th May only)	26·7	10·7	6·2

The 7th Battery C.F.A., whose records are available, fired an average of 248·6 per gun per day during the first five days ; the other batteries of the II. Brigade probably fired a like amount.

122nd Heavy Battery at Frezenberg—the 37th Howitzer 24 April. Battery, pushed up north of Frezenberg,[1] and a section of the 6th Battery C.F.A., with a company of the 8/Middlesex as escort. This last went in even closer, on to Zonnebeke ridge, where it eventually fired over open sights at ranges down to about fifteen hundred yards until it had expended all its ammunition. After it had withdrawn, other sections from the 366th and 367th Batteries (CXLVI. Brigade R.F.A., 28th Division) were brought up. This artillery fire, combined with the fine defence of Locality C, kept the enemy in check, and, as could be seen, caused him very heavy losses.

At 11.35 A.M. General Alderson heard of the retirement of the right of the 3rd Canadian Brigade and of the Germans being on the western end of Gravenstafel ridge. Convinced of the importance of holding on till the 10th Brigade arrived he at once placed the two battalions of the 150th Brigade sent to G.H.Q. Line [2]—the only fresh troops he had in hand—at Br.-General Turner's disposal to counter-attack with energy and stop the enemy. Before these instructions could take effect, a large force of enemy mounted troops and infantry, followed by artillery, was reported by artillery observers to be moving south from Poelcappelle on St. Julien.[3] The order to the two York and Durham battalions was therefore countermanded, and they were sent—being shelled as they marched up—to help the survivors of the 3rd Canadian Brigade organize a front and dig in covering St. Julien.[4] Hitherto, good shooting had stopped the attacks of the German infantry which, after repeated efforts, had desisted to await the result of further artillery bombardment ; but should enemy reinforcements be thrown in at this crisis, as now

[1] This battery—the first howitzer battery of the modern British army, having taken part as such in the Khartum and South African campaigns—when in the 5th Division, had greatly distinguished itself in 1914 at Le Cateau and the Marne. Transferred to the 28th Division, it was on 24th April 1915 with the XXXI. Brigade R.F.A., supporting the 84th Brigade, whilst the CXLVI. Brigade R.F.A. and a Canadian battery supported the 85th Brigade, the artillery having been redistributed to meet the new situation.

[2] The other two battalions of the 150th were still near the canal under the 13th Brigade ; the 149th (Northumberland) Brigade was in Army reserve at Vlamertinghe ; and the 151st (Durham L.I.) Brigade had been attached at 11 A.M. to Allenby's Cavalry Corps.

[3] A mixed column, estimated at a regiment of infantry with some guns, was reported later by an air observer as moving into Poelcappelle from the north-west.

[4] For this, as it proved, they were too late, and by Br.-General Bush's orders they went no further than Potijze.

24 **April.** seemed likely, the effect might well be disastrous. Although the flanks of the breach were still holding, the situation seemed so serious that the G.O.C. 3rd Canadian Brigade, in a telephone conversation at 1 P.M. with General Alderson's Chief General Staff Officer, Colonel C. F. Romer, contemplated the advisability of abandoning St. Julien and the low-lying ground near it, and putting his battalions into G.H.Q. Line, previously notified as the reserve position. Here, besides the companies detailed, many stragglers had already established themselves.

The convenience of the headquarters of the 27th Division at Potijze for command of the new front from St. Julien to the canal was now so evident that a suggestion was made at Second Army headquarters to place General Snow in command of this sector ; but the idea was not acted on, as it was thought that his own division and front would require too much of his attention. At 9 A.M., however, General Plumer had given him command of all troops in corps reserve in the vicinity of Potijze ; and empowered him to use his discretion in employing them to meet unexpected local developments, if communication with V. Corps headquarters happened to be—as it frequently was—interrupted. Thus General Snow was at times responsible for the employment of the corps reserves behind the Canadian Division. Fortunately, he was an old subordinate of General Alderson, and his action when telephone communication was broken was generally in complete consonance with the latter's views. At the time when the right of the 3rd Canadian Brigade retired to the line Locality C—St. Julien and the Germans appeared on the western end of Gravenstafel ridge, there was no corps reserve near Potijze, and General Snow could do no more than send Br.-General Turner his own divisional reserve, the 1/Royal Irish—it had only 356 men in the ranks—which he directed to make good Fortuin, and stop the Germans from coming on. This battalion, which had been brought up from Hooge woods at 9 A.M., moved from Potijze at noon in artillery formation, and after advancing a quarter of a mile came under heavy shell fire, which increased after it passed through the G.H.Q. Line near Wieltje, where it deployed into two lines. It then moved on to the rise of ground north of the Fortuin cross roads angle, receiving fire at a range of six hundred yards from the outskirts of St. Julien, possession of which, as will now be related, was about to pass to the enemy.

THIRD PHASE : THE LOSS OF THE TRENCHES COVERING
ST. JULIEN, AND THE RETIREMENT OF THE 3RD
CANADIAN BRIGADE TO THE G.H.Q. LINE

NOON TO MIDNIGHT

Towards noon, after nearly an hour's bombardment, 24 April.
another effort to push on had been made by the Germans.
They continued their converging attack towards St. Julien
both from the north against the right half of the 3rd
Canadian Brigade and from north-west up the Steenbeek
valley past Kitchener's Wood against the left of that
force. About 12.30 P.M., the commanders of the 10th
(Major D. M. Ormond), 14th and 15th Canadian Battalions
met a quarter of a mile to the south-west of the previous
place of conference. The shelling and machine-gun fire
on the new line, exposed on the flat ground between
Gravenstafel ridge and St. Julien, was now very heavy,
and the 1/Royal Irish had not yet appeared. From where
they stood the three battalion commanders could see
that, on the left flank, an attack was developing from
Kitchener's Wood, and they now received a report,
erroneous as it turned out, that on the right flank the 2nd
Brigade beyond the gap was retiring. Knowing Br.-
General Turner's determination to hold his ground until
fresh troops gave relief, these officers considered whether
a counter-attack should be ordered ; but, in view of the
situation on their flanks, they decided that a further withdrawal of about a thousand yards as far as the Gravenstafel
—Wieltje road was unavoidable. It was none too soon,
for by 12.45 P.M. the enemy had secured the trenches
immediately covering St. Julien, and their defenders of
the 14th and 15th Battalions were beginning to retire
through the village. With the remainder of the right
wing of Turner's brigade they fell back in parties and
small groups to a line just north of the Gravenstafel—
Wieltje road. Warden's company of the 7th Battalion,
however, in Locality C, reinforced by a small party of
the 2nd Canadian Field Company, continued to hold on,
and, having a good field of fire, kept the enemy at bay.[1]
At 1.40 P.M. Br.-General Turner accepted that the
retirement of his right was inevitable, and that his left
must conform. He issued orders to the whole of the 3rd

[1] They remained until about 4 P.M., when, reduced to one officer
(wounded) and 37 men, they were withdrawn via Fortuin.

24 April. Canadian Brigade and attached battalions to occupy the
G.H.Q. Line covering Wieltje, the next defensible position
once the ground north-east of St. Julien was lost. Although
most of it faced east, even south of east, it was the only
solidly prepared line of defence between the original front
and the canal, and he had been directed to hold it at all
costs. His brigade would then prolong to the right the
line already held round Mouse Trap Farm. The right wing
of his force east of St. Julien, however, having come to
the independent decision to drop back straight to the
Gravenstafel—Wieltje road, remained there : and the men
of the 7th and 10th Battalions rallied on its right at the
cross roads immediately south of Fortuin, covering the
temporary headquarters of the 2nd Brigade.

Unfortunately the order for the retirement of the left
wing (2nd and 3rd Battalions) which had been successfully
holding up the enemy west of St. Julien did not reach all
detachments, or came too late for some to comply. Two
companies of the 3rd Battalion, under Major A. J. E.
Kirkpatrick, between St. Julien and Kitchener's Wood
were engaged in successfully holding back the enveloping
attack of the composite brigade of the *XXVI. Reserve Corps*
up the line of the Steenbeek. With six hundred yards of
flat open ground behind them swept by machine-gun and
rifle fire from two sides, it seemed better to stand fast and
kill Germans than to be shot down whilst retiring. So
they fought on. Their action further delayed the enemy
very seriously, but in the evening, of the two companies
only 43 survivors could be mustered, nearly every one
wounded and two totally blind. St. Julien, the houses
being defended by men of the various battalions, held out
for a time, and the Germans did not occupy it until 3 P.M.[1]
From this hour onwards batteries in a position to do so
received orders to fire on St. Julien. Now, as he did on
obtaining possession of Gheluvelt in 1914, the enemy
paused, and, until about 4.30 P.M. when a patrol was seen,
no hostile troops came south of the village.

On the right of the gap the 5th (Western Cavalry)
and 8th (Winnipeg Rifles) Battalions of the 2nd Canadian
Brigade still held their original front, with no infantry

---

[1] According to German accounts, the troops of the northern attack
entered St. Julien at 3 P.M., those from the west at 5 P.M. Rumour, as
will be seen, persisted through the night and early morning of the 25th,
that there were still Canadians in St. Julien ; but for this there seems no
foundation.

between them and Locality C but two platoons of the 24 April.
8th in the French trenches north of Boetleer's Farm. The
defence of this space was maintained by machine-gun and
rifle cross fire and artillery fire. The two battalions had
a covering order from Br.-General Currie to retire to
Gravenstafel if the situation demanded, after informing the
85th Brigade ; but Lieut.-Colonel Lipsett, after consultation with Lieut.-Colonel Tuxford, decided that every effort
must be made to hold on until counter-attack recovered
the ground lost on his left and covered his open flank.[1]

The defence on this side of the battlefield was so successful in holding the enemy back that all three divisional
commanders concerned assumed that the front of the 2nd
Brigade was more or less continuous to Locality C, and
that, St. Julien being lost, the danger spot was Fortuin
—St. Julien, against which, as is now known, the German
effort was actually directed with a view to reaching Zonnebeke ridge. General Snow, as representative of General
Plumer in the salient—all communication by wire being
at the time interrupted—felt it necessary to act. There
were no V. Corps or 27th Division reserves at Potijze, and,
apart from troops in G.H.Q. Line, the nearest reserves
were those of the 28th Division, the 1/Suffolk and 12/London
(Rangers), close to Frezenberg and Verlorenhoek behind
the Zonnebeke front.[2] There was no time to obtain General
Bulfin's consent, although he had detailed a liaison officer
to 27th Division headquarters to facilitate mutual assistance. So in the stress of circumstances General Snow
took the extreme course of using the reserves of the 28th
Division, and sent orders to Lieut.-Colonel W. B. Wallace
of the Suffolks to take the two battalions to Fortuin and
counter-attack any Germans met on the way.[3] He gave
him two companies of the 8/Middlesex as reserve, and
directed the 2/Gloucestershire of his own division, away in
support in Sanctuary Wood, to come to Potijze, where it
arrived between 3 and 4 P.M.[4] At the same time—2.15 P.M.

[1] Company-Sergeant-Major F. W. Hall of the 8th Canadian Battalion,
mortally wounded in a second attempt under heavy fire to reach a wounded
man who was calling for help, was awarded the Victoria Cross posthumously.
[2] They had been relieved in the line by the 2/Cheshire and 1/Monmouth-
shire on the night of the 23rd/24th.
[3] This was entirely in consonance with the views of General Alderson,
who later sent his divisional cyclists to assist in holding Fortuin.
[4] As soon as the 151st (Durham L.I.) Brigade reached him in the
evening, General Snow sent the 2/Shropshire L.I., his last available 27th
Division battalion, and the 8/Durham L.I. to replace the two battalions
he had commandeered from General Bulfin.

24 April. —as the senior officer on the spot, General Snow called on Br.-General Turner to move every man he had to stop any enemy advance via Fortuin at all costs ; notified him that he had the Royal Irish at his disposal ; and directed him to take command in this part of the field.[1]   At 2.30 P.M. General Alderson again urged the 2nd and 3rd Brigades to hold their trenches, as help was on the way, and by 3 P.M., from his reserve near Brielen Bridge, had sent up to Wieltje and St. Jean to support Br.-General Turner the 4th Battalion of the 1st Canadian Brigade, and the 2/K.O.Y.L.I. and Queen Victoria's Rifles of the 13th Brigade.   To Geddes's Detachment he returned the half of the 3/Middlesex which had been guarding the bridges. These battalions marched up under heavy shell fire, as every road was marked by the enemy, and those of the 13th Brigade found the G.H.Q. Line so crowded that they lay out in the open behind it.   For them and other re-inforcements that now arrived in the area there was no cover except such shallow trenches as they could dig for themselves.   By this time the two battalions of the 150th Brigade, the 4th East Yorkshire (Lieut.-Colonel G. H. Shaw) and 4th Green Howards (Lieut.-Colonel M. H. L. Bell) had been assembled near Potijze.   En route, and whilst there, " they received a good many different " orders ".   Br.-General Currie (2nd Canadian Brigade), among others, personally appealed to Br.-General Bush to use them to counter-attack northwards from east of Fortuin, but the latter pointed out that the order to counter-attack

---

[1] 27th Division to 3rd Canadian Brigade, 2.15 P.M., but not received until 4.05 P.M. :—
    " Enemy advance from Fortuin must be stopped at all costs.   You " must move every man you have got to drive him back.   I have directed " two battalions under O.C. Suffolks from Frezenberg against Fortuin. " I am also sending you up the Royal Irish Regiment from here, and " have directed them on cross roads in C.23.c [¼ mile north-east of Wieltje]. " You will get in touch with these troops and take command in that part " of the field and drive enemy north-eastwards.   I am issuing these " orders as I am on the spot and communication appears to be dislocated " and time is of the highest importance.   Act with vigour ".
    General Alderson, on the 27th Division message to the 3rd Canadian Brigade coming to his knowledge at 4.35 P.M., backed it up by the following message :
    " There are in and around Wieltje four battalions York and Durham " Brigade, the Yorks Light Infantry and the Q.V.R. of the 13th Brigade " and part of the 4th Battalion.   With these troops you must make head " against the Germans.   You must push troops up into your front line " and prevent at all costs the Germans breaking through between you and " the 2nd C.I. Bde.   I have no exact knowledge of your situation at the " present moment, but hope that you are still blocking St. Julien and in " close touch with the 2nd C.I. Bde.".

had been cancelled.   About 3 P.M. a staff officer of the
27th Division appeared, and from him the battalions
obtained orders similar to those given to the Royal Irish :—
to make Fortuin good and stop the Germans who were
in St. Julien and probably advancing.   Thus the number
of battalions directed on Fortuin now amounted to five.
But they were not destined to act together.   Although
Br.-General Turner got in touch with the Royal Irish, he
was not to have the services of Colonel Wallace's detachment, which had been diverted, nor of the Yorkshire
battalions, which operated independently.

Wallace's battalions, the Suffolks now under Captain
D. V. M. Balders, had advanced under very heavy shell
fire to make good and hold Fortuin.   But the right wing
of the 3rd Canadian Brigade was now carrying out its
orders to retire from the Gravenstafel—Wieltje road to
the G.H.Q. Line, and, just before reaching Fortuin,
Wallace was further instructed by a staff officer to move
at once north-eastward to cover the flank of the 2nd
Canadian Brigade.   Assured—in error—that St. Julien
was held, and guided by the staff officer himself, the
battalions made the attempt to reach Gravenstafel ridge,
and actually got as far as the Zonnebeke—Keerselare road.
There they were stopped by heavy fire, part undoubtedly
due to British artillery, which had not been warned that
troops were entering the area.   The Suffolks who were
leading lost 280 of all ranks, Lieut.-Colonel A. D. Bayliffe
of the Rangers was amongst the wounded, and sixty of
his battalion were casualties.   Being now eastward of
St. Julien, whence fire was also being received, a portion
of the force was turned to face that way.   Nevertheless,
on an appeal for help from the 2nd Canadian Brigade, two
companies of the Suffolks, under Lieut. S. Bradley, were
despatched eastward to Boetleer's Farm,[1] whither also the
remnants of the 7th and 10th Battalions, about two
hundred strong, were sent from Fortuin cross roads by
Br.-General Currie.

About the time that Colonel Wallace's battalions turned
north-eastward from Fortuin towards Gravenstafel ridge,

[1] It was at first decided to send one company, but all were so weak
that it was thought necessary to detail two—totalling 150 men.   It is
typical of the straits to which battalions had been reduced, and by no means
extraordinary, that a lieutenant of $3\frac{1}{2}$ years' service should be the senior
officer of a half-battalion.   Lieut. Bradley was killed a month later, on
25th May, and no officer or N.C.O. of these two companies of the 1/Suffolk
survived the war.

24 April. the 4/Green Howards and the 4/East Yorkshire of the 150th Brigade, at full strength and in marching order, were arriving at Fortuin. At the cross roads they found, and drove off, a few Germans with a machine gun. Then, seeing other Germans in force advancing southwards out of St. Julien, Lieut.-Colonel Bell changed the front of the Green Howards quarter left towards them, and, Lieut.-Colonel Shaw having been killed, took command of both battalions, and attacked. Assisted greatly by two sections of the 5th and 6th Canadian Batteries (II. Brigade C.F.A.)—which fired over open sights into Germans, of the western attack, approaching deployed from Kitchener's Wood, at about a thousand yards' range—by other guns of Lieut.-Colonel J. J. Creelman's II. Brigade C.F.A. and by Colonel G. R. T. Rundle's CXLVI. Brigade R.F.A. (28th Division), which were in action against St. Julien, the Green Howards and East Yorkshire, coming up past the left of the Royal Irish, drove the enemy back on the village till their foremost lines were stopped by the muddy channel of the Haanebeek, which was under rifle and machine-gun fire. After losing heavily from this and German heavy shell fire directed on friend and foe alike, the two Yorkshire battalions were ordered to desist. But the counter-attack had completely effected its purpose, and the Germans made no further attempt to advance on the 24th, again, like the captors of Gheluvelt on the 31st October 1914, when the 2/Worcestershire and Colonel Lovett's detachment counter-attacked, abandoning their conquest.[1]

Soon after this success a strong patrol of the Buffs was sent from G.H.Q. Line towards St. Julien to get in touch, if possible, with Captain Tomlinson's missing company. It came in contact with Germans, and drove them from some outlying buildings; but, although it remained out until 2 A.M., it did not succeed in picking up any British troops.

At night Colonel Bell's two battalions of the York and Durham Brigade, and the Royal Irish, were returned to the reserve at Potijze. The remaining 1½ battalions of Colonel Wallace's detachment—the London Rangers and half of the Suffolks—were withdrawn from their exposed position to a line a little in front of the Gravenstafel—

---

[1] See "1914" Volume II. pp. 328-331.

The German account (see Note at end of Chapter) states that troops of the *51st Reserve Division* were expelled from St. Julien by a counter-attack about 5.50 P.M., and withdrew to the ridge on the north overlooking St. Julien.

Fortuin road, where they dug in. Here they were in the 24 April. centre of the gap between the 2nd Canadian Brigade on the eastern part of the Gravenstafel ridge and the 3rd in G.H.Q. Line in front of Wieltje.

These movements ended the operations near Fortuin on the western side of the gap. On the eastern side as the day drew to a close the 85th Brigade of the 28th Division was called on to help the 5th and 8th Canadian Battalions, Lieut.-Colonels Tuxford and Lipsett being in constant communication with Major A. V. Johnson of the 3/Royal Fusiliers on their right. The latter was hard pressed himself. The last troops available in the 28th Division, two half companies of the 8/Middlesex, with the Anglesey Siege Company, R.E., already sent to him, had been detailed to dig a line to cover his left, as a precaution in case the Canadian battalions were forced to retire. He suggested calling for help from a detachment of the 28th Division engaged in entrenching on his left rear. This party consisted of one and a half companies of the 2/Northumberland Fusiliers, two companies of the 2/Cheshire and a company of the 1/Monmouthshire of the 84th Brigade, under Major E. M. Moulton-Barrett of the Northumberland Fusiliers. Under 28th Division instructions, it had been sent about 5 P.M., under artillery fire, to dig and hold a line across the Zonnebeke—Langemarck road, south-east of the cross roads between Gravenstafel and Fortuin, as part of a switch line which it was proposed to construct along the Gravenstafel —Fortuin road. At 8.30 P.M., therefore, at the earnest request of Lieut.-Colonel Lipsett, Major Moulton-Barrett moved his men forward, and took up position on the Canadian left, extending the line formed by Lieut. Bradley's Suffolks south-south-west from Boetleer's Farm. The remnants of the 7th and 10th Battalions, under Major Odlum, came up later from the Fortuin cross roads and continued the line westwards to the Haanebeek, and the two half companies of the 8/Middlesex, released by Major Johnson, arrived at Boetleer's Farm. But even as late as 10.30 P.M., there was so much rifle and machine-gun fire up the Stroombeek valley—from a German line formed across it, with its right flank near Locality C— that an attempt by the Monmouthshire company to re-inforce the left of the 8th Canadians completely failed. Nevertheless the line on the right of the gap still held fast.

The Despatch of Further Reinforcements

24 April. During the afternoon various reinforcements for the Canadian Division had been set in motion. At 3.25 p.m. General Plumer ordered his reserve, the 149th (Northumberland) Brigade, now arrived at Brandhoek (between Vlamertinghe and Poperinghe), to Potijze, with the instructions to General Snow : " It is primarily for the purpose of " repelling any advance on the part of the enemy from the " north and north-east. I place it under your orders as " it will be close to you, and if communication is cut and " you cannot refer to me, you will use the brigade at your " discretion ". In consequence of a message from the Second Army, General Snow was informed a little later by telegram that he was " to make every effort to restore the " situation where the Germans are reported to have " broken through ". This, as we know, he had already done. The 149th Brigade marched at 6 p.m. and arrived at Potijze at 10.30 p.m. Soon after orders had been sent to it, General Smith-Dorrien, by direction of G.H.Q., placed all the infantry of the 50th Division under the V. Corps. General Plumer then ordered the remaining brigade, the 151st (Durham L.I.) at Vlamertinghe, to General Snow on the same terms as the 149th. It moved forward at 5 p.m., and reached Potijze between 7 and 10 p.m.[1] The arrival of these very fine Territorial troops, ready to go anywhere and do anything, did much to hearten the troops with whom they came in contact, and their subsequent help and sacrifices were gratefully acknowledged by their Regular comrades.

The 10th Brigade (Br.-General C. P. A. Hull),[2] ordered north to General Smith-Dorrien from the 4th Division of the III. Corps, concentrated near Vlamertinghe by 3 p.m., and after moving half-way towards Ypres, with a view to relieving Geddes's Detachment, was directed to wait until midnight before proceeding further.

The Arrangements for Hull's Attack

The situation obviously required the most serious consideration, as apart from the probable movements of the

---

[1] Of its four battalions, the 8/Durham L.I. was sent to the 85th Brigade, the left of the 28th Division ; the 6th relieved part of the Shropshire L.I., which was covering Potijze, so that the latter battalion could be lent to the 28th Division ; the 7th and 9th bivouacked near Potijze.

[2] Died as Major-General Sir C. P. A. Hull, K.C.B., 24th July 1920.

enemy, so much depended on the action of the French. 24 April. They had promised to counter-attack and recover the lost ground, which would at once ease the strain upon the British confined, gassed and shelled in the narrowed Salient, where during the day even the 27th Division staff at Potijze had been compelled to go below ground. But there was no sign of the French infantry reinforcements, and not a word of the heavy guns so necessary for even hope of success. The first duty of the British commander on the spot, and General Plumer fully realized it, was to hold on as long as possible to give the French time to restore the very awkward situation which the gas attack on their troops had brought about. If they could do nothing, it might be best for the V. Corps to evacuate what was left of the Salient, which the enemy completely dominated by artillery, and to employ the British reinforcements to drive him off the west bank of the canal, on which he had merely a footing. The future course of operations was, however, settled, for Generals Smith-Dorrien and Plumer, by a message from G.H.Q. timed 4.15 P.M.,[1] carried by a staff officer sent to explain Sir John French's views. It ran: "Every effort must be "made at once to restore and hold the line about St. "Julien, or situation of the 28th Division will be jeopard-"ized ".[2]

General Foch soon after brought Sir John French the information that the 153rd Division was detraining at Cassel, and handed to him an autograph note in which he said, "I am calling up a second infantry division, "which will be in the region of Crombeke (5 miles north

---

[1] Appendix 23.

[2] Sir J. French's views, as subsequently reduced to writing by the C.G.S., in a letter to General Smith-Dorrien, and often reiterated, were :— "He does not wish you to give up any ground if it can be helped, but "if pressure from the north becomes such that the 28th Division *ought* to "fall back from its line, then of course it *must* fall back, for such distance "as circumstances necessitate. But we hope the necessity will not arise. "The Germans must be a bit tired by now, and they are numerically "inferior to us as far as we can judge. In fact, there seems no doubt "about it ".

On the front attacked there were the 85th Brigade, Canadian Division, reserves of the 27th and 28th Divisions, 150th (York and Durham) Brigade, 13th Brigade, a Zouave Brigade, with two more brigades of the 50th (Northumbrian) Division, and the 10th Brigade en route, some 52 battalions in all. Opposite to them were the *51st Reserve* and *52nd Reserve Divisions* ; *2nd Reserve Ersatz, 37th* and *38th Landwehr*, and *4th Marine Brigades* ; *2nd Marine Infantry Regiment, 207th Reserve Infantry Regiment* (*XXII. Reserve Corps*) ; and a *XXVII. Reserve Corps* composite brigade, a total of 62 battalions.

24 April. " by west of Poperinghe) very early to-morrow. It is "important that the British have strong reserves near "Elverdinghe, Ypres and Wieltje at the same time. Start- "ing from these four points and eastward of them, we will "take a vigorous offensive against the front Steenstraat, "Pilckem, Langemarck and east of these places". A letter from the C.G.S. at 6 P.M. therefore further informed General Smith-Dorrien that the French reinforcements would leave him free to employ all his infantry east of the canal.

General Smith-Dorrien repeated G.H.Q. instructions to the V. Corps. He had been in communication with General Putz, urging him to use an infantry brigade that he was holding in reserve at Elverdinghe, and had offered to keep his own last brigade at Brielen at French disposal ; and at 4.15 P.M. he placed General Allenby's Cavalry Corps under General Putz's orders to enable the latter to guard his left flank where the French and Belgians joined. The French commander replied optimistically by telephone to General Smith-Dorrien, and asked no more than artillery assistance when General Allenby visited him to obtain orders for his corps. For the remainder of the battle, therefore, the horse artillery batteries co-operated with the French. But, in spite of General Putz's confidence, British anxiety for the left flank both inside and outside the Salient never ceased.

On receipt of Sir John French's orders for the immediate restoration of the line near St. Julien, General Plumer, at 6.30 P.M. instructed General Alderson to make the strongest counter-attack possible towards that place with the fresh forces placed at his disposal :—the 10th and 150th Brigades and six battalions, or such of them as could be assembled, under a selected commander. For artillery support he was to secure all that was possible from all divisions, under arrangements to be made by the C.R.A. Canadian Division.[1] The hour of attack was left to General Alderson to decide, with the proviso that it should not be delayed any longer than he considered necessary for reconnaissance and preparation, although at 6.30 P.M. there was little daylight left for either. General Alderson thereupon selected Br.-General Hull (10th Brigade) to command the counter-attack ; cancelled the arrangements he had in view for the relief of the 3rd Canadian Brigade and Geddes's

[1] The 123rd was now the only Heavy Battery east of Ypres in the area concerned, the 122nd having been withdrawn west of the canal.

Detachment by the 10th and 150th Brigades; and at 24 April. 8 P.M. issued formal orders for the operation. It was to be launched at 3.30 A.M.,[1] in order that their superior artillery might not avail the Germans. Fortuin, " if " occupied by the enemy ", St. Julien and Kitchener's Wood were to be the first objectives; and the general instructions were to drive the enemy as far north as possible. General Alderson placed at Br.-General Hull's disposal :— the 10th Brigade; 150th Brigade (then partly in front line near St. Julien and partly in reserve); the 2/K.O.Y.L.I. and Queen Victoria's Rifles of the 13th Brigade (lying behind G.H.Q. Line); the 1/Suffolk and the Rangers of Wallace's detachment of the 28th Division (in front line just north of the Gravenstafel—Fortuin road); the 4th Canadian Battalion (in reserve near Potijze), and one battalion (the Royal Irish, now back at Potijze, was selected) to be provided by the 27th Division; that is 15 battalions in all,[2] a total exceeding that of the normal infantry units of a division. Thus, like the 4th Division at Le Cateau, Br.-General Hull had infantry and artillery, but no signal company by which to communicate with them, nor any other divisional troops, and only a brigade staff, strengthened at his request by one officer of the Canadian Division staff.

The night was dark, with heavy rain falling, and the situation at the front was to the last degree obscure. Br.-General Hull and his officers did not know the ground, and as there had been no opportunity by daylight for reconnaissance, he had, like General Alderson, to base his plan on the map. It was by no means certain whether all the 15 battalions detailed in orders for the attack could be found and assembled. In darkness, in an area devastated by fire and intersected by trenches, he could not use gallopers to convey his orders. At the rendezvous near the canal north of Ypres—named by General Alderson for the issue of Br.-General Hull's orders—only Br.-General H. E. Burstall (Canadian Divisional Artillery) and, by mistake, Br.-General J. F. Riddell (149th Brigade) appeared. The arrangements for collecting the commanders, not to say their troops, were doomed to failure from the outset owing to the insufficient time available.[3] Br.-General

---

[1] Appendix 24.

[2] The 7/Argyll and Sutherland Highlanders were attached to the 10th Brigade, and made its fifth battalion.

[3] *E.g.,* General Alderson's operation order of 8 P.M. reached 27th Division headquarters at 11.45 P.M.; the commander of the 1/Royal Irish

24 April. Hull therefore proceeded to Wieltje to try and get in touch with the rest of his force. His brigade, leaving kits behind and using their waterproof sheets as capes to cover themselves from the rain, followed at midnight. They had no gas protection of any kind. On arrival at Wieltje, then still under heavy shell fire, and with many houses burning, he established temporary headquarters in the ruins of a cottage, moving them at 3 A.M. to Mouse Trap Farm, where he remained during the attack. Owing to congestion of traffic on the road, and to there being only two gaps in the wire of G.H.Q. Line through which his brigade and half of the 150th would have to defile, he found that it would be impossible to begin the attack before 5.30 A.M., when it would be light; indeed it seemed that unless extraordinary efforts were made to push the troops along they might not even be through the wire of G.H.Q. Line before daybreak.

Thus the day that had begun with the situation more or less in hand ended in hurry and turmoil and the shadow of defeat. The Canadian salient, Locality C, and St. Julien had been lost, and from lack of information the situation was regarded as more serious, perhaps, than the actual state of affairs deserved. The effect of the counterattacks on the enemy was not known, nor of course could it be guessed that his intention to press forward via St. Julien and Fortuin to Zonnebeke ridge had been frustrated.[1]

At Br.-General Hull's headquarters there was little definite news, and he could not ascertain whether St. Julien had fallen or was still partially held. In a defensive battle when retirements occur, it is difficult enough by daylight and almost impossible in the dark, to establish the position of one's own troops reduced by heavy losses and scattered in small detachments. Even more difficult, however, is it to learn anything of the enemy. Actually at midnight both Fortuin and St. Julien, Br.-General Hull's objectives, were clear of any foe; and the German line five hundred yards north of St. Julien, was not continuous and was open to attack. There were however terrible gaps in the British line. The 5th and 8th Battalions of the 2nd Canadian Brigade, with a flank thrown back, were still holding on, their trenches and shelters crowded with

had to be found, and then he had to ride three miles in the dark over roads pock-marked with shell holes to the rendezvous, which he reached at 12.40 A.M.
[1] See p. 211.

gassed and wounded men. But between them and the 24 April. inner flank of the 3rd Canadian Brigade, 2¾ miles away in the G.H.Q. Line north-east of Wieltje, were only two detachments :—one the mixed force of Bradley's Suffolks, Moulton-Barrett's Northumberland Fusiliers, Cheshire and Monmouthshire and Odlum's Canadians, holding about eight hundred yards near Boetleer's Farm ; the other, Wallace's two battalions, holding about twelve hundred yards along the Gravenstafel road, and not in touch with the troops on either side. The 3rd Canadian Brigade and troops that had reinforced it—survivors of the 2nd, 3rd, 14th and 16th Battalions, eleven hundred in all—were in G.H.Q. Line north of Wieltje, whence Geddes's Detachment carried on the front.

As regards reserves, even for a defensive action the situation was far from satisfactory ; there were 2 brigades of the 50th Division near Potijze, strong in numbers, but never before in action ; the 1st and 4th Battalions of the 1st Canadian Brigade, which had already suffered terribly in the counter-attacks of the 23rd ; the remnants of the 13th and 15th Battalions of the 3rd Brigade near St. Jean ; and two battalions of the battered 13th Brigade behind the G.H.Q. Line. Hope lay in the 10th Brigade, fresh and at war strength, now marching up. The Lahore Division was to move next day from reserve to Vlamertinghe. There was no more heavy artillery either arriving or in view, and, as ever, lack of gun ammunition.

Just before midnight General Plumer correctly appreciated the probable extent of the gap, and ordered the Canadian Division—or, as it should now be called from the number and variety of troops in it, Alderson's Force— to take instant action to establish a line as far forward as possible in the direction of St. Julien and in touch with troops on both flanks. General Alderson therefore sent out one of his staff, Lieut.-Colonel G. C. W. Gordon-Hall, who issued orders for the two battalions (the 1st and 4th) of the 1st Brigade to get in touch with the 2nd Canadian Brigade ; the 150th Brigade (already detailed to Hull's Force) to fill the gap between them and the Haanebeek ; and the 3rd Canadian Brigade to establish its right on that stream. The presence of Wallace's detachment was not known to him.

Work was commenced at this time on various switch lines in order to hold up a break-through of the front line. During the morning of the 24th General Alderson

24 April. had directed a line of farms to be put in a state of defence, beginning on the left near Brielen bridge, and running to connect with the G.H.Q. Line east of Wieltje. In the 27th Division area, a switch was prepared from Hooge northwards on the reverse slopes of Verlorenhoek ridge to G.H.Q. Line south of Wieltje ; in the 28th Division a line along the Gravenstafel—Fortuin road, as already mentioned, had been begun ; whilst, to protect the right of the V. Corps, the Second Army ordered the G.H.Q. Line to be continued southwards from Zillebeke Lake.

The progress of the French on the 24th had been negligible, but they had not lost more ground, and on the British left they had completely taken over the sector of the line between Pilckem road and the canal, and established firm touch with the Belgians on their left. During the night news came in that the French had retaken Lizerne, but this was afterwards contradicted. General Codet's men had made an entry, but had been driven out.

NOTE

THE GERMANS ON THE 24TH APRIL 1915

The following is a translation of the summary kindly furnished by the *Reichsarchiv* :—

" The attack of the *51st Reserve Division* was continued on the " morning of the 24th ; it was begun by the release of gas at a few " (*einselnen*) places. To support the *51st Reserve Division*, the " corps reserve of the *XXVI. Reserve Corps* (a composite infantry " brigade) was directed to advance up the west bank of the " Haanebeek.[1]

" The attack encountered strong opposition and progressed but " slowly. Keerselare, from which enemy machine guns were fired, " held out particularly long. In the farms and hedges round " St. Julien, too, the enemy resisted stoutly in spite of heavy " artillery bombardment.

" Keerselare was captured early in the afternoon. Towards " 5 P.M. [British time] the left wing of the corps reserve which was " advancing west of the Haanebeek [Steenbeek] got possession of " the first houses of St. Julien, two hours after parts of *Reserve* " *Infantry Regiment No. 204* had entered the locality from the north.

" At 5.50 P.M. there was a strong counter-attack which compelled " the *51st Reserve Division* to evacuate St. Julien again. The " division retired to the line of the two Heights 15 north of St.

[1] Steenbeek on Map 7 and Sketch 12 : it was to advance towards St. Julien between the stream and Kitchener's Wood. The dead bodies of men of the *242nd* and *244th Reserve Infantry Regiments* (*53rd Reserve Division* of the *XXVII. Reserve Corps*) were found south-west of St. Julien on the 25th, in addition to those of men of the *XXVI. Reserve Corps*.

" Julien.[1] An order to retake the place again that evening was not 24 April.
" carried out on the 24th. When darkness fell the division stood
" on the line Kitchener's Wood—Height 15 north of St. Julien—
" Height 30 east of St. Julien. [This must be the contour near
" Locality C.]. The attack was to be continued on the 25th.

" The right wing of the *XXVII. Reserve Corps* also took part in
" the attack on the 24th April with a composite brigade,[2] and
" reached Height 32 west of Gravenstafel. [There is a Point 32
" near Locality C.].

" The attack of the *XXIII. Reserve Corps* made no further
" progress [against the French and Belgians] on the 24th. The
" corps lay in an extraordinarily unfavourable position. The bridge-
" head formed near Lizerne ran from the northern edge of Steen-
" straat to the northern edge of Lizerne, then bent sharply round
" that village, followed for a time the course of the Lizerne—
" Boesinghe road, and then turned eastwards to Het Sas. The
" bridgehead was continuously under very heavy artillery fire,
" which was often interrupted by counter-attack ".

The narrative in Schwarte ii. pp. 262-3 adds the following
details :—

" The *XXVI. Reserve Corps*, to which was attached parts of the
" *53rd Reserve Division* [the composite brigade], *2nd Reserve Ersatz*
" *Brigade* and *4th Marine Brigade*, made good progress on its left
" flank. The composite brigade of the *53rd Reserve Division* suc-
" ceeded in gaining ground in the direction of Gravenstafel, in
" crossing the Haanebeek, in taking Height 32 [Locality C], and
" in rolling up the British position. Stout resistance was offered in
" the small wood west of Gravenstafel. This supporting point was
" not taken until the 3rd May.[3] *Reserve Infantry Regiment No. 234*
" valiantly supported by a section of field guns brought up into
" the open 200 yards from the enemy, took Keerselare and de Rode
" Carrière [a farm to the east of Oblong Farm, south of Kitchener's
" Wood] and St. Julien. On the 25th the greatly-reduced-in-
" numbers battalions of the *51st Reserve Division* had again to
" receive a sharp counter-attack ".

The German bulletin for the 24th April 1915, like that for the
22nd, contains no mention of gas. It is :—

" The ground gained north of Ypres on the 23rd [*sic*] was held
" yesterday [24th] against enemy attacks. Further to the east we
" continued our attacks, stormed Solaert Farm [Oblong Farm], as
" well as St. Julien and Keerselare and pressed forward victoriously
" against Gravenstafel ".

---

[1] There is one Point 15 about 500 yards north of the bridge in the
village, and a Point 16 a little east of it ; the only other 15 is west of the
village.

[2] According to prisoners taken on 29th, it was formed of one battalion
each of *241st, 245th, 246th, 247th* and *248th Reserve Infantry Regiments*.

[3] This is evidently Berlin Wood (lost on 3rd May), a small wood *east*
of Gravenstafel held by the 3/Royal Fusiliers. " Kitchener's Wood " in
the German narrative is described as " the wood 1,000 metres west of St.
" Julien ", and was lost on the 24th.

CHAPTER XII

THE BATTLES OF YPRES 1915 (*continued*)

BATTLE OF ST. JULIEN (*continued*)

25TH APRIL

(Map 7 ; Sketch 13)

HULL'S ATTACK [1]

Map 7.
Sketch
13.
SUNDAY the 25th April, the day of the landing of Sir Ian Hamilton's expedition on the Gallipoli peninsula, was overcast and cloudy until the afternoon, when there were occasional spells of sunshine. Day had dawned and rain had ceased, but the morning mist had not cleared away, when the battalions of the 10th Brigade passed through the wire of G.H.Q. Line in fours and, forming into line, faced the front St. Julien—Kitchener's Wood. They were, now, like those of the 13th Brigade two days before—but with the difference that they were well rested and up to war strength, whilst Br.-General Wanless O'Gowan's men had been exhausted and reduced in numbers by previous fighting at Hill 60—called on to attempt the impossible. Without adequate artillery preparation and support, on ground unknown and unreconnoitred, they were sent to turn an enemy well provided with machine guns out of a position which had ready-made cover in houses and a wood, and splendid artillery observation from higher ground behind it. Hull's force actually got less artillery assistance than anticipated ; for information of the postponement of the attack from 3.30 to 5.30 A.M. did not reach the batteries of the 27th and 28th Divisions which were ordered to

---

[1] It seems better, for reasons given in the case of the attack of Geddes's Detachment and the 13th Brigade on the 23rd, to use the word "attack" rather than "counter-attack".

SKETCH 13.

YPRES, 1915.
BATTLE OF ST JULIEN.
SITUATION AT NIGHT SUNDAY.
25TH APRIL.

assist. These guns carried out a preliminary bombardment 25 April. from 2.45 to 3.15 A.M., and were silent when the advance began; whilst the batteries of the II. and III. Brigades C.F.A. were allotted targets so distant that their fire not only passed over the German front line, but failed to catch the reserves. The artillery fire affected the enemy so little that in the morning mist it provoked a reply only from a couple of 5·9-inch batteries.

Br.-General Hull placed his four Regular battalions, 1/Royal Irish Fusiliers (Lieut.-Colonel A. R. Burrowes), 2/Royal Dublin Fusiliers (Lieut.-Colonel A. Loveband), 2/Seaforth Highlanders (Lieut.-Colonel R. S. Vandeleur), and 1/Royal Warwickshire (Lieut.-Colonel A. J. Poole) in first line, with the 7/Argyll and Sutherland Highlanders (Lieut.-Colonel D. A. Carden) in support behind the left. They were to attack against St. Julien and Kitchener's Wood, whilst two battalions of the 150th Brigade — the 5th Green Howards and 5th Durham L.I. — were sent orders to move on their right through Fortuin. The 2/K.O.Y.L.I. (down to 250 of all ranks) and Queen Victoria's Rifles and 1/Royal Irish, were detailed to the reserve. Behind the right was the 149th (Northumberland) Brigade, not originally detailed to Hull's Force, but lent from the corps reserve, as the situation on the right flank was still very obscure. It had been impossible to get into touch with all the units allotted by General Alderson to the attack, and some that had been warned were delayed on the road or absent from their places at 5.30 A.M.[1] Thus it came about that the attack was actually made by five battalions only, Br.-General Hull's own brigade, and not by fifteen.

The battalions of the 10th Brigade were able to pass the wire of G.H.Q. Line under cover of the mist, but, before they could open out, they came under rifle and machine-gun fire, though they were still screened from the artillery; and it was at once obvious that snipers were out in the rye grass and other crops that gave cover from view, and that some of the farms between Wieltje and St.

---

[1] During the night the 149th Brigade had been moved forward from Potijze to Wieltje, where it arrived at 4.30 A.M. In view of a probable enemy attack, the 1st and 4th Canadian Battalions had been directed, as we have seen, at 1.50 A.M. by a staff officer of the Canadian Division to help close the gap between the 2nd and 3rd Canadian Brigades ; but they had been ordered off the road by Br.-General Hull to enable his brigade to get through, and were thus delayed. They eventually entrenched astride the angle of the two roads running north-east from Wieltje in front of G.H.Q. Line, to support the 10th Brigade attack.

25 April. Julien were in the hands of the enemy. The brigade, therefore, shook out into fighting formation somewhat earlier than intended. Its advance, visible from many points, was carried out in faultless order, worthy of the traditions of its home at Shorncliffe, where Sir John Moore had trained the battalions that became the nucleus of the celebrated Light Division. The fire now came mainly from machine guns hidden in the houses of St. Julien and the upper stories of farm buildings, with cross fire from Kitchener's Wood, and particularly from two farms south of it (Oblong and Juliet, captured by the Germans on the previous day). There was no great amount of rifle fire, and only a moderate amount of artillery fire; for the *51st Reserve Division*, having been ordered to retake St. Julien and finding it unoccupied, was making preparations for a further advance, and was not at first fully disposed to meet an attack. By rushes the leading lines advanced more than a quarter of a mile till they were within one hundred yards of the outlying houses of St. Julien. Then, though the fifth battalion was thrown in on the left, the lines paused and became stationary, and for twenty minutes the Germans deluged them with machine-gun fire, very effective and very heavy. A few men tried to crawl back into cover, but the majority of those in the leading lines never returned; mown down, like corn, by machine guns in enfilade, they remained lying dead in rows where they had fallen. The following lines were pinned to the ground by fire, and after several efforts to advance, as if by common accord, rose and surged back to cover in the folds of the ground and hedges behind them.

The Germans made no attempt whatever to exploit their fire success, except by the weak counter-attack of a company from the Fortuin side. They were probably intensely relieved by the arrest of an attack so nearly successful: they hardly fired a shot once it came to an end, and did not advance. The supports of the battalions were pushed up, and it was possible for officers of the 10th Brigade to move about unmolested, and for parties to go out and bring in the wounded. A new line was quickly organized with its apex at Vanheule Farm, five hundred yards from the southern edge of St. Julien, and echelonned back on the right to the Haanebeek, and on the left to the northernmost part of Mouse Trap Farm, where it joined on to the general line.

The losses of the 10th Brigade in its magnificent but

hopeless attempt had been heavy, totalling 73 officers and 25 April. 2,346 other ranks, mostly irreplaceable, well trained men. In compensation for the disaster that had overtaken them, the battalions had the satisfaction of knowing later that they had stopped any possible enemy advance in the St. Julien quarter ; for they held the position they had now taken up until withdrawn in the general retirement to a reduced salient on the 4th May.

Just before the annihilation of the 10th Brigade front lines, Br.-General Hull had noted the absence of the York and Durham battalions which were supposed to be on the right of the attack. He therefore ordered two battalions of the 149th Brigade, the 4/ and 7/Northumberland Fusiliers, to reinforce that flank ; but, owing to a fortunate mistake in direction, instead of attempting to thicken the line, they extended it to the right. Still, they were not in touch with the 5/Green Howards and 5/Durham L.I. It was not until 10 A.M. that Br.-General Hull at last got into communication with these units at Verlorenhoek, when it transpired that the mistake was due to the postponement of the attack. After advancing unopposed, at the hour originally fixed, to the old trenches in front of Fortuin, they had found themselves in the air, and had fallen back. They now went up again to help fill the gap between the Northumberland battalions and Colonel Wallace's detachment. In the evening, it may be added, after losing 4 officers and 284 men, they were relieved by the 1/Royal Irish (27th Division), which took up position west of Fortuin to the right of the 10th Brigade. The 3rd Canadian Brigade was at the same time withdrawn from G.H.Q. Line to bivouacs west of the canal, south of Brielen.[1]

THE ATTACK ON THE 85TH AND 2ND CANADIAN BRIGADES

Br.-General Hull's report of the failure of his attack, concluding with the expression of opinion that it should not be renewed, reached V. Corps headquarters about 9.15 A.M. Very soon afterwards news of enemy attacks on the 28th Division and on the front and flank of the 2nd Canadian Brigade, on its left, added to the anxiety.

---

[1] Br.-General Turner's headquarters at Mouse Trap Farm, whence Br.-General Hull had witnessed the attack of his force, were shelled and burnt down during the afternoon, and the brigade staff moved three hundred yards nearer to Wieltje.

25 April. The 28th Division held a front including the northern half of Polygon Wood, whence it ran along the top of the main Ypres ridge to about half a mile north of Broodseinde, then turning westward and north-westward down a spur to the shallow valley of the Stroombeek, to stop short of that watercourse. The 5th Canadian Battalion (Lieut.-Colonel G. S. Tuxford) then carried the line down to the Stroombeek, from which point the 8th Battalion (Lieut.-Colonel L. J. Lipsett) continued it with three companies on the northern side of the beek along the reverse slope of Stroombeek ridge. When the 15th Battalion, on the left of the 8th, was driven back in consequence of the gas attack on the morning of the 24th, the 8th Battalion, using its fourth company and another of the 5th Battalion for reinforcements, had done its best to defend the ground between the left of its line and Locality C by sapping a flanking trench back from the front and occupying French trenches in front of Boetleer's Farm, covering the intervening spaces by fire. In the evening, as we have seen, two companies of the Suffolks, under Lieut. Bradley, 1½ companies of the North-umberland Fusiliers and two of the Cheshires under Major Moulton-Barrett, and a party of 300 of the 7th and 10th Canadian Battalions under Major Odlum, formed a line from Boetleer's Farm south-westwards to the Haane-beek, whilst a company of the 1/Monmouthshire and two half companies of the 8/Middlesex had been used to reinforce. At 3 A.M. on the 25th the 8/Durham L.I. (Lieut.-Colonel J. Turnbull) of the 151st Brigade also arrived at the farm. Sent by General Snow from the corps reserve at Potijze to assist the 85th Brigade, the battalion had been passed on by Br.-General A. J. Chapman to help the hard-pressed Canadians, who were greatly reduced in numbers, cumbered in the trenches with many wounded and gassed men, weak from want of food, and worn out by 48 hours' incessant fighting and bombardment. Even more serious was the fact that the special small-arm ammunition they required was running short and difficult to obtain.[1] The Germans, though close up to the gap at its extremities—some two hundred and fifty yards from the flank of the original front trench, and four or five hundred from Boetleer's Farm—had not been able to push

---

[1] The Canadian infantry was armed with the Ross rifle, which required special ammunition. The Lee-Enfield ammunition, though of the same calibre, caused jams. The Ross rifle was officially discarded in June 1915.

further, and, as usual at night, were engaged in improving 25 April. the trenches they had found, and in wiring. On the arrival of the 8/Durham L.I. it was therefore decided to relieve the 8th Canadians during the remaining hours of darkness. The operation was successfully carried out by two companies as regards the left of Lipsett's battalion ; but there was not time before daylight to get the relief up to the right Canadian company, which therefore remained in the line. The other two Durham companies took such cover as they could find near Boetleer's Farm. The 8th Canadian Battalion (less its one company) was then taken into reserve behind the farm. The exposed flank of the 2nd Canadian Brigade having thus been reinforced, Major Moulton - Barrett, leaving the company of the 1/Monmouthshire behind, withdrew his detachment to the trenches it had begun across the Zonnebeke—Langemarck road.

It was upon the 85th Brigade (Br.-General A. J. Chapman) of the 28th Division, on the right of the Canadians, occupying the spur between the main Ypres ridge and the Stroombeek, that the German attack on the morning of the 25th first fell. The brigade had the 2/East Surrey (Lieut.-Colonel C. C. G. Ashton) and 3/Royal Fusiliers (Major A. V. Johnson) in front line. At 5 A.M., just as the movement of the 10th Brigade against St. Julien was getting under way, the enemy opened organized fire, sweeping and searching the bare slopes with shrapnel for four hours. Then he changed to a heavy bombardment with gas shell and high explosive, so much gas shell being fired that the fumes seriously affected many of the men. Finally at 1 P.M., from trenches only 70 yards away the Germans charged the right sector of the East Surreys— some quarter of a mile long, between the top of the ridge and the railway cutting—and broke in at several places. In hand-to-hand fighting, which made artillery support by either side impossible, on the right of the sector an officer and 28 men of the *244th Reserve Regiment* (*XXVII. Reserve Corps*) [1] were captured and the rest of the intruders killed ; in the centre, with the help of a support company of the 8/Middlesex, they were driven off ; but on the left, owing to the fall of all officers, the enemy remained in occupation of sixty yards of breastwork. The East Surreys were too exhausted and reduced in numbers, and

[1] According to information supplied by the *Reichsarchiv*, the right of the *XXVII. Reserve Corps* was engaged in this attack.

25 April. too short of bombs, to dislodge him at once; and two attempts, organized by Lieut.-Colonel R. J. Bridgford at midnight, and at 3.30 A.M. on the 26th, with two companies of the 2/Shropshire L.I. sent up by the 27th Division, failed to regain the lost ground. To prevent any further enemy progress, a trench was dug round three sides of his capture.

In the Royal Fusilier sector on the left of the East Surreys, where No Man's Land was two hundred yards wide, the enemy was unable to close.

In the adjoining sector, from early morning onwards, the 5th Canadians, the company of the 8th Canadians, the 8/Durham L.I., and the company of the 1/Monmouthshire had been subjected to rifle fire, but mostly to shelling, which gradually increased in volume, being particularly heavy on the front line between 9 A.M. and noon, when 45 to 68 shells per minute were counted. Then it died down somewhat, and the closer fire of trench-mortars and sniping continued its work; but towards 2 P.M. it increased again, and the enemy infantry began to press close. No reinforcements appeared in the gap on the west of Boetleer's Farm, though both the 1st Canadian Brigade and the rest of the 151st (Durham L.I.) Brigade were expected. Ammunition began to run short. About 3.30 P.M. the German infantry, which included men of the *Marine Corps*, in blue, attacked from both north and west. All attempts on Boetleer's Farm were repelled, but the machine gun in the flank covering the left of the front line being knocked out, the Germans were able to penetrate behind the companies of the Durham L.I. The reinforcements sent to help them were unable to reach the front line over the shallow open valley and received a terrible shelling as they retired again on Boetleer's Farm, the German gun fire following them step by step. Receiving no answer to the message as to whether to hold on or come back, the survivors of the two companies about 6 P.M. withdrew to the farm and occupied some shallow trenches on the right of it. The company of the 8th Canadians in the line was rushed and surrounded, only 42 of its men escaping.

Very soon after this loss of another sector of the left of the line, a message reached Br.-General Currie at Gravenstafel from the Canadian Division that the 151st Brigade would neither be sent to the assistance of the 5th and 8th Battalions, nor be used for counter-attack, but was to occupy the line dug along the Gravenstafel— 25 April. Fortuin road, thus permitting Wallace's detachment to be returned to the 28th Division. He further learnt that the 9/Durham L.I. (151st Brigade) had already moved in this direction. Conceiving from the message that the switch line was occupied and his situation was considered hopeless, about 5 P.M. Br.-General Currie ordered the 2nd Canadian Brigade (5th, 7th, 8th and 10th Battalions) to retire southwards at dusk to the line of the Haanebeek on the right of the new position. These orders were sent to Lieut.-Colonel Turnbull of the 8/Durham L.I., but he, being in doubt as to which commander he was under, remained in action along the road through Boetleer's Farm eastwards to Gravenstafel. He was reinforced at this time by a company of the 8/Middlesex and two half companies of the 1/Monmouthshire sent up by Br.-General Chapman (85th Brigade). The Canadian companies began to retire soon after, but on reaching the line designated Lieut.-Colonels Tuxford and Lipsett found that the Royal Fusiliers had received no orders to retire, and were not conforming; the 5th and 8th Canadians therefore went forward again and occupied the trenches of the French supporting point covering Gravenstafel. They remained there until the early morning of the 26th. The 2nd Canadian Brigade eventually moved back to Wieltje and St. Jean on the orders of Br.-General Hasler (11th Brigade) after he had been placed in command of the sector.[1]

The 85th Brigade was now left with its flank exposed, just as in succession the 3rd Canadian Brigade had been on the disappearance of the Algerians and the 2nd Canadian Brigade on the withdrawal of the 3rd. To protect this flank, to which in the darkness the nearest force was the 400-500 Canadians at Gravenstafel, Major A. V. Johnson reinforced the left of the 3/Royal Fusiliers with half a support company and, abandoning a short length of front, swung back his left into the trench which had been prepared the previous night by the party of engineers and 8/Middlesex, and the small wood, later known as Berlin Wood. This line the 85th Brigade continued to hold until the 3rd May.

Thus, when night fell on the 25th, the front between

[1] See page 248. The 8th Battalion reassembled at dawn on the 26th at Wieltje. The 5th Battalion reached St. Jean at 4 A.M. The composite 7th and 10th Battalion remained west of Boetleer's Farm covering the withdrawal until 3.30 A.M. and then marched to Wieltje.

25 April. the 85th Brigade and Fortuin—although Br.-General Hasler with the 11th Brigade was on the way to fill it and establish unity of command—was not only very thin, but filled by various bodies of troops not under one control. There were but isolated detachments of wearied men—the Canadians at Gravenstafel, the 8/Durham L.I. and parties with it near Boetleer's Farm, Moulton-Barrett's companies and part of the 2nd Canadian Brigade south-west of them along the Haanebeek, and Wallace's two battalions between them and Fortuin—unable to establish touch with the troops on either side.[1] Fortunately, this state of affairs was unknown to the enemy, who, as usual, made no movement during the night.

THE REORGANIZATION OF THE V. CORPS LINE

During the morning of the 25th the 11th Brigade (Br.-General J. Hasler) had arrived at Vlamertinghe, and had been placed by the Second Army at the disposal of the V. Corps. General Plumer thereupon decided to re-organize the troops on the front attacked, and at 2.30 P.M. ordered that as from 7 P.M. the front should be redivided between Generals Bulfin and Alderson. The former, with the newly arrived 11th Brigade allotted to him, was to take over command of the frontage next to his own division held by the 2nd Canadian Brigade and the troops on its left up to the flank of Br.-General Hull's command, that is to say to the Fortuin—St. Julien road. General Alder-son's sector was reduced to the front between the Fortuin road and the French.[2] Both divisional commanders were directed to reorganize their commands, putting battalions under their proper brigadiers if possible, or at any rate under a definite general. Any troops they could spare were to be sent to corps reserve at Potijze to be under General Snow.[3] The situation at 2.30 P.M., when the instructions were issued, was assumed to be easy, as a very detailed air report, from an aviator who flew at a thousand feet owing to clouds, 10.30 to 11 A.M., had stated

[1] The 1/Royal Irish was the next unit on the left.
[2] Bulfin's force therefore included his own 28th Division (with Wallace's detachment that belonged to it), 11th Brigade, 2nd Canadian Brigade, 150th (York and Durham) Brigade, 8/Durham L.I. ; Alderson's force, his own Canadian Division (less the 2nd Brigade), 10th Brigade, 13th Brigade, 149th (Northumberland) Brigade and Geddes's detachment.
[3] The reorganization of the artillery commands took place next day, and is referred to in the next Chapter.

that there was a continuous and intact line, and that it 25 April. ran east and west along the top of Gravenstafel ridge, and thence " fairly straight to St. Julien ". Germans in evacuated trenches must in some cases have been mistaken for British. The only gap mentioned was near Fortuin, where there actually was undefended ground on the left of Wallace's detachment, later filled by the 5/Green Howards and 5/Durham L.I.[1] In the absence of news to the contrary—the corps diary records that the information from parts of the front line was " scrappy "—the air report was accepted. The incident is typical of the difficulties under which the higher commanders laboured.

Br.-General Hasler (11th Brigade) on arriving at the 28th Division headquarters at Vlamertinghe at noon, was instructed by General Bulfin to take command of the 2nd Canadian Brigade, and of all detachments found in the sector, from the left of the 85th Brigade to the St. Julien —Fortuin road. He was to move the 11th Brigade so as to reach St. Jean at dusk.[2] It was not until 10 P.M. that the many conflicting reports of the situation could be cleared up, and the plan put into effect. Br.-General Hasler decided to approach the gap between the 85th and 10th Brigades from its known two ends. Whilst the main body of the 11th Brigade moved off from St. Jean at 10.30 P.M. making for Fortuin, the 1/Hampshire (Lieut.-Colonel F. R. Hicks) was sent off half an hour earlier towards Zonnebeke to get in touch with the 85th Brigade, and, having done so, to extend westwards down the Gravenstafel — Fortuin road to meet the rest of the 11th Brigade.

It was a race with dawn. Finding their way by the map in pitch darkness, the Hampshire reached the headquarters of the Royal Fusiliers shortly before 1.30 A.M., but the guides obtained there failed to lead them across country to the flank of the battalion, and at 2.25 A.M., with only one hour to daylight before him, Colonel Hicks decided to dig in where he was, in some of the many old trenches facing north. He soon afterwards discovered that he was only four hundred yards from the left of the Royal Fusiliers at Berlin Wood, and, as the morning mist gave him two hours of protection from view, his men were able to establish themselves, extending on the left to the nearest houses of Gravenstafel. The position proved a good one

---

[1] See page 243.
[2] Appendix 25. For order of battle of the 11th Brigade, see Appendix 4.

25 April. and prevented the enemy from getting round the left of the Royal Fusiliers.

The main body of the 11th Brigade was not so fortunate. At Fortuin corner information was given to Br.-General Hasler that there were very few troops between Fortuin and Gravenstafel, and that hostile patrols were at least up to the road connecting these localities. He therefore turned the column southwards from Fortuin, although in reality the road to Gravenstafel was covered by Wallace's detachment. The result was that 2.30 A.M. on the 26th found his three battalions on Zonnebeke ridge, near and west of Point 37, where they dug in actually some seven hundred yards behind Wallace's detachment. In the course of the night therefore, the situation had been somewhat improved, though not to the extent intended : the 1/Hampshire at full strength had taken the place of the greatly reduced 5th and 8th Canadians, and there were now some battalions in reserve. But there were still gaps in the line : a quarter of a mile between the Royal Fusiliers and the Hampshire ; half a mile between the left of the Hampshire and the 8/Durham L.I. and companies with it still holding out on Gravenstafel ridge near Boetleer's Farm ; and a larger gap of some thousand yards between the Durhams and Wallace's detachment on their left, with the 11th Brigade behind Wallace. It was soon obvious that the Durhams could not remain in their exposed position, which had not only both flanks unsecured, but was in advance of the general line. Orders to rejoin their units reached the companies of the Monmouthshire and Middlesex co-operating with the Durhams ; but it was not until 4 A.M. when the Germans—some of them said to be dressed in khaki [1]—after being beaten off several times, came on in large numbers and tried to close, that the 8/Durham L.I. fell back to the Haanebeek, with such effective resistance as to keep off all pursuit. Later, by instructions of the 85th Brigade, the battalion withdrew to Zonnebeke ridge. Moulton-Barrett's detachment was also pressed by the enemy and took up a new position near a farm (Otto Farm) midway between the left of the Hampshire near Gravenstafel and the right of the main body of the

---

[1] Accusations of wearing the other's uniform were made by both sides. Possibly individuals may have put on enemy headdresses to keep them as souvenirs, or overcoats for the sake of warmth, but it was a risky proceeding, as they exposed themselves to the fire of their friends. On one occasion when the Germans were reported to be in Highland dress, it was found that the supposed kilts were merely their own overcoats.

11th Brigade at Hill 37.[1]   The 8/Durham L.I. had lost 19 25 April. officers and 574 men, and was reorganized into a fighting company of 6 officers and 140 men.[2]

On receipt of General Plumer's 2.30 P.M. orders to reorganize his line, General Alderson directed Br.-General Hull to hold his front from Fortuin to Mouse Trap Farm, with his own brigade and the 1/Royal Irish ; Br.-General Wanless O'Gowan to take over the front of Geddes's Detachment from Mouse Trap Farm to the French with the 13th Brigade, then in reserve west of the canal, the K.O.Y.L.I. and Queen Victoria's Rifles having rejoined it, and the 4/Rifle Brigade of the 27th Division being attached. Geddes's four battalions in front line were to go back to Potijze, but his reserve of three battalions was to remain at St. Jean.   The 149th Brigade was ordered to the south of Wieltje, as General Alderson's reserve.   The 1st Canadian Brigade was sent back across the canal to replace the 13th Brigade at the bridges ; the 2nd Canadian Brigade remained at the disposal of General Bulfin, and it assembled, as already noticed, at Wieltje ; the 3rd was ordered to La Brique (west of St. Jean), but actually in error went for the night west of the canal to bivouac south of Brielen. The reliefs ordered were effected during the hours of darkness of the 25th/26th, with the exception of that of the 2/Buffs, the right of Geddes's detachment, by the 4/Rifle Brigade, the latter battalion being kept in the line near the canal owing to the weakness of the Zouaves in that quarter.   The change was, however, carried out twenty-four hours later.[3]

Sir John French in a special message expressed his admiration of the gallant stand and fight that the Canadian infantry had made, and he might have added the persistence of the Canadian artillery, against overwhelming

[1] Major Moulton-Barrett was wounded about this time, and Captain R. T. K. Auld, adjutant of the 2/Northumberland Fusiliers, was sent to command his detachment. The losses of the 1/Hampshire on the 25th/26th were 6 officers and 157 other ranks.

[2] General Bulfin (28th Division) placed on record : " The greatest " possible credit is due to the 8/Durham L.I. and the small detachment " who, in spite of having their flanks turned and being enfiladed, remained " in the northern line, beating off all attacks and inflicting heavy loss on " the enemy, and thereby saved the flank of the 85th Infantry Brigade ".

[3] Of the 150th Brigade, the 5/Green Howards and 5/Durham L.I., which had been with Br.-General Hull, were sent to reserve trenches south of Fortuin ; the 4/E. Yorkshire and 4/Green Howards stayed in G.H.Q. Line. Of the 151st Brigade, the 8/Durham L.I. was left with the 85th Brigade, the rest of the brigade remaining in corps reserve at Verlorenhoek.

25 April. odds. New to war, and in trenches taken over from the French only five days before they were attacked, in a most difficult position, when coloured troops on their left stampeded, the battalions had held on and gained time. " With " less gallant and determined troops, the disaster which " occurred outside the line they were holding might have " been converted into a serious defeat for our troops ".[1] The Canadians only yielded ground when driven off by gas, against which they had little protection, or by weight of artillery, to which they could not reply.[2]

THE GENERAL SITUATION ON THE 25TH

During the day little had occurred to throw light on the general situation ; the weather was unfavourable for air reconnaissance, but such observation as was possible at intervals in certain areas revealed no movement except one small column approaching St. Julien, although forty trains, double the usual quantity, were noticed at Tourcoing (north-east of Lille). That the enemy wished it to be believed that important movements were on hand was evident ; for news was received from Holland that 125 train loads of troops had gone through Liège on the 23rd and 24th, travelling westwards, a greater number than had passed in a similar period in 1914. Prisoners stated, however, that only two *Landwehr* regiments had been brought up to reinforce the *XXVI. Reserve Corps* and these had been set to dig a second position. They also said that the *44th Reserve Division* had been relieved at Nieuport by units of the *Marine Corps* for the same purpose. These

[1] General Sir H. Smith-Dorrien to Lieut.-General Sir H. Alderson, 6th May 1915.

[2] The losses of the infantry of the Canadian Division, summarized for the period 22nd April-4th May (but mostly incurred during the 22nd to the 25th) were very heavy :—

	Killed.	Died of wounds.	Wounded.	Prisoners (including wounded and prisoners).	Total.
Officers . .	57	8	104	39	208
Other Ranks	1,438	234	1,822	1,767	5,261
					5,469

The total was nearly evenly distributed between the three brigades, the 1st having slightly more casualties than the 2nd, the 2nd than the 3rd.

For devoted attention to wounded under fire 22nd to 25th April, particularly during the evacuation of his dressing station on the 25th, when it was heavily shelled, Captain F. A. C. Scrimger, Canadian Army Medical Service, Medical Officer of the 14th Battalion, received the V.C.

precautions did not seem to indicate any serious plan to 25 April. break through.

On the French wing of the battle the German offensive seemed to have been completely arrested ; [1] there was, however, no counter-movement except from the canal bank near Ypres, and that by a single Zouave battalion about noon and again at 1 P.M. The French Territorials were too greatly fatigued for further action, and no reinforcements had arrived except the leading regiment of the 153rd Division. General Putz had therefore postponed the attack until next day, and to execute it reorganized his forces into two wings under Generals Quiquandon (45th Division) and Deligny (153rd Division), dividing the 87th Territorial Division between them. News came that the IX. Corps (General Curé), consisting of the 152nd Division (General Joppé) [2] and 18th Division (General Lefèvre) were on the way from Artois.

G.H.Q. issued no orders during the day, except to warn the Indian Cavalry Corps to be ready to move at one hour's notice after 5 A.M. on the 26th. At Second Army headquarters there was still considerable doubt as to the scope of the German attack ; the only certain factors seemed to be, that by releasing gas and concentrating an artillery attack on the shoulder of each new successive flank as he gained ground, the enemy might gradually nibble away the front ; and that hasty, isolated attacks by infantry of the best quality without sufficient artillery backing failed to dislodge him. Another offensive in front of Ypres seemed a doubtful remedy unless in combination with a powerful one undertaken by the French, and carefully prepared.

Towards noon the Lahore Division (Major-General H. D'U. Keary) arrived at the huts north-east of Ouderdom (5 miles south-west of Ypres), and plans were then discussed for its employment in another effort northwards east of the canal, provided the French would attack. Possibly, in theory, the best tactical use that could have been made of the division would have been to have sent it to give direct support to the French, or, better still,

---

[1] According to German accounts, it was stopped by order of the *Fourth Army*. See Note at end of Chapter.

[2] Formed, like the 153rd, 1st-12th April 1915 of " unités de nouvelle " formation ". It also contained one Moroccan brigade (the 4th, consisting of one regiment of Moroccan colonial infantry and one of native tirailleurs). Thus the reinforcements were not entirely first-class troops. French Order of Battle, Tome X. ii. p. 832.

25 April. to the Belgians, so as to smash and capture by a flank attack the strip of bridgehead held by the *XXIII. Reserve Corps* on the west side of the canal. This operation should have been a comparatively easy matter, as the enemy depended on the precarious communication afforded by eight pontoon bridges and 16 plank bridges. For this, however, not only were time and space lacking, but difference of language and methods made an enterprise of such a kind conducted by three different nationalities— four, counting the Indians—without a common commander, extremely hazardous ; and so sure was General Putz that his own reinforcements of three divisions would suffice that, whilst retaining the horse artillery, he returned to General Smith-Dorrien one of the British cavalry divisions lent to him. After having seen the effect of a gas cloud on African native troops, the G.O.C. Second Army was in any case determined not to commit the Lahore Division until the French had matured their plans, and he could be sure that they intended to employ sufficient troops to drive home an attack. Meantime officers of the Indian division were sent to reconnoitre routes towards, and the ground near, Wieltje. During the evening General Smith-Dorrien motored to Hazebrouck, and in a personal interview was given the Commander-in-Chief's instructions. These were to the effect that he did not wish any ground given up if it could possibly be avoided ; but, unless the French regained what they had lost, or a good portion of it, it might be impossible to retain the present very salient position in front of Ypres. It was essential, however, that the situation should be cleared up and the area quieted down as soon as possible, so that the offensive of the First Army might be carried out even if this involved the Second Army withdrawing to a still more retired line. The impression formed at G.H.Q. and at General Foch's headquarters was, he said, that the enemy hoped by continuing attacks at Ypres to render the contemplated Allied offensive impossible. Both British and French commanders, however, were determined that their plans should not be disturbed. Sir John French added that as the French had got the Second Army into the difficulty, they ought to get it out. General Putz's ideas did not have this large scope. At 10 P.M., when his orders were received at Second Army headquarters, it was found that his attack was not to be made until 5 P.M. on the 26th, and then only by the 18th Division (less a brigade) and troops of the 45th and 153rd Divisions already in the

line, only 17 battalions in all. Nevertheless, in view of 25 April.
G.H.Q. orders, General Smith-Dorrien, after asking for a
slight change of boundary—that the French should be
astride the Ypres—Langemarck road instead of west of it
—agreed to participate with the Lahore Division, and
issued preliminary orders for that purpose. When, late at
night, zero hour was advanced by the French from 5 P.M.
to 2 P.M., he protested through G.H.Q., as the change
curtailed the already short and inadequate time available
for the preparations of the Indian division, and for the
rest needed by the troops, who would have been on the
march all night. He was definitely instructed by Sir John
French to proceed. In consequence of the late notice and
the subsequent change, it was impossible to issue the
Army operation orders and instructions before 2.15 A.M.
on the 26th.

NOTE

THE GERMANS ON THE 25TH APRIL 1915

The following is a translation of the information kindly furnished
by the *Reichsarchiv* :—
    " On the 25th April, by order of the Army commander, the
" attack of the *XXIII. Reserve Corps* [against the French] was
" stopped ; but the ground that had been gained was to be held.
" The left wing of the corps, however, pushed slowly forward to the
" canal.
    " Simultaneously with the decision to stop the offensive west of
" the Ypres canal, the *Fourth Army* gave orders that from the 25th
" April onwards the weight of the attack should be shifted to the
" sector of the *XXVI. Reserve Corps* [that is the front of the 85th
" Brigade and thence nearly to the canal], as here it seemed possible
" to cut off the enemy position in the Ypres Salient. The attacks
" did not, however, succeed on this day. The corps encountered
" considerable resistance, and part of it was counter-attacked.
    " At 4.35 A.M. on the 25th it was reported to the *51st Reserve
" Division* that the enemy had evacuated St. Julien during the
" night and that the German troops had followed up. The position
" at first ran through that locality, passing through the church.
" It was held on the 25th and 26th against several enemy counter-
" attacks.
    " On the right wing of the *XXVII. Reserve Corps* the successes
" of the previous day were improved ".
    Schwarte ii. says very little about the 25th :
    " On the 25th St. Julien was taken ; the severely thinned
" battalions of the *51st Reserve Division* had again to defend them-
" selves against a sharp counter-attack. The *XXIII. Reserve Corps*
" made no further progress ".

CHAPTER XIII

THE BATTLES OF YPRES 1915 (*continued*)

BATTLE OF ST. JULIEN (*continued*)

26TH APRIL

(Map 8 ; Sketch 14)

THE ATTACK OF THE LAHORE DIVISION

Map 8.
Sketch 14.
THE Second Army operation orders for the 26th April were issued at 2.15 A.M.[1] on that day, but they merely put on paper what had been settled twelve hours earlier after a conference at Poperinghe, at which General Smith-Dorrien had presided. The subordinate commanders concerned had therefore had an opportunity in the interval at least to see the ground over which they were to advance. The orders directed the Lahore Division (Major-General H. D'U. Keary) to move from Ouderdom to an area near Wieltje—St Jean and there to deploy. At 2 P.M., in co-operation with the French, it was to attack northwards against Langemarck, on a front of a thousand yards, through the sector of the V. Corps line held by the 13th Brigade, east of the Ypres—Langemarck road.[2] The V.

---

[1] Appendix 26.
[2] The orders of General Putz (poste de commandement near cross roads 2 miles west of Elverdinghe), issued at 10.15 P.M. on the 25th, were slightly different from those sent earlier to Second Army headquarters, and directed :—

General Joppé with the 152nd Division (less a brigade, not arrived) and Colonel Mordacq's detachment of the 45th Division, to attack on the east side of the canal towards Pilckem in co-operation with the British.

General Quiquandon, with the rest of the 45th Division and the 87th Territorial Division, west of the canal south of Het Sas, to be ready to debouch at Boesinghe as soon as General Joppé's advance permitted.

General Curé, with the 18th Division (less a brigade in general reserve) and the 153rd Division, to dislodge the Germans on the western bank at Lizerne, Steenstraat and Het Sas, and push towards Bixschoote.

SKETCH 14.

YPRES, 1915
BATTLE OF ST. JULIEN.
The British Counter-attacks on the 26th April.

Corps was directed to co-operate in the attack on the 26 April. right of the Indian division. As there was not time to find places for so many batteries in the salient, the Lahore Divisional artillery, except such guns as were required for the close support of the infantry, was to be disposed on the west bank of the canal, and was placed under the B.G.R.A. V. Corps (Br.-General S. D. Browne), who thus had at his orders all the guns in the area.[1] General Plumer in V. Corps orders gave instructions that the artillery bombardment to prepare the advance should begin at 1.20 P.M. and continue for 40 minutes, followed by five minutes' rapid fire, after which a barrage was to be formed 200 yards ahead, and the assault would take place. He directed Alderson's command [2] to co-operate in the attack and the 27th and 28th Divisions to engage the enemy with fire.[3]

To comply with these instructions, General Alderson ordered [4] the 149th (Northumberland) Brigade (Br.-General J. F. Riddell), with the special support of the Canadian artillery, to attack against St. Julien astride the Wieltje road, that is north-eastwards. To fill the gap between this and the divergent attack of the Lahore Division northwards, the 10th Brigade was to detail a battalion. Geddes's Detachment at St. Jean, now ordered to the north of Wieltje, and the 3rd Canadian Brigade, at the strength of a battalion, now reassembled south of Wieltje, were warned they would form the reserve. At 10 A.M. G.H.Q. gave formal orders for an attack to be made at the same time as the French took the offensive, with the caution,

[1] At 8.30 A.M. on the 26th he simplified the artillery commands by placing all the field batteries of the 28th and Canadian Divisional artillery west of the canal under the O.C. VIII. Field Artillery Brigade, and the 122nd Heavy, North Midland Heavy and 459th Howitzer Batteries under the O.C. XIII. Heavy Brigade ; and later the above divisional field artillery, the Belgian III. " Groupe " and the Lahore Divisional artillery were placed by him under Br.-General A. W. Gay, commanding the 28th Divisional artillery, with headquarters at Brielen. The field artillery east of the canal, including the Belgian 98th and 102nd Field Batteries, was left under Br.-General A. Stokes, commanding the 27th Divisional artillery, at Potijze, where also were headquarters XI. Heavy Brigade with the 123rd Heavy Battery.

Of the 14 batteries of the 28th Division (including two howitzer batteries originally belonging to the 5th), 9 were supporting the east front, 2 facing north, and 3 were on the west bank north of Ypres. Ten of the Canadian batteries (including two howitzer batteries R.F.A.) were on the east bank between Potijze and the canal.

[2] Now consisting of the 10th, 13th, 149th, 1st Canadian and 3rd Canadian Brigades, Geddes's Detachment and the Canadian divisional troops.

[3] Appendix 27.   [4] Appendix 28.

somewhat difficult to observe, that it was not to take place before the French advanced. General Keary established his headquarters at Potijze, where he had the benefit of General Snow's communication system. General Smith-Dorrien at noon removed his headquarters from Hazebrouck to Poperinghe; whilst General Plumer went into residence at Goldfish Chateau, hitherto only used as an advanced headquarters, a mile west of Ypres railway station. General Alderson's and other divisional headquarters remained unchanged.

The artillery of the Lahore Division took up its position early on the west bank; [1] but on the 26th April, as on other days of fighting near Ypres in April-May 1915, the number and calibre of the guns, the amount of ammunition, and the advantages of observation, both ground and air, were all in favour of the enemy. Apart from this, the length of time allowed for the British artillery preparation, fixed by the amount of ammunition available, was wholly insufficient; whilst wire cutting and proper support of the infantry was practically impossible owing to the absence of good observation posts and the long distance from the front of so many of the batteries.

At 11.20 A.M. G.H.Q. telephoned a sorely needed message of encouragement to the Second Army, adding that the enemy could not be very strong or numerous, as he must have lost heavily and be exhausted. As will be seen, the British and Indian infantry was never able to close, and the fighting resolved itself into valiant but vain attempts to advance against well-placed machine guns and superior artillery that had observation over nearly every square inch of ground.

The Lahore Division marched off from Ouderdom at 5.30 A.M., its three infantry brigades, each consisting of a British battalion and three Indian battalions—all of low strength owing to sickness and lack of reinforcements—with an attached Territorial battalion. The Jullundur and Ferozepore Brigades, passing by the south and north of Ypres, though they suffered some loss by artillery fire on the way, reached their places of assembly in the shallow valley between St. Jean and Hill Top ridge at 11 A.M. They were immediately located by enemy aircraft and fired on by artillery. The Sirhind Brigade, with the divisional troops, followed the northern route to Potijze. At

[1] Two batteries (one 18-pdr. and one howitzer) of the division accompanied the infantry.

12.30 P.M. the brigades moved to the place of deployment 26 April. and formed up : Jullundur (Br.-General E. P. Strickland) on the right,[1] Ferozepore (Br.-General R. G. Egerton) on the left,[2] facing north, just north of La Brique, between Wieltje farm (500 yards west of Wieltje) and the Ypres— Langemarck road, with the Sirhind (Br.-General W. G. Walker) in reserve behind the right.[3] Their orders were to attack northwards and assault the enemy's trenches wherever met with, the first objective being a frontage from Oblong Farm to the Langemarck road. At 1.20 P.M., when the artillery opened, the brigades immediately advanced in order to reach the position from which to deliver the assault at 2.5 P.M. The front line carried little yellow flags to show its progress to its own—and equally to the enemy's—artillery.

The ground over which the advance was to be made was the scene of the fighting of Geddes's Detachment three days earlier, so that the division had to ascend a gentle rise to Hill Top ridge, then cross a shallow valley, in which lay the front line held by the left of the 2/Buffs (Geddes's Detachment) and the 1/R. West Kent and 2/K.O.S.B. (13th Brigade),[4] and, passing through it, ascend the gentle slopes of Mauser ridge, held by the enemy's infantry.

Directly the leading lines crossed Hill Top ridge they came under heavy artillery fire, and were badly mauled between the support and front lines of the 13th Brigade, particularly by 5·9-inch howitzer shell, which knocked out whole platoons at a time, British and Indians falling literally in heaps.[5] The two British battalions in the front line, the 1/Manchester (Lieut.-Colonel H. W. E. Hitchins) and the Connaught Rangers (Lieut.-Colonel S. J. Murray), on the flanks of the attack, nevertheless continued

[1] Front line : 1/Manchester, 40th Pathans, 47th Sikhs ;
Second Line : 59th Rifles and 4/Suffolk (T.F.).
The 40th Pathans had arrived from China on the 8th April.
[2] Front Line : 129th Baluchis, 57th Rifles, Connaught Rangers ;
Second Line : 4/London (T.F.). Reserve : 9th Bhopal.
[3] 1/Highland L.I., 15th Sikhs, 1/1st Gurkhas, 1/4th Gurkhas and 4/King's (S.R.).
[4] These last 2 battalions had relieved the 5/King's Own, 1/York and Lancaster, and 2/D.C.L.I. in the mist of the early morning.
[5] The three batteries of the *Guard Cavalry Division* fired over two thousand rounds against this attack from in front of Langemarck, though enfiladed themselves from Boesinghe and having several ammunition wagons blown up. Just as the British complained that the enemy aircraft were prying everywhere, so does the historian of the *Guard Cavalry.* Vogel, p. 246.

26 April. on most gallantly through the 13th Brigade front line, giving a splendid example to the Indian battalions between them. Despite heavy machine-gun fire from the small farms at the head of the valley, north-east of Canadian Farm, which drove the whole movement to the left, the leading lines of the Manchester and the Connaught Rangers reached within a hundred to a hundred and twenty yards of the German line before they came to a standstill. Some parties of the other units kept up with them, whilst others passed through the 13th Brigade line into No Man's Land and there held on.

General Joppé's attack had been launched from the support trenches punctually at 2 P.M., although the advance of the 18th and 153rd Divisions on Het Sas was postponed to 3 P.M. owing to difficulties of artillery registration. Some progress was made at the outset. Then, at the critical moment, 2.20 P.M., just as the leading British attackers had actually reached the wire, and the guns had lifted beyond the front enemy trench, the Germans released gas opposite the right French battalion.[1] Drifting from west to east across the front of the Ferozepore Brigade, the cloud broke the advance everywhere, whilst the enemy immediately redoubled his fire. Some of the Indian troops, who were without any means of protection and suffered very heavily, fell back in confusion, but the survivors of the Manchesters and Connaughts with the 40th Pathans and 47th Sikhs held on,[2] though the slightest movement provoked a torrent of enemy machine-gun fire.

The French troops had hesitated on the appearance of gas, and as it blew away from them had gone forward again; but in the end they fell back to their support line, from Belle Alliance Farm to South Zwaanhof Farm. As the left of the 13th Brigade line near Turco Farm was exposed by this retirement, the Sirhind Brigade was moved forward from reserve towards La Brique. The enemy however showed no signs of taking advantage of his success, and the French sent notice to the Lahore

---

[1] See Note at end of Chapter. The gas cylinders had been dug in preparatory for another attack, and were opened on the initiative of some local commander.

[2] Acting-Corporal I. Smith, 1/Manchester, received the Victoria Cross for conspicuous bravery in bringing in wounded men under heavy fire.

Jemadar Mir Dast, 55th Rifles, attached 57th Rifles, Ferozepore Brigade, received the Victoria Cross for great gallantry in leading his platoon and rallying men when no British officers were left, and carrying off wounded officers under very heavy fire.

Division that they would counter-attack to recover their
lost trenches.   Preparations were therefore made to co-
operate.   As the Jullundur Brigade had lost so heavily
two battalions of the Sirhind, the 1/Highland L.I. (Lieut.-
Colonel E. R. Hill) and the 1/4th Gurkhas (Major B. M. L.
Brodhurst), and later the 15th Sikhs (Lieut.-Colonel J. Hill)
were sent up to Br.-General Strickland to reinforce the
brigade.   About 7 P.M. some French black troops advanced,
but with such noise and shouting that they early drew
fire.   They came nearly abreast of the Lahore Division,
but they went no further.   At night the Jullundur and
Ferozepore Brigades were relieved by the Sirhind, which
then, with the help of the 3rd Sappers & Miners and a company of the 34th Sikh Pioneers, proceeded to consolidate
the line.   The parties of the Manchesters and Connaughts
still clinging to the ground they had reached a hundred
yards from the German line were withdrawn, and eventually
the bulk of the Sirhind Brigade was brought back to the
13th Brigade support trenches, leaving a minimum garrison
in the old front line.   This was now held, from the left of
the 4/Rifle Brigade (which had relieved the 2/Buffs at
Hampshire Farm), by the 1/Highland L.I., and 15th Sikhs,
the last named being in touch with the French at the
bottom of the slope behind Turco Farm.[1]

The Attack of the 149th (Northumberland) Brigade

The Northumberland Brigade [2] fared even worse than
the Lahore Division.   Though the brigade was in reserve
at Wieltje, Br.-General J. F. Riddell did not receive General
Alderson's orders to advance and participate in the attack

---

[1] The losses of the attacking battalions had been :—

	British officers.	Native officers.	Other ranks.
1/Manchester . . .	12	..	277
40th Pathans . . .	8	12	300
47th Sikhs	9	8	331
129th Baluchis . . .	7	7	217
57th Rifles	7	10	258
Connaught Rangers . .	15	..	351

Of the commanding officers Lieut.-Colonels H. W. E. Hitchins (Man-
chester) was killed, F. Rennick (40th Pathans) mortally wounded, and
S. J. Murray (Connaughts), Majors J. A. Hannyngton (129th) and T. J.
Willans (57th) wounded.

[2] Only the 4/, 6/ and 7/Northumberland Fusiliers were available, as
the 5/ had been sent up during the morning to Fortuin, where it had been
reported, incorrectly, that the enemy was breaking in.

26 April. at 1.20 P.M. until ten minutes after that hour. Neither he nor his officers knew the ground and were unaware that the belt of wire entanglement of G.H.Q. Line ran obliquely between them and St. Julien. As the Indian division had already begun operations, General Riddell decided, in spite of the very short notice, that he must not fail to co-operate. By 1.50 P.M. his three battalions were on the move, without having had time to load up extra ammunition, and with no more information as to what was required of them than the direction of attack pointed out on the map. A quarter of an hour afterwards they reached the G.H.Q. Line. As they threaded their way through the passages in the wire, they came under heavy fire, but nevertheless managed to deploy :—4/Northumberland Fusiliers (Lieut.-Colonel A. J. Foster) on the right, 6th (Lieut.-Colonel G. R. B. Spain) on the left, and the 7th (Lieut.-Colonel G. Scott Jackson) behind the 4th. They advanced steadily over the practically flat ground in two lines in artillery formation, suffering heavily, not only from an enemy barrage, but also from machine guns in Kitchener's Wood, against which no attack was proceeding. When, about 2.45 P.M., the battalions reached the line of the 10th Brigade, with the 7/Northumberland Fusiliers already absorbed into the attack, the unit of the 10th Brigade, that was to connect them on the left with the attack of the Lahore Division, was not to be seen.

Br.-General Hull of the 10th Brigade had received his copy of General Alderson's orders at 1.25 P.M. Owing to heavy losses on the 25th, all his battalions were engaged in holding his front line, and telephone connection with them was broken, so he informed General Alderson that it was impossible to comply, for it was already past the hour named for the start. He personally went, however, up to the firing line to his left battalion, the 7/Argyll and Sutherland Highlanders, reaching it at 2.30 P.M., and arranged that it should leave its trenches and go forward as soon as he saw the attack of the Lahore Division develop against Kitchener's Wood. This, as we know, never took place. Notwithstanding the lack of protection on the left, the Northumberland Brigade—the first Territorials to go into battle as a brigade—pushed through the 10th Brigade line with the greatest dash, but, like General Hull's men on the previous day, it was met by machine-gun fire from the houses. Without artillery support, it could only advance a short distance beyond the British front trenches.

About 3.40 P.M. Br.-General Riddell was killed, and when, 26 April. soon after, the leading lines reached some old trenches it was obvious that no further progress could be made. Although the task set to the brigade had been impossible and its losses devastating, it had not hesitated to obey. Having arrived at a line beyond which no one might pass and live the men got shelter where they could, but there was no thought of retiring. Colonel Foster then reported the situation in writing to brigade headquarters, and begged for ammunition. On learning that by General Riddell's death he was in command, he ordered the battalions to dig in as best they could. Thus they remained until early morning, when, after Colonel Foster had consulted with Br.-General Hull, they were withdrawn to the 10th Brigade line and subsequently sent back to Wieltje. The brigade had lost 42 officers and 1,912 other ranks, over two-thirds of its strength.[1]

The Attack on the 85th and 11th Brigades

Whilst opposite the left of the British the enemy had remained quiescent—merely beating off attacks, mainly by artillery fire, and declining to exploit his advantage— on the right he had made the most desperate efforts against the 85th Brigade and 1/Hampshire at the new shoulder of the front athwart Gravenstafel ridge, endeavouring to sweep them away, as he had swept the 3rd Canadian Brigade. Between 1 and 2 A.M., in the misty moonlight, a large party of Germans advanced against the Hampshire, some calling out " We are the Royal Fusiliers ". They caught a patrol that was out, but were then dealt with by the fire of a company whose commander had detected a foreign accent. Surprise having failed, as soon as the mist lifted in the morning the point of the shoulder was over- whelmed with fire, front, enfilade and reverse, accurately observed from the ridges north and east, which commanded every scrap of the ground. This shell fire continued not only all day, but for the following eight days : for each sixteen hours of daylight the 85th and 11th Brigades, and particularly the Royal Fusiliers and Hampshire and units

---

[1] Sir John French took the first opportunity of thanking the Northumberland Brigade personally for its services, explaining the emer- gency which had caused its being ordered on such a desperate enterprise. Br.-General G. P. T. Feilding succeeded Br.-General Riddell in command of the brigade.

26 April. aiding them, crouched in their trenches, like their comrades at First Ypres, listening to the burst of the shell and waiting for the bombardment to cease that they might stand up and face the attackers ; for eight hours of darkness, when the enemy ceased all but desultory fire and busied himself with strengthening his defences and bringing up supplies, they too toiled at repairing and extending their lines. On the 26th the Germans on the front between Berlin Wood and the cross roads 1,500 yards south-west of Gravenstafel, aided by observation from the top of the ridge known by that name, made repeated efforts to break in at the gaps between the Royal Fusiliers and the Hampshire, and between the Hampshire and Moulton-Barrett's (now Auld's) detachment; and shelled Wallace's detachment so severely that the officers destroyed all maps and papers, and prepared for a last stand.

A company of the 8/Middlesex despatched to the first of these gaps on the 25th, managed to check the enemy, but was itself almost entirely destroyed ; two companies of the 2/King's Shropshire L.I., with the 6/Durham L.I., under Lieut.-Colonel R. J. Bridgford of the former unit, were sent about 10 A.M. on the 26th to support Auld's detachment, which was reported surrounded and nearly cut off. The advance was made under heavy shell fire, but no infantry was encountered and the detachment was found to be holding its own. Bridgford's detachment was then ordered to return and hold the subsidiary line on Zonnebeke ridge from the right of the main body of the 11th Brigade at Hill 37 south-eastwards to the railway. Well supported by the 149th and 366th Field Batteries of the 28th Division, the latter of which stopped an enemy advance at 800 yards and in the afternoon alone fired 1,740 rounds, the infantry held on steadfastly till night.[1] It was then possible for the 11th Brigade to join up with the Hampshire, to relieve the small detachments and to fill the gaps, and for the 5/Green Howards and 5/East Yorkshire (150th Brigade) to relieve Wallace's detachment (1/Suffolk and 12/London) on the left of the brigade east of Fortuin. Auld's detachment was reinforced with a company of the Welch and some machine guns, and withdrawn to the next

---

[1] The G.O.C. 84th Brigade (Br.-General L. J. Bols) in reporting to the 28th Division recorded the brilliant services of Moulton-Barrett's (Auld's) detachment of Northumberland Fusiliers, Cheshires and Monmouthshires, in holding the enemy and preventing penetration ; and at night the Commander-in-Chief addressed a special message of appreciation to the 28th Division for the manner in which it had borne itself on this day.

farm (Dochy Farm) about four hundred yards in rear, but 26 April. still remained out in front of, and flanking, the general line. The 1/Royal Irish was withdrawn slightly and dug in between the 11th and 10th Brigades.

GENERAL SITUATION AT EVENING

Neither British nor Germans had therefore bettered their position by their attacks. By forcing the 8/Durham L.I. to evacuate the salient on Gravenstafel ridge, at Boetleer's Farm, the enemy had indeed strengthened the British position. The British counter-attacks, unfortunately, had hardly done more than pass the front line. The French, also, east of the canal, had done little more than recover the position lost earlier in the day; whilst on the west bank, although the Belgians co-operated, and desperate fighting continued into the night, only slight progress had been made : parts of Het Sas and Lizerne had been recovered, but Steenstraat remained wholly in German hands and the *XXIII. Reserve Corps* still held its bridgeheads, though they were endangered by French airmen bombing the floating bridges on the canal which connected them with the east bank.

Reports from the air showed that there were no signs of enemy activity and fewer trains at Tourcoing than on the previous day : 17 against 40. The general inference continued to be that no fresh enemy troops were arriving ; but to hamper the movement by rail of a German division reported to be in Ghent, No. 7 and No. 8 Squadrons of the R.F.C. during the afternoon dropped twenty-four 20-lb. bombs on the stations of Thielt, Staden, Ingelminster and Roulers, whilst No. 1 bombed Lille and Courtrai with 100-lb. bombs. The bombing machines sent to Roubaix and Tourcoing failed to reach their objectives.[1] The anxiety of the Germans to gain time either to complete their defences, or to make preparations for another attack, was confirmed in the evening by their acquiescence, as on the preceding evening, in the British walking about undisturbed in front of the 11th and 10th Brigade lines. The only sounds heard were those of the enemy apparently digging and strengthening his trenches—actually he was

---

[1] 2nd Lieut. W. B. Rhodes-Moorhouse received the first Victoria Cross bestowed on an airman, for bombing Courtrai station from a height of 300 feet, and, though mortally wounded, flying 35 miles home at a low altitude to report the success of his mission.

26 April. installing gas cylinders. The alarming factor in the situation was that his guns were now so well situated round three sides of the reduced Salient that they might make life in it impossible, and there were no counter-batteries, except the 123rd Heavy Battery, already sorely stricken, to deal with them. The British fighting in the Salient, with a canal behind them, were in this dilemma : if General Plumer kept the bulk of his troops in reserve west of the canal, the enemy might put down such a barrage on the few routes into the Salient, that the garrison east of the canal would be isolated and could be dealt with at leisure ; whilst if sufficient troops were kept in the Salient, they were bound to be huddled together, with no more protection than cover from view in shallow trenches and in the woods. If General Plumer kept his guns west of the canal they were too far back to render effective assist-ance ; in the Salient they were little better than targets. It was already difficult, as it was said, for the enemy to avoid hitting something or somebody with every shell.

The dangers and hazards of getting ammunition and supplies into, and wounded out of, the Salient each night were immense. The columns were brought to certain rendezvous and then taken over by guides who knew how to avoid the areas most favoured by German artillery.[1] By careful observation of the areas and routes that the Germans shelled—of course on a methodical programme—it was possible after a little time for the R.A., R.A.S.C., and R.A.M.C., and the regimental transport, which had to go back across the canal to the refilling points, to bring their columns through without heavy casualties ; but shelled the enemy never so furiously, the transport moved slowly and deliberately, without lights, never pausing on its way except to avoid a shell hole or clear a lorry that had been hit. So ammunition and supplies were brought up and wounded got away. It was a marvellous display of cold-blooded courage and discipline, which greatly im-pressed those who heard, although they could seldom see, the long processions of vehicles that went up night after night.

In view of the coming First Army offensive, G.H.Q. was

---

[1] At this time there was a collecting station for wounded at St. Jean ; motor ambulances came nightly as far as Zonnebeke and Wieltje, and horsed ambulances collected from the aid posts on portions of the roads inaccessible to motor transport. By midnight, as a rule, three-quarters of the aid posts had been cleared.

not very disposed to weaken still further General Haig's 26 April. force in order to aid the Second Army, and did no more than warn the Indian Cavalry Corps to be prepared to move and the 7th Division to have two brigades and part of the divisional artillery ready to march north at two hours' notice. The Second Army warned the 2nd Cavalry Division to be ready to go east of the canal, and after all the reports of the day had come in, at 10.30 P.M. gave orders to cease attacks and consolidate the positions held. It placed the 2nd Cavalry Division (Major-General C. T. McM. Kavanagh) at the disposal of the V. Corps, which ordered the 3rd and 5th Cavalry Brigades (Br.-Generals J. Vaughan and Sir P. W. Chetwode) dismounted, to proceed to the G.H.Q. Line beyond Wieltje.

NOTE

THE GERMANS ON THE 26TH APRIL 1915

The following is the translation of the account furnished by the *Reichsarchiv* :—

" It was settled that the continuation of the attack of the *XXVI.* " *Reserve Corps* should be carried out in combination with another " gas attack. The installation of the gas cylinders, which had been " begun in the sector of the *52nd Reserve Division* as early as the " evening of the 24th, took several days, and they were placed in " the portion of the front from the Ypres—Pilckem road eastward " to the heights north-west of Gravenstafel. On completion of the " installation the attack had to be postponed on account of un- " favourable weather. It was finally carried out on the 2nd May " towards 5 P.M.

" In the interval there was no cessation of activity on the front " of attack, enemy counter-attacks alternating with German local " offensives. In particular there was little rest on the right flank of " the *XXVII. Reserve Corps* [opposite the 85th Brigade].

" Incidentally during an enemy counter-attack on the 26th April " in the area south-east of Pilckem, the detachments of the gas " cylinder batteries released gas from a few cylinders for defensive " purposes ; with good results, so far as can be gathered from the " records ".[1]

Schwarte ii. p. 263, adds :—

" Lively attacks were made against both corps [*XXIII. Reserve* " and *XXVI. Reserve*] on the 26th, but repelled with heavy loss. " The *XXIII. Reserve Corps* held its position against Foch's counter- " attacks ; a British officer (*sic*) summoned the garrison of Lizerne " to surrender—of course in vain. In the *XXVI. Reserve Corps* all

[1] In a further communication it was stated that east [? south] of Pilckem by Struyve Farm [Hindenburg Farm, 1,000 yards north of Turco Farm] some gas cylinders were opened at the request of a company or battalion commander or possibly by the men of a gas battery on their own initiative.

" was prepared for counter-attack, but it was not carried out.   In
" the late evening Lizerne was taken by the French after heavy
" artillery bombardment ; a break-through was feared, and a counter-
" attack to recapture the place was ordered, but the *204th Reserve*
" *Infantry Regiment* would not attempt it.   ' The infantry again
" ' evidently lacks the right offensive spirit ' (war diary of the
" *XXIII. Reserve Corps*).   The enemy seemed superior in numbers,
" so the corps commander decided to retire the front line ".

CHAPTER XIV

THE BATTLES OF YPRES 1915 (*continued*)

THE BATTLE OF ST. JULIEN (*concluded*)[1]

THE PREPARATIONS FOR RETIREMENT AND THE FORMATION OF PLUMER'S FORCE, 27TH-30TH APRIL

27TH APRIL

(Map 9; Sketch 15)

THE SECOND ATTACK OF THE LAHORE DIVISION

THE operations of the day again depended on the French; but when General Smith-Dorrien received a copy of General Putz's orders, and, a little later, the divisional orders of General Joppé, now commanding on the immediate left of the British, he discovered that no more French troops were to be employed than on the previous day, in fact a battalion less. Although a brigade of the 18th Division in General Putz's reserve had been given to General Joppé, the latter had to hand back to the reserve two battalions of Chasseurs and a regiment of Zouaves, and he proposed to send only one new regiment east of the canal. Thus nothing more serious than a repetition of the local offensives of the previous day seemed intended. General Smith-Dorrien at once despatched a note to General Putz pointing out that the British troops were by themselves insufficient in number and too handicapped

---

[1] This official battle name covers the period up to the 4th May, but historically seems appropriate only up to the 28th April, when a fresh phase of the operations begins.

27 April. by their cramped position in the Salient to achieve anything except in co-operation with the French. General Putz thereupon ordered General Joppé to employ his whole force.[1] The G.O.C. Second Army communicated to the Chief of the General Staff, in a lengthy letter in which he gave the situation fully,[2] a summary of the French orders and a copy of his note. He requested Sir W. Robertson to let the Commander-in-Chief know that no expectation must be entertained of the French doing anything very great, and that he was pretty sure that the line at night would not be much in advance of what it was at the moment. If this proved to be the case—and it did—he meant to reorganize and consolidate the new front, withdrawing superfluous troops to the west of Ypres. It was indeed patent, he continued, that there were far too many troops and too much transport in the narrowed Salient— mere targets for the German artillery, without much cover from fire and little from view. As soon as it was clear that the French could not restore the situation, there was no other course but to withdraw the British line to a position at least fairly defensible. In giving his opinion, General Smith-Dorrien expressly stated that he was not in the least pessimistic, and added " the big " offensive elsewhere would do more to relieve the situation " than anything else ". In reply to his letter, he received at 2 P.M. a telephone message from the Chief of the General Staff informing him that Sir John French did not regard the situation as nearly so unfavourable, and wished him to act vigorously in conjunction with the French.[3] Major-General E. M. Perceval, Sub-Chief of the General Staff, was sent to instruct him verbally to the same effect, and Br.-General F. B. Maurice (Operations Section)[4] carried a similar message to General Plumer.

Nothing, however, but a carefully prepared offensive requiring much time to organize, could—as Neuve Chapelle had indicated—possibly dislodge the Germans from the ground they had gained and had been steadily fortifying for several nights. The French high command was already

---

[1] The liaison officer with the Lahore Division reported that the attack was actually made with a Moroccan brigade and one " régiment de ligne " of Colonel Mordacq's force ; the enemy artillery fire prevented more troops from crossing the floating bridges over the canal. The break-up of divisions and the formation of temporary commands made the rapid execution of operations very difficult for the French as for the British.
[2] Appendix 29.   [3] Appendix 30.
[4] Successor to Br.-General G. M. Harper now G.O.C. 17th Brigade.

organizing a great offensive in Artois; Sir John French was 27 April. engaged to assist in it, and neither he nor General Foch was inclined to abandon this operation or to risk success in both places by dividing between Artois and Flanders the small balance of resources of which they disposed.[1] Yet they could not bring themselves to relinquish the Ypres Salient. They had to bear in mind the special political and sentimental value attaching to every acre of the small portion of Belgium remaining unconquered, and the moral effect created amongst neutrals, if not the belligerent nations themselves, by the German pæans of victory on the gain of the smallest parcel of ground.[2] Otherwise it would probably have been best to have regarded the mishaps of the 22nd and 24th April as no more than serious local incidents—as before the battles of the Somme in 1916, the loss of a substantial part of Vimy Ridge by the IV. Corps (Lieut.-General Sir H. H. Wilson) was judged by Sir Douglas Haig—which, if they could not be repaired at once by the local troops must be accepted. To resume the offensive vigorously before Ypres without serious reinforcements was to invite failure and run the risk of heavy casualties without any compensatory success; while to make a really serious effort with large forces to recover all the lost ground might react adversely on the planned offensive further south, and would to that extent be playing into the enemy's hands.

For ill now, although for weal in the last year of the war, General Foch was the very spirit of the offensive. Sir John French, apart from the desire to conform to his wishes as far as possible, could not fail to be influenced by him; but at heart he was most anxious to withdraw

[1] A French official pamphlet, " Opérations Franco-Britanniques dans les Flandres ", p. 111, puts it clearly : " The greater part, and the best, " of the available shock troops were assembled in the region of Arras in " view of the principal offensive to be launched at the beginning of May. " This explains why the neighbouring sectors, themselves drained of troops, " were unable to lend sufficient reinforcements in spite of the urgency. " This is similarly the explanation of the momentary artillery inferiority " on the Flanders front ". It would appear that General Foch had at once come to the conclusion that the loss of ground near Ypres must be regarded as one affecting the British more than the French. In fact, had not the 29th Division been diverted to Gallipoli, all French troops would have left the neighbourhood of the Salient weeks before.

[2] Certain British authorities even were affected by the German claims, as the telegrams between London and G.H.Q. of this time demonstrate. They appear to have accepted the enemy news in preference to G.H.Q. reports, which were alleged to be prejudiced.

from the impossible position in the Salient and to avoid,
if possible, involving the divisions of the New Army in a
losing battle as their first experience of war. The struggle
at Ypres was therefore continued, and in deference to the
French pre-war doctrine of the offensive on all occasions
and in all situations, the local commanders, both French
and British, were encouraged, nay ordered, to recover by
infantry attack the localities they had lost, without even
the amount of artillery support which pre-war teaching
would have regarded as necessary, let alone what experience
had shown to be indispensable.

General Joffre on this day provided two " groupes " of
3·6-inch guns and a " groupe " of 4·8-inch (long) guns, but
no further reinforcements, General Putz being informed by
General Foch that his forces were sufficient to carry the
affair to a successful conclusion.[1] General Putz resumed
his attempts. He ordered the preparatory bombardment
of the enemy's front trenches to be begun at 12.30 P.M.,
and the infantry assault to take place at 1.15 P.M., when
the guns would lift on to the second line and roads beyond.
General Smith-Dorrien, pending further instructions from
G.H.Q., directed the Lahore Division and all available
artillery to conform to the French programme, with the
proviso that the infantry should take advantage of any
progress made by the French to gain ground, but should
not be committed to the assault until the advance of our
Allies had assured the safety of the left flank of the Indian
troops. The Ypres—Langemarck road remained, as before,
the boundary between the two contingents.

In direct liaison with General Joppé, Major-General
Keary arranged that the Ferozepore Brigade, from shelter
trenches between St. Jean and La Brique, should advance
at 12.30 P.M. and come up on the right of the Sirhind,
the main body of which was in the second line trenches
behind Hill Top ridge. The two brigades would then move
forward simultaneously with the French, who had their
own native troops on their right wing. Br.-General W. G.
Walker (Sirhind Brigade) did not, however, wait, but, in
order to get the benefit of the artillery preparation, moved
forward as soon as the bombardment commenced.[2]

---

[1] " Pour poursuivre l'affaire et la résoudre ".

[2] The 1/4th Gurkhas (Major B. M. L. Brodhurst, killed) on right,
1/1st Gurkhas (Lieut.-Colonel W. C. Anderson) on left, 4/King's (Lieut.-
Colonel J. W. Allen) in support. They passed through the line of the
1/H.L.I. and 15th Sikhs, on the left of the 13th Brigade line, when these
two units followed in support.

As before, immediately the leading lines crossed the low 27 April. crest of Hill Top ridge, they came under heavy artillery fire from many directions, but although skilful use was made of the natural features of the ground and of existing trenches, they could make little progress until reinforced by the supports, and then only part of them reached Canadian Farm and the bottom of the valley in front. The Ferozepore Brigade, reduced to 38 British officers and 1,648 rifles, of which the three Indian battalions furnished only 688,[1] also moved at 12.30 P.M. from its trenches near St. Jean to La Brique,[2] to come up on the right of the Sirhind. It met with the same reception from the enemy as its predecessor as soon as it appeared on the open ridge near Mouse Trap Farm, but, persevering, passed through the lines of the 4/Rifle Brigade, in the 2/Buffs' old trenches, and got up abreast of the Sirhind, from Canadian Farm north-eastwards. Then it was held up.

The French pinned to the ground by a heavy barrage put down on their infantry in its position of assembly did not make an attack.

All the morning Second Army headquarters had been endeavouring to find a brigade to support the Lahore Division. This proved to be impossible, as every formation in the Salient was very reduced in numbers, and either in the line or too exhausted to permit of its employment without nearly certain danger of failure. Eventually, therefore, it was decided to form a composite brigade, and one hardly stronger than a battalion,[3] with Lieut.-Colonel H. D. Tuson of the D.C.L.I. in command, was collected from the V. Corps reserves. At 2.40 P.M. this was placed at General Keary's disposal. He sent Colonel Tuson to support the Sirhind Brigade, with instructions to report whether further bombardment of the German position was necessary. As the front lines proved to be still at least three hundred yards from the enemy, another artillery preparation, to begin at 5.30 P.M., was ordered. At this hour, before the British were ready, the French on their

---

[1] The figures for the Sirhind are not available; its losses at this time had not been heavy. The Jullundur Brigade was down to 1,216 rifles, of which only 451 were Indians.

[2] 4/London and 9th Bhopals leading, Connaught Rangers in support, 129th Baluchis and 57th Rifles in reserve.

[3] 2/D.C.L.I. (82nd Brigade), 260 strong; 1/York and Lancaster (83rd), 280 strong; 5/King's Own (83rd), 400 strong; 2/Duke of Wellington's (13th), 350 strong. Total 1,290.

27 April. left advanced, but the attack withered away under heavy fire before it got level with the front of the Sirhind Brigade. The French commanders, nevertheless, remained optimistic,[1] as General Curé by 4 P.M. had reconquered the whole of Lizerne, taking 250 prisoners, Het Sas, and the line of the canal up to Steenstraat, where well supported by fire from the east bank the Germans still clung to their bridgehead.

A further more or less combined attack was made at 6.30 P.M. by the two Indian brigades and Tuson's detachment, which the Germans met with a terrific burst of fire of all kinds. There was hope for a few minutes nevertheless that the leading lines would reach the wire. Then the word was passed along the front, in the mysterious way that bad news travels in battle, that gas had been turned on against the Turcos—actually they had been severely dosed with gas shell—and that they were fleeing in panic. This unfortunately proved to be the case, the rumour being soon confirmed by the sight of the Africans crowding back across the bridges, and by an appeal to the V. Corps by General Putz for a British cavalry brigade to stem their flight. For this intervention there was no need : two battalions of Chasseurs from the reserve were sent up and effectively rallied the native troops. The garrisons of the French front line from Turco Farm along the road towards Boesinghe, from which the attack had started, fortunately held on. In the failing light this was not discovered, and it was supposed that all the French had retired ; so although an order came through from the Second Army to consolidate the line gained, the survivors of the attack were brought back to the line held in the morning, as both flanks of the Indian brigades were thought to be in the air. The Sirhind Brigade again covered the front with the 1/1st Gurkhas in touch with the 13th Brigade on the right, and the 15th Sikhs nearly at right angles, facing west, in touch with the French on the left. The rest were withdrawn behind Hill Top ridge. Again the Germans did not

---

[1] At 4 P.M. General Foch despatched a message to G.H.Q. as follows :— " We have made fresh progress at Lizerne. Besides 150 men, 5 machine " guns and bomb throwers taken yesterday, we have taken about 100 " prisoners, a machine gun and a bomb thrower, which latter has been " turned against the enemy. To the north of Moorslede Farm [not " discoverable, possibly Turco Farm, called by the French Mortelje Farm, " is meant] on the west of the Ypres—Langemarck road, the attack is " reported to have advanced several hundred metres, and to be moving " forward. The English are reported to have got into Bois des Cuisiniers " [Kitchener's Wood. This was incorrect.] "

pursue but left their opponents in peace to reorganize and 27 April. clear up the battlefield.[1]

The situation on the right in the areas of the 85th, 11th and 10th Brigades was in hand all day, and though heavy shelling continued, the line was unshaken, and no infantry advance was attempted by the enemy.[2] After dark the 11th Brigade took over the whole line from Berlin Wood, the left of the 85th Brigade, to near Fortuin, the right of the 10th Brigade, and relieved Moulton-Barrett's, the 150th Brigade and other detachments in it, and filled all the gaps.[3] Thus the line was now held from right to left by the following brigades: the 85th (28th Division), 11th, 10th (both of the 4th Division) and 13th (5th Division), part of the Sirhind; and thence by the French from Turco Farm towards Boesinghe.

The Reorganization of the Ypres Command

At 4.35 P.M., in the midst of the fighting, whilst General Perceval was discussing with General Smith-Dorrien the 2 P.M. message he had brought from the Chief of the General Staff,[4] a telegram came through " in clear " from G.H.Q.[5] directing the G.O.C. of the Second Army to hand over the command of all troops engaged around Ypres to General Plumer, and to send to him his Chief Staff Officer, Major-General G. F. Milne. The actual transfer of authority was made at 5.30 P.M., and General Milne, with Major-General J. E. W. Headlam, commanding the artillery of the Second Army, and four General Staff officers, Lieut.-Colonel R. H. Hare, Major C. J. C. Grant, Captain W. G. S. Dobbie and Captain R. J. Collins, were attached to the new staff, and reported at V. Corps headquarters at 8 P.M. From this hour General Plumer acted both as G.O.C. "Plumer's

---

[1] The losses of the battalions of the two Indian brigades had been :

	British officers.	Native officers.	Other ranks.
4/King's	9	..	374
1/H.L.I.	2	..	108
4/London	8	..	197
15th Sikhs	3	9	86
9th Bhopals	3	2	117
1/1st Gurkhas . . .	5	2	95
1/4th Gurkhas . . .	5	5	175

[2] He was preparing a gas attack, as we know now. See Note at end of Chapter XIII.

[3] General Bulfin lent Br.-General Hasler two General Staff officers to assist him in this task.

[4] See page 270.   [5] Appendix 31.

27 April. Force " and G.O.C. V. Corps, General Milne being his Chief General Staff Officer in the former capacity and Br.-General H. S. Jeudwine remaining Br.-General General Staff of the V. Corps, and at the same time assisting General Milne. Every effort was made to avoid dislocation of staff duties until the change of command became generally known, and the Lahore Division, the principal formation affected, was not therefore informed until 11 P.M. As most of the other troops engaged were already under General Plumer, the real effect of the change was that he reported direct to G.H.Q. instead of through the Second Army, which was now reduced to one corps, the II., as on the 6th April the III. Corps had been withdrawn from it and placed for operations directly under G.H.Q.

Written instructions were subsequently handed to General Plumer,[1] directing him to consolidate the line then held, to prepare another line east of Ypres ready for occupation in case it became advisable to withdraw from the existing Salient—he was in fact ordered to carry out what had been proposed by General Smith-Dorrien—but to co-operate with and assist General Putz should he, as ordered by General Foch, renew the attack next day.

After dark the reorganization of the troops was taken in hand ; Colonel Geddes's battalions were ordered to return to their own brigades.[2] General Snow (27th Division) recovered control of all his own battalions, still keeping the corps reserve, now down to two battalions. General Bulfin (28th Division) was given, in addition to his own troops, the 11th,[3] 150th (York and Durham) and 151st (Durham L.I.) Brigades ; General Alderson, the 10th, 13th and 149th (Northumberland) Brigades.

At 9.15 P.M. Colonel Desticker, General Putz's Chief of the Staff, visited V. Corps headquarters to confirm the report of the reconstitution of the French front east of the canal, and announce that it was intended to renew the

[1] Appendix 32.
[2] Colonel Geddes closed his headquarters on the night of the 27th, and called at 13th Brigade headquarters at St. Jean on his way to Potijze. As it was very late, he stayed the night. When leaving early on the 28th he found he had lost his map, and asked Br.-General Wanless O'Gowan for one. Whilst the latter was getting it, a shell burst in the room, killing Colonel Geddes and severely wounding his staff officers, Major H. C. Maitland Makgill Crichton (R. Scots Fusiliers) and Lieut. J. Nichols (Q.V.R.).
[3] Br.-General J. Hasler, commanding the 11th Brigade, was killed in St. Jean by a shell about 7 P.M. He was succeeded temporarily by Lieut.-Colonel F. R. Hicks and then by Br.-General C. B. Prowse (Somerset L.I.), who was killed on 1st July 1916.

YPRES, 1915.

The Salient, on the 30th April, as it was established before the withdrawal.

SKETCH 15.

attack next day, but not until the afternoon, by which 27 April. time the three " groupes " of artillery that had arrived would be better able to co-operate.   There was certainly temptation to attack again ; for signs were not lacking that the German infantry was beginning to waver, and although the enemy artillery fire was more intense than ever, it was perhaps the last flare up before the end.   St. Jean, Wieltje, Potijze and other villages had been reduced to ruins : there was not a safe spot in the Salient ; and during the day a long-range 15-inch gun shelled General Smith-Dorrien's advanced headquarters in Poperinghe, besides Bergues and Dunkirk (each about 24 miles range) and only just failing to reach Cassel,[1] which was equally distant.   The weather on the 27th had been too unfavourable for air reconnaissance, but there was good evidence that no reinforcements had arrived : the prisoners taken to date belonged to the corps originally around Ypres, the *XXII. Reserve, XXIII. Reserve, XXVI. Reserve* and *XXVII. Reserve Corps*, and the *Ersatz* and *Landwehr Brigades* normally attached to them ; and all prisoners, except one whose statement was easily disproved, agreed in stating that no new formations had come up, although part of the *XXII. Reserve Corps* had moved nearer Ypres. Sir John French in telegraphing home the result of the day's operations could only say that the Allied troops were in the same position as in the morning, and that the casualties had been very heavy.

28TH APRIL

PLUMER'S FORCE FORMED.   PREPARATIONS FOR A WITHDRAWAL.   GENERAL FOCH'S PROTEST AND A PAUSE

During the night of the 27th/28th April, at 2.40 A.M., a Sketch further attempt was made in the moonlight by two com- 15. panies (230 strong) of the 2/King's Shropshire L.I. (27th Division) to recover the trench of the East Surrey Regiment near Broodseinde.   Received with fire at 30 yards range it was repulsed with the loss of 3 officers and 51 other ranks.   Otherwise the night was comparatively quiet, and the reorganization of the troops under V. Corps was carried out undisturbed.   Except for the continual shelling of all parts of the Salient, and particularly of the 85th Brigade

[1] It was fired from Kattestraat, 4,000 yards south-east of Dixmude. Schwarte ii. p. 263.

28 April. area (north of Zonnebeke), the town of Ypres, the canal crossings and the roadways into Ypres, there was for a few days a lull in the fighting.[1] At 7.50 A.M. on the 28th G.H.Q., to emphasize the new arrangement of command, directed by telegram that the troops under General Sir H. Plumer should be known as " Plumer's Force ".[2]

At 10 A.M. General Plumer was instructed in writing by the Chief of the General Staff that the Commander-in-Chief thought it would " in all probability be necessary " to-night to commence measures for the withdrawal from " the Salient to a more westerly line ", and he was directed to " take such preliminary measures for commencing retire- " ment to-night, if in the C-in-C's opinion it proves neces- " sary ".   He was to report early the line that he proposed eventually to occupy.

Soon after the despatch of Br.-General F. B. Maurice with these instructions, Sir John French went to Cassel to visit General Foch, and inform him of his plans. He particularly emphasized the fatigue of his troops, and the difficulties

---

[1] The enemy, as is now known, was waiting for a wind favourable for a gas attack.

[2] The organization of the British Expeditionary Force was now :—

Plumer's Force :	Cavalry Corps ; V. Corps (27th, 28th and Canadian Divisions), Lahore Division, 10th and 11th Brigades (4th Division) ; 149th, 150th and 151st Brigades (50th (Northumbrian) Division) ; 13th Brigade (5th Division) ; two field cos. R.E. of the 7th Division.
First Army :	I. Corps (1st, 2nd and 47th (2nd London) Divisions) ; IV. Corps (8th Division and 1 brigade of 7th Division) ; Indian Corps (less Lahore Division).
Second Army :	II. Corps (3rd, 5th—less 13th Brigade—and 46th (North Midland) Divisions).
G.H.Q. Troops :	III. Corps (6th and 48th (South Midland) Divisions ; 50th Division (less infantry brigades) ; 4th Division (less 10th and 11th Brigades) ; Indian Cavalry Corps ; 7th Division (less a brigade and two field companies R.E.).

The R.F.C. was also regrouped, No. 8 Squadron going to the 2nd Wing to work with Plumer's Force.

The approximate number of rifles in Plumer's Force was on the morning of the 28th as follows :—

27th Division, 11,401 ; 28th Division, 11,430 ; Canadian Division, 6,650 ; 2nd Cavalry Division, 4,030 ; 50th Division 8,445 ; 10th Brigade, 1,770 ; 11th Brigade, 3,050 ; 13th Brigade, 1,450. Total 48,226. Lahore Division and Cavalry Corps, numbers not recorded for this date. 2,000 reinforcements arrived on 28th.

Heavy artillery of Plumer's Force :—one 9·2-inch gun, four 6-inch howitzers ; eight 60-pdrs. ; twelve 4·7-inch guns (of these only the 123rd Heavy Battery was east of Ypres).

Field Artillery :—18-pdrs., 198 guns ; 13-pdrs., 28 ; 4·5-inch howitzers, 8 ; Belgian 75 mm., 8 ; anti-aircraft, 2.

of supplying them with food and ammunition in the Salient. 28 April.
General Foch protested vehemently against any thought
of withdrawal. To the British Commander-in-Chief's
arguments that the fighting around Ypres was a secondary
matter compared with the coming offensive near Arras,
which was " la grosse affaire " of the moment, he replied
that the lost ground could be retaken with the troops
already available, as he had told General Putz on the
previous day ; that to withdraw was to invite the enemy
to come on and repeat his attack ; and that to win a
second battle it was not necessary to lose a first. He
begged Sir John French before giving orders for retirement
to wait until he had seen the results of the French attacks
to be made next day with the help of heavy artillery that
was being brought up.[1] To this course the British Field-
Marshal agreed, and again instructed General Plumer to
co-operate with General Putz, but to send forthwith out
of the Salient, as General Smith-Dorrien had proposed, all
troops and material that he did not require, and specially
to reconnoitre through-roads north and south of Ypres, so
as to keep clear, if possible, of the main Ypres—Poperinghe
road.

General Foch subsequently sent to G.H.Q. a written
protest embodying the arguments he had put forward
verbally.[2] To this Sir John French replied that they were
agreed that the situation was a dangerous one, but the
only remedy for it was for the British to withdraw from
part of the exposed position, or for the French to retake
the ground they had originally lost, and thus re-establish
the line.

The line on which General Plumer selected to retire
retained Hill 60, then ran to a point on the Menin road in
front of Hooge, included Frezenberg ridge, and then
continued to Mouse Trap Farm, whence it turned west to
the canal as before. Thus the greater part of it was on
the forward slopes of Frezenberg and Mouse Trap ridges,
and therein differed from the switch line begun on the
night of the 26th/27th, which was sited behind the crest
of Frezenberg ridge. By withdrawing to the selected line,
an area would be abandoned about five miles across the
base, a mile deep near Hooge, and two and a half miles
deep near Frezenberg ; but once it was decided to leave

---

[1] The heavy artillery amounted to " two groupes " of 3·6-inch and
one " groupe " of 4·8-inch guns, as we have seen.
[2] Appendix 33.

28 April. Gravenstafel ridge, this line was the first on which a stand could be made. In forwarding his proposals,[1] General Plumer gave it as his opinion that the existing front could not be permanently held ; that unless the French regained practically the whole of the ground they had lost, the British situation could not be improved without the employment of a very large force ; that local attacks would only cause further heavy loss without effecting any material improvement in the situation ; and that the longer the retirement was delayed, the more difficult and costly it would become. He calculated that the withdrawal to the new line would probably take four nights to carry out.[2]

General Plumer was early in communication with General Putz ; but the latter's plan did not seem to offer much prospect of success considering the means at his disposal, and particularly the small number of guns capable of counter-battery work. The French left was to capture Steenstraat and expel the Germans from the west bank of the canal ; then the centre was to join in and cross at Boesinghe ; on which the right, east of the canal, was to move forward. The attacks of the 28th gave " peu de resultats ", says the French account. An artillery bombardment, assisted by Belgian and British guns, was begun at dawn and continued spasmodically till 3.30 P.M., when three French regiments left their trenches to attack Steenstraat. They found the German defenders ready for them, and, in spite of very heavy losses, did not get within five hundred yards of the front trenches. The French right and centre fired but did not advance. German accounts relate that, as on previous occasions, the attacks were stopped by gun fire alone.[3] The British situation remained unchanged ; for as the French on the east bank did not move, the Sirhind Brigade, which had been warned to co-operate with them, did not stir either.

The enemy made no attacks, and very little movement was seen by the Flying Corps either on the roads or railways ; but there were signs of more heavy guns being brought up and mounted in Houthulst Forest. Dead of the *Marine Corps* were found near the Haanebeek east of Fortuin, definitely identifying the presence of part of that formation, and the French captured in Lizerne men of units of the *XXII. Reserve Corps*, thus, as already men-

---

[1] Appendix 34.
[2] Full moon, as it fortunately happened, occurred on the 29th.
[3] " Artillery Regt. No. 46 " v. 50.

tioned, proving a shift southwards of the flank of that 28 April.
corps; but a report of the arrival of 8,000 reinforcements
at Ghent, to replace casualties, was the only news of any
addition of troops to the Ypres—Nieuport front.

The 1st Cavalry Division (less its artillery) was released
by General Putz from his reserve, and was sent back to
the Proven area (6 miles north-west of Poperinghe), to
which district the Indian Cavalry Corps was also moved.
The 3rd Cavalry Division was drawn back from Vlamertinghe to the south-west of Poperinghe.[1]

Having nothing but cavalry under its hand, G.H.Q.
drew from the First Army into reserve at Fletre (8 miles
S.S.W. of Poperinghe) the 7th Division (less a brigade and
a proportion of artillery left in the line), already warned for
this purpose, and sent its field companies, the 54th and
55th, to help to organize the new Ypres lines.

The Lahore Division was ordered at 3.34 P.M. by
Plumer's Force to consolidate the line, generally coinciding
with that of the 13th Brigade, that it had reached on the
27th, and later the 1st Canadian Brigade from the reserve
was placed at General Keary's disposal as a working party.
It so happened that officers of the 20th and 21st Companies, 3rd Sappers & Miners having reconnoitred No Man's
Land, had discovered that a more forward line could be
taken up in the bottom of the valley concealed from the
German trenches, which were on rising ground, by a con-
vexity of the slope. A more ambitious programme was
therefore undertaken by Major G. H. Boileau, R.E., one of
the field engineers of the division, and this forward line laid
out, from the west of Mouse Trap Farm, by Canadian Farm,
to Turco Farm. It was dug and wired under protection
of a Canadian covering party. Canadian Farm itself was
prepared for all-round defence by the Sappers & Miners,
and communication trenches were made by the 34th Sikh
Pioneers. Although it was bright moonlight, and the
Germans could be seen on the skyline 300 to 500 yards
away busily engaged in wiring, so occupied were they that
they did not hinder British work by fire. The only
casualty was an engineer officer, wounded by a sentry in
mistake for a German. Thus a gain of ground was made
without a long casualty list. On completion, the line was
handed over to the 13th Brigade.

[1] The 2nd Cavalry Division (dismounted) remained in Plumer's reserve
at Potijze.

A POSTPONEMENT OF THE WITHDRAWAL. CONTINUA-
TION OF PREPARATIONS

29 April.   Early in the morning of the 29th, General Putz's orders
for yet another attack, at noon, were received ; but there
was no mention in them of fresh troops or additional guns.
At 9.30 A.M., however, General Foch sent a notification
that the operations were postponed until next day for the
reason that the artillery recently arrived had not had time
to register.[1]

Sir John French at once consented to maintain his
troops in position for another day, and to co-operate on the
30th. He further agreed to withhold his order for the
withdrawal from the tip of the Salient until the result of
these operations became known. In a written memorandum
transmitting a copy of General Putz's orders, General Foch
insisted that no result could be obtained except by
" simultaneous, not successive, efforts of the British and
" French troops ". He therefore asked that orders might
be given to Plumer's Force, as they had been to his troops,
" to attack with the greatest energy and the most complete
" co-operation ".

The Germans, as if in preparation for an assault,
devoted special attention on this day to bombarding with
guns and trench mortars the two extremities of the Ypres
front :—the 85th Brigade, against which sapping was also
employed, and the Belgian 6th Division : but both held
their ground. The French spent the day in reorganizing,
but at 6 P.M. their left wing made an independent attack
on Steenstraat. It had greater success than any previous
attempt and obtained possession of the village, but was
unable to drive the Germans over the canal, and they still
remained in possession of a narrow strip of ground on the
west side, from Steenstraat to Het Sas. The French
counter-attacks fell short of complete success from lack of
thorough artillery preparation, though, unlike the British,
they needed guns rather than ammunition.

Again on this day very little movement on the enemy
side could be detected, and there were no signs of the
arrival of reinforcements, so that the encouragement to

---

[1] Of the nine batteries, two 4·8-inch were assigned to support the
attack east of the canal.

make one more attempt to dislodge the few remaining 29 April.
Germans is readily comprehensible.

In the course of the 29th April, General Plumer issued
to his divisional commanders a preparatory order [1] explaining the general arrangements for a retirement from the
tip of the Salient. Under flank protection of the artillery
posted on the western bank of the canal, the Lahore,
50th (Northumbrian), and 2nd Cavalry Divisions, were to
be withdrawn, and the new front occupied by three Old
Army divisions, the 27th, the 28th and the 4th.[2] Large
parties of the 28th and 50th Divisions, with all available
engineer companies—amounting sometimes to 22—were
meantime employed every night under Br.-General R. D.
Petrie, Chief Engineer of the V. Corps, in preparing the
new line of defence and in multiplying the passages over
the canal. By this time engineer parks had been formed,
and there was a sufficiency of engineer stores for summer
work.

30TH APRIL

A SECOND POSTPONEMENT OF THE WITHDRAWAL. RELIEF
OF THE 13TH BRIGADE BY THE 12TH BRIGADE

The enemy did not attack on the 30th April. Again 30 April.
no movement of importance could be detected on or behind
his front, but his bombardment of the Salient and its
approaches was practically continuous.

At 3 A.M. General Putz's orders for an attack to begin
at 8 A.M., which he had been pressed by General Foch to
make, were received by General Plumer. On account of
the mist, zero hour was subsequently postponed until
11.15 A.M. Taking into account the direction of the wind,
which would favour the discharge of gas by the enemy
against the Steenstraat and Het Sas front, the French commander had reversed his previous arrangements, and
decided to begin the attack this time with his right wing,
nearest the British. General Plumer's orders for artillery
co-operation had been issued on the previous evening, and

---

[1] Appendix 35.
[2] The Canadian Division (that is Alderson's command : the Canadian
Division plus the 10th and 11th Brigades of the 4th Division), and not the
4th Division was mentioned in the orders ; but later General Plumer
was informed that the 12th Brigade and all the 4th Divisional troops except
the artillery were being sent to him at once. The artillery would follow,
and the reconstituted 4th Division, General H. F. M. Wilson relieving
General Alderson, would then definitely take the place of the Canadian
in his Force, the latter division going into rest.

30 April. on the receipt of General Putz's communication he directed that the Sirhind Brigade should take part in any advance made by the French, protect their right flank, and maintain connection between the two armies. Although some slight progress was made by General Joppé's left near the canal, his right next to the British did not move, as the wire in front of it had not been sufficiently cut. The Sirhind Brigade therefore remained stationary behind Hill Top ridge. The French centre was unable to debouch from Boesinghe, and though the left wing made a further attack near Steenstraat, progress was " slow ". The French and Belgian artillery, in spite of their orders to concentrate fire on the small German bridgehead, could assist very little, as the opposing infantries were dug in so close to each other. General Curé, commanding the French left wing west of the canal, came to the conclusion [1] that, owing to lack of sufficient heavy artillery, no advantage could be gained by the continuation of the general offensive. He had lost 120 officers and 3,853 other ranks between the 26th and 29th in recovering Lizerne ; he suggested, therefore, limiting future operations to partial attacks, carefully prepared, so as to keep the enemy on the alert, and recovering ground when possible. In this suggestion General Putz concurred, and in the evening sent a liaison officer to General Plumer to propose a convergent attack next day on Hill 29, the highest portion of Mauser ridge, due north of Turco Farm. He asked that the Sirhind Brigade should participate from the south-east. As this did not appear in consonance with the plans for a general offensive in a north-easterly direction formulated to the British Commander-in-Chief by General Foch, General Plumer reported the proposal to G.H.Q. with a request for instructions. In reply, he was given permission to support any attack with fire, but was definitely ordered not to engage his infantry in one, unless it formed part of a general offensive of the French troops east of the canal. Of this decision General Putz was at once informed ; but as there was obviously some misunderstanding, General Plumer himself in the early morning of the 1st May proceeded to General Putz's headquarters and made it clear to him that the Sirhind Brigade would attack simultaneously against Hill 29, but only if the French line advanced. Sir John French during the 30th April had warned General Foch in writing that, if the attacks of the

[1] Palat, ix. p. 257.

day did not sufficiently restore the situation, he would 30 April. that night begin his withdrawal from the tip of the Salient, the troops of his left wing maintaining their position in touch with the French.   In the evening after the very disappointing news of the day had come in, General Foch motored from Cassel to Hazebrouck, and at his urgent request the British commander agreed a second time to a postponement of 24 hours, though this meant leaving his troops exposed on three sides to artillery fire and suffering heavy wastage with little opportunity for reply.

During the evening, however, one relief was carried out : the 12th Brigade (4th Division) (Br.-General F. G. Anley) arrived, and, passing the canal under heavy fire, took over the left sector of the front of the 10th Brigade and the whole of that of the 13th Brigade.   By this change the three infantry brigades of the 4th Division, re-united, occupied the left of the British line supported by the artillery of the Canadian Division, which still remained in action.   Br.-General Wanless O'Gowan on relief withdrew the 13th Brigade west of the canal, eventually collecting it in the wood a mile north-west of Vlamertinghe. Its numbers, after its battles at Hill 60 and before Ypres, in spite of reinforcements totalled barely fourteen hundred of all ranks.

CHAPTER XV

THE BATTLES OF YPRES 1915 (*continued*)

THE WITHDRAWAL TO THE FREZENBERG LINE
1ST-3RD MAY

(Maps 4, 10 ; Sketches 8, 16)

1ST MAY

THE FIRST STAGE OF THE WITHDRAWAL

Map 10.
Sketch
16.
VERY complete arrangements were made by General Plumer to co-operate with the French on 1st May. The leading units of the Sirhind Brigade—which, though it bore an Indian title, now contained a majority of British troops—were moved up into the front trenches of the 12th Brigade ready to advance at 3.10 P.M., the hour fixed by General Putz. The infantry of the 28th and 4th Divisions were warned to take part if the Sirhind Brigade went forward. General Putz also made specially careful arrangements, reinforcing both General Joppé on the right and General Quiquandon in the centre, from his reserve. But at 3.10 P.M., though fire was opened, the French infantry did not leave its trenches. A second attempt, timed for 4.40 P.M., equally failed to materialize, the British liaison officer with the Détachement de Belgique reporting that the men were too tired for any further serious effort.

Before, however, reports of the original failure to advance reached G.H.Q., General Foch had again visited the British Commander-in-Chief to state that his views had been over-ridden by General Joffre, and, by the latter's direction, he presented a note. This began : " In the " present situation the principal object which the Command " of the Allied armies has in view is the preparation of " operations on the front Arras—Neuve Chapelle. The

SKETCH 16.

YPRES, 1915.
THE NEW SALIENT.
Situation on the 4th May.

" intention is to attack on that front and to act on the 1 May.
" defensive about Ypres ". It went on to suggest that
the forces near Ypres could be reduced in favour of the
attack further south, though the offensive attitude, with
partial attacks, should be maintained until the main operations had been commenced. To these proposals, as they
were entirely in consonance with his own views which
he had put aside in order to co-operate with General Foch,
Sir John French of course agreed ; and he informed General
Foch that the retirement from the tip of the Salient would
be begun that night by the withdrawal to the west of
Ypres of troops, services and material not required for
defence. He, however, pointed out that the safety of the
British troops even in the reduced Salient, and the retention
of the town of Ypres, would depend largely on the maintenance of the ground between the Langemarck road and
the canal by the French, and he asked that " the troops
" should be of the best quality, in sufficient strength,
" and that adequate measures of defence should be
" taken ".

At 3.45 P.M., therefore, when the first failure of the
French to attack at 3.10 P.M. became known, a definite
order was issued from G.H.Q. to General Plumer :—" You
" will begin to-night to carry out the withdrawal of your
" troops on the eastern part of the Salient ". Immediately
on its receipt at 4 P.M., General Plumer issued his instructions, which were drawn up and ready, for the first
stage of the retirement to begin at 8 P.M.

By these instructions, the Lahore Division (less its artillery, the bulk of which had never crossed) was brought back
over the canal and assembled at Ouderdom (4½ miles S.S.W.
of Ypres); about half of the batteries of the II. and III.
Canadian Field Artillery Brigades and CXVIII. (Howitzer)
Brigade still in the Salient rejoined the I. C.F.A. Brigade
east of Brielen, the 123rd Heavy Battery took position
near the 122nd west of that place ; and half the artillery
of the 27th Division was retired to positions closer to the
canal. When these moves, which left the front line
untouched, had been carried out, there would be remaining
of Plumer's Force in the front line of the Salient, the
27th and 28th Divisions and the three infantry brigades
of the 4th Division ; [1] and in reserve the 2nd Cavalry

[1] Under command of Lieut.-General E. A. H. Alderson of the Canadian
Division until the arrival on 4th May of Major-General H. F. M. Wilson.
To give some idea of the difficulties of the administrative arrangements,

1 May. Division (Potijze), 149th (Northumberland) Brigade (south of Verlorenhoek), 151st (Durham L.I.) Brigade (Frezenberg), the 150th (York and Durham) Brigade (two battalions attached to the 11th Brigade, two battalions near Vlamertinghe), and the Canadian Division (Brielen).

Separate instructions [1] were issued at the same time as a warning order for the next stage of the retirement to take place on the night of the 3rd/4th May.

The movements ordered for the first stage were carried out during the night of the 1st/2nd May without incident. At 7.30 P.M. General Plumer's headquarters were moved back, and by G.H.Q. instructions established at Abeele, 9 miles S.S.W. of Ypres ; Poperinghe, his old headquarters, now continuously shelled by a long range 15-inch (38 cm.) gun, was no longer suitable, and Sir John French, when visiting General Plumer, had told him that he considered Goldfish Chateau, just behind Ypres, was too far forward. It had, indeed, been shelled for some days, but it was not until orders were received from G.H.Q., that General Plumer could be persuaded to move. Major-General Keary, the withdrawal of the Lahore Division having been completed, vacated his headquarters at Potijze on the morning of the 2nd ; a few minutes later his dug-out was struck by a heavy shell and demolished.

HILL 60. THE FIRST FAILURE OF A GAS ATTACK—
ATTACK BY THE GERMAN *XV. Corps* ON THE 15TH
BRIGADE

Map 4.   During the 1st May a gas attack was made against
Sketch 8. Hill 60 ; it marks a stage in history, as it was the first by which the enemy gained no advantage. The hill, in the sector of the 15th Brigade (Br.-General E. Northey), was held at the time by the 1/Dorsetshire, under Major H. N. R. Cowie. About 7 P.M., after a severe bombardment, the Germans, from less than a hundred yards off, released gas on a front of a quarter of a mile. It shot over in thick volumes so quickly that very few men had time to adjust their extemporized respirators, and one company that was in the act of practising putting them on was caught with them dry. As soon as the cloud reached the

---

on the 30th, it should be recorded that parts of the 4th Division were attached to six different divisions, and were under five different administrations.

[1] Appendix 36.

Dorsetshire trenches the enemy opened rifle fire, attacked 1 May.
both flanks of the battalion with bombing parties, and
concentrated the guns to form a barrage on the approaches
to the hill. A few of the Dorsets, all suffering from gas,
jumped on to the firestep, and, under 2/Lieut. R. V.
Kestell-Cornish,[1] opened rapid fire. This for the moment
saved the situation and just gave time for the supports
of the Dorsets, which were close at hand, the 1/Devonshire
(14th Brigade), which was led up by Lieut.-Colonel E. G.
Williams on his own initiative, and reinforcements of
the 1/Bedfordshire (15th Brigade), to charge through the
gas cloud and reach the front before the Germans gained
a footing, when bombers of the Devons and Dorsets drove
them back.[2] The forbidden weapon had been faced and
defeated for the first time. But the Dorsets by sticking
to their posts had suffered heavily : 90 men died from
gas poisoning in the trenches or before they could be got
to a dressing station ; and of the 207 brought to the
nearest stations, 46 died almost immediately and 12 after
long suffering ; and of 2,413 cases from all fronts admitted
in this period, 227 died in hospital.

2ND MAY

RESUMPTION OF THE ENEMY OFFENSIVE.   REPULSE OF A
    GAS ATTACK BY THE 4TH DIVISION.   THE SECOND
    STAGE OF THE WITHDRAWAL

During the morning of Sunday 2nd May—the day on Map 10.
which the great Austro-German offensive against the Sketch
Russians, known as Gorlice–Tarnow, was begun — the 16.
enemy before Ypres was quiescent. Hopes were therefore
entertained that the withdrawal so successfully begun
would be carried out in its entirety without interference.
At 10.45 A.M., therefore, General Plumer issued orders
for the first part of the second series of moves, already
notified to commanders, to take place during the ensuing
night. These moves included the retirement across the
canal of the 2nd Cavalry Division, the 149th and 151st
Brigades, half the batteries of the 28th Division, an

[1] Died of wounds as a captain, 17th June 1918.
[2] Private E. Warner, 1/Bedfordshire, was awarded the Victoria Cross
for conspicuous bravery in recovering and holding a vacated trench. He
died shortly afterwards from gas poisoning.

2 May. artillery brigade of the 27th, and the five batteries of the Canadian Division still in the Salient.[1] Soon after 12 noon, however, the enemy violently bombarded the front of the three infantry brigades of the 4th Division now holding the north face of the Salient from Berlin Wood to Turco Farm, and the right wing of the French. At 4 P.M. the enemy changed to gas shelling, and at 4.30 P.M. released cloud gas from the north on a 3-mile front across a No Man's Land only a hundred to a hundred and fifty yards wide, whilst the *XXVI. Reserve Corps* attacked.[2] The gas took two or three minutes to reach the British parapets, and about fifteen minutes to pass. The weight of it struck the left of the 10th Brigade— the right only got " a small dose "—and the whole front of the 12th Brigade, that is the line from Fortuin to Turco Farm, and the French right, east of the canal. The wind was not steady and distributed the gas unevenly, some men were quicker than others in getting on their respirators; but in the general result the 10th Brigade (Br.-General C. P. A. Hull) [3] stood steadfast, though every man was affected more or less, and many who remained at duty had to ·go sick during the succeeding days. In the 12th Brigade (Br.-General F. G. Anley) [4] one company of the Lancashire Fusiliers (Lieut.-Colonel C. J. Griffin), which, owing to a delay in passing a message, was not warned in time to put on its improvised respirators, was driven from its trenches, and the battalion had 18 officers and 431 other ranks gassed so badly that they had to be admitted to hospital.[5] It was immediately reinforced by the 7/Argyll and Sutherland Highlanders (Lieut.-Colonel D. A. Carden), hurried up by Br.-General Hull, and a

[1] Arrangements were also made for the disposal of the formations not required for the defence of the reduced Salient ; the 50th (Northumbrian) Division to G.H.Q. Reserve, the Canadian Division to III. Corps, but not to be put into the line, and the 13th Brigade to the II. Corps. The exchange of the 4th and Canadian Division artillery was also ordered. The Cavalry Corps remained under General Plumer.

[2] The attack had nothing to do with the British withdrawal in progress ; the *Fourth Army* had been waiting for a favourable wind. See Note at end of Chapter.

[3] 1/Royal Irish (still attached from 27th Division), 1/Royal Irish Fusiliers, 2/Dublin Fusiliers, 2/Seaforths, with the 1/Royal Warwickshire and 7/Argyll and Sutherland Highlanders in reserve.

[4] 2/Lancashire Fusiliers, 1/King's Own and 2/Essex in the line, with 2/Royal Irish and 3rd Canadian Brigade in the second line, and 2/Monmouthshire and 5/South Lancashire in reserve.

[5] Private J. Lynn, 2/Lancashire Fusiliers, was awarded the Victoria Cross for continuing to serve his machine gun and moving it on to the parapet during the gas attack. He died next day of gas poisoning.

company of the 5/South Lancashire (Lieut.-Colonel L. E. 2 May. Pilkington) from the 12th Brigade reserve, followed soon after by the 4th Hussars and 5th Lancers (2nd Cavalry Division) from General Snow's reserve near Potijze.[1] The brigade reserves charging through the gas—billowy waves three feet high with a fringe of fumes rising above them—were in time to anticipate the Germans and help the Lancashire Fusiliers to drive them off with fire.   The King's Own (Lieut.-Colonel T. D. Jackson), next on the left, not only held their ground, beating back an attack by rifle and machine-gun fire, but moved out a platoon to some buildings in No Man's Land to flank the gap caused by the retirement of the company of Fusiliers.   Part of the Essex (Captain L. O. W. Jones), though they had their respirators on in time, were forced back; but their own supports advancing through the gas cloud at once recovered the trenches, and were then reinforced by two companies of the 2/Monmouthshire (Lieut.-Colonel E. B. Cuthbertson).[2] The French repulsed the attacks without leaving their trenches.

Directly gas appeared, the artillery in support, and the French artillery on the left, had opened fire and shelled the area behind the gas so as to catch the advancing infantry, and the rifles and machine guns of the 4th Division and the French did the rest.   They stopped with heavy loss every attempt made by the Germans to utilize the surprise.   For the second time in two days a gas attack had failed to achieve any result, and the brigades of the 4th Division were fully entitled to the congratulations sent by the Commander-in-Chief.   To put a finish to this day's performance, aviators flying over the area spotted just before 7 P.M. a German column on the Poelcappelle— St. Julien road, and a massed body near Keerselare, and, this being immediately reported, the 9·2 howitzer was turned on to them with accuracy and effect.   The enemy was, it turns out, puzzled by the ill-success of his poison waves, and attributed it to the gas not being strong enough ; as at " First Ypres ", he got the impression that " the enemy position was very strongly fortified and pro-" tected by deep entanglements.   Another gas attack was " therefore planned ".[3]

[1] At night the 2/Royal Irish relieved the 7/Argyll.
[2] The 2/Essex casualties were 8 officers and 265 other ranks, including 3 and 175 gassed.
[3] Schwarte, ii. p. 264.   See Note at end of Chapter.

2 May.   By 8 P.M. all was again quiet. The action had illustrated
once more the value of deep formation in defence ; supports
were at hand to assist the front line when in difficulties,
and were used boldly without a moment's delay.[1] Reserves
were ready at suitable spots to move up and take the
place of the supports when they were drawn into the
fight, whilst brigade headquarters were well forward in the
villages of Wieltje and La Brique.[2]

So calm was the night after the fighting had died down
that at 9.45 P.M. General Plumer directed that the various
moves in retirement that he had ordered should be executed.
Conditions were at first favourable, for light was afforded
not only by the moon, but by the flames of the fires raging
in Ypres, which illuminated the whole country side ; but
as the night advanced a ground mist greatly embarrassed
both movement and communication. Except that the
2nd Cavalry Division was a little late—some of its units
having been engaged in the fighting—all the moves were
performed according to plan, and the reserves withdrew
across the canal, in spite of a good deal of shelling of the
roads that was continued throughout the night. Nothing
now remained but to bring back the infantry of the 27th,
28th and 4th Divisions to the new line which on the
1st May had been reported " habitable ", though the wire
was weak. Actually its trenches were but 3 feet wide and
hardly as many deep.

In the course of the day General Putz reorganized his
command so as to comply with General Foch's orders to
hand back one division, the 18th. The 152nd (General
Joppé) remained next to the British ; and the 45th and
153rd Divisions, with the 87th Territorial divided between
them, were assembled west of the canal. The two battalions of Zouaves and " groupes " of artillery borrowed
from Nieuport were sent back there.

---

[1] That there should be no doubt about what was expected of the
supports of the 4th Division their trenches had signboards bearing the
legend " Counter-attack trenches ".

[2] The brigade headquarters here consisted of a 5-feet deep hole in the
ground, with a splinter-proof roof, on the lee side of a house, the walls of
the building acting as a shell burster. The hole was divided into two by
a sandbag barrier, with an opening through which messages could be
handed. In one compartment was the staff, in the other the signallers.
There were two entrances, on the Ypres side.

3RD MAY

THE ATTACK ON THE 85TH AND 11TH BRIGADES NEAR
GRAVENSTAFEL. SUCCESSFUL COMPLETION OF THE
WITHDRAWAL

The spasmodic hostile shelling that had gone on all 3 May.
night became methodical as it grew light and was continued
right through the 3rd May, and, reinforced by trench
mortars—to reply to which the British still only had
improvised weapons—was directed particularly on the
85th Brigade (Br.-General A. J. Chapman) and the 11th
Brigade (Br.-General C. B. Prowse) next to it, in the
apex of the front near Berlin Wood, below Gravenstafel
ridge. Unfortunately, owing to a proportion of the
British guns having been moved back during the night
to the new positions, the two infantry brigades had only
a small amount of artillery support :—the 85th Brigade,
four 18-pdr. guns and one field howitzer battery, and the
11th Brigade, one 18-pdr. and two field howitzer batteries.
Moreover the position of these guns had been located by
the enemy's vastly superior artillery, and when they
attempted to fire they were soon smothered. Two received
direct hits and were destroyed. The enemy bombardment
was not the only sign of possible attack ; for at 7 A.M.
a long hostile column was seen by the 85th Brigade moving
westwards towards Passchendaele from Moorslede, and
the Germans opposite the 12th Brigade, having cut their
own wire, left their trenches and lay out in the open
ready to advance. Here and elsewhere, however, as in
1914, any attempt of the Germans to close was, in spite
of the shell fire, completely checked by the never-failing
rapidity and accuracy of trained British rifle fire, soon to
become a thing of the past. A large number of them who
massed in a hollow north of Mouse Trap Farm were caught
by artillery fire and dispersed.

At 11.45 A.M., therefore, General Plumer felt it safe
to issue orders for the instructions already handed to his
subordinates to take effect, and for the final withdrawal
of the infantry of the 27th, 28th and 4th Divisions to
begin. Pivoting on the left of the II. Corps near Hill 60,
the new position to be occupied was :—Sanctuary Wood,
front of Hooge, Frezenberg, Mouse Trap Farm, and thence
to Turco Farm as before. The retirement that was
involved averaged 4,000 yards, and by it were abandoned

3 May. localities that had become famous during the First Battle of Ypres, such as Shrewsbury Forest, Nonne Bosschen, Polygon Wood and Zonnebeke. What remained of the artillery was to move off at 8.30 P.M.; then half the infantry at 9 P.M., followed by half of the remainder at 10.30 P.M., with a halt half-way at an intermediate position. The last troops to go were to begin their retirement at midnight, following the same method of dividing and leaving smaller and smaller bodies till the last files of the rear parties were free to follow. All movements were regulated by the 28th—the centre division. It was decided to carry out the operation of retirement completely during the night, without leaving parties to dispute the advance of the enemy when at daylight he should discover the withdrawal. He could certainly have been made to pay heavily for every yard of advance in the wooded sector held by the 27th Division, but in the open ground north of this a fight in retreat might have been very difficult to control. An attempt made by the 27th Division to burn out the tree stumps of Clonmel Copse, in front of the southern end of Sanctuary Wood, so that it should not afford cover to the enemy, unfortunately failed.

Soon after General Plumer's orders had been sent out the enemy's pressure, with great concentration of heavy artillery, began to increase near the junction of the 85th and 11th Brigades at Berlin Wood. Here there were in line the 2/Buffs (Major R. E. Power)—which on the night of the 28th/29th April had taken over from the 3/Royal Fusiliers (Major A. V. Johnson), the battalion that had held the position so long—the 1/Hampshire (Lieut.-Colonel F. R. Hicks) and the 1/Rifle Brigade (Lieut.-Colonel W. W. Seymour), with the Fusiliers now in support behind the junction of the brigades. The British heavy artillery on the west bank of the canal was ordered to support the sector, but it was five miles away; towards 2.55 P.M. every German gun seemed to be concentrated on Berlin Wood, and at 3 P.M. when an infantry attack developed at two points against the Buffs and the Rifle Brigade, they had to rely on the rifle. The men of the former battalion, in Berlin Wood and the front trenches near the salient, were all killed or wounded and the defence was taken up in the support line; but the 1/Rifle Brigade, though reduced to one man to every twelve yards of trench, maintained a resistance in its front line. Reinforcements were rushed up through the shelled zone:

half the 1/York and Lancaster and half the 5/King's 3 May. Own ; later the 2/East Yorkshire from the 28th Division reserve, and the 2/Shropshire L.I., 2/Cameron Highlanders and 9/Royal Scots from the 27th Division. The 3rd Cavalry Division of the corps reserve was moved up close to Ypres, and the 13th Brigade from the north-west of Vlamertinghe to south-west of Brielen, in case they might be required. It was not necessary to engage any of these troops ; for although the Germans, from their footing in Berlin Wood, could enfilade the 11th Brigade line and take in reverse the 85th, they were unable to advance further.[1] Fighting did not die down until 9 P.M. and there was grave anxiety as to whether the withdrawal could be continued ; but it was eventually decided to proceed with it. Although the 85th and 11th Brigades were in such close contact with the enemy that in places the opposing sides were within a few feet, they were able to draw off under cover of darkness, and the whole retirement was carried out as planned and without a hitch, favoured by the usual ground mist. When the reports came in, it was found that only one soldier of the three divisions was missing, and he rejoined next morning. He had fallen asleep in the front trench, and had wakened at 6 A.M. to find his comrades gone, but the enemy still at a distance. A few wounded whom it was dangerous to move had to be left behind in charge of Royal Army Medical Corps personnel, and all were taken prisoner in the German advance on the 4th May ; but by the devotion of the Royal Army Medical Corps and of the Army Service Corps transport attached to that Corps, which pushed up fearlessly into the most forward areas, all who could be moved were brought away. At last, too, 27th Division headquarters left the Salient, General Snow moving from Potijze, where he had been throughout the battle, and where his G.S.O.I., Lieut.-Colonel H. L. Reed, had been wounded on the 29th April, to a farm a mile south of Vlamertinghe. Like the original divisions of the B.E.F.— of which the 4th Division was one—in August-September 1914 the 27th and 28th Divisions had successfully passed through the highest test of the discipline of an army, and withstood the greatest strain on the nerves of individual

---

[1] The unsuccessful attack was made by units of the *51st Reserve* and *53rd Reserve Divisions*. The attack was abandoned by the enemy, but was regarded as so important that a battle honour was given for it. See Note at end of Chapter.

3 May. soldiers—a retirement from close contact with the enemy. And this they accomplished undetected after nearly a fortnight of fighting and, in the case of the 28th Division, of desperate fighting in a desperate position at the point of a salient.

The German communiqué for the day claims no more than " Heavy British losses near Ypres ". The two brigades engaged had certainly suffered severely in their repulse of two divisions, still more perhaps from the steady shelling of their hastily scraped trenches, but their casualties on 3rd May were trifling to what they had visibly inflicted on the enemy.[1] There was no action of importance by the French on 3rd May ; as the British were giving up ground they were less than ever interested in recovering what they had lost.

With the successful completion of the retirement in the early morning of the 4th May, the phase of the fighting officially called the Battle of St. Julien closes. The German attacks in the battles of Ypres 1915 never had the weight or quality behind them that made those of October-November 1914 so dangerous. The enemy relied on overwhelming artillery superiority from a position of vantage on the high ground, and on the surprise of gas. The infantry forces that he employed were not formidable in numbers. But by an amazing piece of luck for him, coloured battalions and elderly third-line troops had just replaced a first-class French division in the sector where he first elected to discharge the gas. His success in opening a gap was complete, but he made little use of the tremendous advantage he had gained, and his delay saved the situation for the Allies. So surprised, or elated, was the commander of the German *Fourth Army*, that he, like Ludendorff after his unexpected success against Sir Hubert Gough in March 1918, set about following two divergent objectives, when to have pursued one or other of them and concentrated either against the French or the British would certainly have achieved, if not a

---

[1] The 85th Brigade, 22nd April to 3rd May, lost :—

Brigade Staff, 11 ; 2/Buffs, 18 officers, 450 other ranks ; 3/Royal Fusiliers, 19 and 490 ; 2/E. Surrey, 11 and 440 ; 3/Middlesex, 8 and 280 ; 8/Middlesex, 13 and 266.

The 11th Brigade, 26th April to 3rd May, lost :—

1/Somerset L.I., 8 officers and 204 other ranks ; 1/Hampshire, 11 and 341 ; 1/Rifle Brigade, 7 and 545 ; London Rifle Brigade, 14 and 332. The casualties of the 1/E. Lancashire are not recorded for this period.

decisive victory, at least an important success, at small cost.

The division of the line at the point of attack between French, Belgians and British made a proper control of the counter-stroke well nigh impossible. The situation of the French, when once they were across the canal, was safe and secure for the moment; far otherwise was that of the British in the Salient with an open flank. Something had to be done, and that speedily; the inertia of the Germans could not be counted on. There were many among the commanders of lower rank in the actual fighting line, brigadiers and commanding officers of battalions, who advocated a retirement back to the ramparts of Ypres and the canal, to get in line with the French. Without doubt, this was the true tactical solution; the reduced Salient was one huge artillery target, far too small a bridgehead for even infantry, far less supporting artillery to be massed in it to break the German line. But, apart from the political and sentimental reasons already referred to, Sir John French was bound to hold what remained of the Salient, at least for a time, to give the French opportunity to recover their abandoned share. His troops, however, were too handicapped by their position in a basin surrounded on three sides by German guns, and with a canal behind them, to expect to be able to do much more than exploit a French success. Command was embarrassed also by the situation of the various headquarters, which had been selected for a front facing southeast and east, and now by the retirement of the French were ill-placed and unsuitable for the new front facing north. Every cable and air line from corps and divisional headquarters to the front—except those from the 27th Division at Potijze and, later, those of the Lahore Division — passed through Ypres and was singularly liable to damage. This greatly increased the always considerable difficulties of command and slowness of communication incident to a modern battle, and was largely responsible for the lack of information as to what was happening at the front. These disadvantages militated also against the effective co-operation of the small amount of artillery available, which was otherwise singularly well placed to assist with enfilade fire.

Seldom was unity of command more needed than at the junction of the British and French fronts after the first German gas attack. It was obvious that the ground lost by the French should be recovered if possible. A combined plan was necessary. For the moment General Putz was powerless: he had lost a very large proportion of his artillery; his infantry, except for a few Zouave battalions, was at best second-class, and for the moment demoralized, and had taken refuge behind the canal. The British reserves in and near the Salient, even the local reserves of battalions, were at once used up in merely filling the long gap, and the three divisions of the V. Corps were placed in a highly dangerous situation. Their defences, for lack of the men thus withdrawn, were reduced to the front position, a shallow zone, without any depth whatever. A single command for the V. Corps and the Groupe d'Elverdinghe was required, and the proximity of the headquarters of General Plumer and General Putz, and the constant communication between them did not compensate for the lack of it. A high decision was at once necessary whether with the Arras offensive in preparation, any forces should be expended in counter-offensives at Ypres. On this point, apparently, both General Foch and Sir John French were at first agreed, and they ordered counter-attacks. Then came the question whether the means for these were adequate; this, too, seems to have been decided in the affirmative, and the instant recapture of St. Julien was recommended. But when and where—except for the one instruction that it was to be immediate—the counter-offensive was to develop was left to the local commanders. Co-operation was promised by each of the two contingents, but unfortunately the French reinforcements, having some way to come, were slow in arriving—slower than General Foch evidently anticipated. The British reinforcements, the 10th Brigade of the 4th Division, the infantry of the 50th (Northumbrian) Division and the Lahore Division had to be thrown in by G.H.Q. order as they arrived, without adequate artillery support, to stem the attack, and their offensive force was exhausted before the weight of the fresh French divisions could be felt. But by the 26th April reconnaissance had revealed that the Germans had consolidated their new position; and while the British reinforcements on the ground were adequate to hold the enemy should he essay a further advance, the time for immediate local counter-attacks had passed, and only a carefully co-ordinated plan, taking many days to mature, had any chance of success.

It is now known that so little effect had the British

efforts that the Germans were able to shift the greater part of a division [1] from the British front to reinforce against the later French counter-attack.

Sir John French, though at first he had whole-heartedly complied with General Foch's wishes, appreciated the small result of the French efforts—or rather the smallness of the first efforts—and the heavy losses of his own troops crowded together in the small place d'armes of the narrowed Salient. He began to doubt. The orders that the British were only to attack if our Allies actually left their trenches were perhaps natural, but could hardly lead to decisive results as the French possibly had their eyes on the British front with similar thoughts in mind.[2] The British effort, however, was over and finished before the serious French offensive against the German bridgehead on the west bank began, and this left General Putz with small means to help on the east bank. It must be confessed that the result of the Allied combination was very poor. Sir John French then became convinced that he must withdraw his troops, and passed from optimism to pessimism. It was naturally most difficult for his subordinates to follow his moods, particularly when his mind was on the border line between one phase of thought and the next, and when, at the entreaty of General Foch he waived his own views and more than once agreed to wait a little longer before withdrawing his men and to order one more counter-attack.

Pinned as they were in the narrow Salient and on Hill 60, shelled night and day from three sides, the conduct of the troops was magnificent. Seldom have there been finer displays of courage than the fighting of the 13th, 14th and 15th Brigades of the 5th Division; the advance in daylight of the 1st and 4th Battalions of the 1st Canadian Brigade, Geddes's Detachment and the 13th, 10th and 149th Brigades; the stands against gas attacks made by the 8th Canadian Battalion, and the 15th, 10th and 12th Brigades; and the defence of the 11th and 85th Brigades. Unfortunately, from lack of heavy artillery and shortage of ammunition and other apparatus, this living valour was expended without compensating victory; like the

---

[1] Part of the *53rd Reserve Division* and half of the *38th Landwehr Brigade*.

[2] It was again a case of :—
"Lord Chatham with his sword undrawn
Kept waiting for Sir Richard Strachan :
Sir Richard, longing to be at 'em,
Kept waiting too,—for whom ? Lord Chatham."

men of the first seven divisions those who fought at
" Second Ypres " paid heavily for want of national preparation in peace.

NOTE

THE GERMANS ON THE 2ND AND 3RD MAY 1915

2 May.   It will be recalled that after the actions of the 26th April the
Germans stopped further attacks until they could be again assisted
by gas, and preparations for installing the cylinders were taken in
hand on the front between Locality C, north-west of Gravenstafel
and the Ypres—Pilckem road. The account kindly furnished by
the *Reichsarchiv* continues as follows :—
    " After the completion of the installation, the attack had to be
" postponed on account of unfavourable weather conditions. It was
" finally carried out on the evening of the 2nd May towards 5 P.M.,
" when the wind became favourable. The objectives were the same
" as before.[1]   Again they were not attained."
    " The troops employed were :—
" Of the *51st Reserve Division* :
    " *102nd Reserve Brigade* (No. *235, 236 R.I. Regts.*) at Vanheule
    " Farm and south of St. Julien.
    " *101st Reserve Brigade* (No. *233* and *234 R.I. Regts.* and *23rd R.*
    " *Jäger Bn.*) at Fortuin.
    " *2nd Reserve Ersatz Brigade* (No. *3* and *4 R.E. Regts.*) at point
    " B.9 on the Langemarck—Zonnebeke road. [This point on
    " the Belgian 1 : 20,000 map is just south of Locality C.]
    " Reserve : A marine infantry regiment.
" Of the *53rd Reserve Division* :
    " *38th Landwehr Brigade* (No. *77 Landwehr Regt.* only, the other,
    " No. *78,* was with the *XXVII. Res. Corps* reserve) south-west
    " of St. Julien.
    " *105th Reserve Brigade* (No. *241* and *242 R.I. Regts.*) westward
    " to the Ypres—Langemarck railway.
    " Reserve :
    " *XXVII. Reserve Corps,* reserve of two composite infantry regi-
    " ments : behind right wing at Wallemolen [1 mile north of
    " Gravenstafel]."
    General Balck (Schwarte, ii. p. 264) adds :—
    " The British order for a further retirement synchronized with
" the *Fourth Army* order for attack. This was again to be begun
" by discharge of gas. Unfavourable wind compelled its postpone-
" ment to the 2nd May, although the situation required an early
" offensive, for the *52nd Reserve Division* had had to repel a serious
" French counter-attack. On the 2nd [1st] May the *XV. Corps*
" attacked Hill 60 with gas without effect. The attack of the
" *XXVI. Reserve Corps,* which was to be assisted by its neighbouring
" corps (*XXVII. Reserve Corps*), was premature, for owing to the
" squally wind, the right wing of the *XXVII. Reserve Corps* could
" not take part. The unevenly distributed gas clouds were not
" strong enough for the great distance the assault had to cross.

---

[1] See page 267.

" Besides, the enemy was obviously ready and in possession of better
" gas protection than on the 22nd. Yet the *51st Reserve Division*
" succeeded in capturing Vanheule Farm [this is a mistake] and the
" first houses in Fortuin [not occupied by the British], although in
" the evening the farm was lost again. The *52nd Reserve Division*
" prepared for an attack on the position covering Vlamertinghe
" Farm [a small farm between Mouse Trap and Canadian Farms].
" The attack was not carried out ; a night attack of the *234th*
" *Reserve Infantry Regt.* (*51st Reserve Division*) which had been
" begun was stopped and the troops dug in. The right flank of the
" *XXVII. Reserve Corps* was considerably behind and the *Marine*
" *Regt. No. 5* was pushed up into the gap to make connection.
" The Army commander had the impression that the enemy position
" was very strongly fortified and protected by deep entanglements.
" Another gas attack was therefore planned which required four
" days to prepare. The distance from the enemy was from 100 to
" 150 metres."

For the 3rd May the *Reichsarchiv* narrative says :— **3 May.**

" On the 3rd May the *51st Reserve Division* was to capture the
" ridge 30—35—37 (north of the Zonnebeke stream) [Zonnebeke
" ridge between the two branches marked Haanebeek]. The *53rd*
" *Reserve Division*, its right wing in touch with the *51st Reserve*
" *Division*, was to attack via Point 33 [north-west of Graven-
" stafel] in the direction of Point 37.

" The action was stopped on the 3rd, and the continuation of the
" offensive was only to be resumed after further preparations.
" Local combats took place and progress was made on the right of
" the *XXVII. Reserve Corps*."

In S.u.G. two official battle honours are awarded for the 3rd
May, and throw further light on the fighting. They are :—

(1) " The Storming of Vanheule Farm " by the *51st Reserve*
Division, a place which Schwarte, ii. p. 264, mentions was captured
and lost again on 2nd May during the gas attack (see above). It
was certainly not captured on the 3rd, for there was no attack on
it on that day, and on the 2nd the diary of the 2/Dublin Fusiliers,
whose battalion headquarters were actually in the farm, records,
" enemy did not reach our trenches ". Another battle honour is
given 7th-9th May to the *Marine Regiment No. 2* for " The Storming
of Vanheule Farm " [it was abandoned by the British in the retirement on the night of the 3rd/4th May].

(2) " The Assault of Gravenstafel " by the *XXVII. Reserve*
Corps. Gravenstafel may have been assaulted on the 3rd May ; but
it had been evacuated a week before, on the 26th April. Berlin
Wood, the scene of the attack, is, however, near Gravenstafel.

CHAPTER XVI

THE BATTLES OF YPRES 1915 (*continued*)

A PAUSE, 4TH TO 7TH MAY

(Maps 4, 10 ; Sketches 8, 16)

OCCUPATION OF THE FREZENBERG LINE

Map 10.
Sketch
16. THE retirement of the three divisions during the night of the 3rd/4th May had been so little expected by the enemy and so skilfully carried out, that next morning the Germans shelled the abandoned British trench lines as usual, quite unaware that they were no longer occupied.[1]

At 10 A.M. on the 4th Major-General H. F. M. Wilson took over command of the infantry brigades of the 4th Division from General Alderson ; the latter left the 2nd Canadian Brigade and divisional artillery at his disposal, but otherwise the return of all brigades and units to their own divisions proceeded as laid down.

The new line now established formed a semi-circle of 3 miles radius round Ypres. The 27th Division held the sector from near Hill 60 to half a mile short of the Roulers railway ; the 28th Division across the railway to Mouse Trap Farm ; and the 4th Division a short front from Mouse Trap Farm (inclusive) to Turco Farm. General Plumer issued orders for the construction of a second line, with a row of strong points in rear ; and a third line along the ramparts of Ypres and the canal bank was taken in hand by the engineers of the Second Army. All the heavy artillery, except two batteries, was now west of the canal. For the first time, the systematic organization of a gas alarm by means of gongs, bells, Klaxon horns, etc., was ordered.

About noon, according to the now settled plan of

---

[1] See Note at end of Chapter.

minor operations, the French made some partial attacks 4 May.
with the centre and left, but General Joppé next to the
British, was not able to take part, owing to the strength of
the German wire.

When in the course of the morning the Germans made
the discovery that the British had withdrawn, their
infantry began a cautious advance. A German who was
present [1] has described the abandoned territory as the
enemy found it : " The whole countryside is yellow . . .
" the battlefield is fearful. A curious sour, heavy, pene-
" trating smell of dead bodies strikes one. . . . Bodies of
" cows and pigs lie, half decayed ; splintered trees, the
" stumps of avenues ; shell crater after shell crater on the
" roads and in the fields." Under cover of the infantry,
some guns were brought forward, batteries being seen
trotting up and unlimbering in the open, whilst the exposed
position of the 28th Division on Frezenberg ridge was at
once heavily shelled with every kind of gun. The bombardment continued as long as there was light, and the
new position was methodically registered. It was so badly
knocked about that several battalions had at night to
dig new trenches behind the original ones. The British
artillery could do very little in reply, as owing to the long
continued battle, the 4·7-inch guns were getting worn out,
and were shooting shorter and more erratically than ever,
whilst the field guns in the Salient although they were
fought gallantly were often overpowered and smothered.[2]
As it grew dark, the Germans set about entrenching at
distances varying from two to six hundred yards from the
new line.[3]

During the next three days, 5th to 7th May, Plumer's
Force continued to improve its defences. General Putz's
detachment, under instructions from General Foch, settled
down to a policy that was directed to keeping the enemy
on its front engaged, and preventing him from detaching
troops whilst the Arras offensive was taking place. The
enemy was busy mainly in making preparations for further

---

[1] R. G. Binding, " Aus dem Kriege ", pp. 89-91. He was at the time
an officer of divisional cavalry.

[2] To make up for their short range, the 122nd and 123rd Heavy
Batteries (4·7-inch), which had been sent west of the canal, returned to
the Salient on the night of the 3rd/4th, and resumed their position near
Potijze.

[3] The operations of this day figure in the list of German battles,
" S.u.G.", p. 98, as " The Pursuit Fighting at Zonnebeke, Westhoek
" [a mile north-east of Hooge], Frezenberg and Eksternest [close to
" Westhoek] ".

5 May. attack ;[1] but he did not cease to shell the British trenches, particularly those exposed to direct view on Frezenberg ridge, using a large proportion of gas shell, but also flattening out the parapets with 5·9-inch and 8-inch, and turning his 17-inch on to Potijze, no longer a divisional headquarters, but where the 122nd and 123rd Heavy Batteries in a practically open position were in action. Encouraged by the withdrawal he also made a number of infantry attacks after special bombardment with heavy howitzers. No less than four small advances were directed against Mouse Trap Farm, on the 12th Brigade right flank, which he had recognized as an important pivot,[2] and a particularly determined one was made on the 5th May against the 83rd Brigade astride the Frezenberg road. Here two companies of the 3/Monmouthshire had to be sent by daylight down the forward slope to reinforce the 2/East Yorkshire and 5/King's Own. The casualties of these two battalions were so severe that they were relieved at night by the 3/Monmouthshire and 2/King's Own. But the Germans were beaten off on each occasion with heavy loss.

Loss of Hill 60

Map 4. Sketch 16.

In one attack, against Hill 60, however, the enemy was successful. The mound, even by the 21st April, has been described as a mere rubbish heap of shell and mine-torn earth, timber and dead bodies, and the fighting of the ensuing days had but churned up and pulverized the surface of this scene of desolation. The British trenches were shapeless cavities ; there was no other kind of shelter, and the enemy was less than a hundred yards away. The position, which, with the trenches on either side of the hill, formed a front of a mile and a quarter, was still held by the 15th Brigade (Br.-General E. Northey).[3] At 8.45 A.M. on the 5th May, when, after a wakeful night, most of the trench garrison except the usual guards, were asleep tired out, the enemy released gas from two points against the hill, held by the Duke of Wellington's (Captain B. J. Barton in command). With a favouring wind, it slowly drifted, not across but along the trenches. Only

---

[1] Schwarte, ii. p. 265.   [2] See Note at end of Chapter.
[3] With the 1/Norfolk, 2/Duke of Wellington's (of the 13th Brigade) and 1/Bedfordshire in front line ; 1/Dorsetshire in local reserve in shelters in Larch Wood, 400 yards behind Hill 60, near the railway cutting ; and 1/Cheshire and 6/King's in reserve in dug-outs on the south-west bank of Zillebeke lake.

one sentry saw the gas coming, and he at once sounded the
alarm. Orders had been given that, in case of attack by
gas, the men were to move to the flanks to avoid it, and
let the supports charge ; but the manner in which the
gas was released from a flank rendered this plan of little
avail, as it affected a great length of front. Further the
gas hung about the trenches so thickly that even with a
cotton respirator, that had constantly to be redamped, it
was impossible to stay in them. Some men ran back to
the support line and those who remained were overcome :
thus when the Germans advanced after the gas had been
flowing fifteen minutes, they secured all but a small portion
of the front line on the lower slopes of the hill.[1] The
Dorsets [2] rushed their strongest company, supported by
the others, along the railway cutting to a trench on the
right of the Duke's, whence they started bombing. They
gained a communication trench leading to the hill and
became engaged in a combat that ebbed and flowed all
day. Br.-General Northey had at once ordered up the
1/Cheshire and 6/King's from the reserve ; but before
they could arrive on the scene the Germans, at 11 A.M.,
released more gas, and now against the Bedfordshire
north-east of the hill. The right, in the Zwarteleen salient,
yielded, thus increasing the gap left by the Duke's, but
the left held on, and sufficient men continued firing to
keep the enemy at bay till about 12.30 P.M., when the
Cheshire, who had been digging a second line near Hooge,
arrived, with a company of the 6/King's, under Lieut.-
Colonel A. de C. Scott,[3] and reinforced the line, having
marched up through a heavy " barrage ", and gas clouds
that still hung about. But it was only gradually and
by repeated counter-attacks that the Germans, who
had pressed forward between the Dorsets and the left
section of the Bedfordshire, were forced back by the
Duke's, Dorsets, Cheshires and King's, and some of the
lost trenches regained, the Dorsets holding the trench
they had originally seized. The actual crest of the
hill remained in the enemy's hands. At 7 P.M. he
again released small quantities of gas, but it had little
effect and the infantry attack that followed was stopped

[1] " S.u.G.", p. 96, says the attack was made by the *30th Division*
(*XV. Corps*).
[2] Under Captain A. L. Ransome, Major H. N. R. Cowie having been
mortally wounded about 6 A.M. The battalion was 450 strong and had
280 casualties this day.
[3] He was soon afterwards mortally wounded.

May. by rifle fire. At 9 P.M., Br.-General Wanless O'Gowan, with three battalions of the 13th Brigade (1/R. West Kent, 2/K.O.S.B. and 2/K.O.Y.L.I.) — which had taken part in the original capture of the hill and retrieved so many desperate situations, and was now just back from the Ypres fighting—arrived with orders from the 5th Division (Major-General T. L. N. Morland) to counter-attack and retake the hill. At 10 P.M., after twenty minutes' bombardment, an attempt was made by the West Kent and Scottish Borderers. But, in addition to the difficulties of darkness and of the broken surface of the ground, the enemy was ready, and little was gained in spite of the devotion of the troops. One party of the K.O.S.B. actually got as far as the top of the hill where the front line had been, but it was driven off about 1 A.M. by enfilade fire from The Caterpillar and Zwarteleen. Hill 60, even if it could be captured, could not be held unless a wide extent of the enemy's front on either side of it was also secured.

Both belligerents, worn out and exhausted, spent next day consolidating their new positions ; but one further attempt to recover the hill was made at dawn on the 7th by the K.O.Y.L.I. and the bombers of the 2/R. Irish Rifles (attached from the 7th Brigade) and of the 1/Cheshire. It resulted in complete failure. Two weak companies of the Yorkshiremen went forward, and all were either killed or taken prisoner.

With this last desperate effort, fighting at Hill 60 came to an end, and this much disputed ground remained in German hands, continuing so until the battle of Messines in June, 1917. Beside the three hundred casualties in the 13th Brigade, the losses of the 15th Brigade from 1st to 7th May had been 33 officers and 1,553 other ranks. In all, the fighting at Hill 60 had cost the 5th Division over 100 officers and 3,000 other ranks. The gallant behaviour of the infantry had almost compensated for lack of heavy artillery and high-explosive shell ; but in the close fighting for one particular small patch of ground like Hill 60, the use of gas with a favourable wind proved the determining factor.

General Sir H. Smith-Dorrien Leaves the Second Army

Under G.H.Q. orders of the 2nd May, a large portion of Plumer's Force had been dispersed to rejoin other formations, and the command reduced to the three divisions 6 May. of the V. Corps and a cavalry division ; but Plumer's Force had not been returned to the Second Army. For a considerable time the relations between General Smith-Dorrien and the Commander-in-Chief had been strained, and the notoriety which attended this unfortunate state of affairs had been aggravated by the order which removed, in the midst of a battle, the troops fighting in front of Ypres from the control of the Second Army, and, although General Smith-Dorrien was the senior of the Army commanders, reduced his command to a single corps. On the morning of the 6th May he therefore felt it his duty to write to Sir John French, in order to facilitate any further step that the Commander-in-Chief might have in his mind. He set forth in his letter that the evident lack of trust in him constituted a seriously weak link in the chain of command, and for the good of the cause it were better he should serve elsewhere, and someone else command the Second Army in his place. The same evening Sir Horace Smith-Dorrien received written instructions from G.H.Q. to hand over his command to Sir Herbert Plumer and return to the United Kingdom. No reason or explanation was vouchsafed. After addressing personal letters of thanks to the corps and divisional commanders who had served under him in the battle he left the Second Army. Orders were subsequently issued by which Lieut.-General Sir Edmund Allenby succeeded General Plumer in the V. Corps. The designation of " Plumer's Force " was discontinued from 6 A.M. next day, when the V. Corps, with its three divisions, reverted to the Second Army, and General Plumer assumed command of that Army, opening new headquarters at 5 P.M. at Oxelaere on the south side of the base of Cassel hill. Major-General the Hon. Sir Julian Byng took over the Cavalry Corps, Br.-General C. J. Briggs following him in the command of the 3rd Cavalry Division.

NOTE

THE GERMANS ON THE 4TH-7TH MAY 1915

The following is the account kindly furnished by the *Reichs-archiv* :—

" During the night of the 3rd/4th May the enemy evacuated his " position in front of the *XXVII. Reserve Corps* and the right of " the *XV. Corps*. Without resistance worth mentioning [it had " been decided there should be none], the *XXVII. Reserve Corps*

4 May. " took Zonnebeke in the early morning and advanced towards
" Frezenberg.   Towards midday the *XXVI. Reserve Corps, XXVII.*
" *Reserve Corps* and *XV. Corps* reached the line : cross roads east
" of Fortuin—Point 37 [on Zonnebeke Ridge]—Point 22·73 [north-
" west of Polygon Wood]—Westhoek—Nonne Bosschen. The enemy
" offered strong resistance on the line Point 28 [¾ of a mile south of
" Fortuin cross roads]—Frezenberg—Eksternest [Westhoek].   In
" the course of the day the *XXVI. Reserve Corps* succeeded in taking
" Vanheule Farm [evacuated] and the *XXVII. Reserve Corps*
" pressed forward to the west of Eksternest [1 mile north-east of
" Hooge] ".

General Balck (Schwarte, ii. p. 264) in his account of the 3rd May
states :—

" Again the attack had come to a standstill, the troops, whose
" strength had not been kept up, were at the end of their powers.
" The companies of the *51st Reserve Division* [commanded by General
" Balck] averaged barely 90 men.[1]   On the morning of the 4th May,
" from the left flank of the *XXVII. Reserve Corps* came the un-
" expected tidings that the enemy had begun to evacuate his
" position, and very soon the same news was reported from other
" quarters.   The line Fortuin—Broodseinde—Klein Zillebeke, a
" width of 9 miles [under 5 miles] was abandoned by the British ".

The following from the report of Great Headquarters is then
quoted :—

" There was again a scene of mobile warfare, which had not
" been witnessed for so long, as our leading lines in open order,
" followed by closed supports, broke in on the Flemish landscape ;
" long trains of artillery and ammunition columns were brought up
" at a trot and reserves lay in the green meadows and abandoned
" British position.   Everywhere in the devastated sector were the
" mighty results of our weapons to be seen.   In the west and centre
" sectors of the north front, as also in the western portion of the
" south front, the Allies held on to their position stoutly, in order
" to cover the retirement of the rest.   The area east of the Canal
" in possession of the enemy, which at the beginning of the battle
" was 15 miles wide and 5 deep had shrunk to 8 miles wide and
" 3 deep ".[2]

Balck then continues :—

" Contrary to expectation, the German attack progressed very
" slowly.   The movement was begun by the *XXVII. Reserve Corps* ;
" Polygon Wood was traversed, Zonnebeke taken, then Nonne
" Bosschen ; it became more and more evident that it was not a
" matter of rear guards at Frezenberg and Westhoek, but a forward
" position of the enemy, behind which stood his main forces.   The
" German attack came to a standstill.   It was the same with the
" *XXVI. Reserve Corps*.   The *51st Reserve Division* once more
" captured Vanheule Farm.   As the day came to an end it was
" recognized that the new position could not be taken without a
" thorough artillery preparation.

" The *XV. Corps* reported progress against the hotly contested

---

[1] They had been made up before the battle to " 180 to 250 " (see
p. 191), so British rifle fire must have been fairly effective.

[2] An 8 wide and 3 deep area was reduced to 5 wide and 2 deep, see
Sketch 16.

" Hill 60. On the front of the *XXVI. Reserve Corps*, Wieltje 4 May.
" Chateau (Mouse Trap Farm) surrounded by its 10-feet moat, was
" recognized as an important strong-point. Heavy howitzer fire
" was concentrated on it, yet surprise attacks attempted against it
" on the 6th and 7th failed ".

CHAPTER XVII

THE BATTLES OF YPRES 1915 (*continued*)

THE BATTLE OF FREZENBERG RIDGE
8TH-13TH MAY

(Maps 11, 12; Sketches 17, 18)

8TH MAY

THE ATTACK ON THE 27TH AND 28TH DIVISIONS AND
THE LOSS OF FREZENBERG RIDGE

Map 11.
Sketch
17.

THE enemy had by no means abandoned the hope of obliterating the Ypres Salient. No doubt encouraged thereto by the British withdrawal from the apex, as General Foch had forecast, he made another most determined effort to gain ground. There ensued some of the most desperate fighting that ever took place in the Salient. Known as " The Battle of Frezenberg Ridge ", it lasted for a period of six days, 8th-13th May,[1] and during its course the British situation more than once became very critical, and exceedingly heavy losses were suffered.

Having spent four days in moving forward his heavy artillery and completing final preparations, Duke Albrecht von Württemberg succeeded in massing the greater part of three corps of the German *Fourth Army* opposite two divisions, the 27th and 28th of the V. Corps, astride the Menin and Frezenberg roads, which converge on Ypres.[2]

---

[1] This is the definition of the official Battle Nomenclature, but the German bombardment of the position began on the 4th and the infantry attacks on the 5th (see previous Chapter), and the battle might well be called a ten-days' one.

[2] *XV. Corps* from " Zillebeke to Bellewaarde Lake ", that is against the 27th Division ; *XXVII. Reserve Corps* from right of *XV.* to Frezenberg (apparently inclusive), that is principally against the 83rd Brigade of the 28th Division ; *XXVI. Reserve Corps*, Frezenberg to Mouse Trap Farm, that is against the 84th Brigade (Schwarte, ii. pp. 265-6). Portions of these three corps, to which the *37th* and *38th Landwehr*, *2nd Reserve Ersatz* and *4th Marine Brigades*—more than the equivalent of another

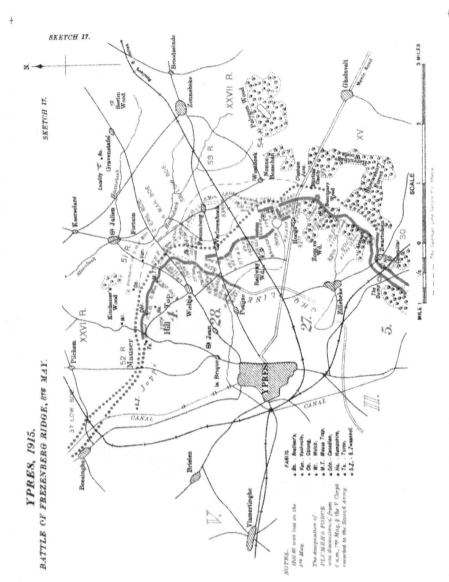

YPRES, 1915.

BATTLE OF FREZENBERG RIDGE, 8TH MAY.

SKETCH 17.

SKETCH 17.

NOTES.—

Hill 60 was lost on the
5th May.

The designation of
PLUMER'S FORCE
was discontinued from
6 a.m., 7th May, & the V Corps
reverted to the Second Army.

FARMS.

Bu.— Budfrom's.
Van.— Vanheule.
Gu.— Gluing.
Wi.— Welch.
M.T.— Mouse Trap.
Cdn.— Canadian.
Ha.— Hampshire.
Tu.— Turos.
S.Z.— S.Zwaanhof.

Ordnance Survey, 1925.

SCALE

MILE 1   ½   0   1   2   3 MILES

——— The German Line before the Attack

The new position of the V. Corps was by no means a 8 May. good one throughout.   In a long continuous line of defence there must usually be weak places; even the Hindenburg Line of 1917, sited under the peace conditions of a back area, was not without them.   The edge of Bellewaarde Wood (on the east of the Lake) and the front slopes of Frezenberg ridge were recognized as being in this category. But it was hoped that infantry although without adequate artillery assistance would be able to hold out; even in May 1915 the power of the German heavy guns was not fully realized.   To have gone back at once to the reverse slopes of Verlorenhoek, Mouse Trap Farm and Mauser ridges— roughly half a mile behind—would however have meant an abandonment of ground, which was to be avoided if possible, a further sacrifice of observation over a consider- able area, and a gift to the enemy of facilities of observation over the basin in front of the ramparts of Ypres.

Beginning in a wooded area, which still provided some cover from view, and passing through Armagh Wood, Sanctuary Wood and the Hooge Woods—the sector held by the 27th Division,[1] which was fairly sheltered, except on the left where the Patricia's stood—the new front ran in the 28th Division sector[2] across the open on a reverse slope to the Ypres — Zonnebeke railway; but it then passed on to the long forward slope of Frezenberg ridge, round Frezenberg village to Mouse Trap Farm.   This sector was not only commanded by Zonnebeke and Graven- stafel ridges in front, but every scrap of it was visible and could be enfiladed on the right from the main Ypres ridge.   The portion from the railway to Frezenberg, held by the 3/Monmouthshire, was particularly exposed and open, and made more so by a slight undulation of the ground; the very few traverses in it were soon demolished, thus offering long stretches of trench to machine-gun fire. From Frezenberg almost up to Mouse Trap Farm the line, though still on a forward slope, was not exposed to the

---

corps—were still attached, had to provide for the front opposite the 5th Division, II. Corps, as far as the Comines canal in the south, and opposite the 12th Brigade and the French as far as the Ypres canal in the north ; but this would leave available certainly the equivalent of six out of the eight and a half divisions.

[1] The 27th Division had the 82nd, 81st and 80th Brigades in line, each with two or more battalions in front line, and the rest in support and reserve.

[2] The 28th Division had the 83rd Brigade on the right and 84th on the left ; the 85th was in reserve near Vlamertinghe.

8 May. same extent to enfilade fire. The farm itself was on the summit or slightly behind it and therefore a stronger defensive position. From Mouse Trap Farm westwards to the canal—the sectors held by the 4th Division [1] and the French, with their junction at Turco Farm—the line was again sheltered on a reverse slope. It may be pointed out that in siting a defence line on a reverse slope facilities for artillery observation are all-important. A reverse slope is of little value in itself, although trenches sited near the bottom of it are usually screened from the enemy's observed fire; but if there is suitable observation over a reverse slope, the ground in front of the trenches can be defended and—given sufficient ammunition—made practically impassable by artillery fire, if there is a minimum field of fire of two hundred yards. Where such a reverse slope position does not exist, the infantry has usually to be on a forward slope to cover the artillery observers near the crest behind them. Actually where the reverse slope was adopted, there was observation on to a belt of the ground in front of the trenches of about three hundred yards and upwards, although it had not been cleared of ruins of houses and other shelter-places for enemy machine guns.

The trenches of the new line, as already mentioned, were narrow and only three feet deep—they were difficult to improve, as some even with that slight excavation reached water level. The soil was treacherous; the trenches fell in even without bombardment, and there was a great lack of sandbags to repair them. The wire was slight. There were support trenches of the same character, mostly well sheltered on reverse slopes; but there were practically no communication trenches, and the dug-outs—of course only designed as the splinter-proofs of the 1915 period—had hardly been begun. In fact, the position, though defensible, was a framework on which much still required to be done. Without deep dug-outs to shelter the men during bombardment, it does not seem probable that any troops could have held it for long.

Behind the front of the 27th and 28th Divisions there was still the G.H.Q. Line, from Zillebeke Lake, in front of Potijze and Wieltje to Mouse Trap Farm, and beyond that point the 4th Division had taken in hand a divisional back line. Under Second Army arrangements, Major-General F. M. Glubb, now its Chief Engineer, with all the

---

[1] It had the 12th Brigade in the line, 10th in reserve near La Brique, 11th in corps reserve at Brielen.

engineer companies and labour procurable, was pushing 8 May. on with the preparation of the " Canal Line ". This, beginning on the north at a point where it joined on to a French line near Brielen bridge, ran along the east bank, then round the eastern ramparts of Ypres, rejoining the canal about a thousand yards south of the town. Behind this again was the so-called "G.H.Q. 3rd Line," a series of strong points in course of construction, which passed through Brandhoek (4 miles west of Ypres), and between these lines there were various intermediate lines in the process of being marked out.

The only heavy artillery support for the three divisions of the V. Corps was furnished by six 60-pdrs. and twelve 4·7-inch guns, of which eight 4·7-inch (XI. Brigade) were pushed up into the Salient in order to make up for their uncertain range by being close to the enemy.[1] These were reinforced on the 7th May by two 5-inch howitzer batteries of the 50th (Northumbrian) Division.[2] This meagre allowance was of course totally inadequate to subdue the large number of German guns concentrated round the Salient, although from time to time the British managed temporarily to silence some of the batteries. The way in which they were " outgunned " from first to last by the Germans was one of the characteristic features of the fighting, and it affected the result far more than any other, including even the use of gas.

General Plumer's instructions to the Second Army circulated on the morning of 8th May, directed it to hold tenaciously to the present position, and contain as many of the enemy as possible, and on no account to occasion the necessity for calling for reinforcements from the forces of the First Army in the south, which were to be engaged next day—in the Battle of Aubers Ridge. He directed that local reserves should be kept at hand to deal with the

[1] One 4·7-inch battery and a section of 60-pdrs. were allotted to each of the three divisions. Of the field artillery the 27th Division had 3 brigades in the Salient ; the 28th, one ; the rest were west of the canal.

[2] The total heavy artillery with the Second Army on 9th May was, 9·2-inch howitzers, 2 ; 6-inch howitzers (old), 4 ; 5-inch howitzers (old), 16 ; 60-pdrs., 8 ; 4·7-inch guns (old), 44.

The 5-inch howitzers, first issued in 1896, used at Omdurman, and like the 4·7-inch gun, relics of the South African War, had a range of about 4,000 yards ; they had a buffer, giving a short recoil, and drag-shoes, but had to be run up between rounds. During 1915 their 50-lb. shell was replaced by a 40-lb., with increased charge, which lengthened their range to 6,100 yards. They were gradually replaced by the service 4·5-inch howitzers, which had a range of 7,500 yards (new 6-inch howitzers had a range of 11,000 yards). As the 5-inch had so small a range, they were sent forward into the Salient, and allotted to the 28th Division.

8 May. local attacks that might be expected, and a corps reserve maintained in each corps ready to cope with any serious development.

THE BREAK IN THE 83RD BRIGADE FRONT

During the night of the 7th/8th May there had been many indications of the coming storm. German patrols had been active and units of the *Marine Division* made a definite assault on the trenches of the 2/Northumberland Fusiliers (84th Brigade) near Mouse Trap Farm, but only to be beaten off with very heavy loss. At 5.30 A.M. on the 8th, a very violent bombardment of the whole V. Corps front was opened, but it was concentrated particularly on the 83rd Brigade, which had suffered heavily in the attacks on the 5th May, and had been badly mauled by artillery on the 7th. Its trenches lay on the exposed forward slopes of Frezenberg ridge on either side of the Zonnebeke railway to beyond Frezenberg village; and its units, to use the words of a battalion war diary, "suffered a hard, cruel time ".[1]

By 7 A.M. the German bombardment was intense on the whole front of the 80th, 83rd and 84th Brigades and the right of the 12th,[2] that is from the Menin road to Mouse Trap Farm. The enemy seemed determined to hammer his way through by weight of metal; even his field artillery fired high - explosive shell, of which the British had practically none. Between 7.10 and 9.10 A.M. the bombardment was terrific, and soon the greater part of the parapets were flattened out and the trenches destroyed.[3] Nevertheless, when at 8.30 A.M. the enemy guns lifted on to the support trenches and roads of approach, and the German infantry rose and assaulted the exposed

---

[1] The greatest pressure was to be against Frezenberg. Schwarte, ii. p. 265.

[2] 80th Brigade line : 4/K.R.R.C. and Patricia's.
83rd   „   „   B Co. of 3/Monmouthshire, 1/K.O.Y.L.I., rest of 3/Monmouthshire, 2/King's Own.
84th   „   „   1/Suffolk, 2/Cheshire, 1/Monmouthshire, 2/Northumberland Fusiliers.

The three brigades had been in the line since 17th April, and were greatly reduced in numbers. It will be noticed that as the 2/Monmouthshire was with the 12th Brigade all three battalions of this regiment were in the Salient.

[3] *Reserve Regiment No. 242 (53rd Reserve Division)* which attacked near Frezenberg states (p. 23 of its history) : " The effect of the heavy " artillery was devastating, one shell crater ran into another . . . only a " few desperate survivors defended themselves obstinately ".

front of Frezenberg ridge—the brunt of the onslaught 8 May.
falling on the 3/Monmouthshire, 2/King's Own, 1/Suffolk
and 2/Cheshire—the attack was driven off. After another
half-hour's bombardment, a second attempt failed in like
manner ; but by this time practically all the men in the
front trenches had been killed, wounded or buried. It
was impossible to send reinforcements down the exposed
front slope, and a third assault at the same place—on
either side of Frezenberg village—about 10 A.M., succeeded,
for just at this moment brigade orders for the evacuation
of the front line reached battalions. The remnants of the
3/Monmouthshire, after a counter-attack led by Lieut.-
Colonel H. W. Worsley-Gough, retired to its support
trenches on the reverse slope 400 yards behind. The
King's Own, on its left, the front line having held out
until overwhelmed, and Lieut.-Colonel A. R. S. Martin
killed, now also defended its support trench. The
Germans after this success at once tried to press forward
on the whole front from the Menin road to Mouse Trap
Farm ; but, held in front by shrapnel and rifle fire whenever
they topped the ridge, they soon desisted and began to
pursue their well-known practice of widening the gap.
On the right they enfiladed the 1/K.O.Y.L.I., and on the
left attacked the Monmouthshire and the King's Own in
front at short range, at the same time creeping round
their rear.

There was fortunately no sign of German reinforcements,
the only movement of note seen from the air on this day
being intense road traffic, mostly of ambulance wagons.

Immediately after ordering the retirement of his
battalions from the exposed front line, Br.-General R. C.
Boyle (83rd Brigade) directed the 2/East Yorkshire (Major
H. H. Powell) in reserve near Potijze, to advance to
assist the 3/Monmouthshire, and Major-General Bulfin at
the same time ordered his divisional reserve, the 85th Brigade at Vlamertinghe, to push up two battalions to Potijze
to be at Br.-General Boyle's disposal. Twenty minutes
later, however, Major C. R. I. Brooke, commanding the
1/K.O.Y.L.I. on the right of the main body of the 3/Mon-
mouthshire, arrived wounded at 83rd Brigade headquarters
in St. Jean, and reported that his trenches, the left sector of
which was badly exposed, were untenable, the Germans
round his left flank and his men coming away. It subsequently turned out that two of his companies (under Captain
H. Mallinson) and B Company (under Captain K. F. D.

8 May. Gattie, the adjutant) of the 3/Monmouthshire with them, sheltered by the lie of the ground, were holding on—and did so until nightfall. There was also a report that the left of the 80th Brigade was retiring. As a large number of stragglers was seen coming back, and the smoke and dust of bursting shell made personal observation of the front practically impossible, pending further information Br.-General Boyle at 11.10 A.M. ordered the 2/East Yorkshire to stop their advance and not go beyond the G.H.Q. Line, behind which the 2/King's Own (now under Major H. K. Clough) and 3/Monmouthshire would, if necessary, retire. The 2/East Yorkshire (commanded on this day in succession by Majors H. H. Powell and W. N. Pike, both of whom were wounded), though only 7 officers and 221 other ranks strong, had, however, acted promptly, and was already advancing. The brigade message passed on was interpreted to mean that not only the East Yorkshire but the King's Own and the Monmouthshire still fighting in the support line and holding up any direct advance, were at once to retire to the G.H.Q. Line. As a result, some parties of these two battalions received the order, although the majority did not and fought on until they were surrounded. Only one officer and 40 men of the 2/King's Own and one officer and 29 men of the two companies of the 3/Monmouthshire from the original front line answered the roll call at night. The battalions of the 27th and 28th Divisions had certainly done their best to carry out to the letter General Plumer's instructions to cling tenaciously to their position ; many of the officers and men with which their ranks were now filled might be half-trained and inexperienced ; but in a crisis with their backs to the wall they did not fail.[1] As soon as Br.-General Boyle heard of the misinterpretation of his message, he ordered the 2/East Yorkshire to advance again from the G.H.Q. Line, and with the 5/King's Own (Lieut.-Colonel Lord R. Cavendish), also from brigade reserve, to re-occupy the lost trenches. The total strength of the two battalions was only 550, yet in spite of severe losses in advancing over ground already completely dominated by enemy artillery fire, they were able to carry their attack more than a thousand yards beyond the G.H.Q. Line. But this was only half-way to the old front line. Whether their efforts

---

[1] The 1/K.O.Y.L.I. on this day lost 10 officers and 417 other ranks ; the 3/Monmouthshire mustered at night 4 officers and 130 other ranks ; of the 2/King's Own only 4 officers and 94 other ranks remained.

prevented a further advance of the enemy is uncertain ; **8 May.** at any rate, he made no attempt in this area to exploit his initial success.

The Stand of the 80th Brigade and the Right of the 83rd Brigade

On the right of the 83rd Brigade, the two battalions of the 80th Brigade (Br.-General W. E. B. Smith) in the line —the 4/K.R.R.C. (Major B. J. Majendie) and the Patricia's (Major A. H. Gault) [1]—holding Hooge woods and Belle-waarde ridge, a front of 1,200 yards, had suffered equally from the bombardment, the woods being described as a " perfect inferno " from shell bursting in them. But, fed by reinforcements from the 4/Rifle Brigade and by Patricia's bringing up signallers, pioneers, orderlies and batmen, they managed to check any break-in, defending sometimes the front trenches, sometimes the support trenches. Unsuccessful attacks continued until 4 P.M., but one party of Germans crept up and took possession of the top of an exposed summit left unoccupied in front of the junction of the two battalions, to have included which in the line would have involved the formation of a dangerous salient. When their left was forced back to the support line Patricia's, after thrice re-establishing it, lost touch with B Company 3/Monmouthshire and the K.O.Y.L.I. and believed the 83rd Brigade had entirely disappeared. On this being reported to General Snow, to fill the gap on Patricia's left, he ordered the 80th Brigade line to be extended north-westwards towards the railway behind Bellewaarde ridge and the K.O.Y.L.I. position, and a flank was formed by the 2/King's Shropshire L.I. (Lieut.-Colonel R. J. Bridgford). This was later reinforced by the 1st Battalion (Lieut.-Colonel H. B. Kirk) and half the 9th Battalion (Lieut.-Colonel J. Clark) of the Argyll and Sutherland Highlanders, whilst the rest of the 9th was brought up in support in front of Hooge Chateau, and the 3/K.R.R.C. (Lieut.-Colonel C. Gosling) to Railway Wood behind the left flank. Finally, the battalions of the 80th Brigade, greatly aided by the devoted stand of the K.O.Y.L.I., and B Company 3/Monmouthshire, were able to clear their front of all Germans except a few snipers lying out in the long grass and ruins of buildings.

---

[1] Major A. Hamilton Gault was twice wounded on this day ; on his being hit the second time, the command passed to Captain A. S. A. M. Adamson.

8 May.   No infantry attack took place on the rest of the 27th Division south of the Menin road, although the 81st Brigade (Br.-General H. L. Croker) next to the road suffered severely from the bombardment and was included in the front of the *XV. Corps* attack.[1] Thus the situation of General Snow's division remained secure.

THE STAND AND ANNIHILATION OF THE 84TH BRIGADE. COUNTER-ATTACK OF THE 12/LONDON REGIMENT (RANGERS)

On the other or northern flank of the 83rd Brigade, the front of the 84th Brigade (Br.-General L. J. Bols) from near Frezenberg to Mouse Trap Farm was also on the front slopes, in view of Zonnebeke ridge; but as has been pointed out, it was not exposed to enfilade fire. In spite of the retirement of the 83rd, which laid bare their right flank, the 1/Suffolk (Lieut.-Colonel W. B. Wallace)—except its extreme right which was driven back with the 83rd Brigade—the 2/Cheshire (Major A. B. Stone), the 1/Monmouthshire (Lieut.-Colonel C. L. Robinson) and the 2/Northumberland Fusiliers (Lieut.-Colonel S. H. Enderby) hung on to their trenches, losing heavily from artillery fire but keeping the enemy's infantry at a distance. It was obvious however that they must eventually be overwhelmed, and at 11.15 A.M. Br.-General Bols sent up the 12/London (Rangers) from brigade reserve—in which there was now left only the 1/Welch (Lieut.-Colonel T. O. Marden) barely 200 strong—to reinforce the 1/Monmouthshire over the ridge, about the same time that the 2/East Yorkshire and 5/King's Own, as already described, were trying to advance to fill the gap in the 83rd Brigade front. After the wastage of three weeks in the Salient, and the heavy losses in their counter-attack of the 24th April and during the 4th to 7th May, the Rangers (under Major H. G. Challen) were barely two hundred strong, and they began to suffer casualties as they passed through the gaps in the wire of G.H.Q. Line, on which the enemy about a mile away had machine guns trained. Directly they approached the flat crest of Frezenberg ridge, they were overwhelmed with shell fire of all kinds. Nevertheless, the survivors gallantly struggled forward, some actually reaching that part of the front line where the 1/Monmouthshire were still holding on. The one machine gun, worked independently—by a Monmouthshire officer after

[1] See footnote 2, p. 310.

its Ranger crew fell—greatly assisted with enfilade fire to 8 May. cover the exposed right flank of the 1/Monmouthshire, until it was disabled. As a unit, however, this most determined Territorial battalion, whose survivors held the line they had gained until 6 P.M., was annihilated.[1] Only 53 men of the Rangers, mostly pioneers and signallers, under Sergeant W. J. Hornall, answered the roll call that night.[2]

Although a frontal break-through had been delayed by the action of the 2/East Yorkshire, 5/King's Own and 12/London, the gap to the right of the 84th Brigade remained open, and from it the Germans proceeded gradually to roll up the line, whilst still engaging it in front. It is impossible to fix the exact sequence of the events which followed, as little news came back, except what was carried by the dribble of stragglers from the front, who, with circumstantial detail, told the tale that their battalion was annihilated and they were the last survivors. In the 2/Cheshire the front was broken about 1 P.M. by a fierce infantry attack in overwhelming numbers, and with few exceptions the whole of the battalion head-quarters and the men of the three companies in the front line were killed or taken prisoner, including Major A. B. Stone, commanding, who was killed.[3] The survivors of the battalion, just over a hundred men, under two second-lieutenants, were assembled in G.H.Q. Line. The Suffolks held out desperately in isolated detachments well into the afternoon, when with all communications cut, they were surrounded. Lieut.-Colonel W. B. Wallace, 11 officers, and 432 other ranks became casualties, so that only one officer and 29 men of the fighting line were present next day.[4]

The 1/Monmouthshire, on the left of the Cheshire, managed to repair a break in its front, but eventually found the Germans appearing both in right flank and rear. Lieut.-Colonel C. L. Robinson informed the Northumberland Fusiliers on his left that he intended to wheel back to form a flank, as a defensive flank improvised in a com-

[1] A captured British officer of another unit who saw the advance of the Rangers from the German lines records that they came through a barrage of H.E. shells which struck them down by dozens, but they never halted for a minute, and continued to advance until hardly a man remained.

[2] The 13 officers were all casualties. Sergeant Hornall was killed in action in 1916.

[3] The total losses of the 2/Cheshire on this day were 13 officers and 382 other ranks.

[4] From the 18th April to the 8th May the 1/Suffolk had lost all but one of its officers and 947 other ranks.

8 May. munication trench was enfiladed, and was requested by
Lieut.-Colonel Enderby, if he did so, to occupy a rise of
ground so as to protect the right of his Fusiliers. But
whilst the movement was in progress Colonel Robinson's
second-in-command was killed, and then he himself fell:
and the 1/Monmouthshire, like the battalion on its
right and its own 3rd Battalion in the neighbouring
brigade, in spite of a very gallant counter-attack, was
about 5 P.M. enveloped, only two officers and 120 other
ranks escaping.[1] The six battalions of the 84th Brigade
mustered 1,400 men next day and were organized into two
composite units.

On the extreme left a German advance against the
left of the 4th Division in a less exposed position, next
the French, was completely obliterated by fire, and the
12th Brigade (Br.-General F. G. Anley) received the congratulations of both the French and British commanders-
in-chief.

Up to nearly 2 P.M., therefore, the resistance offered
by the 80th, 83rd and 84th Brigades had enabled some sort
of line to be maintained, although the artillery could do
little to help, as all communication was cut, and there was
great uncertainty as to what the situation really was.
By that hour, however, except where the companies of
the 1/Monmouthshire and the last parties of the Suffolks
and Rangers were holding out, there was a gap of
over two miles in the front where the 28th Division
had stood, between the Patricia's and K.O.Y.L.I. near the
Zonnebeke railway and the 2/Northumberland Fusiliers
east of Mouse Trap Farm. On the right of the gap the
80th Brigade had formed a flank, and was resisting well,
and General Snow was prepared to counter-attack through
it should the Germans come on; on the other side the
Northumberland Fusiliers were immovable.

THE COUNTER-ATTACKS OF THE 85TH BRIGADE

The two leading battalions ordered up by General
Bulfin, the 3/Middlesex (500 strong under Major G. H.
Neale) of the 85th Brigade and the 1/York and Lancaster
(950 strong [2] commanded by Lieut.-Colonel F. E. B. Isher-

---

[1] The casualties were :—21 officers and 439 other ranks.
[2] Shown as 600 strong on the 1st May. Thus, after its heavy losses
in April whilst in Geddes's Detachment, many men in its ranks must have
been recent reinforcements.

wood) of the 83rd, under Br.-General Chapman (85th **8 May.** Brigade), were now arriving at Potijze, and at 2.40 P.M. were directed to counter-attack on either side of the railway and recover the lost trenches. Half an hour later the 2/East Surrey (Lieut.-Colonel C. C. G. Ashton) of the 85th Brigade arrived and was sent up about 4 P.M. to the left of the York and Lancaster, together with the survivors of the previous advance of the 2/East Yorkshire, 2/ and 5/King's Own then in the G.H.Q. Line ; and when, about 5 P.M., the last available battalion of the 85th Brigade, the 3/Royal Fusiliers (Major A. V. Johnson), came up, it also was thrust in behind the right of the York and Lancaster.

The advance of the 85th Brigade and the battalions with it brought them in touch with the left of the 80th Brigade ; but, although it was continued until 8 P.M., owing to the heavy shell fire they could not reach the Germans. The enemy, instead of pushing on, had entrenched in the gap, no doubt in anticipation of a frontal counter-attack, to which by now he must have become well accustomed. Secure with complete air supremacy, his very powerful artillery in no way neutralized, he was able to break up the British infantry reinforcements before they reached positions from which they could launch a counter-attack. On the right of the gap where the 85th Brigade had gone in, he however desisted from any further infantry effort ; and when a little later the 10th Brigade, as will be related, advanced towards the left of the gap, he abandoned what he had gained. The payment for this negative success was heavy : the 1/York and Lancaster was reduced to 83 rifles under a sergeant, and Lieut.-Colonel Isherwood was killed ; the 2/East Yorkshire was down to 3 officers and 200 men ; the 2/East Surrey, to 8 and 300 ; the 3/Middlesex to a trench strength of 289 ; and the 5/King's Own, to 91 rifles, Lieut.-Colonel Lord R. Cavendish being wounded.

On the left of the gap, the Northumberland Fusiliers, in spite of bombardment and attack in front and flank, were still clinging to their ground. On the annihilation of the 1/Monmouthshire, the situation, apart from the exposure of their flank, became very much worse, as the enemy was able to concentrate more artillery on them. Lieut.-Colonel Enderby managed to get a message through to 84th Brigade headquarters, and received a reply that the 85th Brigade had begun a counter-attack, and the battalion was to hang on if possible, but if it was not

8 May. possible to do so to retire to the G.H.Q. Line. He therefore decided to remain, and a small parapet was thrown up on the right at right angles to the line, and men placed there to defend that flank. Nothing, however, was seen of the counter-attack, which, as we know, was attempted nearly two miles away at the other extremity of the gap. No further message reaching Colonel Enderby, he determined, if the 1/Monmouthshire trenches were not retaken, to withdraw when it grew dark; and about 6.15 P.M. he proceeded towards the left of his line to make arrangements for the retirement from that flank. About 7 P.M., however, Germans appeared from the Monmouthshire trenches, and machine-gun and rifle fire was opened from the rear on the stretcher parties, who were getting the wounded away prior to the retirement. Shortly after a concentrated bombardment was opened, which, on the firing of a signal rocket, suddenly ceased, and the Germans assaulted. But they could not, even now, overwhelm the Northumberland Fusiliers, for A Company under Captain A. C. Hart[1] on the left continued to hold out, and eventually they abandoned all attempts to settle with it. Fifteen officers of the battalion, including Lieut.-Colonel Enderby, who was taken prisoner, and 482 other ranks were casualties; only two officers and 65 men of A Company, and 51 of the other three companies remained.

The stand of the 4/K.R.R.C., the Patricia's,[2] 1/K.O.Y.L.I., B Company 3/Monmouthshire and 2/Northumberland Fusiliers is indeed worthy to rank, with the counter-attack of the Rangers, among the historic episodes of the war.

THE NIGHT ADVANCE OF THE 10TH BRIGADE; RETIREMENT OF THE GERMANS, AND CONSOLIDATION OF THE NEW BRITISH LINE

After putting in the 12/London Regiment (Rangers) about midday, Br.-General Bols (84th Brigade) had only the 1/Welch, under the strength of a company, in reserve, and he moved it into G.H.Q. Line to make a last stand. General Bulfin was at a loss to find him reinforcements;

---

[1] Captain A. C. Hart was killed covering the flank of his company after shooting with his revolver a German officer who called on him to surrender.

[2] Patricia's were reduced to 4 officers and 150 other ranks; their casualties on the 8th May were 10 officers and 382 other ranks.

for the 85th Brigade, his divisional reserve, had gone to 8 May.
the assistance of the 83rd.   He was therefore obliged to
call on the 4th Division for help.   Major-General Wilson's
reserves were beyond the canal, and, as the bombardment
of all exits of Ypres was intense, and it was impossible to
use the roads, units coming up were compelled to move
across country opened out in artillery formation, a slow
method of advance.   General Wilson, in consequence, first
gave Br.-General Bols the assistance of such of the 4th
Division troops east of the canal as could be spared from
local reserve :—half of the 5/South Lancashire and half
the 1/R. Irish Fusiliers.   These arrived at 3 P.M., and were
sent to hold G.H.Q. Line and Wieltje.   At 3.30 P.M., when
the break in the 84th Brigade line became known for
certain, the 1/R. Warwickshire (Lieut.-Colonel A. J. Poole)
and 2/R. Dublin Fusiliers (Lieut.-Colonel A. Loveband)
of the 10th Brigade, from the west of the canal, and the
remaining two companies of the Irish Fusiliers, were put
at General Bols's disposal.   He determined to use them
to sweep obliquely from Mouse Trap Farm across the space
between the 2/Northumberland Fusiliers and G.H.Q. Line,
so as to take the enemy in flank ; but they did not
arrive at G.H.Q. Line until 7.30 P.M., and it was then too
late, and too dark, to do more than extend in front of the
wire and make a short advance.   However this last effort
following on the counter-attack of the 85th Brigade was
sufficient.   It not only dislodged the Germans from Hill 33,
east of Wieltje, to which they had penetrated, and drove
them back from Frezenberg, but produced the extraordinary
result that the *XXVI. Reserve* and *XXVII. Reserve Corps*,
according to German accounts,[1] abandoned the positions
they had captured, and the German *Fourth Army* was
thrown on the defensive.   Still more significant, the
enemy made no further effort at the same place for five
days.

The 7/Argyll and Sutherland Highlanders (Lieut.-
Colonel D. A. Carden) of the 10th Brigade and 1/East
Lancashire (Lieut.-Colonel G. H. Lawrence) of the 11th—
the Territorial battalion only 350 strong—hurried up across
the canal by the 4th Division, did not reach the front
near St. Jean until between 9 and 10 P.M. ; and then, owing
to a false report that Wieltje was in the enemy's hands,
they were given orders, subsequently countermanded, to
turn him out with the bayonet.   Based on this report,

---

[1] See Note at end of Chapter.

8 May. however, a message, timed 9 P.M., from the V. Corps
reached the 27th and 28th Divisions directing that a
counter-attack to retake the original trenches was to be
made and pushed home at all costs.   But when this filtered
down to the battalion commanders they, for once, made
a protest ; for an attack cannot be made on a dark night
over absolutely unknown country with much hope of
success.   It was besides too late, the situation too confused, and the troops too scattered for an operation of
this kind.   In the end, towards 1 A.M., the V. Corps
orders were cancelled ; the 83rd and 85th Brigades, and
the 4th Division battalions with them, were directed to
organize a retrenchment across the gap, the 83rd Brigade
then to remain in G.H.Q. Line, and the 84th Brigade
to go back to Ypres as reserve.   The two companies of
the 1/K.O.Y.L.I, under Captain H. Mallinson, and B
Company of the 3/Monmouthshire with them, which had
held out all day in their original place, now came back to
the G.H.Q. line.

The new front was formed in the back line behind
Verlorenhoek ridge, that had been begun on the 27th
April by the 27th Division.   This was some three-quarters
of a mile behind that held in the morning.[1]   The line was
continued northwards by the 84th Brigade front round
Wieltje,[2] and joined up with the 12th Brigade at Mouse
Trap Farm, held by part of the 2/Monmouthshire.
Company A of the 2/Northumberland Fusiliers remained
unconquered in its original position near the farm.

The 80th Brigade, on the right of the 28th Division,
in order to regain touch with and conform to the retirement
of the 83rd Brigade, had to swing back the left of its line.[3]
The defence was deprived of the assistance of the eight

[1] The front was reported at the time as held by the 3/R. Fusiliers (85th
Brigade), 1/York and Lancaster (1 officer and 150 men strong), 2/East
Yorkshire (3 and 120), 5/King's Own (24), 2/East Surrey (85th Brigade);
with the 1/K.O.Y.L.I. (1 and 120) and 3/Monmouthshire (1 and 30) in
support, and there were parties of each of the above in G.H.Q. Line.   The
six battalions of the 83rd Brigade had lost since 23rd April 128 officers
and 4,379 men.

[2] The 84th Brigade front was held by 1/R. Warwickshire (10th Brigade),
detachments of survivors of the various battalions of the brigade, 2/R.
Dublin Fusiliers (10th) and 1/East Lancashire (11th).

[3] The front was held by the 4/K.R.R.C. in the trenches they had
defended all day, the 3/K.R.R.C. (in relief of Patricia's), and 2/Shropshire
L.I.   The losses of the original front line battalions had been : 4/K.R.R.C.,
5 officers and 300 other ranks; Patricia's, 10 and 373 ; and the commanding
officers of Patricia's, Shropshire and 4/Rifle Brigade, Major A. H. Gault,
Lieut.-Colonel R. J. Bridgford, and Major J. Harington, had been wounded.

4·7-inch guns of the XI. Heavy Brigade (Lieut.-Colonel 8 May. B. M. Bateman), which had been brought forward again to Potijze to compensate by their nearness to the front for lack of range. Six were useless for further service, having exceeded their average " life " of 2,700 full rounds [1] by over a thousand, and the remaining two were withdrawn to the moat on the eastern side of Ypres, being manned on alternate days by the survivors of the 122nd and 123rd Heavy Batteries.

Except in loss of life the day was far from being as disastrous as at first appeared. In the end, the 28th Division lost only a small amount of ground, and that much too exposed to artillery fire to be held permanently. As will be seen in the enemy's account which follows, he himself claims no success : in fact, states that he was thrown on the defensive. Unfortunately, the British casualties had been extraordinarily heavy ; no less than 11 battalion commanders had fallen, and a very large proportion of the other officers, an indication that the men required much personal leading—and little wonder, for of the original fully trained N.C.O.'s and men, few now survived. The ranks of old battalions bearing great names, had been filled with new drafts—half trained, only partially disciplined and new to battle. These had stood the test well as far as courage and fighting spirit went, but they naturally had neither the skill with the rifle nor the resource in battle of old soldiers. The Territorials fought more than well, but unfortunately with ever decreasing numbers ; for, as a result of the intensive recruiting for the New Armies, and the failure to foresee that the Territorial Army might be employed overseas and suffer serious wastage, few Territorial reinforcements were forthcoming. The Germans claimed 800 prisoners in their communiqué. That these were so few when so large a breach was made in the line and such heavy casualties were suffered, is a sign that most men fought it out to the bitter end.

There was still no weight of large numbers behind the German attacks ; the enemy was pursuing his policy of gaining what ground he could with his local troops, after it had been swept clear of defenders by his guns. In a memorandum dated on this day, Sir William Robertson, the Chief of the General Staff, pointed out that " the " circumscribed and unsupported nature of the attacks " delivered by the enemy during the last few days, the

[1] With the M.D. cordite in use ; only 900 with Mk.I. cordite.

" use of guns of a sensational nature, the employment of " asphyxiating gases and other illegitimate means of " warfare, all intended to appeal to the imagination, " point to an attempt on this front to impress us with " the idea of a vigorous German offensive which has in " reality no serious basis in fact. The probability is, " therefore, that whilst maintaining an offensive attitude, " the enemy has really thinned out his line in the West " to the minimum strength with which he thinks it can " be maintained, whilst he is throwing every man he can " collect against the Russians ".[1] The obvious answer to such a policy was for the Allies to attack in the West, but to do so required men and munitions, and meantime the question was, could the successors of the original B.E.F. hold the line even against equal numbers backed up by very superior artillery and apparently unlimited ammunition.

The V. Corps (Lieut.-General Sir E. Allenby), in reporting the situation in the early hours of 9th May, did not anticipate, considering the battered state of the brigades, that they would be able to hold the new line for long, and in case of necessity proposed to occupy the G.H.Q. Line, the left of the II. Corps being thrown back to that line and the switch which continued it through Vormezeele. Measures had already been taken by General Bulfin to withdraw some of the artillery of the 28th Division : at 8.30 P.M. on the 8th the two 5-inch howitzer batteries of the 50th (Northumbrian) Division were ordered to the west bank, and half an hour after midnight they were followed by the field guns ; only the 69th and 100th Field Batteries were left east of Ypres.[2]

9TH-12TH MAY

UNSUCCESSFUL ATTACKS ON THE 27TH DIVISION NEAR THE MENIN ROAD. RELIEF OF THE 28TH DIVISION BY THE " CAVALRY FORCE ". AMMUNITION CRISIS

The operations of the Germans in front of Ypres were without doubt affected by the commencement of the French offensive known as the Battle of Artois—when the

---

[1] The Germans would probably have done better had they fallen back in France, as they did in 1917, to shorten their line, and thus have provided more men for Russia.

[2] Some batteries were brought back to the Salient next day.

villages of Carency, Souchez and Neuville St. Vaast, between 9 May. Arras and Lens, were captured—and the simultaneous British Battle of Aubers Ridge fought by the First Army. But the attacks of the Germans on Ypres were not discontinued.[1] They left the 28th Division alone whilst it remained in the line and made no attempt until the night of the 12th/13th May to recover the ground they had abandoned in the face of the counter-attack of the 85th Brigade and the night advance of the Royal Warwickshire, Royal Irish Fusiliers and Royal Dublin Fusiliers. In view of the very weakened state of the 28th Division, the 1st Cavalry Division on the 9th May was sent by the V. Corps to support it, the 1st and 2nd Cavalry Brigades going up to the G.H.Q. Line, and one regiment, the 4th Dragoon Guards, into the line of the 85th Brigade, whilst the 9th Cavalry Brigade was employed to dig trenches behind Wieltje to connect the G.H.Q. Line to the 4th Division second line.   On the evening of the same day the company of the 2/Northumberland Fusiliers (now 1 officer, wounded, and 65 men) which had held its position near Mouse Trap Farm throughout, was relieved by the 12th Brigade, which extended its line to take over this additional piece of frontage.

It was to the 27th Division, south of the 28th, in the vicinity of the Menin road, that the Germans devoted their attention on the 9th, 10th and 11th May, and there tried to hammer their way through, though never ceasing to bombard the whole of the Salient at certain hours, and making attempts at infantry attacks on the 4th Division, all of which were repelled by rifle fire.   From 5.30 A.M. to 2 P.M. on the 9th they shelled the front of the 27th Division from Zwarteleen to the Ypres—Zonnebeke railway, killing an entire platoon of the 2/Gloucestershire, which held an advanced flanking trench in the form of a flèche or arrow head opposite Stirling Castle, and occupying the ground.   In an unsuccessful counter-attack to recover it, Lieut.-Colonel G. S. Tulloh and 40 men of the Gloucestershire were killed and 90 wounded.   At 2 P.M. the shelling ceased for half an hour and then recommenced with systematic sweeping up and down the line.   At 4 P.M. the fire rose to its highest intensity for twenty minutes, every kind of shell from 8-inch to field gun falling in the British trenches ; and then a line of Germans appeared

---

[1] Schwarte, ii. p. 266, says, " the following days [after the 8th] brought " a further continuation of the battle ".

9 May. 250 yards away. They made a desperate effort to close
with the left of the 27th Division, two other almost continuous lines following the first, but they were driven off
by the fire of the 3/ and 4/K.R.R.C., 4/Rifle Brigade and
2/Shropshire L.I., leaving dead and wounded reckoned by
hundreds, whilst the living turned and ran. Once again
they rallied and came forward, but they could not
face the British rifle fire and in the end fled in disorder.
After a personal reconnaissance, Br.-General H. L. Croker,
however, decided to abandon any further attempts to
regain the advanced trench, as it was surrounded by an
enemy-made obstacle of fallen trees and shell holes that
made movement in any direction most difficult and
reinforcement under fire almost impossible.

10 May.   On the 10th May the enemy devoted most of his
ammunition to an adjacent part of the 27th Division front,
the trenches astride the Menin road, held by the 2/Cameron
Highlanders (Lieut.-Colonel J. Campbell), the 4/K.R.R.C.
(Major B. J. Majendie) and 4/Rifle Brigade (Capt. F. H. A.
Wollaston) of the 81st and 80th Brigades.[1] From 10.30 A.M.
to nearly 1.30 P.M. the bombardment with heavy howitzers
was intense, and from noon onwards infantry was seen to
be massing. The front trenches were by this time practically destroyed and many of the men buried, but the
support trenches of the K.R.R.C. and Rifle Brigade 300
yards behind, though only waist deep, were secure from
observation, and these became their line of defence, the
Camerons still sticking to Sanctuary Wood. The 9/Argyll
and Sutherland Highlanders—whose commanding officer,
Lieut.-Colonel J. Clark, was shortly afterwards killed—
was now moved up to support the Camerons, and part of
the 1/Argyll sent to reinforce the K.R.R.C., just as the
Germans advanced. Their first attack, covering the
whole front of the 81st and 80th Brigades, was repulsed
by rifle fire, and they were unable to close. After a further
bombardment and the discharge of a small amount of
gas against the Camerons and the 1/Royal Scots on their
right, the Germans tried again ; but the improvised
respirators proved sufficiently effective, and they were
repulsed. They repeated this form of attack at 6 P.M.,
advancing in loose masses, but lying down as soon as the
defenders rose from the battered trenches to fire.

[1] The line ran along the front of Sanctuary Wood, crossed the Menin
road by a trench cut in it, with a traverse at either end, held by the
Camerons, and then along the front of Hooge woods to Bellewaarde Lake.

The question of a counter-attack was now considered, **10 May.** but in view of the shell-beaten state of the ground, and the trees brought down by artillery fire forming an almost impassable entanglement, General Snow, like Br.-General Croker on the previous day, decided against offensive action, and it was of course equally difficult for the enemy to undertake it. The 1st and 2nd Wessex and 17th Field Companies R.E. were brought up to construct a new line as close as possible to the old 4/K.R.R.C. front, so as to avoid having to give up any trenches south of the road in re-adjustment of the line. But this plan had to be abandoned for the same reason as the counter-attack, as the state of the ground made it impossible to complete the necessary digging before dawn. It was therefore decided to occupy the second line behind Bellewaarde Lake, as far south as Sanctuary Wood, and thence a communication trench south of and parallel to the Menin road, to connect with the Cameron front trench. This alteration was carried out without interference.[1]

On the following day, 11th May, the Germans followed **11 May.** their previous procedure, and again attacked the 27th Division, and again at another place—this time south of the Menin road, held by the 2/Cameron and 1/Argyll and Sutherland Highlanders (Lieut.-Colonel H. B. Kirk).[2] After a bombardment beginning at 7.30 A.M. they shortly before 11 A.M., attacked the angle of the Cameron front, using gas. Owing to a sudden change of wind, the gas blew back on them and exposed two of their battalions in fairly close order, which, caught by a machine gun, suffered severely. Lieut.-Colonel Campbell of the Camerons was now wounded and Lieut.-Colonel Kirk took command of the defence, General Snow sending him up two companies of the 1/Leinster from his reserve. The enemy again resorted to bombardment, and after the Camerons and Argylls had repulsed a second attack, the former were

---

[1] The battalions principally engaged had lost :—4/K.R.R.C. in the three days' fighting 8th-10th 15 officers and 478 other ranks, leaving it with 3 officers and 100 men ; the 4/Rifle Brigade 13 officers and 450 other ranks ; the Camerons, on the 10th, 3 officers and 150 men ; and the 9/Argyll and Sutherland on the 9th and 10th about 350.

[2] The Order of Battle was :—
81st Brigade : 9/Royal Scots, 1/Royal Scots, 2/Cameron Hrs., 1/Argyll (less one company), which extended across, and a little north of, the Menin road, with the 9/Argyll (200 strong) in Zouave Wood, converting it into a strong point.
80th Brigade : 4/Rifle Brigade, 3/K.R.R.C. and 2/Shropshire L.I., with one company each of 1/Argyll and 2/Shropshire L.I. in support.

11 May. compelled by the complete destruction of their trenches
to withdraw to their support line. The Germans were
then able to seize the highest point of the ground marked
by the ring-contour 55 at the bend of the Menin road,
and the north-east corner of Sanctuary Wood. A fight
with alternate attack and counter-attack went on well
into the night for the possession of this locality, in which
portions of the 1/Royal Scots and 2/Gloucestershire and
the other half of the Leinsters took part, Lieut.-Colonel
C. Conyers of the Royal Irish Fusiliers, lent to the last
named, being mortally wounded; but it remained in
enemy hands.

12 May.   Except for heavy shelling of the 27th Division, the
12th May was uneventful. As the division had only two
much worn battalions, the 4/K.R.R.C. and the Patricia's,
in reserve, the 150th (York and Durham) Brigade at
Vlamertinghe was placed at General Snow's disposal,
and one battalion of it, the 5/Durham L.I., was at once
sent up to strengthen the line, its companies being divided
between the Camerons, Argylls and 1/ and 9/Royal Scots.[1]
The IV. Durham (5-inch) Howitzer Brigade and a 60-pdr.
battery were also sent to him.

There was good news from the air as regards the Ypres
sector, as streams of railway traffic were observed moving
through Valenciennes towards Douai and Lens, and there
were detrainments at night at these places. This seemed
to indicate that the pressure of the French attack in the
Arras district was drawing reinforcements from the north.

During the night of the 12th/13th May the line of the
28th Division was reorganized. Its artillery and engineers
remained, but its infantry, and the 1/R. Warwickshire
and 2/R. Dublin Fusiliers of the 10th Brigade, which had
reinforced it, were relieved by the 1st and 3rd Cavalry
Divisions under Major-General de Lisle, the new combination being given the name of the " Cavalry Force ". It
took over the front also of the northernmost battalion of
the 27th Division, the 2/Shropshire L.I., near the railway.
The infantry of the 28th Division went into Army reserve
around the villages east and south of Poperinghe. General
Bulfin's men had been in the thick of the fighting since the
beginning of the Second Battle of Ypres, having lost more
than 15,000 men :[2] now in spite of fairly numerous rein-

---

[1] The 50th (Northumbrian) Division at this time was furnishing large
parties each night for work on rear lines of defence.
[2] See p. 356.

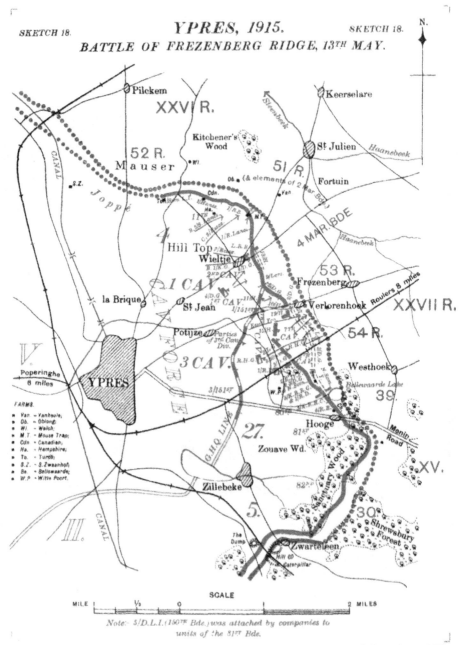

YPRES, 1915.

BATTLE OF FREZENBERG RIDGE, 13TH MAY.

FARMS.
Van = Vanheule;
Ob. = Oblong;
Wl. = Welch;
M.T. = Mouse Trap;
Cdn. = Canadian;
Ha. = Hampshire;
Ta. = Turco;
S.Z. = S.Zwaanhof;
Be. = Bellewaarde;
W.P. = Witte Poort.

SCALE

MILE 1 ⅓ 0 1 2 MILES

Note:- 5/D.L.I.(150TH Bde.)was attacked by companies to
units of the 31ST Bde.

Ordnance Survey, 1926.

forcements—except in the attached Territorials—its 17 13 May.
battalions were reduced to 200 officers and 8,000 men.

During this period the ammunition crisis became very
serious. On 9th May the weekly report to the War Office
showed that there was practically no 4·5-inch howitzer
ammunition remaining, though the Second Army was
urgently demanding more.[1] The figures had hardly been
put on paper before an order was received from the
Secretary of State for War for the despatch to the Dardanelles of 2,000 rounds of 4·5-inch howitzer ammunition
and 20,000 rounds of 18-pdr. ammunition. On a definite
promise that it should be at once replaced, Sir John
French protested and complied with the order; the
18-pdr. shell was replaced on the 12th and 13th, but as
regards the howitzer rounds the promise was not fulfilled
until 16th May.

It was brought to notice at the time that the B.E.F.
was short of 42 machine guns, and that the stock was
completely exhausted; the reserve of small arm ammunition was down to 93 rounds per rifle, and rifles were so
few at home that it was suggested that drafts should come
out without them; whilst the sending of the 14th (Light)
Division was for the moment delayed owing to there being no
gun or rifle ammunition for it. Of grenades, trench mortars
and trench stores, too, the B.E.F. was still woefully short.

On the other hand, on 9th May the 9th (Scottish)
Division, the first of the New Army divisions, began to
detrain in St. Omer district, completing the operation on
the 14th. It may be added here that it was immediately
followed by the 14th Division, and before the end of the
month by the 12th (Eastern) Division. On 11th May the
first Kite Balloon Section, with material and personnel
provided by the Admiralty, proceeded to Steenvoorde for
work with the Second Army. It made its first ascent at
Poperinghe on the 20th.

13TH MAY

THE ATTACK ON THE 27TH DIVISION, "CAVALRY FORCE" AND 4TH DIVISION

According to a German account,[2] a great attack, Map 12.
planned for the 13th May, had to be suspended on account Sketch 18.

[1] 800 rounds at First Army railhead; none at Second Army; 2,800
at G.H.Q. Base; none at the Base.
[2] Schwarte, ii. p. 266.

13 May. of shortage of ammunition. All British narratives, however, are unanimous in recording that from 3.30 A.M. to 1 P.M. on that day the bombardment of the trenches and back areas with heavy shell was incessant, and the V. Corps diary specifically states that it was the heaviest yet experienced. Even after 1 P.M. it was continued intermittently until nightfall.

The relief of the infantry of the 28th Division had been carried out without incident during the night of the 12th/13th, and the Cavalry Force was disposed from Bellewaarde Lake, to a point 600 yards south-east of Mouse Trap Farm, where the 4th Division took up the line.[1]

The trenches taken over, having been dug in haste after the 28th Division was forced back, were poor, had no communication trenches, and practically no wire. Though every effort was made to improve the defences during the night there was little time, and unfortunately the engineers and infantry parties sent up to assist failed to find the rendezvous. The 3rd Cavalry Division was specially handicapped as its field squadron R.E. was absent working on Army back lines.

The heaviest bombardment, shrapnel and high-explosive, was directed on the 13th May on the front between Hooge and the Ypres—St. Julien road, a sector held by the 80th Brigade (27th Division) and the Cavalry Force, where shell fire and the rain, which fell without ceasing from early dawn until night, soon reduced the trenches to a quagmire. About 8 A.M. the enemy broke in on the front of the 7th Cavalry Brigade (right to left the Leicestershire Yeomanry, 2nd and 1st Life Guards, each about 300 strong), which, being exposed on a long gentle forward slope, was held very lightly. Having secured a footing in the line the enemy gradually bombed out the remaining defenders, who had no hand-grenades with which to reply, the two squadrons of the Leicestershire Yeomanry being driven southwards into the sector of the 6th Cavalry Brigade. The third squadron, however, in

---

[1] 3rd Cavalry Division (Major-General C. J. Briggs) on the right, with the 6th (Br.-General D. Campbell), and the 7th (Br.-General A. A. Kennedy) Cavalry Brigades in front line ; and the 8th (Br.-General C. B. Bulkeley-Johnson) in reserve. 1st Cavalry Division (Major-General H. de B. de Lisle) on the left, with the 1st (Colonel T. T. Pitman) and the 2nd (Br.-General R. L. Mullens) Cavalry Brigades in front line ; and the 9th (Br.-General W. H. Greenly) in reserve. Each brigade furnished about fifty officers and between 800 and 900 rifles, and a machine-gun detachment.

support trenches three hundred yards behind, by steady 13 May. fire—although the rain and mud made the use of rifles very difficult—covered the gap and prevented any further advance by the enemy, who thereupon set about building up a firing line opposite it.

The 5th Dragoon Guards (1st Cavalry Brigade) in the centre of the 1st Cavalry Division front and a squadron of the 18th Hussars (2nd Cavalry Brigade) on the extreme left nearest the 4th Division, were also shelled out of their front line. In the 4th Division itself [1] the front trenches of the 5/London (London Rifle Brigade) and the 1/East Lancashire were flattened out and had to be evacuated.[2] But these gaps made in the line, except in the 7th Cavalry Brigade sector, were almost immediately repaired by the local commanders sending up supports—part of the 11th Hussars and the 2/Essex. This battalion, under Captain L. O. W. Jones, which was in support, had to advance over nearly half a mile of open country, losing 180 men in the operation, but reached the front line, the 1/Rifle Brigade, to the left, standing up and cheering it. Two platoons of the latter battalion holding Mouse Trap Farm on which, it was counted, over a hundred shells a minute were falling, were annihilated; but the farm was re-occupied in the evening, with the assistance of the East Lancashire, although the Germans had sapped up to within 30 yards. Various infantry attacks on the 4th Division front followed, from trenches two to three hundred yards away, particularly against the Hampshires [3] and Somerset L.I. In some cases the Germans reached the wire, but were driven off by rifle fire; and when the shelling ceased at times, men of the 11th Brigade stood up and dared them to come on. But it was soon obvious, as on the previous day, that they would not do so until the ground had been swept clear of defenders by artillery fire. The 80th Brigade on the right of the cavalry, with the 4/Rifle

---

[1] Right to left, 11th Brigade :—London Rifle Brigade (two companies), 1/East Lancashire, 1/Rifle Brigade (holding Mouse Trap Farm and to the left of it), 1/Hampshire, 1/Somerset L.I. In support London Rifle Brigade (two companies) and 2/Essex (of 12th Brigade).

[2] Lance-Sergeant D. W. Belcher with a handful of men of the London Rifle Brigade remained and held his position all day, opening rapid fire on the Germans 150 to 250 yards distant, whenever they showed signs of attacking. His bold attitude averted an attack on the flank of the division and he received the Victoria Cross, the second bestowed on a Territorial.

[3] Now commanded by Major the Hon. L. C. W. Palk. Lieut.-Colonel F. R. Hicks had received wounds near La Brique on 5th May, of which he subsequently died.

13 May. Brigade and 3/K.R.R.C. in front line, reinforced at 2 P.M. by the 2/Royal Irish Fusiliers (82nd Brigade), maintained its position in spite of all bombardment.

Thus it was only in the sector of the 7th Cavalry Brigade that the situation was doubtful. Communication with the front was difficult, and dense black smoke from the very intense shelling prevented any part of the line being seen : so neither the actual extent of the gap nor the fact that it was blocked by the Leicester Yeomanry squadron was known for some time. Right and left of it the North Somerset Yeomanry (6th Cavalry Brigade) and Queen's Bays (1st Cavalry Brigade) held on.

As a first step to remedy the situation, the 8th Cavalry Brigade (Royal Horse Guards, 10th Hussars and Essex Yeomanry) was deployed behind the gap ; and, about 10 A.M. General Briggs, who had come up to Potijze, ordered Br.-General Bulkeley-Johnson to make a definite counter-attack. An artillery bombardment was promised to begin at noon, but the preliminaries could not be completed until 2 P.M. and the counter-attack followed at 2.30. Part of the 9th Cavalry Brigade supported the 8th, and the survivors of the Leicester Yeomanry joined in led by Captain the Hon. D. P. Tollemache, the brigade major of the 7th Cavalry Brigade, both the commanding officer, Lieut.-Colonel the Hon. P. C. Evans-Freke and the second-in-command, Major W. F. Ricardo, having fallen. In spite of very heavy shrapnel fire, the original line was regained in places, and the Germans who had taken possession of the ground were turned out and in some cases pursued. But shrapnel and machine-gun fire made it impossible for all to reach the old line or for any one to remain there, and a new line a thousand yards in rear, consisting chiefly of shell holes on a long reverse slope, was occupied. It extended from Railway Wood on the right to the trenches of the 1st Cavalry Brigade on the left, with a flank along the railway. Towards evening the 151st (Durham L.I.) Brigade arrived to hold the G.H.Q. Line behind the threatened front ; but the Germans did not advance again, and did not even take possession of the ground vacated.

In the very severe fighting thus briefly summarized, the cavalry lost very heavily, no less than one brigadier and seven commanding officers becoming casualties.[1]

[1] Killed :—Lieut.-Colonels E. R. A. Shearman (10th Hussars); Hon. P. C. Evans-Freke (Leicestershire Yeomanry); E. Deacon (Essex Yeomanry). Wounded :—Br.-General D. Campbell ; Colonel A. F. H. Ferguson

In consequence of the reduced strength of the Cavalry 13 May. Force, the 27th Division took over the right of its line up to the railway, relieving the 6th Cavalry Brigade ; the 4th Division took over the left, closing to within five hundred yards of the Ypres—Verlorenhoek road, relieving the 2nd Cavalry Brigade. Thus General de Lisle's front was reduced by half.

Both General Joffre and the Second Army commander, General Plumer, sent their congratulations to the cavalry and the 4th and 27th Divisions, to which General Allenby (V. Corps) added a special compliment to the 80th Brigade on its success. The Germans had shelled the V. Corps off the untenable position on the front slopes of Frezenberg ridge and in six days had gained a slice of ground between Hooge and Mouse Trap Farm a little over a thousand yards deep in the centre, but that had ended their advance. Assisted by less than a dozen modern heavy guns, handicapped by lack of ammunition, the miserable condition of the trenches, and the unquestioned domination of the German artillery, the British had, by their endurance and tenacity, made even such a small success too costly to be continued ; they were worthy successors of the men of " First Ypres ". From the German account, which is given below, it would appear that if even one really fresh brigade could have been sent up on any single day in the period to attack at dusk, when the German guns were neutralized by darkness, a great result might have been achieved.

The total casualties of the V. Corps in the battle of Frezenberg 8th-13th May had been 456 officers and 8,935 other ranks.[1]

(2nd Life Guards) ; Lieut.-Colonels O. B. B. Smith-Bingham (3rd Dragoon Guards) ; G. F. Steele (Royals); G. C. Glyn (North Somerset Yeomanry).

The Leicester Yeomanry lost 12 officers and 175 other ranks killed and wounded, out of a total strength of 281. For the divisional casualties see footnote below.

[1]	Officers.			Other Ranks.		
	Killed.	Wounded.	Missing.	Killed.	Wounded.	Missing.
1st Cavalry Division	9	28	..	86	335	20
3rd „ „ .	31	59	3	195	768	175
4th Division . .	15	39	6	342	833	203
27th „ . .	27	61	8	350	1,412	339
28th „ . .	30	72	61	237	1,148	2,341
50th „ . .	1	4	..	16	111	..
Corps Troops . .	1	1	..	2	22	..
	114	264	78	1,228	4,629	3,078
		456			8,935	

NOTE

THE 8TH-13TH MAY 1915 FROM THE GERMAN SIDE [1]

8TH MAY

The attack made by the three German corps after several days' preparation was intended to be a very serious one. Of the *XV. Corps* it is said that it " took possession of Hill 60 east of Hooge, " and had to content itself with this ". The Hill mentioned may be the small elevation marked " 50 ", north of Hooge, near the junction of the fronts of the 4/K.R.R.C. and P.P.C.L.I., which, as related, was too exposed to German artillery fire to be held. The *XXVII. Reserve Corps*, whose right extended as far as Hill 28, north of Frezenberg (exclusive) had therefore the 83rd Brigade opposite to it. The account of its operations is that " the enemy did not await " assault,[2] but retired to a prepared position, so that the German " infantry secured Frezenberg, Verlorenhoek and also Westhoek " [already outside the British line] ". The *XXVI. Reserve Corps*— opposite the 84th Brigade—" took Hill 28, north of Frezenberg and " Hill 33 north of Verlorenhoek [this was the extreme point reached " by the Germans before the counter-attack], but could make no " progress against Chateau Wieltje [Mouse Trap Farm] ". The narrative then goes on : " A great counter-attack [? the advance of " the Royal Warwickshire, R. Irish Fusiliers and R. Dublin Fusiliers] " that was only stopped at Frezenberg [it did not go much further " than Verlorenhoek], threw the *Fourth Army* on the defensive, and " compelled the *XXVI. Reserve Corps* and also the *XXVII. Reserve* " *Corps* to abandon the position captured. Only the *XV. Corps* " held its ground ".

9TH-13TH MAY

" The next few days brought a further continuation of the " battle. The lack of ammunition made itself very seriously felt ; " but the ammunition allotted had from the 9th May onward to be " sent to the *Sixth Army* in consequence of the fighting at La " Bassée and Loos [Artois front]. Troops also, the *38th Landwehr* " *Brigade* and the *202nd R.I. Regt.*, had to be given up to the sister " Army. But the necessity of rest for the troops of the *Fourth* " *Army* made itself more and more felt ; the *37th Landwehr Brigade* " had to be relieved by a part of the Army reserve, and the *2nd* " *Reserve Ersatz Brigade* taken out of the line. The effect of the " fighting was particularly marked in the *XXVI. Reserve Corps* ".[3] The narrative then passes to 24th May

[1] Schwarte, ii. pp 265-6.
[2] The British front line battalions were, as has been seen, mostly annihilated by fire. The German bulletin claims only 800 British prisoners wounded and unwounded in the Ypres area, 1st to 8th May.
[3] A footnote states :—

FIGHTING STRENGTH OF THE INFANTRY
51st Reserve Division

20th April .	. 343 officers ;	12,993 men ;	33 machine guns ;
11th May .	. 224 ,,	8,712 ,,	37 ,, ,,

52nd Reserve Division

20th April .	. 343 officers ;	13,551 men ;	26 machine guns ;
11th May .	. 247 ,,	9,234 ,,	21 ,, ,,

[The reinforcements received are not stated.]

CHAPTER XVIII

THE BATTLES OF YPRES 1915 (*concluded*)

THE BATTLE OF BELLEWAARDE RIDGE, 24TH-25TH MAY [1]

(Map 13; Sketches 19 and B)

14TH-23RD MAY

A PAUSE. EXPULSION OF THE GERMANS FROM THE WEST
BANK OF THE YPRES CANAL BY THE FRENCH

WHILST the defensive wing of the B.E.F., the Second
Army, first under General Sir H. Smith-Dorrien and then
under General Sir H. Plumer, had been holding on against
German attacks, the right wing, the First Army, under
General Sir D. Haig, had been engaged in an offensive in
co-operation with the French, without obtaining the hoped
for success. On the 9th May the First Army had fought
the Battle of Aubers Ridge, which had been broken off,
the limited number of heavy guns and small amount of
artillery ammunition available being wholly insufficient
to breach the greatly strengthened German defences.
The French offensive, commenced on the same day, though
it had a fine initial success, also brought about neither a
break-through nor a decisive victory, though it was continued officially until the 18th June. In further co-
operation with the French, the offensive of the First Army
was renewed in the battle of Festubert, 15th-27th May:
the enemy's first line of defence was carried, but his
resistance in the second could not be overcome with the
means at General Haig's disposal, and this battle was
also brought to a close without any decision being reached.
In point of date these operations should now be described,
but, bearing in mind that they were taking place further

---

[1] The spelling "Bellewaerde" in the Battle Nomenclature Report has
not been officially accepted, and the Battle Honour has been awarded as
"Bellewaarde".

14 May. south, it is simpler from the narrative point of view first to follow to a close the battles of Ypres—the operations of Sir John French's defensive wing in the north—and then to deal with the offensive in the southern theatre.[1]

On the 14th May enemy shell fire in the Ypres sector moderated considerably, but the Germans attempted two small attacks. In the course of the morning they massed in the trenches opposite Mouse Trap Farm, held by two platoons of the 1/East Lancashire, where their sap-heads had been pushed to within thirty yards of the British line. By persistent effort they eventually succeeded in occupying a portion of the enclosure, but were expelled without offering much resistance by two platoons of the 5/South Lancashire, which had two companies in a retrenchment behind the farm. In the afternoon Germans were seen collecting opposite Hooge and Bellewaarde, but here their assembly was broken up by fire. Then for nine days, except for minor enterprises and desultory firing, the situation of the II. and V. Corps remained unchanged, and it was judged that the "Second Battle of Ypres" had come to an end. But there was still to be another serious fight.

Advantage was taken of the pause to improve the trenches and construct additional back lines, all the available engineers and large working parties, mainly from the Cavalry Corps and 50th (Northumbrian) Division, being employed. Defensive measures against gas were improved by the issue of vermoral sprayers—to neutralize any gas left hanging about the trenches—and of the first batch of helmets (flannel bags with eye-pieces), enough to provide each battalion with 16, which were distributed to the machine gunners. The heavy artillery of the V. Corps, now slightly augmented and consisting of one 15-inch howitzer, three 9·2-inch howitzers, four old 5-inch howitzers, eight 60-pdrs. and twenty 4·7-inch guns, was reorganized into three brigades—the V., XI. and XIII., under Br.-General H. C. C. Uniacke.[2]

[1] The battles of Aubers Ridge and Festubert will be narrated in the opening chapters of the next volume.

[2] Owing to the constant variation of infantry commands, the divisional artillery was by now allotted to zones and supported the troops holding definite sectors, irrespective of the formations to which they belonged. Thus, one artillery brigade covered the front between the Wieltje—Fortuin road and a line joining Mouse Trap Farm to St. Julien. The expression "feu de barrage" appears frequently in orders. In addition to the artillery telephone system, which was very liable to interruption, certain signal offices just west of the canal were selected as centres to which

Various other changes of organization were carried 14 May. out : the " Cavalry Force " was dissolved and absorbed again into the Cavalry Corps, which now held the centre of the V. Corps front, with the 28th Divisional artillery administratively attached to it. The 50th (Northumbrian) Division was still not engaged as a whole, its three infantry brigades, reinforced by drafts after their heavy losses, being distributed for instruction : 149th Brigade to the 4th Division, 150th to the Cavalry Corps, and 151st to the 28th Division. The 2nd Cavalry Division relieved the 1st and 3rd, and advanced the line occupied on the 13th May up the reverse slope to within three hundred yards of the trenches lost on that day. The remnants of these trenches were now used as posts for cavalry snipers.

Between the 17th and 19th May the 1st Cavalry Division gradually relieved the infantry of the 27th Division, and took over its front. The three brigades : the 80th (Br.-General W. E. B. Smith), 81st (Br.-General H. L. Croker) and 82nd (Br.-General J. R. Longley) and the divisional troops, which had been in the line without relief for four weeks, were congratulated anew by the Commander-in-Chief on their steadfastness and endurance, the 80th Brigade, reduced, in spite of drafts, to a bare 1,628, being singled out as deserving, if ever a brigade did, the epithet of " Stonewall ". The losses of the division in the period 22nd April to 15th May had been over 200 officers and 6,000 other ranks.[1]

On the 15th May the French on the British left again took the offensive with the 153rd Division, and secured the houses on the eastern bank at Steenstraat and the canal bridge there, but the Germans still held out on the western bank in a farm south of the village. To exploit this success, General Putz ordered the 153rd Division to continue the operation, and the 45th and 152nd to

---

messages sent by orderly from observing and liaison officers at the front could be transmitted to the various headquarters and batteries.

The heavy batteries, all on the west bank (except one battery of the XI. Brigade manned alternately by the men of the 122nd and 123rd Batteries, on the east bank of the moat of Ypres between the Menin and Lille gates), and controlled from corps headquarters, were given specific targets as required : for instance, " enemy batteries ", " bridge in St. Julien ". In the latter part of the battle a number of enemy batteries—called officially by such names as " Alphonse ", " Bertie ", etc.—were located by aeroplane and fixed on the map by co-ordinates ; but there was only a small amount of registration by aeroplanes and wireless, owing to the enemy's air superiority.

[1] See p. 356 for total British casualties.

15 May. attack on the east bank. In spite of violent counter-attacks the farm was stormed, and during the night the remaining Germans retired over the canal, leaving numerous dead on the ground. The French were now in complete possession of the western bank, and the Belgians were in their original position. On the 22nd the French reorganized their forces in Flanders ; the name Détachement d'Armée de Belgique was abolished, that of **XXXVI.** Corps substituted, and the command given to General Hély d'Oissel.[1]

The arrival or imminent arrival of New Army divisions has been referred to. Besides these important additions, drafts to fill up to establishment the units of the Old Army were coming along fairly well, but, owing to the lack of Territorial recruits, the engagement of whom had been interfered with by enrolments for the New Army, it was found necessary on the 18th to withdraw three of the weakest Territorial battalions — the 5/London (London Rifle Brigade), the 12/London (Rangers), and 13/London (Kensingtons)—to the lines of communication ; to organize as half-battalions the 7/ and 9/Argyll and Sutherland Highlanders ; and to amalgamate into a single battalion the hard hit 1/, 2/ and 3/Monmouthshire.[2]

Although the news from Russia was far from favourable and the Austro-German forces were daily gaining ground in Galicia and Poland, and in the Gallipoli Peninsula little progress was being made—despite repeated attacks Sir Ian Hamilton's force had failed to reach Krithia—the B.E.F. was cheered by the news that on the 23rd May Italy had declared war against Austria.

THE BATTLE OF BELLEWAARDE RIDGE

24TH-25TH MAY

THE GAS ATTACK ON THE V. CORPS

Map 13.
Sketch 19.

On the morning of the 24th May—Whit Monday and a fine, hot day—the V. Corps front, some 5½ miles, after various reliefs had taken place, was held from right to left, that is from near Hill 60 to the flank of the French

[1] The 152nd, 153rd, 45th and 87th Territorial Divisions, about 33,000 rifles, were on the immediate British left ; the 38th and 81st Territorial, and the Marine Brigade, about 14,000 rifles, at Nieuport.

[2] The three lieutenant-colonels having become casualties, Major W. S. Bridge was in command.

YPRES, 1915.

BATTLE OF BELLEWAARDE RIDGE, 24TH MAY.

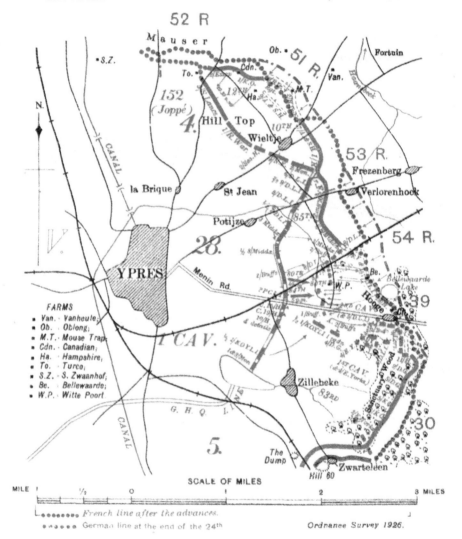

FARMS
- Van. · Vanheule;
- Ob. · Oblong;
- M.T. · Mouse Trap;
- Cdn. · Canadian;
- Ha. · Hampshire;
- To. · Turco;
- S.Z. · S. Zwaanhof;
- Be. · Bellewaarde;
- W.P. · Witte Poort

SCALE OF MILES

MILE   ½   O   1   2   3 MILES

●●●●●● French line after the advances.
●●●●●● German line at the end of the 24th

Ordnance Survey 1926.

at Turco Farm, by the 83rd Brigade (28th Division) ; 24 May. the 1st Cavalry Division, with the 1st and 2nd Cavalry Brigades astride the Menin Road, just east of Hooge ; the 85th Brigade (28th Division) across the railway and Zonnebeke road ; and the 10th Brigade (4th Division), covering Wieltje and up to Mouse Trap Farm (inclusive), with the 12th Brigade (4th Division) beyond it. In reserve were the 84th Brigade (28th Division) behind Ypres, the 2nd Cavalry Division and the 11th and 13th Brigades near Vlamertinghe, and further west the 27th Division and 3rd Cavalry Division.[1]

Nothing special was noticed during the night of the 23rd-24th except the rumbling of transport going south ; but it would be light about 2.30 A.M. and the troops on duty stood to arms, as usual, some fifteen minutes earlier. At 2.45 A.M. the enemy sent up four red lights, followed by two others, whereupon heavy fire was opened by guns, machine guns and rifles, and cloud gas on the largest scale yet experienced was released on nearly the whole length of the V. Corps front, from just south of Hooge to just short of Turco Farm, a front of $4\frac{1}{2}$ miles. So close were the German trenches, except on the 85th Brigade front, where there was a wide No Man's Land, that the hissing of the gas as it emerged from the cylinders was plainly heard. The wind was light and the gas clouds

---

[1] As already mentioned, the infantry of the 50th (Northumbrian) Division was distributed, and to save frequent mention of small units in the narrative the allotment is here given :

149th Brigade with 4th Division :
    4/Northumberland Fusiliers in the divisional second line : it sent a half company to the 2/Essex, and one company to the 2/R. Dublin Fusiliers.
    5/Northumberland Fusiliers had a company each with the 5/South Lancashire, 1/King's Own, 2/Essex and 2/Royal Irish. It lost 9 officers and 283 men on the 24th.
    6/ and 7/Northumberland Fusiliers in reserve.

150th Brigade with the Cavalry Corps :
    4/Green Howards with 9th Lancers. The battalion had 5 officers and 198 men casualties.
    5/Green Howards in reserve and sent at 11 P.M. to G.H.Q. Line.
    4/East Yorkshire with 1st Cavalry Brigade.
    5/Durham L.I. with 2nd Cavalry Brigade.

151st Brigade with 28th Division :
    6/Durham L.I. in G.H.Q. Line.
    7/Durham L.I. had two companies with 3/Royal Fusiliers, remainder in G.H.Q. Line.
    8/Durham L.I. closed gap between 3/Royal Fusiliers and 2/East Surrey, and reinforced them. It lost 14 officers and 241 other ranks.
    9/Durham L.I. had two companies with the East Surrey and lost 10 officers and 204 other ranks.

24 May. in consequence moved very slowly, and from the air seemed almost stationary over the trenches. They rose 40 feet high from the ground and were so dense as to blot out houses; in the course of time their effect was felt twenty miles behind the line, and, it is recorded, was still very bad on the canal bank at 6 A.M.

There was no surprise, for the trench garrisons were on the alert, and many officers expected an attack as the wind seemed favourable for one; but, the gas cylinders being in most cases so close, there was little time to put on respirators. Many men were overcome before they could protect themselves, and on this occasion the German infantry [1] assaulted almost immediately after the gas was released. But no sensational results were achieved, as there had been on the 22nd April.

The first onslaught of the Germans was driven back by rifle and machine-gun fire with heavy loss, except at Mouse Trap Farm, held by two platoons of the R. Dublin Fusiliers. Here the trenches were only thirty yards apart, and the enemy at once captured the moated farm, now a mere heap of mud and rubbish. On the rest of the front the struggle was long; the units of the Old Army of the 1st Cavalry Division and the 4th and 28th Divisions, though diluted beyond recognition by partially trained reinforcements, again demonstrated for all time that the great traditions of the past were not lost with the men who fell in 1914. For $4\frac{1}{2}$ hours the enemy bombardment was continued with full intensity, but fortunately the lachrymatory gas used in a proportion of the shells did little more than make the eyes water. All telephone communication was soon cut, observation was nearly out of the question, as the enemy had the advantage of the higher ground, and the front line was shrouded in a black pall of smoke and dust formed by the continuous shelling with heavy howitzers. As in the worst days at " First Ypres ", information could only be gathered and communications forwarded by using patrols and runners, who only too often became casualties. It is therefore more than usually difficult to determine the exact sequence of events in different parts of the field, especially as the units that suffered most had little leisure to record times.

[1] According to "S.und.G.", p. 98, the *39th Division (XV. Corps)* attacked opposite Hooge, the *53rd Reserve* and *54th Reserve Divisions (XXVII. Reserve Corps)* from Bellewaarde to Wieltje and the *51st Reserve Division (XXVI. Reserve Corps)* north-west of Ypres. If this is correct four enemy divisions attacked four brigades.

THE BREAK IN THE LINE NORTH AND SOUTH
OF BELLEWAARDE LAKE

The line of the 85th Brigade (since the 18th May com- 24 May.
manded by Br.-General C. E. Pereira) between Bellewaarde Lake and the Ypres—Zonnebeke road lay on the
reverse slope of Verlorenhoek ridge.[1] The trenches here
and elsewhere, owing to the rain and storms of the preceding
days, were knee-deep in mud, and, apart from the effects
of shelling, the sides, undercut by water, were constantly
falling in. In the course of a couple of hours the two
companies of the 8/Middlesex and the company of the
2/East Surrey next to them, on whom the fiercest attack
fell, were after a magnificent defence overwhelmed[2] and
practically annihilated. The rest of the East Surrey and
the 9/Durham L.I. (Lieut.-Colonel A. Henderson), reinforced about 7.30 A.M. by the 8/Durham L.I. (Lieut.-
Colonel J. Turnbull), stuck to their positions all day, it
being specially recorded by the 28th Division that there
were few stragglers to the rear and none from one of its
battalions. Foiled in the north, the enemy soon set about
exploiting the gap southwards. Although the 3/Royal
Fusiliers sent half a company to its left to cover that
flank, by about 8 A.M.—Major A. V. Johnson commanding
being wounded, all the officers casualties and the majority
of its men and those of the 7/Durham L.I., with it, gassed,
wounded or killed—the battalions were forced from their
trenches. Br.-General C. E. Pereira sent up first a half-
company and then 1½ companies of the 2/Buffs from
brigade reserve ; but, owing to the heavy fire, few of these
reinforcements ever reached the front. With the aid of
the third remaining company of the Buffs,[3] the survivors
were rallied in the third line trenches behind what had
been Railway Wood. There they managed to hold on
all day.[4] On the receipt of a report of the loss of the front

---

[1] Half the 7/Durham L.I. and 3/Royal Fusiliers were south of the
railway, and the 2/East Surrey, with two companies 8/Middlesex and two
companies of 9/Durham L.I. north of it.
[2] The 2/East Surrey (Lieut.-Colonel C. C. G. Ashton) records that
there was no trace of its company. Of the total four companies of the
8/Middlesex (Major E. D. W. Gregory), 14 officers and 374 men strong,
11 and 200 were casualties.
[3] The fourth was with the 2nd Cavalry Brigade.
[4] The 3/Royal Fusiliers lost 16 officers and 536 men, only 3 officers,
including the quartermaster, and 244 other ranks being left. The
casualties of the 2/Buffs (Major C. A. Worthington in command, Major

24 May. line, Br.-General Pereira immediately organized and set in motion a counter-attack to recover it with every available man of the 85th Brigade although this amounted to no more than 2 weak companies of the 3/Middlesex and a few of the 2/Buffs ; but he stopped the operation when he heard from General Bulfin (28th Division) that the 84th and 80th Brigades were being sent up for the purpose ; and, whilst thus waiting, his brigade repulsed all further endeavours of the enemy to advance.

Further to the right near Hooge in the 1st Cavalry Division sector, the gas clouds had passed a few yards north and clear of the 1st Cavalry Brigade [1] (Lieut.-Colonel T. T. Pitman in temporary command), and that formation had no great difficulty in holding its own ; it was troubled mainly about the happenings on its left. Here the 2nd Cavalry Brigade (Br.-General R. L. Mullens)[2] held the Menin road, Hooge, and as far as Bellewaarde Lake, and except on the extreme right the whole of its front was badly affected by gas, which hung about the Hooge woods. But the line still held, any gaps being immediately filled by the supports, and the enemy's efforts to advance were stoutly resisted. Nevertheless, the pressure continued and it became necessary gradually to strengthen the 2nd from the 9th Cavalry Brigade (Br.-General W. H. Greenly), the divisional reserve.[3] The 85th Brigade sent a company of the 2/Buffs, and the 83rd contributed two companies from the 1/York and Lancaster, the battalion in support in Sanctuary Wood. Before these reinforcements arrived, Br.-General Mullens and his brigade major were overcome by gas, and Major-General de Lisle directed Br.-General Greenly to take command of the 2nd Cavalry Brigade and the medley of units fighting in its line.

Until about 10 A.M. the cavalry line held good, and then the German *39th Division*, aided by units of the *XXVII. Reserve Corps*, which came down through the gap on the left where the 3/Royal Fusiliers had stood,

---

Power having been wounded on 3rd May) in the period 21st-29th May—but mostly on the 24th—were 6 officers and 389 other ranks.

[1] It had the Queen's Bays, 5th Dragoon Guards, and 11th Hussars in the line.

[2] It had the 9th Lancers and 18th Hussars, with the 4th Green Howards (Lieut.-Colonel M. H. L. Bell)—450 strong—and 120 men of the 5/Durham L.I. in the line.

[3] Two squadrons of the 15th Hussars were sent to the 9th Lancers and two of the 19th to the 18th Hussars.

broke through the 18th Hussars' front between Hooge **24 May.** and Bellewaarde.[1]   The 9th Lancers (Major D. J. E. Beale-Browne) and infantry with them, were not, however, to be moved, and organizing a flank in a communication trench south of and parallel to the Menin road, kept the enemy off.   Br.-General Greenly did not attempt to restore the line by a frontal counter-attack ; he brought his only reserve, the 4th Dragoon Guards, to the G.H.Q. Line behind the gap, where there were already about four hundred men ;[2] but the two remaining companies of the York and Lancaster, with a company of the 4/East Yorkshire and a squadron of 15th Hussars, he placed in Zouave Wood—now little more than stumps and without a green leaf in it—in order that they might fall on the southern flank of the Germans should they push on.   On the northern side of the gap, Br.-General Pereira formed some of the 3/Royal Fusiliers along the railway, safe-guarding the flank on that side, and all available guns of the 27th and 28th Divisions were concentrated on the lost ground.   The enemy, whether he had intended to come further or not, did not advance from the trenches of the 18th Hussars and Royal Fusiliers that he had occupied.

The Break in the Line at Mouse Trap Farm

In the 4th Division on the left of the British front the line was held by the 10th and 12th Brigades (Br.-Generals Hull and Anley).[3]   Mouse Trap Farm had been lost at the first rush of the enemy, as already mentioned, and a certain number of recently joined men straggled back, but the enemy for a time gained no other advantage.

[1] The 18th Hussars had suffered heavy losses on the 13th May.   Of the 15 officers and 273 men present on the 24th, 8 and 160, more than half, were reinforcements received since the 13th which had never previously been under fire.   The regiment came out of action with 6 officers and 57 men, Lieut.-Colonel C. K. Burnett being amongst the wounded.

[2] Belonging to the 15th and 19th Hussars, 4/Green Howards and 5/Durham L.I.

[3] 10th Brigade : The 1/Royal Irish Fusiliers, 7/Argyll and Sutherland Highlanders (2 companies), and 2/Royal Dublin Fusiliers in line, the last of which had occupied the much disputed Mouse Trap Farm and right of it.   The 9/Argyll, organized as two companies, supported the R. Dublin Fusiliers and 7/Argyll.

The 5/Border Regiment (Lieut.-Colonel T. A. Milburn) was attached by companies, for instruction, to the battalions of the 10th Brigade.   Most of its men were miners and showed great unconcern as regards gas ; their example is reported to have done much to fortify the confidence of the other troops.

12th Brigade : 2/Royal Irish, 1/King's Own and 2/Essex in line.

24 May. The 1/Royal Irish Fusiliers (Lieut.-Colonel A. R. Burrowes), the right battalion, owing to good gas discipline, had very few men incapacitated, and though heavily engaged, beat off all attacks ; but further to the left matters were not so satisfactory. By 4 A.M. the 2/Dublin Fusiliers, beyond the St. Julien road with the 7/Argyll and Sutherland Highlanders between it and the Royal Irish Fusiliers, was very hard pressed, and Lieut.-Colonel Loveband called on the 9/Argyll (now a half-battalion), which was at his disposal and occupying a retrenchment a few hundred yards back. Charging up through the gas under Major G. J. Christie, the Highlanders reached the support trench about fifty yards behind the front, and covered the junction of the Fusiliers with the 7/Argyll (Lieut.-Colonel D. A. Carden) [1] on their right, where a gap had been made. The difficulties in which the Dublins found themselves had reacted on the Argylls and their left had been driven in ; but the Royal Warwickshire, in brigade reserve, were sent up in support, and, the 9/Argyll assisting, the line was recovered. Further reinforced by two companies of the 2/Seaforth Highlanders, the 7/Argyll sector, in spite of attacks and bombardment, was maintained for the rest of the day.

Shortly after the recovery of the line, Major-General Wilson placed the three available battalions of the 149th (Northumberland) Brigade at Br.-General Hull's disposal, and part of them was moved forward to the canal bank ; but, further calls for immediate reinforcement coming from the Dublin Fusiliers, and the Royal Irish having lost some of the trenches on the left of Mouse Trap Farm, Br.-General Hull ordered the 1/R. Warwickshire (Lieut.-Colonel A. J. Poole), still in support, to counter-attack at once.

The 2/Royal Irish (Lieut.-Colonel R. G. S. Moriarty) of the 12th Brigade, next on the left of the Dublin Fusiliers, held the angle—practically a right angle—where the front turned westwards. It had received the full force of the gas, and in spite of all precautions having been taken, many men were overcome. From their footing in the line at Mouse Trap Farm, the Germans now started a bombing attack along the Irish trench and began to gain ground. Lieut.-Colonel C. J. Griffin of the 2/Lancashire Fusiliers, in the switch trench behind the angle of the front, immediately sent up a company, which found three com-

---

[1] It was only 373 strong, but had a company of the 5/Border Regiment attached.

panies of the Royal Irish still in position, and helped 24 May. them to recover the lost trenches. But the Germans soon renewed their attacks.

Simultaneously with Br.-General Hull's order to the Warwickshire to assist the Dublin Fusiliers, Br.-General Anley had despatched instructions to the Lancashire Fusiliers to support the Royal Irish, and by arrangement the counter-attacks of the two battalions were combined. Owing, however, to machine-gun fire, principally from part of the Royal Irish trenches again in German possession, no progress could be made, and at 12.30 P.M. the two brigadiers met, and decided to stand fast and make another combined effort at 2 P.M., after the artillery had concentrated fire on Mouse Trap Farm and trenches near. But before that hour arrived it became evident that all the Royal Irish trenches were in German hands, and, a little later, that the enemy was in the Dublin Fusiliers' front line, and the whole angle of the front lost. Thus there was a second large gap in the British front line.

The 2/Royal Dublin Fusiliers had continued to resist until about noon, when, 10 officers (including Lieut.-Colonel Loveband) being killed and the rest wounded, organized defence came to an end.[1] The 9/Argyll, however, continued to hold out in the support trench. The 2/Royal Irish was also overwhelmed, only one officer and two platoons in a supporting point a thousand yards behind the line being left of the trench strength.[2] The company of the Lancashire Fusiliers with the Royal Irish was also annihilated, only one officer and eight men escaping.

As the signal lines from divisional headquarters at Brielen forward had been constantly cut, General Wilson had by now placed Br.-General Anley in command of all 4th Division troops east of the canal. The latter had to make many decisions on his own responsibility, but was in constant touch with Br.-General Hull, whose head-quarters were close to his on the canal bank. He came to the conclusion that the forces at his disposal were inadequate to carry out the large operation—far more than a local counter-attack—which was necessary. For, in addition

---

[1] Of other ranks, 583 were casualties, leaving little more than the headquarters details and transport men. Most of the men in the ranks were reinforcements, as the battalion had lost 15 officers and 495 other ranks on 25th April. The 9/Argyll and Sutherland Highlanders mustered at night, 3 officers and 85 men, Major Christie being severely wounded.

[2] It lost 17 officers, including Lieut.-Colonel R. G. S. Moriarty killed, and 378 other ranks.

24 May. to the increased front to be recaptured, the right flank of the advance, instead of being protected by British forces on the eastern end of Hill Top ridge south-west of Mouse Trap Farm, would be enfiladed by the Germans on it. He therefore decided that he must remain on the defensive pending reinforcements ; withdraw, if compelled, the troops still holding out on the flanks of the gap ; and be prepared to occupy the divisional second line. This line ran a thousand yards behind Mouse Trap Farm, from about Wieltje Farm to Hill Top Farm, and thence was continued to Turco Farm by a trench connecting to the French, known as the " French Switch ". Br.-General Anley asked Br.-General Hull to be ready to make similar dispositions.

Meanwhile, in the centre of the British front, between the two gaps made in it at Bellewaarde and Mouse Trap Farm, the left wing of the 85th and right wing of the 10th Brigades held fast. On the right of the first gap Greenly's Cavalry Brigade maintained its position ; whilst on the left of the new one the 1/King's Own (Lieut.-Colonel T. D. Jackson) and 2/Essex (Captain L. O. W. Jones), with the invaluable aid of the French 75 mm. batteries on the west bank,[1] though heavily bombarded, had beaten back all infantry attacks. This was one of those fine feats in defence of which, because it was so entirely successful, there is little to be said except that the accuracy of British musketry told. Nevertheless the position of the King's Own with an exposed flank was perilous. Fortunately the Germans made no attempt to envelop it. Perhaps made cautious by fire from the French Switch trench behind the flank, occupied by the 5/South Lancashire, they confined themselves to holding the left wing of the 12th Brigade by fire in front, and sending bombing parties to attack in flank from the Royal Irish trenches. Although the King's Own were very short of hand-grenades, these parties were time after time driven back ; but as the day wore on the German pressure, far from diminishing, tended to increase.

THE COUNTER-ATTACK OF THE 84TH AND
80TH BRIGADES

At the Bellewaarde gap the 2nd Cavalry Brigade on the right, with its left broken, and the 85th Brigade on

---

[1] The 12th Brigade had a telephone line to the French artillery, and an officer who understood French to speak on it.

the left, with its right forced back to Railway Wood, had 24 May.
been waiting for the 84th and 80th Brigades to arrive
and recover the ground between them that had been
lost. By divisional orders, the 84th Brigade (Br.-General
L. J. Bols), the reserve of the 28th Division—very weak
after its heavy losses of the 8th-13th May, and sadly
lacking in trained officers and N.C.O.'s—had been assembled
at 8.45 A.M., and by 9.45 A.M. it was east of Vlamertinghe,
where its last battalion, the 1/Welch, rejoined it on relief
from the trenches.[1] At 10.5 A.M. the brigade was ordered
to prepare dinners, but before the cooking could be finished,
at 12 noon, it was directed to counter-attack between
Bellewaarde Lake and the railway, and recover the lost
trenches of the 85th Brigade, without waiting for its
food or the arrival of the 80th Brigade. Br.-General Bols,
therefore, moved the battalions in succession across
country south of Ypres, in which operation they suffered
considerable loss from shell fire, to the G.H.Q. Line, which
here ran from the middle of the north side of Zillebeke
Lake, by Hell Fire Corner, and then east of Potijze.
Although all guns of the 28th Division and many of the
27th[2] were ordered to keep up a heavy fire and prepare
the way, it was 5 P.M. before the counter-attack could be
launched[3]—the enemy then being in Hooge and almost
up to Railway Wood. There had been the usual unfortunate delays in getting through the wire of G.H.Q. Line,
and the companies which passed first suffered both from
gas and heavy shelling whilst lying waiting in front of the
wire for the others to arrive. The first stage of the counter-
attack was nevertheless successful ; the enemy was turned
out of Witte Poort Farm (half-way between the Menin
road and Railway Wood) and off the small ridge below
which the farm stands. The 84th Brigade then dug in

---

[1] This battalion was over 600 strong. The remaining battalions of
the 84th Brigade were very weak, and each organized as two companies :
the fighting strength consisting almost entirely of recruits who had joined
during the previous ten days. One of them contained a large number
of men lacking both in training and discipline, the last draft of 215 received
a week before being reported on : " discipline bad, marching bad ".
The total strength of the brigade (5 battalions)—the 12/London (Rangers)
had left for G.H.Q.—was 60 officers and 2,300 other ranks.

[2] All the 27th Division artillery east of Ypres—I. Brigade R.F.A.,
61st Howitzer Battery and 4th and 5th Durham (5-inch) Howitzer
Batteries—were placed under Lieut.-Colonel W. B. Emery for this purpose.

[3] First Line:—2/Northumberland Fusiliers and 2/Cheshire, with 1/Suffolk
in echelon behind the right.

Second Line :—1/Welch. Reserve, G.H.Q. Line :—Monmouthshire
composite battalion.

24 May. east of the road which passes there, to await the arrival of the 80th Brigade.

The 80th Brigade (Br.-General W. E. B. Smith), of the 27th Division, which was in corps reserve, had at 6.30 A.M. been ordered forward to Brandhoek (between Vlamertinghe and Poperinghe), and at 1 P.M. General Allenby placed it at the disposal of the 28th Division. General Bulfin at once sent it forward to Kruisstraat, in the southern outskirts of Ypres, which it reached at 3 P.M. But it was not until 4.30 P.M. that orders reached it to counter-attack south of the 84th Brigade supported by the artillery of the 27th Division. Then, owing to the difficulties of the advance, it was 7 P.M. before it arrived at the G.H.Q. Line and lay down behind it, and endeavoured to get in touch with the cavalry and the 84th Brigade. Eventually the headquarters of the latter were found and Br.-Generals Bols and Smith met and decided to make a joint night attack.

By 11 P.M., the moon being up—full moon was four days later—the 80th Brigade had filed through the wire of G.H.Q. Line, and was in a position to advance, its two left battalions being sent to reinforce the 84th.[1] Although detected in the bright moonlight, the brigades actually got within a few yards of the German trenches without severe losses ; but in the end they were forced back by rifle and machine-gun fire at point-blank range, and retired to the line originally gained by the 84th Brigade along the road just east of Witte Poort Farm. Connection was then established with the cavalry by extending parties to the right towards Zouave Wood. Of this line the 80th and 84th Brigades remained in possession, although heavy casualties had been suffered, and the men were very exhausted, and no water or rations could be got to them.[2]

In the cavalry sector there was a small successful night operation to record. As soon as it was dusk, Br.-General

[1] 4/Rifle Brigade on the right, then 3/K.R.R.C., 4/K.R.R.C. and 2/Shropshire L.I., with the Patricia's in brigade reserve.

[2] In the 84th Brigade the losses were about 60 per cent of the strength : 2/Northumberland Fusiliers lost Captain C. W. Wreford-Brown, commanding, 12 other officers and 350 men ; 2/Cheshire, Captain G. R. Barton, commanding, wounded, 9 other officers and 279 men ; 1/Suffolk, Major F. W. O. Maycock, commanding, killed, 9 other officers and 135 men ; 1/Welch, Lieut.-Colonel T. O. Marden, commanding, wounded, 14 other officers and 418 men.

The casualties of the 80th Brigade were 16 officers and 490 other ranks ; it had lost since the 22nd April 102 officers and 3,110 other ranks.

Greenly directed Major Bayley, commanding the 1/York 24 May. and Lancaster, to send one of his two companies in Zouave Wood to the Menin road to drive the Germans out of the houses. This it did with great effect, the Germans who escaped running back in the dark and being fired on and killed by their own people. The situation then became so quiet that the relief of the 1st Cavalry Division by the 2nd, leaving the 4/Green Howards and 4/East Yorkshire in the line, was carried out.[1] As is now known, on the evening of the 24th, the German *Fourth Army* issued orders that operations should be stopped : [2] the German battalions were quite as worn out and had suffered nearly as many casualties as the British.

The Withdrawal of the 4th Division Line

It remains to relate what had happened on the left where Br.-General Anley had abandoned the idea of a counter-attack to recover the trenches lost near Mouse Trap Farm unless reinforcements were forthcoming. Some little time after—at 4.50 P.M.—a staff officer of the V. Corps brought him instructions that three battalions of the French 152nd Division were placed at his disposal to take part in a counter-attack which he was directed to make after dark. But about 7.40 P.M., Captain W. C. Garsia, G.S.O. 3 of the 4th Division, who had been sent to the French to arrange for the co-ordination of the counter-attack, appeared at 12th Brigade headquarters with the information that the French troops were not to be employed except in support. At this moment, Lieut.-Colonel A. A. Montgomery, G.S.O. 1 of the 4th Division, was also with Br.-General Anley, having been sent by General Wilson to settle with the brigade commanders on the spot the details of the counter-attack. Since this was ordered by General Wilson the situation had been completely altered by the limitation as regards the use of the French. A decision had to be made at once, as the hours of darkness were few, and if the operation was to be proceeded with, the troops must be placed in position at once and artillery support arranged for. On the other hand, if any withdrawal was to be made, that must be ordered at once, so that the new line in rear might be organized and occupied

---

[1] The losses of the 1st Cavalry Division 22nd-25th May had been 37 officers and 620 other ranks.
[2] See Note at end of Chapter.

24 May. before daylight broke. The matter could not be referred to General Wilson without delay, as all lines were cut and divisional headquarters were a two-mile walk distant. The gap in the front of the 4th Division was a wide one, and the only troops available to take part in the counter-attack now that the French would not assist were two companies of the Lancashire Fusiliers and two battalions of the 11th Brigade (Br.-General C. B. Prowse) all of whom were weak in numbers, and, although ready to make a last effort, in reality not in a fit state to do so. Lieut.-Colonel Montgomery, therefore, at 8 P.M. gave orders for a withdrawal of the 7/Argyll and the King's Own and Essex to the Divisional Line and French Switch, behind and parallel to the road from Wieltje towards Turco Farm. This meant giving up the angle of the front near Mouse Trap Farm, a triangular wedge a thousand yards deep, but almost impossible to hold, as the ground was so waterlogged that trenches dug in it at once filled with mud. To form a new continuous front, it was arranged that a connecting trench should be dug by the Monmouthshire from the original trenches of the Royal Irish Fusiliers, which they still held, to Wieltje Farm to join on to the new front there.

On being informed of the decision, Major-General H. F. M. Wilson, commanding the 4th Division, immediately confirmed it, and the Commander-in-Chief subsequently expressed his approval of it. The French, to whom the change was reported, readjusted their line at Turco Farm to conform. All the 4th Division wounded were removed and the withdrawal was successfully carried out during the night without interference.[1] By order of Lieut.-General Allenby, advanced posts of the new line were established in front of Wieltje village, and at Cross Road Farm (on Hill Top ridge midway between Wieltje and Turco Farm). In view of the ill-success and heavy losses in the counter-attack of the 80th and 84th Brigades, and in the many others of the previous four weeks, made in haste and with totally inadequate artillery backing, the decision come to by the 4th Division appears to have been a thoroughly sound one. It was concurred in by all officers who were up at the front, and was fully in accord with the views held by the French brigade and battalion

---

[1] Possibly this inactivity of the enemy was due to the warning order for the counter-attack sent to a battalion having fallen into his hands; but his infantry was usually quiescent at night.

commanders who, like their forefathers of Crimean days, 25 May. had for some time regarded the desperate counter-attacks made by the British as magnificent, but not war.

The Close of the Battles of Ypres

After the night counter-attack of the 80th and 84th Sketch Brigades, the day of the 25th May passed without very B. much shelling, and with no sign of attack.[1] During the night of the 25th/26th, by divisional orders, the 80th Brigade, assisted by 2/Royal Scots of the 8th Brigade —which had been moved up from La Clytte (5 miles south - west of Ypres) in reserve to the V. Corps — dug a trench from the Menin road to Zouave Wood to complete the connection with the cavalry, and the 84th handed over its line to the 80th, and was withdrawn into reserve. On the following night, the 26th/27th, the 80th was relieved by the 8th Brigade ; on the night of the 28th/29th the 85th Brigade—Br.-General C. E. Pereira had been wounded on the 26th—was relieved by the 9th Brigade.[2] Of the 27th and 28th Divisions this left only the 83rd Brigade in the line. Onward to the end of the month there was little to record. The Cavalry Corps re-occupied Hooge village, and the stables of Hooge Chateau, and the line north of that point was gradually pushed forward and consolidated.[3]

The ammunition situation was now most desperate. At the close of the fighting on the 25th May there was practically nothing but a little shrapnel available,[4] and on the 27th Sir John French brought the First Army's Battle of Festubert to an end and telegraphed to the

---

[1] On this day Mr. Asquith formed his Coalition Ministry : on the 26th Mr. Winston Churchill resigned the office of First Lord of the Admiralty.

[2] The total losses of the 85th Brigade in this period were 28 officers and 1,578 other ranks.

[3] The losses for the period 21st-30th May were :—

	Officers.	Other Ranks.
V. Corps . . .	323	8,936
II. „ . . .	35	1,171
	358	10,107

[4] At noon on 26th the total rounds of H.E. and Lyddite for field and heavy guns of the whole B.E.F. on the lines of communication were :— 18-pdr., 272 ; 4·5-inch, 536 ; 4·7-inch, 2,338 ; 5-inch howitzer, 1,620 ; 60-pdr., 379 ; 6-inch howitzer, nil ; 6-inch B.L.C., nil ; 8-inch howitzer, nil ; 9·2-inch howitzer, 612 ; 15-inch howitzer, 10.

War Office that, until the ammunition reserve recovered he must cease offensive operations.

The Germans seem to have arrived at much the same conclusion, for the Battles of Ypres 1915 came to an end. Apart from lack of ammunition, both sides were in need of rest, thoroughly exhausted by a long effort lasting over a month, and carried out mainly by the divisions already in the area. These, without relief, were engaged again and again until practically annihilated. The step by step advance of the Germans, supported by an overwhelming strength of heavy artillery, and often initiated by discharge of poison gas, had accomplished nothing decisive. But the balance was so nice that a couple of fresh German divisions suddenly appearing, as they did on 11th November 1914, might well have brought about a very serious situation. The German reserves fortunately were in Russia, employed on the barren labour of gaining territory there, equally failing to inflict a decisive defeat on their opponents.

It will have been observed that the higher Allied commanders in this defensive battle were generally unable to influence the course of events beyond passing on the instructions of General Foch and Sir John French for counter-attacks to be made to recover the lost positions, and supplying for that purpose reinforcements which were handed down from Army to corps, from corps to division, and from division to brigade, without any general plan for their employment or detailed orders for the objectives to be attained. These methods are in such contrast to those employed in the offensive battle of Neuve Chapelle that it seems desirable to recapitulate for those not cognizant of the conditions obtaining at the time, the limitations under which the commanders on the defensive laboured. The problems before them will then be duly appreciated.

Trench or immobile warfare had only recently become the established type, and it was a type for which, as a nation and through no fault of the higher commanders, the British were totally unprepared. Air observation, aeroplane photography and signal communications suitable to such warfare, were in the infancy of their development. Communication trenches, if existent, were muddy ditches, without trench boards or revetment. German artillery fire, aided as it often was by balloon observation; fire from machine guns of which the enemy had a great preponderance ; and rifle fire by picked marksmen, a matter in which he had specialized, combined to make movement near the front by daylight impossible. Consequently all leaders found great difficulty in ascertaining the positions of even their own troops, and the trace or situation of the trenches, often disconnected and fragmentary, which they occupied. The fact that neither they nor their troops knew the names of the farms and small localities was a further handicap. But to locate accurately the enemy's positions was even more difficult. If a break-in occurred and changes of position took place these difficulties were enhanced ; whilst continual interruption of the telegraph and telephone lines prevented such information as there was from being communicated to the rear. The use of the Flying Corps for the purpose of reporting the situation had not yet been organized, and the infantry had no means of communicating with aeroplanes. The higher leaders rarely had more than vague data on which to form a plan, and the only course open to them was to supply the subordinate leaders on the spot with the means, in the shape of reinforcements, to influence the combat.

As in the course of time the front stabilised, these difficulties were lessened ; and when eventually air observation, aeroplane photography, and an elaborate system of signal communication were perfected, the higher leaders were enabled to assume a measure of control. But, even so, after long experience—and experience was the only possible teacher — it was generally admitted that in spite of the help afforded by these scientific developments, commanders, from brigadiers upwards, could best influence the combat in defence or counter-attack by a humbler, yet essential, function : by preparing plans beforehand for every reasonable contingency, and ensuring that these plans were understood and rehearsed, as far as possible, by all elements down to the platoon. The control by higher commanders of the actual fighting when once it had begun remained almost negligible ; and their efforts were then best directed to ensuring the provision of ammunition, rations, water, and the special stores and material required, so that their men might fight to best advantage.

The total British losses in the fighting at Hill 60 and the battles of Ypres, for the period 22nd April to 31st May, 1915, were very heavy and amounted to 2,150 officers and 57,125 other ranks.

Unit.	Officers.			Other Ranks.			Grand Total.
	K.	W.	M.	K.	W.	M.	
1st Cav. Div. .	17	59	9	151	638	329	1,203
2nd ,, ,, .	4	7	—	36	180	17	244
3rd ,, ,, .	31	60	3	273	1,057	194	1,618
4th Division .	87	224	36	1,566	5,476	3,470	10,859
5th Division .	71	209	13	1,068	5,478	1,155	7,994
27th Division .	55	166	13	1,122	4,980	927	7,263
28th Division .	97	300	98	3,177	5,548	6,313	15,533
50th Division (less divisional troops)	40	121	25	596	2,963	1,459	5,204
Canadian Div..	65	104	39	1,672	1,822	1,767	5,469
Lahore Div. {	B. 28 I. 6	105 57	— 1	B. 180 I. 177	1,096 1,684	345 209	}3,888
Total . .	501	1,412	237	10,018	30,922	16,185	59,275

2,150   57,125

59,275

These casualties were certainly heavier than the German, but in view of the infantry attacks and counter-attacks made in haste and without adequate support from guns, and of enemy preponderance in artillery this is not extraordinary.[1] That the line was held at all was due to the heroic sacrifice of the infantry, cavalry and engineers, a very large proportion of whom were untrained soldiers, who could be relied on for defence, but hardly, with their lack of military training, to win a battle. They were well seconded, under the most disadvantageous conditions by the artillery,[2] short of ammunition throughout, and in the case of the Territorial and the 4·7-inch batteries, armed with obsolete weapons. Inkerman, the fight of a few hours between man and man, has gone down to history as a soldiers' battle; "Second Ypres" was fought by the brigadiers and the regimental officers and soldiers. But, instead of lasting a few hours, it was drawn out over 33 days and

[1] The German losses before Ypres for the period are given as 860 officers and 34,073 other ranks (see Note at end of Chapter for details). This includes the casualties of the XXIII. Reserve Corps (211 and 10,381) the greater part of which was engaged against the French, but does not include the losses of the detachments of the XXII. Reserve Corps and Marine Corps which took part. Exact comparison, however, is not possible, for reasons already mentioned (page 20, fn. 2).

[2] The batteries of the 2nd groupe of the 7th Regiment of Belgian artillery were still with the V. Corps.

nights, and accompanied by the overwhelming employment by the enemy of high explosive shell from heavy artillery, field artillery and *Minenwerfer*, and poison gas. It was indeed the first of the new nature of battle — of which Verdun was to be the type—in which the enemy planned that his infantry should merely have to occupy ground from which his guns had driven every living creature, and in which man was not pitted against man, but against material. But, as ever, it was with the man—not the weapons—that the decision rested. Wonderful devices and inventions for causing death and destruction may prolong the agony of a conflict, but they will never of themselves win a war against a brave and determined nation.

This volume may suitably close with the words addressed by Field-Marshal Sir John French to a brigade of the 28th Division, and which, with slight variations, he repeated to the Cavalry Corps and to the other brigades of the 4th, 27th and 28th Divisions :—

" I came over to say a few words to you and to tell
" you how much I, as Commander-in-Chief of the army,
" appreciate the splendid work that you have all done
" during the recent fighting. You have fought the Second
" Battle of Ypres, which will rank amongst the most
" desperate and hardest fights of the war. You may have
" thought, because you were not attacking the enemy,
" that you were not helping to shorten the war. On the
" contrary, by your splendid endurance and bravery you
" have done a great deal to shorten it. In this, the Second
" Battle of Ypres, the Germans tried by every means in
" their power to get possession of that unfortunate town.
" They concentrated large forces of troops and artillery,
" and, further than that, they had recourse to that mean
" and dastardly practice, hitherto unheard of in civilized
" warfare, namely, the use of asphyxiating gases. You
" have performed the most difficult, arduous and terrific
" task of withstanding a stupendous bombardment by
" heavy artillery, probably the fiercest artillery fire ever
" directed against troops, and warded off the enemy's
" attacks with magnificent bravery. By your steadiness
" and devotion both the German plans were frustrated.
" The enemy was unable to get possession of Ypres—if
" he had done this he would probably have succeeded
" in preventing neutral Powers from intervening—and he
" was also unable to distract us from delivering our attack

" in conjunction with the French in the Arras—Armentières
" district. Had you failed to repulse his attacks and made
" it necessary for more troops to be sent to your assistance
" our operations in the south might not have been able to
" take place, and would certainly not have been as successful
" as they have been. Your Colours have many famous
" names emblazoned on them, but none will be more
" famous or more well deserved than that of the Second
" Battle of Ypres. I want you one and all to understand
" how thoroughly I realize and appreciate what you have
" done. I wish to thank you, each officer, non-commis-
" sioned officer and man, for the services you have rendered
" by doing your duty so magnificently, and I am sure
" that your country will thank you too."

NOTE I

THE GERMANS ON 24TH/25TH MAY 1915

The Germans claim no success in this fighting, and no battle-
honour is given for it.

The following is the account given by General Balck (Schwarte,
ii. pp. 266-7).

" The attack was resumed on the 24th [having been brought to
" an end on the 13th May owing to lack of ammunition and the
" fatigue of the troops]. According to German reports, it achieved
" no great success, though the British report an almost annihilating
" defeat of their forces.[1] The gas struck the newly arrived 1st and 3rd
" Cavalry Divisions. Towards noon the *51st Reserve Division* took
" Wieltje Chateau [Mouse Trap Farm] and the ' Wasserburg ' [not
" identified] west of it. This done, the troops were at an end of their
" powers.

" On the evening of the 24th orders arrived from *Fourth Army*
" headquarters, that no more major operations should be undertaken.
" The fighting died down. The British also wanted rest ; their
" attention was directed to the battlefields of Artois and their
" position on the Yser required building up. But raids and mining
" did not cease on either side.

" The battles of the *XXII. Reserve Corps* had come to an end,
" as on the night of the 16th/17th the west bank was abandoned.
" The losses of the troops, particularly in officers, had been very
" heavy."

NOTE II

THE GERMAN LOSSES

The following figures as regards the German losses before Ypres
have kindly been furnished by the *Reichsarchiv*.

---

[1] In a footnote General Balck gives particulars which refer not to the
24th, but to the 13th May. This mistake is confirmed by his mention of
the 3rd Cavalry Division.

The figures are given in ten-day periods, as rendered in the German Army.

	Officers.			Other Ranks.		
	Killed.	Wounded.	Missing.	Killed.	Wounded.	Missing.
XXIII. Reserve Corps						
21st-30th April . .	40	89	13	977	3,862	1,780
1st-10th May . .	3	8	0	161	524	0
11th-20th May . .	14	23	5	279	1,349	515
21st-30th May . .	9	7	0	193	694	47
Total . .	66	127	18	1,610	6,429	2,342
XXVI. Reserve Corps [1]						
21st-30th April . .	50	119	4	998	4,247	813
1st-10th May . .	19	45	2	519	2,408	208
11th-20th May . .	14	20	2	380	1,079	323
21st-30th May . .	8	26	1	346	1,144	70
Total . .	91	210	9	2,243	8,878	1,414
XXVII. Reserve Corps [2]						
21st-30th April . .	16	38	2	319	1,121	144
1st-10th May . .	24	121	0	660	2,785	74
11th-20th May . .	4	21	2	346	1,120	185
21st-30th May . .	12	27	1	331	1,242	57
Total . .	56	207	5	1,656	6,268	460
XV. Corps						
21st-30th April . .	7	10	1	101	437	28
1st-10th May . .	13	26	0	269	900	15
11th-20th May . .	3	6	0	129	397	4
21st-30th May . .	2	2	1	91	397	5
Total . .	25	44	2	590	2,131	52

Total officers, 860   Other ranks, 34,073

[1] Includes the *37th Landwehr* and *2nd Reserve Ersatz Brigade.*
[2] Includes the *38th Landwehr Brigade.*

APPENDICES

COMPOSITION OF THE HIGHER STAFFS

OF THE

BRITISH EXPEDITIONARY FORCE

10TH FEBRUARY 1915 [1]

GENERAL HEADQUARTERS

Commander-in-Chief . .	Field-Marshal Sir J. D. P. French, G.C.B., O.M., G.C.V.O., K.C.M.G.
GENERAL STAFF BRANCH :	
Chief of the General Staff	Lieut.-General Sir W. R. Robertson, K.C.V.O., C.B., D.S.O.
Sub-Chief of the General Staff	Br.-General E. M. Perceval, D.S.O.
Br.-General G.S. (Operations)	Br.-General G. M. Harper, D.S.O.
Br.-General G.S. (Intelligence)	Br.-General G. M. W. Macdonogh.
ADJUTANT-GENERAL'S BRANCH :	
Adjutant-General . .	Lieut.-General Sir C. F. N. Macready, K.C.B.
Deputy Adjutant-General (at the Base) . . .	Major-General E. R. C. Graham, C.B.
QUARTERMASTER-GENERAL'S BRANCH :	
Quartermaster-General .	Lieut.-General R. C. Maxwell, C.B.
Deputy Quartermaster-General	Br.-General C. T. Dawkins, C.M.G.
ATTACHED :	
Br.-General, Royal Artillery	Br.-General J. P. Du Cane, C.B.
Chief Engineer, Forces in the Field . . .	Br.-General G. H. Fowke.
Headquarters G.H.Q. Troops	Br.-General R. S. Oxley.
Provost-Marshal . .	Colonel V. T. Bunbury, C.B., D.S.O.

[1] Extracted from " Composition of the Headquarters of the Forces in the Field ", dated 10th February 1915, the first issued after Lieut.-General Sir W. R. Robertson had become Chief of the General Staff.

HEADQUARTERS OF ADMINISTRATIVE SERVICES AND DEPARTMENTS :

Director of Army Signals	Br.-General J. S. Fowler, D.S.O.
Director of Ordnance Services	Br.-General H. D. E. Parsons, C.M.G.
Director of Transport	Br.-General W. G. B. Boyce, D.S.O.
Director of Railway Transport	Br.-General J. H. Twiss
Director of Remounts	Br.-General F. S. Garratt, C.B., D.S.O.
Director-General, Medical Services	Surgeon-General Sir A. T. Sloggett, Kt., C.B., C.M.G., K.H.S.
Deputy Director-General, Medical Services	Surgeon-General T. J. O'Donnell, D.S.O.
Director of Army Postal Services . . .	Colonel W. Price, C.M.G.
Paymaster-in-Chief . .	Br.-General C. A. Bray, C.B., C.M.G.

FIRST ARMY

Commander	General Sir D. Haig, K.C.B., K.C.I.E., K.C.V.O., A.D.C. General.
Br.-General, General Staff .	Br.-General J. E. Gough, V.C., C.M.G., A.D.C.
D.A. and Q.M.G. . . .	Br.-General P. E. F. Hobbs, C.M.G.
Major-General, Royal Artillery	Major-General F. D. V. Wing, C.B.
Director of Medical Services	Surgeon-General W. G. Macpherson, C.M.G., M.B., K.H.P.

SECOND ARMY

Commander	General Sir H. L. Smith - Dorrien, G.C.B., D.S.O.
Br.-General, General Staff .	Br.-General G. T. Forestier-Walker, A.D.C.
D.A. and Q.M.G. . . .	Br.-General W. H. Rycroft, C.B.
Br.-General, Royal Artillery	Br.-General H. F. Mercer, C.B., A.D.C.
Director of Medical Services	Surgeon-General R. Porter.

THE ROYAL FLYING CORPS

Commander	Major-General Sir D. Henderson, K.C.B., D.S.O.
G.S.O. 1	Colonel F. H. Sykes

CAVALRY CORPS

Commander	Lieut-General E. H. H. Allenby, C.B.
Br.-General, General Staff .	Br.-General J. F. N. Birch.
Br.-General, Royal Artillery	Br.-General H. D. White-Thomson, D.S.O.

INDIAN CAVALRY CORPS

Commander	Lieut. - General M. F. Rimington, C.V.O., C.B.
Br.-General, General Staff .	Br.-General H. J. M. Macandrew, D.S.O.
Br.-General, Royal Artillery	Br.-General R. St. C. Lecky.

I. Corps

Commander	Lieut.-General C. C. Monro, C.B.
Br.-General, General Staff .	Br.-General R. D. Whigham, D.S.O.
Br.-General, Royal Artillery	Br.-General R. A. K. Montgomery, C.B., D.S.O.
Br.-General, Royal Engineers	Br.-General S. R. Rice, C.B.

II. Corps

Commander	Lieut.-General Sir C. Fergusson, Bt., C.B., D.S.O., M.V.O.
Br.-General, General Staff .	Br.-General W. T. Furse, D.S.O.
Br.-General, Royal Artillery	Br.-General A. H. Short.
Major-General, Royal Engineers	Major-General A. E. Sandbach, C.B., D.S.O.

III Corps

Commander	Lieut.-General W P. Pulteney, C.B., D.S.O.
Br.-General, General Staff .	Br.-General G. F. Milne, C.B., D.S.O.
Br.-General, Royal Artillery	Br.-General E. J. Phipps-Hornby, V.C., C.B.
Br.-General Royal Engineers	Br.-General F. M. Glubb, C.B., D.S.O.

IV. Corps

Commander	Lieut.-General Sir H. S. Rawlinson, Bt., C.V.O., C.B.
Br.-General, General Staff .	Br.-General A. G. Dallas.
Br.-General, Royal Artillery	Br.-General A. H. Hussey.
Br.-General, Royal Engineers	Br.-General R. U. H. Buckland, A.D.C.

V. Corps

Commander	Lieut.-General Sir H. C. O. Plumer, K.C.B.
Br.-General, General Staff .	Br.-General H. S. Jeudwine.
Br.-General, Royal Artillery	Br.-General S. D. Browne.
Colonel, Royal Engineers .	Colonel R. D. Petrie.

Indian Corps

Commander	Lieut. - General Sir J. Willcocks, K.C.B., K.C.S.I., K.C.M.G., D.S.O.
Br.-General, General Staff .	Br.-General H. Hudson, C.B., C.I.E.
Colonel, Royal Engineers .	Br.-General H. C. Nanton.

Inspector-General of Communications :

I.G.C.	Major-General F. T. Clayton, C.B.
Deputy I.G.C. . . .	Br.-General J. E. Capper, C.B.

BRITISH ORDER OF BATTLE

NEUVE CHAPELLE 1915

ARTILLERY

Heavy Artillery :

Southern (No. 1) Group—Br.-Gen. G. McK. Franks.
  I. Bde. R.G.A. : 109th & 110th Heavy Btys.⎫
  Independent : 114th Heavy Bty. . . .⎭ 12—4·7″ guns.
  IV. Bde. R.G.A. : 8th Siege Bty. R.G.A.· . 4—6″ guns.
      4th Sub-Sec. 10th Siege
      Bty. R.G.A. . . . 1—9·2″ how.
Northern (No. 2) Group—Br.-Gen. H. C. C. Uniacke.
  III. Bde. R.G.A. (111th, 112th Heavy Btys.) .⎫
  VIII. Bde. R.G.A. (113th, 118th, 119th Heavy ⎬20—4·7″ guns.
  Btys. . . . . ⎭
  10th Siege Bty. R.G.A. (less 3rd & 4th Sub-
  Secs.) . . . . 2—9·2″ hows.
  One 15″ howitzer (R.M.A.).
  H.M. Armoured Train " Churchill " (1—6″ gun ; 1—4·7″ gun ;
  1—4″ gun).

IV. Corps—(Br.-Gen. A. E. A. Holland, C.R.A 8th Div.) :
  (1) Horse Artillery Group :
      V. Bde. R.H.A. (O & Z Btys.) of 8th Div. .⎫
      XIV. Bde. R.H.A. (F & T Btys.) of 7th Div. . ⎬ 42—13-pdr.
      A, Q & U Btys. R.H.A. of 1st Indian Cav. ⎮ guns.
      Div. . . . . ⎭
  (2) " A " Group :
      XXXIII. Bde. R.F.A. (32, 33, 36 ⎰ of 8th ⎱ 36—18-pdr.
      Btys.) . . . . . ⎱ Div. ⎰ guns.
      XLV. Bde. R.F.A. (1, 3, 5 Btys.) .
  (3) " B " Group :
      N, V, X Btys. R.H.A. of 2nd Indian Cav.
      Div. . . . . 18—13-pdr.
                                                    guns.
      XXII. Bde. R.F.A. (104, 105, 106 ⎰ ⎱
      Btys.) . . . . . . ⎮ of 7th ⎮ 36—18-pdr.
      XXXV. Bde. R.F.A. (12, 25, 58 ⎬ Div. ⎭ guns.
      Btys.) . . . . . ⎭
  (4) Siege Howitzer Group :
      4th, 6th, 59th & 81st Siege Btys. R.G.A. . 16—6″ hows.
      5th Siege Bty. R.G.A. . . . . . 4—6″ hows.

(5) Field Howitzer Group :

XXXVII. Bde. R.F.A. (31, 35, 55 Btys.) of
7th & 8th Divs. . . . . . . 18—4·5" hows.
Battery of 4" and 3·7" trench howitzers.
5th Mountain Bty. R.G.A. from 3rd Div. at-⎫
tached (less one section) 25th Inf. Bde. One ⎬ 6—2·75" guns.
section with 23rd Inf. Bde. . . . ⎭

Indian Corps—(Br.-Gen. A. B. Scott, C.B., D.S.O.) :

2nd Siege Battery, R.G.A. . . . . . 4—6" hows.
IV. Bde. R.F.A. (7, 14, 66 Btys.) . ⎧ of ⎫
IX. Bde. R.F.A. (19, 20, 28 Btys.) . ⎨ Meerut ⎬
XIII. Bde. R.F.A. (2, 8, 44 Btys.) . ⎩ Div. ⎭ 108—18-pdr.
V. Bde. R.F.A. (64, 73, 81 Btys.) . ⎧ of ⎫ guns.
XI. Bde. R.F.A. (83, 84, 85 Btys.) . ⎨ Lahore ⎬
XVIII. Bde. R.F.A. (59, 93, 94 Btys.) ⎩ Div. ⎭
XLIII. (How.) Bde. R.F.A. (30, 40, 57 Btys.) of
Meerut & Lahore Divs. . . . . . . 18—4·5" hows.
One Section 7th Mountain Bty. R.G.A., from
2nd Div., attached Garhwal Bde. . . . 2—2·75" guns.

7TH DIVISION : Major-Gen. T. Capper.

20th Brigade : Br.-Gen. F. J. Heyworth.
1/Grenadier Gds. 2/Border Regt. 6/Gordons (T.F.).
2/Scots Gds. 2/Gordons.

21st Brigade : Br.-Gen. H. E. Watts.
2/Bedfordshire. 2/R. Scots Fus.
2/Green Howards. 2/Wiltshire.

22nd Brigade : Br.-Gen. S. T. B. Lawford.
2/Queen's. 1/R. Welch Fus. 8/R. Scots (T.F.).
2/R. Warwickshire. 1/S. Staffordshire.

Field Coys. R.E. : 54, 55 & 2/Highland (T.F.).

Mtd. Troops : A Sqdn. Northd. Hussars. Cyclist Co.

8TH DIVISION : Major-Gen. F. J. Davies.

23rd Brigade : Br.-Gen. R. J. Pinney.
2/Devonshire. 2/Scottish Rifles.
2/W. Yorkshire. 2/Middlesex.

24th Brigade : Br.-Gen. F. C. Carter.
1/Worcestershire. 1/Sherwood Foresters. 5/Black Watch (T.F.).
2/E. Lancashire. 2/Northamptonshire. 4/Camerons (T.F.).

25th Brigade : Br.-Gen. A. W. G. Lowry Cole.
2/Lincolnshire. 1/R. Irish Rifles. 13/London (T.F.).
2/R. Berkshire. 2/Rifle Brigade.

Field Coys. R.E. : 2, 15 & 1/Home Counties (T.F.).
1st (Siege) Coy. R. Anglesey R.E. (S.R.).

Mtd. Troops : Northamptonshire Yeo. Cyclist Co.

LAHORE DIVISION : Major-Gen. H. D'U. Keary

Ferozepore Brigade : Br.-Gen. R. G. Egerton.
    Connaught Rangers. 57th Wilde's Rifles.   4/London (T.F.).
    9th Bhopal Infty.   129th Baluchis.

Jullundur Brigade : Br.-Gen. E. P. Strickland.
    1/Manchester.   59th Scinde Rifles.
    47th Sikhs.   4/Suffolk (T.F.).

Sirhind Brigade : Br.-Gen. W. G. Walker, V.C.
    1/Highland L.I.   1/1st Gurkhas.   4/King's (S.R.).
    15th Sikhs.   1/4th Gurkhas.

Engineers : 20 & 21 Coys. 3rd Sappers & Miners.

Pioneers : 34th Sikh Pioneers.

Mtd. Troops : 15th Lancers.

MEERUT DIVISION : Lieut.-Gen. C. A. Anderson.

Dehra Dun Brigade : Br.-Gen. C. W. Jacob.
    1/Seaforths.   1/9th Gurkhas.
    2/2nd Gurkhas.   4/Seaforths (T.F.).

Garhwal Brigade : Br.-Gen. C. G. Blackader.
    2/Leicestershire.   2/39th Garhwalis.   3/London (T.F.).
    1/39th Garhwalis.   2/3rd Gurkhas.

Bareilly Brigade : Br.-Gen. W. M. Southey.
    2/Black Watch.   41st Dogras.   4/Black Watch (T.F.).
    6th Jats.   58th Vaughan's Rifles. 2/8th Gurkhas.[1]

Engineers : 3 & 4 Coys. 1st Sappers & Miners.

Pioneers : 107th Pioneers

Mtd. Troops : 4th Cavalry.

[1] Divisional Troops.

GERMAN ORDER OF BATTLE[1]

NEUVE CHAPELLE 1915

Sixth Army (part of)

Commander : Crown Prince Rupprecht of Bavaria.

Chief of the Staff : Major-General Krafft von Dellmensingen.

VII. Corps (General von Claer) :
  13th Division (Lieut.-General von dem Borne) :
    25th Brigade : 13th and 158th Regiments.
    26th Brigade : 15th and 55th Regiments.

  14th Division (Lieut.-General von Ditfurth) :
    27th Brigade : 16th and 53rd Regiments.
    79th Brigade : 56th and 57th Regiments.

  Corps Troops : 11th Jäger Battalion.

6th Bavarian Reserve Division (Lieut.-General von Scanzoni) :
  12th Bavarian Reserve Brigade : 16th and 17th Bavarian Res. Regts.
  14th Bavarian Reserve Brigade : 20th, 21st and 9th Bavarian Res. Regts.

XIX. (Saxon) Corps (part of) :

  24th Division :
    47th Brigade : 139th and 179th Regiments (one battalion each).
    48th Brigade : 106th and 107th Regiments (one battalion each).

  40th Division :
    88th Brigade : 104th Regiment (one battalion).
    87th Brigade : 133rd Regiment (one battalion).

[1] Infantry formations and units only.

BRITISH ORDER OF BATTLE

HILL 60 AND THE BATTLES OF YPRES 1915

3RD DIVISION : Major-Gen. J. A. L. Haldane.

7th Brigade : Br.-Gen. C. R. Ballard.

3/Worcestershire.	1/Wiltshire.	Hon. Art. Coy. (T.F.).
2/S. Lancashire.	2/R. Irish Rifles.	4/S. Lancashire (T.F.).

8th Brigade : Br.-Gen. A. R. Hoskins.

2/R. Scots.	4/Middlesex.	4/Gordons (T.F.).
2/Suffolk.	1/Gordons.	

9th Brigade : Br.-Gen. W. Douglas Smith.

1/Northumberland Fus.	1/Lincolnshire.	10/King's (T.F.).
4/Royal Fus.	1/R. Scots Fus.	

R.F.A. Bdes.

XXIII. (107, 108, 109 Btys.).	XLII. (29, 41, 45 Btys.).
XL. (6, 23, 49 Btys.).	XXX. (How.) 128, 129 Btys.

R.G.A. : 5/Mountain Battery.

Field Coys. R.E. : 56 & 1/Cheshire (T.F.).

Mtd. Troops : C Sqdn. N. Irish Horse.   Cyclist Coy.

4TH DIVISION : Major-Gen. H. F. M. Wilson.

10th Brigade : Br.-Gen. C. P. A. Hull.

1/R. Warwickshire.	1/R. Irish Fus.	7/Argyll & Sutherlands
2/Seaforths.	2/R. Dublin Fus	(T.F.).

11th Brigade : Br.-Gen. J. Hasler.

1/Somerset L.I.	1/Hampshire.	London Rifle Brigade
1/E. Lancashire.	1/Rifle Brigade.	(T.F.).

12th Brigade : Br.-Gen. F. G. Anley.

1/King's Own.	2/Lancashire Fus.	5/S. Lancashire (T.F.)
2/Royal Irish.	2/Essex.	2/Monmouthshire (T.F.).

R.F.A. Bdes.

XIV. (68, 88 Btys.).	XXXII. (27, 134, 135 Btys.).
XXIX. (125, 126, 127 Btys.).	

R.G.A. : 2/Mountain Battery.

Field Coys. R.E. : 9 & 1/W. Lancashire (T.F.).

Mtd. Troops : A Sqdn. Northants Yeo.   Cyclist Coy.

5TH DIVISION : Major-Gen. T. L. N. Morland.

13th Brigade : Br.-Gen. R. Wanless O'Gowan.

| 2/K.O.S.B. | 1/R. West Kent. | 9/London (Queen Victoria's Rifles) (T.F.). |
| 2/Duke of Wellington's. | 2/K.O.Y.L.I. | |

14th Brigade : Br.-Gen. G. H. Thesiger.

| 1/Devonshire. | 1/D. of Cornwall's L.I. | 5/Cheshire (T.F.). |
| 1/E. Surrey. | 2/Manchester. | |

15th Brigade : Br.-Gen. E. Northey.

| 1/Norfolk. | 1/Cheshire. | 6/King's (T.F.). |
| 1/Bedfordshire. | 1/Dorsetshire. | |

R.F.A. Bdes.

XV. (52, 80 Btys.).   XXVIII. (122, 123, 124
XXVII. (119, 120, 121 Btys.).   Btys.).
                                         130th Bty. of XXX.
                                         (How.) Bde.

Field Coys. R.E. : 59, 2/Home Counties (T.F.) & 1/N. Midland (T.F.)

Mtd. Troops : C Sqdn. Northants Yeo.   Cyclist Coy.

27TH DIVISION : Major-Gen. T. D'O. Snow.

80th Brigade : Br.-Gen. W. E. B. Smith.

| 2/K. Shropshire L.I. | 4/K.R.R.C. | Princess Patricia's Canadian Light Infantry. |
| 3/K.R.R.C. | 4/Rifle Brigade. | |

81st Brigade : Br.-Gen. H. L. Croker.

| 1/Royal Scots. | 2/Camerons. | 9/R. Scots (T.F.). |
| 2/Gloucestershire. | 1/Argyll & Sutherlands. | 9/Argyll & Sutherlands (T.F.). |

82nd Brigade : Br.-Gen. J. R Longley.

| 1/Royal Irish. | 2/R. Irish Fus. | 1/Cambridgeshire (T.F.). |
| 2/D. of Cornwall's L.I. | 1/Leinster. | |

R.F.A. Bdes.

I. (11, 98, 132, 133 Btys.).[1]   XX. (67, 99, 148, 364
XIX. (39, 59, 96, 131 Btys.).[1]   Btys.).[1]
                                            61st Bty. of VIII.
                                            (How.) Bde.

Field Coys. R.E. : 17, 1/Wessex (T.F.) & 2/Wessex (T.F.).

Mtd. Troops : A Sqdn. Surrey Yeo.   Cyclist Coy.

[1] 4-gun batteries.

28TH DIVISION : Major-Gen. E. S. Bulfin.

83rd Brigade : Br.-Gen. R. C. Boyle.

2/King's Own.	1/K O.Y.L.I.	5/King's Own (T F.)
2/E. Yorkshire.	1/York & Lancaster.	3/Monmouthshire
		(T.F.).

84th Brigade : Br.-Gen. L. J. Bols.

2/Northumberland Fus.	2/Cheshire.	12/London (Rangers) (T.F.).
1/Suffolk.	1/Welch.	1/Monmouthshire.
		(T.F.).

85th Brigade : Br.-Gen. A. J. Chapman.

2/Buffs.	2/E. Surrey.	8/Middlesex (T.F.).
3/Royal Fus.	3/Middlesex.	

R.F.A. Bdes.

III. (18, 22, 62, 365 Btys.).[1]   CXLVI. (75, 149, 366, 367 Btys).[1]
XXXI. (69, 100, 103, 118 Btys.).[1]   VIII. (How.) 37 & 65 Btys.

Field Coys. R.E. : 38, 1/Northumbrian (T.F.).

Mtd. Troops : B. Sqdn. Surrey Yeo.   Cyclist Coy.

50TH (1/NORTHUMBRIAN) DIVISION (T.F.) :

Major-Gen. Sir W. F. L. Lindsay.

149th Brigade (1/Northumberland) : Br.-Gen. J. F. Riddell.

4/Northumberland Fus.	6/Northumberland Fus.
5/Northumberland Fus.	7/Northumberland Fus.

150th Brigade (1/York & Durham) : Br.-Gen. J. E. Bush.

4/E. Yorkshire.	5/Green Howards.
4/Green Howards.	5/Durham L.I.

151st Brigade (1/Durham L.I.) : Br.-Gen. H. Martin.

6/Durham L.I.	8/Durham L.I.
7/Durham L.I.	9/Durham L.I.

R.F.A. Bdes.

I. Northumbrian.[2]	III. Northumbrian.[2]
II. Northumbrian.[2]	IV. Northumbrian (How.) [3]

Field Coy. R.E. : 2/Northumbrian.

Mtd. Troops : A Sqdn. Yorks. Hussars.   Cyclist Coy.

1ST CANADIAN DIVISION : Lieut.-Gen. E. A. H. Alderson.

1st Canadian Bde. : Br.-Gen. M. S. Mercer.

1st Bn. (Western Ontario Regt.).   3rd Bn. (Toronto Regt.).
2nd Bn. (Eastern Ontario Regt.).   4th Bn.

2nd Canadian Bde. : Br.-Gen. A. W. Currie.

5th Bn. (Western Cavalry).   8th Bn. (Winnipeg Rifles).
7th Bn. (1st British Columbia   10th Bn. (10th Canadians).
Regt.).

---

[1] 4-gun batteries.   [2] 15-pdrs.   [3] 5″-hows.

3rd Canadian Bde. : Br.-Gen. R. E. W. Turner, V.C.

13th Bn. (Royal Highlanders of   15th Bn. (48th Highlanders of
  Canada).   Canada).
14th Bn. (Royal Montreal Regt.).   16th Bn. (Canadian Scottish).

Canadian F.A. Bdes.
    I. (1, 2, 3, 4 Btys.).[1]   III. (9, 10, 11, 12 Btys.).[1]
    II. (5, 6, 7, 8 Btys.).[1]

R.F.A. Bde. : CXVIII. (How.) 458 & 459 Btys.

Canadian Field Coys. : 1, 2, 3.

Mtd. Troops : Service Sqdn. 19th Alberta Dragoons. Cyclist Coy.

LAHORE DIVISION : Major-Gen. H. D'U. Keary.

Ferozepore Bde. : Br.-Gen. R. G. Egerton.
  Connaught Rangers. 57th Wilde's Rifles.   4/London (T.F.).
  9th Bhopal Infty. 129th Baluchis.

Jullundur Bde. : Br.-Gen. E. P. Strickland.
  1/Manchester.   47th Sikhs.   4/Suffolk (T.F.).
  40th Pathans.   59th Scinde Rifles.

Sirhind Bde. : Br.-Gen. W. G. Walker, V.C.
  1/Highland L.I.   1/1st Gurkhas.   4/King's (S.R.).
  15th Sikhs.   1/4th Gurkhas.

R.F.A. Bdes.
  V. (64, 73, 81 Btys.).   XVIII. (59, 93, 94 Btys.).
  XI. (83, 84, 85 Btys.).   XLIII. (How.) 40 & 57 Btys.

Engineers :   20 & 21 Coys. 3rd Sappers & Miners.

Pioneers :   34th Sikh Pioneers.

Mtd. Troops :   15th Lancers.

1ST CAVALRY DIVISION : Major-Gen. H. de B. de Lisle.

1st Cavalry Bde. : Br.-Gen. C. J. Briggs.
  Queen's Bays.   5/Dragoon Guards.   11/Hussars.
2nd Cavalry Bde. : Br.-Gen. R. L. Mullens.
  4/Dragoon Guards. 9/Lancers.   18/Hussars.
9th Cavalry Bde. : Br.-Gen. W. H. Greenly.
  15/Hussars.   19/Hussars.
R.H.A. Brigade : VII. (H, I & Warwickshire (T.F.) Btys.).
Field Sqdn. R.E. : No. 1.

2ND CAVALRY DIVISION : Major-Gen. C. T. McM. Kavanagh.

3rd Cavalry Bde. : Br.-Gen. J. Vaughan.
  4/Hussars.   5/Lancers.   16/Lancers.

[1] 4-gun batteries.

4th Cavalry Bde. : Br.-Gen. Hon. C. E. Bingham.
  6/Dragoon Guards. 3/Hussars.   Oxfordshire Hrs.
                                             (Yeo.).
5th Cavalry Bde. : Br.-Gen. Sir P. W. Chetwode.
  R. Scots Greys.   12/Lancers.   20/Hussars.
R.H.A. Brigade : III. (D, E, J Btys.).
Field Sqdn. R.E. : No. 2.

  3RD CAVALRY DIVISION : Major-Gen. Hon. J. H. G. Byng.
6th Cavalry Bde. : Br.-Gen. D. Campbell.
  3/Dragoon Guards. 1/Royal Dragoons.   N. Somerset Yeo.
7th Cavalry Bde. : Br.-Gen. A. A. Kennedy.
  1/Life Guards.   2/Life Guards.   Leicester Yeo.
8th Cavalry Bde. : Br.-Gen. C. B. Bulkeley-Johnson.
  Royal Horse Guards. 10/Hussars.   Essex Yeo.
R.H.A. Brigade : XV. (C, K, G Btys.).
Field Sqdn. R.E. : No. 3.

ORDER OF BATTLE

OF THE

DÉTACHEMENT D'ARMÉE DE BELGIQUE
APRIL 1915 [1]

Commander : General Putz.

Composition

20th April 1915 : Groupement de Nieuport (38th Division and 81st Territorial Division), 45th Division and 87th Territorial Division.

23rd April 1915 : As above ; plus the 153rd Division.

25th April 1915 : As above ; plus the 18th and 152nd Divisions. (The 18th and 153rd Divisions formed the IX. Corps, commanded by General Curé.)

22nd May 1915 : 38th, 45th, 152nd and 153rd Divisions and 81st and 87th Territorial Divisions. (Now the XXXVI. Corps, commanded by General Hély d'Oissel.)

Composition of Divisions

18th Division

Commander : General Lefèvre (Justinien).
  35th Brigade :   32nd and 66th Infantry Regiments.
  36th Brigade :   77th and 135th Infantry Regiments.
  One squadron. 3 groupes of artillery (75 mm.).

45th Division

Commander : General Quiquandon.
  90th Brigade :   2nd *bis* Zouaves de marche ; 1st Tirailleurs de marche ; 1st and 3rd Bns. d'Afrique.
  91st Brigade :   7th Zouaves de marche ;
                      3rd *bis* Zouaves de marche.
  One squadron. 3 groupes of artillery (75 mm.).

[1] The Détachement existed as such from 22nd October to 16th November 1914 : from that date to 4th April 1915, it was called the Eighth Army, and from 4th April to 22nd May, was again given its original appellation. On the latter date it became the XXXVI. Corps.

152nd Division

Commander : General Joppé.

304th Brigade :　　268th and 290th Infantry Regiments.
4th Moroccan }　　1st Moroccan Infantry; 8th Tirailleurs de
　Brigade }　　　marche.
　Two squadrons. 2 groupes of artillery (75 mm.).

153rd Division

Commander : General Deligny.

306th Brigade :　　418th Infantry Regiment; 2nd and 4th Bat-
　　　　　　　　　talions Chasseurs à pied.
3rd Moroccan }　　1st mixte Zouaves et Tirailleurs ;
　Brigade }　　　9th Zouaves de marche.
　Two squadrons. 2 groupes of artillery of 90 mm. and 1 groupe
　　　　　　　　　(2 batteries) of 95 mm.

87th Territorial Division

Commander : General Roy.

173rd Brigade :　　73rd and 74th Territorial Regiments.
174th Brigade :　　76th, 79th and 80th Territorial Regiments.
186th Brigade :　　100th and 102nd Territorial Regiments.
　Two squadrons. 2 groupes of artillery (90 mm.).

GERMAN ORDER OF BATTLE[1]

HILL 60 AND THE BATTLES OF YPRES 1915

FOURTH ARMY (part of)

Commander : General Duke Albrecht von Württemberg

Chief of the Staff : Major-General Ilse.

XV. Corps (General von Deimling) :
30th Division :
60th Brigade : 99th and 143rd Regiments.
85th Brigade : 105th and 136th Regiments.

39th Division :
61st Brigade : 126th and 132nd Regiments.
82nd Brigade : 171st and 172nd Regiments.

XXII. Reserve Corps (part of) (General von Falkenhayn) :
43rd Reserve Division :
85th Reserve Brigade : 201st and 202nd Reserve Regts.
86th Reserve Brigade : 203rd and 204th Reserve Regts.
15th Reserve Jäger Battalion.

44th Reserve Division :
207th Reserve Regiment (of 88th Reserve Brigade) only.

XXIII. Reserve Corps (General von Rathen) :
45th Reserve Division :
89th Reserve Brigade : 209th and 212th Reserve Regts.
90th Reserve Brigade : 210th and 211th Reserve Regts.
17th Reserve Jäger Battalion.

46th Reserve Division :
91st Reserve Brigade : 213th and 214th Reserve Regts.
92nd Reserve Brigade : 215th and 216th Reserve Regts.
18th Reserve Jäger Battalion.

[1] Infantry formations and units only.

XXVI. Reserve Corps (General von Hügel) :

51st Reserve Division :
  101st Reserve Brigade : 233rd and 234th Reserve Regts.
  102nd Reserve Brigade : 235th and 236th Reserve Regts.
  23rd Reserve Jäger Battalion.

52nd Reserve Division :
  103rd Reserve Brigade : 237th and 238th Reserve Regts.
  104th Reserve Brigade : 239th and 240th Reserve Regts.
  24th Reserve Jäger Battalion.

XXVII. Reserve Corps (General von Carlowitz) :

53rd Reserve Division (Saxon) :
  105th Reserve Brigade : 241st and 242nd Reserve Regts.
  106th Reserve Brigade : 243rd and 244th Reserve Regts.
  25th Reserve Jäger Battalion.

54th Reserve Division (Württemberg) :
  107th Reserve Brigade : 245th and 246th Reserve Regts.
  108th Reserve Brigade : 247th and 248th Reserve Regts.
  28th Reserve Jäger Battalion.

37th Landwehr Brigade : [1]
73rd and 74th Landwehr Regiments.

38th Landwehr Brigade : [2]
77th and 78th Landwehr Regiments.

2nd Reserve Ersatz Brigade : [1]
3rd and 4th Reserve Ersatz Regiments.

2nd Marine Brigade :
2nd Marine Regiment only.

4th Marine Brigade :
4th and 5th Matrosen Regiments.

[1] Attached to XXVI. Reserve Corps.
[2] Attached to XXVII. Reserve Corps.

APPENDIX 7.

O.A. 816.

INSTRUCTIONS FOR OPERATIONS COMMENCING 14TH DECEMBER 1914

1. It is the intention of the Commander-in-Chief that an offensive Map 4. will be commenced on December 14th by the II and III Corps in Sketch 1. conjunction with the French on the left, with the object of reaching the line Le Touquet [3 miles S.S.E. of Warneton]—Warneton—Hollebeke.

2. For this purpose the French are to be responsible for the capture of Hollebeke and Wytschaete; the British Forces for the capture of Messines and Warneton respectively.

3. The attack on the line Wytschaete Ridge—Messines to be conducted by General Sir H. Smith-Dorrien.

The attacking troops will be the II Corps.

The attack to commence from the line of the present entrenchment.

Left to be kept forward with the object of securing Wytschaete high ground and then Hill 75 [2,000 yards S.E. of Wytschaete] before Messines is taken.

The left of the attack to be in touch with the French on the line Vandenberghe Farm—Wytschaete Hospice.

Right to be directed on the Hospice at Messines.

The dividing line between the II and III Corps will be the Ploegsteert—Messines Road which will be allotted to the III Corps.

4. The attack on the line Messines Ridge—Warneton will be conducted by Lieut.-General W. P. Pulteney.

The attacking troops will be the III Corps (less whatever troops are required to assist the 19th Brigade in holding the trenches apportioned to the III Corps south of Le Touquet) and one Infantry Brigade of the IV Corps.

The attack to start from the line of the trenches now held by the III Corps from opposite Messines to Le Touquet.

The left of the attack will be directed on Messines. The right will be held back. The advance on Warneton to be delayed until Messines is taken, when further orders will be issued to meet the situation which the course of the action will have then produced.

5. The attack will be supported by a powerful artillery bombardment and by the Cavalry Corps.

Major-General W. Lindsay will control the fire of the 7th and 8th Siege Batteries.

6. The IV and Indian Corps will carry out active local operations with a view to containing the enemy now in their front.

I Corps and Indian Cavalry Division will remain in reserve under orders of the Commander-in-Chief and held ready to move at short notice.

G.H.Q.
12/12/14
7 P.M.

A. J. MURRAY, Lieutenant-General,
Chief of the General Staff.

APPENDIX 8.

ARMY OPERATION ORDER No. 40 [1]

BY

FIELD-MARSHAL SIR JOHN FRENCH, G.C.B., ETC.,
Commander-in-Chief, British Forces in the Field.

General Headquarters,
17th December 1914.

1. It is the intention of the Commander-in-Chief to attack vigorously all along the front to-morrow with the II, III, IV and Indian Corps. The I Corps and Cavalry Corps, less 3rd Cavalry Division now under the orders of II Corps, will remain in reserve, ready to move at short notice.

The II Corps will resume the attack in conjunction with General Grossetti and will be responsible for the front as far south as the River Douve.

The artillery of III Corps now detailed to assist II Corps will remain under orders of II Corps.

The 3rd Cavalry Division remains under orders of II Corps.

A powerful French attack is being made in the neighbourhood of Arras and to assist that attack the III, IV and Indian Corps will demonstrate and seize any favourable opportunity which may offer to capture any enemy's trenches in their front.

The 21st and 24th Infantry Brigades will come under orders of IV Corps forthwith.

2. Operations will commence at 10.0 A.M.

3. The following maximum expenditure of ammunition will be allowed :—

13-pr., 60-pr., 6-inch, 9·2-inch as required.

18-pr. 40 rounds, 4·5-inch 20 rounds, 4·7-inch 40 rounds, 6-inch howitzer 30 rounds.

4. Reports to Bailleul from 10.0 A.M.

A. J. MURRAY, Lt.-Genl.,
Chief of the General Staff.

Issued at 9 P.M.[2]

[1] It will be noticed that the last Army Operation Order, issued on 24th October, also bore this number. (" 1914 " Vol. II., Appendix 83.)

[2] Clock stamp shows time of issue as 10.40 P.M.

APPENDIX 9.

O.A. 918.   21st December.

(1) 1st Corps will relieve the Indian Corps which will be gradually withdrawn into General Reserve. General Sir Douglas Haig with 1st Corps and such troops of Indian Corps as may be available will be responsible for restoring in so far as it has not been done the situation on front originally held by Indian Corps.

Time for change of command and details of operations and relief to be mutually arranged between Corps Commanders.

(2) The remainder of 1st Corps will move early to-morrow.

1st Corps will notify Cavalry Corps, IV Corps and Indian Corps of roads required and hours of march, in order that roads may be kept clear.

If billets are required in Cavalry or IV Corps area, arrangements will be made between Corps concerned.

A. J. MURRAY, Lt.-General,
C.G.S.

G.H.Q.
6.30 P.M.

APPENDIX 10.

Chantilly,
21/1/15.

At a meeting of General Joffre and F.M. Sir John French held at Chantilly on 21st January it was agreed :—

(a) That the F.M. should relieve the IX. Corps and then XX. Corps as soon as reinforcements from England permit (probably early in March), and that when these reliefs are carried out the I. Corps will be relieved by French troops.

(b) That the F.M. should lend some cavalry to Genl. Foch to permit of portion of the IX. Corps being given a few days rest, and not for permanent relief. Arrangements for this operation being made between the F.M. and Genl. Foch.

(c) The F.M. having informed Genl. Joffre of the conversations he had held with the King of the Belgians to obtain the loan of a portion of the Belgian artillery with a view to reinforcing the English troops (more especially those which were coming out without artillery), Genl. Joffre said he had no objection, nor could he see any, to the King of the Belgians giving to the Field-Marshal all the guns which were not necessary to himself. The same applies to any part of the Belgian Army.

(d) That Genl. Joffre should keep on the left of the line now held by the XX. Corps a force equivalent to that which is now there (one Active Division as well as the Territorial Troops which will be attached to it), as well as those now at Nieuport at their present effectives.

J. JOFFRE.   J. D. P. FRENCH, F.M.

APPENDIX 11.

1ST ARMY OPERATION ORDER No. 9

AIRE,
8th March 1915.

Map 1. 1.   The Expeditionary Force will resume the offensive on 10th March.

The 1st Army will attack north of the La Bassée canal, the 2nd Army and Xth French Army will co-operate by offensive action on their respective fronts.   Our cavalry will be held in readiness to co-operate in the attack of 1st Army.

2.   The G.O.C., 1st Army intends to force the enemy's lines in the vicinity of Neuve Chapelle and drive back any hostile forces from the line Aubers—Ligny le Grand, with the object of cutting off the enemy's troops which are now holding the front between Neuve Chapelle and La Bassée.

3 (*a*) The artillery will complete such registration as is necessary by 7.30 A.M., at which hour the preliminary bombardment will commence.   At 8.5 A.M. the infantry assaults on the enemy's trenches will be carried out simultaneously at all points.   The artillery fire on Neuve Chapelle will be maintained until 8.35 A.M., when the village will be assaulted.

(*b*) The attack will be carried out by the Indian Corps and 4th Corps in accordance with special instructions which have been issued to Corps Commanders.   The left of the Indian Corps and the right of the 4th Corps will be directed on the general line :—road junction at southern end of Neuve Chapelle—La Cliqueterie Farm.

The capture of Bois du Biez is assigned to the Indian Corps and of Aubers and La Cliqueterie Farm to the 4th Corps.

Allotment of roads west of our line of trenches will remain as at present ; east of this line the road junction Pont Logy—road junction south end of Neuve Chapelle — road junction north of Bois du Biez and all roads to the north, are allotted to the 4th Corps.

(*c*) The 1st Corps will assault the enemy's lines north east of Givenchy under special instructions which have been issued to G.O.C. 1st Corps, and will take advantage of any ´weakening or retirement of the enemy in its front, north of the canal, or on right of Indian Corps by assuming a vigorous offensive in the direction of Violaines.

(*d*) The Canadian Division will, simultaneously with the above attacks, co-operate by a fire attack along its entire front, and will be prepared to assume the offensive under orders from 1st A.H.Q.

4.   The 1st, 4th and Indian Corps will each respectively detail one brigade as Army Reserve under the orders of G.O.C., 1st Army.

5.   1st Army Headquarters Report Centre will be established at Merville at 6 P.M. on 9th March.

R. BUTLER, Brig.-Genl.
General Staff, 1st Army.

Issued at 9 P.M.

APPENDIX 12.

INDIAN CORPS OPERATION ORDER No. 56

St. VENANT,
9-3-15.

1. The Expeditionary Force is resuming the offensive on March Map 1. 10th, and the Xth French Army is co-operating.   The G.O.C., 1st Army intends to force the enemy's lines in the vicinity of Neuve Chapelle and drive back any hostile forces from the line Aubers— Ligny le Grand, with the object of cutting off the enemy's troops now holding the front between Neuve Chapelle and La Bassée.

2. The 4th and Indian Corps are to capture Neuve Chapelle and to push on east of that village.   The dividing line between the two Corps is :—Road junction at southern end of Neuve Chapelle—La Cliqueterie Fe.   The capture of the Bois du Biez is assigned to the Indian Corps and of La Cliqueterie Fe. to the 4th Corps.

The 1st Corps is assaulting the enemy's lines north-east of Givenchy.

3. The Indian Corps will attack vigorously from the front on the La Bassée—Estaires road between the following limits :—Road junction in square S.4.d.,[1] and the left of the line held by the Indian Corps.   The objectives are successively :—

   (a) Enemy's front and support trenches.
   (b) Road from Port Arthur round east side of Neuve Chapelle.
   (c) East edge of the Bois du Biez.
   (d) Line through Le Hue and Ligny le Grand to La Cliqueterie Fe. (exclusive).

4. The attack will be carried out by the Meerut Division reinforced by the artillery of the Lahore Division.   It will also be assisted by No. 1 Group Heavy Artillery under the orders of the 1st Army.

5. The artillery will complete such registration as is necessary by 7.30 A.M., at which hour a bombardment will commence in accordance with special orders as to times and objectives.   At the hour fixed for the assault, the artillery will not cease fire but will lengthen range and fuze.

6. The infantry will assault the enemy's trenches at 8.5 A.M. under detailed instructions already communicated to the Meerut Division. The artillery fire on Neuve Chapelle will be maintained until 8.35 A.M. when the village will be assaulted.

---

[1] That is the Port Arthur salient inclusive.

7. The Lahore Division (less artillery and Ferozepore Bde.) will be disposed as under on the date of the assault and will remain in a state of constant readiness :—

>*Jullundur Bde.* in area Vieille Chapelle—La Couture, clear of the roads by 7.30 A.M.
>
>*Remainder of Division* in area La Tombe Willot—Les Lobes— Lestrem (exclusive) by 10 A.M.

8. The Ferozepore Bde. will remain at Calonne and form part of the 1st Army Reserve.

9. Supply depots for use in emergency have been established at Richebourg St. Vaast and La Couture for 6,000 British and 10,000 Indian rations, half at each place.

10. Reports to La Cix. Marmuse.

H. HUDSON, Brig.-Genl.
General Staff.

Indian Corps.
Issued to Signals at 9.15 A.M.

APPENDIX 13.

OPERATION ORDER No. 21

BY

LIEUT.-GENERAL SIR CHARLES ANDERSON, K.C.B.,

Commanding Meerut Division, 9th March 1915.

Map 1.   1. The 4th and Indian Corps are to attack Neuve Chapelle on March 10th, with the immediate object of capturing the enemy's trenches west of that village and the occupation of a line to the east of the eastern boundary of the " diamond " round Neuve Chapelle.[1]

The general object of the attack is to enable the 4th and Indian Corps to establish themselves on a more forward line to the east, the eventual objective being the high ground from Aubers to Ligny le Grand, with the object of cutting off the enemy's troops now holding the front between Neuve Chapelle and La Bassée.

The 8th and Meerut Divisions, reinforced by the artillery of the Lahore Division and heavy guns, are to carry out the attack.

The Lahore Division will be in Indian Corps Reserve.

The 1st Corps is assaulting the enemy's lines North East of Givenchy.

2. The Meerut Division will as its first objective attack the German

---

[1] See Smith-Dorrien trench.

trenches extending from the front of Port Arthur to opposite the left of the line held by the Meerut Division (C to H), and push on to the north side of the cross roads F.D., forming the base of the triangle with its apex at Neuve Chapelle Village, till the line C.O.G.H. is reached.

Subsequent objectives will be :—

(a) The best available line on the east side of Port Arthur—Neuve Chapelle Road.

(b) The eastern edge of the Bois du Biez.

(c) Line through Le Hue and Ligny le Grand to La Cliqueterie Fe. exclusive.

During these various advances all commanders must bear in mind the necessity for being prepared to specially protect the right flank of the movement.

3. The artillery reinforced by that of the Lahore Division and Heavy Artillery, 1st Army, will carry out a preliminary bombardment for thirty-five minutes commencing at seven-thirty A.M. to destroy obstacles, defences and machine guns on the front to be assaulted, to render hostile observing stations untenable, and prevent arrival of reinforcements. Batteries have also been detailed to demonstrate against enemy's trenches on the Rue du Bois front. The range and fuze will then be increased to cover the infantry assault at 8.5 A.M. on enemy trenches.

Artillery fire will be maintained on Neuve Chapelle village from 8.5 A.M. to 8.35 A.M. when the village will be assaulted.

4. The Garhwal Brigade will assault the enemy's trenches as in para 2. The assault will be delivered at 8.5 A.M. The assault by the 8th Division on the village of Neuve Chapelle will commence at 8.35 A.M. and the Garhwal Brigade will advance to the eastern boundary of the Neuve Chapelle diamond in conjunction with the advance of the 8th Division on its left. It will form for the assault in Port Arthur, Advanced Post No. 2, the trenches along the Estaires—La Bassée Road and in the two new lines of breastwork immediately in rear of them.

Blocking parties to close all enemy trenches, and bombing parties to work outwards and clear enemy's trenches on both flanks, will be organized by G.O.C. Garhwal Brigade and will accompany the assault.

5. The Dehra Dun Brigade will be in support and will be formed up in positions of readiness in work A.1, works D.6 and D.7, and the breastwork connecting them, E.7 and E.8, and E.9 and 10, and work about cross roads at St. Vaast. It will move into the position of assembly in rear of the Garhwal Brigade and the parties of S. & M. and Pioneers mentioned in paragraph 7, and will be careful not to block any of these units.

As the attack progresses the Brigade will be closed up to the position occupied by the Garhwal Bde. prior to the attack.

6. The Bareilly Brigade will continue to hold the present line of trenches. During the artillery bombardment a heavy rifle fire will

be maintained on the enemy's trenches, and the assault by the Garhwal Brigade will be assisted by heavy fire on both flanks. The progress of the attack by the 8th Division must be watched to avoid fire from our left flank striking it.

Troops holding the line from Port Arthur exclusive to the extreme left of front held by Meerut Division will be prepared to move forward to take over a portion of such new line as may be established by the action of the attack. Port Arthur will remain garrisoned as a keep.

7. The following parties will be formed under detailed orders of the C.R.E. :—

(a) Half Company S. &. M. and two companies 107th Pioneers to assemble in the southern of the three lots of small breast-works " Z " close in rear of D Sub-section of the Bareilly Brigade Front.

(b) Half Company S. & M. and one Company 107th Pioneers to assemble in two northern lots of breastwork referred to above—" X " and " Y ".

These parties, each under a R.E. Officer and equipped with necessary tools and material, will follow the Garhwal Brigade into their position of assembly and will be ready to advance when ordered to respectively put localities " C " and " D " in a state of defence.

8. All trench guns will be disposed under instructions already issued to the Divisional Trench Gun Officer. He will hold eight of these guns at disposal of G.O.C. Garhwal Brigade.

9. The troops as per margin will be formed up under cover in vicinity of bridge over Loisne River, and will form the Divisional Reserve under Lieut.-Colonel Stainforth, 4th Cavalry. One Company 2/8th Gurkhas will be sent forward to Bareilly Brigade Report Centre to take over prisoners, when called for by the G.O.C. Bareilly Brigade.

4th Indian Cavalry.
1 Coy. S. & M. Hd.
Qrs. & 1 Company
107th Pioneers.
2/8th Gurkha Rifles
(less 1 Coy. to be de-
tailed for work under
C.R.E.).

10. All troops will be in position by 4.30 A.M. on the 10th March.

11. Wire in front of our trenches will be cut and necessary bridges placed over ditches in front of our trenches, under orders of the G.O.C. Bareilly Brigade, under cover of darkness during night 9th/10th March.

C. NORIE, Colonel,
Issued at 1 P.M. by Signal Coy.   General Staff, MEERUT DIVISION.

APPENDIX 14.

ARMY CORPS OPERATION ORDER No. 10

BY

LIEUT.-GENERAL SIR H. S. RAWLINSON, Bart., K.C.B., C.V.O.,

Commanding IVth Army Corps

Headquarters, IVth Corps,
7th March, 1915.

1. In accordance with instructions received from the General Map 1. Officer Commanding 1st Army, the IVth Corps and Indian Corps will carry out a vigorous attack on the enemy on a date and at an hour to be notified later.[1] The Village of Neuve Chapelle will be attacked and captured by assault after which a further advance will be made to gain the line Aubers—Le Plouich—La Cliqueterie Ferme—Ligny le Grand.

2. The attack on the Village of Neuve Chapelle will be carried out in two stages by the 8th Division. Detailed instructions have already been communicated to G.O.C. 8th Division.

First objective. The enemy's front and support trenches opposite " B " lines.

Second objective. Eastern edge of Neuve Chapelle Village on the right to orchard and the Moated Grange on the left. The point of junction with the Indian Corps will be at the S.E. corner of the Village.

3. For the attack on the first objective, namely Neuve Chapelle Village, the artillery of the 7th and 8th Divisions, less the 4·7″ heavy batteries, will be grouped under the orders of the G.O.C. 8th Division ; the 4·7″ batteries of the 7th and 8th Divisions together with certain heavy batteries will form a group under the orders of the 1st Army.

A simultaneous attack on Neuve Chapelle Village will be carried out by the Indian Corps from the south.

4. When Neuve Chapelle Village has been captured and made good, the 7th and 8th Divisions supported by the Indian Corps on their right will be ordered by the Corps Commander to press forward to capture the high ground about Aubers—La Cliqueterie Ferme and Ligny le Grand.

5. When the 7th Division is ordered by the Corps Commander to move forward to the attack, the following artillery units will come under the orders of the G.O.C. the 7th Division :—

The 81st Battery of the 7th Siege Brigade, 6″ howitzer,
4th Siege Battery 6″ howitzer,

---

[1] Contained in a message to 7th and 8th Divisions on March 8th.

The 59th Battery 7th Siege Brigade, 6″ howitzer,
31st 4·5 Howitzer Battery,
111th Heavy Battery R.G.A. (4·7″),
" A ", " F ", " O ", " Q ", " T ", " U ", and " Z " batteries
R.H.A.

One Section Pack Artillery attached to 23rd Infantry Brigade.

6. The 20th Brigade will be held in Corps Reserve and will not advance beyond the Rue de Bacquerot without the direct orders of the Corps Commander.

7. The Canadian Division will maintain its position and will open artillery, rifle, and maxim gun fire on the enemy's positions in their immediate front, and on Fromelles village, in order to hold the enemy to his ground, and prevent reinforcements being sent to Aubers.

8. IVth Corps Report Centre will be at Pont Levis, half a mile West of Estaires after 6.0 A.M. on the morning of the attack.

A. G. Dallas,
Brigadier General,
General Staff, IVth Corps.

Issued at 11.50 P.M.

APPENDIX 15.

8TH DIV. OPERATION ORDER No. 12

8/3/15.

Map 1. 1. In accordance with instructions received from the General Officer Commanding 1st Army, the IVth Corps and Indian Corps will carry out a vigorous attack on the enemy on a date and at an hour to be notified later. The village of Neuve Chapelle will be attacked and captured by assault, after which a further advance will be made to gain the line—Aubers—Le Plouich—La Cliqueterie Ferme—Ligny le Grand.

2. The attack on the village of Neuve Chapelle will be carried out in two stages by the 8th Division.

First Objective. The enemy's front and support trenches opposite " B " Lines.

Second Objective. Eastern edge of Neuve Chapelle village on the right to orchard No. (6) and the Moated Grange on the left. The point of junction with the Indian Corps will be at the S.E. corner of the village.

3. For the attack on Neuve Chapelle village, the artillery of the 7th and 8th Divisions, less the 4·7″ heavy batteries, will be grouped under the orders of the G.O.C. 8th Division ; the 4·7″ batteries of the 7th and 8th Divs. together with certain heavy batteries will form a group under the orders of 1st Army.

A simultaneous attack on Neuve Chapelle village will be carried out by the Indian Corps from the South.

4. 8th Div. will attack with the 23rd and 25th Inf. Bdes. in front line.

The dividing line between the two Bdes. will be the road (14) (17) (18) (19) (31) for which the Left Bde. will be responsible.

24th Inf. Bde. less 2nd North'n Regt., 5th Black Watch and 4th Cameron Highrs. will be in Div. Reserve.

Div. Mtd. Troops, 2nd North'n R. and 4th Cameron Highrs. will hold the trench line B.C.D.

The Div. will assemble for attack in accordance with the Div. Instructions issued herewith.

5. Details of attack as follows :—

(a) *Right attack* : G.O.C. 25th Inf. Bde.
>25th Inf. Bde.
>Mountain Btty. (less 1 section).
>2nd Field Coy. R.E.

First objective—House at (27) and the trenches immediately west of it, thence the German trenches to the road (14) (17) (18) exclusive.

Second objective—The village.

(b) *Left attack* : G.O.C. 23rd Inf. Bde.
>23rd Inf. Bde.
>1 Section Mountain Btty
>15th Fd. Coy. R.E.

First objective—German trenches (17) (21) to (77).

Second objective—The house at (19) and the trench system round it, Orchard No. (6)—Moated Grange.

(c) *Divisional Reserve.*
>(i) Royal Engineers : Commander—C.R.E.
>Rl. Anglesey R.E. (less 1 section).
>Home Counties R.E. (less 1 section).

>(ii) Infantry : Commander—G.O.C. 24th Inf. Bde.
>1st Worcestershire R.
>1st Sherwood Foresters.
>2nd East Lancashire R.
>Brigade Grenadier Coy. less 1 platoon.

The Infantry of the Divisional Reserve will move forward so as to take the place of the 25th Inf. Bde. in the trenches as they are vacated by that Bde., and will remain there under the orders of the G.O.C. 8th Div.

(d) *B. Lines.*
>Commander—Lt.-Colonel Pritchard, D.S.O.
>2nd Northamptonshire R.
>5/Black Watch.
>One section Rl. Anglesey R.E.
>One section Home Counties R.E.
>Machine guns 4/Cameron Highrs.

O.C. B. Lines will be responsible for at once joining up our trenches to the captured trenches, taking charge of prisoners, and passing them to the rear.

(e) *C. and D. Lines* :[1] Commander Lt.-Col. Wickham.
Div. Mtd. Troops.
4/Cameron Highrs.

Troops in C. and D. lines will keep up a heavy rifle and machine gun fire on the enemy's trenches in their front from the moment the Artillery bombardment begins.

6. As soon as a body of troops leaves our front line of trenches its place in that trench must be taken by a supporting body.

7. As each objective is captured it will at once be placed in a state of defence.

8. The advance to attack on the first and second objectives respectively will take place at an hour to be notified later.

9. Details of the action of the Artillery will be communicated confidentially to. G. Os. C. Inf. Bdes.

10. 21st Inf. Bde. 7th Div., will occupy the trenches and breastworks in rear of the left of B. Lines, when they are vacated by 23rd Inf. Bde.

11. As soon as the village of Neuve Chapelle has been captured and made good, the 7th and 8th Divisions, supported by the Indian Corps on their right, will be ordered by the Corps Commander to press forward to capture the high ground Aubers—La Cliqueterie Ferme— and Ligny le Grand.

W. H. ANDERSON, Colonel,
General Staff,
8th Division.

Issued at 11 P.M.

APPENDIX 16.

ARTILLERY TIME TABLE

NEUVE CHAPELLE, 10TH MARCH 1915

FIRST PHASE

	Description of Gun.	Objective.	Time. Commence.	Cease.
Map 3.	15″ howitzer.	Aubers and guns round Aubers and Pommereau.	7.30 A.M.	
	9·2″ howitzers. Three.	Neuve Chapelle & outskirts.	7.30 A.M.	8.5 A.M.
	6″ howitzers.	One battery, Ind. Corps. To shell selected spots.	7.30 A.M.	7.40 A.M.
	18 pounders.	Nine batteries, Ind. Corps. Wire-cutting.	7.30 A.M.	7.40 A.M.

[1] Front from opposite Moated Grange to left flank of 8th Div.

Description of Gun.	Objective.	Time.	
		Commence.	Cease.
18 pounders.	Six batteries, 4th Corps. Wire-cutting.	7.30 A.M.	7.40 A.M.
6″ howitzers.	4th Corps. Shell selected spots.	7.30 A.M.	7.40 A.M.
13 pounder. 1 baty. }	Three roads & trench running		
4·7″. One section. }	N.W. from Bois du Biez.	7.35 A.M.	8.5 A.M.
4·7″. One section.	" Gap " between Corps.	7.40 A.M.	8.5 A.M.
4·5″ howitzers.	Three batteries, 4th Corps. Enemy trenches.	7.40 A.M.	8.5 A.M.
-Ditto-	Three batteries, Ind. Corps. Enemy trenches & flank.	7.40 A.M.	8.5 A.M.
6″ howitzers.	Five batteries, 4th Corps. Enemy trenches.	7.40 A.M.	8.5 A.M.
-Ditto-	One battery, Ind. Corps. Enemy trenches.	7.40 A.M.	8.5 A.M.
18 pounders.	Twelve batteries, 4th Corps. Covering areas & flank.	7.40 A.M.	8.5 A.M.
-Ditto-	Eighteen batteries, Ind. Corps. Covering areas & flank.	7.40 A.M.	8.5 A.M.
13 pounders.	Three batteries, 4th Corps. Covering areas.	7.40 A.M.	8.5 A.M.
-Ditto-	Six batteries, 4th Corps. Belt of fire East.	7.40 A.M.	8.5 A.M.
4·7″. One battery.	Trenches 4th Corps. Point 27.	7.55 A.M.	8.5 A.M.
	Roads & trench from Bois du Biez.	8.5 A.M	To end.

COUNTER BATTERIES

6″ B.L. gun.	Counter batteries, Aubers Ridge.	7.35 A.M.	
60 pr. gun.	Counter batteries, under 1st. Corps. Area N. of Canal to Beau Puits.	7.35 A.M.	
4·7″. 6 batteries.	Counter batteries.	7.30 A.M.	
4·7″. 1 battery.	Counter battery.	8.5 A.M.	
One 6″ gun } One 4·7″ gun } (Armoured Train) One 4″ gun }	{ Aubers and guns near { there. }	7.35 A.M.	

PACK ARTILLERY : 4th Corps. Two Sections Right Column, one Section Left Column and to push forward.
   Ind. Corps. Two guns close up, and both push forward.

APPENDIX 17.

Handed in at 2.53 P.M. Received 3.6 P.M.
To 7th Division.
G.41. 10.3.15.

 The IV Corps will move forward from the line captured this Map 2. morning towards Aubers. The 7th Division first objective Moulin du Pietre second objective Rue d'Enfer 8th Division first objective points 85 86 88 second objective Pietre. The leading troops of both divisions will cross the line 1. 2. 3. 4. 54. 31 at 3.30 P.M.   Addressed 7th Division, repeated 8th Division and First Army.

From IV. Corps.

[Message to 8th Division identical, handed in 2.55 P.M., received 3.4 P.M.]

APPENDIX 18.

1ST ARMY OPERATION ORDER No. 11

G.713   10th March 1915.

Map 1.   The 4th Corps and Indian Corps will continue their advance to-morrow in accordance with the orders already issued.   Objectives 4th Corps Aubers La Cliqueterie Fm both inclusive.   Indian Corps Bois du Biez and thence to the line La Cliqueterie Fm exclusive Ligny le Grand inclusive.   Advance to commence at 7-0 A.M. at all points.   1st Corps will continue its attack on German trenches East of Givenchy under arrangements to be made by 1st Corps and will in co-operation with the right of the Indian Corps attack southward from the vicinity of Richebourg L'Avoue with the object of capturing the German trenches in front of 1st Corps as far south as the La Bassée Canal.   The 5th Cavalry Brigade now about Pont du Hem will be ready to march at any time after 9-0 A.M.   Indian Corps will retain two brigades as Army Reserve under the orders of G.O.C. 1st Army.   Acknowledge.   Addressed 1st, 4th, Indian Corps, 5th Cavalry Brigade.

From First Army.
11.30 P.M.

APPENDIX 19.

WIRE No. G–20 DATED 11TH MARCH 1915

Map 1.   Fourth and Indian Corps will continue their advance to-day in accordance with orders already issued.   Fourth Corps advances seven A.M., objectives Aubers and La Cliqueterie Farm both inclusive and Meerut Division with Jullundur Brigade and Artillery of Lahore Division, supported by No. I. Group G.H.Q. Artillery will continue its advance at seven A.M., objectives Bois du Biez and thence to line La Cliqueterie Farm exclusive Ligny le Grand inclusive.   It will also take advantage of any opportunity which offers of advancing from Rue du Bois southwards in co-operation with First Corps which continues its attack on enemy trenches east of Givenchy.   Copies to Meerut and Lahore Division, 1st Army, 1st and 4th Corps.

From Indian Corps.

[Received by Meerut Divn. 2.30 A.M.]

Appendix 20.

1st ARMY OPERATION ORDER No. 12

G.735.   11th March 1915.

The Indian and Fourth Corps will continue the offensive to- Map 2.
morrow in accordance with the general plan of operations already
ordered.   Artillery fire will be concentrated on the enemy's positions
about 95, 93 and about 85, 86 from 10 to 10-30 A.M.   At 10-30 A.M.
the Fourth Corps will assault and secure the above positions and
continue its advance simultaneously with the advance of the Indian
Corps.   The 4th Corps will be responsible for the capture of the
cross roads at point 98.   From 10-30 to 11 A.M. artillery fire will be
concentrated on the enemy's position along the road on the North
West of the Bois du Biez from the cross roads at point 98 inclusive
to the road junction south east of Port Arthur inclusive.   At 11-0
A.M. the Indian Corps will assault the above position and secure Bois
du Biez.   The First Corps will continue offensive operations in their
front under Corps arrangements.   The Indian Corps and First Corps
will each retain one brigade as Army Reserve under the orders of
the G.O.C. 1st Army.   Acknowledge.   Addressed First, Fourth,
Indian Corps, Canadian Division, 5th Cavalry Brigade.

From First Army.
11.45 P.M.

Appendix 21.

1st ARMY OPERATION ORDER No. 13

G.766.   12th March 1915.

The 4th and Indian Corps will continue to hold the advanced
line reached by them to-day.   This line to be established as a
defensive line and secured against attack including wiring.   The
general advance will not be continued to-morrow morning without
further orders and reliefs may be carried out within Corps accordingly.   Acknowledge.   Addressed First Corps, Fourth Corps, Indian
Corps, Canadian Division, Gough's Detachment,[1] 2nd Echelon, 1st
Army Aire.

First Army.
10-40 P.M.

[1] Consisting of 2nd Cavalry Div. and an infantry brigade of 46th
(N. Midland) Div.

APPENDIX 22.

O.A.M. 950.

Second Army.

(By Colonel Montgomery) [1]

Maps 4,   Evidently not much reliance can be placed on the two French
7.   Divisions on your left.   We do not know where the division ordered
from Arras is at the present, but it ought to be in action by noon
somewhere N.E. of Poperinghe.   We are enquiring.

It is of course of the first importance that our left should not be
turned, and your dispositions should be such as to safeguard the
left.   The Chief is not fully aware of your dispositions or of the
details of the situation, but he considers the whole of the cavalry
should be used N. of the line Ypres—Poperinghe, supported by the
two brigades from the 4th Division.   This will enable you to use
the Northumbrians E. of the Canal.   The Chief thinks that vigorous
action E. of the Canal will be the best means of checking the enemy's
advance from the line Lizerne—Boesinghe.

The Lahore Division is being ordered to proceed in the direction
of Poperinghe.   Further information regarding it will be sent you
later.

W. R. ROBERTSON,
Lieut.-General, C.G.S.

9.30 A.M.
24.4.15.

APPENDIX 23.

Priority

To Second Army.

O.A. 959.   24th April.

Every effort must be made at once to restore and hold line about
St. Julien or situation of 28th Division will be jeopardised.   Am
sending General Staff officer to explain Chief's views.   Acknowledge.

F. MAURICE, Br.-General
G.S.

From G.H.Q.
4.15 P.M.

[1] Bt. Lieut.-Colonel H. M. de F. Montgomery.

APPENDIX 24.

OPERATION ORDER No. 10

BY

LIEUT.-GENERAL E. A. H. ALDERSON, C.B.,
Commanding Canadian Division

24th April 1915.

1. By orders of the Corps commander a strong counter-attack will be made early to-morrow morning in a general direction of St. Julien with the object of driving the enemy back as far north as possible and thus securing the left flank of the 28th Division. Maps 4, 7.

2. Br.-General Hull commanding the 10th Brigade will be in charge of this counter-attack.

3. The following troops will be placed at the disposal of Br.-General Hull for this purpose, viz. :

10th Infantry Brigade, York & Durham Brigade, K.O.Y.L.I. and Queen Victoria's Rifles of the 13th Brigade, 1st Suffolks and 12th London Regiment of the 28th Division, 4th Canadian Battalion, and one battalion of the 27th Division.

4. The O's C. these units will report for instructions at 9 P.M. to-night to General Hull, whose Hqrs. will be at the road junction in I.l.c. and d.[1] up to midnight.

5. The Northumberland Brigade and Durham Light Infantry Brigade of the Northumbrian Division, forming the Corps reserve and now at Potijze, can be called upon for support by Gen. Hull.

6. The first objectives of the attack will be Fortuin (if occupied by enemy), St. Julien and the wood in C.10. and 11.[2] After these points have been gained, General Hull will advance astride of the St. Julien—Poelcappelle road and drive back the enemy as far north as possible. All units holding the front line of trenches will follow up the attack and help to consolidate the ground gained.

7. The C.R.A. Canadian Division will arrange for artillery support of the counter-attack and get into touch with the C.R.A.'s of the 27th and 28th Divisions regarding all possible artillery support from these Divisions.

8. The counter-attack will be launched at 3.30 A.M.

9. Divisional hqrs. will remain at the Chateau de Trois Tours near Brielen.

C. F. ROMER,
Colonel,
General Staff.

8 P.M.

[1] West of the canal just north of Ypres.
[2] Kitchener's Wood.

Appendix 25.

To : Eleventh Infantry Brigade, Canadian Div
  Eighty-third ,,   ,,
  Eighty-fourth ,,   ,,
  Eighty-fifth ,,   ,,

G.L. 882.   Twenty-fifth.

Maps 4, 1. Eleventh infantry brigade has been placed under orders of G.O.C.
7. twenty-eighth division. This brigade will move so as to reach
Fortuin not later than nine P.M. to-night marching via road running
north in square H.12.c. [a road 1200 yards west of Ypres]—north
side of Ypres—St. Jean—Wieltje—Fortuin. One platoon divisional
cyclists has been ordered to report to eleventh infantry brigade at
five-thirty P.M. and will remain attached to the brigade. This
platoon will provide a guide for the road to Fortuin. Canadian
division report present line runs from original trenches in D.2.d.10.0
—D.8.b.9.9.—D.8.a.0.7 [1]—thence straight to Fortuin—thence due
west. Brigadier commanding eleventh infantry brigade will be
responsible for this line from original trenches on the right to the
road running south-east in square C.18.d. [St. Julien—Fortuin road],
and will if possible occupy it to-night and hold it strongly as security
of the whole trench line southwards depends on the enemy being
kept well to the north of this line. If the line named cannot be
occupied a new line will be dug in best position north of the Fortuin
road in touch with the original trench line on the right and tenth
infantry brigade on the left. The line will be immediately reconnoitred and reorganised. Brigadier commanding eleventh brigade
will assume command of all troops at present holding or supporting
this line—these include second Canadian brigade one battalion first
Canadian brigade three battalions Durham Light Infantry brigade
two battalions York & Durham Brigade two battalions eighty-fourth
infantry brigade besides various companies entrenched on south
side of the Fortuin road. As soon as the situation permits all
detached units will be withdrawn and collected in rear of the line
these units will be returned to the brigades to which they belong if
they belong to the twenty-seventh twenty-eighth or Canadian
divisions with the exception of the second Canadian brigade which
will remain under orders of the eleventh infantry brigade till such
time as it can be dispensed with. Such territorial units as can be
spared will be sent to Potijze to report to twenty-seventh division
and eleventh infantry brigade will report to twenty-eighth division
stating what units are sent back. Brigadier commanding eleventh
infantry brigade will report situation every three hours through
eighty-fifth infantry brigade headquarters commencing at nine P.M.
Position of eleventh brigade headquarters will be given in first
report. Guides will be provided at second Canadian brigade headquarters C.27.d.7.6. [in St. Jean].

                 LOCH, Lt.-Col.

From Twenty-eighth Division. [Note on Canadian Division Copy,
Time 6.25 P.M.   " received 7.20 P.M."]

[1] That is a point south of the Stroombeek, 550 yards north-east of
Boetleer's Farm—a point 100 yards south-west of the first point, whence
the line runs facing nearly north-east, and 400 yards north of, the farm.

APPENDIX 26.

2ND ARMY OPERATION ORDER No. 8

Headquarters, 2nd Army,
26th April 1915.

1. The present line of the V Corps runs from where the original Maps 4, line of trenches crosses square D.9. [about Gravenstafel] by the 8. North of Fortuin, to the Farm in C.15.c [Turco Fm.] ; thence the French line continues by the road in C.7.c. [N.N.W. to Canal] and along the West bank of the Canal to the West of Lizerne.

2. The French troops, strongly reinforced, are attacking the Germans on their front, with their right on the Ypres—Langemarck road.

3. That portion of the 2nd Army facing North will assume the offensive, in conjunction with the French, in order to drive the enemy back from the positions he now occupies.

4. For this purpose the Lahore Division will move to-day from about Ouderdom via Vlamertinghe and Ypres to an area North of Wieltje—St. Jean where it will deploy (with its left flank on the Ypres—Langemarck road). Thence it will move to the line occupied by the V. Corps, and echeloned slightly in rear of the French advance will attack the enemy on a front of 1,000 yards, driving him back on Langemarck. North of our present line the Ypres—Langemarck road is allotted to the French.

5. Such artillery as is necessary for close support will accompany the Infantry. The remainder will be disposed on the West bank of the Canal under the general control of the V. Corps.

The arrangements for the advance will be made by the V. Corps and the Lahore Division acting in direct communication, and will be timed so that the attack can commence at 2 P.M. As many bridges as possible over the canal at Ypres will be allotted to the Lahore Division.

6. The V. Corps will co-operate in the attack, directing its main efforts on the right of the Lahore Division, and will arrange for the co-ordination of the necessary Artillery bombardment and support.

7. Cavalry Corps, less one Division and Artillery will remain in Army Reserve in their present positions, ready to move at half an hour's notice after 2 P.M.

8. An Army Report Centre will open at 12 noon near the Station in the Rue d'Ypres Poperinghe.

G. F. MILNE,
Major-General,
General Staff, II Army.

Issued at 2-15 A.M.

2nd Army.
V Corps.   G.444.

Reference paragraph 6, Operation Order No. 8 of 26th instant, it is considered advisable that the artillery at present in position should be employed in support of the counter attack, and the Army Commander desires that the Artillery Adviser on your Staff should co-ordinate the work of the various Artillery Commands. He should arrange, in conjunction with the G.O.C., Lahore Division, for the preliminary bombardment of the enemy's positions and the subsequent artillery support, paying special attention to the wood in C.10 (d) and C.11 (c) from which the advance can be enfiladed.

G. F. MILNE,
M.G.G.S.,
26th April 1915.   2nd Army.

APPENDIX 27.

V. CORPS OPERATION ORDER No. 12

V. Corps H.Q.
26.4.15.

Maps 4, 8.

1. The French troops strongly reinforced are attacking the Germans on their front with their right on the Ypres—Langemarck road.

The Lahore Division is to attack this afternoon on the right of the French.

2. The V. Corps will co-operate in the attack.

3. The Lahore Division is assembling as follows :—

Jullundur Brigade on right and
Ferozepore Brigade on left assemble about Wieltje and St. Jean and will be deployed ready to begin an advance by 1.20 P.M. from an east and west line from Farm in C.28.a [Wieltje Farm] to Ypres—Langemarck road.

The Sirhind Brigade will be in reserve about Potijze.

4. At 1.20 P.M. an artillery bombardment will begin and will be continued till 2 P.M. During this time the two brigades of the Lahore Division will advance.

At 2 P.M. rapid fire will begin and continue till 2.5 P.M. when the assault will take place on the German line between the wood in C.10.d [Kitchener's Wood] and the Ypres—Langemarck road.

5. The Canadian Division will co-operate by pushing forward on the right of the Lahore Division in accordance with special instructions which have been given to G.O.C. Canadian Division.

The 27th and 28th Divisions will engage the enemy in their front with fire.

6. The artillery of all divisions not required on Divisional fronts will co-operate under instructions which have been issued separately.

7. Reports to Chateau in H.11.a. [Goldfish Chateau] after 1 P.M.

H. S. JEUDWINE,
B.G., G.S.
Issued at 10.30 A.M.   V. Corps

APPENDIX 28.

OPERATION ORDER No. 10

BY

LIEUT.-GENERAL E. A. H. ALDERSON, C.B.,

Commanding Canadian Division

26th April 1915.

1) French troops strongly reinforced are attacking with their right Maps 4, on the Ypres—Langemarck road. The Lahore Division which will 8. be deployed by 1.20 P.M. from the farm in C.28.a [Wieltje Farm] to Ypres—Langemarck road will attack with its right on the wood in C.10.d [Kitchener's Wood]. The V. Corps will co-operate in the attack.

2) An artillery bombardment will begin at 1.20 P.M. and be continued until 2 P.M., during which time the Lahore Division will advance. At 2 P.M. rapid fire will begin and continue until 2.05 P.M., after which the assault will take place.

3) A battalion of the 10th Brigade will advance in co-operation with the Lahore Division between the wood in C.10.d. [Kitchener's Wood] and the Wieltje—St. Julien road. The Northumbrian Brigade will attack St. Julien and advance astride the Wieltje—St. Julien road at the same time as the Lahore Division moved forward.

4) The troops holding the front line of the Canadian Division will assist the attack by fire.

5) Colonel Geddes will move the three battalions now in reserve at St. Jean to the G.H.Q. 2nd Line in C.23.c and 29.a [that is covering Wieltje] as soon as the Northumbrian Brigade clears the ground.

6) The 3rd Canadian Infantry Brigade will move to position south of Wieltje and form the divisional reserve as soon as the Lahore Division commences its advance.

7) The artillery of the Canadian Division will support the attack of the battalion of the 10th Brigade and Northumbrian Brigade by the heaviest possible artillery fire on the German position between the wood in C.10.d [Kitchener's Wood] and St. Julien inclusive.

8) Reports to Chateau des Trois Tours.

C. F ROMER, Colonel, G.S.

Issued at 12.30 P.M.

APPENDIX 29.

Advanced Headquarters, 2nd Army,
27th April, 1915.

My dear Robertson,

Maps 4,   In order to put the situation before the Commander-in-Chief, I
8.   propose to enter into a certain amount of detail.

You will remember that I told Colonel Montgomery [H. M. de F.,
General Staff, G.H.Q.] the night before last, after seeing General
Putz's orders, that as he was only putting in a small proportion of
his troops (and those at different points) to the actual attack, I did
not anticipate any great results. You know what happened—the
French right, instead of gaining ground, lost it, and the left of the
Lahore Division did the same, but the British regiment on the right
of the Lahore Division, the Manchesters, did very well and took
some enemy trenches and held them for a considerable time.

The Northumberland Brigade to their right made a very fine
attack on St. Julien and got into it, but were unable to remain there.

Away to the right, between St. Julien and our old trenches about
square D.10 [85th Brigade area], there was a good deal of fighting,
but with fairly satisfactory results—the Germans eventually retiring.

The enemy's losses are very heavy. Artillery observing officers
claim to have mown them down over and over again during the day.
At times, the fighting appears to have been heavy, and our casualties
are by no means slight.

I enclose you on a separate paper the description of the line the
troops are on at this moment. I saw General Putz last night about
to-day's operations, and he told me he intended to resume the
offensive with very great vigour. I saw his orders, in which he
claims to have captured Het Sas, but on my asking him what he
meant he said the houses of that place which are to the west of the
canal. He told me also that the success at Lizerne had been practically nil—in fact, that the Germans were still in possession of the
village or were last night.

From General Putz's orders for to-day, he is sending one brigade
to cross the river east of Brielen to carry forward the troops on the
east of the canal in the direction of Pilckem, and he assured me that
this brigade was going to be pushed in with great vigour.

It was not till afterwards that I noticed that, to form his own
reserve, he is withdrawing two battalions from the east of the canal
and another two battalions from the front line in the same part to
be used as a reserve on that bank of the river, so the net result of
his orders is to send over six fresh battalions to the fighting line and
to withdraw four which had already been employed.

I have lately received General Joppé's orders. He is the general
commanding the attack towards Pilckem on the east of the canal,
and I was horrified to see that he, instead of using the whole of this
brigade across the canal for this offensive, is leaving one regiment
back at Brielen, and only putting the other regiment across the canal
to attack—so the net result of these latter orders with regard to the
strength of the troops on the east of the canal for the fresh offensive
is the addition of one battalion.

I need hardly say that I at once represented the matter pretty strongly to General Putz, but I want the Chief to know this as I do not think he must expect that the French are going to do anything very great—in fact, although I have ordered the Lahore Division to co-operate when the French attack, at 1.15 P.M., I am pretty sure that our line to-night will not be in advance of where it is at the present moment.

I fear the Lahore Division have had very heavy casualties, and so they tell me have the Northumbrians, and I am doubtful if it is worth losing any more men to regain this French ground unless the French do something really big.

Now, if you look at the map, you will see that the line the French and ourselves are now on allows the Germans to approach so close with their guns that the area east of Ypres will be very difficult to hold, chiefly because the roads approaching it from the west are swept by shell fire, and were all yesterday, and are being to-day. Again, they are now able to shell this place, Poperinghe, and have done it for the last three days ; all day yesterday at intervals there were shells close to my Report Centre and splinters of one struck the house opposite in the middle of the day, and splinters of another actually struck the house itself about midnight—in other words, they will soon render this place unhealthy.

If the French are not going to make a big push, the only line we can hold permanently and have a fair chance of keeping supplied, would be the G.H.Q. line passing just east of Wieltje and Potijze with a curved switch which is being prepared through Hooge, the centres of Squares I.18.d., I.24.b. and d. [that is by Hooge and Sanctuary Wood], to join on to our present line about a thousand yards north-east of Hill 60.

This, of course, means the surrendering of a great deal of trench line, but any intermediate line, short of that, will be extremely difficult to hold, owing to the loss of the ridge to the east of Zonnebeke, which any withdrawal must entail.

I think it right to put these views before the Chief, but at the same time to make it clear that, although I am preparing for the worst, I do not think we have arrived at the time when it is necessary to adopt those measures. In any case, a withdrawal to that line in one fell swoop would be almost impossible on account of the enormous amount of guns and paraphernalia which will have to be withdrawn first, and therefore, if withdrawal becomes necessary, the first contraction would be, starting from the left, " our present " line as far as the spot where the Haanebeke stream crosses the " road at the junction of Squares D.7 and D.13 [1,500 yards east of " St. Julien], thence along the subsidiary line which is already " prepared, as far as the South-East corner of Square J.2 [1,500 " yards south-east of Frezenberg], from whence a switch has been " prepared into our old line on the east side of J.14.b., *i.e.* just " excluding the Polygone Wood ". I intend to-night if nothing special happens to re-organize the new front and to withdraw superfluous troops West of Ypres.

I always have to contemplate the possibility of the Germans gaining ground west of Lizerne, and this, of course, would make the situation more impossible—in fact, it all comes down to this, that unless the French do something really vigorous the situation might become such as to make it impossible for us to hold any line east of Ypres.

It is very difficult to put a subject such as this in a letter without appearing pessimistic—I am not in the least, but as an Army Commander I have of course to provide for every eventuality and I think it right to let the Chief know what is running in my mind.

More British troops, of course, could restore the situation—but this I consider to be out of the question, as it would interfere with a big offensive elsewhere which is after all the crux of the situation and will do more to relieve this situation than anything else.

Since writing above, our Cavalry report that the French actually took the whole of Lizerne last night capturing 120 Germans, and are now attacking the bridgehead covering the bridge leading over the canal to Steenstraat.

General Putz has answered my protest and has ordered General Joppé to put in the whole of the fresh Brigade and not to leave one Regiment of it in reserve at Brielen. The attack is to commence at 1.15 P.M. and we are to assist with heavy artillery fire, and the Lahore Division is only to advance if they see the French troops getting on.

Our Cavalry is where it was last night, one division west of Lizerne, one dismounted in reserve holding G.H.Q. trenches east of Ypres, one dismounted in huts at Vlamertinghe.

I am still at my Advanced Headquarters in Poperinghe. Whether I remain here to-night again I do not know, the main advantage of my being here is my close touch with General Putz and my being able to impress my views upon him.

Yours sincerely,
H. L. SMITH-DORRIEN.

APPENDIX 30.

Telephoned Message [1]

2.15 P.M. 27th April.

C.G.S. TO SECOND ARMY

Chief does not regard situation nearly so unfavourable as your letter represents. He thinks you have abundance of troops and especially notes the large reserves you have. He wishes you to act vigorously with the full means available in co-operating with and assisting the French attack having due regard to his previous instructions that the combined attack should be simultaneous. The French possession of Lizerne and general situation on Canal seems to remove anxiety as to your left flank. Letter follows by Staff Officer.

[1] The record is in the writing of the C.G.S., Lieut.-General Sir W. R. Robertson.

APPENDIX 31.

Advanced Second Army
V Corps

O.A. 976   27th [April]

Chief directs you to hand over forthwith to General Plumer the command of all troops engaged in the present operations about Ypres. You should lend General Plumer your Brigadier-General General Staff and such other officers of the various branches of your staff as he may require. General Plumer should send all reports direct to G.H.Q. from which he will receive his orders. Acknowledge. Addressed Second Army repeated V. Corps.

R. HUTCHISON, Major, G.S.

From G.H.Q.
4.35 P.M

APPENDIX 32.

Lieut.-General Sir H. Plumer, K.C.B.   O.A. 983.

1. With reference to the failure of the French attack to-day and to the Chief's instructions given you by Brig.-General Maurice,[1] the Chief wishes you to consolidate the line you now hold so as to render it more secure against attack.

2. You are also requested to prepare a line east of Ypres joining up with the line now held north and south of that place ready for occupation if and when it becomes advisable to withdraw from the present salient. Please report early as to the position of the line you select for this purpose. It should be such as to avoid withdrawal from Hill 60. The necessary instructions, if any, will be sent by G.H.Q. to Second Corps on receipt of your report.

3. [Not reproduced. It refers to an attack to be made by the French subsequently modified.]

F. MAURICE, B.G., G.S.,
G.H.Q.   for Lieutenant-General,
27/4/15   Chief of the General Staff.

[1] See page 270.

APPENDIX 33.

General adjoint
to the Commander-in-Chief.

Headquarters,
28th April 1915.

Groupe Provisoire
du Nord.

NOTE

FOR THE FIELD MARSHAL COMMANDER-IN-CHIEF
OF THE BRITISH FORCES

Maps 4, 8. (1) In continuation of the interview of this morning, 28th April 1915, General Foch has the honour to put in writing for the Field Marshal the arguments which he developed verbally.

(2) The Field Marshal indicated to General Foch the necessity in which he might find himself to retire to the line : Fortuin, Frezenburg, the Ypres—Menin road between Hooge and Veldhoek, old front Hill 60, for the reasons that

(a) the British troops established east of this line are very tired, have suffered heavily and are difficult to supply ;

(b) the fighting round Ypres is a secondary matter in comparison to the scheme further south. It should absorb neither troops nor resources.

(3) Without denying the value of these arguments General Foch has the honour to observe :

(a) the new position selected for the British Army is at the foot of the ridges, and will be more difficult to hold than the present one on the crest

(b) the enemy, master of the abandoned crest will be able to attack under favourable conditions ; he will be able to bring his artillery nearer to Ypres from the east and thus shell from a new direction that junction of communication

(c) As long as the enemy occupies the Langemarck region and further south he holds under his guns Ypres, Vlamertinghe, Poperinghe, the British line of supply. Thus, the supply of troops facing east will remain difficult. To sum up, the supply can only be assured by the recapture by the Allies of the Langemarck region and not by a simple retirement.

(d) If we retire voluntarily to the line Fortuin—Hill 60 it may be anticipated that we shall be driven further back on Ypres and the Canal. The withdrawal will be over ground where the positions are less and less strong.

(e) The withdrawal of the present line to the line Fortuin—Hill 60 will be a confession of impotence, it will simply invite a very strong German effort. Besides the important tactical considerations already enumerated, the moral ascendency will pass to the Germans. A new battle of Ypres will be provoked and that under conditions materially and morally worse than those under which the former was fought.

(*f*) Even if the battle further south, towards Neuve Chapelle—Arras ought to be considered as more fertile in strategic results and more important, the preparation for it by a retirement is not to be thought of : for this would be the beginning of a set-back whose extent might well become very large.

(4) The conclusions to be drawn from the above in the eyes of General Foch are :

(*a*) The retirement should not be ordered for the moment ; it should be forbidden. If the enemy infantry does not attack in the region under consideration it should not be provoked to one by a retreat. His artillery alone is in action ; its effects can be reduced by defensive arrangements.

(*b*) It is absolutely necessary for the Allied Armies to maintain their present attitude : the attack towards Langemarck ; to make fresh efforts to recover the ground lost there, the possession of which alone permits the holding of Ypres and its environs.

(5) The 28th April may not be important but the 29th, thanks to the arrival of a strong force of heavy artillery, will without doubt give results if the British Army co-operates fully with the French effort.

(6) General Foch in consequence has the honour to request the Field Marshal not to consider any further the retirement from the line on account of the serious consequences which would ensue, but to be good enough to keep to his present intention, and to support the French *offensive to retake the Langemarck region at all costs*, beginning at noon on the 29th

F. Foch.

Appendix 34.

G. H. Q.

1. I beg to report that in accordance with instructions con- Maps 4, tained in telegram O.A. 976, dated 27th inst., I assumed Command 8. of the troops in the Ypres area last night, 27th inst.

2. I have received G.H.Q. letter 983 (Secret) dated 27th inst. [Appendix 32]. With reference to it :—

3. I had already given orders to G.O.C. Divisions to consolidate and strengthen the line we now hold.

4. Major Hutchison has on his map the rough line I propose to occupy when it becomes advisable to withdraw from the present salient.

5. I note that para. 3 of the letter has been modified by telegram O.A. 964 dated 28th inst.

I have given instructions that the subsidiary French attack is to be supported by the Artillery and Infantry fire of the troops under the Command of the G.O.C. Lahore, Canadian, and 28th Divisions.

6. All the units which have been engaged have suffered heavy losses and have had repeated and continuous calls upon them, and in my opinion the support I have indicated is all they should be called upon to give until the French have made appreciable progress and gained some material ground.

Further local attacks which were necessary in the first instance to keep back the enemy and to retain as much ground as possible, will now only cause further heavy losses without effecting any material improvement in the general situation.

7. With regard to the situation generally, and especially in the retirement indicated in para. 2 of G.H.Q. letter 983 of the 27th inst., I consider that :—

(1) The present line we are now holding cannot be held permanently.

(2) Unless the French regain practically the whole of their trenches, the situation will not be improved materially from our point of view, without the employment of a very large force.

(3) If the retirement is to be carried out the longer it is delayed the more difficult and costly it will be.

(4) The French should be given a certain time to regain their trenches, and then we should begin our retirement on to the second line I have referred to.

(5) It will take probably four nights to complete the retirement.

(6) If and when the retirement is carried out, there must be a complete understanding with the French as to their point of junction with us, and a definite undertaking on their part to hold and retain the section of the ground East of the Canal they now occupy.

HERBERT PLUMER, Lieut.-General,
Commanding PLUMER'S FORCE.

28th April 1915.

APPENDIX 35.

PREPARATORY ORDER FOR WITHDRAWAL
FROM TIP OF SALIENT

Maps 4, 9.   1. In case it should be considered necessary to shorten our present line east of Ypres, the following is a general outline of the withdrawal :—

(a) The north and north-east fronts will be maintained as long as possible unchanged, the movement of artillery commencing from the south and south-east.

(b) A reserve will be kept about Potijze throughout

(*c*)   Arrangements will be made so that during the movement flank protection by artillery posted west of the canal will be available.

2.   During the withdrawal the following formations will be moved west of Ypres in the order stated :—

(*a*) Lahore Division ;

(*b*) Northumbrian Division ;

(*c*) 2nd Cavalry Division.

3.   The line to be finally occupied will be as follows :—

From present trench line in I.30.b.[1] due north to Hooge Chateau, I.18.b., thence north-west to G.H.Q. line about C.29.a.c.[2] along G.H.Q. line to farm in C.22.b.,[3] and thence along present British and French trench line.

A tracing of this line, which has been reconstructed during the last few days, is attached.

4.   This line will be held, in order from south to north, by the following divisions :—

(*a*) 27th Division ;

(*b*) 28th Division ;

(*c*) Canadian Division

5.   The allotment of the new line will be as follows :—

27th Division : From left of II. Corps in I.30.d.[1] to level crossing in I.6.c.[4] (exclusive of railway line).

28th Division : From level crossing in I.6.c.[4] (inclusive of railway line) to farm in C.22.b.[3] (exclusive).

Canadian Division : From farm in C.22.b.[3] (inclusive) to French right at farm in C.15.c.[5] (exclusive).

6.   The allotment of roads for carrying out this move will be as follows :—

27th Division : All roads to south and exclusive of road running west from cross roads Westhoek (J.7.b.).

28th Division : The above road (inclusive) and all roads up to and including the Passchendaele—Ypres road, but that part of the road from Wieltje (C.22.b.) to Ypres will be common to both 28th and Canadian Divisions under the control of 28th Division.

Canadian Division : St. Julien—Wieltje road, with part use of that portion from Wieltje to Ypres, and all roads and bridges west of it, excepting road leading to No. 4 Bridge (C.25.a.).[6] This last road only to be used by arrangement with the French.

7.   It is proposed, if the tactical situation permits, to carry out the withdrawal in four nights.   In view of the fact that the move-

---

[1] In front of Armagh Wood.　　　　　[2] East of Wieltje.
[3] Mouse Trap Farm.
[4] 1,000 yards south-west of Frezenberg.　　　[5] Turco Farm.
[6] Bridge east of the northern end of Brielen

ment will probably commence to-night, all preparations and plans should be considered.

8. The final withdrawal from the present trench line to the one detailed above in paragraph 8 will take place in one night. Arrangements will be made by divisions to make use of the " Subsidiary Line ", in order to ensure co-operation as regards timing. The advisability of leaving a strong outpost line on the present front line should be seriously considered.

9. Detailed orders will be issued day by day

G. F. MILNE, Major-General,
C.G.S. Plumer's Force.

29th April 1915.
9.30 A.M.

APPENDIX 36.

27th Division.
28th Division.
Canadian Div.[1]

Maps
4, 9, 10.
1. In order to shorten the line now held to the East of Ypres, 27th, 28th and Canadian Divisions will withdraw on the night 3rd/ 4th May to a line which has been prepared connecting the Subsidiary Line about Westhoek through Frezenberg with the fortified farm in C.22.b.7.7. [Mouse Trap Farm]. On the right, this line connects by means of the Subsidiary Line with the present right of the trench line of the 27th Division.

2. This line will be held as follows :—

From the right to the track (exclusive) just west of West-hoek by the 27th Division.

From the above track (inclusive) to the fortified farm in C.22.b. [Mouse Trap Farm] (exclusive) by the 28th Division.

From the above farm (inclusive) to farm in C.15.c. [Turco Farm] (exclusive) by the 1st Canadian Division.

From this farm (inclusive) to the North by the French.

3. Roads and tracks will be available as under :—

27th Division and attached troops

Cross roads J.l.d. 7.2. [500 yds. N.W. of Westhoek]—Camp I.10.c. [near White Chateau]—Menin Gate—Grande Place Rue de Stuers—Railway Station—Kruisstraat—Groenen Jager and roads and tracks South of this.

[1] This as regards infantry meant the three brigades of the 4th Division.

28th Division and attached troops

Roads and tracks north of the above as far as and including Fortuin—Wieltje—La Brique—No. 2 bridge, I.1.b. [S.W. of La Brique]—road junction I.1.c. 10.8. [due W. to Boesinghe road]—road junction B.29.d. 9.1. [400 yds. S.E. of Brielen]—Vlamertinghe road; but the Canadian Division to have joint use of this road under control of 28th Division.

(N.B.   This is a new road not shown on maps)

Canadian Division

Road as above under control of 28th Division and No. 3 [E. of Brielen] bridge and roads approaching it. Also road running parallel to canal on west bank as far north as and including road on west bank from No. 4 bridge to Brielen.

4.   Artillery will begin withdrawal at 8-30 P.M.

5.   The withdrawal of the Infantry of 27th Division and 28th Division will take place in three successive parties, viz. :

First parties   —Half the troops in the trench line

Second parties—Half the remainder

Third parties   —The troops still remaining followed by rear parties as required.

(*a*) *First parties*

At 9 P.M. half the Infantry of the 28th Division will begin to withdraw ; it will reach the following line by 10 P.M. :—

North-western corner of Polygon Wood thence by Subsidiary Line to where the latter meets the present trench line about D.20.b. 8.8. [Zonnebeke—Keerselare road].

Half the Infantry of 27th Division manning trenches in South face of Polygon Wood will be withdrawn in conjunction with right of 28th Division so as to reach the North-western corner of Polygon Wood at 10 P.M.   On this line there will be a halt till 10.30 P.M. during which time any connection which has been lost will be regained along the whole of this line and maintained during the remainder of the withdrawal.

At 10-30 P.M. the withdrawal will be continued by both 27th and 28th Divisions, the former withdrawing detachments in succession from the right, but leaving half the troops to hold the trenches.

No troops will be withdrawn from the Canadian Division line East of farm C.22.b. [Mouse Trap Farm] at this date.

(*b*) *Second parties*

At 10-30 P.M., the withdrawal of Second parties will begin. It will be carried out in the same sequence as first parties, troops reaching subsidiary line at 11-30 P.M. halting there till 12 midnight, and completing withdrawal by 1 A.M.

After it is completed First parties of troops of Canadian Division holding the trench line East of Farm C.22.b. [Mouse Trap Farm] will withdraw.

(c) *Third parties*

The withdrawal of third parties will begin at 12 midnight in the same order as First parties, troops reaching subsidiary line at 1 A.M. halting there till 1-30 A.M. and completing withdrawal by 2-15 A.M. After it is completed the Second and Third parties of Canadian troops holding trench line East of farm C.22.b. [Mouse Trap Farm] will withdraw.

6. The disposal of troops after they have reached the new trench line is in the hands of Divisional Commanders, but all movements must be completed by 3-30 A.M.

7. 28th Division will be responsible for the timing of this retirement, and will keep 27th and Canadian Divisions frequently informed of the progress of it, and will give these Divisions adequate warning of the commencement of withdrawal of the units on its extreme right and left respectively.

27th and Canadian Divisions will regulate their retirement by that of the 28th Division, and will keep in close touch with it.

If before or after the retirement has begun the action of the enemy makes it advisable to postpone or delay it, the Division which becomes aware of the reasons for such delay will immediately inform both other Divisions as well as Force Headquarters, and failing special instructions, will conform to the movements of 28th Division.

8. The following points require regulation by Divisional Commanders, and instructions to every officer, N.C.O., and man concerned :—

(a) Reconnoitring new trench line and determining exact extent of front to be occupied by each unit.

(b) Reconnoitring and marking routes from old to new trench line.

(c) Maintenance of communication between divisional and brigade and between brigade and battalion H.Q. during retirement.

9. No move in an easterly direction of troops or vehicles will be permitted East of the Canal, either North or South of Ypres, after 6 P.M.

All transport and horses not indispensable to the operations will be moved West of Ypres on the preceding night.

10. Areas for accommodation will remain as allotted to Divisions at present, with recent additions West of Poperinghe.

11. Divisional Commanders will inform Force Headquarters by 6 P.M. 2nd where their Report Centres will be during the operations, and of any subsequent changes they contemplate.

12. Reports to Advanced Report Centre, H.11.a. [Goldfish Chateau].

G. F. MILNE, Major-General,
C.G.S., PLUMER'S FORCE.

1st May 1915.

GENERAL INDEX

411

INDEX TO
ARMS, FORMATIONS AND UNITS

HISTORY OF THE GREAT WAR

BASED ON OFFICIAL DOCUMENTS, BY DIRECTION OF THE HISTORICAL
SECTION OF THE COMMITTEE OF IMPERIAL DEFENCE

Vol. I. **Military Operations—France and Belgium: Mons
—the Retreat to the Seine—the Marne and the
Aisne, August–October, 1914.** Compiled by
Brigadier-General J. E. EDMONDS, C.B., C.M.G.
With 15 Sketches. 8vo. 12s. 6d. net.

Separate Case, containing 34 General, Battle, and
Situation Maps. 12s. 6d. net.

Vol. II. **Military Operations—France and Belgium:
Antwerp—La Bassée—Armentières—Messines,
and Ypres, October–November, 1914.** Compiled
by Brigadier-General J. E. EDMONDS, C.B., C.M.G.
With 18 Sketches. 8vo. 12s. 6d. net.

Separate Case, containing 40 General, Battle, and
Situation Maps. 5s. 6d. net.

Vol. III. **Military Operations — France and Belgium,
Winter 1914–15: Battle of Neuve Chapelle—
Battle of Ypres.** Compiled by Brigadier-General
J. E. EDMONDS, C.B., C.M.G., and Captain G. C.
WYNNE. With 21 Sketches. 8vo. 12s. 6d. net.

Separate Case, containing 13 Maps. 5s. 6d. net.

SOME PRESS OPINIONS

VOL. I

THE ARMY, NAVY, AND AIR FORCE GAZETTE.—" The
first volume is a finished treatise of a convincing character, giving the
facts from the crucible of long test and clearing up debatable matter
without fear or favour. This work, when completed, will be the most
important military history ever written. . . . It is not a book solely for
the library where the masses can consult it, but rather is it a history
which should find a place in the homestead, for is it not the record of
each man's war life handed down to his sons' sons? . . . Brigadier-
General J. E. Edmonds and his great work will rank with the famous
historians and their histories down through Napier to Fortescue."

LONDON: MACMILLAN AND CO., LTD.

SOME PRESS OPINIONS

Vol. I.—*Continued*

THE ARMY QUARTERLY.—" This volume has only to be read to silence completely any complaints on the score of the delay in its appearance. It has been worth waiting to get as thorough and careful a story as this. It is abundantly clear that an earlier appearance would have robbed it of much of the authoritative and, in some respects, definitive character which it possesses."

Mr. JOHN BUCHAN in *THE OBSERVER.*—" General Edmonds and his colleagues seem to me to have triumphed over almost insuperable difficulties, and to have achieved a signal success. Their first volume is a real book . . . a history which has shape, and colour, and light, as well as fidelity to fact. It is the only official history of military operations known to me in which there is a strong and sustained narrative interest. . . . The book is admirably planned . . . acumen and a strong good sense are manifested on every page."

THE TIMES LITERARY SUPPLEMENT.—" Though so complete, the picture is never overloaded with detail ; the compiler's sense of proportion has served him well, and is one of the most admirable features of a work which, let it be said at once, has been excellently done."

VOL. II

THE DAILY MAIL.—" The second volume of this the official history of the British Army in the Great War is even better than the first. It is written with a rare freedom from technical terms, so that it can be understood by the least sophisticated. The coloured maps are quite excellent and exceedingly clear, and the book itself is a remarkably cheap one. Its editors deserve the public gratitude for a very fine piece of work."

THE TIMES LITERARY SUPPLEMENT.—" Enough has been said to show the great interest of the story this volume relates, and to give some indication of the excellence with which it has been told. It is military history at its best—lucid, impartial, and graphic. The maps, both those bound in the volume and those in a separate cover, are extremely well done."

LONDON : MACMILLAN AND CO., LTD.

ADDENDA AND CORRIGENDA TO
" 1915 " Vol. I

(Kindly pointed out by various correspondents)

Page 31, line 20.   For " 80th Brigade " read " 82nd Brigade ".

Page 31, footnote.   For " 20th " read " 20th March."

Page 164, footnote 1, line 18.   After " ' promoted lieutenant.' " add :
> " The following appears in ' Eyewitness's ' letter of 6th April 1915 (printed in " The Times " of 9th April 1915) :
>   ' It has been reported that in the Argonne, where the ' trenches are very close, the Germans have on several ' occasions pumped blazing oil or pitch on to the French, ' but, according to the statements of our prisoners, they ' are preparing a more novel reception for us in front of ' parts of our line.   They propose to asphyxiate our men if ' they advance by means of poisonous gas.   The gas is con- ' tained under pressure in steel cylinders, and, being of a ' heavy nature, will spread along the ground without being ' dissipated quickly '."

Page 286, line 5.   For " into the front trenches " read " behind the front trenches ".

Page 286, line 13.   After " did not leave its trenches." add :   " although part of the Sirhind Brigade advanced a short distance."

Page 318.   Delete the last 5 words and the first 4 words on page 319—not 5 lines and 4 lines as printed in a previous correction.

Page 333, line 20.   Add :   " B Company of the 1/King's Own (the battalion was also in support) took part in the counter-attack of the 2/Essex."

Maps 9, 10, 11.   The front of the 1/King's Own did not extend so far to the west, its left being in front of the westernmost buildings of Canadian Farm, where it was in touch with the 2/Essex.

ADDENDA AND CORRIGENDA TO
"1915" Vol. I

(Kindly pointed out by various correspondents)

Page 220, line 10 (end of first para.). Addendum issued with "1915" Vol. II should be amended to read :
Add footnote :
"The second order did not reach the battalions concerned until much later, for it was about noon when the 5/Durham L.I. crossed the canal and the 5/Green Howards followed some time afterwards."

Page 276, line 22. After "next day." add footnote :
"With regard to the supersession of General Sir H. Smith-Dorrien by General Sir H. Plumer see General Sir C. Harington's 'Plumer of Messines' containing an extract from one of Lord Plumer's letters, dated 30th April 1915, in which he says :
'It is not fair because Smith-Dorrien and I were in
'absolute agreement as to what should be done, and I am
'only doing now exactly what I should have been doing if
'I had remained under Smith-Dorrien.'"

ADDENDA AND CORRIGENDA TO
VOLUME III. (1915*)

(Kindly pointed out by various correspondents.)

Page 8, footnotes, line 10 from bottom. For what is said about the " Egg " grenade substitute : ' The " Egg " grenade, after trial, was introduced in place of the " Ball " grenade on 1st March 1916, and was first noticed by the British at Ovillers about the middle of July 1916.'

Page 12. Add after line 2 :
"On the 22nd January 1915 an Army Order was issued which directed that dismounted officers of Royal Engineers and infantry should no longer be armed with a sword on active service in the field, and should be equipped with the same accoutrements as the rank and file, except as regards the bayonet frog, entrenching implement and carriers. Actually the wearing of the sword by dismounted officers had been abandoned, as in the S. African War, very soon after the first actions."

Page 13, lines 4-5. For " but it was some time before the Intelligence Branch could state with any certainty ' substitute :
" but by the 17th December, in a memorandum to the War Office, the Intelligence Branch could state with certainty ".

Page 18, lines 12-14. For the sentence : " In other respects . . . scale was made." substitute : " No arrangement was made nor were orders issued for a combined artillery preparation."

Page 31, line 11. After " 13th and 15th Brigades " add : " , and the artillery of the 27th and 28th Divisions was strengthened at different times by the loan of five batteries from the 3rd, 4th and 5th Divisions ".

Page 44, line 1. After " the problem." add footnote : " This solution had been evolved by the Munitions Committee of the Leeds Engineering Employers assembled by Sir Algernon Firth, Bt. as President of the Associated Chambers of Commerce. Leeds was the first of the new districts to be organized on the basis of a national factory for the production of munitions."

Page 83, footnote 3, line 2. For " Sir Roger Bacon " read " R. H. S. Bacon ".

2

Page 87, Note II., lines 9-10. For " The two divisions were weaker than the British Intelligence could know at the time ; " substitute : " The two divisions were each short of an infantry regiment, as the British Intelligence suspected at the time, although what had become of the six battalions withdrawn was not known ; "

Page 95, line 6. For " some two hundred yards in rear." read : " fifty to sixty yards in rear in brigade support."

Page 143, footnote 1, line 3. For " Ypres sector " substitute : " Ypres front (it came from rest billets at Tourcoing, where it had only just arrived) ".

Page 158. Delete footnote 4.

Page 177, footnote 2, line 6. For " 1st Bridging Train " read " 2nd Bridging Train ".

Page 184, line 2. After " Cavalry Corps " add footnote : " A 9th Cavalry Brigade had been formed on the 14th April of the 15th and 19th Hussars. These regiments had provided the divisional squadrons of the first six divisions, and were replaced in this duty by a squadron each from the Northumberland Hussars, South Irish Horse, and North Irish Horse, and 3 squadrons of the Northamptonshire Yeomanry. The remaining two squadrons of the Northumberland Hussars formed the divisional squadrons of the 7th and 8th Divisions. The third regiment of the 9th Cavalry Brigade, the Bedfordshire Yeomanry, joined on the 11th June 1915."

Page 196, footnote 1. Add : " It was commanded by a Frenchman."

Page 220, line 10 (end of first paragraph). Add footnote : " The orders apparently did not reach the battalions of the 150th Brigade until nearly noon, for the 5/Durham L.I. crossed the canal about that time followed later by the 4/East Yorkshire and 4/Green Howards."

Page 264, line 5 from bottom of text. For " 5/Green Howards and 5/East Yorkshire " read " 4/Green Howards and 4/East Yorkshire."

Page 265, line 11 from bottom. For " Ingelminster " read " Ingelmunster."

Page 275, line 10. After " 150th Brigade " add footnote : " The 4/Green Howards and 4/East Yorkshire relieved the 5/D.L.I. and 5/Green Howards and remained attached to the 11th Brigade."

Page 288, line 22. For " resultats " read " résultats."

Page 345, line 11. After " Yorkshire " add " , a company of the 5/Durham L.I."

Page 370 et seq. To Order of Battle add the names of the commanders of divisional artillery : " 3rd Division, Br.-General H. G. Sandilands ; 4th Division,

ADDENDA AND CORRIGENDA TO VOLUME III (1915 *)

Additional to those issued with Vol. IV.

Page 9, line 7 from bottom. After " modern battle." add footnote :
" See ' 1914 ' Vol. II. pp. 11-12, where the reserve of ammunition is discussed."

Page 21, line 6 from bottom. After " difficult." add footnote :
" On this day occurred the first recorded case of bombing down a trench. Captain R. G. G. Robson, R.E. (killed three days afterwards), 3rd Company 1st K.G.O. Sappers & Miners, had taken a load of jam-pot bombs into the front line trench in order to instruct the infantry in their use. He found himself on the flank of a length of trench just captured by the enemy, and initiated a system of attack by lobbing a bomb into the next bay, and, as soon as the explosion had taken place, rushing round the traverse between him and the enemy with two or three infantrymen. By continuing this process a considerable length of trench was recovered."

Page 24. Add to Note II : " Falkenhayn's plans for 1915 are given in full in the German official account, Volume VII. (published 1931). He did intend to attack on the Western Front in the spring of 1915, but circumstances prevented him from doing so. The first reserve of 6 corps (4½ new organizations) which he collected for the purpose was taken from him by the Kaiser's order, under Hindenburg's influence, to reinforce the Eastern Front as the Tenth Army, and fight in the Winter Battle in Masuria. The second reserve, 14 divisions, which he organized by April, by reducing the number of battalions in a division from 12 to 9 and various other economies, eked out by new units, was to be assembled in France. The crisis in Turkey brought about by the landing of the Mediterranean Expeditionary Force on Gallipoli compelled him, however, to decide that before he could attack again in the West a way through Serbia to Constantinople must first be forced. Even this had to be postponed ; for Austria, in fear of declaration of war by Italy, declared that she would make her peace with Russia, even at the cost of surrendering Galicia. In consequence, Falkenhayn's striking force, as the Eleventh Army, was sent to the Austrian front and made the successful breakthrough at Gorlice-Tarnow.
" During the discussions regarding the theatre in which the Eleventh Army should be employed, Falkenhayn had directed some of the greatest of the German strategists, Generals von Kuhl, von Seeckt, Krafft von Delmensingen Wild von Hohenborn, and Tappen to consider where best an offensive could be made on the Western Front. The Aisne, Roye and Arras sectors and northwards of Arras were examined : Verdun was not. The schemes prepared are of interest because they appear to have had some influence on Ludendorff in 1918. Seeckt's plan contemplated a break-through on a front of 15 to 20 miles, north of the Somme, somewhere between the river and Arras, Ficheux—Thiepval being recommended.

ADDENDA AND CORRIGENDA

This accomplished, the Allied line was to be rolled up north-wards, the line of the Somme being used to hold off French assistance. Krafft's and Wild's plan was much the same on a smaller scale, and it laid down ' in the first place, the British ' army must be broken and crushed.' If the forces available were not sufficient to extend to the Somme, the line Albert—Doullens and thence the course of the Authie was to be held, instead of the Somme, to protect the left of the operation. The main attack was to be made on either side of Arras and then directed north-westwards to the coast. Kuhl decided against an attack in the Roye area (the line taken by Hutier's Army in March 1918), as it could not be decisive, and selected the Aisne front (the Chemin des Dames offensive of 1918). What Falkenhayn's decision would have been is not known."

Page 32, footnote 1. Substitute for the last four lines :
" appears to be that carried out by order of the Garhwal Brigade on the night of the 9th/10th November 1914 by two parties of fifty men each from the 1st and 2nd Battalions 39th Garhwal Rifles, under Major G. H. Taylor, in order to render unfit for occupation an enemy trench fifty yards from its right flank, which enfiladed the line of the 1st Battalion."

Page 157. Add at end of Note : " The actual dispositions of the German attack seem to have been slightly changed (*vide* pp. 131-6)."

Page 165, line 24. Add footnote :
" It appears from the paper " Volonté," 25th April 1929, that the prisoner mentioned on p. 163 was captured by the 11th Division, and the warning he gave was not passed on to the 45th or 87th Divisions."

Page 259. Before the last paragraph, beginning " Directly . . ." add :
" It was supposed that the German trenches were not more than four hundred yards distance, and a formation in lines, suitable for a charge, was ordered."

Page 259, line 8 from bottom. After " artillery fire," add : " and discovered that the German trenches were at least six hundred yards further on and that the ground to be traversed was devoid of cover. The charging lines scattered in the long advance,"

Page 294, line 14 from bottom. After " W. W. Seymour)," add : " each of the two last-named reinforced by two companies of the 4/East Yorkshire,"

Page 317, line 13. After " batmen," add : " and supported by the fire, sometimes at 1,600 yards' range, of the 39th Battery (XIX. Brigade R.F.A.), the 1/Wessex Field Company R.E., acting as escort and carrying ammunition,"

Page 318, last line. Delete last five lines and first four on page 319.

Page 369. Under " 14th Bavarian Reserve Brigade " delete " 9th Bavarian Reserve Regiment."

Br.-General R. F. Fox ; 5th Division, Br.-General J. G. Geddes ; 27th Division, Br.-General A. Stokes ; 28th Division, Br.-General A. W. Gay ; 50th Division, Br.-General C. G. Henshaw ; 1st Canadian Division, Br.-General H. E. Burstall ; Lahore Division, Br.-General F. E. Johnson."

SKETCH B.

YPRES, 1915
The Stages of the Battle.

FARMS:—
Bo. = Boetleers.
Van. = Vanheules.
Ok. = Oblong.
Wl. = Welsh.
MT. = Mouse Trap (Shell Trap).
Cd.ⁿ = Canadian.
Ha. = Hampshire.
Tu. = Turcos.
S.Z. = S.Zwanhof.
Be. = Bellewaarde.
WP. = White Poerte.

Line on 22nd April
New Line on 23rd April
New Line on 30th April
New Line on 4th May
New Line on 13th May
Final Line

French Blue; Belgians Brown;
British Red.

Scale of miles

Prepared in the Historical Section (Military Branch).

Ordnance Survey, 1926.